MANAGERIAL ECONOMICS

MANAGERIAL ECONOMICS

Economic Tools for Today's Decision Makers

PAUL G. KEAT
American Graduate School of International Management
PHILIP K. Y. YOUNG
Pace University

MACMILLAN PUBLISHING COMPANY
NEW YORK
MAXWELL MACMILLAN CANADA
TORONTO
MAXWELL MACMILLAN INTERNATIONAL
NEW YORK OXFORD SINGAPORE SYDNEY

Editor: Jill Lectka
Production Supervisor: Publication Services, Inc.
Production Manager: Aliza Greenblatt
Cover Designer: Sheree Goodman
Cover Illustration: Tim Foley

This book was set in Palatino by Publication Services, Inc.,
and was printed and bound by Arcata Graphics.
The cover was printed by Lehigh Press.

PRINTED IN THE UNITED STATES OF AMERICA

Macmillan Publishing Company
866 Third Avenue, New York, New York 10022

Macmillan Publishing Company is
part of the Maxwell Communication
Group of Companies.

Maxwell Macmillan Canada, Inc.
1200 Eglinton Avenue East
Suite 200
Don Mills, Ontario M3C 3N1

LIBRARY OF CONGRESS CATALOGING-IN-PUBLICATION DATA

Keat, Paul G.
Managerial economics : economic tools for today's decision makers
/ Paul G. Keat, Philip K.Y. Young.
p. cm.
Includes index.
ISBN 0-02-362295-4
1. Managerial economics. I. Young, Philip K.Y. II. Title.
HD30.22.K39 1992
338.5′024658–dc20 91-21085
CIP

Printing: 1 2 3 4 5 6 7 Year: 2 3 4 5 6 7 8

To my wife, Sheilah, and my children, Diana and Andrew
P.G.K.

To my wife, Ilse, and my children, Christopher and Adriana
P.K.Y.Y.

Preface

One day after class, a student in one of our courses commented on the managerial economics text then being used: "This book is very dry. What it needs is a plot!" To a large extent, the idea for this text stemmed from this remark. Having taught courses in managerial economics for over 15 years, we obviously believe that this course is a vital part of management education. However, we felt that there was a need for a textbook that would excite readers about the subject matter as well as inform them. We hope that this book will meet this need. Each chapter begins with a "situation" in which managers in the soft drink industry must make certain key decisions. After the relevant economic concepts or tools of analysis are presented, each chapter ends with a suggested way in which these concepts or tools can help managers make the correct decision.

The heart of managerial economics is the microeconomic theory of the firm. Much of this theory was formalized in a textbook about 100 years ago by Professor Alfred Marshall of Cambridge University. Indeed, if readers were to refer back to his *Principles of Economics* (1890), they would find many of the diagrams and equations presented in this text as well as all other texts in managerial economics. To be sure, the world has greatly changed since Marshall's ideas were developed. Market structures other than the "perfectly competitive model," have also become important. Technology moves at such a rapid pace that the rate of obsolescence of a product is now often measured in months rather than years. Competition among firms is frequently conducted on a global scale rather than a local or national one. Multinational firms invest, manufacture, and sell around the world. In so doing, they sometimes buy out their global competitors or form alliances or joint ventures with them.

Yet through all of these changes, basic microeconomic principles such as supply and demand, elasticity, short-run and long-run shifts in resource allocation, diminishing returns, economies of scale, and pricing according to marginal revenue and marginal cost continue to be important tools of analysis for managerial decision makers. In fact, the overall objective of this text is to demonstrate to our readers that microeconomic theory has stood the test of time and is just as relevant today as it was when it was first developed in Victorian England. Two brief examples should demonstrate what we mean.

The manufacturing and selling of computers is one of the most competitive and "technology-driven" industries today. At the time this preface is being written, the newest and fastest-growing part of this business is the workstation. One of the first firms to develop and produce this product, Sun Microsystems, Inc., continues to be a leader in the field, despite a flurry of new entrants into the market. In explaining why, one analyst stated: "Scott [the CEO of Sun] keeps changing the rules of the game. He's like a chess player. He understands that you have to consistently seize a temporary advantage in markets where you know your power will eventually erode."[1] As you will see in Chapter 3 of the text (on supply and demand), this remark is indicative of the long-run shift of new entrants into a market where economic profit is being earned. Managers such as the CEO of Sun who understand this fundamental aspect of competition and are prepared to take appropriate actions will succeed in spite of the inevitable pressures from the new entrants.

Another example of the relevance of microeconomic theory to today's decision makers can be found in a conversation that one of us recently had with a student. This particular student worked as a manager for a large life insurance company. During the classes in which the theory of production was discussed (see Chapter 7), she continually asked about the relevance of production isoquants and isocosts as well as the importance of dealing in such a quantitative fashion with the production process. On the last day of class, she said that, to her surprise, the concepts learned in the study of the production function had actually been applied in a recent business case. It seems that some of the executives of the company wanted to store documents on compact discs (CD-ROM) instead of on microfilm, as was the current practice. One of the managers, who was opposed to this move, claimed that this would be far too costly for the firm. The student remarked that, upon hearing this argument, she immediately thought about the isoquant-isocost example. She recalled that the main teaching point was that a firm should reallocate its resources if the extra product relative to the extra cost was greater in one activity than in another. She immediately ordered a study to ascertain what her firm would gain in productivity by switching to compact discs. As she expected, the study found that fewer people would be required to handle the discs compared to the microfilm and that the retrieval time is much faster for discs than for microfilm. Thus, switching to compact discs may be more costly to the firm, but it would also be more *cost-effective*. She summarized the story by saying that "knowledge of the production theory gave me the insight to ask the right questions and to tell my staff what data I needed to make a decision."

We present these examples here because we are well aware of the reputation that economics courses have among some business students of being "too theoretical and not practical enough for the real world." In our opinion, biased as

---

[1] "The Smart Alecks at Sun Are Regrouping," *New York Times*, April 28, 1991.

it may be, nothing could be further from the truth. We know that the instructors in managerial economics will agree with us on this matter. We hope that this text will serve as a solid supplement to their classroom efforts to demonstrate to their students the importance and utility of economic theory for everyday decision making.

This text is designed for upper level undergraduate courses and first year MBA courses in managerial economics and applied economics. Very often, we have found that students enter the managerial economics course with varying degrees of knowledge of the subject. Some have undergraduate majors in economics; others have not studied economics at all in college. The majority of students have had at least one year of study in economic principles (macro and micro) but have forgotten many of the details since taking these courses as freshmen or sophomores. The first two chapters are a general introduction to economics and economic reasoning, and Chapter 3 reviews the basic elements of supply and demand theory. The appendix in Chapter 2 reviews the mathematics that will be used throughout the text.

We have purposely limited the use of calculus in this text. By and large, we will rely on numerical tables and graphs to illustrate the quantitative aspects of the economic terms and concepts. For those instructors and students who desire the economy of expression gained by using calculus, we have presented a brief mathematical appendix at the end of a chapter or a brief mathematical section within a chapter when the use of calculus is indicated.

In addition to discussing the applications of economic theory to the firm, our text (as is the custom with all texts in managerial economics) includes chapters on various tools of analysis that are helpful to managerial decision making but are not a part of the core of traditional microeconomic theory. They are demand, production and cost estimation using regression analysis, forecasting, linear programming, capital budgeting, and risk analysis. Given the constraints of space as well as the scope of this text, we can only present general introductions to these topics. Readers are probably well aware that these subjects are a substantial part of other courses in the business curriculum. Regression analysis is a key part of a course in advanced statistics or forecasting, linear programming is an important part of a course in operations research, and capital budgeting and risk analysis are important topics in managerial finance classes. (Certain advanced courses in finance may devote an entire semester to capital budgeting.) Another subject, the role of government, can often be found in microeconomic texts under the heading of market externalities. However, this topic is also a major part of another course (usually a course on "business and society"). But here, again, we have space enough only to treat this material in an introductory manner (see chapter 16).

We first met at IBM's International Finance, Planning, and Administration School (IFPA) in Briarcliff, New York. (Paul Keat was a manager of academic courses—including managerial economics—and Philip Young was on leave from Pace University, serving as the first visiting professor to IBM/IFPA.) Part of our responsibility at the school was to teach a course in managerial economics to IBM managers and professionals both in the United States and in Europe. Many of the examples and approaches to explaining the material in this text were developed while we worked together teaching the course.

Ancillary Materials

A computer diskette with more than two dozen programs will be furnished to each adopter. These programs, which are intended to help students solve some of the questions raised in text discussions, are written in Lotus 1-2-3™. The program on the diskette, entitled Intro, provides an index of the various programs.

An instructor's manual and test bank is available. The volume provides answers to all questions and problems in the text, as well as a group of multiple choice and short-answer questions. Also, it includes a description of the soft drink industry with additional information about "situations" and "solutions" contained in the text. This will enable instructors to use the situations more extensively in class.

Acknowledgments

We wish to thank our colleagues at the American Graduate School of International Management (AGSIM), Pace, IBM, and other firms where we have worked as consultants for their assistance and encouragement. In particular, Professor Hassan K. Hosseini of AGSIM provided a helpful review of Chapter 9. Professor Farrokh Hormozi of Pace was very helpful in the preparation of Chapter 5. Brad Fox of Pacific Bell and Gary Carr of NYNEX provided us with key data and insights into the changing regulatory environment in the telecommunications industry. We are especially grateful to William Spellman (former director of the International Finance, Planning, and Administration School of IBM) and Tony Bonaparte (former Dean of the Lubin Schools of Business at Pace University) for giving us the opportunity to work together and to become good friends as well as colleagues.

We also wish to thank the following reviewers:

Lewis Freiberg, Northeastern Illinois University
Richard A. Jenner, San Francisco State University
Peter Brust, University of Tampa
Yale L. Meltzer, College of Staten Island
Daryl N. Winn, University of Colorado
Edward H. Heinze, Valparaiso University
Jerry Manahan, Midwestern State University
Yien-I Tu, University of Arkansas
Frederica Shockley, California State University–Chico
Jan Palmer, Ohio University–Athens
Leila J. Pratt, The University of Tennessee at Chattanooga
Mo-Yin Tam, University of Illinois at Chicago
Al Holtmann, University of Miami
L.B. Pulley, University of Virginia
Richard Winkelman, Arizona State University

John Conant, Indiana State University
Robert Britt, West Virginia University
George Hoffer, Virginia Commonwealth University
Roy Savoian, Lynchburg College
Charles Callahan, State University of New York at Brockport
William Doyle Smith

In closing, we would like to express our appreciation to Jill Lectka, our acquisitions editor at Macmillan, and Rebecca Tan, her assistant, for all their help and encouragement. We are also most grateful to Sarah Troutt, production editor, and Dave Mason, copy editor. We would also like to acknowledge Everett Berling, Beverly Boswell, Alicia Latkovski, and Christopher Vukich, graduate students at AGSIM, and Wayne Chu, George John, and Mayura Tatachar, of Pace University, for their research assistance; and Frances Young, for her work in preparing the manuscript.

About the Authors

Paul G. Keat is currently Associate Professor of World Business at the American Graduate School of International Management at Glendale, Arizona. Prior to assuming this position he was, for many years, associated with the International Business Machines Corporation in professional and managerial capacities.

His education includes a B.B.A. in accounting from the Baruch School of the City University of New York, an M.A. from Washington University, and a Ph.D. in economics from the University of Chicago.

He began his IBM career in the department of economic research and then moved into the long-range planning area. Later, as a member of the finance function, he spent several years at IBM's European headquarters in Paris, as manager in the financial planning area, and then as the financial manager for the company's European software business. After his return to the United States he served as manager in the pricing area of one of the company's manufacturing groups. Before leaving IBM in 1987 he was associated with the company's International Finance, Planning and Administration School (IFPA), where he taught managerial economics, lectured on finance in a number of company-related courses, and managed academic courses. He also taught at the IBM's IFPA school at La Hulpe, Belgium.

He has taught at several U.S. universities, including Washington University, CUNY, and Iona College. He was an adjunct professor of finance at the Lubin Graduate School of Business at Pace University, and he also taught in Pace's Executive MBA program.

Philip K. Y. Young is currently Professor of Economics at the Lubin Graduate School of Business of Pace University (New York). His experiences at Pace include serving as the Executive Director of Corporate Programs for the Lubin Schools of Business. In this capacity, he was responsible for the management and development of Pace's Executive MBA Program and all of Pace's corporate educational and training programs. He is also the recipient of Pace University's outstanding teacher award.

He served as the first visiting professor at the International Finance, Planning, and Administration School of the IBM Corporation, where he developed and taught courses for IBM both in the United States and in La Hulpe, Belgium.

He has published articles in a number of areas, including ethnic entrepreneurship, investment prospects in the Pacific Basin, and computers and office productivity. In addition to his teaching and research, he is an active participant in training and education programs for major corporations in the telecommunications, computer, and financial services industries. He teaches these courses in the United States, Europe, and Latin America. He also teaches courses for IBM on television via its interactive satellite network.

He has a B.A. from the University of Hawaii, a master's in international affairs from Columbia University, and a Ph.D. in economics from New York University.

Contents

CHAPTER 9

Linear Programming 336

CHAPTER 10

The Estimation of Production and Cost Functions 360

CHAPTER 11

Market Structure and Output and Pricing Decisions 400

CHAPTER 15

Risk and Uncertainty 548

CHAPTER 16

The Role of Government in the Market Economy 580

Appendix 617

Index 633

MANAGERIAL ECONOMICS

"Nobody cares whether I drink Coke or Pepsi."

CHAPTER 1

Introduction

The Situation

The last of the color slides was barely off the screen when Bob Burns, the CEO of Global Foods, Inc., turned to his board of directors to raise the question that he had been waiting all week to ask. "Well, ladies and gentlemen, are you with me in this new venture? Is it a 'go'? Shall we get into the soft drink business?"

"It's not that easy, Bob. We need some time to think it over. You're asking us to endorse a very major *decision,* one that will have a long-term impact on the direction of the company.

"I appreciate your wish to deliberate further, Dr. Breakstone," Bob responded, "but I would like to reach a decision today. As the president of a major university, you have been especially valuable in advising this company in matters relating to social and governmental policies. But we must diversify our business very soon in order to maintain the steady growth in profits that we have achieved in recent years. As my presentation showed, the manufacturing and marketing of our own brand of soft drink is one of the best ways to do this. It represents a significant diversification, yet it is very closely related to our core business: food.

"The *economics* of the soft drink market tell us that we would be foolish to pass up the kind of *investment return* that the market offers to those newcomers willing to take the *risk.* The food business is generally a mature one. On the other hand, our *forecast* indicates that there is still a lot of room for growth in the soft drink market. To be sure, there is a tremendous amount of *competition* from the 'red team' and the 'blue team.' But we already have expertise in the food business, and it should carry over into the beverage market."

"That's just it, Bob," interjected another board member. "Are we prepared to take this risk? You yourself acknowledged that the *market power* wielded by the two dominant companies in this business is not to be taken lightly. Others have tried to take market share from them and have failed miserably. Moreover, the projections that you

(Continued)

have shown for a growing soft drink market are based on the *assumption* that the growth rate will remain the same as it has been in the past 10 years or so. As we all know, the soft drink market has been growing, but it has also been very fickle. Only recently, Americans were on a health kick, and fruit juices and bottled waters along with health foods were in fashion. Now it seems that soft drinks are back in style again. Who knows what people will want in the 1990s? Maybe we'll all go back to drinking five cups of coffee a day. And what about all the money that we're going to have to spend up front to *differentiate* our product? As you well know, in the processed-food business, establishing brand recognition—not to mention brand loyalty—can be extremely difficult and costly."

"Well, ladies and gentlemen, all your concerns are certainly legitimate ones, and believe me, I have given much thought to these drawbacks. This is one of the biggest decisions that I will have made since becoming CEO. My staff has spent hundreds of hours analyzing all available data to arrive at a judgment. Our findings indicate a strong probability of earning an above-average return on an investment in the soft drink business, a return commensurate with the kind of risk we know exists in that market. But if we could make all our decisions with 100 percent certainty simply by feeding numbers into a computer, we'd all be out of a job. To be sure, details on production, cost, pricing, distribution, advertising, financing, and organizational structure remain to be ironed out. However, if we wait until all these details are worked out, we may be missing a window of opportunity that might not appear again in this market for a long time. I say that we should go ahead with this project as soon as possible. And unanimity among the board members will give me greater confidence in this endeavor."

Introduction: Economics and Managerial Decision Making

Economics is "the study of the behavior of human beings in producing, distributing, and consuming material goods and services in a world of scarce resources."[1] Managerial economics is a discipline that combines economic theory with managerial practice. Joel Dean, the author of the first managerial economics textbook, defined this field of study as the "use of economic analysis in the formulation of business policies." A noted academician as well as a business consultant, Dean observed that there was a "big gap between the problems of logic that intrigue economic theorists and the problems of policy that plague practical management [that] needs to be bridged in order to give executives access to the practical contributions that economic thinking can make to top-management policies."[2]

[1] Campbell McConnell, *Economics*, New York: McGraw-Hill, 1987, p. 1.

[2] Joel Dean, *Managerial Economics*, Englewood Cliffs, N. J.: Prentice-Hall, 1951, p. vii.

To be sure, a textbook on the use of economic theory in managerial decision making does present a considerable challenge in light of the abstract nature of the subject matter. Most students who have taken economics courses (particularly those beyond the introductory level, such as intermediate microeconomics) will attest to the highly complex and quantitative nature of their content. But the authors of this volume firmly believe that economic theory has much to offer in the managerial decision-making process. Let us briefly discuss the reasons for this belief.

To start with, it is important for managers to be versed in economics because it is part of the basic vocabulary of business analysis and problem solving. In the situation presented at the beginning of this chapter, many economic terms and concepts were used in the discussion between the CEO and the board of directors. (These terms are italicized for your reference.) In this situation, the CEO of the hypothetical Global Foods, Inc., is asking the board of directors to ratify a decision to enter the soft drink market. He feels that the "economics"[3] of his analysis supports this decision. That is, the company can expect to be rewarded for its efforts in a manner consistent with the risk that it will be taking in the project. Among the factors taken into account in assessing the desirability of this venture were (1) the anticipated market demand for soft drinks, (2) the degree of competition in the market, (3) the extent of the market power held by existing firms, and (4) the importance of establishing product differentiation in order to compete with the other firms in the market. In addition, one of the board members strongly felt that much of the success of this venture hinged on the validity of the assumption made about the future tastes and preferences of consumers.

But there is no need to rely on a hypothetical situation to be convinced of the importance of economic literacy in managerial decision making. Economic terms and concepts can be found in virtually all periodicals that report business news, including such standards as the *Wall Street Journal*, *Business Week*, *Fortune*, and the *New York Times*. Take, for example, an interview with various analysts of the "hospitality" industry (i.e., hotels and motels) reported in the *Wall Street Journal*. When asked about the prospects for the industry in 1989, three analysts had this to say:

> Analyst #1: "Look for continuing problems due to supply exceeding demand and an increase in the cost of capturing occupancy as the industry remains competitive."
>
> Analyst #2: "There will be a reasonably healthy, modest room rate increase of 3–4 percent and flat to slightly higher occupancy levels."

---

[3]Experience in industry indicates that the word *economics* is often used in conjunction with a particular product, industry, or business practice (e.g., the "economics of the travel and entertainment business" or the "economics of hiring supplemental workers"). Used in this manner, it becomes a sort of shorthand phrase for "desirability" or "undesirability," as the case may be. For example, one might hear a manager say, "I don't think that the economics of the travel business justifies expanding the number of our branch offices."

> Analyst #3: "Supply and demand are roughly in equilibrium. While the rate of new construction has slowed dramatically since the mid-1980s, this in all likelihood will be offset by a slowdown in the growth of the economy."[4]

Apparently, the three were not in agreement about the prospects for the industry in 1989. As you can see, their forecasts were based on key assumptions about such economic factors as supply and demand and the state of the overall economy.

In addition to providing a useful vocabulary, the theory of economics itself can provide much assistance to managerial decision making. William Baumol, a well-respected economist and an active consultant to industry stressed this point in an article appropriately entitled "What Can Economic Theory Contribute to Managerial Economics?" In Baumol's view, an economic theorist is a model builder *par excellence* and can use this ability to take any business problem, no matter how complex, break it down into essential components, and describe the relationship among the components, thereby facilitating a systematic search for an optimal solution. In short, Baumol believes economic theory is helpful to managers because it offers them a set of analytical methods to solve their problems. Furthermore, in his extensive experience as an advisor to government and industry, every problem that he has worked on was helped by the "method of reasoning involved in the derivation of some economic theorem."[5]

William H. Meckling, the former dean of the Graduate School of Management at the University of Rochester, expressed a similar sentiment in an interview conducted by the *Wall Street Journal.* In Meckling's view, "Economics is a discipline that can help students solve the sort of problems they meet within the firm." Recalling his experience as the director of naval warfare analysis at the Center for Naval Analysis and as an economic analyst at the Rand Corporation, one of the nation's most prominent think tanks, Meckling stated that these institutions are "dominated by physical scientist types, really brilliant people." But he went on to say that "the economists knew how to structure the problems . . . the rest of the people knew a lot about technical things but they had never thought about how you structure big issues."[6]

The third type of contribution that economics can make to managerial decision making entails certain quantitative techniques often employed in economic analysis. For example, statistical techniques such as regression analysis are used by economists to estimate demand, production, and cost functions. (Indeed, a major field of study in economics is *econometrics,* the application of statistical techniques to economic problems.) Another aspect of statistical analysis, probability theory, is used in the economic analysis of risk. In addition, economists use various optimization techniques such as linear programming in their study

---

[4]"Analysts Examine Key Market Indicators," special section on business travel, *Wall Street Journal,* January 9, 1989.

[5]William Baumol, "What Can Economic Theory Contribute to Managerial Economics?" *American Economic Review,* 51, 2 (May 1961), p. 144.

[6]"Economics Has Much to Teach the Businessman," *Wall Street Journal,* May 3, 1983.

	Economic terms and concepts	*Economic models*	*Quantitative analysis*
Managerial decisions	Supply, demand, competition, cost structure, economies of scale, etc.	Determination of equilibrium price and output, setting of a profit-maximizing level of output, etc.	Regression analysis, linear programming, model building with the use of calculus, etc.

Figure 1.1 Managerial Economics—A Blend of Economics and Management Decision Making

of the behavior of a firm. They have also found it most efficient to express their models of behavior by firms and consumers in terms of the symbols and logic of calculus.

Figure 1.1 summarizes our discussion of the three principal ways in which economics relates to managerial decision making, forming the basis for managerial economics as a distinct area of study.

A Brief Review of Important Economic Terms and Concepts

For purposes of study and teaching, economics is divided into two broad categories, microeconomics and macroeconomics. The former concerns the study of individual consumers and producers in specific markets, and the latter deals with the aggregate economy. Topics in microeconomics include supply and demand in individual markets, the pricing of specific outputs and inputs (also called factors of production, or resources), production and cost structures for individual goods and services, and the distribution of income and output in the population. Topics in macroeconomics include analysis of the gross national product (also referred to as "national income analysis"), unemployment, inflation, fiscal and monetary policy, and the trade and financial relationships among nations.

Microeconomics is the category that is more utilized in managerial economics. However, certain aspects of macroeconomics must also be included because decisions by managers of firms are influenced by their views of the current and future conditions of the macroeconomy. In the example cited earlier, the third analyst of the hospitality industry noted the adverse impact that the anticipated slowdown in the economy would have on this particular industry. As another example, we can well imagine that the management of a company producing capital equipment (e.g., computers, machine tools, trucks, or robotic instruments) would indeed be remiss if they did not factor into their sales forecast some consideration of the macroeconomic outlook. For these and other companies whose businesses are particularly sensitive to the business cycle, a recession would have a very unfavorable effect on their sales, whereas a robust period of economic expansion would be beneficial. But for the most part, managerial economics is based on the variables, models, and concepts that embody microeconomic theory.

As defined in the previous section, economics is the study of how choices are made regarding the use of scarce resources in the production, consumption, and distribution of goods and services. The key term is *scarce resources.* Scarcity can be defined as a condition in which resources are not available to satisfy all the needs and wants of a specified group of people. Although scarcity refers to the supply of a resource, it makes sense only in relation to the demand for the resource. For example, there is only one Mona Lisa. Therefore, we can safely say that the supply of this particular work of art by da Vinci is limited. Nevertheless, if for some strange reason no one wanted this magnificent work of art, then in purely economic terms it would not be considered scarce. Let us take a less extreme and certainly more mundane example: broken glass on the streets of New York City. Here we have a case of a "resource" that is not scarce not only because there is a lot of broken glass to be found, but also because nobody wants it! Now suppose there is a new art movement inspired by the use of materials retrieved from the streets of urban areas, with broken glass from the streets of New York being particularly desirable. The once-plentiful resource would fast become a "scarce" commodity.

The relative nature of scarcity is represented in Figure 1.2 As can be seen in the figure, the supply of resources is used to meet the demand for these resources by the population. Because the population's needs and wants exceed the ability of the resources to satisfy all the demands, scarcity exists.

In an introductory economics course, the concept of scarcity is usually discussed in relation to an entire country and its people. For example, you will probably recall from your first course in economics the classic example of "guns" (representing a country's devotion of resources to national defense) versus "butter" (representing the use of resources for peacetime goods and services). To be sure, scarcity is a condition individual consumers and producers must also deal with. This text is primarily concerned with the way in which managers of the producing organizations contend with scarcity. But before discussing this particular aspect of the problem, let us review the condition of scarcity from the perspective of an entire country.

The intent of the "guns versus butter" example is to illustrate that scarcity forces a country to choose the amounts of resources that it wishes to allocate

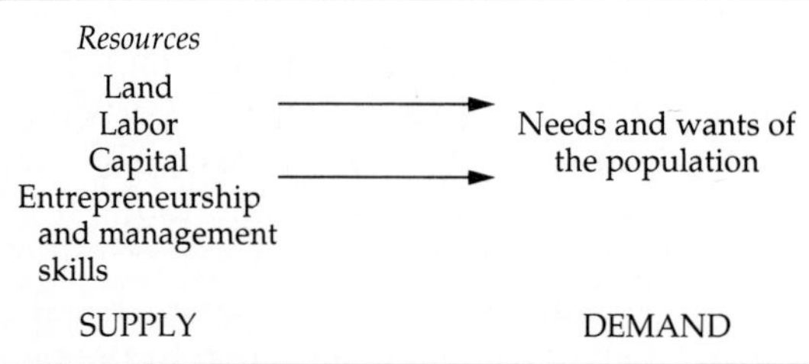

Figure 1.2 Supply, Demand, and Scarcity

between defense and peacetime goods and services. In so doing, its people must reckon with the *opportunity cost* of their decision. This type of cost can be defined as the amount or subjective value that must be sacrificed in choosing one activity over the next best alternative. In the "guns versus butter" example, one activity involves the production of war goods and services, and the other pertains to peacetime goods and services. Because of the scarcity of resources, the more that the country allocates to guns, the less it will have to produce butter, and vice versa. The opportunity cost of additional units of guns are the units of butter that the country must forgo in the resource allocation process. The opposite would apply as resources are allocated more for the production of butter than for guns.

In the presence of a limited supply relative to demand, countries must decide how to allocate their scarce resources. This decision is central to the study of economics. In fact, economics has been defined as "the science which studies human behavior as a relationship between ends and scarce means which have alternative uses."[7] Essentially, the allocation decision can be viewed as comprising three separate choices:

1. *What* goods and services should be produced and in what quantities?
2. *How* should these goods and services be produced?
3. *For whom* should these goods and services be produced?

These are the well-known *what, how,* and *for whom* questions found in the introductory chapter of all economic principles textbooks.

The first question incorporates the "guns versus butter" decision. Should a country with scarce resources produce guns? Should it produce butter? If so, how much butter and how many guns? The same applies to the countless other goods and services or product groups that a country is capable of producing.

The second question involves the allocation of a country's resources in the production of a particular good or service. Suppose a country decides to produce a certain amount of butter. What amounts of land, labor, capital, and entrepreneurial efforts should it devote to this end? Should it use more workers than machinery (a labor-intensive process) or vice versa (a capital-intensive process)? The important point to remember about this question is that it is an economic and not a technical one. It is not asking which formula or recipe should be used to make butter; it is asking what combination of the factors of production should be used in producing a given amount of the product.

The meaning of the third question should be readily apparent. It is a decision that must be made about the distribution of a country's output of goods and services among the members of its population.

All countries must deal with these three basic questions because all have scarce resources. Scarcity is a more serious problem in some countries than in others, but all have needs and wants that cannot be completely met by their

[7] Lionel Robbins, *An Essay on the Nature and Significance of Economic Science*, 2nd ed., London: Macmillan & Co., Ltd., 1935, p. 16. Interested students are encouraged to read this classic in the literature of microeconomics.

existing resources. Precisely how these countries go about making allocation decisions is the question to which we now turn.

There are essentially three ways a country can answer the questions of what, how, and for whom. These ways, referred to as *processes*, are as follows:

1. *Market process*: The use of supply, demand, and material incentives to answer the questions of what, how, and for whom.
2. *Command process*: The use of the government or some central authority to answer the three basic questions. (This process is sometimes referred to as the *political process.*)
3. *Traditional process*: The use of customs and traditions to answer the three basic questions.

Countries generally employ a combination of these three processes to allocate their scarce resources. The market process is predominant in the United States, although the command process plays an important role. Hence, the United States is said to have a mixed economy. Based on the levels of spending by the federal, state, and local governments, we can state that approximately one-fifth of the goods and services produced in the United States are influenced by the command process.[8] The command process does not necessarily mean that a government literally orders the production of certain amounts of guns, butter, or other goods or services; rather, a government may use the material incentives of the market process to allocate resources in certain ways, a process often referred to as *indirect command*. For example, the government offers defense contractors the opportunity to earn a profit by producing military goods and services. In addition, the government can control the allocation of resources in a more direct way through various laws governing the actions of both consumers and producers. For example, the government controls manufacturing and distribution through such agencies as the Food and Drug Administration. It attempts to control consumer use of certain foods and drugs through various laws and regulations. A simple but important example of this pertains to the tobacco industry. Over the past several decades, the U.S. government has made determined efforts to convince people to stop smoking. These efforts range from warnings on cigarette packages to the banning of smoking on airline flights. Prohibition during the 1920s offers another example of the government's efforts to stop the consumption of certain goods or services.

In addition to using rules and regulations and its fiscal power, the government can also influence the allocation of scarce resources through subsidies, tariffs, and quotas. Further discussion of these aspects of the command process in the U.S. economy is found in other sections of this chapter and throughout the rest of the text. In fact, the final chapter is devoted to a discussion of the role of government in the market economy.

---

[8]Spending by the federal government for goods and services for fiscal year 1990 was about $440 billion. State and local spending during this time period was approximately $700 billion. The nominal GNP in 1990 was $5.5 trillion. (*Economic Report of the President*, 1991.)

The traditional process is also at work in the U.S. economy, but this process can be better understood by considering its impact on different countries throughout the world, particularly those whose economies are still developing. Examples of the traditional process are found in the eating habits, and in the patterns of work and social interaction in such countries. Two examples of how the traditional process influences the allocation of scarce resources are religious restrictions on certain foods, such as beef and pork, and hiring practices based primarily on familial relationships. A branch of anthropology called economic anthropology is particularly concerned with the impact of customs and traditions on the economic questions of what, how, and for whom. In the business curriculum, students will find this subject of particular importance in courses on international business.

Because of the predominance of the market process in the U.S. economy, our discussion of the allocation of scarce resources is based on the assumption that managers operate primarily through the mechanisms of supply, demand, and material incentive (i.e., the profit motive). Their decisions about what goods to produce, how they should be produced, and for whom they should be produced are essentially market-oriented. That is, firms choose to produce certain goods and services because, given the demand for these products and the cost of using scarce resources, they can earn sufficient profit to justify their particular use of these resources. Moreover, they combine their scarce resources to produce maximum output in the least costly way. Finally, they supply these goods and services to those segments of the population expected to provide the most material reward for their efforts.

Table 1.1 compares the three basic questions from the standpoint of a country and from the standpoint of a company. From the firm's point of view, question 1 is the product decision. At some particular time, a firm may decide to provide new or different goods or services or to stop providing a particular good or service. For example, in 1986 General Electric decided to withdraw from the small appliances business and sold this part of the company to Black and Decker. Late in 1988 IBM decided to stop producing telecommunications equipment and sold its Rolm division to Siemens, the German multinational conglomerate. The decision by the Coca-Cola Company to replace its mainstay product with "New Coke" and its subsequent decision to produce the old product once again under the label "Coca-Cola Classic" is another example of the product decision.

Question 2 is a basic part of a manager's responsibility. It involves personnel practices such as hiring and firing as well as questions concerning the purchase

Table 1.1 The Three Basic Economic Questions

From the Standpoint of a Country	*From the Standpoint of a Company*
1. What goods and services should be produced?	1. The product decision
2. How should these goods and services be produced?	2. The hiring, staffing, procurement, and capital-budgeting decisions
3. For whom should these goods and services be produced?	3. The market segmentation decision

of items ranging from raw materials to capital equipment. For example, the decision to automate certain clerical activities using a network of personal computers results in a more capital-intensive mode of production. The resolution to use more supplementary, part-time workers in place of full-time workers is another example of a management decision concerning how goods and services should be produced. A third example involves the selection of materials in the production of a certain item (e.g., the combination of steel, aluminum, and plastic used in an automobile).

The firm's decision concerning question 3 is not completely analogous to that of a country. Actually, a firm's decision regarding market segmentation (a term used in the marketing field) is closely related to question 1 for a country. In deciding what segment of the market to focus on, the firm is not literally deciding who gets the good or service. For example, suppose a firm decides to target a certain demographic segment by selling only a "high-end" or premium version of a product. In a free-market economy, this would not prevent anyone from buying the product. However, the way in which a company markets the product (which includes its pricing and distribution policies) makes certain segments of the market more likely to purchase the product.[9]

Perhaps one of the best ways to link the economic problem of making choices under conditions of scarcity with the tasks of a manager is to consider the view put forth by Professor Robert Anthony that a manager is essentially a person who is responsible for the allocation of a firm's scarce resources.[10]

It is interesting to note that "managers" or "management skills" was not delineated as a separate factor of production by early economic theorists. The four traditional categories of resources are land, labor, capital, and entrepreneurship. The last category can be treated as broad enough to include management, but the two classifications do involve different characteristics or skills.

The term *entrepreneurship* is generally associated with the ownership of the means of production. But in addition, it implies an owner's willingness to take certain risks in the pursuit of his or her goals (e.g., starting a new business, producing a new product, or providing a different kind of service). Management, on the other hand, involves the ability to organize and administer various

---

[9] A decision by the Corning Glass Works regarding its production of sunglasses illustrates this point. Some time ago the firm made a decision to stop producing low-priced glasses, usually sold in pharmacies and discount stores, and to develop and sell a high-priced product generally sold by specialty department stores, sunglass boutiques, and opticians. The product, given the brand name "Serengeti," is sold at an average retail price of $80 and is meant to appeal to an "upscale" segment of consumers (presumably those who drive expensive sports cars and wear fashionable clothing).

[10] Actually, Anthony divided the planning and control process in a firm into three activities: strategic planning (i.e., setting the firm's overall objectives), management control (i.e., making sure that scarce resources are obtained and used effectively and efficiently in the firm's accomplishment of its objectives), and operational control (i.e., making sure that specific tasks are carried out effectively and efficiently). These ideas were first put forth in R. N. Anthony, *Planning and Control Systems: A Framework for Analysis*, Boston: Harvard Business School, Division of Research, 1965.

tasks in pursuit of certain objectives. An important part of a manager's job is to monitor and guide people in an organization. In the words of Peter Drucker, who has been called "the founding father of the science of management,"

> It is "management" that determines what is needed and what has to be achieved [in an organization].... Management is work. Indeed, it is the specific work of a modern society, the work that distinguishes our society from all earlier ones.... As work, management has its own skills, its own tools, its own techniques.[11]

Part of being a good manager involves taking risks, so experts have advised managers to become more "entrepreneurial." By the same token, entrepreneurs may require professional management expertise to run their venture more effectively. One of the more celebrated examples of this can be seen in the replacement of Steven Jobs, the cofounder of the Apple, Inc., by John Scully as the CEO of the corporation. Jobs is perhaps the quintessential entrepreneur in today's world of high technology. Yet, for reasons beyond the scope of this text, it was decided that the task of running the company was better carried out by a professional manager. Eventually, Jobs left Apple to start new ventures in the computer field.[12]

Some economists cite management skills as a separate factor of production. Others include them in the general category of entrepreneurship. Still others combine entrepreneurship and management skills into one category, as we have done. An interesting treatment of the subject was given by Alfred Marshall, whose work in economic theory about 100 years ago still provides much of the foundation for modern microeconomics. Marshall used the building trade to illustrate certain differences between managerial and entrepreneurial skills and activities. According to Marshall, an individual may well be able to manage the construction of his own home even though he is less efficient than a professional contractor. However, it is another matter when housing construction is carried out on a large scale.

> When this [housing construction] is done on a large scale, as for instance in opening a new suburb, the stakes at issue are so large as to offer an attractive field to powerful capitalists with a very high order of general business ability, but perhaps with not much technical knowledge of the building trade. They rely on their own judgment for the decision as to what are likely to be the coming relations of demand and supply for different kinds of houses; but they entrust to others the *management of details* [emphasis added]. They employ architects and surveyors to make plans in accordance with their general directions; and then enter into contracts with professional builders for carrying them out. But they themselves *undertake the chief risks of the business* [emphasis added], and control its general direction.[13]

---

[11] Peter Drucker, *Management*, New York: Harper & Row, 1973, p. xi.

[12] See Lee Butcher, *Accidental Millionaire: The Rise and Fall of Steve Jobs at Apple Computer*, New York: Paragon House, 1988.

[13] Alfred Marshall, *Principles of Economics*, 8th ed., Philadelphia: Porcupine Press, 1920, reprinted 1982, pp.245–46. (First edition published in 1890.)

You may be somewhat surprised at the freshness of observations made a century ago. You may also feel that Marshall was referring simply to management tasks and responsibilities at different levels. Putting Marshall's ideas in terms of today's large corporation, what he refers to as "the decision as to what are likely to be the coming relations of demand and supply" most likely involve strategic decisions made by upper management. What he terms "the management of details" are usually carried out by lower levels of management (e.g., by first-line supervisors).

Regardless of how the classification is handled, it is important to be aware of the distinction between the two factors. Obviously, the content of this text is devoted to developing management skills. Nonetheless, a mastery of the economic principles presented in this book could well lead to a sharpening of one's entrepreneurial skills, to an extent that would help one to assess the market conditions and risks involved in a particular venture.

The Case of Global Foods, Inc.: Situations and Solutions

Prior sections of this chapter cited various reasons why an understanding of economics is important to managerial decision making. An effective way of demonstrating this importance is to cite real-world examples gleaned from the popular press and distilled from the findings of research studies on the use of economics in managerial decision making. All other texts in managerial economics do this, and this book is no exception. But in addition, we hope to show how economic terms and concepts can be applied to managerial decision making through the use of a series of hypothetical situations such as the one presented at the beginning of this chapter. In fact, each chapter will begin with a *situation* requiring some sort of decision or action relating directly to the subject matter of the chapter. For example, in this chapter, a decision must be made about whether to enter the soft drink market. This is a fundamental business decision involving the allocation of a firm's scarce resources, a major theme of this chapter.

At the end of each chapter, a *solution* for the situation will be presented based on the knowledge gained from reading the chapter. We use the term *solution* rather loosely because it may not involve a specific answer, as one might expect in the solution to a mathematical problem. In our view, the ambiguity of a solution is very much in keeping with conditions in the real world. Very often in an actual business problem, there is no unique formula that one can use to compute the answer. Either the formula does not exist or is not entirely applicable to the problem, or the problem itself is not amenable to a straightforward quantitative solution technique. And even when a specific numerical solution is arrived at—as is the case in Chapter 14, on capital budgeting—there may be other considerations of a qualitative nature that temper the acceptability of the solution. Therefore, the solutions offered at the end of the chapters are only suggested outcomes of the situations. (You may wish to consider alternative ways for the managers depicted in the situations to deal with their tasks or problems.)

The situations used throughout the book are based on one industry and one firm in that industry. As you have already learned, we will be using the soft drink industry. Moreover, we will be following the trials and tribulations of the managers of Global Foods, Inc., and, in certain cases, the managers of firms that do business with Global. This will help to tie together the disparate aspects of economic analysis. Also, it is felt that a focus on one firm in one industry will create added interest in the events depicted in the situations, further motivating mastery of each chapter's material.

A number of industries were initially considered. The soft drink industry was chosen based on the following criteria:

1. The industry should be one that all readers can relate to as consumers.
2. The goods or services sold in the industry should be essentially nontechnical, and the means of production should be relatively easy for the layperson to understand.
3. The competitive environment should be very intense.
4. Information about the industry should be readily available (e.g., from trade journals and research monographs), and news about current activities in this industry should be frequently reported in the popular media.

The soft drink industry closely meets all of these criteria. Just about everyone consumes this product, and the product itself is rather simple: carbonated water, sweeteners, and various flavorings. The packaging is also uncomplicated. Soft drinks are sold today in 12-ounce aluminum cans, in 1- and 2-liter plastic bottles, and in glass bottles. The making of the syrup and the bottling of the beverage involve various manufacturing processes that are relatively easy to understand. The two most important trade publications in the soft drink industry are *Beverage World* and *Beverage Digest*. We found them to be excellent sources of background information on the industry. Moreover, the major soft drink companies are constantly reported on in major periodicals. Recent articles from these sources will be cited throughout the text.

The situations used in each chapter, along with the characters portrayed at Global, are entirely fictitious. However, the features of each situation closely resemble actual business problems or circumstances with which managers must often deal. The verity of the issues involved in each situation is based on the authors' experiences in private industry as well as on extensive interviews with managers from various companies in the soft drink business.[14] The following section gives a summary of the situations and solutions presented in the chapters. The main decisions to be made by the characters portrayed in the situations are included under the heading "Key Question."

---

[14]The authors are greatly indebted to various managers from a leading soft drink manufacturer and a major producer of high-fructose corn syrup. At their request, neither their names nor the names of their companies will be cited.

Summary of the Situations and Solutions

1 Introduction

Situation. Bob Burns, CEO of Global Foods, Inc., asks the board of directors to approve a decision to enter the soft drink business.

Key Question. "Should we enter the soft drink business?"

Solution. The Board approves the decision, and Global Foods enters the soft drink business.

2 The Goals of a Firm

Situation. Bob Burns, recently appointed CEO of Global Foods, must clarify and communicate the goals of the firm to its employees and shareholders.

Key Question. "What should our firm's goals be over the next three to five years?"

Solution. Bob establishes five key objectives for the firm to accomplish over the next three years.

3 Supply and Demand

Situation. Ross Harris, senior purchasing agent for Global Foods, and Kathy Martinez, staff associate for a major producer of high-fructose corn syrup (HFCS), must prepare studies for their respective companies as a prelude to a major contract negotiation between the suppliers and users of HFCS.

Key Question. "What is the best time period within which to lock in the price of HFCS?"

Solution. The suppliers and users of HFCS agree to a compromise in which the price of HFCS is to be established every 3 months instead of every 12 months.

4 Demand Elasticity

Situation. Henry Caulfield, the proprietor of a "Gas 'n Go" convenience store, must evaluate the desirability of various pricing schedules for soft drinks set by the major beverage companies.

Key Question. "For what price should I sell this new soft drink?"

Solution. He decides that the relative inelasticity of the products in question makes it difficult to increase sales by lowering the price.

5 Demand Estimation

Situation. Jennifer Harrah, senior research associate of a market research firm, is assigned the task of producing a statistical model that will help to explain the determinants of soft drink consumption. Her firm's client is Global Foods, Inc.

Key Question. "What are the key determinants of demand for soft drinks, and what are their quantitative impact on sales?"

Solution. Jennifer estimates the quantitative impact of a selected number of factors on soft drink sales with the use of multiple regression analysis.

6 FORECASTING

Situation. Frank Robinson, newly appointed head of Global's forecasting department, is asked to estimate the next year's sales of Citronade, the company's lemon-lime soda.

Key Question. "What will next year's sales for Citronade be?"

Solution. Frank uses a trend analysis, adjusted seasonally as well as cyclically to forecast the coming year's sales.

7 PRODUCTION

Situation. George Ernest, vice president of manufacturing, is concerned that the enthusiasts in the marketing department who favor the firm's entry into the soft drink market are not fully informed about the special challenges posed in the manufacturing of soft drinks. In George's view, their naiveté is evidenced by their desire to package the firm's product in returnable bottles as a means of differentiating it from the competition.

Key Question. "Should we package our soft drinks in returnable and refillable glass bottles?"

Solution. George recommends that the company not use this type of packaging because it is much more costly than nonreturnable aluminum cans and plastic bottles.

8 COST

Situation. Marie Jacobs, newly hired MBA, is assigned the task of identifying ways in which the company can be the industry's low-cost producer.

Key Question. "How can we become a low-cost producer in the industry?"

Solution. Marie identifies various short- and long-run measures to reduce the firm's cost of production. Of particular interest is her suggestion on the reshaping of the 12-ounce can to reduce the aluminum content of this particular packaging.

9 LINEAR PROGRAMMING

Situation. Jim Benson, distribution manager of the beverage division of Global Foods, is asked to evaluate the company's distribution system with an eye toward adding new warehouses to the system.

Key Questions. "What is the least costly distribution system? Should we add new warehouses?"

Solution. A linear programming approach to the problem indicates that it is not economically justifiable to add new warehouse capacity. However, Jim is asked by the management committee to consider other factors.

10 THE ESTIMATION OF PRODUCTION AND COST FUNCTIONS

Situation. Jill Corey is asked by the director of manufacturing to utilize available data to ascertain whether there is an optimal-size bottling plant, that is, a plant size with minimum unit cost.

Key Question. "Is there a plant size that will achieve the lowest possible unit cost?"

Solution. Jill utilizes cross-sectional regression analysis, which indicates that there is an optimal plant size.

11 MARKET STRUCTURE AND OUTPUT AND PRICING DECISIONS

Situation. Frank Robinson is appointed product manager of the new soft drink. One of his first tasks is to recommend a price for the product.

Key Question. "What price should we charge for our new soft drink?"

Solution. After analyzing the demand elasticity and short-run cost structure of the product, Frank recommends a price based on the MR = MC rule.

12 BREAK-EVEN ANALYSIS: VOLUME-COST-PROFIT

Situation. Suzanne Prescott, a senior analyst for the diet cola line of the firm's soft drink division, is asked to prepare a profit plan for the coming year.

Key Question. "What is the profit outlook for the coming year for our diet cola?"

Solution. She uses break-even analysis to forecast the coming year's profit for this particular product. She also uses sensitivity analysis to provide best-case and worst-case scenarios.

13 SPECIAL PRICING PRACTICES

Situation. Rebecca James must decide what price bid she should submit to a large airport caterer that wishes to award a contract to a single supplier.

Key Question. "How should bid price be set to give Global Foods a good shot at obtaining the large caterer's contract?"

Solution. Since demand elasticities differ in different markets, the price offered in this price-sensitive market will have to be sufficiently low to give Global a good chance of winning the contract.

14 CAPITAL BUDGETING

Situation. George Kline, the manager of Global's capital planning department, is considering two new project proposals. One involves the expansion of company activities into a new geographical region, and the other involves the purchase of a new depalletizing machine to replace the one currently in use.

Key Questions. "Should we expand into a new geographical area? Should we replace one of our depalletizers?"

Solution. Using capital budgeting techniques involving the calculation of net present value and internal rates of return, George recommends that the firm accept the first project proposal and reject the second one.

15 RISK AND UNCERTAINTY

Situation. George is asked by the firm's treasurer to consider the risk involved in going ahead with the project to expand into a new geographical area.

Key Question. "What is the extent of our risk in expanding our geographic area?"

Solution. After considering various acceptable ways to adjust a capital project for risk, George decides to rely primarily on sensitivity analysis. In addition to his original findings, George presents the treasurer with an optimistic and a pessimistic set of results.

16 THE ROLE OF GOVERNMENT

Situation. Bill Adams, the director of data and voice communications, believes Global Foods should consider using the telecommunications services of the local telephone company, rather than its own internal switching services.

Key Question. "What impact do government regulation and deregulation have on management decisions?"

Solution. Because of the changing regulatory environment of the telecommunications industry, the local phone company is able to offer Global Foods a full complement of telecommunications services at competitive prices.

The Solution

After about an hour of heated debate, Bob had a suggestion to make to the board. "Look, we've been discussing this to such an extent that perhaps the key arguments I made in my presentation have gotten lost or confused. Let me summarize the seven key reasons why we want to enter the soft drink business, and then let's vote on this matter.

1. *Outlook for the industry:* Prospects for growth in the industry continue to be strong. Therefore, we can expect the demand for our products to be a part of this positive industry trend.

2. *Market size and structure:* Although the industry is dominated by Coca-Cola and Pepsi-Cola, we believe there is still room for the entry of niche marketers. A number of regional and specialty companies have emerged over the past few years, particularly those offering sparkling fruit juices. We believe we can be as successful, if not more successful, than these new entrants.

3. *Manufacturing, packaging, and distribution:* Our experience in the manufacturing of food products will give us a significant head start when we enter the soft drink business. Moreover, we do not plan to build bottling facilities from scratch. Instead, we look to purchase and consolidate existing bottling plants currently owned and operated by independent firms or by multiple franchise operations. We are also encouraged by the number of new cost-reducing technologies that have been introduced and the fact that the cost of the artificial sweetener aspartame should decline when Monsanto's patent expires.

4. *Transportation and distribution:* We already have a well-managed fleet of vehi-

(Continued)

cles that deliver our food products. We also have important influence and contacts in the retail food business. These will be essential in establishing a presence on the shelves of supermarkets and convenience stores throughout the country.

5. *Pricing, advertising, and promotion:* As the "new kid on the block," we recognize that we will have to enter the market as a price follower. However, in time, as our products are developed and marketed, we should be able to establish some independence either to raise or lower our prices in comparison with the rest of the industry. As far as advertising and promotion are concerned, we have an excellent advertising agency that has served us well with our current product line. However, we shall be flexible enough to consider other agencies if the need arises. Moreover, our experience with various promotional programs (e.g., discount coupons through direct mail and magazine inserts) should be transferable to the soft drink industry. Most important, all advertising and promotional efforts should be greatly aided by the fact that our company name—Global Foods—enjoys a high degree of consumer recognition (along with the specific brand names of our products).

6. *New products:* As you have seen in the detailed report, we have exciting plans for several new products as well as a full line of naturally and artificially sweetened carbonated drinks. Through an independent market research company, we have tested consumer preferences for our new offerings. The results have been most satisfactory.

7. *Financial considerations:* As stated at the very beginning of this presentation, our main goal is to create value for our shareholders. We must continue to grow in a profitable manner if we are to continue satisfying the financial expectations of our shareholders. We compete in a mature industry that enables us to generate a considerable amount of cash from our current line of products with well-entrenched brand names. We believe that we should use this cash to expand into the soft drink business. As all our financial projections and analysis indicates, this effort should yield a rate of return that is more than enough to compensate us for the investment and its associated risk."

After hearing this executive summary, Bob Burns asked the board for a final decision. "All right, let's vote. All those in favor of entering the soft drink market? Opposed? Great, it's unanimous. Ladies and gentlemen, we're going into the soft drink business."

Summary

Managerial economics is a discipline that combines microeconomic theory with management practice. Microeconomics is the study of how choices are made to allocate scarce resources with competing uses. An important function of a manager is to decide how to allocate a firm's scarce resources. Examples of such decisions are the selection of a firm's products or services, the hiring of personnel, the assigning of personnel to particular functions or tasks, the purchase of materials and equipment, and the pricing of products and services.

This text will show how the application of economic theory and concepts help managers to make allocation decisions that are in the best economic interests of their firms.

Throughout the text, numerous examples will be cited to illustrate how economic theory and concepts can be applied to management decision making. References will also be made to business cases and economic events that have been reported in the popular press. However, a unique feature of this book is a unifying case study of a food and beverage company, Global Foods, Inc. Each chapter begins with a situation in which the managers of this firm have to make key economic decisions. The solutions that end the chapters suggest ways that economic analysis can assist in the decision-making process.

Important Concepts

Command process: The use of central planning and the directives of government authorities to answer the questions of *what, how,* and *for whom.*

Economic decisions for the firm: "What goods and services should be produced?"—the product decision. "How should these goods and services be produced?"—the hiring, staffing, and capital budgeting decision. "For whom should these goods and services be produced?"—the market segmentation decision.

Economics: The study of how choices are made under conditions of scarcity. The basic economic problem can be defined as: "What goods and services should be produced and in what quantities?" "How should these goods and services be produced?" "For whom should these goods and services be produced?"

Efficiency: In economic analysis, efficiency can be divided into two types: *economic efficiency* and *allocative efficiency* (also referred to as *effectiveness*). The former refers to the production of goods and services in the least costly manner. The latter refers to the production of goods and services in close accordance to consumer wants and needs.

Market process: The use of supply, demand, and material incentive to answer the questions of *what, how,* and *for whom.*

Opportunity cost: The amount or subjective value forgone in choosing one activity over the next best alternative. This cost must be considered whenever decisions are made under conditions of scarcity.

Resources: Also referred to as *factors of production* or *inputs,* economic analysis usually includes four basic types: land, labor, capital, and entrepreneurship. This chapter also included managerial skills as well as entrepreneurship.

Scarcity: A condition that exists when resources are limited relative to the demand for their use. In the market process, the extent of this condition is reflected in the price of resources or the goods and services they produce.

Traditional process: The use of customs and traditions to answer the questions of *what, how,* and *for whom.*

Questions

1. Define *scarcity* and *opportunity cost*. What role do these two concepts play in the making of management decisions?
2. Elaborate on the basic economic questions of *what, how,* and *for whom*. Provide specific examples of these questions with respect to the use of a *country's* scarce resources.
3. Following are examples of typical economic decisions made by the managers of a firm. Determine whether each is an example of *what, how,* or *for whom*.
   a. Should the company make its own spare parts or buy them from an outside vendor?
   b. Should the company continue to service the equipment that it sells or ask customers to use independent repair companies?
   c. Should a company expand its business to international markets or concentrate on the domestic market?
   d. Should the company replace its telephone operators with a computerized voice messaging system?
   e. Should the company buy or lease the fleet of trucks that it uses to transport its products to market?
4. Define the market process, the command process, and the traditional process. How does each process deal with the basic questions of *what, how* and *for whom*?
5. Discuss the importance of the command process and the traditional process in the making of management decisions? Ilustrate specific ways in which managers must take these two processes into account.
6. Explain the differences between management skills and entrepreneurship. Discuss how each factor contributes to the economic success of a business.
7. Compare and contrast microeconomics with macroeconomics. Although managerial economics is based primarily on microeconomics, explain why it is also important for managers to understand macroeconomics.
8. What do you think is the key to success in the soft drink industry? What chance do you think Global Foods has in succeeding in its new venture into the soft drink market? Explain. (Answer these questions on the basis of the information provided in the chapter as well as any other knowledge you might have about the food and beverage business.)
9. (Optional) Have you been personally involved in the making of a decision for a business concerning *what, how,* or *for whom*? If so, explain your rationale for making such decisions. Were these decisions guided by the market process, the command process, or the traditional process? Explain.

CHAPTER 2

The Goals of a Firm

The Situation

After the meeting, Bob Burns called in his staff for a quick debriefing as well as a rundown of all the tasks necessary to implement the decision to go into the soft drink business. He summoned his two administrative assistants, Karen Williams and John Depaoli, and his trusted advisor, Jeff Hartley, the chief financial officer of Global Foods, Inc.

Jeff began the discussion. "Well, Bob, if you want the honest truth, I thought everything went very well. However, if you stop and think about why some of the members of the board were resisting our proposal, you will realize that it wasn't because they were opposed to going into the soft drink business per se. It was because they didn't quite see how this move would fit into Global's overall objectives, both in the short run and in the long run."

"Karen, John, what do you think about Jeff's observation?" asked Bob.

Karen, somewhat hesitantly, spoke first. "I think that Jeff is right, Mr. Burns. We had a more difficult time convincing the board of directors about the wisdom of going into the soft drink market because they could not see clearly how it fit into the company's strategic goals. Even before our presentation, it should have been made very clear to them that the only way for food companies like ours to survive and create value for shareholders in an increasingly competitive industry is to grow at least as fast as the competition."

"I agree," John added. "As we showed the board in our presentation, the soft drink market has been growing much faster than the food-processing business. In looking for new sources of growth for our company, the soft drink business has to be considered as a top priority. But this would have been as obvious to the board as it is to us if they considered a primary goal of this firm to be a rate of growth that at least matches the rest of the industry.

"Of course, there are other goals besides growing faster than your competitors," continued Jeff. "What you have to do, Bob, is to state these goals as clearly and as simply as possible, not only to the board of directors, but to everyone in the company. After all, if

(Continued)

people know where they are headed, it's a lot easier to motivate them to work at their best for the company."

"All of you are quite right." Bob responded. "Ever since I took over the helm of this company, I've been totally preoccupied with increasing its profitability and finding new sources of growth. I just assumed everyone was clear on what I was trying to do. As basic as it might sound, what we need is a clearcut statement of our company's goals.

Introduction

Chapter 1 explained that managerial economics deals primarily with the problem of deciding how best to allocate a firm's scarce resources among competing uses. The best, or "optimal," decision is the one that enables the firm to meet its desired objectives most closely. This chapter will elaborate on the process of making decisions under conditions of scarcity by discussing the goals of a firms and the economic significance of the optimal decision. The appendix to this chapter explains the role of marginal analysis in economic decision making. This appendix also presents a review of the mathematics used in this text to illustrate key economic concepts and methods of analysis.

The Economic Goal of the Firm and Optimal Decision Making

Every business has a goal. Most students would assert that the primary goal of a business is to earn a certain amount of profit (i.e., to "make money"), and, in fact, the economic theory of the firm—the foundation on which much of managerial economics rests—assumes that the principal objective of a firm is to maximize its profits (or minimize its losses).[1] Thus, throughout this text, unless otherwise stated, we will assume this same objective.

To be sure, there are many other goals that a firm can pursue, relating to market share, revenue growth, return on investment, technology, customer satisfaction, and shareholder value (i.e., maximizing the price of its stock). It is crucial to be aware of precisely what a firm's goals are. Different goals can lead to very different managerial decisions given the same limited amount of resources. For example, if the main goal of the firm is to maximize market share rather than profit, the firm might decide to reduce its prices. If the main goal is to provide the most technologically advanced products, the firm might well decide to allocate more resources to research and development. The added

[1] As we will see in Chapter 11, a firm may lose money in the short run and still be better off than it would be if it were to shut down operations, as long as its losses are less than its fixed costs. However, if it is going to lose money, from an economic standpoint it is optimal to minimize its losses.

research and development expenses would most likely reduce the amount of profit the firm earns in the short run but may result in increased profits over time as the company increases its technological lead over its competitors. If the main goal of the firm is to carry a complete line of products and services, it may choose to sell certain products even though they might not be earning a profit.

Given the goal (or goals) that the firm is pursuing, we can say that the optimal decision in managerial economics is one that brings the firm closest to this goal. For example, as you will see in Chapter 11, to maximize its profit (or minimize its loss), a firm should price its product at a level where the revenue earned on the last unit of a product sold (called *marginal revenue*) is equal to the additional cost of making this last unit (called *marginal cost*). In other words, the optimal price equates the firm's marginal revenue with its marginal cost.

One additional concept should be presented in our discussion of a firm's goals. In economics, a distinction is made between the "short-run" time period and the "long-run" time period. As explained in greater detail in later sections of this text (see Chapters 3, 6, and 7), these time periods actually have nothing directly to do with calendar time. During the short run, we assume that a firm can vary the amount of certain resources (e.g., labor hours) but must operate with a fixed amount of at least one of its resources (e.g., factory space). Theoretically, in the long run, a firm is able to vary the quantities of all resources being utilized. In this text, we will look at both short-run and long-run decisions made by the firm. Whenever short-run decisions are being considered, we will assume that the firm's goal is to maximize its profit (or minimize its loss). Unless otherwise stated, the same will be true for our analysis of a firm's long-run decisions. In reality, the short- and long-run objectives of a firm may not always be the same. For example, when entering the U.S. market, certain Japanese firms have been known to pursue the short-run objective of maximizing market share (with the expectation of lower profits) while anticipating that, in the long run, profits will increase.[2]

Economic Goals Other Than Profit

The concept of profit maximization has been attacked as incomplete by many writers. They point out that companies may have other economic objectives, some of which may actually be inconsistent with the maximization of profit.

For the time being, we will omit discussion of the objective of "value" or "shareholder wealth" maximization and consider some of the other alternatives concerning a company's activity during a single period of time (such as a year). It is readily admitted that profit maximization is a rather vague term. How does a company know that its profits in a given period are the largest they can

---

[2]A good example are the Japanese manufacturers of copying machines. Also note that in reference to the possibility of an actual firm having diverging short- and long-run objectives, "short" and "long" do not literally refer to the way they are defined in economic theory. Instead, the usual connotation of calendar time applies. We use this example simply as a way of cautioning readers about the difference in short-run and long-run objective, regardless of the way these terms are defined.

be? Or, more correctly (from an ex ante, or planning, viewpoint), how does a company know that the actions it is taking in this time frame will result, if all goes as expected, in the greatest possible profit?

Let us look at the objectives set out by a company's chief executive officer (or a committee representing the company's top management). It is not unusual for the CEO or his or her representatives, having decided on the achievable results for the next fiscal period, to distribute objectives to the various operating heads at the beginning of the planning cycle. Now imagine this memorandum from the firm's CEO to the general manager of one of the company's operating units:

> Dear Joe:
>
> We have had a pretty good year in 1991, and we believe that 1992 should be even better.
>
> I am therefore issuing the following objective for your unit in 1992: Take any and all actions that will ensure that your profit is maximized.
>
> Corporate management is confident that you will not disappoint us. We know that the objective we have given you is challenging. We also are convinced that it is achievable.
>
> John, CEO

This memorandum is obviously an extreme simplification, but what is Joe to do with his marching orders to maximize profit? What resources does he have to do this? And how can his performance be measured at the end of the year? What is his maximum profit?

Now let us look at another "objective" memorandum:

> Dear Joe,
>
> We have had a pretty good year in 1991, and we expect that 1992 should be even better. We are assigning specific objectives to each of our operating units in such a way that the total result will be a financial posture consistent with our economic and industry forecasts, our available resources, and good increases in productivity. With this in mind, we want you to build your 1992 plan to correspond to the following objectives for your unit:
>
> 1. Your revenue should increase by 10 percent from 1991.
> 2. The profit margin of your unit should increase from 8 percent to 9 percent, and your return on assets should be 10 percent.
> 3. Your division will receive $10 million of company funds for expansion projects whose minimum internal rate of return should be 12 percent.
> 4. The head count of your unit can increase by no more than 2 percent.
>
> Corporate management is confident that you will not disappoint us. We know that the objective we have given you is challenging. We also are convinced that it is achievable.
>
> John, CEO

Assuming that this memorandum makes more sense (which it certainly should, for otherwise our point has been lost), does this mean that the company's objective is not really profit maximization at all, but rather a growth rate, a profit margin, or a return on its assets? This is what many writers on this subject say.

Such a conclusion is, however, misleading. Any of these measures in itself is incomplete, and each should be seen as a realistic target consistent with the ultimate objective of maximizing the firm's overall profits. Management, in this example, advised by its expert staff regarding the company's economic environment, competition, technological advances, and market potential, has come to the conclusion that maximum profits can be achieved by the combination of growth and profit measures included in its memorandum.

Thus, the specific objectives assigned to an operating unit are really proxies for the overall objective of profit maximization. The achievement of these proxies is also measurable at the end of the fiscal period; the division executive's performance and contribution toward the company's profits can be evaluated, and rewards in terms of bonuses or incentive plans can then be determined.

Noneconomic Objectives

In this complex world, companies may have objectives that are not strictly economic or at least do not appear to be governed by economic thinking. Indeed, some large companies have published statements of principles that, if accepted at face value, would indicate that making profits is the last thing they strive for. Profits may be mentioned as only one of several objectives, and they may actually be listed last. Furthermore, the statements do not mention any maximum but rather concentrate on such measures as "adequate" or "reasonable" return to stockholders. Such modesty is certainly more palatable to the public. What, then, are some of the guiding principles such companies publish?

1. *"A good place for our employees to work."* What does this mean? It is obviously very broad and can include a multitude of factors, including wages and benefits, hiring and layoff policies, physical plant characteristics, and work satisfaction. Are these really noneconomic objectives? If so, there would be no cost-benefit considerations, and obviously, this is not the case. Such considerations clearly apply to wages and employee benefits. Good physical working conditions also have a price. General satisfaction—which may relate to certain psychological benefits derived from organized employee functions or facilities for recreation and family activities—does not come free. Apparently, the employer makes certain economic choices in creating employee goodwill. The employer knows that a happy work force tends to be more productive and more loyal (employees will be more reluctant to leave the employer). Certain benefits are purchased at a certain cost, and thus surely come within the definition of profit maximization: the employer will pay for employee "happiness" only to the extent that there is a return in terms of productivity.

For various reasons (e.g., union organization, legal requirements, and the fact that the work force is better informed about working conditions elsewhere), employers are more concerned with employee satisfaction than they were in the past. This does not mean, however, that employee satisfaction is inconsistent with the firm's objective of maximizing profits. Today's environment imposes an institutional constraint on the employer's freedom of action, and certain requirements create costs not in existence 50 years ago, thus lowering the company's profits. Even so, the company's objective of profit maximization is not weakened. The company may go to even greater lengths to offset these costs in order to preserve profit levels.

2. *"Provide good products/services to our customers."* Much of what we have discussed in regard to the first objective applies to the second. Customer satisfaction does not come without cost, and without customer satisfaction there are no profits (unless we are talking about an entrepreneur aiming at a quick killing and an equally quick disappearance). Thus, a company will plan to spend sufficient resources to achieve its sales and to create and preserve customer satisfaction to the point where additional expenditures no longer create additional profits.

A typical company today pays greater attention to satisfying customers than in the past. This is due to legal requirements (e.g., safety regulations), warranty requirements (often brought about by competition), and consumer organizations, not to mention the greatly increased level of consumer knowledge and sophistication. The cost of maintaining a satisfied customer population has risen over time. Thus, like employee satisfaction, customer satisfaction is by no means a noneconomic objective. A company must weigh costs and benefits. Given the costs of providing satisfactory products and services to customers in today's competitive environment, this objective certainly qualifies as profit-maximizing behavior.

3. *"Act as a good citizen in our society."* The question of a business's role in our society and the firm's responsibility toward society are at the forefront of today's policy discussions. The concept of social responsibility has many facets. The dumping of wastes or the pollution of air are problems about which we read daily. In these instances the costs incurred by the company in manufacturing the product are less than the costs incurred by society as a whole. Even if a company's smokestacks cause soot to form on residences in the plant's surrounding area, the firm's costs ordinarily include only the usual production costs necessary to bring its merchandise to market. They do not include the cost borne by the home or store owners forced to clean or paint their premises more frequently because of the soot. This situation is usually described as the difference between private costs (for the resources utilized by the firm) and social costs (which include the private costs and the costs imposed on the home and store owners).[3]

We could say that this firm, to be a responsible citizen, should take voluntary steps to minimize such social costs or compensate those who are victims of this situation. However, it is because firms generally do not concern themselves with the differences between social costs and private costs that environmental regulations have been enacted, imposing standards of behavior on companies and penalizing them for not adhering to these standards. Therefore, a company's objectives are to work within the rules imposed on them by local, state, or fed-

[3]For a more detailed discussion about these "market externalities," see Chapter 16.

eral authorities. But again we come back to the question: Does the existence of such restrictions invalidate the profit maximization principle? Not at all. The company is operating within a constraint erected by society. This constraint by necessity raises operating costs and thus may lower the maximum obtainable profit level, but it certainly does not prevent a company from trying to achieve a maximum within the limits of the constraint.

A company's quest for profits may lead it to another type of antisocial behavior. It is an entrepreneur's natural motivation to try to gain economic power at the expense of other firms, that is, to monopolize and, as we shall see later in this book, thereby achieve greater profits than it would obtain if surrounded by competing firms. That is the reason for the existence of antitrust laws in the United States. Thus, companies are restricted from certain practices that would enhance their profits at the expense of others—companies as well as consumers. Given the antitrust constraints (whether prohibiting coercion, collusion, or predatory pricing), companies generally behave as good, responsible citizens to ensure that they do not run afoul of these laws and get involved in long, costly litigation and possible penalties. (Of course, this is not always so; sometimes companies miscalculate and do face government action.) The result is the same as we have discussed previously. Antitrust regulations impose costs and decrease the potential level of profits for some companies (while protecting the rest of society); but, given the rules and a company's need to operate within them, the profit maximization objective is not rendered invalid.

Social responsibility and corporate behavior come up in still another context. This has to do with corporate support of eleemosynary and educational institutions. Since companies are supposed to maximize profits for their owners, is corporate giving not a direct contradiction of the maximization principle? Some authors believe this to be the case. But, at the risk of creating a tautology, we submit that corporate donations involve the creation of goodwill with the public and the employees, and ultimately of potential sales and profits. The underwriting of a program on public television brings the company's name forth in a very favorable light. Has it ever happened to you, as you sat in a symphony hall reading the printed program and waiting for your favorite orchestra to play your favorite music, that you saw the name of a company listed among the orchestra's contributors? Were you favorably impressed, or if this happened to be the company that was your employer, did you feel a sense of pride? By the same token, if a company contributes funds to a university, is it not possible that its recruiting efforts at this school will be more welcome and successful? The benefits obtainable by a company that donates computer equipment or other scientific machinery to a university are even more obvious. Thus, judicious donations by a corporation can be beneficial to society and at the same time offer profit potentials.

We could continue this discussion of so-called noneconomic objectives, but the point has been made. Today's markets and institutions constrain companies in many ways that did not exist in the past. Therefore, companies must concern themselves with creating employee and customer satisfaction and maintaining social responsibility to a much higher degree. But these considerations do not contradict the profit maximization principle. If companies were maximizers in the past, under less restrictive conditions, they are still maximizers today but have to operate within the requirements imposed by current standards and the costs that accompany them.

Once Again—Do Companies Maximize Profits?

We have discussed some possible alternative objectives to profit maximization and concluded that none of these objectives is necessarily inconsistent with our basic principle. Now let us look at another criticism that has recently been leveled at the view of profit maximization as the primary objective.

The argument is that today's corporations do not maximize at all. Instead, their aim is to "satisfice." To understand this argument, we have to consider two parts of this idea:

1. The position and power of stockholders in today's corporation.
2. The position and power of professional management in today's corporation.

Years ago the owner or owners of a business also managed it. Businesses were predominantly quite small and lent themselves to being operated as individual proprietorships, partnerships, or small, closely held corporations. Modern businesses, particularly medium-sized or large corporations, of course, cannot be managed by the owners, who are the shareholders and number in the thousands or even hundreds of thousands. Many stockholders own only minute pieces of a corporation. Further, stockholders tend to diversify their holdings; thus, they may hold small interests in many different corporations. The argument asserts that most stockholders are not well informed on how well a corporation can do and will be satisfied with an adequate dividend and some reasonable growth. And since they own different stocks, poor performance on one of their holdings may be offset by some of their other assets; the stockholder is more concerned with the portfolio of stocks than with any individual stock. Shareholders may not be capable of knowing whether corporate management is doing its best for them and they actually may not be very concerned as long as they receive what they consider a satisfactory return on their investment—hence "satisficing."

Second, in a modern corporation professional managers—the chairman of the board, the president, a group of vice presidents, and other high-level managers—direct the operations of a company. Although they are overseen by a board of directors (which usually includes a large number of insiders), they are responsible for major decision making. It is claimed by a number of writers that managers (who commonly hold a relatively small number of shares) have their own objectives, which do not include maximization of shareholder earnings. Indeed, it is often said that managers tend to be much more conservative—that is, risk-averse—than stockholders would be, since their jobs will most likely be safer if they turn in a competent and steady, if unspectacular, performance. They could probably benefit stockholders in the long run by taking some well-calculated risks. However, they may be too cautious to do so, and thus they miss out on opportunities. They fear that they may not survive the reverses that could result from risk taking. If stockholders need only be satisfied, this may be the appropriate way for management to go.

Further, management's interests may actually be contrary to those of stockholders. For instance, management may be more interested in revenue growth than profits. Why? It has been claimed that management remuneration tends to be a function of revenue size rather than profits. Several studies have been made on this subject, but the evidence is considerably less than overwhelming. Also, company management may be more interested in maximizing its own income, may indulge in various perquisites, and in general may not act in the best interest of the widely dispersed, somewhat disinterested and lethargic stockholder population.[4]

The two sides in this relationship tend to complement one another. The owners of the corporation—the stockholders—are not interested in maximization, or even if they are, they are not well enough informed and have too little power. The corporation's management, whose selfish motives lead them to act in their own favor when stockholder and management goals differ, will manage in a way that serves their interest while keeping the stockholder satisfied with adequate return and moderate growth.

Like all ideas presented by intelligent people, this one probably contains a certain amount of truth. Each of the points seems eminently reasonable and, for all we know, could be valid over limited periods of time. But let us look at some of the realities of life and also some recent events in the business world that tend to contradict this argument.

You, the reader of this book, may be among that group of far-flung stockholders owning a hundred shares in a company with millions of shares outstanding. However, particularly in the case of large corporations, much of the outstanding stock is held by institutions and in professionally managed accounts. Among these are banks that manage large pension funds, insurance companies with their extensive portfolios, and mutual funds. These organizations employ expert analysts (who are only human and therefore, at least occasionally, make mistakes) who study companies and pass judgment on the quality of their management and their promise for the future. Of course, they deal mostly with stock prices, but after all, stock prices are a reflection of a company's profitability.[5] These analysts make recommendations to their management on which stocks

---

[4]A formal theory dealing with the potential conflicts between shareholders and management has been developed by Michael C. Jensen and William H. Meckling in their article "Theory of the Firm: Managerial Behavior, Agency Costs and Ownership Structure" (*Journal of Financial Economics* October 1976, pp. 350–60). These conflicts arise whenever managers own less than 100 percent of the stock, which is, of course, the predominant situation in today's large corporation. To ensure that managers act on behalf of the stockholder, the latter will have to incur "agency costs," which are expenditures to monitor managers' actions, to structure the organization in such a way as to limit management's action, and so forth.

[5]The connection between profits and stock prices will be examined in the next section, when we expand the maximization principle to include the wealth of stockholders.

to buy and which to sell. Companies that underperform would be weeded out of these institutional portfolios, with a consequent drop in their stock prices.

Now, what happens when certain stocks tend to underperform in the market? They become targets for takeovers by others. We really do not have to belabor this point, since anyone reading the business sections of daily newspapers or other business publications is very much aware of recent events in the takeover and buyout arenas. In addition to the accumulation of stock and subsequent tender offers by outside financiers, we have also witnessed the existence of proxy fights by dissident large stockholders. Thus, it appears that management in today's corporation is not insulated from outside pressures. Management is constrained to act in agreement with stockholders, who look for increases in stock values and returns and who act to "punish" the managements of those companies that appear to underperform.

Another argument leads to a similar conclusion. Competitive pressures also act to stimulate management to performance. If a company's results lag behind those of competitors, those lethargic stockholders who do not challenge the company directly will tend to sell its shares and turn to those companies providing better returns and better prospects of returns. The price of the company's stock will suffer relative to prices of the others; such a scenario will not go unnoticed in financial markets. Company management will come under the gun to improve performance, and ultimately management may be replaced because of pressure by outside board members, a successful proxy fight, or even a takeover.

Management has another, more direct, motivation to act in concert with the objectives of stockholders. Parts—frequently large parts—of an executive's remuneration are tied to performance in terms of operating profits for the corporation or for units supervised by the particular executive.[6] Furthermore, an executive's compensation package is usually enhanced by the issuance of stock options. Since the value of stock options depends on the price of the company's stock, which in turn is a function of the company's profit performance, a self-serving company manager may find that his objectives (less than miraculously) coincide with those of the stockholders.

Thus, there appears to be a strong convergence of management and stockholder objectives, contrary to the claims of some well-known writers.

Profit Maximization, Restated

It is readily agreed that the existence of the profit maximization objective can never be proven conclusively. We must note, however, that lack of financial success by a company is not necessarily a contravention of the principle. The best of plans may go awry, and management's judgment certainly is not error-

[6]The fact that these performance incentives may be tied to near-term profits can create a problem, since the executive's horizon may be shortened. More about this will be discussed later.

proof. Under certain circumstances, the aim for loss minimization may replace the goal of profit maximization, but this too supports our basic premise. As difficult as it is to point to acts of profit maximization by management, none of the alternative constructions lends itself as well as a yardstick by which to measure business activity. As long as a corporation strives to do better, that is, prefers higher profits to lower profits and lower costs to higher costs, and acts consistently in those directions, the assumption of profit maximization serves as a better basis for judging a company's decisions than any of the other purported objectives. And, incidentally, this "striving to do better can include a multitude of decisions, including those that lead to a revenue increase greater than a cost increase, a revenue decrease smaller than a cost decrease, or a constant revenue with decreased costs. All of these decisions involve an increase in profits.

However, maximizing profits in the very short term (e.g., one year) can always be accomplished by management. If, for instance, revenue in the coming year is expected to decline, a company can keep up its profits by cutting expenses. If management seeks to do this without an immediate further reaction on revenue, it can eliminate some development projects. The effect of a lack of new products will not be felt right away, but the shortsightedness of this management decision will come home to roost only a few years hence. This is the decision area in which the objective of period profit maximization can be attacked more logically. Profit maximization for one period is an incomplete measure from the viewpoint of a business organization that is expected to operate into the infinite—or at least the foreseeable—future.

Maximizing the Wealth of Stockholders

Because period profit maximization is an extremely useful way to look at day-to-day decision making in the firm, we will use it as our model throughout most of this book. However, as was just mentioned, there is another view of maximization that is usually adopted in finance textbooks and that takes into consideration a stream of earnings over time. This concept includes not only the evaluation of a stream of cash flows; it also considers the all-important idea of the time value of money.[7] Since it is an obvious fact that a dollar earned in the future is worth less than a dollar earned today, the future streams must be discounted to the present. Both the shape of these streams through time and the interest rate at which they are discounted affect the value of the stockholders' wealth today. The discount rate in particular is affected by risk, so risk becomes another component of the valuation of the business. Financial theorists differentiate various types of risk, with the two major types commonly identified as business risk and financial risk.

---

[7]Time value of money and discounting of flows will be discussed in much greater detail in the appendix to Chapter 14.

Business risk involves variation in returns due to the ups and downs of the economy, the industry, and the firm. This is the kind of risk that attends all business organizations, although to varying degrees. Some businesses are relatively stable from period to period, whereas others incur extreme fluctuations in their financial returns. For instance, public utilities (i.e., suppliers of electricity and gas as well as the operating telephone companies) tend to have more stable earnings over time than do industrial companies, particularly those in industries that are highly cyclical (e.g., steel, automobiles, and capital goods), or companies in high-tech fields.

Financial risk concerns the variation in returns that is induced by leverage. *Leverage* signifies the proportion of a company financed by debt. Given a certain degree of leverage, the earnings accruing to stockholders will fluctuate with total profits (before the deduction of interest and taxes). The higher the leverage, the greater the potential fluctuations in stockholder earnings. Thus, financial risk moves directly with a company's leverage.

How do we obtain a measure of stockholders' wealth? By discounting to the present the cash streams that stockholders expect to receive out into infinity. Since we know today's price of a company's stock, we can—given the expected dividends to be received by the stockholders—determine the discount rate the investment community applies to the particular stock. This discount rate includes the pure time value of money as well as the premiums for the two categories of risk. The dividend stream is used to represent the receipts of stockholders because that is all they really receive from the company. Of course, a stockholder also looks for a capital gain, but selling the stock at some point involves someone else buying it; thus, this payment represents only a trade, an exchange of funds. However, dividends represent the returns on the stock generated by the corporation. In equation form, we have the following:

$$P = \frac{D_1}{(1+k)} + \frac{D_2}{(1+k)^2} + \frac{D_3}{(1+k)^3} + \cdots + \frac{D_n}{(1+k)^n}$$

where P = Present price of the stock

D = Dividends received per year (in year 1, year 2, . . . , year n)

k = Discount rate applied by the financial community, often referred to as the cost of capital of the company

Multiplying P by the number of shares outstanding gives the total value of the company's equity.

Thus, under this construction, maximizing the wealth of the shareholder means that a company tries to manage its business in such a way that the dividends over time paid from its earnings and the risk incurred to bring about the stream of dividends always create the highest price and thereby the maximum value for the company's stock.

The wealth maximization hypothesis tends to weaken even further the management-versus-stockholder argument. Corporate executives, for whom stock options represent a significant portion of remuneration, now have an even greater incentive to aim at results that conform to the objectives of the stockholders.

This is a rather complex if quite obvious development of the maximization principle. As stated previously, we will work primarily with the profit maximization hypothesis because it is quite sufficient for most of our purposes. We will return to the wealth maximization rule in Chapter 14 when we discuss a company's investment and replacement decisions involving expenditures for which the resulting payoffs flow into the corporation over a considerable period of time. In that chapter we will also briefly discuss how the market tends to determine the rate of return it requires from a company (and thus sets the discount rate k, the company's cost of capital). In Chapter 15 we will examine the question of risk and uncertainty and attempts to find ways to deal with it.

Economic Profits

Throughout this chapter we have been using the term *profit* and assumed that it has some kind of meaning. But we have not defined it. We only said that profit—and its maximization—is uppermost in the company owner's and manager's minds. In a way, profit is easy to define. Every company that closes its books annually and whose accountants construct a statement of earnings (whether this company is public, so that everybody can see the published statement and its "bottom line," or whether it is private) knows what its profits are. The accountants report the level of profits, and they also affirm that everything in the financial statements has been done in conformance with generally accepted accounting principles (GAAP).

Unfortunately, things are not quite that simple. Profits, as reported on an earnings statement, are not necessarily definitive. Accountants have certain amounts of freedom in recording items leading to the "bottom line."[8] A few examples will suffice:

1. There are different ways of recording depreciation. In the past the straight-line method, the sum-of-the-years'-digits method, the declining balance method, and probably others have been used. Under present tax law the Accelerated Cost Recovery System (ACRS) is most frequently employed.
2. There are various ways of recording inventories, the famous FIFO (first-in, first-out) and LIFO (last-in, first-out) being just two alternatives.
3. Amortization of such items as goodwill and patents can be recorded differently.

[8]Some writers in this field have said that accountants take too many liberties. Professor Abraham Briloff has written a number of books and articles on this subject.

This is just a small sample of the better-known alternative treatments by accountants, and any of these are in conformance with GAAP. Moreover, the tax return that a company completes and sends to the IRS may be quite different from the published statement of a public company.

As if the question of what accounting profits really are were not enough, the economist compounds this problem even further. Everybody agrees that profit equals revenue minus costs (and expenses). But economists do not agree with accountants on the concept of costs. An accountant reports costs on a historical basis. The economist, however, is concerned with the costs that a business considers in making decisions, that is, future costs. We will concern ourselves with this concept more thoroughly later in this book, but we must touch on the subject now, albeit briefly. Basically, economists deal with something they call *opportunity costs* or *alternative costs;* this means that the cost of a resource is what a business must pay for it to attract it into its employ or, put differently, what a business must pay to keep this resource from finding employment elsewhere. To get down to specific examples, we can mention the following:

1. *Historical costs vs. replacement costs.* To an economist, the replacement cost of a piece of machinery (and, therefore, the level of periodic depreciation on the replacement cost) is important, whereas an accountant measures cost—and depreciation—on a historical basis.
2. *Implicit costs and normal profits.*
   a. The owners' time and interest on the capital they contribute are usually counted as profit in a partnership or a single proprietorship. But the owners could work for someone else instead and invest their funds elsewhere. So these two items are really costs to the business and not profit.
   b. The preceding item is not relevant in the case of a corporation, since even top executives are salaried employees, and interest on corporate debt is deducted as an expense before profits are arrived at. However, the payments made to the owners/stockholders—dividends—are not part of cost; they are recorded as a distribution of profits. But surely a part of the shareholder's return is similar to the interest on debt, since the stockholder could have invested his or her funds elsewhere and requires a certain return in order to leave the investment with the corporation. Thus, on this account, corporate profits as recorded by accountants tend to be overstated.

It appears, therefore, that an economist includes costs that would be excluded by an accountant. Indeed, the economist refers to the second category of costs—which are essential to obtain and keep the owners' resources in the business—as "normal profits,"which represent the return that these resources demand to remain committed to a particular firm.

Thus, "economic" costs include not only the historical costs and explicit costs recorded by the accountants, but also the replacement costs and implicit costs (normal profits) that must be earned on the owners' resources. In the rest of this book, profits are considered to be economic profits, which are defined as total revenue minus all the economic costs we have described in this section.

The Solution

The day after the presentation to the board of directors, Bob Burns drew up a set of objectives that he believed best defined the goals of the company. Bob believed that all of the objectives were important for Global Foods, Inc., but that some priority could be established for them. Following, in order of Bob's view of their relative importance, are the "Goals of the Global Foods Corporation."

- To be the fastest-growing company in the industry.
- To provide our customers with food and beverages of the highest quality.
- To respond to our customers' changing tastes and preferences in a timely and efficient manner.
- To be among the lowest-cost producers in the industry.
- To be the most profitable firm in the industry, as measured by return to shareholder equity.

Bob decided to convey these goals to the company by sending a note to all of Global's employees. He also decided to use this opportunity to inform everyone about the decision to enter the soft drink business.

Memorandum to: All employees of Global Foods, Inc.
From: Robert A. Burns, CEO
Subject: Entry into the soft drink business.

As you may have already heard, the Board of Directors has approved our plans for entering the soft drink industry. The Board and I felt that this action is necessary to ensure our continuing success into the foreseeable future.

The decision that was made can be understood in light of the goals we have set for our company. I want to state these goals here in what the Board and I believe is the order of priorities:

1. We wish to be the fastest-growing company in our industry. Since soft drink sales have been rising more quickly than food sales, the entry into this new business will be helpful.
2. We wish to supply goods of the highest quality. In this way, we will ensure the corporation's growth.
3. We wish to respond to customer's changing preferences in a timely manner. This means that our market research and product development efforts must be given high priority.
4. We wish to be the industry's low-cost producer. Every decision we make must be accompanied by thorough analysis of the cost involved. It is easy for a company intent on fast growth to lose sight of the need for efficient operations. We must never do that.
5. We wish to be the most profitable company in the industry. In a way, this could be stated as the first of our objectives. However, I firmly believe that if we accomplish the first four goals, this fifth goal will surely follow. Because of our effort for rapid expansion, profitabil-

(Continued)

ity may lag somewhat in the short run. But the financial community will be convinced that our direction is correct for the achievement of profitability in the longer run.

More information about our entry into this new, exciting business will become available shortly. I know that all of you will commit yourselves to seeing that we will achieve great success.

Summary

In this text we will generally assume that a firm's short-run and long-run objective is the maximization of its profit or the minimization of its loss. Although a firm can select from a number of other goals, both in the short run and the long run, the assumption of profit maximization provides us with a clear-cut model for explaining how firms can use economic concepts and tools of analysis to make optimal decisions. In presenting these concepts and tools of analysis, a certain amount of mathematics will be employed. Thus, before proceeding to the next chapter, we believe that a brief review of the mathematics used in this text will be helpful. This review is contained in the following appendix.

Important Concepts

Business risk: The variability of returns (or profits) due to fluctuations in general economic conditions or conditions specifically affecting the firm.

Economic cost: All cost incurred to attract resources into a company's employ. Such cost includes explicit cost usually recognized on accounting records as well as opportunity cost.

Economic profit: Total revenue minus total economic cost. An amount of profit earned in a particular endeavor above the amount of profit that the firm could be earning in its next best alternative activity. Also referred to as *abnormal profit* or *above-normal profit*.

Financial risk: The variability of returns (or profits) induced by leverage (the proportion of a company financed by debt). The higher the leverage, the greater the potential fluctuation in stockholder earnings for a given change in total profits.

Noneconomic objectives: A company's objectives that do not appear to be governed by economic thinking but rather define how a business should act. "Acting as a good corporate citizen" is an example of a noneconomic objective.

Normal profit: An amount of profit earned in a particular endeavor that is just equal to the profit that could be earned in a firm's next best alternative activity. When a firm earns normal profit, its revenue is just enough to cover both its accounting cost and its opportunity cost. It can also be considered as the return to capital and management necessary to keep resources engaged in a particular activity.

Optimal decision: The decision that enables the firm to meet its desired objective most closely.

Profit maximization hypothesis: One of the central themes in economics, the claim that a company will strive to attain the highest economic profit in each period.

Satisficing: A concept in economics based on the principle that owners of a firm (especially stockholders in a large corporation) may be content with adequate return and growth since they really cannot judge when profits are maximized.

Wealth maximization: A company's management of its business in such a manner that the cash flows over time to the company, discounted at an appropriate discount rate, will cause the value of the company's stock to be at a maximum.

Questions

1. The following is a quote from a *New York Times* article: "If a company makes product donations to the school—computers for instance—then the image of a company goes up as graduate students use the company's products." Does such action square with a company's objective of profit maximization? Discuss.
2. Is the maximization of profit margin (profit as a percent of total sales) a valid financial objective of a corporation? Discuss.
3. "The growth of consumer information organizations, legal requirements, and warranty requirements has caused significant increases in the cost of customer satisfaction. Thus it is no longer useful to talk about profit maximization as a company objective." Comment on this quote.
4. Discuss the difference between profit maximization and shareholder wealth maximization. Which of these is a more comprehensive statement of a company's economic objectives?
5. Explain the term *satisfice* as it relates to the operations of a large corporation.
6. Why may corporate managers not specifically aim at profit (or wealth) maximization for their companies?
7. What are some of the forces that cause managers to act in the interest of shareholders?
8. Do you believe that profit (or shareholder wealth) maximization still represents the best overall economic objective for today's corporation?
9. Because of inflation, a company must replace one of its (fully depreciated) machines at twice the nominal price paid for a similar machine eight years ago. Based on present accounting rules, will the company have covered the entire cost of the new machine through depreciation charges? Explain by contrasting accounting and economic costs.
10. How do implicit costs lead to a difference between accounting and economic profits?
11. You have a choice of opening your own business or being employed by someone else in a similar type of business. What are some of the considerations in terms of opportunity costs that you would have to include in arriving at your decision?

12. Various depreciation methods can be used to arrive at an accounting profit number. From the viewpoint of the economist, how should annual depreciation charges be determined?

APPENDIX 2A
Review of Mathematical Concepts Used in Managerial Economics

Economics is the most mathematical of all the social sciences. Indeed, to the uninitiated reader, many academic journals in economics resemble a mathematics or physics journal. Because this text is intended to show the practical applications of economic theory, this presents something of a dilemma. On one hand, the economic theory of managerial decision making has evolved along with the rest of economics to a point where it can be (and usually is) profusely expressed in mathematical terms. On the other hand, industry experience indicates that managers seldom use the more advanced mathematical expressions of economic theory. They do, nonetheless, rely quite often on many of the concepts, graphs, and relatively simple numerical examples that are used throughout this text to assist them in their decision making.

But the dilemma does not end here. Regardless of the role of mathematics in managerial decision making, it certainly serves as an important instructional vehicle for economics professors. Using calculus enables the very concise expression of complex functional relationships and the quick solution of problems involving the optimal allocation of scarce resources. Moreover, students with extensive academic backgrounds or work experience in applied mathematics (i.e., engineers and scientists) often find that they are able to discern the essential nature of an economic problem more easily with equations and calculus than with narratives and tabular examples.

The dilemma has been resolved in the following way. The explanations of economic terms, concepts, and methods of analysis rely primarily on verbal definitions, numerical tables, and graphs. As appropriate, chapter appendixes will present the same material using algebra and calculus. At times, algebra and calculus will be employed in the main body of a chapter. Moreover, problems and exercises at the end of the chapter will give students ample opportunity to reinforce their understanding of the material with the use of algebra and calculus, as well as with tables and graphs.

The authors' experience as teachers indicates that many students have already learned the mathematics employed in this text, both in the main body and in the appendixes. However, some students may have studied this material some time ago and may therefore benefit from a review. Such a review is offered in the balance of this appendix. It is intended only as a brief refresher. For a more comprehensive review, readers should consult any of the many texts and review books on this subject.[9] In fact, any college algebra or calculus text would be just as suitable as a reference.

Variables, Functions, and Slopes: The Heart of Economic Analysis

A variable is any entity that can assume different values. Each academic discipline focuses attention on its own set of variables. For example, in the social sciences, political scientists may study power and authority, sociologists may study group cohesiveness, and psychologists may study paranoia. Economists study such variables as price, output, revenue, cost, and profit. The advantage that economics has over the other social sciences is that most of its variables can be measured in a relatively unambiguous manner.[10]

Once the variables of interest have been identified and measured, economists try to understand how and why the values of these variables change. They also try to determine what conditions will lead to optimal values. Here the term *optimal* refers to the best possible value in a particular situation. *Optimal* may refer to the maximum value (as in the case of profit), or it may refer to the minimum value (as in the case of cost). In any event, the analysis of the changes in a variable's value, often referred to as a variable's "behavior," is almost always carried out in relation to other variables. In mathematics, the relationship of one variable's value to the values of other variables is expressed in terms of a function. Formally stated in mathematical terms, Y is said to be a function of X (i.e., $Y = f(X)$, where f represents "function" if for any value that might be assigned to X a value of Y can be determined). For example, the demand function indicates the quantity of a good or service that people are willing to buy, given the values of price, tastes and preferences, prices of related products, number of buyers, and future expectations. A functional relationship can be expressed using tables, graphs, or algebraic equations.

---

[9]See, for example, Bodh R. Gulati, *College Mathematics with Applications to the Business and Social Sciences*, New York: Harper & Row, 1978; and Donald and Mildred Stanel, *Applications of College Mathematics*, Lexington, Mass.: D.C. Heath, 1983.

[10]To be sure, variables in the other social sciences are measurable, but in many instances, the measurement standards themselves are subject to discussion and controversy. For example, psychologists may use the result of some type of IQ test as a measure of intelligence. But there is an ongoing debate as to whether this result is reflective of one's native intelligence or socioeconomic background. In other cases, no readily available measure may exist for a particular variable of interest to the social scientist, and one may therefore have to be artificially devised. For example, political scientists employ various indexes of power based on data available on other variables. Fortunately for the economist, most variables of interest can be measured in a straightforward manner. However, even economists may encounter the measurement problem. For example, as will be seen in Chapters 3, 4, and 5, "tastes and preference" is an important variable in the demand equation but is not an easy variable to measure. Therefore, such variables as advertising expenditures may be used as proxies for consumer tastes and preferences. Also, a variable representing some trend factor could be utilized.

Table 2A.1 Tabular Expression of the TR Function

Units Sold (Q)	*Total Revenue (TR)*
0	$ 0
1	5
2	10
3	15
4	20
5	25

To illustrate the different ways of expressing a function, let us use the total revenue function. Total revenue (or sales) is defined as the unit price of a product *(P)* multiplied by the number of units sold (*Q*). That is, $TR = P \times Q$. In economics the general functional relationship for total revenue is that its value is dependent on the number of units sold. That is, $TR = f(Q)$. Total revenue, or TR, is called the *dependent variable* because its value depends on the value of *Q*. *Q* is called the *independent variable* because its value may vary independently of the value of *TR*. For example, suppose a product is sold for $5 per unit. Table 2A.1 shows the relationship between total revenue and quantity over a selected range of units sold.

Figure 2A.1 shows a graph of the values in Table 2A.1. As you can see in this figure, we have related total revenue to quantity in a linear fashion. There does not always have to be a linear relationship between total revenue and quantity. As you will see in the next section, this function, as well as many other functions of interest to economists, may assume different nonlinear forms.

We can also express the relation depicted in Table 2A.1 and Figure 2A.1 in the following equation:

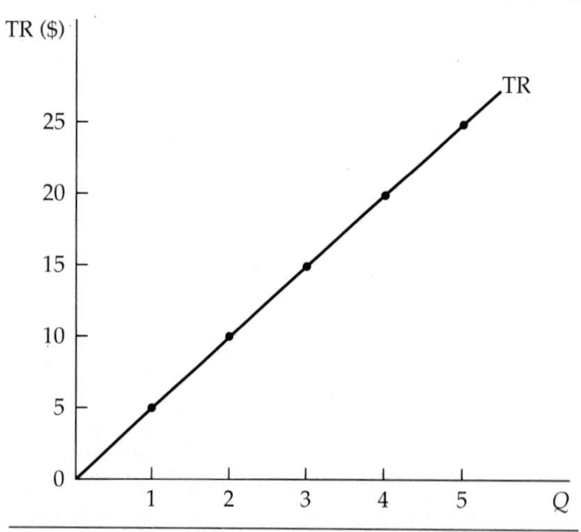

Figure 2A.1 Total Revenue Function

$$\text{TR} = 5Q \tag{2A.1}$$

where TR = Dependent variable (total revenue)
Q = Independent variable (quantity)
5 = Coefficient showing the relationship between changes in TR relative to changes in Q

This equation can also be expressed in the general form:

$$Y = a + bX \tag{2A.2}$$

where Y = Dependent variable (i.e., TR)
X = Independent variable (i.e., Q)
b = Coefficient of X (i.e., the given P of \$5)
a = Intercept term (in this case, 0)

In a linear equation, the coefficient b (which takes the value of 5 in our total revenue function) can also be thought of as the change in Y over the change in X (i.e., $\Delta Y/\Delta X$). In other words, it represents the slope of the line plotted on the basis of Equation (2A.2). The slope of a line is a measure of its steepness. This can be seen in Figure 2A.1, which, for purposes of discussion, we have reproduced in Figure 2A.2. In this figure, the steepness of the line between points A and B can be seen as BC/AC.

The slope of a function is critical to economic analysis because it shows the change in a dependent variable relative to a change in a designated independent variable. As explained in the next section of this appendix, this is the essence of *"marginal analysis."*

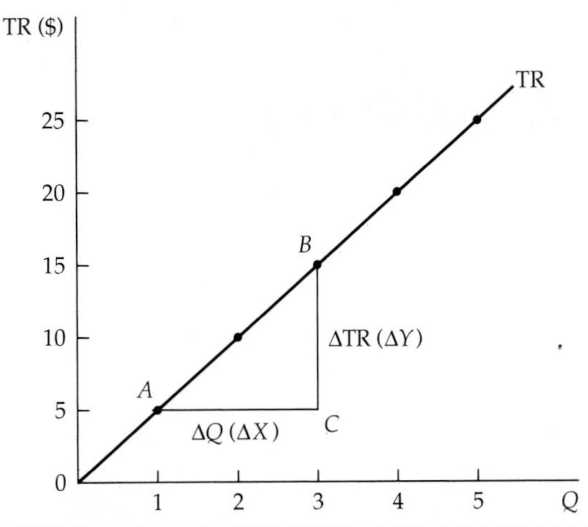

Figure 2A.2 The Slope of the Total Revenue Line

The Importance of Marginal Analysis in Economic Analysis

One of the most important contributions that economic theory has made to managerial decision making is the application of what economists call *marginal analysis*. Essentially, marginal analysis involves the consideration of changes in the values of variables from some given starting point. Stated in a more formal mathematical manner, marginal analysis can be defined as the amount of change in a dependent variable that results from a unit change in an independent variable. If the functional relationship between the dependent and independent variables is linear, this change is represented by the slope of the line. In the case of our total revenue function, $TR = 5Q$, we can readily see that the coefficient, 5, indicates the marginal relationship between TR, the dependent variable, and Q, the independent variable. That is, total revenue is expected to change by five units for every unit change in Q.

Most economic decisions made by managers involve some sort of change in one variable relative to a change in other variables. For example, a firm might want to consider raising or lowering the price from $5 per unit. Whether or not it is desirable to do so would depend on the resulting change in revenues or profits. Changes in these variables would in turn depend on the change in the number of units sold as a result of the change in price. Using the usual symbol for change, Δ (delta), this pricing decision can be summarized via the following illustration:

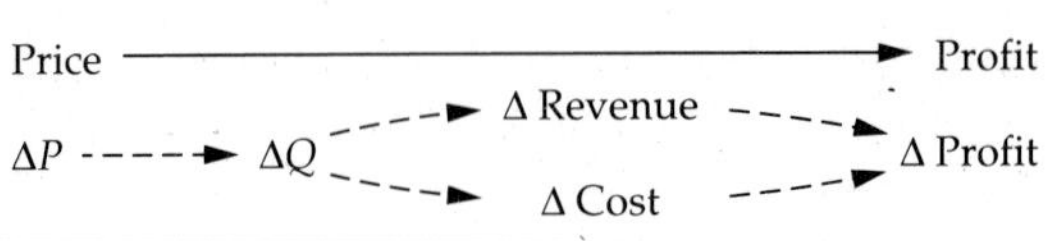

The top line shows that a firm's price affects its profit. The dashed arrows indicate that changes in price will change profit via changes in the number of units sold (ΔQ), in revenue, and in cost. Actually, each of the dashed lines represents a key function used in economic analysis. ΔP to ΔQ represents the demand function. ΔQ to ΔRevenue is the total revenue function, ΔQ to ΔCost is the cost function, and ΔQ to ΔProfit is the profit function. Of course, the particular behavior or pattern of profit change relative to changes in quantity depends on how revenue and cost change relative to changes in Q.

Marginal analysis comes into play even if a product is new and being priced in the market for the first time. When there is no starting or reference point, different values of a variable may be evaluated in a form of sensitivity or what-if analysis. For example, the decision makers in a company such as IBM may price the company's new workstations by charting a list of hypothetical prices and then forecasting how many units the company will be able to sell at each price. By shifting from price to price, the decision makers would be engaging in a form of marginal analysis.[11]

Many other economic decisions rely on marginal analysis, including the hiring of additional personnel, the purchase of additional equipment, or a venture into a new line of business. In each of these cases, it is the change in some variable (e.g., profit, cash flow, productivity, or cost) associated with the change in a firm's resource allocation that is of importance to the decision maker. Consideration of changes in relation to some reference point is also referred to as *incremental analysis.* A common distinction made between incremental and marginal analysis is that the former simply considers the change in the dependent variable whereas the latter considers the change in the dependent variable relative to a one-unit change in the independent variable. For example, suppose lowering the price of a product results in a sales increase of 1,000 units and a revenue increase of $2,000. The incremental revenue would be $2,000, and the marginal revenue would be $2 ($2,000/1,000).

Functional Forms: A Variation on a Theme

For purposes of illustration, we will often rely on a linear function to express the relationship among variables. This is particularly the case in Chapter 3, on supply and demand. But there are many instances when a linear function is not the proper expression for changes in the value of a dependent variable relative to changes in some independent variable. For example, if a firm's total revenue does not increase at the same rate as additional units of its product are sold, a linear function is clearly not appropriate. To illustrate this phenomenon, let us assume that a firm has the power to set its price at different levels and that its customers respond to different prices on the basis of the following schedule:

P	*Q*
$7	0
6	100
5	200
4	300
3	400
2	500
1	600
0	700

The algebraic and graphical expressions of this relationship are shown in Figure 2A.3. As implied in the schedule and as shown explicitly in Figure 2A.3, we have assumed a linear relationship between price and quantity demanded.

[11]One of the authors was a member of the pricing department of IBM for a number of years. This type of sensitivity analysis involving marginal relationships is indeed an important part of the pricing process. Much more about pricing will be said in Chapters 11, 12, and 13.

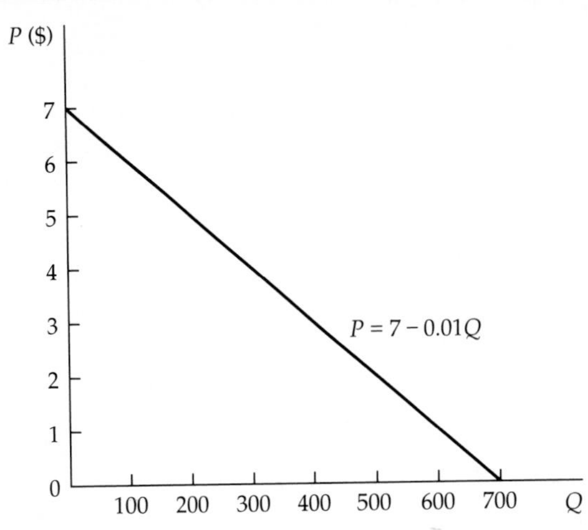

Figure 2A.3 Demand Curve

Based on the definition of total revenue as $TR = P \times Q$, we can create a total revenue schedule as well as a total revenue equation and graph. These are all shown in Figure 2A.4.

Since we know that the demand curve is $Q = 700 - 100P$ and $TR = P \times Q$, we can arrive at the values of the coefficient and intercept terms as well as the functional form in a very straightforward manner. First, we need to express P in terms of Q so that we can substitute this relationship into the total revenue equation:

$$Q = 700 - 100P \tag{2A.3}$$

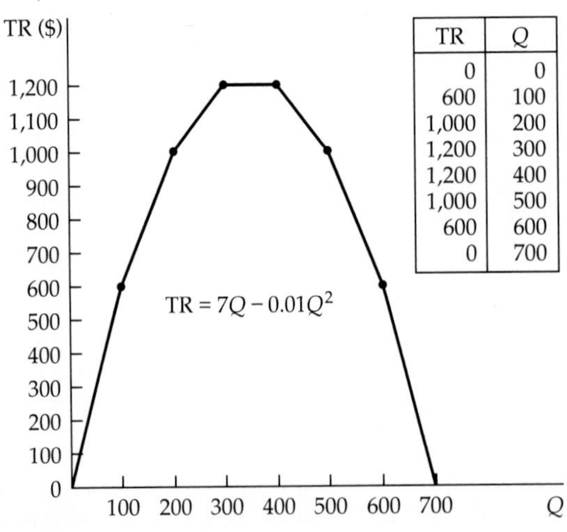

TR	Q
0	0
600	100
1,000	200
1,200	300
1,200	400
1,000	500
600	600
0	700

Figure 2A.4 Total Revenue

or

$$P = 7 - 0.01Q \tag{2A.4}$$

Substituting the Equation (2A.4) into the total revenue equation gives

$$\begin{aligned} TR &= P \times Q \\ &= (7 - 0.01Q)Q \\ &= 7Q - 0.01Q^2 \end{aligned} \tag{2A.5}$$

As can be seen, a linear demand function results in a nonlinear total revenue function. More precisely, the functional relationship between total revenue and quantity seen here is expressed as a quadratic equation. Basically, this particular functional relationship is obtained whenever the independent variable is raised to the second power (i.e., squared) as well as to the first power. Graphically, quadratic equations are easily recognized by their parabolic shape. The parabola's actual shape and placement on the graph depend on the values and signs of the coefficient and intercept terms. Figure 2A.5 shows four different quadratic functions.

If, in addition to being squared, the independent variable is raised to the third power (i.e., cubed), the relationship between the dependent and independent variables is called a cubic function.[12] Figure 2A.6 illustrates different cubic functions. As in the case of quadratic equations, the pattern and placement of these curves depend on the values and signs of the coefficients and intercept terms.

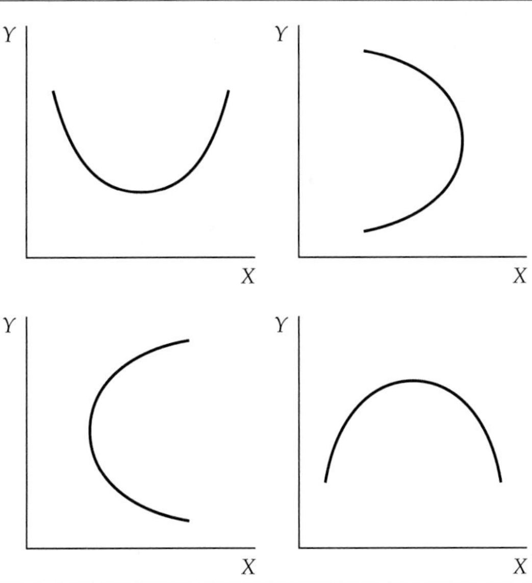

Figure 2A.5 Examples of Quadratic Functions

[12]Readers already familiar with the mathematics discussed here will recognize the linear, quadratic, and cubic equations as polynomials of different degrees.

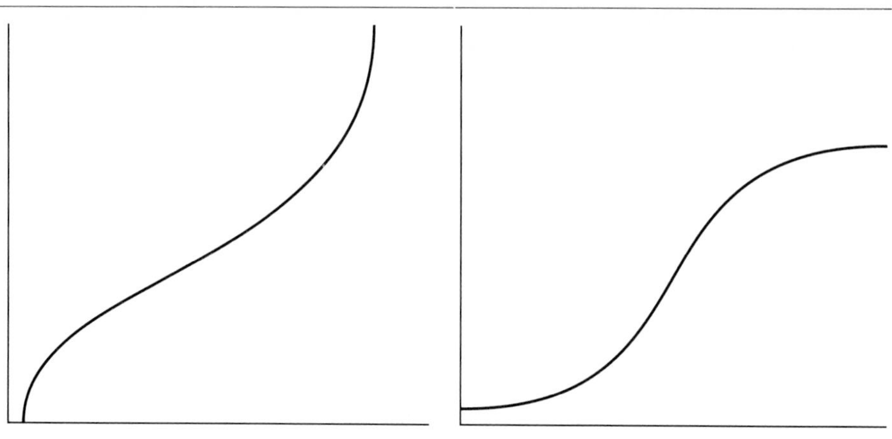

Figure 2A.6 Examples of Cubic Functions

The independent variable can also be raised beyond the third power. However, anything more complex than a cubic equation is generally not useful for describing the relationship among variables in managerial economics. Certainly, there is no need to go beyond the cubic equation for purposes of this text. As readers will see in ensuing chapters, the most commonly used forms of key functions are as follows: (1) linear demand function, (2) linear or quadratic total revenue function, (3) cubic production function, (4) cubic cost function, and (5) cubic profit function. Some variations to these relationships will also be used, depending on the specifics of the examples being discussed.

There are other nonlinear forms used in economic analysis besides those just listed. These forms involve the use of exponents, logarithms, and reciprocals of the independent variables. Simple examples of these types of nonlinear form are shown in Figure 2A.7. These forms are generally used in the statistical estimation of economic functions, such as the demand, production, and cost functions, and in the forecasting of variables based on some trend over time (i.e., time series analysis). More will be said about these particular functional forms in Chapters 5, 6, 9, and 10.

Continuous Functional Relationships

In plotting a functional relationship on a graph, we have assumed that changes in the value of the dependent variable are related in a continuous manner to changes in the independent variable. Intuitively, a function can be said to be continuous if it can be drawn on a graph without taking the pencil off the paper.[13] Perhaps the best way to understand a continuous function is to observe its opposite, a function with discontinuity. Suppose the admission price to an amusement park is established as follows: Ages 1 through 12 must pay $3, ages

[13]This particular way of explaining a continuous is taken from Gulati, op. cit. To be sure, the author provides a much more rigorous definition of this concept.

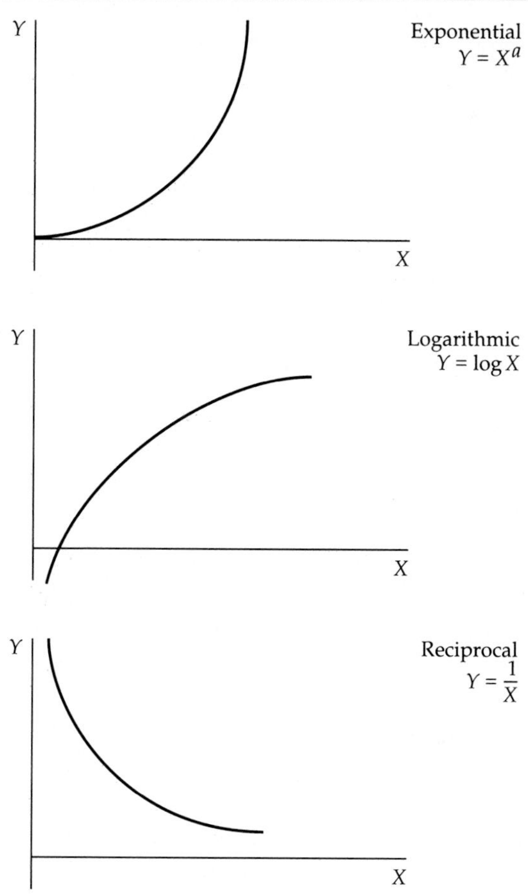

Figure 2A.7 Examples of Selected Nonlinear Functions

13 through 60 must pay \$8, and ages 61 and above must pay \$5. A graph of the relationship between admission price and age is shown in Figure 2A.8. Notice that there is a jump or break in the graph at the level separating children from adults and the level separating adults from senior citizens. Because of these breaks in the relationship between the independent and dependent variables, this discontinuous relationship is also referred to as a *step function*.

Unless otherwise specified, the functional relationships analyzed in this text are considered to be continuous. Looking back at our example of the demand and total revenue functions, we can see that they indeed indicate a continuous relationship between price and quantity and between total revenue and quantity. (See Figures 2A.1 and 2A.4.) However, a closer look at the intervals used in the examples might lead you to question the applicability of a continuous function in actual business situations. For instance, let us observe again in Figure 2A.9 the relationship between total revenue and quantity first shown in Figure 2A.4.

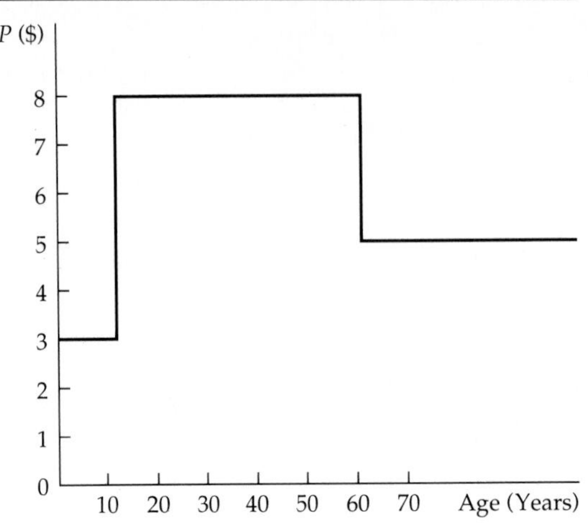

Figure 2A.8 Example of a Step Function: Age Groups and Admission Price

The inquiring reader might ask whether or not this relationship, $TR = 7Q - 0.01Q^2$, is in fact valid for points *within* each of the given intervals. For example, if the firm sold 150 units, would it earn $825? Even if the answer is affirmative, to be a truly continuous function, the relationship would have to hold no matter how small the intervals of quantity considered.[14] For example, if the firm sold 150.567 units, its revenue would be $827.265.

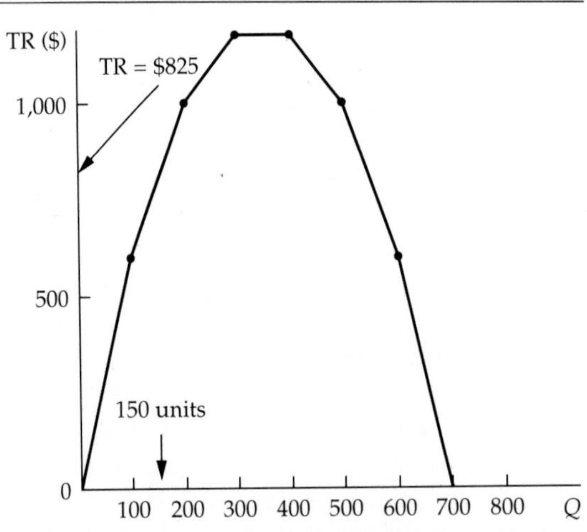

Figure 2A.9 Discrete Intervals in a Continuous Functions: The Example of Total Revenue

[14] According to mathematicians, "A function is said to be continuous over an open interval if it is continuous at *every* point in that interval" (Gulati, op. cit., p. 505).

But at this point, an adjustment to strict mathematics must be tempered with common sense. There are many instances in economic analysis in which continuous functions are assumed to represent relationships among variables, even though the variables themselves are subject to limitations in how finely they can be subdivided. For example, a firm may only be able to sell its product in lots of 100 or, at the very least, in single units. A firm might not want to consider price changes in terms of cents, but only in terms of dollars. In other cases, it might not be a matter of a firm's choice but of what resources are available. For example, suppose we have a function relating persons hired to the output they produce. (In Chapter 7, this is referred to as the short-run production function.) Let us further suppose that labor resources are measured in terms of units of people (as opposed to hours, minutes, or even seconds of work time). Many economic activities in business involve variables that must be measured in discrete intervals (e.g., people, units of output, monetary units, machines, factories). For purposes of analysis, we will assume that all the economic variables are related to each other in a continuous fashion but are valid only at stated discrete intervals.

Using Calculus

Calculus is a mathematical technique that enables one to find instantaneous rates of change of a continuous function. That is, instead of finding the rate of change between two points on a plotted line, as shown in Figure 2A.2, calculus enables us to find the rate of change in the dependent variable relative to the independent variable at a particular point on the function. However, calculus can be so applied *only* if a function is continuous. Thus, we needed to establish firmly the validity of using continuous functions to represent the relationships among economic variables.

Our brief introduction to calculus and its role in economic analysis begins with the statement that if all functional relationships in economics were linear, there would be no need for calculus! This point may be made clearer by referring to an intuitive definition of calculus. To quote the author of an extremely helpful and readable book on this subject:

> Calculus, first of all, is wrongly named. It should never have been given that name. A far truer and more meaningful name is "SLOPE-FINDING."[15]

It is not difficult to find the slope of a linear function. We simply take any two points on the line and find the change in Y relative to the change in X. The relative change is, of course, represented by the b coefficient in the linear equation. Moreover, because it is linear, the slope or rate of change remains the

[15]Eli S. Pine, *How to Enjoy Calculus,* Hasbrouck Heights, N.J.: Steinlitz-Hammacher Company, 1983. Pine's definition is, of course, a simplification since it leaves out integral calculus. Nevertheless, we recommend this book highly for those who wish a "user-friendly" review of differential calculus.

same between any two points over the entire range of intervals one wishes to consider for the function. This is shown in the algebraic expression of the linear function by the constancy of the *b* coefficient.

However, finding the slope of a nonlinear function poses a problem. Let us arbitrarily take two points on the curve shown in Figure 2A.10 and label them *A* and *D*. The slope or rate of change of *Y* relative to the change in *X* can be seen as *DL/AL*. Now, on this same curve let us find the slope of a point closer to point *D* and call it *C*. Notice that the slope of the line between these two points is less than the slope between *D* and *A*. (The measure of this slope is *DM/CM*.) The same holds true if we consider point *B*, a point that is still closer to *D*; the slope between *B* and *D* is less than the two slopes already considered. In general, we can state that in reference to the curve shown in Figure 2A.10, the slope between point *D* and a point to the left decreases as the point moves closer to *D*. Obviously, this is not the case for a linear equation because the slope is constant.

To understand how calculus enables us to find the slope or rate of change of a nonlinear function, let us resume the experiment. Suppose we keep on measuring changes in *Y* relative to smaller and smaller changes in *X*. Graphically, this can be represented in Figure 2A.10 by moving point *B* toward point *D*. As smaller and smaller changes in *X* are considered, point *B* moves closer and closer to point *D* until the limit at which it appears to become one and the same with point *D*. When this occurs, the slope or rate of change of *Y* relative to *X* can be represented as point *D* itself. Graphically, this is represented by the slope of a line tangent to point *D*. In effect, this slope is a measure of the change in *Y* relative to a very small (i.e., infinitesimally small) change in *X*. To

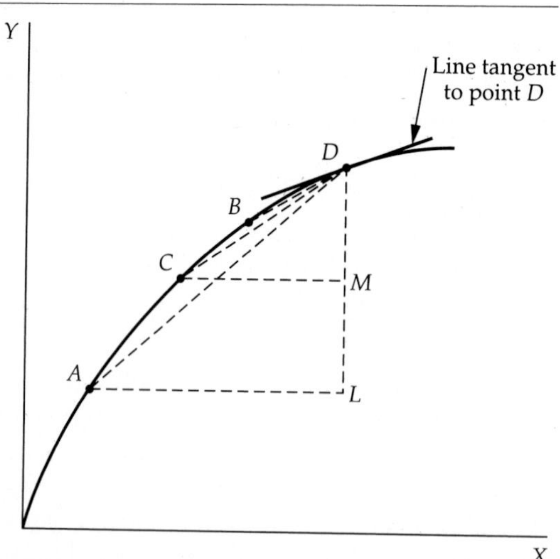

Figure 2A.10 Finding the Slope of a Nonlinear Function

find the magnitude of the slope of tangency to any point on a line, we need to employ calculus, or more specifically, a concept used in calculus called the *derivative.*

In mathematics, a derivative is a measure of the change in Y relative to a very small change in X. Using formal mathematical notation, we can define the derivative as:

$$\frac{dY}{dX} = \lim_{\Delta X \to 0} \frac{\Delta Y}{\Delta X}$$

This notation can be expressed as: "The derivative of Y with respect to X equals the limit (if such a limit exists) of the change in Y relative to the change in X as the change in X approaches zero."[16] As you can see from the discussion in the previous two paragraphs, the derivative turns out to be the slope of a line that is tangent to some given point on a curve. By convention, mathematicians use d to represent very small changes in a variable. Hence, dY/dX means "changes in Y relative to very small changes in X." For changes between two distinct points, the delta sign (Δ) is used.

Finding the Derivatives of a Function

There are certain rules for finding the derivatives of a function. We shall present in some detail two rules that will be used extensively in this text. The other rules and their use in economic analysis will be only briefly mentioned. Formal proofs of all of these rules are not provided. Interested students may consult any introductory calculus text for this information.

CONSTANTS The derivative of a constant must always be zero. Derivatives involve rates of change, and a constant, by definition, never changes in value. Expressed formally, if Y equals some constant, (e.g., $Y = 100$), then

$$\frac{dY}{dX} = 0$$

The null value of the derivative of a constant is illustrated in Figure 2A.11. Here we have assumed Y to have a constant value of 100. Clearly, this constant value of Y is unaffected by changes in the value of X. Thus, $dY/dX = 0$.

POWER FUNCTIONS A *power function* is one in which the independent variable, X, is raised to the power of one or more. This type of function can be expressed in general terms as

[16]The concept of *limit* is critical to understanding the derivative. We have tried to present an intuitive explanation of this concept by considering the movement of point B in Figure 2A.10 closer and closer to point D, so that in effect the changes in X become smaller and smaller. *At the limit,* B becomes so close to D that, for all intents and purposes, it is the same as D. This situation would represent the smallest possible change in X. For a more formal explanation of *limit,* readers should consult any introductory calculus text.

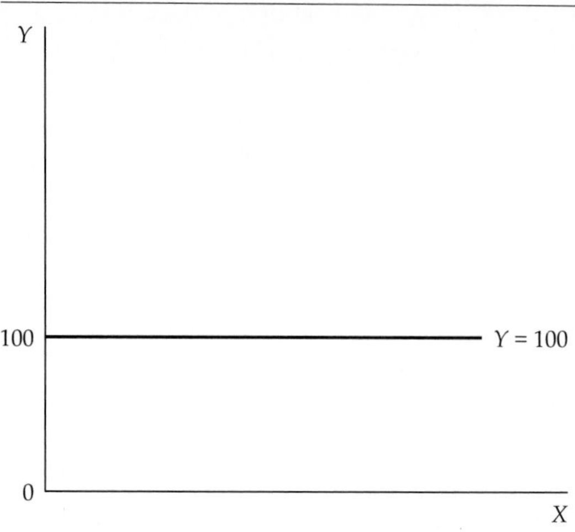

Figure 2A.11 The Derivative of a Constant Equals Zero

$$Y = bX^n \tag{2A.6}$$

where Y = Dependent variable
b = Coefficient of the dependent variable
X = Independent variable
n = Power to which the independent variable is raised

The rule for finding the derivative of this type of function is

$$\frac{dY}{dX} = nbX^{(n-1)} \tag{2A.7}$$

Thus, suppose we have the equation

$$Y = 10X^3 \tag{2A.8}$$

The derivative of this equation according to this rule is

$$\begin{aligned} \frac{dY}{dX} &= 3 \times 10X^{(3-1)} \\ &= 30X^2 \end{aligned} \tag{2A.9}$$

Thus, at the point where $X = 5$, the "instantaneous" rate of change of Y with respect to X is $30(5)^2$, or 750.

SUMS AND DIFFERENCES For convenience in presenting the rules in the remainder of this appendix, we will use the following notations:

$U = g(X)$, where U is an unspecified function, g, of X
$V = h(X)$, where V is an unspecified function, h, of X

Given the function $Y = U + V$, the derivative of the sum (difference) is equal to the sum (difference) of the derivatives of the individual terms. In notational form,

$$\frac{dY}{dX} = \frac{dU}{dX} + \frac{dV}{dX}$$

For example, if $U = g(X) = 3X^2$, $V = h(X) = 4X^3$, and $Y = U + V = 3X^2 + 4X^3$, then

$$\frac{dY}{dX} = 6X + 12X^2$$

PRODUCTS Given the function $Y = UV$, its derivative can be expressed as follows

$$\frac{dY}{dX} = U\frac{dV}{dX} + V\frac{dU}{dX}$$

This rule states that the derivative of the product of two expressions (U and V) is equal to the first term multiplied by the derivative of the second, plus the second term times the derivative of the first. For example, let $Y = 5X^2(7 - X)$. By letting $U = 5X^2$ and $V = (7 - X)$, we obtain

$$\begin{aligned}\frac{dY}{dX} &= 5X^2\frac{dV}{dX} + (7 - X)\frac{dU}{dX}\\ &= 5X^2(-1) + (7 - X)10X\\ &= -5X^2 + 70X - 10X^2\\ &= 70X - 15X^2\end{aligned}$$

QUOTIENTS Given the function $Y = U/V$, its derivative can be expressed as follows:

$$\frac{dY}{dX} = \frac{V(dU/dX) - U(dV/dX)}{V^2}$$

For example, suppose we have the following function:

$$Y = \frac{5X - 9}{10X^2}$$

Using the formula and letting $U = 5X - 9$ and $V = 10X^2$, we obtain the following:

$$\frac{dY}{dX} = \frac{10X^2 \times 5 - (5X - 9)20X}{100X^4}$$
$$= \frac{50X^2 - 100X^2 + 180X}{100X^4}$$
$$= \frac{180X - 50X^2}{100X^4}$$
$$= \frac{18 - 5X}{10X^3}$$

APPLYING THE RULES TO AN ECONOMIC PROBLEM AND A PREVIEW OF OTHER RULES FOR DIFFERENTIATING A FUNCTION There are several other rules for differentiating a function that are used in economic analysis. These involve differentiating a logarithmic function and the "function of a function" (often referred to in mathematics as the *chain rule*). We will present these rules as they are needed in the appropriate chapters. In fact, almost all of the mathematical examples involving calculus will require only the rules for constants, powers, and sums and differences. As an example of how these three rules are applied, we return to the total revenue and demand functions presented earlier in this appendix. Recall that

$$\text{TR} = 7Q - 0.01Q^2 \tag{2A.10}$$

Using the rules for powers and for sums and differences, we find that the derivative of this function is

$$\frac{d\text{TR}}{dQ} = 7 - 0.02Q \tag{2A.11}$$

The derivative of the total revenue function is also called the *marginal revenue function* and plays a very important part in many aspects of economic analysis. (See Chapter 4 for a complete discussion of the definition and uses of marginal revenue.)

Turning now to the demand function first presented in Figure 2A.3, we recall that

$$Q = 700 - 100P \tag{2A.12}$$

Using the rules for constants, powers, and sums and differences, we see that the derivative of this function is:

$$\begin{aligned} \frac{dQ}{dP} &= 0 - 1(100)P^{(1-1)} \\ &= -100P^0 \\ &= -100 \end{aligned} \tag{2A.13}$$

Notice that, by the conventions of mathematical notation, variables such as P that have no stated exponent are assumed to be raised to the first power (i.e., $n = 1$). Thus, based on the rule for the derivative of a power function, $(n - 1)$ becomes $(1 - 1)$, or zero.[17] Therefore, dQ/dP is equal to the constant value 100.

[17]The rule in algebra is that any value raised to the zeroth power is equal to unity.

Recall our initial statement that there is no need for calculus if only linear functions are considered. This is supported by the results shown in Equation (2A.13). Here we can see that the first derivative of the linear demand equation is simply the value of the *b* coefficient, 100. That is, no matter what the value of *P*, the change in *Q* with respect to a change in *P* is 100 (i.e., the slope of the linear function, or the *b* coefficient in the linear equation). Another way to express this is that for a linear function, there is no need to take the derivative dY/dX. Instead, we can use the slope of the line represented by $\Delta Y / \Delta X$.

PARTIAL DERIVATIVES Many functional relationships in this text will entail a number of independent variables. For example, let us assume that a firm has a demand function represented by the following equation:

$$Q = -100P + 50I + P_s + 2N \tag{2A.14}$$

where Q = Quantity demanded
P = Price of the product
I = Income of customers
P_s = Price of a substitute product
N = Number of customers

If we want to know the change in *Q* with respect to a change in a particular independent variable, we can take the partial derivative of *Q* with respect to that variable. For example, the impact of a change in *P* on *Q*, with other factors held constant, would be expressed as

$$\frac{\delta Q}{\delta P} = -100 \tag{2A.15}$$

The conventional symbol used in mathematics for the partial derivative is the lower-case Greek letter delta, δ. Notice that all we did was use the rule for the derivative of a power function on the *P* variable. Because the other independent variables, I, P_s, and N, are held constant, they are treated as constants in taking the partial derivative. (As you recall, the derivative of a constant is zero.) Thus, the other terms in the equation drop out, leaving us with the instantaneous impact of the change in *P* on *Q*. This procedure applies regardless of the powers to which the independent variables are raised. It just so happens that in this equation, all the independent variables are raised only to the first power.[18]

Finding the Maximum and Minimum Values of a Function

A primary objective of managerial economics is to find the optimal values of key variables. This means finding "the best" possible amount or value under certain circumstances. Marginal analysis and the concept of the derivative are very helpful in finding optimal values. For example, given a total revenue function, a firm might want to find the number of units it must sell to maximize its

[18]An expression such as this is referred to in mathematics as *linear additive equation.*

revenue. Taking the total revenue function first shown in Equation (2A.5), we have

$$\text{TR} = 7Q - 0.01Q^2 \tag{2A.16}$$

The derivative of this function (i.e., marginal revenue) is

$$\frac{d\,\text{TR}}{dQ} = 7 - 0.02Q \tag{2A.17}$$

Setting the first derivative of the total revenue function (or the marginal revenue function) equal to zero and solving for the revenue-maximizing quantity, Q^*, gives us[19]

$$\begin{aligned} 7 - 0.02Q &= 0 \\ Q^* &= 350 \end{aligned} \tag{2A.18}$$

Thus, the firm should sell 350 units of its product if it wants to maximize its total revenue. In addition, if the managers wish to know the price that the firm should charge to sell the "revenue-maximizing" number of units, they can go back to the demand equation from which the total revenue function was derived, that is,

$$P = 7 - 0.01Q \tag{2A.19}$$

By substituting the value of Q^* into this equation, we obtain

$$\begin{aligned} P^* &= 7 - 0.01(350) \\ &= \$3.50 \end{aligned} \tag{2A.20}$$

The demand function, the total revenue function, and the revenue-maximizing price and quantity are all illustrated in Figure 2A.12.

To further illustrate the use of the derivative in finding the optimum, let us use an example that will play an important part in Chapter 11. Suppose a firm wishes to find the price and output levels that will maximize its profit. If the firm's revenue and cost functions are known, it is a relatively simple matter to use the derivative of these functions to find the optimal price and quantity. To begin with, let us assume the following demand, revenue, and cost functions:

$$Q = 17.2 - 0.1P \tag{2A.21}$$

or

$$P = 172 - 10Q \tag{2A.22}$$

$$TR = 172Q - 10Q^2 \tag{2A.23}$$

$$TC = 100 + 65Q + Q^2 \tag{2A.24}$$

By definition, profit (π) is equal to total revenue minus total cost. That is,

$$\pi = \text{TR} - \text{TC} \tag{2A.25}$$

---

[19]Henceforth, all optimal values for Q and P (e.g., values that maximize revenue or profit or minimize cost) will be designated with an asterisk.

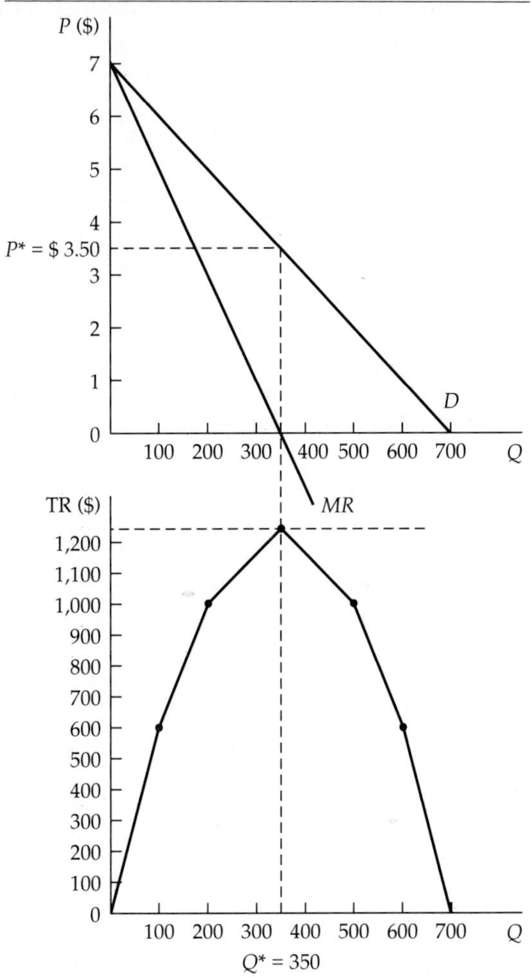

Figure 2A.12 Demand Function, Total Revenue Function, and Revenue-Maximizing Price and Quantity

Substituting equations (2A.23) and (2A.24) into (2A.25) gives us:

$$\pi = 172Q - 10Q^2 - 100 - 65Q - Q^2 \tag{2A.26}$$
$$= -100 + 107Q - 11Q^2$$

To find the profit-maximizing output level, we simply follow the same procedure used to find the revenue-maximizing output level. We take the derivative of the total profit function, set it equal to zero, and solve for Q^*:

$$\frac{d\pi}{dQ} = 107 - 22Q = 0 \tag{2A.27}$$

$$22Q = 107$$

$$Q^* = 4.86 \tag{2A.28}$$

The total revenue and cost functions and the total profit function are illustrated in Figure 2A.13*a* and *b*, respectively.

DISTINGUISHING MAXIMUM AND MINIMUM VALUES IN THE OPTIMIZATION PROBLEM In economic analysis, finding the optimum generally means finding either the maximum or minimum value of a variable, depending on what type of function is being considered. For example, if the profit or total revenue function is the focus, the maximum value is obviously of interest. If a cost function is being analyzed, its minimum value would be the main concern. Taking the derivative of a function, setting it equal to zero, and then solving for the value of the independent variable enables us to find the maximum or minimum value of the function.

However, there may be instances in which a function has both a maximum and a minimum value. When this occurs, the method described previously can-

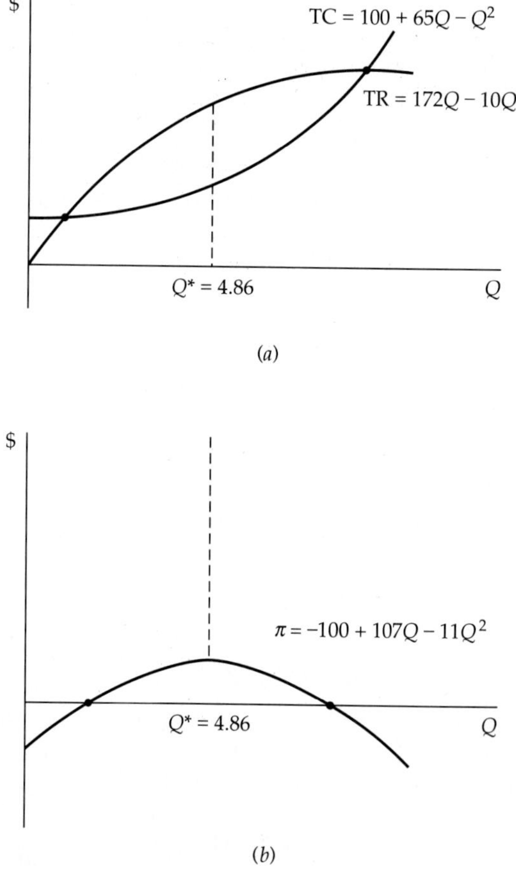

Figure 2A.13 Total Revenue, Total Cost, and Total Profit Functions not tell us whether the optimum is a maximum or a minimum. This situation of indeterminacy can be seen in Figure 2A.14*a*. The graph in this figure represents a cubic function of the general form $Y = a - bX + cX^2 - dX^3$. Clearly, this function has both a minimum (point *A*) and a maximum (point *C*). As a generalization, if we took the first derivative at the four points designated in Figure 2A.14a, we would find that

At point *A*, $dY/dX = 0$.
At point *B*, $dY/dX > 0$.
At point *C*, $dY/dX = 0$.
At point *D*, $dY/dX < 0$.

As expected, the first derivatives of points *A* and *C* are equal to zero, reflecting the fact that their lines of tangency are horizontal (i.e., have zero slope). The positive and negative values of the derivatives at points *B* and *D* are reflective

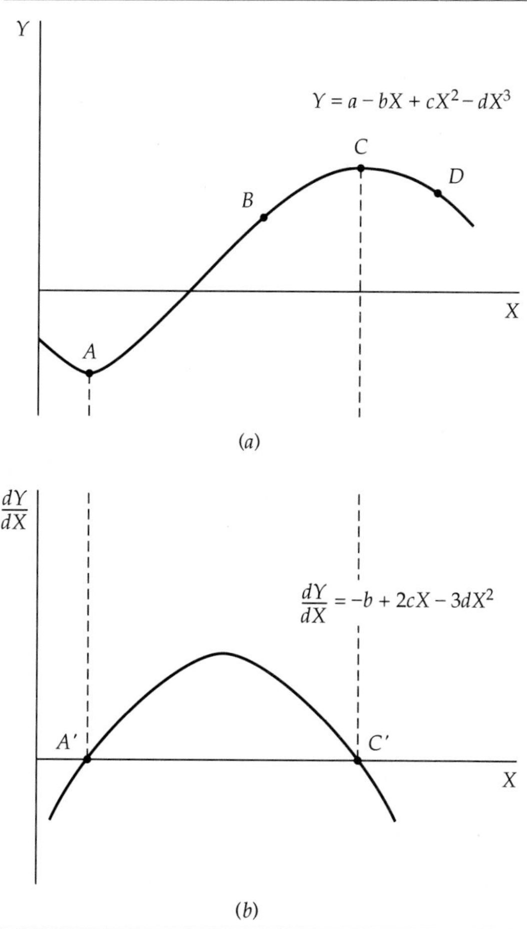

Figure 2A.14 Maximum and Minimum Points of a Cubic Function

of their respective upward and downward lines of tangency. However, because *both* points A and C have first derivatives equal to zero, a problem arises if we wish to know whether these points indicate maximum or minimum values of Y. Of course, in Figure 2A.14 we can plainly see that point A is the minimum value and point C is the maximum value. However, there is a formal mathematical procedure for distinguishing a function's maximum and minimum values. This procedure requires the use of a function's *second derivative.*

The second derivative of a function is the derivative of its first derivative. The procedure for finding the second derivative of a function is quite simple. All the rules for finding the first derivative apply to obtaining the second derivative. Conceptually, we can consider the second derivative of a function as a measure of the rate of change of the first derivative. In other words, it is a measure of "the rate of change of the rate of change."[20]

Let us illustrate precisely how the second derivative is used to determine the maximum and minimum values by presenting a graph of the function's first derivative in Figure 2A.14*b*. As a check on your understanding of this figure, notice that, as expected, the second derivative has a negative value when the original function decreases in value and a positive value when the original function increases in value. But now consider another aspect of this figure. Recall that the second derivative is a measure of the rate of change of the first derivative. Thus, graphically, we can find the second derivative by evaluating the slopes of lines tangent to points on the graph of the *first derivative.* See points A' and C' in Figure 2A.14*b*. By inspection of this figure, it should be quite clear that the slope of the line tangent to point A' is positive and the slope of the line tangent to point C' is negative. This enables us to conclude the following: At the minimum point of a function, the second derivative is *positive.* At the maximum point of a function, the second derivative is *negative.*[21]

---

[20]Mathematics and physics texts often use the example of a moving automobile to help distinguish the first and second derivatives. To begin with, the function can be expressed as $M = f(T)$, or miles traveled is a function of the time elapsed. The first derivative of this function describes the automobile's velocity. As an example of this, imagine a car moving at the rate of speed of 45 miles per hour. Now suppose this car has just entered a freeway, starts to accelerate, and then reaches a speed of 75 mph. The measure of this acceleration as the car goes from 45 mph to 75 mph is the second derivative of the function. Because the car is accelerating (i.e., going faster and faster), the second derivative is some positive value. In other words, the distance (measured in miles) that the car is traveling is increasing at *an increasing* rate. To extend this example a bit further, suppose the driver of the car, realizing that this section of the freeway is closely monitored by radar, begins to slow down to the legal speed limit of 60 mph. As the driver slows down, or decelerates, the speed at which the car is traveling is reduced. In other words, the distance (in miles) that the car is traveling is increasing at a *decreasing rate.* Deceleration, being the opposite of acceleration, implies that the second derivative in this case is negative.

[21]Let us return to the automobile example for an alternative explanation of the second-order condition for determining a function's maximum value. Let us imagine that, at the very moment the car reached 75 mph, the driver started to slow down. This means that at the precise moment the accelerating car started to decelerate, it had reached its *maximum* speed. In mathematical terms, if a function is increasing at an *increasing* rate (i.e., its second derivative is positive), then the moment it starts to increase at a *decreasing* rate (i.e., its second derivative becomes negative), it has reached its maximum value. Similar reasoning can be used to explain the second-order condition for determining the minimum value of a function.

Using mathematical notation, we can now state the *first- and second-order conditions* for determining the maximum or minimum values of a function.

$$\text{Maximum value: } \begin{array}{ll} dY/dX = 0 & \text{(first-order condition)} \\ d^2/dx^2 < 0 & \text{(second-order condition)} \end{array}$$

$$\text{Minimum value: } \begin{array}{ll} dY/dX = 0 & \text{(first-order condition)} \\ d^2/dx^2 > 0 & \text{(second-order condition)} \end{array}$$

We will now illustrate how the first- and second-order conditions are used to find the profit-maximizing level of output for a firm. Suppose this firm has the following revenue and total cost functions:

$$\text{TR} = 50Q \tag{2A.29}$$

$$\text{TC} = 100 + 60Q - 3Q^2 + 0.1Q^3 \tag{2A.30}$$

Based on these equations the firm's total profit function is

$$\begin{aligned} \pi &= 50Q - (100 + 60Q - 3Q^2 + 0.1Q^3) \\ &= 50Q - 100 - 60Q + 3Q^2 - 0.1Q^3 \\ &= -100 - 10Q + 3Q^2 - 0.1Q^3 \end{aligned} \tag{2A.31}$$

Notice that this firm's profit function contains a term that is raised to the third power because its cost function is also raised to the third power. In other words, the firm is assumed to have a cubic cost function, and therefore it has a cubic profit function.[22] Plotting this cubic profit function gives us the graph in Figure 2A.15. We can observe in this figure that the level of output that maximizes the

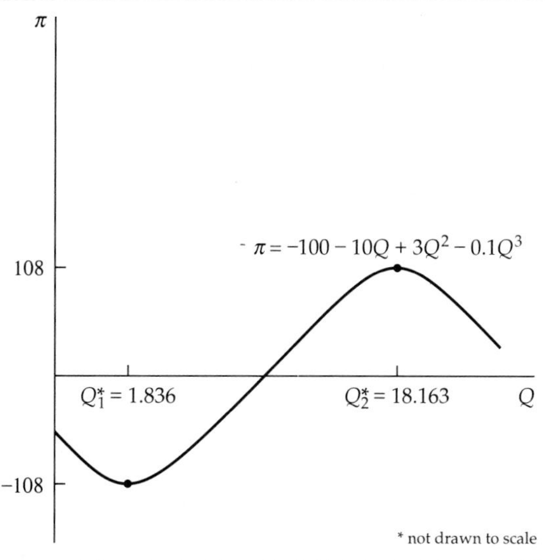

Figure 2A.15 Cubic Profit Function

[22]The economic rationale for cost functions of different degrees is explained in Chapter 8.

firm's profit is about 18.2 units, and the level of output that minimizes its profit (i.e., maximizes its loss) is about 1.8 units.

Let us employ calculus along with the first- and second-order conditions to determine the point at which the firm maximizes its profit. We begin as before by finding the first derivative of the profit function, setting it equal to zero, and solving for the value of Q that satisfies this condition.

$$\pi = -100 - 10Q + 3Q^2 - 0.1Q^3 \tag{2A.32}$$

$$\frac{d\pi}{dQ} = -10 + 6Q - 0.3Q^2$$

$$= -0.3Q^2 + 6Q - 10 = 0 \tag{2A.33}$$

Note that Equation 2A.33 has been rearranged to conform to the general expression for a quadratic equation. Because the first derivative of the profit function is quadratic, there are two possible values of Q that satisfy the equation:[23]

$$Q_1^* = 1.836 \qquad Q_2^* = 18.163$$

As expected Q_1^* and Q_2^* coincide with the two points shown in Figure 2A.13. Although both Q_1^* and Q_2^* fulfill the first-order condition, only one satisfies the second-order condition. To see this, let us find the second derivative of the function by taking the derivative of the marginal profit function expressed in Equation(2A.33):

$$\frac{d^2\pi}{dQ^2} = -0.6Q + 6$$

By substitution, we see that at output level 1.836 the value of the second derivative is a positive number:

$$\frac{d^2\pi}{dQ^2} = -0.6(1.836) + 6 = 4.89$$

On the other hand, we see that at output level 18.163 the value of the second derivative is a negative number:

$$\frac{d^2\pi}{dQ^2} = -0.6(18.163) + 6 = -4.89$$

---

[23]The first derivative of a cubic function is a quadratic function. Such a function can be expressed in the general form

$$Y = aX^2 + bX + c$$

Perhaps you recall from your previous studies of algebra that the values of X that set the quadratic function equal to zero can be found by using the formula for the "roots" of a quadratic equation:

$$X = \frac{-b \pm \sqrt{b^2 - 4ac}}{2a}$$

By substituting the values of the coefficients in Equation 2A.33 (i.e., $a = -0.3$, $b = 6$, $c = -10$) we obtain the answers shown.

Thus, we see that only Q_2^* enables us to adhere to the second-order condition that $d^2\pi/dQ^2 < 0$. This confirms in a formal, mathematical manner what we already knew from plotting and evaluating the graph of the firm's total profit function: Q_2^* is the firm's profit-maximizing level of output.

Five Key Functions Used in this Text

Five key functions will be used in this text: (1) demand, (2) total revenue, (3) production, (4) total cost, and (5) profit. The following diagrams show the algebraic and graphical expressions for these functions. As can be seen, the demand function is linear, the total revenue function is quadratic, and the production, cost, and profit functions are cubic. Note that the last three functions all refer to economic conditions in the short run.

1. Demand

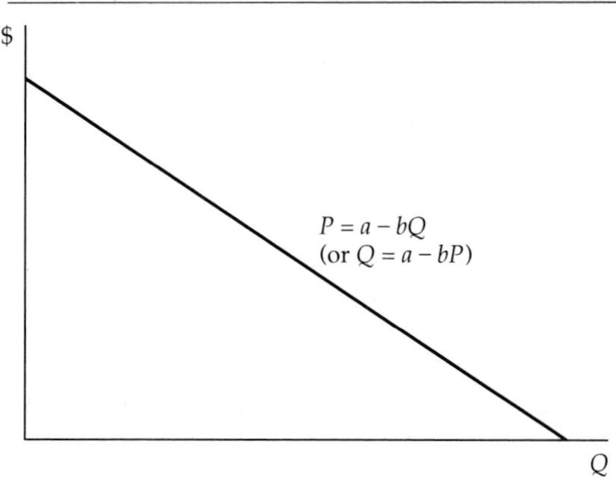

2. Total revenue

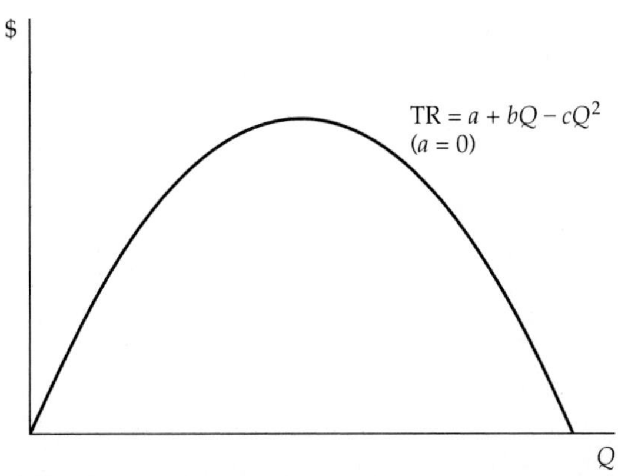

3. Production (short run)

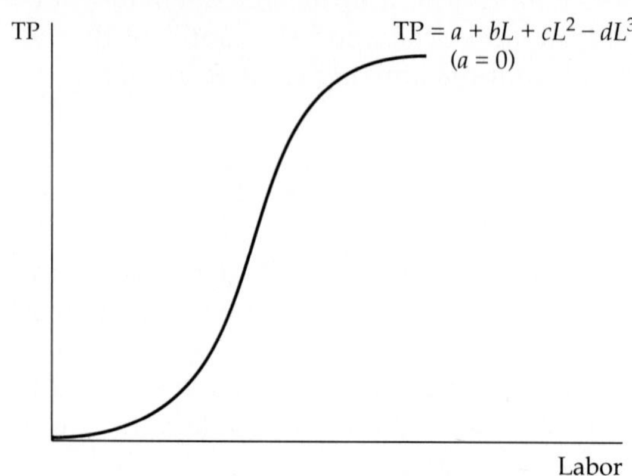

4. Cost (short run)

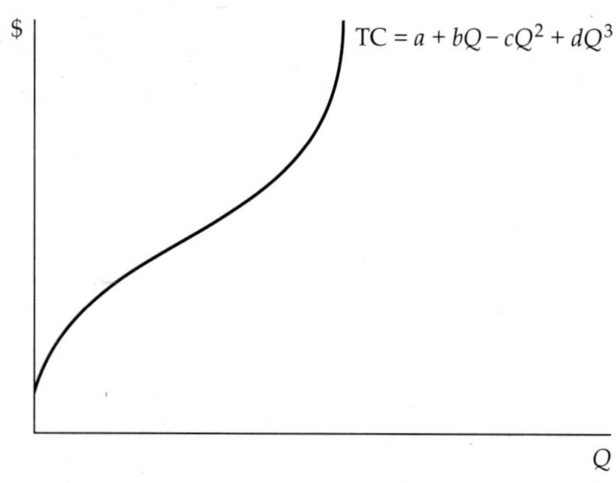

5. Profit (short run)

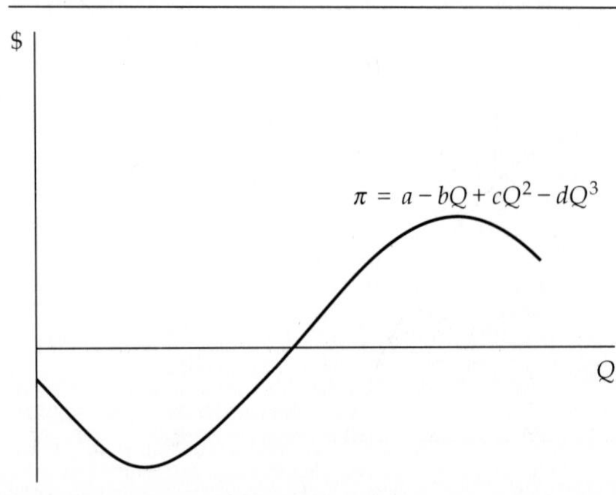

Summary

As you proceed with your study of managerial economics and the reading of this text, you will find that the essence of economic analysis is the study of functional relationships between certain dependent variables (e.g., quantity demanded, revenue, cost, profit) and one or more independent variables (e.g., price, income, quantity sold). Mathematics is a tool that can greatly facilitate the analysis of these functional relationships. For example, rather than simply saying that "the quantity of a product sold depends on its price," we can use an algebraic equation to state precisely how many units of a product a firm can expect to sell at a particular price. Moreover, when we engage in a marginal analysis of the impact of price on quantity demanded, we can use the first derivative of this equation to measure the change in quantity demanded relative to changes in price.[24] Furthermore, as shown in this appendix, the precise algebraic expression of the demand function enables us to derive a firm's total revenue and marginal revenue functions. And with the help of calculus, the optimal price and quantity (e.g., the price and quantity that maximize revenue) can be quickly found.

The more data a firm is able to obtain about its key economic functions (i.e., demand, revenue, production, cost, and profit), the more that mathematics can be employed in the analysis. The more that mathematics can be utilized, the more precise a manager can be about such key decisions as the best price to charge, the best markets to compete in, and the most desirable levels of resource allocation. Unfortunately, in the real world firms do not often have the luxury of accurate or complete data with which to work. This is another aspect of decision making and will be discussed in later chapters.[25]

Questions

1. Define the following terms: function, variable, independent variable, dependent variable, functional form.
2. Briefly describe how a function is represented in tabular form, in graphical form, and in an equation. Illustrate using the relationship between price and quantity expressed in a demand function.
3. Express in formal mathematical terms the following functional relationships. You may use the general form $Y = f(X)$. However, in each case be as specific as possible about what variables are represented by Y and X. (For example, in the first relation, advertising is the X variable and could be measured in terms of the amount of advertising dollars spent annually by a firm.)
   a. The effectiveness of advertising.
   b. The impact on output resulting from increasing the number of employees.

---

[24]In Chapter 4, you will see how this first derivative is incorporated into a formula for *elasticity*, a value indicating the percentage change in a dependent variable, such as units sold, with a percentage change in an independent variable, such as price.

[25]In particular, see Chapter 5 on demand estimation, and Chapter 6, on forecasting.

c. The impact on labor productivity resulting from increasing automation.
d. The impact on sales and profits resulting from price reductions.
e. The impact on sales and profits resulting from a recession.
f. The impact on sales and profits resulting from changes in the financial sector (e.g., the stock market or the bond market).
g. The impact on cost resulting from the use of outside vendors to supply certain components in the manufacturing process.

4. What is a continuous function? Does the use of continuous functions to express economic relationships present any difficulties in analyzing real-world business problems? Explain.
5. Define in mathematical terms the slope of a line. Why is the slope considered to be so important in the quantitative analysis of economic problems?
6. Define marginal analysis. Give examples of how this type of analysis can help a managerial decision maker. Are there any limitations to using this type of analysis in actual business situations? Explain.
7. Explain why the first derivative of a function is an important part of marginal analysis.
8. Explain how an analysis of the first derivative of the function $Y = f(X)$ enables one to find the point at which the Y variable is at its maximum or minimum.
9. (Optional) Explain how an analysis of the second derivative of a function enables one to determine whether the variable is a maximum or a minimum.
10. Briefly explain the difference between $\Delta Y / \Delta X$ and dY/dX. Explain why in a linear equation, there is no difference between the two terms.

Problems

1. Answer the following questions on the basis of the accompanying demand schedule.

Price	*Quantity*
$100	25
80	35
60	45
40	55
20	65
0	75

   a. Express the schedule as an algebraic equation in which Q is the dependent variable. Plot this on a graph.
   b. Express the schedule as an algebraic equation in which P is the dependent variable. Plot this on a graph.

2. You are given the following demand equations:

$$Q = 450 - 16P$$

$$Q = 360 - 80P$$

$$Q = 1{,}500 - 500P$$

a. Determine each equation's total revenue and marginal revenue equations.

b. Plot the demand equation and the marginal and total revenue equations on a graph.

c. Use calculus to determine the prices and quantities that maximize the revenue for each equation. Show the points of revenue maximization on the graphs that you have constructed.

3. You are given the following cost equations:

$$\text{TC} = 1{,}500 + 300Q - 25Q^2 + 1.5Q^3$$

$$\text{TC} = 1{,}500 + 300Q + 25Q^2$$

$$\text{TC} = 1{,}500 + 300Q$$

a. Determine each equation's average variable cost, average cost, and marginal cost.

b. Plot each equation on a graph. On separate graphs, plot each equation's average variable cost, average cost, and marginal cost.

c. Use calculus to determine the minimum point on the marginal cost curve.

4. Given the demand equation shown, answer the following questions:

$$Q = 10 - .004P$$

a. Combine this equation with each of the cost equations listed in question 3. Use calculus to find the price that will maximize the short-run profit for each of the cost equations.

b. Plot the profit curve for each of the cost equations.

CHAPTER 3

Supply and Demand

The Situation

Ross Harris, as a senior purchasing agent responsible for the sweetener used in Global Foods' soft drink product, reported directly to the vice president in charge of purchasing for the entire firm. In two weeks, Ross's firm would be sitting down with the major producers of high-fructose corn syrup (HFCS) to set the price of HFCS for the coming year. Other major soft drink companies would also begin their annual negotiations. Ever since HFCS began replacing sugar (or sucrose) as a sweetener in soft drinks, the major soft drink firms had been negotiating annually with the largest refiners of HFCS on the coming year's price. On balance, the arrangement had worked well for the soft drink industry. Once the price had been determined, soft drink makers were protected from any increase in the spot price for HFCS. Of course, if the price of HFCS fell below the fixed price, the soft drink firms would end up paying more for the product than if they had relied primarily on the spot market for their supply.

This year, however, the major HFCS refiners wanted to change one of the key terms of the pricing agreement. Instead of setting the price on an annual basis, the refiners wanted it to be set every 90 days. "They [the refiners] say they want a more 'market-sensitive' price for their product," Ross's boss explained. "And from the way the spot price of HFCS has been fluctuating in recent years, I don't blame them for this request. As it so happens, most of the agreements have protected us against price increases and have hurt the refiners by preventing them from selling at the higher spot prices.

"Needless to say, this change from an annual to a quarterly agreement puts us in a potentially riskier situation, since we would be able to protect ourselves from possible increases in the price of HFCS for only three months. The management committee does not know whether it is worth 'going to the mat' with the refiners to keep the arrangement on an annual basis. The pro-

(Continued)

posed arrangement may turn out to be beneficial, or at least no different from the current one. Ross, I want you and your staff to do a quick but thorough analysis of the situation. Basically, tell us the pros and cons of a quarterly contract."

Meanwhile, Kathy Martinez, whose company was one of the major refiners that processed corn into the HFCS, was given the assignment of preparing a market analysis for corn, the major ingredient of HFCS. This was to be combined with an analysis of the cost of processing the corn into HFCS. The combined report would then be used by her company's negotiating team as supporting material in the firm's efforts to change the contract pricing period from an annual to a quarterly basis. Kathy had only 10 more days in which to complete her portion of the report.

Introduction

In this chapter, we introduce the basic elements of supply and demand. Although for some of you, this chapter will serve as a review of material covered in an economics principles course, it has been included because it is essential that every reader have a thorough grounding in supply and demand before proceeding to the particulars of managerial economics. There may be situations—such as those described for Ross and Kathy—in which you may be required to conduct or evaluate a study with a considerable use of supply-and-demand analysis. But regardless of how directly this chapter's material may apply to your work, most of the material covered in this book will relate in some way to supply or demand. Indeed, supply and demand can be considered the conceptual framework within which the specifics of managerial economics are discussed.

Many students who study supply and demand for the first time are preoccupied with the mechanics of the analysis (e.g., which way the supply and demand lines shift and the reasons for this shift, how a shortage or a surplus is measured, or the movement from one point of equilibrium to another). To be sure, these mechanics will be covered in this chapter. But as you study supply and demand in preparation for the study of managerial economics, you should focus particular attention on the conceptual and applied aspects of the analysis. For example, in addition to being able to define a shortage or a surplus in the market, you should understand the causes of market shortages or surpluses and the role that price changes play in correcting these market imbalances. Another part of the mechanics of supply and demand involves the division of market changes into short-run and long-run time frames. The direction of price changes depends very much on which time frame is being considered. But the conceptual aspect of short-run and long-run changes in price involve what economists refer to as the *rationing function* and the *guiding* or *allocating function* of price. In upcoming sections of this chapter, both the mechanics and the concepts of these movements of price over time will be discussed.

Market Demand

The demand for a good or service is defined as:

> *Quantities* of a good or service that people are ready to *buy* at various *prices* within some given *time period, other factors* besides price held constant.

There are several key terms in this rather lengthy definition. The key relationship is between the quantity that people are willing to purchase and the price of the product. To be sure, there are other factors, such as personal taste and income. But these other factors are set aside or "held constant" as the relationship between quantity and price is considered.

Also important is the length of time within which the relationship between quantity and price is examined. The longer the time period, the greater the flexibility of people's responses to the list of possible prices. Perhaps the best way to understand the economic definition of demand is to begin with a simple example involving one buyer: yourself.

Suppose you were asked to respond to the following market survey question: "In a one-week period, how many slices of pizza would you be prepared to buy for each of the prices cited below?"

Price (per slice)	Q_{D1}	Q_{D2}	Q_{D3}	Q_{DM}
2.00	___			
1.50	___			
1.00	___			
0.50	___			
0.05	___			

Answer the survey question by filling in the blanks under Q_{D1}. Q_{D2} and Q_{D3} represent other respondents to the survey, and Q_{DM} represents the total response by you and the other two respondents. Assuming that there are only three of you in the market for pizza, this last column represents the market demand.

Typically, students responding to the survey state that they would be willing to buy more slices of pizza as the price falls from $2.00 to $0.05. In fact, some have even mentioned throwing a big party (or buying several pies and freezing them) at a nickel a slice. If your response was similar, then you can be considered a "rational" consumer. In economics, a rational consumer is one who follows the law of demand, which states that the quantity demanded is inversely related to price, other factors held constant. Occasionally, a student will respond that he or she would be willing to buy *less* pizza at lower prices. Further questioning usually reveals that they assume the pizza to be of a lesser quality at lower prices.

There are instances in which consumers behave in an "irrational" manner in response to the price of a good or service. Indeed, an appeal to the notion that "if it costs so much, then it must be good" often underlies the approach to the selling of such items as perfumes, cosmetics, high-fashion clothing, and luxury automobiles.[1] But in the economic analysis of demand, it is assumed that buyers do not associate price with quality and therefore will act in a rational way to changes in the price of a particular good or service.

Suppose that the responses to our pizza survey are as shown in Table 3.1. Notice that although the pattern of response is different for each respondent, they all follow the law of demand by indicating willingness to buy more as the price falls, and vice versa. Person 2 is not affected by price changes between \$2.00 and \$1.00. However, the table indicates that when the price falls to \$0.50, this person would be willing to buy more pizza during the week.[2] Person 3 appears to like pizza much more than the other two respondents. At each possible price, this person would be willing to buy more than the others. Apparently, other factors besides the price influence the willingness of people to buy a particular good or service. It is these factors that can help to account for the differences in response among the three consumers. Person 3 may simply like pizza more than the other two consumers (or the other two may be on a diet) or may have a considerably higher disposable income. If we add up the individual demand schedules, we obtain the market demand schedule. This is shown in the column labeled as Q_{DM}.

Let us now shift the focus to the market demand for pizza. The market demand for any product is the summation of the demand by individual buyers. We have seen that other factors besides price can affect the amount of a good or service that an individual is willing to buy. The same holds true for the entire set of buyers constituting the market demand for this good or service. Nonprice determinants of demand are:

1. Tastes and preferences
2. Income

Table 3.1 Hypothetical Demand Curve for Pizza (3 Individuals, Per Week)

Price (per slice)	Q_{D1}	Q_{D2}	Q_{D3}	Q_{DM}
\$2.00	0	2	3	5
1.50	1	2	5	8
1.00	2	2	8	12
0.50	3	3	10	16
0.05	4	4	12	21

[1]The use of price in creating a "snob appeal" for a particular product is an important part of marketing. An introductory course in marketing as well as a more advanced course in consumer psychology should provide interested readers with much information on this subject.

[2]The reason for this is based on the concept of *pricing elasticity of demand*. This will be explained in detail in the next chapter.

3. Prices of related products (substitutes or complements)
4. Number of buyers
5. Future expectations

To illustrate the impact of price and nonprice factors on demand, we will present a slightly different survey of the demand for pizza.[3] Let us now consider the demand in terms of pies purchased per month. This hypothetical demand schedule for pizza is shown in Table 3.2 as Q_{D1}, along with two others, one depicting a higher level of demand (Q_{D2}) and the other indicating a lower level (Q_{D3}). All three schedules are plotted on the graph shown in Figure 3.1.

Before we proceed further with our discussion, the use of certain terms should be clarified. In economic analysis, the term *quantity demanded* is used in reference to the amount of a good or service that people wish to buy at a particular price. However, if the *entire* list of quantities demanded at different prices is being considered, the term *demand* is used. Thus, in Table 3.2, at the price of $5, the quantity demanded in the first list of responses is 200. At $4, the quantity demanded increases to 300. The demand for pizza consists of all the data shown in columns P and Q_{D1}. In Figure 3.1, we observe that a particular quantity demanded is a point on the demand curve, whereas the demand is the curve itself. Changes in the quantity demanded involve a movement along the demand curve; changes in demand involve shift of the entire demand curve.

Given these distinctions in terminology, the following statements can be made:

Changes in *price* result in changes in the *quantity demanded* (i.e. *movements along* the demand curve).

Changes in the *nonprice determinants* result in changes in *demand* (i.e. *shifts* of the demand curve).

Table 3.2 Market Demand Curve for Pizza

Price (per slice)	Q_{D1}	Q_{D2}	Q_{D3}
$7.00	0	100	0
6.00	100	200	0
5.00	200	300	100
4.00	300	400	200
3.00	400	500	300
2.00	500	600	400
1.00	600	700	500
0	700	800	600

[3]We have modified the numerical example to offer some variety in illustration. Moreover, this numerical example conforms to the examples used in the appendix to Chapter 2 as well as the appendix to this chapter.

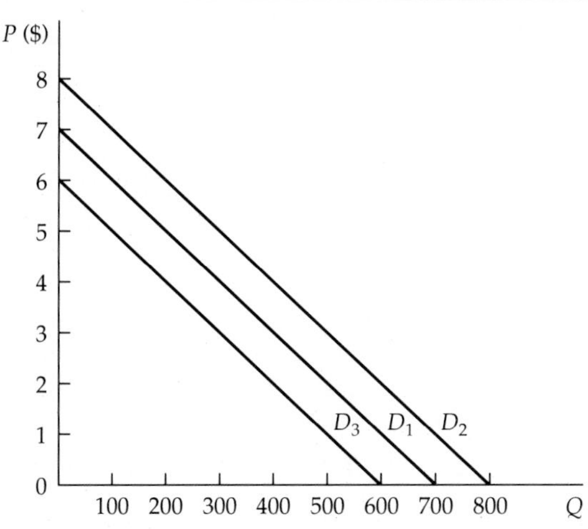

Figure 3.1 Market Demand for Pizza

Suppose the government publishes a report stating that pizza is the most nutritious of all fast foods, and as a result, people's preference for this food increases. This means that they would be willing to buy more pizza at each price. In other words, this would increase their demand for pizza. Column Q_{D2} in Table 3.2 and curve D_2 in Figure 3.1 illustrate the increase in demand resulting from this change in tastes and preferences.

Suppose the price of hot dogs decreased. Assuming that hot dogs are a substitute for pizza, this would cause the demand for pizza to fall from its original level, as represented by column Q_{D3} and curve D_3. You may want to consider other possible changes in the nonprice determinants of the demand for pizza and their impacts on demand. For example, how would an increase in the number of buyers affect the demand schedule and curve? Changes in other factors and their expected impacts on demand are summarized as follows.

1. *Tastes and Preferences.* Why do people buy things? Marketing professors, corporate market researchers, and advertising executives spend their careers trying to answer this question. Economists use a general-purpose category in their list of nonprice determinants called *tastes and preferences* to account for the personal likes and dislikes of consumers for various goods and services. These tastes and preferences may themselves be affected by other factors. Advertising, promotions, and even government reports can have profound effects on demand via their impacts on people's tastes and preferences for a particular good or service.

2. *Income.* As people's incomes rise, it is reasonable to expect their demand for a product to increase and vice versa. In the next chapter, the possibility of demand moving in the *opposite direction* to changes in income will be discussed.

3. *Prices of related products.* A good or service can be related to another by being a substitute or by being a complement. If the price of a substitute product

changes, we expect the demand for the good under consideration to change in the *same direction* as the change in the substitute's price. For example, note the relationship between the price of a hot dog and the demand for pizza in the example cited above.

Now consider what would happen to the demand for software if the price of computer hardware falls, or to the demand for compact discs if the price of CD players falls. It is reasonable to expect that the demand for the two items would *rise* as a result of a *fall* in the price of their respective *complementary* products.

4. *Future expectations.* If enough buyers expect the price of a good or service to rise (fall) in the future, it may cause the current demand to increase (decrease). In markets for various financial instruments (e.g., stocks, bonds, negotiable certificates of deposit, U.S. Treasury bills, etc.) as well as for agricultural commodities and precious metals, expectations of future price changes among both buyers and sellers play an important part in determining the market demand. In most of these types of markets, speculation among buyers and sellers is an important factor to consider. Buyers and sellers act on a current price of a product not for its immediate consumption but because of the possibility of gaining from some future transaction. (Recall the old adage "buy low and sell high.") In fact, for most of these products, a sizable and growing *futures* market has emerged, in which buyers and sellers conduct transactions for these products at some agreed-upon future date. Naturally, expectations of future price movements have an impact on the supply and demand for the future delivery of a commodity. In turn, movements of futures prices could have an impact on the current (also called "spot") supply and demand for the commodity.

This factor can also affect the demand for consumer and commercial products. For example, the demand for video recorders and cameras, home computers, and facsimile machines was probably not as high as sellers expected when these products were first introduced, because buyers were waiting for their prices to come down at a later time.

5. *Number of Buyers.* The impact of the number of buyers on demand should be apparent; as far as sellers are concerned, the more the merrier. What is interesting, nonetheless, is how changing demographics and tastes and preferences within demographic groups can affect the pool of potential buyers for a particular good or service. In other words, sheer numbers (i.e., population) may not be as important as differences within the population. For example, the tracking of the baby boom generation from childhood to adulthood and eventually to retirement age has proven to be a fascinating study for market researchers. One can plainly see the impact on the demand for such items as children's apparel, furniture, and toys during the 1950s and 1960s, when this group was growing up.

As the baby boomers grew into their teen years, the demand for such items as records, stereos, certain types of cars, and admissions to movie theaters went up accordingly. Market researchers are now busy contemplating the impact on the demand for an assortment of goods and services—from health care to retirement condominiums—that will stem from the "graying" of this segment of the population.[4]

We will discuss further how changes in these factors change demand and market price. But first we must introduce the concept of supply. By combining supply with demand, we can conduct a complete analysis of the market, both in the short run and in the long run.

Market Supply

The supply of a good or service is defined as:

> *Quantities* of a good or service that people are ready to *sell* at various *prices* within some given *time period, other factors* held constant.

Notice that the only difference between this definition and that of demand is that in this case the word *sell* is used instead of *buy*. Just as in the case of demand, supply is based on an assumed length of time within which price and the other factors can affect the quantity supplied.

Recall that the law of demand states that the quantity demanded is related inversely to price, other factors held constant. On the other hand, the law of supply states that quantity supplied is related *directly* to price, other factors held constant. Thus, any schedule of numbers representing a relationship between price and quantity supplied would show a *decrease* in the quantity supplied as price falls.

Table 3.3 shows a hypothetical supply schedule. Also shown are two additional supply schedules, one indicating a greater supply and the other showing a reduced supply. These schedules are shown as supply curves in Figure 3.2. The supply curve has a positive slope, reflecting the direct relationship between price and quantity supplied.

In analyzing the supply side of the market, it is important to make the distinction between *quantity supplied* and *supply*. The distinction between these two terms is the same as that used for the demand side of the market:

Changes in *price* result in changes in the *quantity supplied* (i.e., movements along the supply curve).

Changes in *nonprice determinants* result in changes in the *supply* (i.e., shifts of the supply curve).

The nonprice determinants of supply are as follows:

1. Costs
2. Technology
3. Prices of other goods or services offered by a seller

---

[4]The imagery that demographers have used in references to the maturing of the baby boomers is a "rat moving through a python."

Table 3.3 Market Supply for Pizza

P	Q_{S1}	Q_{S2}	Q_{S3}
$7	600	700	500
6	500	600	400
5	400	500	300
4	300	400	200
3	200	300	100
2	100	200	0
1	0	100	0
0	0	0	0

4. Number of sellers
5. Future expectations
6. Weather conditions

Remember that a change in any one or a combination of these factors will change market supply (i.e., cause the supply line to shift to the right or the left). Let us briefly discuss each factor to understand why this is expected to happen.

1. *Costs and technology.* The two factors of costs and technology can be treated as one because they are so closely related. *Costs* refer to the usual costs of production, such as labor costs, costs of materials, rent, interest payments, depreciation charges, and general and administrative expenses—in other words, all of the items usually found in a firm's income statement. *Technology* refers to technological innovations or improvements introduced to reduce the unit cost of production (e.g., automation, robotics, and computer hardware and software

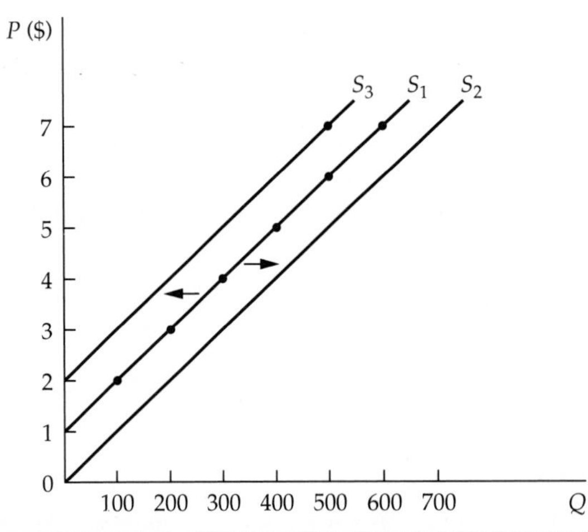

Figure 3.2 Supply Curves for Pizza

utilization). Technological changes that result in entirely new products for final consumption are not considered part of this category. These new products would have to be considered in an entirely different market analysis. In any event, unit cost reductions, whether from technological innovations or simply management decisions, will result in an increase in market supply. Increases in the unit cost of production will have the opposite effect.

2. *Prices of other goods or services offered by the seller.* From the consumer's standpoint, any good or service has other goods or services related to it either as substitutes or as complements. From the producer's standpoint, there can also be substitutes or complements for a particular good or service offered in the market. For example, suppose the sellers of pizza notice that the price of hot dogs increases substantially. In the extreme case, they may drop their line of pizza and substitute hot dogs. Or they may at least reduce the amount of resources (e.g., labor and store space) devoted to the selling of pizza in favor of hot dogs. In either case, the market supply of pizza would decrease. If the sellers were already selling two (or more) products, the change in market conditions would prompt them to reallocate their resources toward the more profitable products. (Given this possibility, it may be more appropriate to say that the sellers consider pizza and hot dogs as "competing" products rather than as "substitute" products.)

Some goods and services are produced jointly by the suppliers. We can consider them "complementary" products. There are a number of ways in which one product may be a complement to another. For example, two goods may be part of the same source (e.g., beef and hides from cattle), or two goods may be offered as part of the same package (e.g., hardware and software). Whatever the particular linkage, the price of a complementary good is expected to affect the supply of the good under consideration in a direct manner: an increase in the price of a complementary good will increase the supply of the good in question, and vice versa. A more complete discussion of this topic can be found in Chapter 13.

3. *Future expectations.* This factor has a similar impact on sellers as on buyers; the only difference is the direction of the change. For example, if sellers anticipate a rise in price, they may chose to hold back the current supply to take advantage of the higher future price, thus decreasing market supply. As we discussed in the section on demand, a rise in price is expected to increase the current demand for a product.

4. *Number of sellers.* Clearly, the number of sellers has a direct impact on supply. The more sellers, the greater the market supply.

5. *Weather conditions.* Bad weather (e.g., floods, droughts, unusual seasonal temperatures) will reduce the supply of an agricultural commodity. Good weather will have the opposite impact.

With this discussion of supply, we are now able to combine supply with demand into a complete analysis of the market.

Market Equilibrium

Now that we have reviewed the definitions and mechanics of demand and supply, we are ready to examine their interaction in the market. Market demand and supply are compared Table 3.4 and Figure 3.3.

You can see in both the table and the graph that at the price of $4, the market is cleared in the sense that the quantity demanded (300) is equal to the quantity supplied (300). Thus, $4 is called the *equilibrium price,* and 300 is referred to as the *equilibrium quantity.* Another way to view this market situation is to imagine what would happen if the price were not at the equilibrium level. For example, suppose the price were at a higher level, say $5. At this price, as you can see in Table 3.4 the quantity supplied would exceed the quantity demanded, a condition called a *surplus*. At a lower price, say $3, the situation is reversed: the quantity demanded exceeds the quantity supplied. This situation is called a *shortage*. Both the surplus and the shortage conditions are indicated in Figure 3.3.

In the event of a surplus or a shortage, various competitive pressures cause the price to change (decrease in the case of a surplus, and increase in the event of a shortage). The price thus serves to clear the market of the imbalance. The clearing process continues until equilibrium (i.e., quantity demanded equals quantity supplied) is arrived at. In the case of a surplus, sellers wishing to rid themselves of the extra items offer the product at a lower price to induce people to buy more. At the same time, as the price falls, suppliers are discouraged from offering as much as before. In the case of a market shortage, as the price rises toward the equilibrium level, the market is cleared because the quantity demanded decreases while the quantity supplied increases. In the event of a shortage, sellers try to take advantage of the situation by raising their prices, and people are thus discouraged from buying as much as before. Also, sellers are induced to offer a greater number of items in the market. Both actions serve to clear the market of a shortage.

Table 3.4 Supply and Demand for Pizza

P	Q_D	Q_S
$7	0	600
6	100	500
5	200	400
→4	300	300
3	400	200
2	500	100
1	600	0
0	700	0

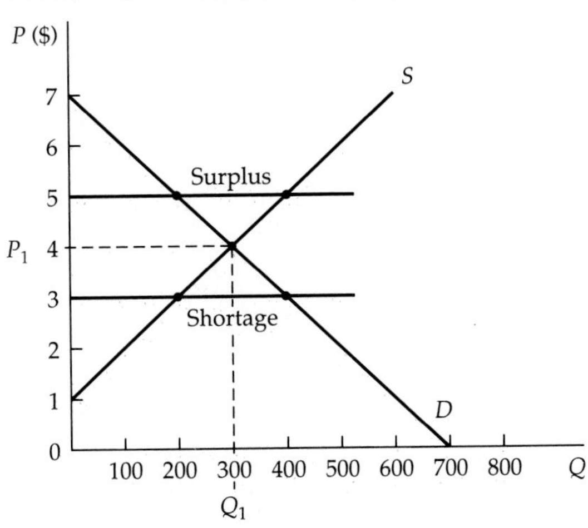

Figure 3.3 Supply and Demand Curves for Pizza, Indicating Market Equilibrium

To summarize the material in this section, remember the following definitions:

Equilibrium price: The price that equates the quantity demanded with the quantity supplied; (i.e., the price that clears the market of a surplus or shortage)

Equilibrium quantity: The amount that people are willing to buy and sellers are willing to offer at the equilibrium price level

Shortage: A market situation in which the quantity demanded exceeds the quantity supplied, *at a price below the equilibrium level*

Surplus: A market situation in which the quantity supplied exceeds the quantity demanded, *at a price above the equilibrium level*

Comparative Statics Analysis

The model of market demand, supply, and equilibrium price and quantity developed in the preceding sections can now be used to analyze the market. The particular method of analysis we will use is called *comparative statics analysis*. This is a commonly used method in economic analysis and will be used throughout the text. In general, this method of analysis proceeds as follows:

1. State all the assumptions needed to construct the model.
2. Begin by assuming that the model is in equilibrium.
3. Introduce a change in the model. In so doing, a condition of disequilibrium is created.
4. Find the new point at which equilibrium is restored.
5. Compare the new equilibrium point with the original one.

In effect, comparative statics analysis is a form of sensitivity analysis, or what business people often refer to as what-if analysis. For example, if we were doing a what-if analysis of a company's cash flow, we would start with a given pro forma income statement adjusted to provide the cash flow for a given period of time. We would then conduct sensitivity analysis by supposing that certain factors changed, such as revenue, cost, or the rate of depreciation. We would then inspect how changes in these factors would change the cash flow of the firm over time. In the same manner, economists conduct a what-if analysis of their models.

The term *statics* alludes to the theoretically stable point of equilibrium, and *comparative* refers to the comparison of the various points of equilibrium. The ensuing sections will explain exactly how comparative statics analysis is used in the analysis of the market.

Short-Run Market Changes: The "Rationing Function" of Price

Let us continue with our analysis of pizza. Following the steps involved in comparative statics analysis, we start by assuming that all factors except the price of pizza are held constant, and the various patterns of response to price among buyers and sellers are represented by the supply and demand lines in Figure 3.3. We make a fresh start by redrawing this graph in Figure 3.4.

As noted in step 2 above, we begin this analysis in the condition of equilibrium. This is denoted in Figure 3.4 as the point where the supply line intersects with the D_1 demand line (i.e., the price level where quantity supplied is equal to quantity demanded).

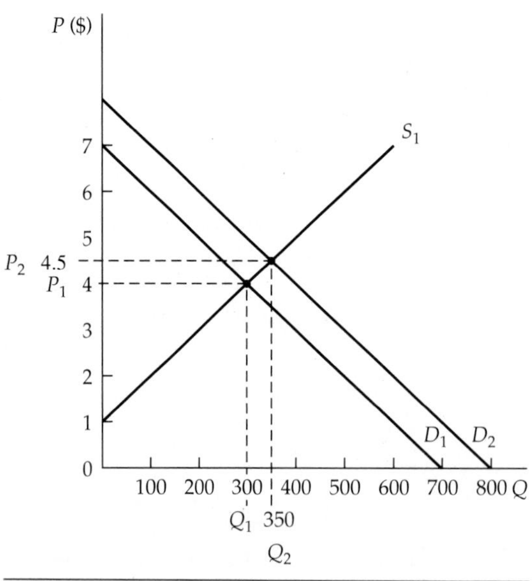

Figure 3.4 Increase in Demand for Pizza and Resulting Impact on Market Equilibrium

Based on step 3 we introduce a change in one or more of the assumptions made when the model was constructed. Let us assume that a new government study shows pizza to be the most nutritious of all fast foods and that consumers substantially increase their demand for pizza as a result of this study.[5] In Figure 3.4, this increase is represented by a shift in the demand curve from D_1 to D_2. As you can see, this shift results in a new, higher equilibrium price of $4.50. Notice also that the new equilibrium quantity is greater than the original equilibrium quantity.

The comparison of the new equilibrium point with the original one (step 5 in comparative statics analysis) leads us to conclude that, as a result of a change in tastes and preferences, the price of pizza rises, and so does the quantity bought and sold.

This analysis can be repeated using other possible changes in market conditions (e.g., the price of cheese rises, the price of soft drinks falls). Each time, the same procedure should be followed. If we consider only one possible change at a time, the effects on equilibrium price and quantity can be illustrated as in Figure 3.5. Instead of using specific numbers, we have designated the prices and quantities with the symbols P and Q along with appropriate subscripts. We can summarize the effects shown in the graphs as follows:

An increase in demand causes equilibrium price and quantity to rise. (See Figure 3.5*a*.)

A decrease in demand causes equilibrium price and quantity to fall. (See Figure 3.5*b*.)

An increase in supply causes equilibrium price to fall and quantity to rise. (See Figure 3.5*c*.)

A decrease in supply causes equilibrium price to rise and quantity to fall. (See. Figure 3.5*d*.)

In Figure 3.5 we observe that the shift in demand or supply has in effect created either a shortage or a surplus at the original price P_1. Thus, the equilibrium price has to rise or fall to clear the market. When the market price changes to eliminate the imbalance between quantities supplied and demanded, it is serving what economists call the *rationing function* of price. The term *rationing* is often associated with shortages, but we have defined it to include a surplus situation as well.

Long-Run Market Analysis: The Guiding or Allocating Function of Price

The comparative statics analysis presented earlier required only that you consider the response of equilibrium price and quantity to a given change in supply or demand. This response was dubbed the "rationing function" of price. Let us

[5]The authors recall that some years ago *Consumer Reports* found that indeed pizza was the most nutritious of all the fast foods on the market (others being hot dog, hamburgers, fried chicken, and fish and chips).

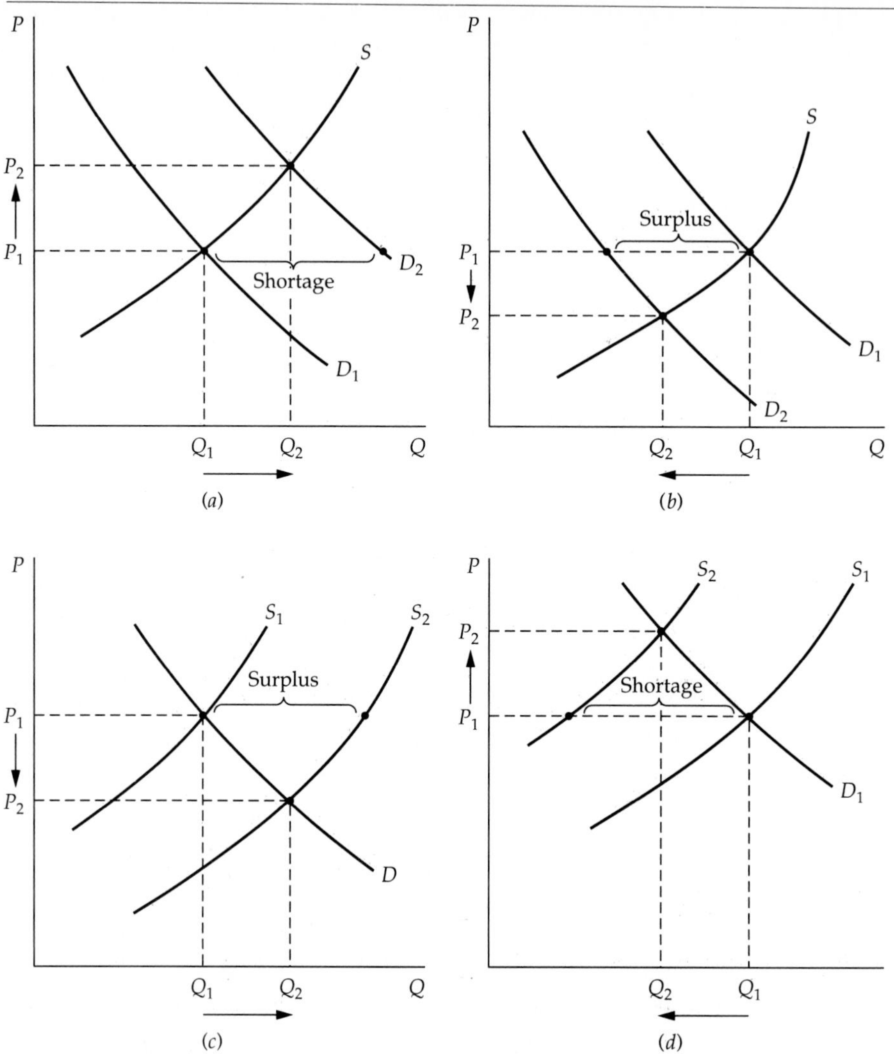

Figure 3.5 Changes in Supply and Demand and Their Short-Run Impact on Market Equilibrium (the Rationing Function of Price)

consider what might happen as a result of this change in market price. To illustrate this, we shall examine the market for hot dogs, a presumed substitute for pizza. The two markets are represented by the supply and demand diagrams in Figure 3.6.

Now let us assume that at the same time people's tastes and preferences change in favor of pizza, their tastes and preferences become more adverse to hot dogs (e.g., for health reasons). The changes in the demand for the two products are shown in Figure 3.6 by a downward shift in the demand for hot dogs and an upward shift in the demand for pizza (D_1 to D_2). This would cause

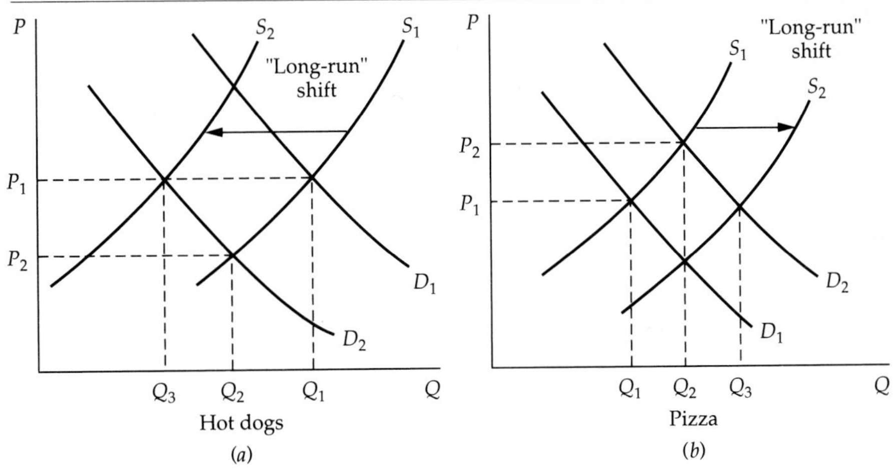

Figure 3.6 Short-Run and Long-Run Changes in Supply (in Response to an Initial Change in Demand)

a shortage in the pizza market and a surplus in the hot dog market. But as we know, the rationing function of price will immediately start to correct these market imbalances. As the price of hot dogs falls, the surplus is eliminated; as the price of pizza rises, the shortage is eliminated. (For the purposes of this analysis, it really does not matter where the price of pizza stands in relation to the price of hot dogs. To simplify matters, we have assumed that the two prices were about equal before the change in tastes and preferences occurred. The point is that after price performs its rationing function, the equilibrium price of pizza will be higher than the equilibrium price of hot dogs in relative terms.)

Now suppose that the prices have indeed changed, and the two markets are once again in equilibrium. What do you suppose will happen next? As you might well imagine, the depressed price of hot dogs will cause the sellers to begin allocating less of their resources to this market. Some may even go out of the business of making or selling hot dogs. On the other hand, the higher price of pizza will induce the allocation of more resources into this market. New pizza stands and restaurants may be opened. Food companies may build new plants to produce frozen pizza for distribution through supermarkets. The effect of these follow-on adjustments to the initial change in equilibrium prices can be seen in the figure as a rightward shift in the supply of pizza and a leftward shift in the supply of hot dogs.

After this "long-run" adjustment is made, equilibrium price and quantity may well return to the levels at which they were before the initial changes in demand took place (i.e., P_3 in each market may be close to or equal to P_1). But the main point is that Q_3 is considerably less than Q_1 in the hot dog market and considerably more than Q_1 in the pizza market. These differences represent the shifting of resources out of the hot dog market and into the pizza market. Several centuries ago, Adam Smith referred to this shifting of resources into and out of markets in response to price changes as the "invisible hand."[6] Another way to express these shifts in supply is that they represent a response to "price signals" sent to the owners of the factors of production. In any event, when resources have been shifted out of the market for hot dogs and into the market for pizza, price is fulfilling its *guiding* or *allocating* function. Defined in a more formal manner, the guiding or allocating function of price is the movement of resources into or out of markets in response to a change in the equilibrium price of a good or service.

The preceding example illustrates a basic distinction made in economic analysis between the "short run" and the "long run." This distinction has nothing to do directly with a specific calendar time. Instead, it refers to the amount of time it takes for sellers and buyers to react to changes in the market equilibrium price. The following descriptions of the short run and the long run will help readers distinguish the two time periods.

1. Short-run time period
   a. Period of time in which sellers already in the market respond to a change in equilibrium price by adjusting the amount of certain resources, which economists call *variable inputs*. Examples of such inputs are labor hours and raw materials. A short-run adjustment by sellers can be envisioned as a movement along a particular supply curve.
   b. Period of time in which buyers already in the market respond to changes in equilibrium price by adjusting the quantity demanded for a particular good or service. A short-run adjustment by buyers can be envisioned as a movement along a particular demand curve.
2. Long-run time period
   a. Period of time in which new sellers may enter a market or the original sellers may exit from a market. This period is long enough for existing sellers to either increase or decrease their *fixed factors* of production. Examples of fixed factors include property, plant, and equipment. A long-run adjustment by sellers can be seen graphically as a shift in a given supply curve.
   b. Period of time in which buyers may react to a change in equilibrium price by changing their tastes and preferences or buying patterns. (The *Wall Street Journal* and other sources of business news may refer to this as a "structural change" in demand.) A long-run adjustment by buyers can be seen graphically as a shift in a given demand curve.

Another good way of distinguishing the short run from the long run is to note that the rationing function of price is a short-run phenomenon, whereas the guiding function is a long-run phenomenon.

[6]For Smith the "visible" hand was that of the government, which might try to dictate the allocation of resources among different markets by the command process rather than by the market process.

Let us summarize the short-run "rationing function " and the long run "guiding function" of price in terms of our example involving pizza and hot dogs:

1. Changing tastes and preferences cause the demand for pizza to increase and the demand for hot dogs to decrease.
2. The changing demand for the two products cause a shortage in the pizza market and a surplus in the hot dog market.
3. In response to the surplus and shortage in the two markets, price serves as a *rationing* agent by decreasing in the hot dog market and increasing in the pizza market. That is, the short-run response by suppliers of the two products is to change their variable inputs (i.e., movement downward along the supply line in the market for hot dogs, and movement upward along the supply line in the market for pizza).
4. In the *long run,* price fulfills its *guiding* function by causing sellers and potential sellers to respond by increasing capacity or entering the market for pizza and by decreasing capacity or leaving the market for hot dogs (i.e., rightward shift in the supply line for pizza and a leftward shift in the supply line for hot dogs).
5. As a result of the shifts in supply, new equilibrium levels of price and quantity are established. The new quantities bought and sold represent shifts in resources out of one market and into the other.

The distinction between short- and long-run changes in the market can also be made in cases that begin with changes in supply rather than in demand. One of the best examples is the case of the Organization of Petroleum Exporting Countries (OPEC) and the world oil market. A complete analysis of this case is beyond the scope of this text. However, the headline of an article in *Newsweek* perhaps best sums up the activities in this market in the decade following the OPEC's major price hike in late 1973: "OPEC, Meet Adam Smith."[7] This reference to the great classical economist Adam Smith pertained to his concept of the "invisible hand," or the guiding function of price.

OPEC conspired to raise the price of oil by limiting production to an amount that would support a price above the current level. The supply-and-demand diagram shown in Figure 3.7 illustrates this action. As we can see, limiting the production of oil can be envisioned as a leftward shift in the supply line to the level where it intersects the demand curve for oil at some designated point above the current market price (i.e., P_2 rather than P_1). The short-run response by consumers to the increase in oil prices was to cut back their consumption of oil. But in the terms specific to our analysis, this reduction can be seen as a decrease in the *quantity demanded* for oil. In other words, the decrease in the supply of oil (i.e., the shift of supply line to the left) prompted a *movement back along the demand curve* for oil.

However, over time consumers began to change their pattern of consumption of oil. They formed car pools, they bought more fuel-efficient cars, they turned

---

[7] *Newsweek*, October 29,1984, p. 93

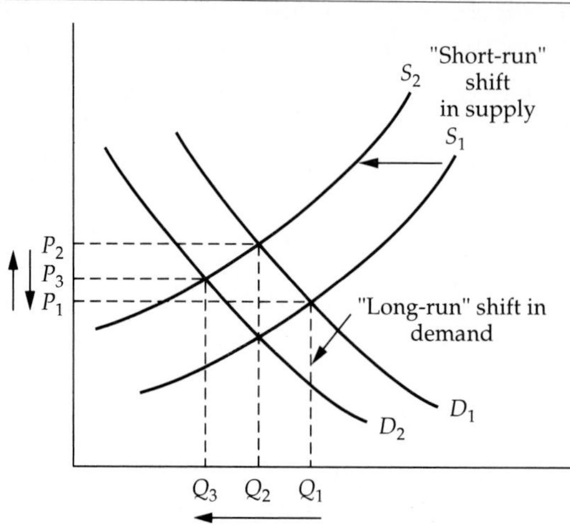

Figure 3.7 Short-Run and Long-Run Changes in Demand (in Response to an Initial Change in Supply)

their thermostats down in their homes, and they even tried to follow the new 55 mph speed limit established on highways throughout the country. Industrial users of oil responded by substituting more fuel-efficient machinery as soon as it became cost-efficient to make these changes. The effect of this *long-run* change in the pattern of oil usage was to cause the demand for oil to gradually fall. Graphically, this is represented by a leftward shift of the demand curve for oil from D_1 to D_2. Notice that as a result of this long-run shift in demand, the equilibrium price and quantity fell. As seen in Figure 3.7, the long-run quantity that is bought and sold (i.e., Q_3) was now even less than it was before this decrease in demand took place. This indicates a further shift of resources out of this market.

As in the case of pizza and hot dogs, price fulfilled its short-run rationing function as well as its long-run guiding function. When the supply line for oil first shifted to the left—in large part due to the OPEC conspiracy—a shortage was created. This imbalance forced the market price up to clear the market of this shortage. The higher price served as a signal to buyers to change their consumption pattern for oil, that is, to become more economical in their use of oil.

Thus, price served to reallocate an economy's resources in the sense that the buyer's long-run response was to rely more on resources other than those in the oil market. In fact, a sizable portion of these alternative resources involved the production of goods and services that helped people to reduce their consumption of oil. For example, resources were shifted into the production of fuel-efficient cars and machinery, wood-burning stoves, kerosene heaters, firewood, sweaters, and flannel pajamas.

An additional facet of this long-run, guiding function of price can be observed. In retrospect, OPEC's efforts to raise the world price of oil by deliberately reducing the supply made it possible for non-OPEC oil producers to justify such projects as drilling for oil in the North Sea and Alaska. Moreover, the oil-producing efforts of Mexico were encouraged by the rising oil prices. Over the long run, these additional sources increased the world's supply of oil, putting further pressures on OPEC to limit their supply to keep oil prices from falling.[8]

Supply, Demand, and Managerial Decision Making

So far in our review of supply and demand, we have assumed that there is little if any market power exercised by buyers and sellers. *Market power* is defined as the power to establish the price of a good or service. As seen in our illustrations, the market price is determined by the forces of supply and demand rather than by any particular buyer or seller. Thus, it would seem that this leaves very little managerial decision-making power as far a price is concerned. (Chapters 11 and 13 will present situations in which sellers exercise various degrees of price-setting power.) Nevertheless, whatever the degree of market power exerted by a firm, there is a need for managers in all types of markets to understand the basic elements of supply and demand and to decide whether or not it is desirable to compete in a particular market.

To begin with, managers must have a thorough knowledge of the elements of supply and demand to understand the nature of the market environment in which they are competing. For example, suppose you are considering starting the first video rental store in your neighborhood. What does economic theory tell you about your prospects for success? It suggests that if your new venture is successful, other video stores will soon open up and take away some of your business. It also indicates that this competition might force you to sell at lower prices or prevent you from raising your prices. Furthermore, even if you are able at first to exercise market power because of the lack of competition, you still must understand the factors that influence the demand for video rentals.

How sensitive are customers to changes in price?[9] If the economy goes into a recession, how will sales be affected? What will happen to the demand for rented videos if the price of purchased videos continues to fall? Will the increase in pay-per-view programming on cable television substantially affect the demand for video rentals? As owner/manager of the video store, you must deal with these kinds of questions.

---

[8]The Gulf Crisis in 1990 caused a temporary rise in oil prices. As the situation stabilized, oil prices fell to their pre-crisis level.

[9]The question of price sensitivity is discussed at length in the next chapter. According to the law of demand, sellers can expect consumers to buy more when the price falls. As you will see in the next chapter, it is important for sellers to know *how much* more in order to determine whether a price reduction will help to increase revenues.

Failure to understand the nature of supply and demand may lead to poor management decisions. For example, the owner of a video store that is earning a considerable amount of profit may be lulled into complacency if the "long-run" advent of competitors is not anticipated. If this complacency is manifested in poor service or an incomplete selection of titles (i.e., not making an effort to satisfy customers), the firm will be particularly hurt when competitors arrive on the scene—as they inevitably will. As an additional example, suppose changes in market conditions cause a decline in demand, and the owner of the video store decides to offset this by lowering prices. As will be explained in detail in the next chapter, if customers are not very sensitive to price changes, this price reduction may actually cause revenues to fall.

The Solution

In his presentation to the management committee, Ross Harris recommended that Global Foods, Inc., acquiesce to the HFCS manufacturers' request to negotiate a pricing and delivery contract on a quarterly basis. "Based on our current projections of demand and supply, we believe that there will be a slight upward trend in HFCS prices in the short run," Ross began. "This means that if we negotiate on a quarterly basis, we may have to pay a bit more for the product, because the negotiated price will reflect the underlying supply and demand conditions in the market. However, if we bought the product in the spot market, we would be operating in an extremely volatile environment. In our business, I strongly believe that continuity of supply and the quality of the product are just as important as the price. By negotiating a contract with the suppliers, we are assured of at least a minimum amount of high-quality product at the contracted price. If we order too much, we can always sell the surplus to other companies in the food industry. If we do not order enough, we can always meet the shortage by purchasing product in the spot market. As you all know, we currently handle our surpluses and shortages of HFCS in this manner. In fact, this is how we know that the product in the spot market is not always of top quality."

"In talking to purchasing agents in the rest of the industry and with some of my contacts in the HFCS manufacturing business," Ross continued, "I am convinced that the HFCS companies are very adamant about setting the price on a quarterly basis. The volatility of supply-and-demand conditions in the market for corn has hurt their profit margins in the past, and they want greater flexibility in pricing the final product in order to compensate for the upward movements in the price of corn."

Ross made a final point. "I stated that our projections call for some upward trend in

(Continued)

the price of HFCS in the near term. However, if we continue the present arrangement of negotiating the price with our suppliers—even if it is done on a quarterly rather than a yearly basis—we will be helping to preserve a relatively stable market environment in which they can project with greater certainty the future demand for HFCS. This will enable them to better plan for their manufacturing capacity requirements. In *the long run,* this should mean fewer chances of supply bottlenecks, shortages, and higher prices.

The report by Kathy Martinez was short and to the point. The market for corn was found to be typical of markets in which agricultural commodities were bought and sold. She presented a chart showing that these markets are characterized by *price volatility* brought on by frequent changes in supply and demand conditions (See Figure 3.8).

Kathy went on to explain that in the market for corn in the United States, the major factors affecting supply are weather conditions, the output of corn in other countries, and the U.S. government's acreage control program. Another factor is the market for alternative uses for corn. The supply available for the HFCS market depends on the supply and demand conditions for these alternative uses.

As far as the demand for HFCS is concerned, she noted that the major factor has been the soft drink industry's increasing use of the sweetener as a substitute for sugar. However, soft drink demand is subject to seasonal fluctuations, being the highest in the summer and lowest in the winter. Pricing on a yearly basis, does not allow the

(Continued)

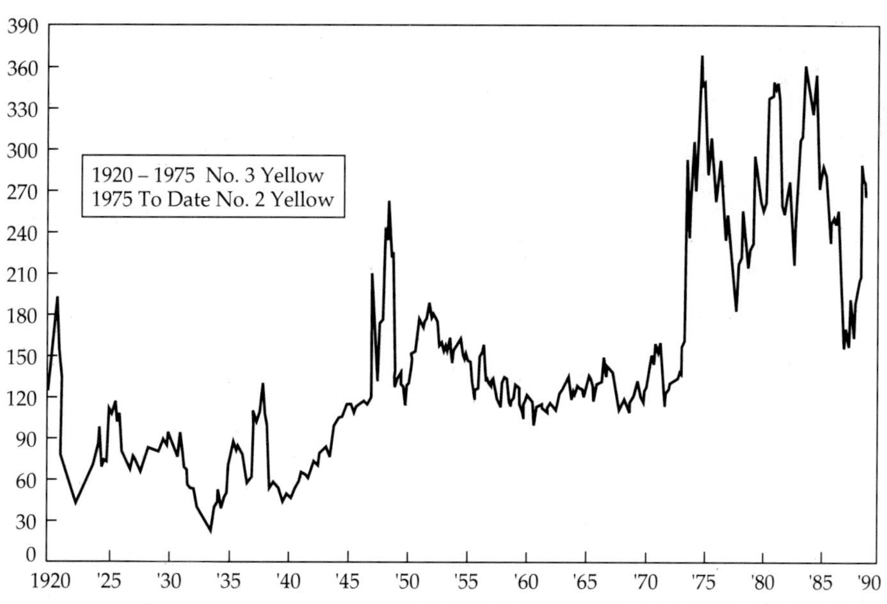

Figure 3.8 Monthly Average Corn Cash Prices, Chicago (*Source*: Economic Research Service, USDA)

flexibility to price according to these seasonal fluctuations. In particular, it does not allow prices to be raised in response to the increase in the summer demand for HFCS.

Kathy's report summarized the situation as follows. On the supply side, the price of corn, the major ingredient of HFCS, is very volatile. On the demand side, the major buyers of HFCS are the soft drink manufacturers, the makers of a product that has seen steady long-term growth, subject to seasonal fluctuations. Thus, HFCS manufacturers must try to protect themselves from adverse corn price fluctuations by establishing greater pricing flexibility vis-à-vis the customers responsible for the major part of the demand.[10]

[10]This "solution" is based on an actual change in the industry that occurred in 1986. Prior to that time, the price if HFCS was established between HFCS manufacturers and the major soft drink companies once a year. The reasons that the HFCS manufacturers wanted to shift to quarterly negotiations are essentially those discussed here. The actual reasons the soft drink companies agreed to go along with the change are not known. (For a detailed account of this, see *Chemical Marketing Reporter,* March 24, 1986.)

Summary

This chapter has presented the basic elements of supply and demand. We began by introducing the *law of demand* and the *law of supply* and the nonprice factors that affect demand and supply. The law of demand states that, other factors held constant, the quantity demanded is inversely related to price. The law of supply states that, other factors held constant, the quantity supplied is directly related to price. Other factors that affect demand are: (1) tastes and preferences, (2) income, (3) prices of related products, (4) number of buyers, and (5) future expectations. Other factors that affect supply are (1) costs, (2) technology, (3) prices of other products that sellers can supply, (4) number of sellers (5) future expectations, and (6) weather conditions. Both numerical and graphical examples of supply and demand and how they interrelate to determine the equilibrium price and quantity were presented. The appendix to this chapter presents the same material in algebraic terms.

We studied how price serves a short-run rationing function and a long-run guiding function in the marketplace. Price serves a rationing function when it increases or decreases to clear the market of a shortage or surplus caused by a change in market conditions (i.e., a shifting of the supply or demand curve). Price changes serve as guiding function signaling producers or consumers to put more or less of their resources in the affected markets.

In explaining the rationing and guiding functions of price, we noted the particular way in which economists define the short run and the long run. We also discussed how comparative statics analysis is used to explain the rationing and guiding functions of the price. This technique, involving the comparison of equilibrium points before and after changes in the market have occurred, is a standard way of analyzing problems and will be used throughout this text.

APPENDIX 3A
The Mathematics of Supply and Demand

This appendix presents the short-run analysis of supply and demand using algebraic equations and graphs. As you will see, the mechanics of supply and demand can be very concisely expressed in algebraic equations. Furthermore, viewing the demand function in terms of an equation will better prepare you for the next two chapters on demand elasticity and estimation.

The demand function for a good or service can be expressed mathematically as:

$$Q_D = f(P, X_1, \ldots, X_n)$$

where Q_D = Quantity demanded
P = Price
$X_1, \ldots, X_n$ = other factors believed to affect the quantity demanded

Using pizza once again as our example, let us assume that price and the nonprice factors affect the demand for pizza in the following way:

$$Q_D = -100P + 1.5P_{\text{hd}} - 5P_{\text{sd}} + 20A + 15\text{Pop}, \qquad (3A.1)$$

where Q_D = Quantity demanded for pizza (pies)
P_{hd} = Price of hot dogs (cents)
P_{sd} = Price of soft drinks (cents)
A = Advertising expenditures (thousands of dollars)
Pop = Percentage of the population aged 10 to 35

Suppose we hold constant all factors affecting the quantity demanded for pizza except price by assuming the values of these nonprice factors to be

P_{hd} = 100 (\$1.00 or 100 cents)
P_{sd} = 75 (\$.75 or 75 cents)
A = 20 (\$20,000)
Pop = 35 (35 percent)

Substituting these values into Equation (3A.1) gives us

$$\begin{aligned} Q_D &= -100P + 1.5\,(100) - 5\,(75) + 20\,(20) + 15\,(35) \\ &= 700 - 100P \end{aligned} \qquad (3A.2)$$

All of the values of the nonprice variables are now included in the constant term, 700. Plotting this equation gives us the demand curve shown in Figure 3A.1.

Those familiar with the graphical presentation of algebraic equations may be puzzled about the way in which economists present the supply and demand equations in graphical form. As a rule, the dependent variable is placed on the vertical or Y axis, and the independent variable is placed on the horizontal or X axis. Given this format, one would expect Q, the dependent variable,

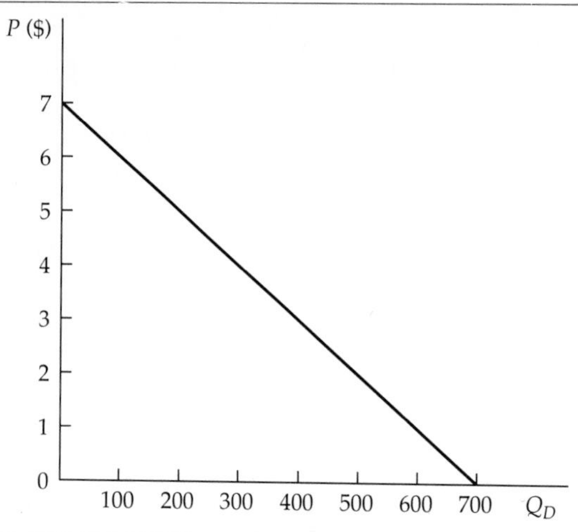

Figure 3A.1 Demand Curve

to be placed on the vertical axis and P, the independent variable, to be placed on the horizontal axis. However, in this chapter, as well as in the next, Q is placed on the horizontal axis, and P on the vertical axis. It seems that the originator of these diagrams, Professor Alfred Marshall, first presented them in this manner.[11] Since then economists have followed this way of presenting supply and demand in graphical form.

Regardless of Marshall's original reasons for reversing the axes, let us simply state that in the analysis of cost, revenue, and profit, the quantity of output is the independent variable. Thus, placing Q on the horizontal axis in the analysis of supply and demand simply prepares us for its subsequent designation as an independent variable.

In the meantime, an adjustment must be made in linking the supply and demand equations to their graphs in order to conform to mathematical convention. In supply-and-demand analysis, whenever an equation such as $Q_D = 700 - 100P$ is plotted on a graph, we must do one of two things. If we wish to be consistent with mathematical convention, we must place Q_D on the vertical axis and the P on the horizontal axis. This is shown in Figure 3A.2*a*. If we wish to follow the usual format in economics, we must rearrange the terms in the equation so that P is expressed in terms of Q_D:

$$\begin{aligned} Q_D &= 700 - 100P \\ 100P &= 700 - Q_D \\ P &= \frac{700 - Q_D}{100} \\ P &= 7 - 0.01Q_D \end{aligned}$$

[11] Alfred Marshall, *Principles of Economics*, 8th ed., Philadelphia: Porcupine Press, 1920, reprinted 1982, p. 288.

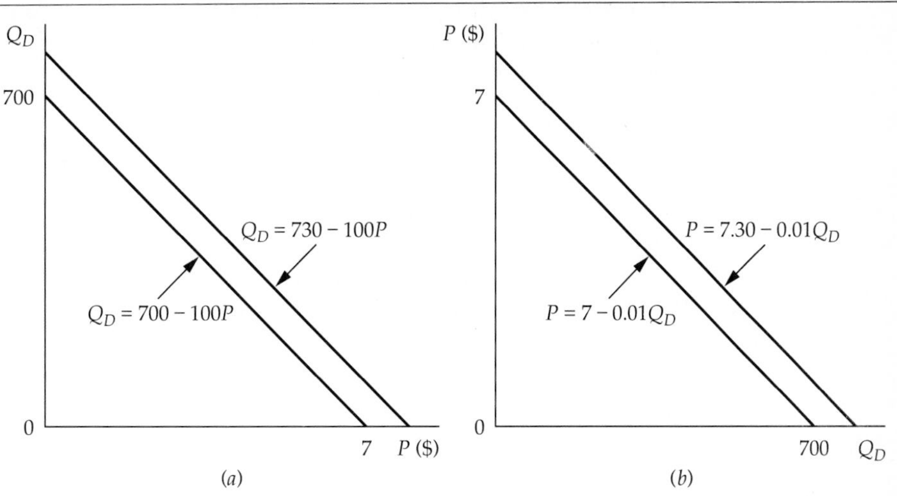

Figure 3A.2 Transforming the Demand Curve

As such, P is now the "dependent" variable and can be plotted on the vertical axis. Q_D is now the "independent" variable and can be plotted on the horizontal axis. This is illustrated in Figure 3A.2*b*.

Let us review this point by assuming that one of the nonprice factors affecting the quantity demanded for pizza has changed. In particular, suppose the price of hot dogs increases to $1.20. In Equation (3A.2), this would increase the constant or "Y intercept" term from 700 to 730. This, in effect, would cause the demand curve to shift from its original position to the new one shown in Figure 3A.2*a*. Figure 3A.2*b* shows the effect of an increase in the price of hot dogs on the transformed demand equation. In this case, the constant term or "Y intercept" increases from 7 to 7.3 and is also shown by a rightward shift in the demand curve.

We now focus on the supply by assuming that the supply equation is the same as the curve used in Table 3.4 and Figure 3.3. This equation can be expressed as:

$$Q_s = -100 + 100P \qquad (3A.3)$$

Once the supply and demand equations are given, there are several ways to find the equilibrium price and quantity. One way is to solve for the supply and demand equations simultaneously. This is done by first setting up the two equations in the following way:

$$Q_D = 700 - 100P$$
$$Q_S = -100 + 100P$$

We can then eliminate P by adding the equations together. This gives us

$$\begin{aligned} 2_Q &= 700 - 100 \\ &= 600 \qquad (3A.4) \\ Q^* &= 300 \end{aligned}$$

To find the equilibrium price (P^*), we simply return to either the demand or the supply equation, insert the value for the equilibrium quantity, (300), and solve for P. Using Equation (3A.2), this would give us

$$300 = 700 - 100P$$
$$100P = 700 - 300$$
$$P^* = 4$$

Notice that when we added the supply and demand equations together, we no longer made the distinction between Q_S and Q_D, because in equilibrium $Q_S = Q_D$. In fact, this brings us to the other way in which the supply and demand equations can be used to determine the equilibrium price and quantity. By definition, market equilibrium occurs when the quantity supplied is equal to the quantity demanded. Thus, we can set equation (3A.2) equal to equation (3A.3) and solve for the unknown P. That is,

$$700 - 100P = -100 + 100P$$
$$200P = 800$$
$$P^* = 4$$

And by inserting the value of 4 into either equation, we obtain the equilibrium quantity, 300.

You now have three ways to view the basic elements of supply and demand. First, there are supply and demand schedules, as shown in Tables 3.1, 3.2, 3.3, and 3.4, in which the equilibrium price is found by matching the quantity supplied with the quantity demanded. Second, there are supply and demand diagrams, as presented in most of the figures in this chapter, in which price and quantity are determined by the intersection of the supply and demand curves. Finally, there are supply and demand equations, which enable one to find equilibrium price and quantity by solving for the unknowns in the two equations. For teaching purposes, the use of graphs is favored. But regardless of the manner in which the concepts of supply and demand are presented, there remains the challenge for business decision makers to ascertain the actual supply and demand data for their particular industries and organizations.

Important Concepts

Change in Demand: The result of a change in one or more of the nonprice determinants of demand, graphically represented by a *shift* in the demand curve (rightward for an increase in demand and leftward for a decrease in demand).

Change in supply: The result of a change in one or more of the nonprice determinants of supply, graphically represented by a *shift* in the supply curve (rightward for an increase and leftward for a decrease).

Change in the quantity demanded: The result of a change in the price of a good or service, graphically represented by a *movement along* a particular demand curve.

Change in the quantity supplied: The result of a change in the price of a good or service, graphically represented by a *movement along* a particular supply curve.

Demand: Quantities of a good or service that people are ready to buy at various prices, other factors besides the price held constant. Demand can be expressed as a numerical schedule, as a demand curve on a graph, or as an algebraic equation.

Equilibrium price: The price that equates the quantity demanded with the quantity supplied; the price that clears the market of any shortage or surplus.

Guiding function of price: Also referred to as the *allocating function of price,* the movement of resources into or out of markets as a result of changes in the equilibrium market price. This is considered to be a long-run function. On the supply side of the market, sellers may enter or leave the market or may vary all of their factors of production. On the demand side, consumers may change their tastes or preferences or find long-lasting alternatives to a particular good or service.

Long run: A time period in which new sellers may enter a market or sellers already in a market may leave. This time period is sufficient for both old and new sellers to vary *all* of their factors of production. From the standpoint of consumers, the long run provides time enough to respond to price changes by actually changing their tastes or preferences or their use of alternative goods and services. For example, suppose bad weather in Brazil results in an increase in the price of coffee. In the short-run, people are expected to buy less coffee because of the higher price. However, in the long-run, they may buy even less coffee because the higher price will have prompted them to drink more tea on a regular basis.

Market equilibrium: A condition that exists in the market when the quantity demanded is equal to the quantity supplied.

Nonprice determinants of demand: (1) tastes and preferences, (2) income, (3) prices of related products (i.e., substitutes or complements), (4) future expectations, (5) number of buyers.

Nonprice determinants of supply: (1) Costs, (2) technology, (3) prices of other products that may be produced by a firm, (4) future expectations, (5) number of sellers, (6) weather conditions.

Rationing function of price: The increase or decrease in price to clear the market of any shortage or surplus. This is considered to be a short-run function because both buyers and sellers are expected to respond only to price changes.

Shortage: A condition that exists in the market when the quantity demanded exceeds the quantity supplied at a price *below* the equilibrium or market-clearing price.

Short run: A time period in which only those sellers already in the market may respond to a change in market price by using more or less of their variable resources. From the standpoint of consumers, the short run is a period in which they respond only to price changes. As a result of a change in price, consumers may change their tastes or preferences or their use of alternative goods or services. However, in economic analysis , these related changes are considered long-run phenomena. (See *Long run.*)

Supply: Quantities of a good or service that people are ready to *sell* at various prices, other factors besides price held constant. Supply can be expressed as a numerical schedule, as a supply curve on a graph, or as an algebraic equation.

Surplus: A condition that exists in the market when the quantity supplied exceeds the quantity demanded at a price that lies *above* the equilibrium or market-clearing price.

Questions

1. Define demand. Define supply. In your answers, explain the difference between *demand* and *quantity demanded* and between *supply* and *quantity supplied.*
2. List the key nonprice factors which influence demand and supply.
3. In defining demand and supply, why do you think economists focus on price while holding constant other factors that might have an impact on the behavior of buyers and sellers?
4. Define comparative statics analysis. How does it compare with sensitivity analysis or what-if analysis used in finance, accounting and statistics.
5. Define the rationing function of price. Why is it necessary for price to serve this function in the market economy?
6. Define the guiding or allocating function of price.
7. Discuss the differences between the short run and the long run from the perspective of producers and from the perspective of consumers.
8. Explain the difference between shortages and scarcity. In answering this question, you should consider the difference between the short run and the long run in economic analysis.
9. Why do you think it is important for managers to understand the mechanics of supply and demand both in the short run and in the long run? Give examples of companies whose business was either helped or hurt by changes in supply or demand in the markets in which they were competing.
10. "If Congress levies an additional tax on luxury items, the prices of these items will rise. However, this will cause demand to decrease, and as a result the prices will fall back down, perhaps even to their original levels." Do you agree with this statement? Explain.
11. Overheard at the water cooler in the corporate headquarters of a large manufacturing concern: "The competition is really threatening us with their new product line. I think we should consider offering discounts on our current line in order to stimulate demand." In this statement, is the term *demand* being used in a manner consistent with economic theory? Explain. Illustrate your answer using a line drawn to represent the demand for this firm's product line.
12. In the demand equation, quantity demanded is the dependent variable and price is the independent variable. However, in plotting a demand equation on a graph, economists generally place quantity demanded on the horizon-

tal axis and the price on the vertical axis. In mathematics, the dependent variable is indicated on the vertical axis, and the independent variable is indicated on the horizontal axis. Why have economists switched the conventional representations of the two axes?

13. "Because of the war in the Gulf, airlines and hotels have been experiencing a substantial drop in demand for their services. Therefore, they should consider raising their prices to compensate for this drop in demand." Do you agree with this statement? Explain. Illustrate your answer with the use of a supply-and-demand diagram.

Problems

1. The following function describes the demand condition for a company that makes caps featuring names of college and professional teams in a variety of sports.

$$Q = 2{,}000 - 100P$$

where Q is cap sales and P is price.
   a. How many caps could be sold at $12 each?
   b. What should the price be in order for the company to sell 1,000 caps?
   c. At what price would cap sales equal zero?
   d. Plot the demand, marginal revenue, and total revenue curves.

2. Consider the following supply and demand curves for a certain product.

$$Q_S = 25{,}000P$$
$$Q_D = 50{,}000 - 10{,}000P$$

   a. Plot the demand and supply curves.
   b. What are the equilibrium price and equilibrium quantity for the industry? Determine the answer both algebraically and graphically. (Round to the nearest cent.)

3. The following relations describe the supply and demand for posters.

$$Q_D = 65{,}000 - 10{,}000P$$
$$Q_S = -35{,}000 + 15{,}000P$$

where Q is the quantiy and P is the price of a poster, in dollars.
   a. Complete the following table.

Price	Q_S	Q_D	*Surplus or Shortage*
$6.00			
5.00			
4.00			
3.00			
2.00			
1.00			

   b. What is the equilibrium price?

4. The following relations describe monthly demand and supply for a computer support service catering to small businesses.

$$Q_D = 3{,}000 - 10P$$
$$Q_S = -1{,}000 + 10P$$

where Q is the number of businesses that need services and P is the monthly fee, in dollars.
 a. At what average monthly fee would demand equal zero?
 b. At what average monthly fee would supply equal zero?
 c. Plot the supply and demand curves.
 d. What is the equilibrium price/output level?
 e. Suppose demand increases and leads to a new demand curve:

$$Q_D = 3{,}500 - 10P$$

 What is the effect on supply? What are the new equilibrium P and Q?
 f. Suppose new suppliers enter the market due to the increase in demand, so that the new supply curve is $Q = -500 + 10P$.
 What are the new equilibrium price and equilibrium quantity?
 g. Show these changes on the graph.
5. The ABC marketing consulting firm found that a particular brand of portable stereo has the following demand curve for a certain region:

$$Q = 10{,}000 - 200P + 0.03\text{Pop} + 0.6I + 0.2A$$

where Q is the quantity per month, P is price ($), Pop is population, I is disposable income per household ($), and A is advertising expenditure ($).
 a. Determine the demand curve for the company in a market in which $P = 300$, Pop $= 1{,}000{,}000$, $I = 30{,}000$, and $A = 15{,}000$.
 b. Calculate the quantity demanded at prices of $200, $175, $150, and $125.
 c. Calculate the price necessary to sell 45,000 units.
6. Joy's Frozen Yogurt shops have enjoyed rapid growth in notheastern states in recent years. From the analysis of Joy's various outlets, it was found that the demand curve follows this pattern:

$$Q = 200 - 300P + 120I + 65T - 250A_c + 400Aj$$

where Q = Number of cups served per week
 P = Average price paid for each cup
 I = Per capita income in the given market (thousands)
 T = Average outdoor temperature
 A_c = Competition's monthly advertising expenditures (thousands)
 A_j = Joy's own monthly advertising expenditures (thousands)

One of the outlets has the following conditions: $P = 1.50$, $I = 10$, $T = 60$, $A_c = 15$, $A_j = 10$.
 a. Estimate the number of cups served per week by this outlet. Also determine the outlet's demand curve.

b. What would be the effect of a \$5,000 increase in the competitor's advertising expenditure? Illustrate the effect on the oulet's demand curve.
c. What would Joy's advertising expenditure have to be to counteract this effect?

7. Illustrate the following situations with the use of supply and demand diagrams. Show the short-run effect on equilibrium price and equilibrium quantity as a result of these changes in market conditions.
   a. *The market for copper:* Because of cutbacks in defense spending, the U.S. Army reduces its demand for copper. At the same time, the price of fiberoptic cable falls.
   b. *The market for phonograph turntables:* The price of compact disc players falls.
   c. *The market for fax machines:* Companies in Korea, Taiwan, and Singapore decide to begin manufacturing fax machines.
8. Over the last several years, the demand for compact discs (CDs) has dramatically increased. What are some of the causes of this increase in demand? According to supply-and-demand theory, price should rise when demand increases. However, in recent years the average price of a CD has actually fallen. Explain this apparent contradiction between the theory and fact.
9. Following are three sample demand equations. Plot them on a graph in which Q is on the vertical axis and P is on the horizontal axis. Then transform these equations so that P is expressed in terms of Q and plot these transformed equations on a graph in which P is on the vertical axis and Q is on the horizontal axis.
   a. $Q = 250 - 10P$
   b. $Q = 1{,}300 - 140P$
   c. $Q = 45 - 0.5P$

CHAPTER 4

Demand Elasticity

The Situation

Henry Caulfield is the owner-operator of a local "Gas 'n Go" gas station and convenience store. Henry chose to locate his store in an area at least ten minutes away by car from the nearest supermarket or grocery store. For the most part, Henry's business has been quite successful.

Then one day he noticed that a new grocery store was opening just one block away. A month later he noticed that a new convenience store had opened for business less than a three-minute drive away. Henry realized that to maintain the status quo in the face of this new competition, he would have to make some tough decisions about his pricing and promotion policies and the mix of items carried in his store.

The items that he carried were typical of those found in retail establishments of this type, with beer, cigarettes, hot coffee, and soft drinks accounting for about 75 percent of total sales. Soft drinks were by far the best-selling item in his store. Essentially, the retail price of soft drinks was based on the wholesale price plus a mark-up of about 400 percent. Henry recognized that this mark-up was considerably higher than the one used by a supermarket, but he believed that people were willing to pay more for the convenience.

On certain occasions, Henry would offer a particular brand of soft drink at a substantial discount. Regardless of whether he lost or made money on soft drinks by this action, he found that it helped to attract additional customers into his store, and gasoline sales actually increased. Several people from an adjacent town told him that they waited until they were in the vicinity of his station to fill their tanks because of his discount on soda. Given the public's responsiveness to special discounts on soft drinks and the ability of this product to promote other products, Henry decided to use the pricing of soft drinks as his main weapon against his new competition. Instead of of-

(Continued)

fering a temporary discount, he decided to reduce the price of soft drinks permanently. However, after a month, despite the lower soft drink prices, there was a noticeable decline in his sales of soft drinks. Henry realized that he would have to reassess his competitive tactic.

The Economic Concept of Elasticity

In the previous chapter we studied the idea of demand and discussed the movement along a demand curve (i.e., change in quantity demanded). We found the demand curve to slope downward to the right; this means, of course, that the lower the price, the greater the quantity of the product consumed. We are now going to discuss the question of how sensitive the change in quantity demanded is to a change in price. The measurement of this sensitivity in percentage terms is called the *price elasticity of demand.* Henry Caulfield made implicit use of this concept when he decided to lower his soft drink prices to compete with the new stores in his area. But this is only one of the elasticity measures with which we will concern ourselves in this chapter. We will also cover the concepts of income elasticity, cross-elasticity, and supply elasticity.

In the most general terms, we can define elasticity as a percentage relationship between two variables, that is, the percentage change in one variable relative to a percentage change in another. In different terms, we divide one percentage by the other:

$$\text{Percent change in } A \div \text{Percent change in } B = \text{Coefficient of elasticity}$$

The result of this division is the coefficient of elasticity. It is then our task to interpret the coefficient and to determine the effects of the change. The meaning of the size as well as the sign of the coefficient (the coefficient may be negative or positive) will be the focus of our inquiry for the remainder of this chapter. Let us first turn to the most frequently encountered elasticity concept, the price elasticity of demand.

The Price Elasticity of Demand

When Henry Caulfield contemplated lowering his price to counteract his new competition, he was dealing with price elasticity of demand. He was determining whether by lowering his prices he would raise his unit sales sufficiently to increase his total revenue.[1]

[1]More important, he was wondering whether he would actually increase his profits with this action. However, we are not yet in a position to deal with this question.

When we speak of the price elasticity of demand, we are dealing with the sensitivity of quantities bought to a change in the producer's price. Thus, this concept describes an action that is within the producer's (or, in this case, the dealer's) control. Other elasticities to be discussed later are outside the producer's control and may evoke other action on the producer's part to counteract them.

Demand price elasticity is defined as a percentage change in quantity demanded caused by a one percent change in price. Let us develop this concept mathematically. We can write the expression, "percentage change in quantity demanded" as

$$\Delta\text{Quantity demanded} \div \text{Initial quantity demanded}$$

where Δ (delta) signifies an absolute change. The second part of this relationship, "percentage change in price," can be written as

$$\Delta\text{Price} \div \text{Initial price}$$

Dividing the first expression by the second, we arrive at the expression for the price elasticity of demand:

$$(\Delta\text{Quantity} \div \text{Quantity}) \div (\Delta\text{Price} \div \text{Price}) = \%\Delta\text{Quantity} \div \%\Delta\text{Price}$$

This is the general expression. We turn now to the actual computation of elasticities, and we will describe two methods of obtaining the price elasticity of demand.

Measurement of Price Elasticity

Let us begin with *arc elasticity,* the method most commonly used in economics textbooks. The formula for this indicator is

$$E_p = \frac{Q_2 - Q_1}{(Q_1 + Q_2)/2} \div \frac{P_2 - P_1}{(P_1 + P_2)/2}$$

where E_p = Coefficient of arc price elasticity
Q_1 = Original quantity demanded
Q_2 = New quantity demanded
P_1 = Original price
P_2 = New price

The numerator of this coefficient, $(Q_2 - Q_1)/[(Q_1 + Q_2)/2]$, indicates the percentage change in the quantity demanded. The denominator, $(P_2 - P_1)/[(P_1 + P_2)/2]$, indicates the percentage change in the price.

Notice that the change in each variable is expressed relative to the *average* of its beginning and ending values. For example, if the price of a product rises from \$11 to \$12, causing a fall in the quantity demanded from 7 to 6, the formula gives the following price elasticity coefficient:

$$
\begin{aligned}
E_p &= \frac{6-7}{(7+6)/2} \div \frac{12-11}{(11+12)/2} \\
&= \frac{-1}{6.5} \div \frac{1}{11.5} \\
&= \frac{-1}{6.5} \times \frac{11.5}{1} \\
&= \frac{-11.5}{6.5} \\
&= -1.77
\end{aligned}
$$

The reason the arc elasticity formula employs the average of the beginning and ending values can be clearly seen. If we had used the beginning values, the coefficient would be:

$$
\begin{aligned}
E_p &= \frac{6-7}{7} \div \frac{12-11}{11} \\
&= \frac{-1}{7} \div \frac{1}{11} \\
&= \frac{-1}{7} \times \frac{11}{1} \\
&= \frac{-11}{7} \\
&= -1.57
\end{aligned}
$$

However, suppose the price fell from \$12 to \$11, causing the quantity demanded to rise from 6 to 7 units. Using the beginning values would give us:

$$
\begin{aligned}
E_p &= \frac{7-6}{6} \div \frac{11-12}{12} \\
&= \frac{1}{6} \div \frac{-1}{12} \\
&= \frac{1}{6} \times \frac{12}{-1} \\
&= \frac{12}{-6} \\
&= -2
\end{aligned}
$$

Thus, the *same* unit changes in price and quantity gives *different* values of elasticity, depending on whether the price increases or decreases.[2] By using the

[2]The reason for this ambiguity is simply that the base number differs between a percentage increase and a decrease between two numbers. A good example of this can be found in the retail trade. Suppose a company buys a dress wholesale for \$100 and marks it up 100 percent, thereby establishing the retail price at \$200. Suppose in a clearance sale it decides to sell it at cost. This would represent a 50 percent markdown (i.e., from \$200 down to \$100).

average of the beginning and ending values, we avoid this ambiguity. The price elasticity coefficient is the same whether price increases or decreases.

An additional source of ambiguity arises in the computation of elasticity when we consider changes over different ranges of price and quantity. For example, suppose that the values of price and quantity provided in the preceding analysis are part of the hypothetical demand schedule shown in Table 4.1.

The numbers in this schedule indicate a linear relationship between quantity demand and price, with a unit change in price resulting in a unit change in quantity over the entire range of the schedule.[3] Suppose we compute the arc elasticity for a price change from \$12 to \$10 rather than between \$12 and \$11. Using the arc elasticity formula gives

$$\begin{aligned} E_p &= \frac{6-8}{(8+6)/2} \div \frac{12-10}{(10+12)/2} \\ &= \frac{-2}{7} \div \frac{2}{11} \\ &= \frac{-2}{7} \times \frac{11}{2} \\ &= \frac{-22}{14} \\ &= -1.57 \end{aligned}$$

Table 4.1 Hypothetical Demand Schedule

Price	*Quantity*
18	0
17	1
16	2
15	3
14	4
13	5
12	6
11	7
10	8
9	9
8	10
7	11
6	12
5	13

[3]The algebraic expression of this demand equation is $P = 18 - Q$, or $Q = 18 - P$.

Notice that the coefficient is different from the previously computed value. In fact, for any given value of price, the arc elasticity coefficient will vary depending on the new price's distance from the original price.[4]

To adjust for the ambiguity inherent in the use of the arc formula, economists recommend the use of *point elasticity,* the second of the two ways to compute the elasticity coefficient. This method of computation is expressed as follows:

$$\epsilon_p = \frac{dQ}{dP} \times \frac{P_1}{Q_1}$$

To compute point elasticity, we employ one of the economist's favorite mathematical devices, the derivative. Students familiar with elementary calculus, or who learned about it in the appendix to Chapter 2, will have no difficulty with this expression. The key is that by assuming very small changes (actually, in calculus the change is "infinitesimally small") in price and quantity around some given level, we avoid the problem of the measure of elasticity differing based on the amount of change.

To find the derivative of Q with respect to P (i.e., dQ/dP), we need the algebraic expression of the demand equation. The equation implied in Table 4.1 is $Q = 18 - P$. The derivative of Q with respect to P is -1. Thus, the point elasticity coefficient at $12 and 6 units is:

$$\begin{aligned}\epsilon_p &= -1 \times \frac{12}{6} \\ &= -2\end{aligned}$$

Actually, whenever the demand equation is linear, the point elasticity formula appears almost too simple because the first derivative of this equation with respect to P is a constant. From a practical standpoint, there is really no need to use calculus for finding the point elasticity of a linear demand function. The first derivative dQ/dP is the same as the (constant) slope of the demand line, $\Delta Q/\Delta P$. Thus, the point elasticity of a linear demand function can be expressed as:

$$\epsilon_p = \frac{\Delta Q}{\Delta P} \times \frac{P_1}{Q_1}$$

The relationship between point elasticity and arc elasticity can be seen with the use of algebraic manipulation. First, let us consider the change in price and quantity from some given points P_1 and Q_1:

$$\epsilon_p = \frac{Q_2 - Q_1}{Q_1} \div \frac{P_2 - P_1}{P_1}$$

[4]Interested readers should try computing the arc elasticity for changes between $12 and $9, between $12 and $8, and so on. They will find that the arc elasticity coefficient decreases as the change in price increases.

Letting $Q_2 - Q_1 = \Delta Q$ and $P_2 - P_1 = \Delta P$ and then rearranging these terms gives us:

$$\begin{aligned}\epsilon_p &= \frac{\Delta Q}{Q_1} \div \frac{\Delta P}{P_1} \\ &= \frac{\Delta Q}{Q_1} \times \frac{P_1}{\Delta P} \\ &= \frac{\Delta Q}{\Delta P} \times \frac{P_1}{Q_1}\end{aligned}$$

Next, let us consider the change in price and quantity in relation to the average or midpoint between the original and new values of these variables:

$$E_p = \frac{Q_2 - Q_1}{(Q_1 + Q_2)/2} \div \frac{P_2 - P_1}{(P_1 + P_2)/2}$$

Letting $Q_2 - Q_1 = \Delta Q$ and $P_2 - P_1 = \Delta P$, canceling out the 2 in the denominator of each term, and then rearranging the formula gives us:

$$\begin{aligned}E_p &= \frac{\Delta Q}{Q_1 + Q_2} \div \frac{\Delta P}{P_1 + P_2} \\ &= \frac{\Delta Q}{Q_1 + Q_2} \times \frac{P_1 + P_2}{\Delta P} \\ &= \frac{\Delta Q}{\Delta P} \times \frac{P_1 + P_2}{Q_1 + Q_2}\end{aligned}$$

As you can see, the only difference between point and arc elasticity is that the former considers P_1/Q_1, whereas the latter considers $(P_1 + P_2)/(Q_1 + Q_2)$.

Of course, in cases where the demand curve is nonlinear, calculus must be employed to compute point elasticity. For example, consider the following demand curve.

$$Q = 100 - P^2$$

Assuming $P_1 = 5$, then $Q = 75$. Then the point elasticity is

$$\begin{aligned}\epsilon_p &= -2P \times \frac{5}{75} \\ &= -2(5) \times \frac{5}{75} \\ &= \frac{-50}{75} \\ &= -0.67\end{aligned}$$

The concept of point elasticity, as well as the use of calculus, will be found to be of particular importance in the next chapter, when the estimation of demand equations will be discussed. However, for now, using discrete changes and the arc elasticity coefficient would appear to be the more realistic thing for

Henry Caulfield (and most other practical business people) to do. He may not be familiar with calculus, but this certainly does not detract from his business acumen. He is dealing with a concrete problem: how much he will sell if he lowers his price by a discrete quantity (i.e., a certain number of cents). Arc elasticity is perfectly suitable for this problem.

Economists, in their neat way, have created categories of elasticity:

1. *Relative elasticity of demand:*

   $$E_p > 1 \text{ (in absolute terms)}$$

   This occurs when a 1 percent change in price causes a change in quantity demanded greater than 1 percent. The coefficient calculated earlier, 1.77, is a case of relatively elastic demand.
2. *Relative inelasticity of demand:*

   $$0 < Ep < 1 \text{ (in absolute terms)}$$

   Here the percentage change in price is greater than the corresponding change in quantity. For example, in Table 4.1 as price is lowered from 8 to 7, quantity rises from 10 to 11, giving a coefficient of 0.71.
3. *Unitary elasticity of demand:*

   $$E_p = 1 \text{(in absolute terms)}$$

   A 1 percent change in price results in a 1 percent change in quantity in the opposite direction.

These are three common measures of elasticity. But there are also two limiting cases at the extremes of the elasticity scale:

1. *Perfect elasticity:*

   $$Ep = \infty \text{ (in absolute terms)}$$

   In this case, there is only one possible price, and at that price an unlimited quantity can be sold. The demand curve for $E_p = \infty$ is a horizontal line. We will encounter a demand curve with this shape later, when we discuss perfect competition.
2. *Perfect inelasticity:*

   $$E_p = 0$$

   Under this condition, the quantity demanded remains the same regardless of price. Such a demand curve may exist for certain products within a particular price range. An example may be the case of salt. Today's price of salt is about 39 cents per pound. If this price were to rise to 49 cents (a significant percentage increase), or fall to 29 cents (a significant percentage decrease), it is very doubtful that the consumption of salt would change at all.

Both of these extreme cases, although possible under certain conditions, will seldom be observed in real life. Still, the two limits should be well understood by every student of economics.

The Determinants of Elasticity

Now that we have described what elasticity is, let us look into the reasons that the demand for some goods and services is elastic, whereas for others it is inelastic. In other words, what determines elasticity? As we look into this question, we must remember that the elasticity for a particular product may differ at different prices. Thus, although the demand elasticity for salt is very low—possibly zero—in the vicinity of its current price, it may not be so inelastic at $5 *or* $10 per pound.

It is often said—and many use this as a rule of thumb—that demand is inelastic for goods considered to be necessities, and it is elastic for luxury products. For example, the demand for furs, gems, and expensive automobiles is probably more elastic than the demand for milk, shoes, and electricity.

Unfortunately, the luxury/necessity dichotomy is ambiguous. Demand for expensive automobiles may be elastic, but if we consider the demand for Mercedes autos, we will probably find that within the prevailing price range, a movement up or down of several thousand dollars would make relatively little difference to those people who are in the market for this particular kind of car. The probable reason for such inconsistencies is relatively simple: One person's luxury is another person's necessity.

Probably the most important determinant of elasticity is ease of substitution. This argument cuts both ways: If there are many good substitutes for the product in question, elasticity will be high; conversely, if this commodity is a good substitute for others, its demand elasticity will also be high. The broader the definition of a commodity, the lower its price elasticity will tend to be, since there is less opportunity for substitution. For instance, the demand elasticity for beer or bread will tend to be less than that for a particular brand of beer or for white bread. There are fewer substitutes for bread in general (particularly if we include in this definition other baked products, such as rolls and bagels) than there are for white bread or, even further, a specific brand of white bread. If the price of bread rises (relative to other products), we may consume somewhat less bread than before. However, if the price of brand A white bread rises, while other white bread prices remain the same, then one would expect the quantity of brand A demanded to drop significantly as consumers switch to other brands.

Henry's convenience store was once the only game in town, so to speak. His nearest competitor was relatively distant. Now customers can substitute for Henry's merchandise by walking one block to the grocery store. And since Henry was most likely selling the same soft drink brands as his close competitor, the substitution effect is extremely strong.

Another major determinant of demand elasticity is the proportion of total expenditures spent on a product. Here we can go back to our salt example. The reason for the low elasticity of demand for salt is that the proportion of a consumer unit's (e.g. an individual, a family, etc.) income spent on salt is extremely small. A hefty price increase (e.g., from 39 cents to 49 cents per pound) would probably cause a shrug of the shoulder but would affect consumption of salt very little.

The spending on soft drinks by a typical individual or a family constitutes a larger portion of income than spending on salt. However, in most circumstances, spending on soda still represents a relatively small percentage of a family's income. Thus, we would not expect a change in price to affect the quantity of demand significantly. Still, in households where large quantities of soft drinks are consumed, a price change could have some effect on quantities sold, although it would probably require a substantial change in price to affect purchases significantly.

However, for a product such as a large appliance, the situation may be entirely different. To most families, a clothes washer represents more than a trivial expense, and a price change could have an important impact on purchases. Thus, we expect the demand elasticity for a clothes washer to be considerably greater than that for salt or soft drinks. There is another possible reason for the relatively high demand elasticity of a clothes washer. An appliance purchase may be postponable, since there is commonly a choice between buying and repairing. Faced with a higher purchase price, a consumer may choose to repair the old appliance.[5]

The Elasticity of Derived Demand

This section of the elasticity discussion represents a small digression, albeit an important one. So far we have discussed demand elasticity for a final product, that is, a product purchased for consumption, such as soft drinks, a clothes washer, salt, white bread or beer.

We are now going to look briefly at the demand for items that go into the production of a final commodity, such as materials, machinery, and labor. The demand for such components of a final product is called *derived demand.* In other words, these components are not demanded for their own sake but because there is a demand for the final product requiring them.

The great British economist Alfred Marshall, about whom previous references were made, described four principles governing the elasticity of the derived demand curve.[6] According to Marshall, the derived demand curve will be more inelastic:

1. The more essential is the component in question
2. The more inelastic is the demand curve for the final product
3. The smaller is the fraction of total cost going to this component
4. The more inelastic is the supply curve of cooperating factors

---

[5]The choice between buying and maintaining becomes even more pronounced for the purchase of an automobile. Here, of course, the price and the proportion of a person's income are considerably higher. In this case, there is a third possibility for the consumer: the purchase of a used car. Thus, recalling what we said about substitutability, we can say that the elasticity of demand for cars in general is lower than the demand elasticity for new cars. Of course, it is also possible to purchase a used washing machine, but there is no organized market for these as there is for cars.

[6]Alfred Marshall, *Principles of Economics,* 8th ed., Philadelphia: Porcupine Press, reprinted 1982, pp. 319–20.

An example will illustrate this concept. Let us consider demand for residential housing (the final product) and the derived demand for one class of labor employed in construction, electricians. After all, the demand for electricians does not exist for its own sake but is due to the demand for housing. Probably all of Marshall's principles apply in this case, but two of them are particularly important. The first is essentiality: you just cannot build a house without employing electricians. Second, the cost of electrical work is probably a relatively small percentage of the entire cost of the house.

Suppose the electricians demand and obtain a substantial wage increase. A contractor may try to cut a few corners with regard to electrical work, but most of it must still be done. Thus, the employment of electricians will not decrease much. The implication here is that the elasticity of demand for electricians is low. Now assume that the work of electricians involves 10 percent of the total cost of construction (this cost is probably overstated). A 10 percent wage increase for electricians represents a 1 percent increase in the total cost of construction. This small addition to the total cost will most likely not trigger a price increase and thus will not affect the employment of electricians to any significant extent. If we also consider the probability that the demand for housing is somewhat inelastic and that the supply elasticity of cooperating factors (i.e., other crafts employed on the project) is rather low, we can conclude that the demand elasticity for electricians is relatively low.

These conclusions tend to hold in the short run much more than in the long run. Over a short period of time, employment of electricians will not drop very much. However, given a longer adjustment period, elasticity of demand will rise as people find ways to substitute for the expensive factor, both on the production side and on the consumption side.[7]

Elasticity in the Short Run and in the Long Run

A long-run demand curve will generally be more elastic than a short-run curve. Here "short run" is defined as an amount of time that does not permit a full adjustment by consumers to a price change. In the shortest of runs, no adjustment at all may be possible, and the demand curve, over the relevant range may be almost perfectly inelastic. As the time period lengthens, consumers will find ways to adjust to the price change by using substitutes (if the price has risen), by substituting the good in question for another (if the price has fallen), or by shifting consumption to or from this particular product (i.e., by consuming more or less of other commodities).

A good example is the case of energy costs. When heating oil prices shot up in the 1970s, the immediate response by consumers was not great. As time passed, however, consumers adjusted their oil consumption. They became used to lower temperatures around the house and at work. They began to dress more warmly

[7] A very interesting analysis of short- and long-run elasticity effects on the economic power of labor unions can be found in Milton Friedman, *Price Theory: A Provisional Text*, Hawthorne, N.Y.; Aldine, 1962, pp. 155-59.

indoors. (Would this result in a higher demand for sweaters? We will look at this particular idea, known as cross-elasticity, later in this chapter.) Over a still longer period, consumers (including one of the authors) converted their homes from oil heat to gas heat. Not only was there conversion, but more newly-built homes were equipped with gas heat. In addition, homes up for resale would advertise gas heating to attract potential buyers, and gas-heated homes commanded a premium price. How can we demonstrate this phenomenon graphically?

We can represent this relationship between the short run and the long run using a series of short-run demand curves intersected by the long-run demand curve, as illustrated in Figure 4.1. Each of the short-run demand curves (D_{S1} to D_{S5}) is rather inelastic. Assume that the original position is point *a*, which represents a price of P_1 and a quantity of Q_1. If the price rises to P_2, consumers will, in the short run, decrease the quantity demanded to point *b*, at quantity Q_2, a relatively small difference in quantity. As time passes, during which consumers adjust to using substitutes, a new short-run demand curve, D_{S2}, will result, and demand will take place at point *c*, at Q_3, which represents a much larger decrease in quantity. Thus, we can connect points *a* and *c* to illustrate the change in quantity demanded in the long run. Then, for constantly increasing prices, we can generate new short-run demand curves, D_{S3}, D_{S4} and D_{S5}, and connect points *d*, *e* and *f* to create a long-run demand curve.

In other words, in the short run, price changes increase or decrease the quantity demanded very little, up or down each of the short-run curves. However, over time, adjustment permits movement to another short-run curve, and a long-run demand curve is created. And the long-run demand curve formed from a point on each short-run curve is obviously far more elastic.

The lengths of the short run and the long run depend on how quickly an adjustment can be made. In the case of heating oil, the long run represented several years. But let us return to the case of Henry Caulfield. Once Henry cuts

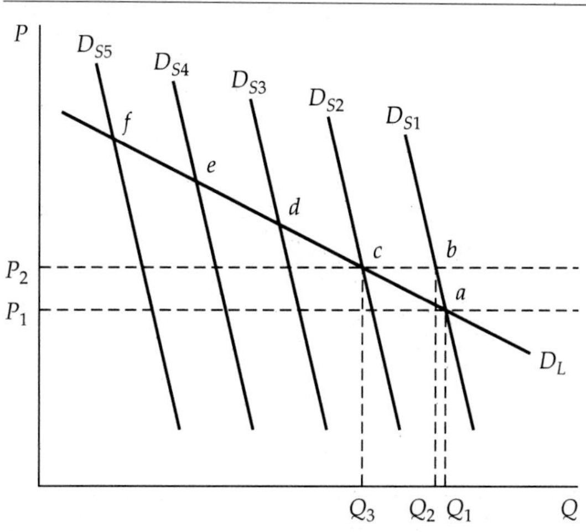

Figure 4.1 Short-Run versus Long-Run Elasticity

his price (if he decides to do so), the news will probably spread quite quickly around the community. The adjustment from the short run to the long run will probably be a matter of days, or weeks at most.

Demand Elasticity and Revenue

Demand elasticity in itself is a rather interesting concept. However, if all it meant was the responsiveness of quantity to price change, it could be easily dismissed. But there is an aspect of demand elasticity that is terribly important to Henry Caulfield or any other businessperson in the throes of a pricing decision (in either direction).

There is a relationship between the price elasticity of demand and revenue received. A decrease in price would decrease revenue if nothing else were to happen. But since demand curves tend to be downward-sloping, a decrease in price will increase the quantity purchased, and this will increase receipts. Which of the two tendencies is stronger? Remember that elasticity is defined as the percentage change in quantity divided by percentage change in price. If the former is larger (and, therefore, the coefficient will be greater than 1 in absolute terms), then the quantity effect is stronger and will more than offset the opposite price effect.

What does that entail for revenue? If price decreases and, in percentage terms, quantity rises more than price has dropped, then total revenue will increase. We summarize the rules describing the relationship between elasticity and total revenue (TR) in Table 4.2.

Let us return to the example of a straight-line demand curve and see what happens to revenue. You will remember that elasticity on such a curve decreases as we move down and to the right. Total revenue and arc elasticity at each price interval are calculated in Table 4.3. Figures 4.2 and 4.3 show graphically the relationship between elasticity and revenue. It is obvious that as price decreases, revenue rises when demand is elastic, falls when it is inelastic, and reaches its peak (i.e., is level) when elasticity of demand equals 1.

At this point we can formally introduce a term we will use a great deal throughout this book: *marginal revenue*. This concept can be defined as the change in total revenue as quantity changes by one unit[8]

$$\Delta TR \div \Delta Q$$

Now we can add to the previous table a *marginal revenue* column. The amended table is shown in Table 4.4.[9] Marginal revenue is positive as total revenue rises

[8]Readers with knowledge of calculus will see that we are dealing again with a derivative, $d\text{TR}/dQ$, the derivative of total revenue with respect to quantity.

[9]In this table only a subset of the prices and quantities is shown. This should be sufficient for an understanding of the concept of marginal revenue.

Table 4.2 The Relationship between Price Elasticity and Total Revenue (TR)

	Demand		
	Elastic	*Unitary Elastic*	*Inelastic*
Price increase	TR↓	$\overline{TR}$	TR↑
Price decrease	TR↑	$\overline{TR}$	TR↓

Table 4.3 Demand Schedule Showing Total Revenue and Elasticity Values

Price	*Quantity*	*Elasticity*	*Revenue*
18	0		0
17	1	−35.0	17
16	2	−11.0	32
15	3	−6.2	45
14	4	−4.1	56
13	5	−3.0	65
12	6	−2.3	72
11	7	−1.8	77
10	8	−1.4	80
9	9	−1.1	81
8	10	−0.9	80
7	11	−0.7	77
6	12	−0.6	72
5	13	−0.4	65
4	14	−0.3	56
3	15	−0.2	45
2	16	−0.2	32
1	17	−0.1	17
0	18	0	0

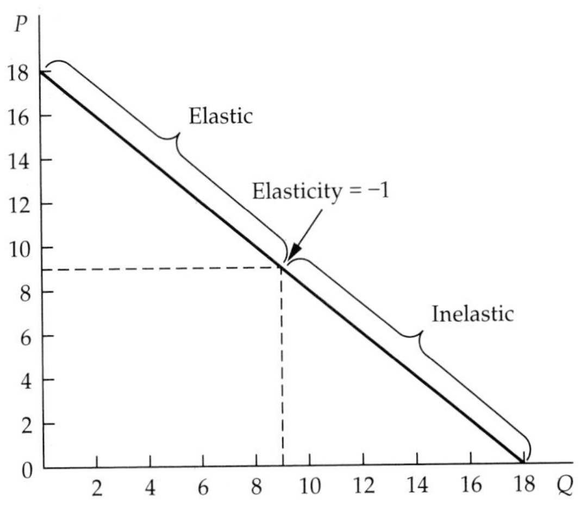

Figure 4.2 The Elasticity-Demand Relationship

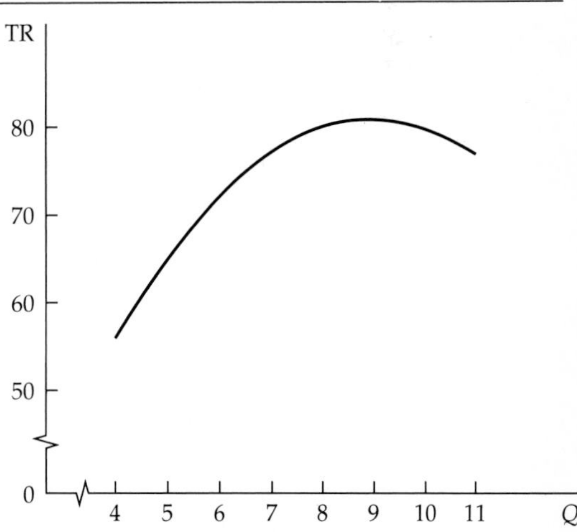

Figure 4.3 The Effect of Elasticity on Total Revenue

Table 4.4 Demand Schedule with Marginal Revenue Added

Price	*Quantity*	*Total Revenue*	*Marginal Revenue*	*Elasticity*
13	5	65	9	−3.0
12	6	72	7	−2.3
11	7	77	5	−1.8
10	8	80	3	−1.4
9	9	81	1	−1.1
8	10	80	−1	−0.9
7	11	77	−3	−0.7

(and the demand curve is elastic). When total revenue reaches its peak (elasticity equals 1), marginal revenue reaches zero.[10]

Figure 4.4 shows the mathematical and graphic relationship between the demand curve and marginal revenue (MR). It turns out that when the demand curve is described by a straight line, the marginal revenue curve is twice as steep as the demand curve. Under these circumstances, the marginal revenue curve can be drawn by bisecting the distance between the Y-axis (vertical axis) and the demand curve. Of course, at the point where marginal revenue crosses the

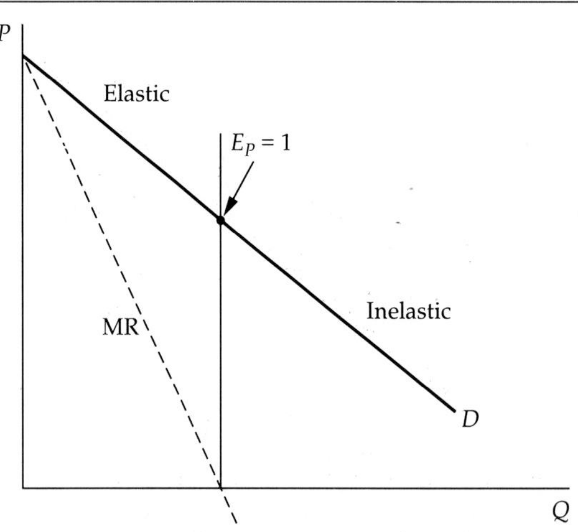

Figure 4.4 The Relationship between Demand and Marginal Revenue

[10] Again, elementary calculus will be of help. As was shown in the appendix to Chapter 2, where the mathematics of managerial economics was explained, if $d\text{TR}/dQ$ equals zero, we can solve for the maximum revenue.

X-axis (horizontal axis), the demand curve is unitarily elastic (and total revenue reaches its maximum).[11]

All of this is going through Henry's mind as he is deciding how to counteract his competition. For him to benefit at all from decreasing his price, the demand curve for soft drinks from his store must be elastic. A price cut leading to a decrease in revenue would be self-defeating (or even disastrous). But this is not his only concern. If Henry is a profit maximizer, then it is profit, not revenue, that concerns him. If the demand for his product is elastic, revenue will increase. But as he sells more units, his total cost will, of course, rise. Will the increase in revenue more than offset the additional cost? That is the question uppermost in Henry's mind. Unfortunately, we are not ready to answer at this point. We first have to study production functions and cost functions, and then link demand and cost in Chapter 11.

The Mathematics of Elasticity

It is now time to apply some of the calculus you have learned. Point elasticity was mentioned earlier in this chapter and was said to require the use of differential calculus. The formula for point elasticity was given as:

$$dQ/dP \times P/Q$$

For this formula to be employed, the demand curve has to be stated in the form of an equation. The equation for the demand curve represented in Table 4.1 is

$$Q = 18 - P$$

Therefore, dQ/dP equals -1. This is the slope of the straight- line demand curve.

As stated in the discussion of arc elasticity, elasticity changes along the demand curve. So does point elasticity, of course. Thus, the point at which elasticity is measured must be specified. For example, the point elasticity at $Q = 5$ and $P = 13$ is

$$-1 \times 13 \div 5 = -2.6$$

In Table 4.3 the arc elasticity was shown to be -3 in the interval between $P = 13$ and $P = 14$ and between $Q = 4$ and $Q = 5$, and -2.3 in the next interval. Point elasticity, as should be expected, is somewhere between the two arc elasticities.

---

[11] In mathematical terms, the path from the demand curve to the marginal revenue curve can be traced as follows:

Demand curve:	$P = a - bQ$
Total revenue:	$PQ = aQ - bQ^2$
Marginal revenue:	$dTR/dQ = a - 2bQ$

At $Q = 10$ and $P = 8$, the result is

$$-1 \times 8 \div 10 = -0.8$$

We are now in the inelastic section of the demand curve.

We also mentioned the use of calculus in reference to marginal revenue, which was defined as $d\text{TR}/dQ$. For this purpose, we will reverse our demand function so that quantity becomes the independent variable.

Demand:	$P = 18 - Q$
Total revenue:	$\text{TR} = PQ = 18Q - Q^2$
Marginal revenue:	$d\text{TR}/dQ = 18 - 2Q$

At $Q = 5$ and $TR = 65$, marginal revenue is

$$18 - (2 \times 5) = 8$$

Again, since we are measuring TR at a point rather than over an interval, the result (MR=8) will be somewhat different from the marginal revenue obtained in Table 4.4, where discrete differences were used in the calculation.

At $Q = 10$, $\text{MR} = 18 - (2 \times 10) = -2$. We are now in the area of negative marginal revenue (relative inelasticity on the demand curve), or at a quantity higher than the one that produces maximum revenue.

If we wish to find the point where revenue is maximized, we look for the point at which MR=0. Thus,

$$\begin{aligned} 18 - 2Q &= 0 \\ 18 &= 2Q \\ 9 &= Q \end{aligned}$$

This result, again, is not the same but is very similar to the number found in Table 4.4, where discrete intervals rather than infinitely small differences were used.

Empirical Elasticities

In the next chapter we will explain how economists estimate demand curves and elasticities from industry and product data. But it may be of interest at this point to reinforce the meaning of price elasticity by mentioning briefly the results of some studies published in recent years.

A recent study of the demand for coffee estimated the price elasticity to be between −0.14 and −0.19.[12] Apparently, the demand for coffee is not very sensitive to price.

A study of the demand for kitchen and other household appliances stated that the elasticity was -0.63. There is sensitivity to price changes, but for a 1

[12] C.H. Huang, J. J. Siegried, and F. Zardoshty, "The Demand for Coffee in the United States: 1963–77, *Quarterly Review of Economics and Business*, 20, 2 (Summer 1980), pp. 36–50.

percent change in price, quantity demanded will change only 0.63 percent. Demand is inelastic.[13]

Meals (excluding alcoholic beverages) purchased at restaurants have a demand elasticity of −2.27.[14]

During the 1960s, Gregory Chow studied the demand for computers and concluded that price elasticity was −1.44.[15] Here demand is relatively elastic, and quantity demanded will rise 1.44 percent for every 1 percent decrease in price.

The Cross-Elasticity of Demand

The previous discussion dealt with the influence of a price change on the quantity demanded of the product subject to the price change. *Cross-elasticity* deals with the impact (again, in percentage terms) on the quantity demanded of a particular product created by a price change in a related product (while everything else remains constant). What is the meaning of "related" products? In economics we talk of two types of relationships: substitutes and complements.

In Henry Caulfield's case, we are dealing with substitutes. The sodas sold by the new grocery store are substitutes for those sold by Henry. They probably are the same products (same brands) but are sold by different suppliers, and one supplier can be considered a substitute for the other. Of course, there are also substitutes on Henry's own shelves—he stocks different brands of cola, for example.

Much of the time when we consider cross-elasticity we are dealing with similar products (not just different brands of the same product) in a more general sense. Thus, chicken and beef can be considered to be substitutes; a change in the price of chicken will have an effect on the consumption of beef. Other instances of substitutes come to mind easily: coffee and tea, butter and oleomargarine, aluminum and steel, and glass and plastic.

Complements are products that are consumed or used together. Henry sells potato chips, pretzels, and other "munchies" that are consumed together with soft drinks. Other cases of complementary products are peanut butter and jam, stereo sets and tapes, tennis rackets and tennis balls, and personal computers and floppy disks.

The definition of cross-elasticity is a measure of the percentage change in quantity demanded of product A resulting from a 1 percent change in the price of product B. The general equation can be written as

$$E_X = (\Delta Q_A \div Q_A) \div (\Delta P_B \div P_B)$$

[13]H. S. Houthakker and L. D. Taylor, *Consumer Demand in the United States: Analysis and Projections*, 2d ed., Cambridge, Mass.: Harvard University Press, 1970, p. 81.

[14]Ibid., p. 63.

[15]G. C. Chow, "Technological Change and Demand for Computers," *American Economic Review*, December 1967, pp. 1117–30.

Again, we run into a little problem regarding the denominator in this expression, and arc elasticity comes to the rescue:[16]

$$E_X = \{(Q_{2A} - Q_{1A}) \div [(Q_{2A} + Q_{1A}) \div 2]\} \div \{(P_{2B} - P_{1B}) \div [(P_{2B} + P_{1B}) \div 2]\}$$

What about cross-elasticity coefficients? First, let us look at the sign. A decrease in the price of the supermarket's soft drinks will cause the quantity of soft drinks sold by Caulfield to decrease. And, of course, if the supermarket raises prices, Caulfield's sales will rise. Thus, the sign of cross-elasticity for substitutes is positive. On the other hand, the coefficient sign for cross-elasticity of complements is negative. For instance, a decrease in the price of tapes could lead to increased purchases of stereo consoles.

To measure the strength of the elasticity coefficient, we employ a more arbitrary definition than for demand elasticity. As a rule of thumb in business, two products are considered good substitutes or complements when the coefficient is larger than 0.5 (in absolute terms, since the coefficient for complements is negative).

Empirical Elasticities

Again, it should be useful to briefly mention some study results:

The cross elasticity of Florida Indian River oranges and Florida interior oranges was shown to be between +1.16 and +1.56 in a study conducted in Grand Rapids, Michigan, supermarkets. The coefficients are very high and positive, signifying strong substitutability. On the other hand, the cross elasticities between the two Florida oranges and California oranges were between +0.01 and +0.19; obviously, California oranges are not good substitutes for Florida oranges, and vice versa.[17]

A study of the residential demand for electric energy found the cross-elasticity with respect to prices of gas energy to be low, about 0.13.[18]

---

[16]The following equation, obtained by arithmetic manipulation, may be easier for some readers:

$$E_x - [(Q_{2A} - Q_{1A}) \div (P_{2B} - P_{1B})] \times [(P_{2B} + P_{1B}) \div (Q_{2A} + Q_{1A})]$$

Or, if point elasticity is of interest, the use of calculus gives

$$dQ_A/dP_B \times P_B/Q_A$$

The calculations would proceed similarly to those for demand elasticity.

[17]M. B. Goodwin, W. F. Chapman, Jr., and W. T. Hanley, *Competition between Florida and California Valencia Oranges in the Fruit Market*, Bulletin 704, Agricultural Station, Institute of Food and Agriculture Services, University of Florida, December 1965.

[18]R. Halvorson, "Residential Demand for Electric Energy," *Review of Economics and Statistics*, 57 (February 1975), pp. 12–18.

Income Elasticity

Before the arrival of his competitors, Henry Caulfield saw his sales grow, not only as the number of households in the area increased, but also as the household income level in the area rose. This represents quantity of sales as a function of (i.e., influenced by) consumers' income. As a measure of the sensitivity of this relationship, economists use the term *income elasticity of demand.* The general expression for this elasticity is

$$E_Y = \%\Delta Q \div \%\Delta Y$$

where Y represents income.[19] The definition of income elasticity is a measure of the percentage change in quantity consumed resulting from a 1 percent change in income.

As before, we shall turn to arc elasticity for the actual calculation of income elasticity:[20]

$$E_Y = \{(Q_2 - Q_1) \div [(Q_2 + Q_1) \div 2]\} \div \{(Y_2 - Y_1) \div [(Y_2 + Y_1) \div 2]\}$$

In the case of income elasticity, the coefficient can be either positive or negative. For most products, one would expect income elasticity to be positive. After all, given a rise in income , a person will spend more. Thus, when the coefficient is positive, we refer to the income elasticity as normal. (Later, this definition will be refined in relation to elasticities for "superior" commodities.)

The coefficient of +1 represents another dividing line. As income rises, people can increase consumption of products (and services) proportionally, less than proportionally, or more than proportionally to the income rise. If the expenditure on product A goes up by 10 percent when income goes up by 10 percent, then the income elasticity coefficient equals 1. That is, the proportion of the consumer's income spent on this commodity remains the same before and after the change in income.[21] Suppose a consumer's annual income is $30,000

---

[19] Again, on terms of calculus, this expression could be written as

$$\epsilon_Y = \partial Q / \partial Y \times Y \div Q$$

This, of course, expresses the point elasticity. Also, as the reader can see partial derivatives have been used. As in all other cases of elasticity, the assumption is that only the effect of income on quantity is being measured, with all other possible variables in the demand relationship, (e.g., price, price of related products, interest rates, advertising) held constant.

[20] As in the case of the other elasticities, the equation can be rewritten in several different forms. The student can select the equation that is most convenient:

$$E_Y = [(Q_2 - Q_1) \div (Q_2 + Q_1)] \div [(Y_2 - Y_1) \div (Y_2 + Y_1)$$

$$E_Y = [(Q_2 - Q_1) \div (Q_2 + Q_1)] \times [(Y_2 + Y_1) \div (Y_2 - Y_1)]$$

$$E_Y = [(Q_2 - Q_1) \div (Y_2 - Y_1)] \times [(Y_2 + Y_1) \div (Q_2 + Q_1)]$$

[21] Remember that, by definition, the price of the product remains the same. Thus, it does not matter whether we measure an increase in quantity of the product or in expenditures on the product.

and spending on clothing is $2,700 per year. If this person's income rises by 10 percent to $33,000, and he or she then spends $2,970 annually on clothing—also a 10 percent increase—the proportion of total income spent on clothing remains at 9 percent.

If the income elasticity coefficient is greater or less than 1, the fraction of income spent on the product in question changes more or less than proportionally with income. Products whose income elasticities exceed +1, taking larger portions of consumers' income as incomes increase, are often referred to as "superior" commodities.

A few examples should help to explain the income elasticity concept. For instance, the short-run income elasticity for food expenditure has been estimated to be about 0.5 and the elasticity of restaurant meals 1.6.[22] In other words, food consumed at home takes up a smaller proportion of income as income rises.[23] When income rises by 10 percent, a consumer will spend more on food than he or she did at the lower income level, but spending on food will increase only by 5 percent; thus, the proportion of total spending on food is less at the higher level of income. The pattern of spending on restaurant meals is significantly different. Here the data show that as income rises, consumers will spend a larger proportion of income on food consumed away from home. For every 1 percent increase in income (or total expenditure), consumers will raise their spending on restaurant meals by 1.6 percent.

The income elasticity for jewelry and watches was estimated in the same study to be 1.0 in the short run.[24] This is a somewhat surprising result since these items are generally considered luxuries. However, the long-run elasticity was estimated at 1.6, which is closer to what we would expect; it may just be a case of an adjustment process that is relatively long.

It is possible that the income elasticity coefficient will be less than zero. This would occur if the quantity bought of (or the expenditure on) a product were to decrease absolutely as the result of an increase in income. Although such a result may at first seem implausible, a little reflection will show that such a condition may very well exist. Some products will be demanded by consumers whose incomes are low; but as incomes rise, and consumers feel "better off," they will shift consumption to goods more commensurate with their new economic status. What types of products would be disfavored ? The usual examples that economists use are potatoes, pork and beans, and canned luncheon meat.[25] Goods of this type are usually referred to as "inferior" commodities.[26]

---

[22]Houthakker and Taylor, op. cit., pp. 62–63.

[23]Actually, this study measured the relationship between spending on food and total expenditures, rather than income. Since the proportion of total expenses to income is relatively stable, this substitution does not significantly change results.

[24]Ibid., p. 72.

[25]With apologies to consumers at all income levels who happen to like these particular items.

[26]The study of coffee demand quoted previously in this chapter also reported that income elasticity of demand for soluble coffee was actually negative. However, the results were not statistically significant, a concept we will discuss in our next chapter.

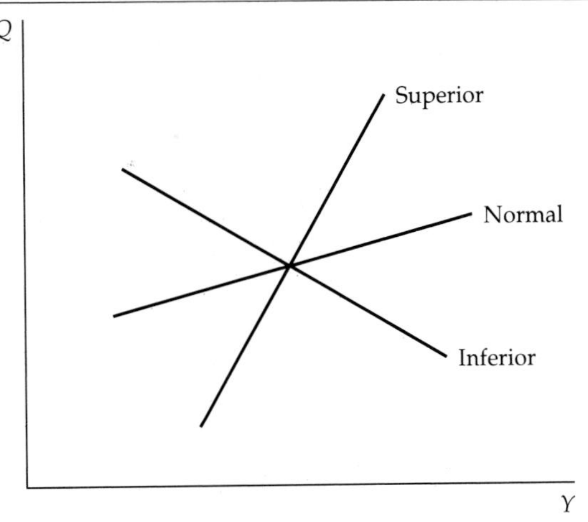

Figure 4.5 Categories of Income Elasticity

So, let us now recapitulate the concept of income elasticity by specifying three categories:

Income elasticity > 1: superior goods
Income elasticity > 0, and < 1: normal goods
Income elasticity < 0: inferior goods

We can depict these situations graphically as shown in Figure 4.5.

Other Elasticity Measures

We have covered the three most common elasticity measures, but there are others. Elasticity is encountered every time a change in some variable affects quantities. For instance, one thing that Henry could do to counteract his competition is to advertise his products. He might speculate how an increase in advertising expenses would affect his total sales. Thus, advertising elasticity can be defined as the percentage change in quantity relative to a 1 percent change in advertising expenses.

Another variable that could have a significant impact on demand—particularly for durable goods—is the interest rate. No one would deny that shifts in mortgage interest rates can cause significant changes in the demand for residential (or nonresidential) construction. Also, the special loan rates offered by automobile manufacturers to customers beginning in the 1980s appear to stimulate car sales, and sales tend to sag when the low rates are terminated.

Elasticity could also be calculated in relation to population size. What is the effect on sales of changes in population? For instance, we could calculate the elasticity of demand for baby carriages as a result of population increases due to the baby boom (and the children of the baby boomers). Or we could investigate the effect of a change in the number of adults (population above the age of 18) on the annual purchases of automobiles (again, as always, holding all other variables constant). And, of course, in Henry Caulfield's case, changes in his community's population will affect his sales. The degree to which sales will be affected is measured by elasticity.

These are just a few examples of possible elasticity calculations. In the next chapter, when we discuss demand estimation, we will see that economists use many variables to explain changes in demand. Although price elasticity, cross elasticity, and income elasticity are the ones most frequently measured, elasticities can be obtained for a large variety of variables.

Elasticity of Supply

Before we close this chapter, it will be useful to devote a little space to the price elasticity of supply. The price elasticity of supply measures the percentage change in quantity supplied as a result of a 1 percent change in price. In other words, this elasticity is a measure of the responsiveness of quantities produced by suppliers to a change in price. In the previous chapter, we developed a supply schedule and a supply curve, and we found that the curve slopes upward and to the right. Thus, the arc coefficient of supply elasticity,

$$E_s = \{(Q_2 - Q_1) \div [(Q_2 + Q_1) \div 2]\} \div \{(P_2 - P_1) \div [(P_2 + P_1) \div 2]\}$$

is a positive number: quantity and price move in the same direction.

The interpretation of the coefficient is the same as for the case of demand elasticity. The higher the coefficient, the more quantity supplied will change (in percentage terms) in response to a change in price.

A Computer Application

This section presents a simple application using Lotus 1-2-3.* It computes the arc elasticity of demand, as well as total and marginal revenue. The actual text as it would appear on a personal computer screen is shown in Table 4.5. The instructions tell you to insert 14 quantities and 14 prices. As this is done, the demand elasticity coefficient will replace the ERRs and zeros. Also, total and marginal revenue will appear.

The results based on the data from Table 4.1 are shown in Table 4.6. Table 4.7 presents the formulas that have been used in each of the cells, for those readers who would like to reproduce this program on their own personal computer. (Table 4.5 shows the columns and rows into which the formulas go.) Figure 4.6 shows the graphs generated by the program, depicting the curves based on the data that were entered.

*Lotus 1-2-3 is a registered trademeark of Lotus Development Corporation.

Table 4.5 Computer Application for Arc Elasticity of Demand: Initial Setup

	A	B	C	D	E	F	G
	INSTRUCTIONS:		Insert 14 prices in even-numbered lines 8–34 in column A				
2			(in descending order)				
3			Insert 14 quantities in even-numbered lines 8–34 in column B				
4							
5			DEMAND	TOTAL	MARGINAL		
6	PRICE	QUANTITY	ELASTICITY	REVENUE	REVENUE		
7							
8				0			
9			ERR		ERR		
10				0			
11			ERR		ERR		
12				0			
13			ERR		ERR		
14				0			
15			ERR		ERR		
16				0			
17			ERR		ERR		
18				0			
19			ERR		ERR		
20				0			

READY

	A	B	C	D	E	F	G
21			ERR		ERR		
22				0			
23			ERR		ERR		
24				0			
25			ERR		ERR		
26				0			
27			ERR		ERR		
28				0			
29			ERR		ERR		
30				0			
31			ERR		ERR		
32				0			
33			ERR		ERR		
34				0			
35							
36							

Table 4.6 Results of Computer Analysis for Data from Table 4.1

```
INSTRUCTIONS:  Insert 14 prices in even-numbered lines 8-34 in column A
                 (in descending order)
               Insert 14 quantities in even-numbered lines 8-34 in column B
```

PRICE	QUANTITY	DEMAND ELASTICITY	TOTAL REVENUE	MARGINAL REVENUE
18	0		0	
		−35.00		17
17	1		17	
		−11.00		15
16	2		32	
		−6.20		13
15	3		45	
		−4.14		11
14	4		56	
		−3.00		9
13	5		65	
		−2.27		7
12	6		72	
		−1.77		5
11	7		77	
		−1.40		3
10	8		80	
		−1.12		1
9	9		81	
		−0.89		−1
8	10		80	
		−0.71		−3
7	11		77	
		−0.57		−5
6	12		72	
		−0.44		−7
5	13		65	

Table 4.7 Formulas Used to Generate the Results in Table 4.6

```
D8:   +A8*B8
C9:   (F2) ((B10-B8)/(B10+B8))/((A10-A8)/(A10+A8))
E9:   (D10-D8)/(B10-B8)
D10:  +A10*B10
C11:  (F2) ((B12-B10)/(B12+B10))/((A12-A10)/(A12+A10))
E11:  (D12-D10)/(B12-B10)
D12:  +A12*B12
C13:  (F2) ((B14-B12)/(B14+B12))/((A14-A12)/(A14+A12))
E13:  (D14-D12)/(B14-B12)
D14:  +A14*B14
C15:  (F2) ((B16-B14)/(B16+B14))/((A16-A14)/(A16+A14))
E15:  (D16-D14)/(B16-B14)
D16:  +A16*B16
C17:  (F2) ((B18-B16)/(B18+B16))/((A18-A16)/(A18+A16))
E17:  (D18-D16)/(B18-B16)
D18:  +A18*B18
C19:  (F2) ((B20-B18)/(B20+B18))/((A20-A18)/(A20+A18))
E19:  (D20-D18)/(B20-B18)
D20:  +A20*B20
C21:  (F2) ((B22-B20)/(B22+B20))/((A22-A20)/(A22+A20))
E21:  (D22-D20)/(B22-B20)
D22:  +A22*B22
C23:  (F2) ((B24-B22)/(B24+B22))/((A24-A22)/(A24+A22))
E23:  (D24-D22)/(B24-B22)
D24:  +A24*B24
C25:  (F2) ((B26-B24)/(B26+B24))/((A26-A24)/(A26+A24))
E25:  (D26-D24)/(B26-B24)
D26:  +A26*B26
C27:  (F2) ((B28-B26)/(B28+B26))/((A28-A26)/(A28+A26))
E27:  (D28-D26)/(B28-B26)
D28:  +A28*B28
C29:  (F2) ((B30-B28)/(B30+B28))/((A30-A28)/(A30+A28))
E29:  (D30-D28)/(B30-B28)
D30:  +A30*B30
C31:  (F2) ((B32-B30)/(B32+B30))/((A32-A30)/(A32+A30))
E31:  (D32-D30)/(B32-B30)
D32:  +A32*B32
C33:  (F2) ((B34-B32)/(B34+B32))/((A34-A32)/(A34+A32))
E33:  (D34-D32)/(B34-B32)
D34:  +A34*B34
```

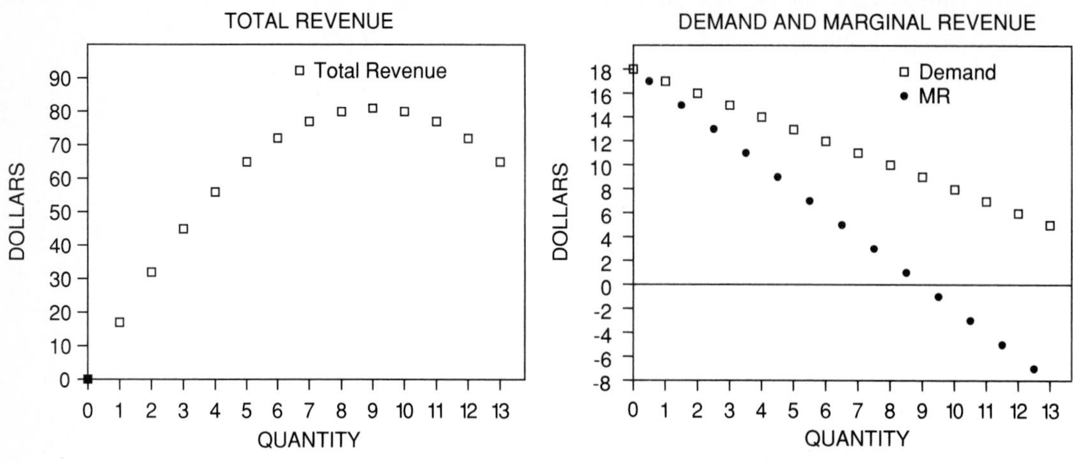

Figure 4.6 Plots of Data from Table 4.6

The Solution

Henry Caulfield is no stranger to the economic concept of price elasticity. He has a bachelor's degree in business administration and was doing well as the regional manager of a large supermarket chain when he decided to leave his job and open his own business. Indeed, it was his understanding of price elasticity that prompted him to reduce the soft drink prices as a way of competing against the two new stores in his area. When he had offered special discounts on soft drinks in the past, he noticed that people were very responsive. In fact, Henry had kept a record of the relationship between price and sales, a part of which is shown in Table 4.8. The "special" price was offered as part of the store's "Fourth of July Celebration" sale.

Table 4.8 Sales Data for 2-Liter Bottles of Soft Drinks

Average Price	Average Weekly Sales	Total Revenue
Regular Price: $1.89	1,050	$1,985
Special Price: $ .89	2,450	2,181

The data indicate an elastic demand for soft drinks at Henry's store. When demand is price-elastic, a reduction in price causes total revenue to increase. This was exactly what had happened when Henry had offered his "Fourth of July" celebration special. He was now puzzled because the permanent price reduction did not seem to be having the same positive effect on his total revenue.

Then, in a flash, it dawned on him. One of the most important aspects of demand elasticity—and, for that matter, of any aspect of economic analysis—is the assumption that certain factors are held constant in the examination of the impact of one variable on another. In this case, it was assumed that other factors besides price did not have an impact (or at least not much of an impact) on quantity when Henry had offered the special holiday price for his soft drink. What other factors besides price might now be taken into account?

To begin with, last summer Henry did not have any close competitors. Therefore, when he offered his discount, there was no other store nearby to match this price reduction. Obviously, the two new stores were not going to stand by idly watching potential customers go to Henry because he had the lowest price for soft drinks. Therefore, the demand for soft drinks at Henry's store was much less elastic than he thought because he was unable to take away their business. To make matters worse, this "price war" among the three stores might have actually reduced their total soft drink revenues. This is because when all three stores dropped their price, they might well have brought the quantity demanded into the inelastic range of their combined demand curves. (We assume here that the three stores constitute the entire local market for soft drinks.)

But regardless of the reaction of his competitors and the possible impact that all of their price cuts might have had on the degree of price elasticity, there was one simple fact that Henry had completely overlooked. Last year's discount took place in summer, a time when the seasonal demand for this product increases anyway. Thus, when Henry cut the price, the demand for his product had already started to increase and his increased revenue may have been caused by the fact that during this time the demand curve was moving to the right.

One final factor had to be considered. In the past, all of his discounts on soft drinks were "specials" and, therefore, temporary in nature. Consumers knew that they had to take advantage of these specials during a designated period. Since they now realized that the price of soft drinks in Henry's store was permanently lowered, they were in no hurry to buy the product. In other words, Henry had failed to take "future expectations" into account.

Thus, to be able to measure elasticity, Henry would have to separate the effects on unit sales of price from all the other, non-price, determinants of demand. Since he had not done this, he had overestimated the degree of responsiveness by his customers to his price reduction. As a result, unfortunately, the reduction in soft drink prices did not provide a solution for Henry. But at least he now understood why it did not.[27] In addition, this analysis reminded

(Continued)

[27]Our example may help you to understand an apparent paradox in the pricing of soft drinks in supermarkets. Very often, substantial discounts on soft drinks are offered at all supermarkets during the summer (i.e., "summer specials"). These discounts either may be offered by the soft drink companies to the supermarkets, which then pass them on to customers, or they may be initiated by the supermarkets themselves. Why should they do this at a time when demand is high? After all, economic theory states that an increase in demand causes prices to rise, other factors held constant. What probably happens is that one of the major soft drink companies decides to take market share away from the other major producers by cutting its price. The others quickly follow. The same is true among supermarkets. These price wars can and do occur at any time during the year. It is just that a "summer special" is a good reason to have a sale.

Henry never to take for granted that "other factors remain constant." In the real world, conditions are changing all the time, and it is important to factor these changes into the analysis. As a small consolation, Henry realized that the entry of additional suppliers into the market was all part of the economics of running a successful business. After all, if people did not think he was making any money, they would probably not be as willing to start a competing enterprise.

Summary

This chapter has dealt with the important concept of elasticity. In the most general terms, elasticity is defined as the sensitivity of one variable to another or, more specifically, the percentage change in one variable caused by a 1 percent change in another. Several forms of elasticity connected with the demand curve were discussed.

The first was price elasticity of demand: the percentage change in the quantity demanded of a product caused by a percentage change in its own price. Since demand curves slope downward and to the right, the coefficient of price elasticity is negative. If the coefficient is less than -1 (or greater than 1 in absolute terms), demand is said to be elastic. On the other hand, the elasticity coefficient can indicate inelasticity or unitary elasticity.

Elasticity is also tied to total revenue. When demand is elastic, revenue rises as quantity demanded increases; revenue reaches its peak at the point of unitary elasticity and descends as quantity rises on the demand curve's inelastic sector. From the concept of revenue, we developed marginal revenue as the change in revenue when quantity changes by one unit. Marginal revenue is positive at quantities where demand is elastic and becomes negative when the demand curve becomes inelastic.

Next, we explained cross-elasticity, the relationship between the demand for one product and the price of another. Products can be substitutes, and their cross-elasticity is then positive; cross-elasticity is negative for products that are complements.

The third major elasticity concept, income elasticity, measures the sensitivity of demand for a product to changes in the income of the population. Goods and services were defined as superior, normal, and inferior, depending on the responsiveness of spending on a product relative to percentage changes in income.

The examples calculated in the chapter used the method of arc elasticity, which measures changes in both variables over discrete intervals, rather than point elasticity, which deals with change over an infinitely small interval and consequently requires knowledge of elementary calculus.

Several other subtopics appeared in this chapter:

Other elasticities, such as advertising and interest elasticity.

Derived demand, which is the demand for inputs to a final product, and the price elasticity of derived demand.

Supply elasticity, the measure of the sensitivity of quantities produced to the price charged by the producers.

In the next chapter, which discusses methods of estimating demand functions, elasticity concepts will be employed again, and they will reappear in various guises in many of the chapters that follow.

Important Concepts

Coefficient of elasticity: The percentage change in one variable divided by the percentage change in the other variable.

Complementary good: A product consumed in conjunction with another. Two goods are complementary if the quantity demanded of one increases when the price of the other decreases.

Cross-elasticity: The percentage change in the quantity consumed of one product as a result of a 1 percent change in the price of a related product.

Derived demand: The demand for products or factors that are not directly consumed but go into the production of a final product. The demand for such a product or factor exists because there is demand for the final product.

Elasticity: The sensitivity of one variable to another or, more precisely, the percentage change in one variable relative to a percentage change in another.

Income elasticity: The percentage change in quantity demanded caused by a 1 percent change in income.

Inferior good: A product whose consumption decreases as income increases (i.e., its income elasticity is negative).

Marginal revenue: The change in total revenue resulting from changing quantity by one unit.

Price elasticity of demand: The percentage change in quantity demanded caused by a 1 percent change in price.

Price elasticity of supply: The percentage change in quantity supplied as a result of a 1 percent change in price.

Substitute good: A product that is similar to another and can be consumed in place of it. Two goods are substitutes if the quantity consumed of one increases when the price of the other increases.

Questions

1. State the general meaning of elasticity as it applies to economics. Define the price elasticity of demand.
2. Explain the difference between point elasticity and arc elasticity. What problem can arise in the calculation of the latter, and how is it usually dealt with? In actual business situations, would you expect arc elasticity to be the more useful concept? Why or why not?

3. It has often been said that craft unions (electricians, carpenters, etc.) possess considerably greater power to raise wages than do industrial unions (automobile workers, steel workers, etc.). How would you explain this phenomenon in terms of demand elasticity?
4. Discuss the relative price elasticity of the following products:
   a. Mayonnaise
   b. A specific brand of mayonnaise
   c. Chevrolet automobiles
   d. Jaguar automobiles
   e. Washing machines
   f. Air travel (vacation)
   g. Beer
   h. Diamond rings
5. What would you expect to happen to spending on food at home and spending on food in restaurants during a decline in economic activity? How would income elasticity of demand help explain these changes?
6. Would you expect the cross-elasticity coefficients between each of the following pairs of products to be positive or negative? Why?
   a. Personal computers and software
   b. Electricity and natural gas
   c. Apples and oranges
   d. Bread and VCRs
7. A study of expenditures on food in northern cities resulted in the following equation:

$$\log E = 0.693 \log Y + 0.224 \log N$$

   where E = Food expenditure
   Y = Total expenditure on all goods and services
   N = Size of family

   Discuss the effect of an increase in income and family size on the expenditure on food. (For explanation of the meaning of logarithms, see page 184.)
8. Why is it unlikely that a firm would sell at a price and quantity where its demand curve is price-inelastic?
9. Which products would exhibit a higher elasticity with respect to interest rates, automobiles or small appliances? Why?
10. The immediate effect of gasoline price increases in the aftermath of the Persian Gulf crisis in August 1990 on gasoline consumption was not very significant. Would you expect the consumption of gasoline to be more severely affected if these higher prices remained in effect for a year or more? Why or why not?
11. In December 1990, the federal tax on gasoline increased by 5 cents. Do you think that such an increase, reflected in the price of gasoline, would have a significant impact on gasoline consumption?
12. Why do you think that whenever governments (federal and state) wish to increase revenues, they usually propose an increase in taxes on cigarettes and alcohol?

13. Could a straight-line demand curve ever have the same elasticity on all of its points?
14. If a demand curve facing a firm is horizontal or nearly so, what does it say about this firm's competition?
15. A company faced by an elastic demand curve will always benefit by decreasing price. True or false? Explain.

Problems

1. The Acme Paper Company lowers its price of envelopes (1,000 count) from \$6 to \$5.40. If its sales increase by 20 percent following the price decrease, what is the elasticity coefficient?
2. The demand function for a cola-type soft drink in general is: $Q = 20 - 2P$, where Q stands for quantity and P stands for price.
   a. Calculate point elasticities at prices of 5 and 9. Is the demand curve elastic or inelastic at these points?
   b. Calculate arc elasticity at the interval between $P = 5$ and $P = 6$.
   c. At which price would a change in price and quantity result in approximately no charge in total revenue? Why?
3. The equation for a demand curve has been estimated to be $Q = 100 - 10P + 0.5Y$ where Q is quantity, P is price, and Y is income. Assume that $P = 7$ and $Y = 50$.
   a. Interpret the equation.
   b. At a price of 7, what is price elasticity?
   c. At an income level of 50, what is income elasticity?
   d. Now assume that income is 70. What is the price elasticity at $P = 8$?
4. Mr. Smith has the following demand equation for a certain product: $Q = 30 - 2P$.
   a. At a price of \$7, what is the point elasticity?
   b. Between prices of \$5 and \$6, what is the arc elasticity?
   c. If the market is made up of 100 individuals with demand curves identical to Mr.Smith's what will be the point and arc elasticity for the conditions specified in parts *a* and *b*?
5. The Teenager Company makes and sells skateboards at an average price of \$70 each. Over the past year they sold 4,000 of these skateboards. The company believes that the price elasticity for this product is about −2.5. If it decreases the price to \$63, what should be the quantity sold? Will revenue increase? Why?
6. The ABC company manufactures AM/FM clock radios and sells on average 3,000 units monthly at \$25 each to retail stores. Its closest competitor produces a similar type of radio that sells for \$28.
   a. If the demand for ABC's product has an elasticity coefficient of −3, how much will it sell per month if the price is lowered to \$22?
   b. The competitor decreases its price to \$24 . If cross-elasticity between the two radios is 0.3, what will ABC's monthly sales be?
7. The Mesa Redbirds football team plays in a stadium with a seating capacity of 80,000. However, during the past season, attendance averaged only

50,000. The average ticket price was $30. If price elasticity is -4, what price would the team have to charge in order to fill the stadium? If the price were to be decreased to $27 and the average attendance increased to 60,0000, what is the price elasticity?

8. The Efficient Software Store had been selling a spreadsheet program at a rate of 100 per month and a graphics program at the rate of 50 per month. In September 1990, Efficient's supplier lowered the price for the spreadsheet program, and Efficient passed on the savings to customers by lowering its retail price from $400 to $350. The store manager then noticed that not only had sales of the spreadsheet program risen to 120, but the sales of the graphics program increased to 56 per month. Explain what has happened. Use both arc price elasticity and arc cross-elasticity measures in your answer.
9. Given the demand equation $Q = 1,500 - 200P$, calculate all the numbers necessary to fill in the following table:

		Elasticity		Total	Marginal
P	*Q*	*Price*	*Arc*	*Revenue*	*Revenue*
$7.00					
6.50					
6.00					
5.50					
5.00					
4.50					
4.00					
3.50					
3.00					
2.50					

10. Would you expect cross-elasticity between the following pairs of products to be positive, negative, or zero?
    a. Automobile wheels and hubcaps
    b. Rye bread and whole-wheat bread
    c. Construction of residential housing and furniture
    d. Breakfast cereal and men's shirts

    Explain the relationship between each pair of products.

APPENDIX 4A
Applications of Supply and Demand

The last two chapters laid the foundation for the student's knowledge of supply and demand and elasticity. Knowing these elements is essential for any further study of economics and is a necessary prerequisite for all the chapters that follow.

Before we discuss the various building blocks that will complete the study of managerial economics, this appendix will endeavor to reinforce the concepts of supply and demand and of elasticity in two ways:

1. Some specific applications of supply and demand will be discussed, including the effects of price controls, excise taxes, and agricultural policies.
2. Various actual situations as reported in the press will be introduced and discussed, and it will be shown that the materials we have just learned can be applied to analyze these situations.

Interference with the Price Mechanism

In Chapter 3, we discussed the movement toward equilibrium in both the short and long runs. A change in demand or supply will call forth actions that will cause equilibrium to occur at a new supply-demand intersection. It was shown that in the short run, price changes will eliminate shortages or surpluses. In the long run, resources in the economy shift from the production of one product to another in response to changes in demand. The shift away from one equilibrium and the move to a new equilibrium will proceed when these movements are permitted to occur freely and are not impeded by any outside interference. Thus, when the supply of corn decreased and price rose so the market cleared at this new price—that is, at the new intersection of supply and demand—there was nothing inhibiting this change from taking place.

However, with present economic institutions, free movement of prices is not always allowed. At least three times in the last 50 years,[28] price controls were imposed in the United States. Prices on various products were set (or fixed at existing levels), and these products could not be sold at prices higher than those prescribed by government. Such a policy is usually referred to as setting a price ceiling. If the price ceiling for a product had been set at the prevailing equilibrium level, then the ceiling would have no effect (until a change in circumstances dictated a higher price). But if the price were set below the equilibrium price,[29] then, as explained in Chapter 3, a shortage would result. In Figure 4A.1, the equilibrium price is P_0, and the quantity sold (and clearing the market) at this price is Q_0. If for some reason the price winds up at P_1 under free-market conditions (i.e., no price controls), the price will rise until the equilibrium price (P_0) is again reached. But if the price is prescribed to be no higher than P_1,[30] the movement toward equilibrium will not take place. Only

[28]During World War II, the Korean War, and again in 1971.

[29]It is obvious that a ceiling set above the equilibrium price would be meaningless.

[30]Price ceilings can be enforced by the government imposing fines or even prison sentences on violators. Such punishment would have appeared rather lenient to some of our ancestors. During the times of price controls in ancient Egypt, Greece, and Rome, the death sentence was the penalty for breaking price control laws. The edict of Diocletian in A.D. 301 imposed the death sentence on those selling at prices higher than decreed, as well as on those buying at such prices (Robert L. Schuettinger and Eamonn F. Butler, *Forty Centuries of Wage and Price Controls*, Washington, D.C.: Heritage Foundation 1979, p. 23).

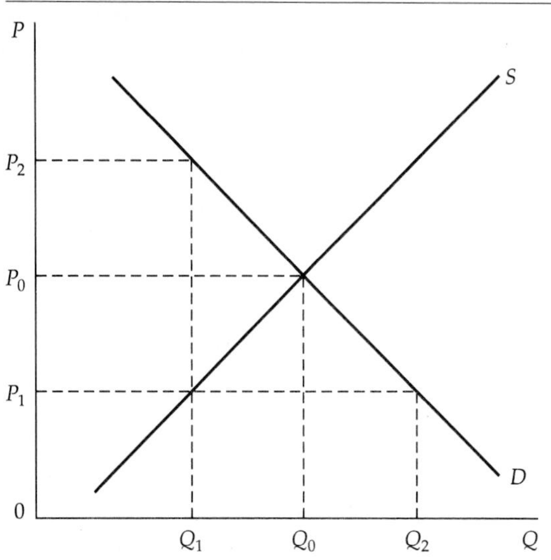

Figure 4A.1 The Effect of a Price Ceiling on Supply and Demand

Q_1 will be supplied while Q_2 is demanded at the lower rate, so a shortage of magnitude Q_1–Q_2 will be established. Thus, only the consumers in the interval 0–Q_1 will be able to buy this particular product. What will be the result of this forced disequilibrium? Possibly consumers will try to shift their demand to other products, causing a pressure on the other products' prices. And if these products are also price-controlled, shortages of these other goods will occur.

There is another possible result. Since only Q_1 units of the product will be supplied at price P_1, these units could be purchased at price P_2 along the demand curve. Consumers would be willing to pay P_2, a price higher than the equilibrium price, P_0, for the limited quantity Q_1. Thus, a strong pressure on the price will be exerted, and somewhere in this process the difference between P_1 and P_2 will be paid to the suppliers.

An example of such a case was the price of automobiles after World War II. A ceiling price below the price level that would have cleared the market was imposed on new cars. This low price caused automobile manufacturers to limit their production. However, consumers were paying high prices for these cars in the way of a dealer's premium. They may also have received lower trade-in prices on their old automobiles or may have bought their new car as a "used" one, since second-hand cars were not price-controlled. The price they actually paid was indeed higher than it could have been if the manufacturers had charged a higher list price.[31] Similarily, where rent ceilings have been imposed many people end up paying a bonus to the superintendent or to a rental agent.

Another example precedes those just discussed by more than 150 years. During the Revolutionary War, the legislature of Pennsylvania imposed limits on

[31] Milton Friedman, *Price Theory: A Provisional Text*, Hawthorne, N.Y.: Aldine 1962, p. 18.

prices of goods sold to the military and was thus instrumental in creating extreme shortages of food for George Washington's army at Valley Forge.[32]

On the other side of the price control coin are price floors. In such cases, a price is established below which the product or service may not be sold. An excellent example of a price floor is the legal minimum wage. Employers are not allowed to pay their workers less than the established minimum, and must, therefore, deal with the disturbance to a price equilibrium.[33]

If the equilibrium wage (e.g., per hour) for some unskilled work were to be at level W_0 as shown in Figure 4A.2, but the law stated that a wage lower than W_1 is illegal, then a surplus of labor Q_1–Q_2 would exist. In the absence of the minimum wage law, wages would drop to W_0, and the quantity supplied and demanded of labor would meet at Q_0. Thus, all workers offering themselves for employment at that wage would be hired.

But if the wage cannot fall below W_1, what will happen? The unemployed will look for work elsewhere. If the minimum wage prevails in all types of employment, they would not be able to find work. However, there are still some forms of employment in the United States that are not covered by law. And, a person can become self-employed, in which case minimum wages do not apply.[34]

Most economists agree that minimum wages above an equilibrium point will tend to cause unemployment among the least skilled workers. Since the

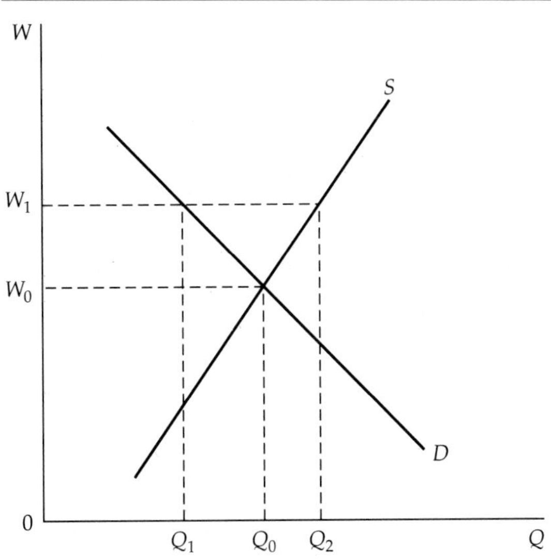

Figure 4A.2 The Effect of a Price Floor on Supply and Demand.

[32]Schuettinger and Butler, op. cit., p. 41.

[33]Wages are, of course, the price of labor, so it is quite correct to discuss minimum wages under the topic of price floors.

[34]And, at the risk of sounding facetious, the extreme case of self-employment is unemployment.

youngest members of the labor force are on average the least skilled, unemployment for many years has been highest among teen-age workers, many of whom have dropped out of school and acquired few if any skills.[35]

Two additional points should be made regarding the impact of minimum wages. First, in referring to Figure 4A.2, the workers in the labor market who are retained after the imposition of the legal minimum will be better off than they were before. These workers can be found in the interval 0–Q_1.[36] Second, the short-run effects of an increased legal minimum are probably stronger than the long-run effects. As time passes, the wage levels in the economy will rise (either due to inflation or in real terms), and at some point the minimum wage may approach the free-market equilibrium wage.

Another example of government controls is in the area of agriculture. We will discuss this subject later.

The Incidence of Taxes

From the viewpoint of the economics of the firm, one important example of applied analysis using supply and demand curves and elasticities is in the area of the incidence or effect of excise taxes on the prices and quantities of products.

An excise tax is a tax imposed as a specific amount per unit of product. It is also sometimes referred to as a specific tax, as compared to a sales tax, which is levied as a percent of the price of the product or service. The federal excise tax on gasoline today is 14 cents per gallon. The sales tax, which is usually collected by states and local communities, in the city of Phoenix, Arizona, for example, is 6.7% of the price of a product. Sales taxes are often referred to as ad valorem taxes. We could discuss the incidence of either ad valorem or specific taxes, but we will choose the latter for our analysis. The principles and applications are similar, but a specific tax provides a simpler and more straightforward illustration.

A numerical example will aid in this exposition. Table 4A.1 shows the demand and supply schedules for a particular product. The equilibrium price is $4. At this price, 15 units will be demanded, and 15 units will be supplied, thus clearing the market.[37] The demand and supply curves are shown in Figure 4A.3*a*, where an equilibrium at $P = 4$ and $Q = 15$ can be observed.

---

[35] A study examining the effects of minimum wages on teenage workers is Thomas Gale Moore, "The Effect of Minimum Wages on Teenage Unemployment Rates," *Journal of Political Economy*, July/August 1971, pp. 897-902.

[36] It is an interesting decision, implicitly made by the U.S. Congress when it passes a law increasing the minimum wage, whether the overall welfare of the country will be increased if some part of the labor force has its wages improved while another part has its income lowered.

[37] An arithmetic solution can be obtained as follows: the equation of the demand curve for the schedule shown in Table4A.1 is $Q_d = 35 - 5P$, and the equation for the supply curve is $Q_S = -5 + 5P$. Solving for $Q_D = Q_S$, we obtain

$$35 - 5P = -5 + 5P$$
$$40 = 10P$$
$$4 = P$$

Table 4A.1 Demand and Supply and Tax Incidence

Unit Price	*Quantity Demanded*	Quantity Supplied *Without Tax*	Quantity Supplied *With Tax*
$6	5	25	20
5	10	20	15
4	15	15	10
3	20	10	5
2	25	5	0
1	30	0	

Now suppose the government imposes an excise tax of $1 per unit, which it will collect from the sellers. The effect is to shift the supply curve up by the unit tax. The shift can be thought of in the following way: Before the enactment of the tax, suppliers offered to sell 20 units at $5. But now, for the producers to obtain $5 per unit, these products will have to be sold at $6 apiece (of which $1 will be remitted to the government).[38] In effect, the production cost for this good has risen by $1 per unit. The last column in Table 4A.1 shows the new supply schedule.

The important question to be asked is what will be the market-clearing price and quantity after the imposition of the new excise tax. An easy answer would be, $1 more than before, or $5. Certainly, the suppliers would prefer not to

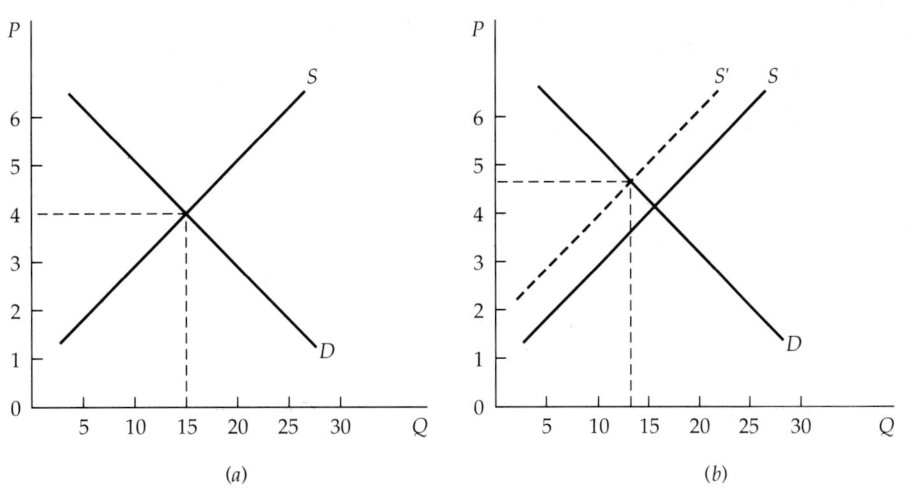

Figure 4A.3 The Influence of an Excise Tax on Supply and Demand

[38]The equation of this new supply curve is $Q_S = -10 + 5P$.

receive less per unit than they had been getting before the tax. But this is not the correct answer, except in very rare cases.[39] The new intersection will be at \$4.50, and the quantity will be 12.5 units.[40]

Thus, sellers will receive only \$3.50 per unit after the imposition of the tax, and consumers will be paying 50 cents more than before. In economic jargon, 50 cents of the tax has been shifted forward to consumers, and 50 cents has been shifted back to the producers. This new equilibrium is shown in Figure 4A.3*b*.

How the incidence of the tax is distributed between the two parties to the transaction depends on the elasticity of the supply and demand curves. The more elastic the demand curve, the larger will be the portion of the tax that the supplier has to bear. In Figure 4A.4*a*, we repeat the demand and supply curves previously shown and add a second demand curve, which (before the tax) also intersects the supply curve at \$4 and 15 units but at all other points is flatter (more elastic) than the original demand function. In Figure 4A.4*b*, the tax is added on to the supply curve. With the new demand curve, the equilibrium price is \$4.42, and the quantity demanded is just above 12 units.[41]

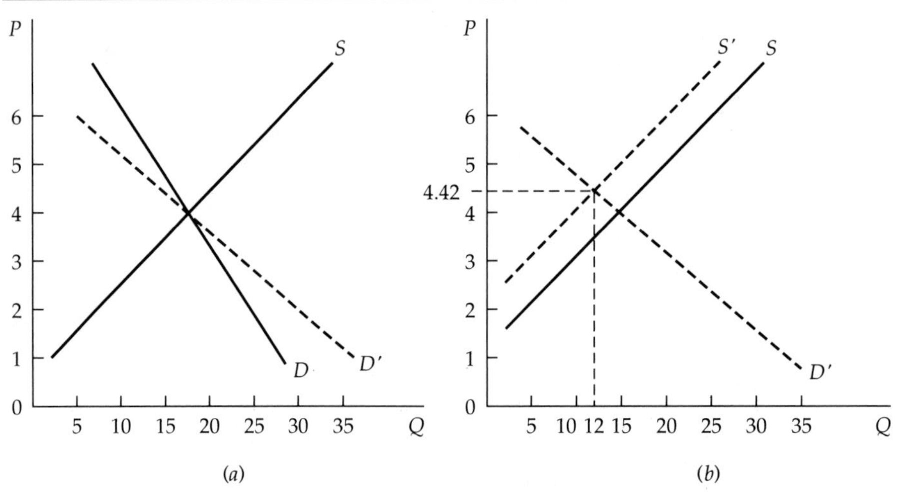

Figure 4A.4 Effect of Demand Elasticity on Equilibrium

[39]This will occur where the demand curve is perfectly inelastic.

[40]Using our equations,

$$\begin{aligned} 35 - 5_P &= -10 + 5P \\ 45 &= 10P \\ 4.5 &= P \end{aligned}$$

[41]The equation for the more elastic demand curve is $Q_D = 43 - 7P$ and the equilibrium price is

$$\begin{aligned} 43 - 7_P &= -10 + 5P \\ 53 &= 12P \\ 4.4167 &= P \end{aligned}$$

The effect of the tax on the equilibrium quantity is of significance to the government unit levying the tax. It is obvious that a government setting a new (or increasing an old) excise tax is taking such action to increase its revenue. However, if the demand curve for the particular product is very elastic, the erosion of the revenue base will cut short the amount of revenue the government expects to collect. In the present case, the government would have collected $12.50 in revenue with the original demand curve and only $12.08 for a more elastic demand curve. Had the demand curve been perfectly inelastic (vertical), then not only would the entire tax have been shifted to the consumer, but government revenue would have been $15 because the number of units sold would have remained at 15. Thus, a government would prefer to enact an excise tax on a product with low demand elasticity. [42]

Some of the more familiar excise taxes are those on tobacco and alcohol. Since the consumption of these products is not considered desirable by today's standards, tobacco and alcohol are very frequently among the first to be selected when additional taxes are contemplated. All states as well as the federal government impose an excise tax on these two products. In some cases, the amount of the tax on each unit is greater than 50 percent of the total price of the product. Because of the low esteem in which these products are held by a large segment of the population, opposition to the imposition of a tax (or an additional tax) is generally not great (except by the two industries involved). These taxes are often referred to as "sin" taxes. But would it have been attractive to levy such high excise taxes on these two products had the demand curve for them been very elastic? Probably not, because the tax base would have eroded significantly. Therefore, the government unit that wants to achieve what is popularly known as a "revenue enhancement" will find it considerably more favorable to enact an excise tax on products whose demand elasticity is low. Tobacco and alcohol seem to fit this category well. Thus, a government unit can claim to be taxing "undesirable" commodities and at the same time help to maximize its revenue.

Among the many proposals to fight the large federal deficits of the late 1980s is the imposition of a very large tax (as much as 30 to 50 cents per gallon) on gasoline. The popular estimate, has been that each cent of tax would decrease the deficit by about $1 billion. However, such calculations may not consider what would happen to the consumption of gasoline over time. The experience with OPEC's price increases in the 1970s and early 1980s shows that the demand curve for gasoline is by no means inelastic.

---

[42] You have certainly been subjected to a tax increase in some product you consume, whether it was tobacco, gasoline, or alcohol, to mention just three products on which excise taxes are levied by both federal and local governments. You will probably recall that on the day the tax was increased, the price of say, gasoline, rose by the precise amount of the tax. This is because, first of all, the increase may have been relatively small in comparison to the total price, so that the demand curve may be quite inelastic in this relatively narrow price range. Second, as we have already learned, demand elasticity tends to be lowest in the very short run, so, the tax may be completely (or almost completely) shifted to the consumer at first. But as time passes, there may be a series of small price decreases, or—and this is the more likely scenario in an inflationary environment—prices may not rise as quickly as they otherwise would have.

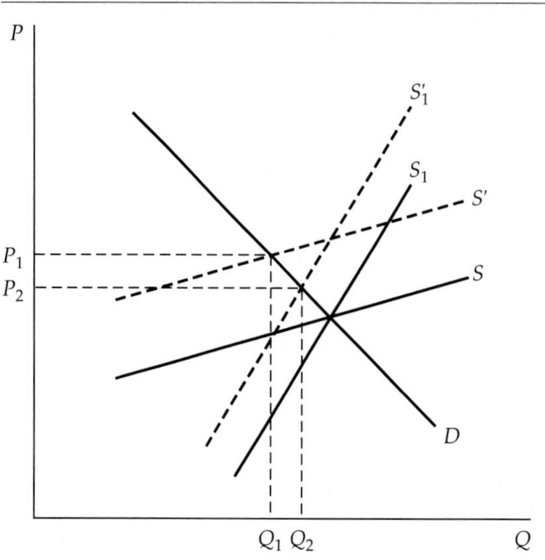

Figure 4A.5 Supply Elasticity and Tax Incidence

The elasticity of supply is also important from the viewpoint of tax incidence. From Figure 4A.5, we can see that the effect on the price and quantity is greater the higher the elasticity of supply. If supply elasticity is relatively low, the producer will bear the greater burden of the tax.[43]

Interference with the Price Mechanism II: Agriculture

It may seem out of place to discuss agriculture in a textbook on managerial economics. But business decisions are made not only in manufacturing or service industries. Farming is a business also, and farmers, whether they own large or small properties, must make decisions that will affect their future, although owners of agricultural enterprises make their decisions under circumstances quite different from those of other businesspeople. In the United States, for many decades, the federal government has had in place a body of laws designed to help farmers. We will not discuss the philosophy or merits of these long-entrenched policies. Instead, our interest lies in the effect these policies have on prices and the production of agricultural commodities.

[43] Again, as in the case of demand, chances are that in the very short run, supply curves will be rather inelastic, as suppliers cannot immediately remove resources from this industry to another pursuit. As time progresses, however, and resources shift out of the affected industry, the supply curve will be become more elastic, and both price and production will be affected to a more significant degree.

Farm incomes in this country, as well as elsewhere, are rather unstable. Both the short-run demand curves and supply curves for food are quite inelastic. Thus, if, for example, some natural disaster decreases the crop of wheat in a given year (i.e., moves the supply curve to the left), the price of wheat will soar. An unexpectedly large crop will drive prices down (and, since the demand curve is inelastic, will bring about a decrease in farm income). On the other side of the coin, since supply curves in agriculture also are inelastic in the short run, a small change in demand will create a significant price response. To protect farmers,[44] the U.S. government has enacted various types of controls.

One of the techniques that has been used is price supports. The government in effect guarantees the farmer that if the entire crop cannot be sold at a stipulated price, the government will buy the unsold (surplus) portion from the farmer. Figure 4A.6*a* illustrates this situation.

You will recognize this situation to be almost identical to the price floor discussed earlier. In this case, of course, to relieve the downward pressure on the price of the product, the government takes care of the surplus by buying it up. Assume that the support price is fixed at P_1, whereas the free-market price would have been P_0. Farmers will then be able to sell quantity Q_1 to consumers; however, given the support price, they will produce quantity Q_2, and thus a surplus $Q_2 - Q_1$ will be created. This surplus will be purchased by the U.S. government at the support price. The cost to the government is $P_1 \times (Q_2 - Q_1)$,

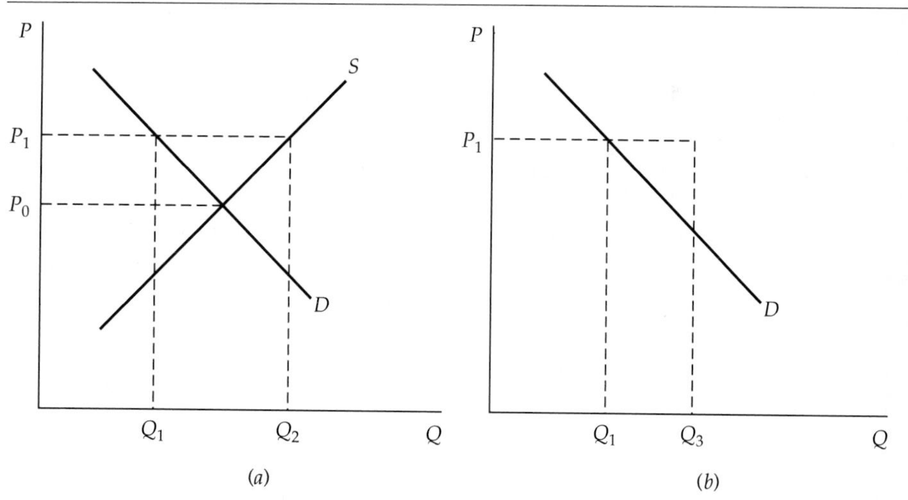

Figure 4A.6 The Use of Price Supports

[44] In the longer run, farm productivity has been rising substantially, moving the supply curve to the right and creating a long-run decrease in farm prices.

and the farmers' total revenue is $P_1 \times Q_2$. This, of course, is also the total cost to consumers and to the government combined.[45]

To reduce the amounts that have to be paid to the farmers, a policy of production controls was instituted. Let us assume that a production quota is at Q_3, as shown on Figure 4A.6*b*; then, the government expenditure will decrease from $P_1 \times (Q_2 - Q_1)$ to $P_1 \times (Q_3 - Q_1)$, and the farmers' income will be $P_1 \times Q_3$.[46]

Another type of policy, which has gained popularity in the last 15 years or so, is the establishment of target prices guaranteed by the government. Such a policy will protect the farmer in the same way as the price support policy; however, instead of selling the product at the supported prices, the producers sell their crops at market prices and collect the difference between the market and target prices for each unit sold from the U.S. government. If we assume the existence of production controls in this case as well, Figure 4A.7 illustrates the results. The price prevailing in the market is now P_2,[47] and the quantity sold is Q_3. Price P_2 is, however, less than the target price P_1, and the government will reimburse the farmer the difference between P_2 and P_1 for each of the units sold, or Q_3. Thus, the cost to the government (actually, the taxpayers) is $Q_3 \times (P_1 - P_2)$. In this case, the consumers bought quantities at a lower price than under the price support system of Figure 4A.6*b*, and the government is not forced to become the owner of these farm products and to bear the cost of the storage.

If the target price in Figure 4A.7 is the same as the support price in Figure 4A.6*b*, then the total amount going to the farmers and paid out by the combined forces of consumers and government (not counting storage costs) will be the same, $P_1 \times Q_3$. But the distribution of the total costs between the government and the consumer will be different, depending on the elasticity of the demand curve. We learned that when total revenue rises in response to a price increase, the demand curve is inelastic. If we concentrate on the total amount paid by the consumer directly for the farm product, we see that with price supports (Figure 4A.6*b*), the total consumer expenditure is $P_1 \times Q_1$, and with target prices it is $P_2 \times Q_3$. Since P_1 is higher than P_2, then if the area $P_1 \times Q_1$ is larger than the area $P_2 \times Q_3$, the demand curve (in this interval) must be inelastic. To recap, if the demand curve is inelastic, the consumer will pay more under the price support program than under the target price policy. And since the total combined expenditures (government and consumer) are the same under both systems, the government portion of this total cost is larger under the

[45] The payments to farmers by the government must be obtained through tax revenues: thus, the consumers as well as business pay for that part of the total food bill.

[46] Actually, to draw the production quota line vertically from the X–axis is not quite correct. At some point, the supply curve drawn in Figure 4A.6*a* will cross the production quota line. Only above that intersection point will the vertical line be effective.

[47] This is not the free-market price, since Q_3 represents the quantity that would be sold under conditions of production controls, a quantity presumably less than would have been produced and sold in the absence of controls.

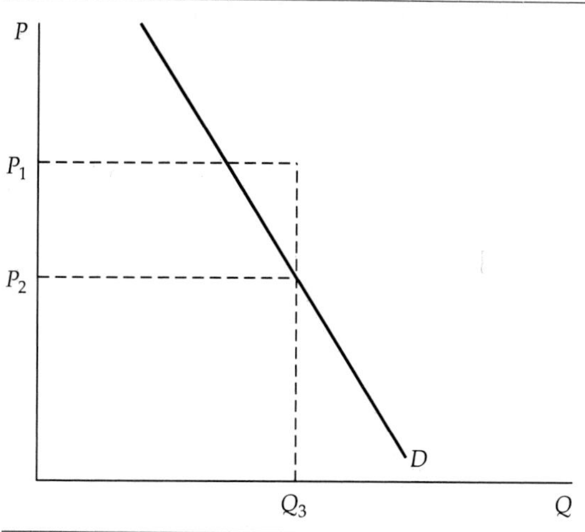

Figure 4A.7 The Effect of Target Prices

target price system. Since most economists agree that demand curves for most agricultural commodities are inelastic, the target price system would tend to be more expensive for the government.[48]

Actual Situations

We will now turn to some actual events, reported in newspapers and journals, that can easily be explained using supply-and-demand analysis.

Voluntary Export Restraints

In 1981 the United States and Japan agreed that Japan would limit its exports of cars to the United States to 1,680,000 annually. The limit was later increased but was still considerably below the number that would have been sold in the United States in the absence of this quota. What was the result? The price of Japanese vehicles rose. The effect of such a limitation can be seen in Figure 4A.8*a*. The original quantity and price of Japanese cars sold in the United States are shown as Q_0 and P_0. The imposition of the "voluntary" export quota on Japan at a limit less than the equilibrium quantity changed the shape of the supply curve. At the level of exports, Q_1, the supply curve becomes vertical, and the demand curve now intersects the supply curve at P_1—a new, higher price.

[48]Storage costs are not being considered in this conclusion. On the other hand, the government may be able at some time to sell some of the stored products and thus recover a part of its original expenditures.

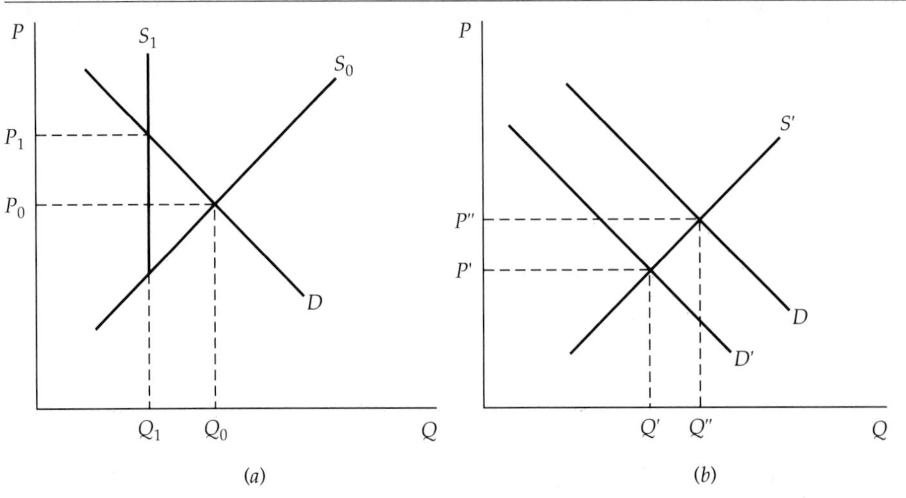

Figure 4A.8 Imposition of Voluntary Export Restraints

Given the restriction, the Japanese began to ship their higher-priced models to the U.S. to satisfy the upper portion of the market. Since the demand for Japanese cars now could not be satisfied, American consumers sought to purchase domestic or other imported automobiles. Such action shifted the demand curve for the rest of the automobile market to the right, as illustrated in Figure 4A.8*b*, thus increasing the number and the price of vehicles purchased. It was estimated by one economist that new car prices in 1984 were $1,500 higher than they would have been had quotas not been in effect. The additional cost to American consumers was $13 billion. The beneficiaries of this increased cost were the big three automobile manufacturers (to the tune of about $6 billion in higher profits), the autoworkers (about $3 billion in overtime payments), and the American dealers of Japanese cars and the Japanese manufacturers themselves (about $4 billion).[49] Subsequently, Japanese automobile manufacturers began to produce their cars in the United States. Since 1985, with the U.S. dollar weakening considerably against the Japanese yen, the prices of Japanese cars have risen significantly, permitting U.S. manufacturers to continue to increase their prices and enjoy higher profits.[50]

The Port of New York

New York was, not so long ago, the United States' great international port of entry. But this is no longer the case. Many events have contributed to its decline. Important among these is the shift in trade from Europe to the Far East, and the ascendance of other ports on the East Coast.

[49]Yoshi Tsurumi, "They're Merely a Subsidy for Detroit," *New York Times*, December 16, 1984.

[50]"Schools Brief," *Economist*, October 25, 1986, pp. 84-85

But there is another major reason for New York's decline. In the 1950s and 1960s containerization was introduced to cargo shipping. Loading and unloading a single, large container onto or from a truck, rather than working with individual pieces of freight, decreased the number of workers required. During the 1960s the International Longshoremen's Association was successful in including a guaranteed annual income provision in its contract for the East and Gulf coasts. The guarantee was based on 2,080 working hours, which is equivalent to 40 hours for 52 weeks. "New York paid a higher price than most of the 35 other International Longshoremen's Association ports in the East. Attrition cut the New York workforce from 20,000 to 7,400, but that was far from enough." In 1986 ". . . only 4,200 were actually working on a daily basis."[51]

A graphic depiction of guaranteed annual wage is similar to the case of minimum wages discussed previously and is shown in Figure 4A.9. If the annual wage is fixed at W_1, then 4,200 workers (Q_0) would be employed. Since 7,400 (Q_1) workers are available, there is a labor surplus of $Q_1 - Q_0$. However, by contract, the employer must pay W_1 to each of the 3,200 workers not utilized. Thus, the supply curve appears as a vertical line.

There were other clauses in the contract that created high costs for New York shipping. For instance, crew sizes were fixed much above the number of workers needed. New York found itself at a competitive disadvantage when

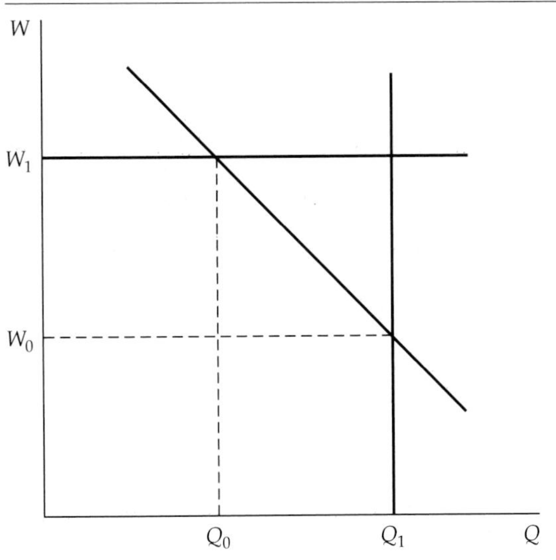

Figure 4A.9 Guaranteed Annual Wage

[51]James Cook, "Losing Jobs by Trying to Save Them," *Forbes*, June 1, 1987 pp. 56–59. This entire section is based on information contained in the article.

man-hour assessments for the guaranteed income amounted to about $204 in New York for unloading a 23-ton container, compared with $42 for the same job in Baltimore. Thus, business at the New York port kept shrinking. Non-ILA ports have sprung up on the East Coast, and some of the other ILA ports have begun to bargain separately, agreeing to lower rates. Recently the union has agreed to review the terms of its contract to reverse the trend in New York. But over the two decades, the increased cost of doing business in New York has shifted the demand to other ports and has caused a significant decline in New York's share of cargo shipping.

The Demand for Beef

Recently there has been a shift away from beef demand. The result has been an increase in the consumption of seafood, but the main beneficiary of this shift in demand appears to be chicken. Table 4A.2 shows data for these consumption changes over 12 years.

Demand for beef was very high into the early 1970s, and prices kept rising. However, the concern raised about the link between red meat and cholesterol levels was instrumental in putting a check on beef demand. Also, around this same time, chicken producers developed new and convenient chicken products that appealed to the public. Table 4A.2 shows that beef consumption per capita dropped 16 percent from 1975 to 1987, while chicken consumption rose 57 percent. Fish consumption also rose significantly, 26 percent, but considerably less than chicken.

During this period, the U.S. cattle population decreased substantially. As discussed previously, a change in supply is a long-run reaction to changes in demand.[52] More recently, however, the beef industry has begun to take steps that appear to have stopped the demand slide. Actually, there has been some increase in the demand for beef, as the industry has had some limited success with advertising campaigns. In 1987 cattle growers voted to establish a $1-per-animal fund for product and nutritional research and a national adver-

Table 4A.2 U.S. Consumption per Capita, in Pounds

	1975	*1987*
Beef	88.0	73.4
Chicken	39.9	62.7
Fish	12.2	15.4

Source: Reprinted by permission of *The Wall Street Journal*, © 1989 Dow Jones and Company, Inc. All rights reserved worldwide.

[52]The discussion in this section is based on the following articles: Marj Charlier, "Beef's Drop in Appeal Pushes Some Packers to Try New Products," *Wall Street Journal*, August 8, 1985; and Marj Charlier, "The U.S. Beef Industry Just Can't Seem to Get the Hang of Marketing," *Wall Street Journal*, January 4, 1989.

tising campaign. One possible way to combat the demand for chicken is to offer branded merchandise, a method chicken producers have been using for years. The beef industry appears to be rather slow in emulating some of the marketing techniques of the chicken producers, but, according to the research director of the beef council, "there is a sense of emergency that we have to become marketers."[53] These trends are graphically depicted in Figure 4A.10. The original equilibrium of beef prices and production was at the intersection of P_0 and Q_0. As consumer preferences shifted from beef to chicken and fish, the demand curve for beef moved to the left, from D_0 to D_1. Quantities produced were less, and prices declined relatively.[54]

Over time, resources shifted out of beef production. According to the National Cattlemen's Association, the number of beef cattle decreased from 130 million in 1975 to about 110 million in 1985.[55] The shift of resources is shown on Figure 4A.10 as a movement of the supply curve from S_0 to S_1. This action tended to stabilize beef prices during the period.[56] In the last few years, as just described, beef producers have begun to fight back, if not always effectively. The various campaigns mounted by the industry to convince consumers of beef's beneficial qualities are intended to move the demand curve to the right, from D_1 and D_2. Whether the new demand curve will be between D_1 and D_0 or even to

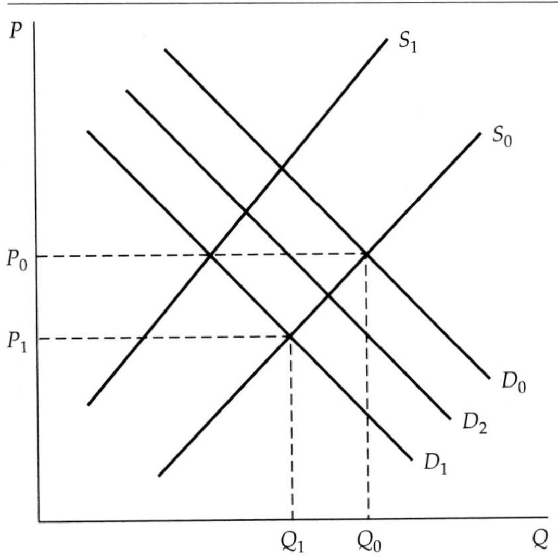

Figure 4A.10 The Downward Shift in Beef Demand

53 Charlier, "U.S. Beef Industry," op. cit.

54 Absolute prices of both chicken and beef may have risen due to inflationary factors, which were very strong in the 1970s and early 1980s.

55 Charlier, "Beef's Drop in Appeal," op. cit.

56 Similarily, increase in chicken-producing resources dampened the price effect of the increased chicken demand.

the right of D_0 cannot be foreseen. The danger lurking in this effort to increase beef demand is that, given the present low level of beef herds,[57] beef prices may soar, thus discouraging consumers. If the supply curve for beef in the short run in rather inelastic, this is what could happen.

The European Community and Wine Consumption

Excess supplies of wine have created a problem for the European Community (EC). In the mid-1980s, members of the EC collectively produced 16.5 billion liters of wine. However, only 13.5 billion liters were consumed.

To protect the almost 2 million wine growers in the area, the EC has offered financial incentives to decrease the amount of land under production. There has been a 10 percent decrease in land used for producing wine in the past decade, but production has continued to grow. Therefore, the EC has been purchasing the surplus. In 1985 these purchases totaled about $872 million.[58]

This situation is nearly identical to our discussion of U.S. agricultural policies, which is illustrated in Figure 4A.6.

Demand for Household Goods

It is a well-known fact that women have significantly increased their participation in the labor force since the end of World War II. After the war, men returned from the armed services, and women, who had taken the men's place in the work force, returned to their traditional pursuits. In 1947, women made up about 28 percent of total employment. Women then began to enter the labor force again, and the proportion of female employment rose to 35 percent by 1965 and to 45 percent by 1987. With the change in women's functions, a change in U.S. living patterns and consumption habits followed. According to a recent *Wall Street Journal* article,[59] homes in the United States are not quite as clean as they were in the past. Whereas women once spent much of their time as housewives, their acceptance into the labor force has changed this traditional role. "Sales of scouring powder, mildew removers, floor wax and dishwashing liquid slipped again last year, continuing a 10-year trend," according to Selling Areas Marketing, Inc., a New York–based research company.[60] On the other hand, sales of paper plates and aluminum baking pans have risen significantly. In addition, new time-saving household products have come to the market, and a new service business—maid services—has sprung up.

All of the preceding examples illustrate shifts that occur in the economy as consumer tastes change. Demand curves for some products move to the left,

---

[57] Beef supplies were further depleted in 1988 because of the severe drought.

[58] Ivo Downey, "Hard to Swallow," *Sphere*, October 1986, p. 19. When this article was written, Spain and Portugal were about to become full EC members. The wine production of these two countries was expected to add about 25 percent to the EC's total output.

[59] Betsy Morris, "Homes Get Dirtier as Women Seek Jobs and Men Volunteer for the Easy Chores," February 12, 1985.

[60] Ibid.

and for others they move to the right. As time passes, supply adjusts until a new equilibrium is reached.

It is extremely important that a manager or entrepreneur understand such cause-and-effect relationships. Demand and supply curves move continually in an economic society. It is management's task to identify such movements, to understand their consequences, and to design strategies and tactics to minimize adverse results and take advantage of new opportunities. Knowledge of economic interrelationships is a tool that will assist decision makers in taking these important actions.

CHAPTER 5

Demand Estimation

The Situation

Jennifer Harrah was assigned the task of developing and testing a statistical model that would help to explain consumer demand for soft drinks. Jennifer worked for a major market research firm that had a worldwide reputation for its work in the "FMCG" (fast-moving consumer goods) sector of the economy. Her firm had just been hired by Global Foods, Inc., to conduct preliminary research into the soft drink market.

As a regular consumer of soft drinks, Jennifer often wondered what affected people's demand for these beverages. Moreover, she had done a case study on Global Foods in graduate school and was looking forward to working with the very company she recalled as very interesting to study at the time. In the study, Global Foods was portrayed as the classic example of a large, multinational company that faced declining profit margins and demand for its products because of the maturity of the markets in which they were being sold. Her class had reached the conclusion that the best way for this company to energize itself was to go into markets where growth in unit sales and profit margins was very high, and that also related to food, its core business.

However, Jennifer was surprised that the company chose soft drinks as its new product line. Her class had decided that microwavable frozen gourmet meals was a logical candidate for the firm's expansion efforts.

In a meeting with the senior partner of her firm and a representative of Global Foods, Inc., Jennifer's assignment was spelled out in greater detail. The partner opened the meeting by saying, "Jennifer, I'm going to put you in charge of the entire project. You decide on the best way to obtain the data, the statistical technique to use to analyze the data, and the most effective way to present the results to our client. Global will give you as much assistance as possible. They have their own internal mar-

(Continued)

ket research group, but the CEO felt that the use of an outside consultant would give the study more objectivity and credibility. Your only constraint is time. This is a top-priority project for our client. In fact, the CEO wants you to produce the results in three weeks, give or take a few days. Can you do it?

"This is an assignment made in heaven," Jennifer thought. "An interesting subject, a large, well-known client, an opportunity for interaction with top management, and a major contract for our firm." She waited a bit so as not to seem too eager and then replied, "No problem. The report will be ready in 20 days."

Introduction

In the previous chapters, we analyzed the demand function from a theoretical standpoint. We showed how each of the determinants of demand—price and the nonprice factors, such as tastes and preferences and income—affects the amount people are willing to purchase of a particular good or service. Hypothetical numerical examples were devised to illustrate the concept of elasticity, a key way in which economists measure the sensitivity of quantity demanded to changes in price and the nonprice determinants of demand. The use of hypothetical data is a convenient way to illustrate the theory. But to put the theory into practice, managers of a firm need to know the true quantitative relationship between demand and the factors that affect it.

What would consumers be willing to pay for a particular good or service? How can we produce a good or service to enable us to sell enough at a certain price to receive an acceptable return on our investment? What impact does advertising have on sales? Can we expect different segments of the market (e.g., by region, income level, occupational category) to react in different ways to our marketing efforts? In short, *"what do consumers really want?"*

For business decision makers, the answer to this question is crucial. We can anticipate that they would be willing to pay considerable sums of money to obtain this information, and, in fact, they do. Many firms have their own market research departments as well as economic research departments. Others hire independent consulting firms, and still others rely on the research arms of their advertising agencies. The actual cost of such services depends on the magnitude and complexity of the subject matter. However, the fee for the services of one consultant could cost a company from $1,500 to $3,000 per day. The services of the principal of a prestigious consulting firm could cost $10,000 per day.

There are a number of ways in which market researchers seek out the "truth" of consumer behavior. They might use the direct approach of a survey, either face to face (e.g., stopping people in shopping centers) or by telephone. Certainly, many of you have at some time been a participant in this type of data gathering.[1]

Another direct approach used by market researchers is the focus group. Consumers are asked to attend a group meeting conducted by the researcher, at which various questions are asked regarding a company's goods and services. Company representatives may be present or may choose to observe the proceedings from behind a two-way mirror. The major problem with such direct methods is that consumers often cannot be realistic about how they would act in actual market situations. For instance, in the example concerning the demand for pizza in Chapter 3, we asked how many slices of pizza you would be willing to buy at various prices within a one-week period. The answer you provided was hypothetical. In an actual situation, how hungry would you be? Would you be with friends or alone? Would this be at lunchtime, or would you be thinking of grabbing a snack on the run? There are so many factors that can influence your actual response that it would in all likelihood be quite different from the one you provided for this text.

To get a more accurate view of the "true" behavior of consumers, researchers conduct market experiments in which different situations are established and the resulting behavior observed. For example, different prices may be set for a product at different intervals of time or in different store locations to determine if this causes differences in the number of units sold. Another type of experiment involves consumers being paid to participate in simulated shopping conditions, allowing researchers to monitor responses to variations in such factors as price, packaging, and shelf location. However, as in the case of consumer surveys, there is no guarantee that consumers will act in real situations as they do in simulated ones. Furthermore, it is very difficult as well as expensive to create a simulated situation that is authentic in every detail.

One way to avoid the high cost of obtaining direct data about consumer behavior is to use existing historical data. These data may be available as part of a company's record-keeping policies or may be obtained from sources such as government agencies, trade publications, and lobby groups.[2] But regardless

---

[1]One of the authors recalls receiving a telephone call around dinnertime from a person seeking attitudinal information about various products made by Black & Decker. The survey lasted approximately 20 minutes. Among the information sought by the interviewer was the perception of Black & Decker as a maker of consumer products other than tools and equipment. About two months after the date of this interview, General Electric announced the sale of its small household appliances division to Black & Decker.

[2]Examples of government sources of business data are the Department of Commerce and the Bureau of Labor Statistics. In fact, the general publications list of the U.S. Government Printing Office is an excellent source of goverment data. Each industry has a number of trade publications catering to the special interests of those in the business. For example, we have relied considerably on information from *Beverage World* and *Beverage Industry*. Among the special-interest groups that have provided us with background data on the soft drink industry are the U.S. Sugar Planters Association and the American Corn Growers Association.

of how the data are obtained, there is still a need to subject them to statistical analysis, particularly when more than one variable is involved and there is considerable interaction among the variables.

The procedure commonly used by economists to estimate consumer demand is regression analysis. As a matter of fact, regression analysis is the preferred statistical procedure for all types of economic analysis, because it is so suitable to the kinds of variables and relationships among variables studied by economists. Besides its application in demand estimation, it is used to estimate production and cost functions (see Chapter 10). It is also used in macroeconomic studies of consumption, investment, international trade, interest rates, and the demand for money. Indeed, the use of regression analysis can be found in the majority of economics articles in academic journals that involve empirical analysis. Given the scope of material generally covered in a managerial economics course, all we can do in this text is to offer an introduction to this subject. Entire courses in "econometrics," ranging from the introductory to the advanced, are devoted largely to regression analysis. Readers wishing to pursue this topic further are encouraged to enroll in these courses.

Regression Analysis

The basic intent of regression analysis is to estimate a quantitative relationship among variables. The first step in this statistical procedure is to specify the regression model (also referred to as the regression equation). The second is to obtain data on the variables specified in the model. The third is to estimate the quantitative impact each of the independent variables has on the dependent variable. The fourth step is to test the statistical significance of the regression results. Finally, the results of the regression analysis may be used as supporting material in the making of business policies and decisions.

Regression analysis involves two basic types of variables: the dependent variable and the independent variables. The latter are also called the explanatory variables. As evidenced by its name, the dependent variable is the one whose value depends on the value of some other variable or variables. The dependent variable is the central focus of any regression study and is the variable that researchers try to explain and predict. In the regression analysis of demand, the dependent variable is the quantity demanded of a particular good or service. If only one independent variable is employed in the analysis, we use the term *simple regression.* If more than one independent variable is involved, we use the term *multiple regression.* As you would expect, the independent variables most commonly used in the regression analysis of demand are price, price of related products, tastes and preferences, income, and the number of buyers. For purposes of explanation and illustration, it is much easier to focus on simple regression. After the simple regression model has been developed and explained, the multiple regression model will be presented.

The Simple Regression Model

Our discussion of simple regression begins with a formal statement of the relationship we hypothesize to exist between the dependent variable and the independent variable. Stated as a mathematical equation, this relationship is as follows:

$$Y = a + bX + u \tag{5.1}$$

where Y = Dependent variable
X = Independent variable
a = Intercept
b = Slope
u = Random factor

Notice that regression analysis seeks the best *linear* relationship between the dependent variable and the independent variable.[3] Thus, a denotes the intercept of the line and b the slope of the line. Note that another term, u, is included in the formal statement of the regression model. It is usually referred to as the "random" or "error" term. Although its value is not actually a part of the estimated impact of X on Y, its inclusion in the formal regression equation is essential. To understand why, allow us to deviate from the main topic to a brief discussion about the difference between *deterministic* and *probabilistic* models in statistical analysis.

Suppose that you want to develop a simple model of the gasoline consumption of your car, with the dependent variable being the amount of gasoline used and the independent variable being the number of miles traveled. If you knew the number of miles per gallon that your car is able to obtain, it would be a matter of simple arithmetic to quantify this relationship. For example, if your car's gas mileage is 20 miles per gallon and you traveled 100 miles, your consumption would be 5 gallons of gasoline. This relationship can be generalized as $Y = 0.05X$. Figure 5.1*a* shows the deterministic relationship between X and Y.

Now suppose that you decide to measure the relationship between miles traveled and gasoline consumed by recording this information for five separate trips, each 100 miles longer than the last, beginning with a 100-mile trip. As you can imagine, the actual amount of gasoline consumed relative to miles traveled would not conform exactly to what is predicted in the deterministic model. Suppose the actual recorded data are those shown in Figure 5.1*b*. As you can see, the plotting of each trip's mileage along with gasoline consumption actually results in a scattering of points rather than a path of points along a straight line. This implies that other factors besides miles traveled (e.g., weather conditions,

[3]The application of regression to economic problems generally assumes a linear relationship between the dependent variable and the independent variable(s). In fact, the term *linear regression analysis* is often used in economic studies. There are more advanced, nonlinear regression techniques that can be used. However, as shown later, economists frequently transform nonlinear relations into equations suitable for linear regression analysis.

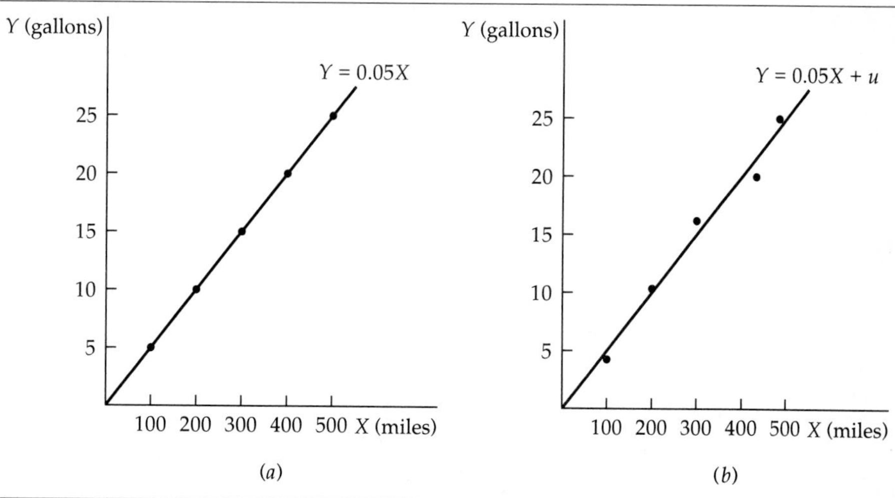

Figure 5.1 Gasoline Consumption Model

traffic patterns, and driving habits) affect gasoline consumption. Our model of gasoline mileage must therefore be restated as $Y = 0.05X + u$, where the value of u accounts for the deviation of the points from the straight line representing $Y = 0.05X$. The variable u represents the factors other than the independent variable that can affect the value of the dependent variable.

We assume in statistical theory that this u factor has a random rather than a systematic impact on the dependent variable. In statistical theory, randomly occurring events are described in terms of the probability of their occurrence. Hence, the term *probabilistic* is used to describe an equation that contains the random u element.[4] You will see why it is important to understand the nature of a probabilisitic model when we arrive at the section discussing the statistical significance of the regression results.

Data Used in Regression Analysis

The data used in regression analysis are divided into two types: cross-sectional and time series. Cross-sectional data provide information on a variable at a given point in time. The different values of the variable represent a "cross section" of observations of such entities as individuals, groups of individuals, and locations (e.g., county, city, metropolitan area, state, or country). Time series data provide information on one entity over time (e.g., the annual per capita income of a state over a period of 20 years). The pizza example used in Chapter 3 involved cross-sectional data, since information was gathered on a cross section of individuals at a given point in time (actually, a one-week period). Information on a time series basis might involve tracking the per-capita purchase of pizza in a given region of the country relative to its price over a period of time. For

[4]A full discussion of the probability distributions of random variables can be found in any statistics or econometrics text. For example, see Thad Miner, *Economic Statistics and Econometrics*, New York: Macmillan, 1988.

example, we could look at the annual per-capita consumption of pizza in the United States.[5]

Estimating the Regression Equation

The estimation of the regression equation involves a search for the best linear relationship between the dependent and the independent variable. Thus, the regression equation we seek to estimate can be expressed as:

$$Y = a + bX \tag{5.2}$$

where Y = Dependent variable
X = Independent variable
a = Intercept of the line with the Y axis
b = Slope of the line

The intercept and slope are usually referred to as the *parameters* or *coefficients* of the regression equation.

Figure 5.2 shows a scatter plot of hypothetical data for Y and X. As indicated in part *a* of this figure, any number of lines could be drawn through the scatter plot to represent the relationship between Y and X. In regression analysis, the most common way to estimate the relationship is called the *method of ordinary least squares* (OLS). Essentially, this method requires that a line be drawn through the scatter of points in such a way that the *sum of the squared deviations of each of the points from the line is minimized.* The least squares line is shown in Figure 5.2*b*. An illustration of the least squares method is shown in Figure 5.3.

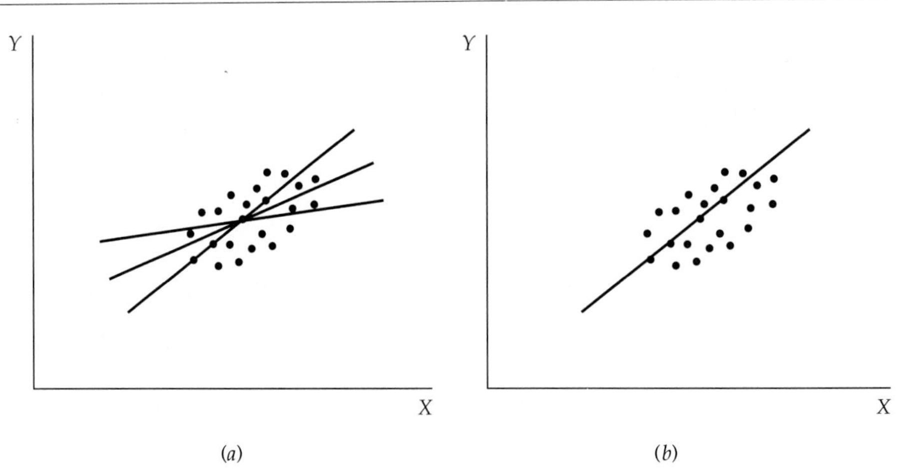

Figure 5.2 Linear Representations of Scatter Plots

[5]Incidentally, here's a bit of "pizza trivia" that may be of interest to you. During a recent National Pizza Week, the U.S. Department of Agriculture reported that Americans eat 11 billion slices of pizza each year, or about 23 pounds per capita. The favorite pizza topping is pepperoni; the least favorite is anchovies (James McNair, *Pizza*, San Francisco: Chronicle Books, 1987).

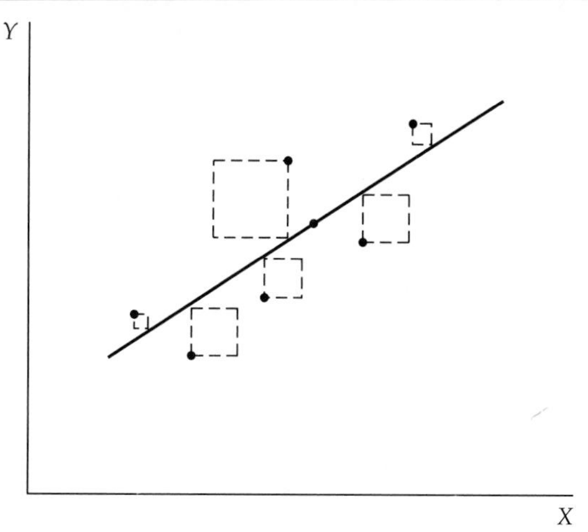

Figure 5.3 Minimizing the Sum of Squared Deviations

The actual estimation of the regression line is a relatively simple matter, given the availability of computers and software packages. Many hand-held calculators contain programs or special function keys for estimating simple regression equations. However, when more than one independent variable is used (i.e., multiple regression analysis), the processing power of a computer is required. In any event, those wishing to review the formulas for estimating the equations as well as the mathematical derivations of these formulas may consult a statistics or econometrics text. Using the method of least squares, we arrive at the regression line indicated in Figure 5.2*b*.

Although the method of least squares provides a good linear representation of the scatter of points, there is clearly a difference in fit of the least squares lines shown in Figure 5.4*a* and *b*. Mere observation indicates that Figure 5.4*b* represents a better fit of the regression line through the scatter of points. This is obviously because of the nature of the scatter of points and not because of the way in which the lines were constructed. Both regression lines were drawn in a manner satisfying the least squares criterion. Thus, it would be useful to have some measure of how well a regression line fits the scatter of points.

The Coefficient of Determination: A Measure of the Explanatory Power of the Estimated Regression Equation[6]

To explain the meaning of the coefficient of determination, we need to introduce a few concepts and notations used in standard statistics and econometrics

[6]This section draws heavily from the explanation presented in H. Kelejian and W. Oates, *Introduction to Econometrics*, New York: Harper & Row, 1989.

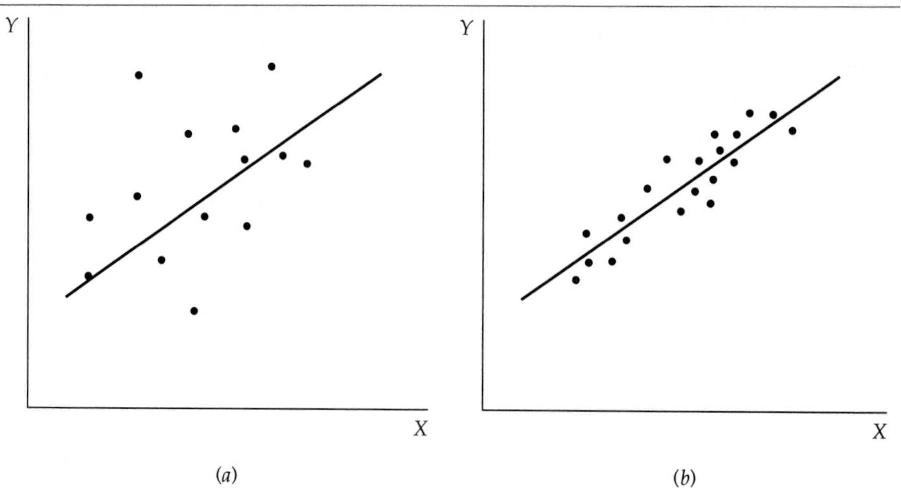

Figure 5.4 Regression Lines with Different Fits through the Scattering of Points

texts. Whenever regression results based on sample data are presented, a "hat" is placed over the estimated values:

$$\hat{Y} = \hat{a} + \hat{b}X \tag{5.3}$$

The hats over Y, a, and b signify that their values are estimated using a sample data set. A reasonable approach to measuring how well this estimated regression equation does in determining the value of Y given the value of X is to compare the values of $\hat{Y}$ with the actual Y values found in the sample.

The scatter plot shown in Figure 5.5 will help to explain this approach. Equation (5.3) represents the estimated regression line through the scatter of points. Let us take one of these points, point A, for purposes of illustration. You can see that the deviation of this point from the regression line is indicated by the distance between A and B in Figure 5.5. If we added up the squared deviations of each of the points from the regression line, we would obtain the smallest possible sum, because the method of least squares was used to estimate the regression line. Thus, in evaluating the fit of this regression line to the scatter plot of actual data, we need some standard of comparison.

Suppose you were asked to predict the amount of pizza demanded by consumers without the help of a regression equation. Would it not be reasonable to use the mean value (i.e., the arithmetic average) of quantity demanded as the predicted value? Statistical theorists, in fact, use the mean value of the dependent variable (Y) as the basis for comparing the relative "goodness of fit" of the regression line to the scatter of actual data points. In effect, this particular measure answers the question: How much better off are we in using a regression line to predict the value of Y than we are in simply using the mean of Y?

In Figure 5.5, the mean of Y (i.e., $\overline{Y}$) is indicated by the dotted line. The deviation of the regression line from the mean value of Y is indicated by the distance

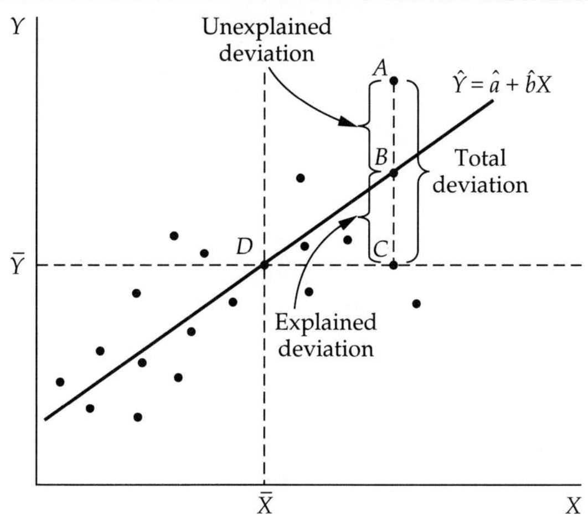

Figure 5.5 Explained and Unexplained Deviations

between points B and C. Note that the regression line always passes through the point representing the mean of X and the mean of Y.[7] This is indicated by point D in Figure 5.5. Thus, we observe in Figure 5.5 that the deviation of a sample value of Y from its mean can be divided into two separate components: AB and BC. More formally, we can state the following:

$$\begin{aligned} AC &= (Y_i - \overline{Y}) = \text{Total deviation of the } i\text{th sample value of } Y \text{ from the sample mean} \\ BC &= (\hat{Y} - \overline{Y}) = \text{Explained deviation of } Y_i \text{ from } Y \\ AB &= (Y_i - \hat{Y}_i) = \text{Unexplained deviation of } Y_i \text{ from } \overline{Y} \end{aligned}$$

BC is the "explained" deviation of the sample value of Y from its mean because it can be accounted for by the regression line. AB is the "unexplained" portion of the total deviation because its value differs from that estimated by the regression line. If the breakdown between the explained and unexplained components is measured for every observation, and the resulting values are squared (to compensate for positive and negative deviations) and then added together, we arrive at the following relationships:

$$TSS = \sum(Y_i - \overline{Y})^2 = \text{Total sum of squares (sum of the squared deviations of the sample values of } Y \text{ from the mean)}$$

$$RSS = \sum(\hat{Y}_i - \overline{Y})^2 = \text{Regression sum of squares (sum of the squared deviations of the estimated values from the mean)}$$

[7]For the proof of why this always is the case when the method of least squares is used, consult a statistics or econometrics text.

$$ESS = \sum(Y_i - \hat{Y}_i)^2 = \text{Error sum of squares (sum of the squared deviations of the sample values from the estimated values)}$$

The abbreviations TSS, RSS, and ESS are commonly used in econometrics books for these relationships, so we will use them here in reference to the total, explained, and unexplained components, respectively, of the variation of the sample values from their mean. To summarize, we can simply say that $TSS = RSS + ESS$. From these relationships, we can construct a measure of the explanatory power of the regression equation.

The most commonly used measure of the explanatory power of the regression equation is called the *coefficient of determination*. The symbol used for this measure is R^2. We define this measure in the following way:

$$R^2 = \frac{RSS}{TSS} = 1 - \frac{ESS}{TSS} \tag{5.4}$$

If RSS is equal to TSS, this means that the total deviation of Y from its sample mean can be "explained" or accounted for by the equation. This also implies that R^2 is equal to 1. Another way to view this situation is to look at the alternative expression of R^2, $1 - ESS/TSS$. If the regression line accounts for the total deviation of Y from its mean, there would be no error sum of squares (i.e., $ESS = 0$). This means $ESS/TSS = 0$, and therefore $R^2 = 1$. Figure 5.6a illustrates a situation in which $R^2 = 1$. You can see in this figure that $R^2 = 1$ means that every point on the scatter plot lies on the regression line.

At the other extreme, if the regression line does not account for any of the variation of Y from its mean, R^2 assumes the value of 0. As you can see from the formula, $R^2 = 0$ means that $RSS/TSS = 0$. Using the alternative formula for R^2, we see that this means $ESS = TSS$ (i.e., $ESS/TSS = 1$). Such a case

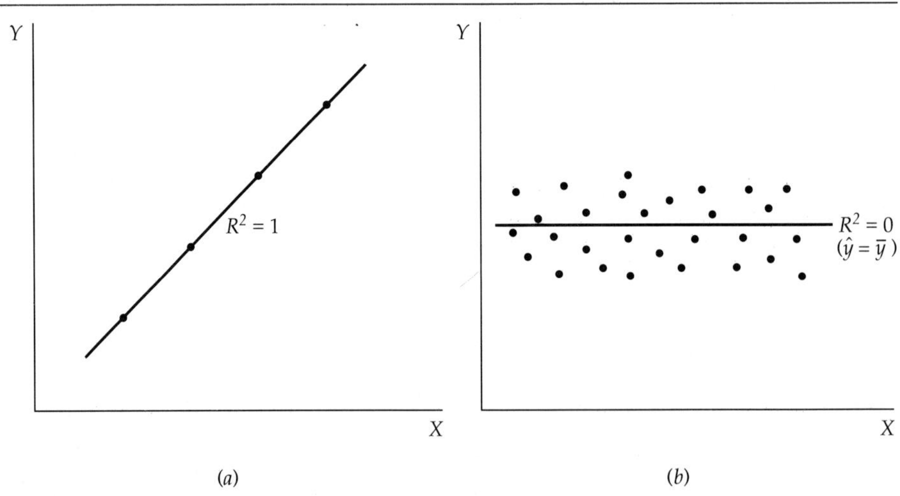

Figure 5.6 The Coefficient of Determination

would indicate that the mean value of Y is just as useful as the least squares regression line in predicting the value of Y (i.e., $\hat{Y} = \overline{Y}$). Figure 5.6*b* illustrates this case.

In actuality, R^2 will assume some value between the two extremes of 0 and 1. Clearly, the closer R^2 is to unity, the greater the explanatory power of the regression equation. For example, an R^2 of .93 indicates a very good fit of the regression line to the scatter of points (see Figure 5.7*a*). This statistic indicates that 93 percent of the variation in Y from its mean can be accounted for by the regression equation. An R^2 close to 0 indicates a regression equation with very little explanatory power. For example, $R^2 = .15$ (i.e., only 15 percent of the variation in Y from its mean is explained) is shown in Figure 5.7*b*.

Whether a given value of R^2 is considered "high" or "low," or "acceptable" or "unacceptable" in statistical analysis depends on the type of data being used (cross-sectional versus time series), the particular standards of the researcher, and the typical R^2 computed in studies of a similar nature. Studies employing cross-sectional data generally have a lower R^2 than those using time series data. This is because time series data—as would be expected—have a built-in trend element that usually causes the Y and X variables to move closely together over time. It is not uncommon for the estimation of demand using time series data to produce an R^2 of .90 or above. Macroeconomic studies of the consumption function usually have an R^2 of .95 or more. Ordinarily, if a researcher estimates a regression equation with $R^2 = .75$, it means that the regression model has rather strong explanatory power. However, since most consumption function studies produce R^2 values of .95 or above, a consumption equation with an R^2 value of .75 would have to be considered relatively low.

One further point should be mentioned about R^2. As additional variables are added to the regression equation (i.e., as we move from simple regression to multiple regression), the regression equation, naturally, will "explain" more of

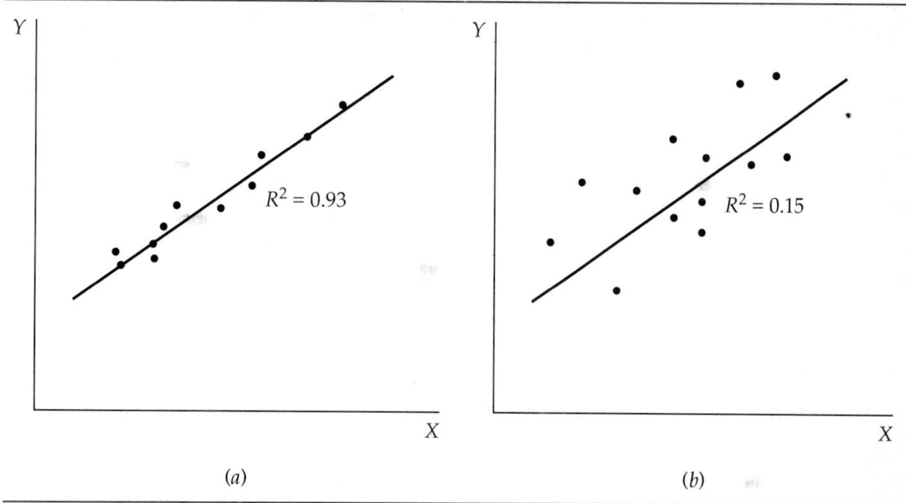

Figure 5.7 Indicator of Regression Line Fit

the variation in the dependent variable. In fact, it can be shown that the addition of some random number or a variable completely unrelated to the regression model will improve the goodness of fit of the regression equation (i.e., will increase the magnitude of R^2). To compensate for the fact that regression equations with more independent variables tend to have higher R^2 values, we can use a measure called the "corrected" or "adjusted" coefficient of determination, $\overline{R}^2$. This measure is defined as

$$\overline{R}^2 = R^2 - \frac{k}{n-k-1}(1 - R^2)$$

where k = Number of independent variables
n = Sample size

By observation, you can deduce that in multiple regression R^2 will always exceed $\overline{R}^2$. The difference between the two measures will depend, of course, on the size of the sample (n) and the number of independent variables (k). For a given sample size, $\overline{R}^2$ will show an increasing adjustment downward from R^2 as the number of independent variables increases. Regardless of the number of independent variables in the equation, the amount of downward adjustment from R^2 will decrease as the sample size increases. At any rate, almost all regression software packages automatically compute $\overline{R}^2$ along with R^2.

Evaluating the Regression Coefficients

Up to this point, we have discussed regression analysis in reference to what is called *descriptive statistics*. Data are gathered on two variables, one dependent and the other independent; a line is fitted through the scatter of points representing the values of the two variables; and a measure of how well the line fits the scatter is developed. But to evaluate the usefulness of the results of the regression analysis for making business decisions, we need to enter the realm of *inferential statistics*.

A researcher seeking certain information about some population can attempt to obtain data either on the entire population or on some sample of the population. In just about all cases, a sample from the population is used because of the prohibitive cost of obtaining information on the whole population. Moreover, in many cases it is simply impossible to obtain complete population data. But if a sample is used instead of the population, the researcher must assess the degree to which the results of the sample reflect the population. In other words, it becomes necessary to *make inferences* about the population based on what is known about the sample and to make a judgment about how good these inferences are.

Suppose we are conducting a study of the demand for pizza on a university campus with a student population of 4,500. The variables under study are income and average quantity of pizza slices demanded per month. Suppose further that we are able to obtain information on the entire population of students. This is shown in Table 5.1, where consumers have been divided into 10 groups according to weekly after-tax income, starting with $100 per week and increasing by $20 intervals to $280. The average number of pizza slices purchased per month is shown in the matrix of numbers. To make this illustration as simple as possible, we have assumed that there are 450 student consumers in each of the 10 income categories. For example, reading *down* in the $100 column, we see that 10 students (i.e., one-tenth of 100) buy an average of 10 slices of pizza per month, 30 students (i.e., one-tenth of 300) buy an average of 10.5 slices per month, and so on.[8] (Note the vertical arrow in Table 5.1.) By reading *across* each row, we can observe the number of pizza slices demanded for the nine frequency categories. (Note the horizontal arrow in Table 5.1.) We observe that the number of pizza slices demanded increases as weekly income increases. For example, in the second row, frequency 300, we see that the 30 individuals (i.e., one-tenth of 300) who have an average weekly income of $100 buy 10.5 slices of pizza per month; the 30 who earn an average of $120 per month buy 12 pizza slices per month, and so on. The most frequently occurring average number of slices for each income category is seen by reading across the row indicated by the frequency of 900. As it turns out, this row also represents the average number of slices per pizza for each income category.[9]

Figure 5.8 shows the distribution of those consumers who earn $200 per week. The entire data set in Table 5.1 is illustrated in Figure 5.9. Notice that we

Table 5.1 Number of Pizza Slices Consumed per Month, by Weekly Income

Frequency	*f*	*$100*	*$120*	*$140*	*$160*	*$180*	*$200*	*$220*	*$240*	*$260*	*$280*
		→									
(1)	100	10.0	11.5	13.0	14.5	16.0	17.5	19.0	20.5	22.0	23.5
(2)	300	10.5	12.0	13.5	15.0	16.5	18.0	19.5	21.0	22.5	24.0
(3)	600	10.8	12.3	13.8	15.3	16.8	18.3	19.8	21.3	22.8	24.3
(4)	800	11.2	12.7	14.2	15.7	17.2	18.7	20.2	21.7	23.2	24.7
(5)	**900**	**11.5**	**13.0**	**14.5**	**16.0**	**17.5**	**19.0**	**20.5**	**22.0**	**23.5**	**25.0**
(6)	800 ↓	11.8	13.3	14.8	16.3	17.8	19.3	20.8	22.3	23.8	25.3
(7)	600	12.2	13.7	15.2	16.7	18.2	19.7	21.2	22.7	24.2	25.7
(8)	300	12.5	14.0	15.5	17.0	18.5	20.0	21.5	23.0	24.5	26.0
(9)	100	13.0	14.3	16.0	17.5	19.0	20.5	22.0	23.5	25.0	26.5
	4,500										

[8]Of course, the point of this example does not depend on this assumption. In situations where the observations in each population category are unequal, the relative frequency or proportion can be used in place of the absolute number. For example, 2.2 percent (10/450) of those who earn $100 per week buy an average of 10 slices per month, 6.6 percent (30/450) of those earning this income buy an average of 10.5 slices per month, and so on.

[9]You should recognize that the frequency of occurrence of 900 represents the arithmetic mean of the distribution for each income category, because it is clearly the median (midpoint of the distribution) as well as the mode (most frequently occurring value) of a symmetric distribution.

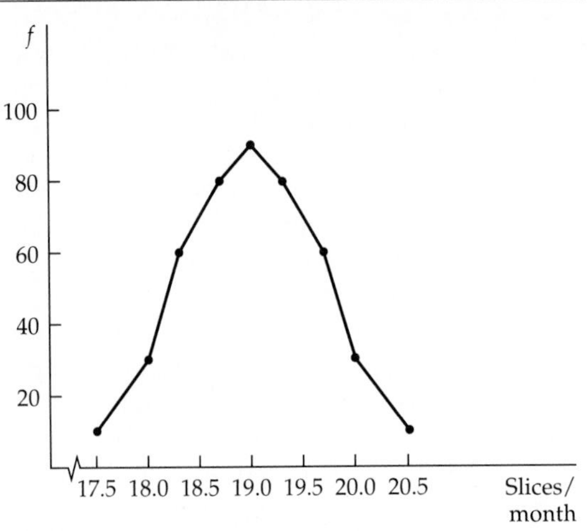

Figure 5.8 Pizza Demand: Distribution of Consumers Earning $200 per Week

assume that there is a normal, continuous distribution for each income level. Each distribution has a different mean or expected value, but all have the same variance.

For such population data, the regression line would be

$$Y = 4 + 0.075X \tag{5.5}$$

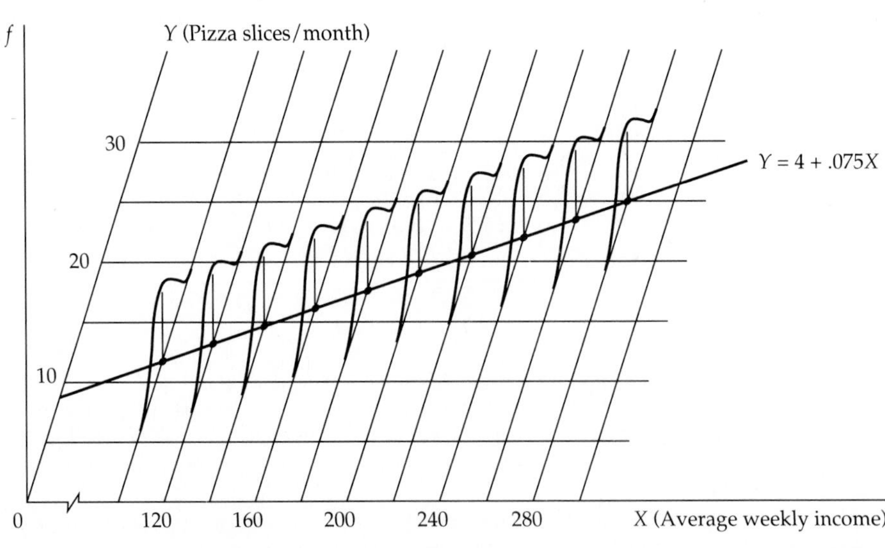

Figure 5.9 Combined Frequency Distributions for Pizza Demand

Now suppose that we select a sample of pizza buyers from this population. As you can well imagine, this sample might indicate a different relationship between income and quantity demanded of pizza. To demonstrate this point, we have drawn a "bird's-eye view" of a portion of Figure 5.9 in Figure 5.10*a*. Notice that the dense cluster of population points symmetrically placed around the mean of each distribution reflects the normal, bell-shaped distribution that we have assumed to exist for each income level. The encircled dots in Figure 5.10b, c, and d indicate different samples drawn from the population. As you can see, a least squares regression line fitted through the sample points in Figure 5.10b would show a positive relationship between income and the demand for pizza. However, because the slope is not as steep as the slope for the population regression line, the magnitude of this relationship is smaller. The sample shown in Figure 5.10c indicates that no relationship exists between income and the demand for pizza. The sample Figure 5.10*d* actually shows a

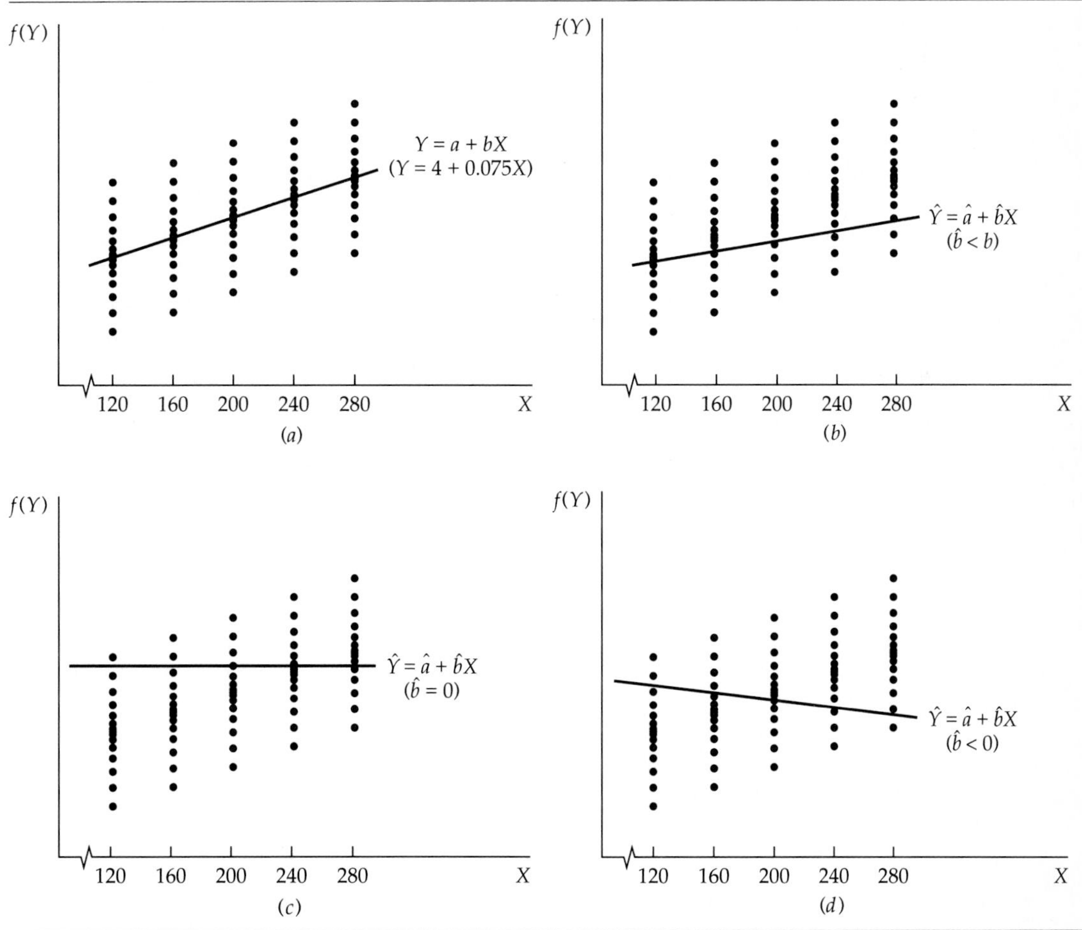

Figure 5.10 Population Regression Line and Three Sample Regression Lines

negative relationship between income and pizza demand, implying that pizza is an "inferior" product.

In reality, data on the population such as those shown in Table 5.1 are unknown to researchers. All they have to work with are sample data of the type illustrated in Figure 5.10 *b*, *c*, and *d*. How confident can a researcher be about the extent to which the regression equation for the sample truly represents the unknown regression equation for the population? The answer to this question is presented in the following section.

A Test for the Statistical Significance of the Estimated Regression Coefficients

The test used to establish, with a certain degree of confidence, that the regression coefficients estimated from sample data are truly reflective of the population is called the test of *statistical significance*. Because this test involves what are called t-values, it is commonly referred to as the t-test.

Our explanation of this test begins with a review of the error term, u, introduced at the beginning of this chapter. In statistical theory, it is assumed that this term is randomly distributed about the population regression line in a normal fashion, with its mean being the value of Y given the value of X and with some amount of variance.[10]

As illustrated in Figure 5.10, a random sample taken from the population may produce regression results that are quite different from a regression line fitted through the population. If we repeatedly selected a random sample of a given size from this population and estimated a regression line for each one of these samples, we would generate a large number of sample regression lines (see Figure 5.11). Each of these sample regression lines has its own intercept and slope coefficients, $\hat{a}$ and $\hat{b}$. In statistical theory, it can be shown that if the error term of the population is normally distributed about its regression line with some constant variance (σ_u^2), then repeated sampling will produce a distribution of estimated regression coefficients, $\hat{a}$ and $\hat{b}$, *that are themselves normally distributed with a mean or expected value equal to the population's regression*

[10]Recall that a normal distribution is the symmetric, bell-shaped curve so often used in statistics. As such, it can be defined by two values, its mean and its variance (or standard deviation, the square root of the variance). The larger the variance, the more "spread out" the normal distribution becomes. For example, distribution I below has the same mean as distribution II but has a larger variance.

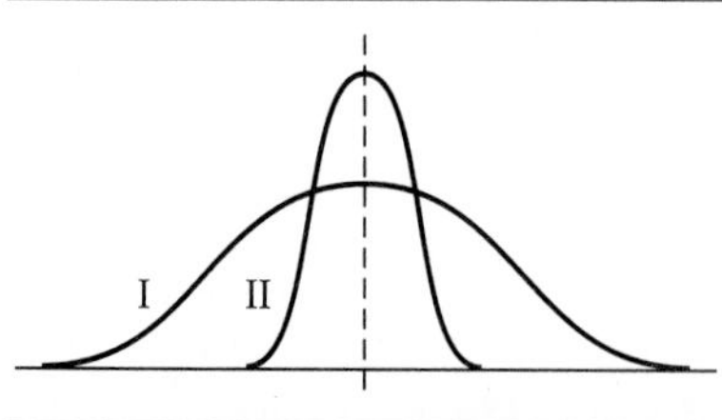

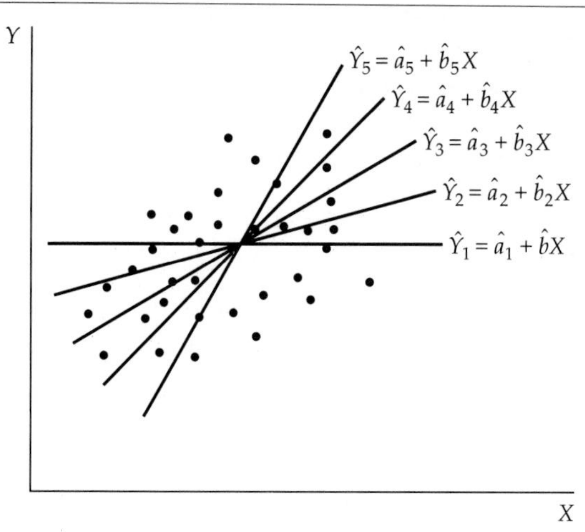

Figure 5.11 Regression Lines Produced from Repeated Sampling

coefficients, and with a variance equal to a number related to the variance of the error term in some systematic fashion.[11] The following equations express this statement in notational form. Because we are primarily interested in the slope coefficient, we shall focus our attention on b. However, the same statements can be made about the intercept term, a.

$$E(\hat{b}) = b \tag{5.6}$$

$$var(\hat{b}) = \sigma_{\hat{b}}^2 = \frac{\sigma_u^2}{\sum(X_i - \overline{X})^2} \tag{5.7}$$

Equation 5.6 is fairly straightforward. It states that the mean or expected value of the estimated coefficient $\hat{b}$ is equal to b, the true (but unknown) regression coefficient for the entire population. Equation 5.7 states that the variance of the distribution of regression coefficients estimated from a repeated sampling of the population is equal to the variance of the population's error term, u, divided by the sum of the squared deviations of each observed value of X minus the mean of X. The verbalization of Equation 5.7 is rather cumbersome, to be sure. But the important thing to keep in mind is that we need to know the variance of the distribution of sample $\hat{b}$ terms to determine the probability of the occurrence of any one particular $\hat{b}$.

Because information about the variance of the population's error term is generally unknown, we resort to the use of an *estimator* of the population variance. In statistical theory, it can be shown that an unbiased estimator of the variance of the distribution of error terms ($\hat{\sigma}_u^2$) is equal to the *sum of the squared residuals*

[11]The proof of this statement can be found in any advanced statistics or econometrics text.

of each of the sample points from the estimated regression line, divided by the sample size minus 2 (i.e., $n-2$). *Residuals* are the differences between the actual values of Y and those estimated from the regression equation (i.e., Y_i minus $\hat{Y}_i$). Expressed in notational form,

$$\hat{\sigma}_u^2 = \frac{\sum(Y_i - \hat{Y}_i)^2}{n-2}$$

In turn, the unbiased estimator of the variance of the sample b terms ($\hat{\sigma}_{\hat{b}}^2$) is equal to the estimator of the variance of the error terms divided by the sum of the squared deviations of each observed value of X minus the mean of X. In notational form,

$$\hat{\sigma}_{\hat{b}}^2 = \frac{\hat{\sigma}_u^2}{\sum(X_i - \overline{X})^2}$$

We obtain the standard deviation of the distribution of sample $\hat{b}$ coefficients simply by taking the square root of the estimated variance of this distribution. That is,

$$SE_{\hat{b}} = \sqrt{\hat{\sigma}_{\hat{b}}^2}$$

As is the custom, we shall refer to standard deviation of the sample regression coefficient as the "standard error of the coefficient" ($SE_{\hat{b}}$). And, as we are about to show, $SE_{\hat{b}}$ plays a central role in the t-test.

In conducting the t-test, we start by hypothesizing that the true (but unknown) regression coefficient for the population is a certain value. In statistical analysis, this is called the *null hypothesis*. Typically in economic research, we hypothesize the population's regression coefficient to be 0, that is, there is no relationship between X and Y in the population. The alternative hypothesis is that there is indeed a relationship between X and Y. Using conventional statistical notation, we can state the null and alternative hypotheses as:

$$H_0 : b = 0$$
$$H_a : b \neq 0$$

If the b or slope coefficient is truly 0, as the null hypothesis states, then for the entire population, changes in X would have no impact on Y.

Suppose the true value of b were indeed 0. Would it still be possible to select a sample that showed a relationship between Y and X? Most certainly it would, and Figure 5.12 shows exactly how this could happen. Notice in this figure that the scatter plot of the population is such that a regression line fitted through the points is horizontal (i.e., has zero slope). But suppose the sample that we selected—indicated by the circled points in Figure 5.12—happened to show a positive relationship when a least squares line is fitted through the sample scatter. Based on the results of the regression analysis of the sample data, we would conclude that for the entire population a direct relationship exists between X and Y, when there really is none. This kind of error would be of obvious concern to decision makers. For example, suppose a regression analysis of sales on advertising expenditures mistakenly showed a positive relationship between the two variables and prompted a firm to increase substantially the

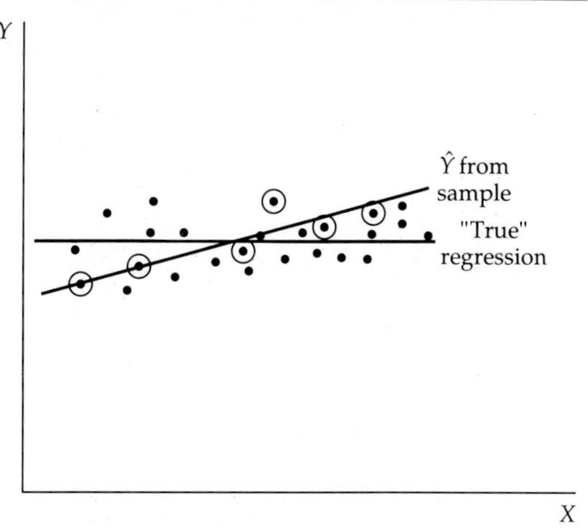

Figure 5.12 False Relationship Indicated by Sample Regression

size of its advertising budget. Since in reality there is no impact of advertising on sales, this decision would lead to a waste of the firm's financial resources.

Earlier, we stated that if the error term of the population regression equation is normally distributed, it can be shown that the estimated sample coefficients are also normally distributed. It can also be demonstrated mathematically that the *standardized deviation* of each sample's estimate from the actual population value has a *t-distribution*.[12] Figure 5.13 illustrates this point. In Figure

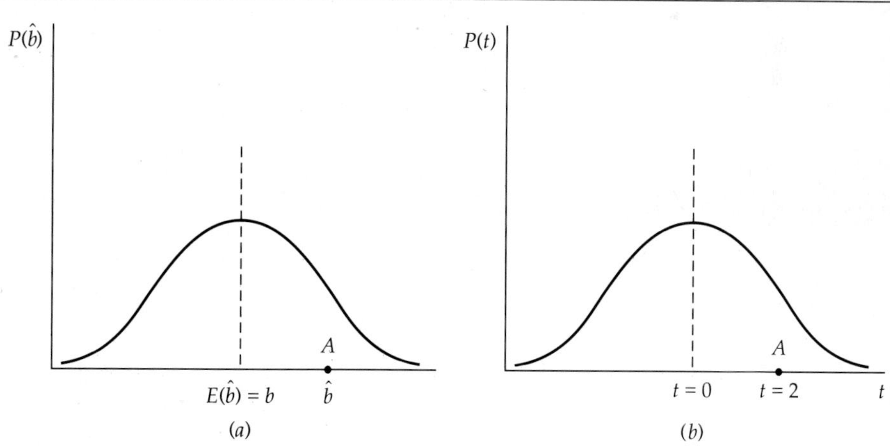

Figure 5.13 The t-Distribution

[12]The t-distribution is a symmetric, bell-shaped distribution that closely resembles the normal distribution. Its precise shape depends on a measure called *degrees of freedom*. In simple regression, there are $n - 2$ degrees of freedom. As the sample size (n) increases, the t-distribution tends toward the standard normal distribution. In the limit, the two become identical.

5.13*a*, we see a normal distribution of estimated $\hat{b}$ coefficients with its midpoint designating the mean or expected value. The vertical axis of the graph measures the probability of the occurrence of the different values of the estimate $\hat{b}$. Obviously, the mean or expected value of $\hat{b}$ has the greatest probability of occurring. Suppose that the estimated sample coefficient $\hat{b}$ is the one shown by point *A* in Figure 5.13*a*. What is the probability of such a point occurring? To find the answer to this question, we "standardize" the differences between any point in the distribution and its expected value. This is done using the following equation:

$$t = \frac{\hat{b} - E(\hat{b})}{SE_{\hat{b}}} \tag{5.8}$$

This value shows how many *t*-units away from the expected value is the estimated coefficient $\hat{b}$. To interpret this *t* value, we also need to know the number of "degrees of freedom" (d.f.) involved in this case. For any given sample, d.f. is defined as $n - k - 1$, where n, k, and 1 represent the sample size, the number of independent variables, and the intercept regression equation with a sample of 62 observations, there would be 60 degrees of freedom. The probability of the occurrence of value *A* (converted into 2 units) can now be found with the help of Table A.4. In this table, we see that for 60 d.f., the probability that *t* will have a value of 1.671 or more is about 5 percent. (See column for "one-tailed, $a = .05$.") Therefore, the probability that *t* will have a value of 2 or more would clearly be less than 5 percent.

After finding the *t*-value for the estimated regression coefficient $\hat{b}$ the researcher must then decide whether or not to reject the null hypothesis that there is no relationship between *X* and *Y* in the population. The standard procedure is to establish what is called the *critical t-value* based on a predetermined point on the *t*-distribution. Usually this point is set at the .05 *level of significance*. We can then turn to the *t*-table to find the critical value of *t* corresponding to this level of significance. For example, the table shows that for 60 degrees of freedom, the range between 2.0 and −2.0 includes about 95 percent of the values of *t*. Another way of saying this is that the chance of obtaining a *t*-value greater than 2.0 or less than −2.0 is only about 5 percent. Figure 5.14 illustrates the .05 level of significance on a *t*-distribution with 60 degrees of freedom. Notice that the values of *t* that are greater or less than the critical *t*-value lie on the two ends or "tails" of the distribution.[13]

The preceding conclusion helps us to understand the rationale for the "rule of 2" often employed by economists in their evaluation of the *t*-test. This rule states that the null hypothesis that $b = 0$ can be rejected if the *t*-value is less than or equal to −2 or greater than or equal to 2. Using the absolute value of *t*, we can state that the null hypothesis can be rejected if:

$$|t^*| > 2$$

---

[13]More will be said about the "one-tail" and "two-tail" *t* tests on pp. 174–175.

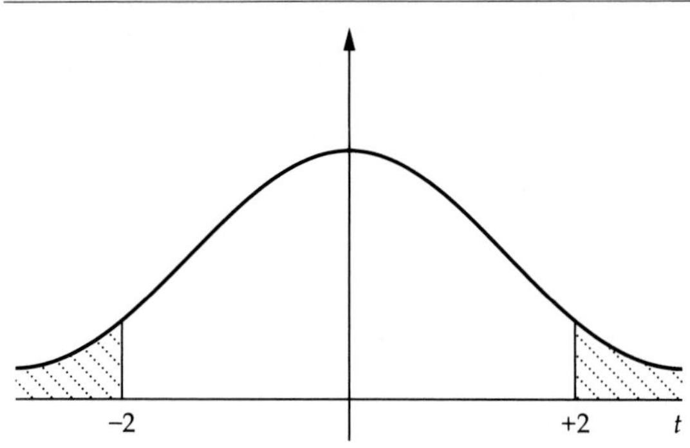

Figure 5.14 Critical t-values for Two-Tail Test, 5 percent Level of Significance, 60 Degrees of Freedom

The implication of this rule of thumb is that the .05 level of significance is being used to select the critical t-value, t^*. As you can see in the t-table at the .05 level of significance, 2 serves as a useful approximation of the critical t-value for about 20 degrees of freedom and above.

A SUGGESTED CLASSROOM EXERCISE TO ILLUSTRATE THE USE OF THE t-TEST At this point, you may still be a bit puzzled about the notion of a t-value and its use in testing the relationship between the sample b and the unknown population b, particularly if you are unfamiliar with statistical theory. We will therefore present a simple exercise that you may wish to try yourselves or along with your classmates and instructor.[14] This exercise deals with the pizza demand example used earlier.

Cut 45 cardboard squares of equal size. According to Table 5.1, there are nine possible levels of demand for pizza for each income category. Thus, each of the squares is to be given a value ranging from 1 to 9. As shown in the first column of Table 5.1, there should be one square labeled 1, three squares labeled 2, six squares labeled 3, and so on. (Note that we have divided the frequencies in each income category by 100. There are 4,500 observations in the population, but we have reduced the number of squares used to 45 simply for convenience. As long as the relative frequencies are the same, it should not matter whether 45 or 4,500 squares are used in this exercise.)

Place all 45 squares in an envelope. Then select one square for each income category. Be sure to put the square back into the envelope after each selection. By doing this, you are generating a random sample of 10 observations, one for each income category. Because the number 5 occurs most frequently (9 times in this exercise and 900 times in the hypothetical population of student consumers)

[14]The authors wish to acknowledge Leo Brand, economics professor at Pace University, for suggesting this exercise.

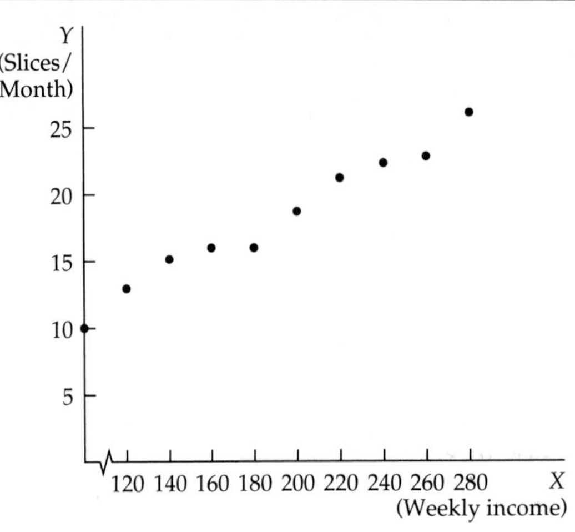

Figure 5.15 Scatter Plot of Sample Data for Pizza Experiment

it is clear that the probability of drawing this number from the envelope is the greatest. In fact, each time a square is selected, there is a 20 percent chance (i.e., 9/45) that the number 5 will be selected. Then combine the number drawn with its income category to determine the corresponding pizza consumption.

Suppose one of these exercises produces the following table of numbers. As a reference to the exercise, the number that was drawn from the envelope is included in parentheses next to the quantities demanded for pizza.

Average Quantity of Pizza Slices Demanded (Y)	*Weekly Income (X)*
10.0 (1)	$100
13.0 (5)	120
15.2 (7)	140
16.0 (5)	160
16.0 (1)	180
18.7 (4)	200
21.2 (7)	220
22.3 (6)	240
22.0 (1)	260
26.0 (8)	280

A scatter plot of these data is presented in Figure 5.15.

The regression equation estimated for this sample is:[15]

$$Y = 3.27 + 0.078X \qquad (5.9)$$
$$(0.86) \quad (0.004)$$

Let us now conduct a t-test for the significance of the estimated sample coefficient, $\hat{b}$. Recall that the null and alternative hypotheses can be expressed in the following manner:

$$H_o : b = 0$$
$$H_a : b \neq 0$$

Clearly, our sample $\hat{b}$ coefficient of 0.078 is greater than zero. Therefore, we must determine the probability of encountering such a sample value from a population whose true value is really zero. We begin by subtracting zero (the hypothesized population value of b) from 0.078 (the estimated sample value, $\hat{b}$), and then we divide this difference by the standard error of $\hat{b}$. By convention, the standard error of an estimated regression coefficient is presented in parentheses under the coefficient. As you can see in Equation (5.9), the standard error of $\hat{b}$ is 0.004, and the standard error of the intercept is 0.86. This procedure is summarized below.

$$t = \frac{0.078 - 0}{0.004} \qquad (5.10)$$
$$t = 19.5$$

Equation (5.10) is referred to as the t-ratio or the t-value.

From the results of the equation, you can see that if the population coefficient, b, were truly zero, then 0.078 would lie 19.5 t-units away from the mean. Turning to Table A.4 in the appendix of this text, we see that the probability of encountering such a value is so remote that it is not even included in the chart. However. this table does show that the probability of obtaining a t-value (with 8 degrees of freedom) greater than 3.355 or less than -3.355 from a distribution whose mean is zero is one out of one hundred (i.e., .01). This implies that the probability of obtaining a value of 19.5 is virtually nil. And so we come to the rather obvious conclusion that the true value of the population coefficient is, in all likelihood, not equal to zero. In terms of statistical theory, we "reject the null hypothesis."

In using regression analysis, economists almost always hypothesize the population coefficient to be equal to zero (i.e., $H_0 : b = 0$). However, the value of the unknown population coefficient can by hypothesized to be any value that the researcher desires. For example, suppose that a number of previous

[15]Any number of readily available software packages for the personal or the mainframe computer can be used to estimate regression equations. In fact, for simple regression, a hand calculator will suffice. The software package used for the examples in this text is Micro TSP, copyright©Quantitative Micro Software, 1982–88. Other commonly used packages are SPSS (Statistical Packages for the Social Sciences), SAS (Statistical Analysis software), and Storm.

studies on the demand for pizza estimated the value of the coefficient of the income variable to be about 0.073. We might then use these previous studies as the justification for hypothesizing that the unknown coefficient is equal to this value:

$$H_o : b = 0.73$$

$$H_a : b \neq 0.73$$

We find the corresponding t-ratio to be

$$t = \frac{0.078 - 0.073}{0.004}$$

$$t = 1.25$$

Suppose we test this hypothesis using the .05 level of significance, two-tail test. Turning again to the t-table in the appendix, we find a critical t-value of 2.306 for a regression with 8 degrees of freedom. Since the t-value of 1.25 is not greater than 2.306, we are *not* able to reject the null hypothesis. Once again, this does not mean that we can now say that the population coefficient is indeed 0.073. However, this failure to "pass the t-test" means that we are unable to say with a high degree of certainty that the population value is *not* 0.073. Until future studies indicate otherwise, researchers may want to assume the working hypothesis that the unknown population coefficient is around 0.073.

THE t-DISTRIBUTION AND THE ONE-TAIL AND TWO-TAIL TESTS In using regression analysis for economic and business research, it is standard for the null hypothesis to state that there is no relationship between a particular independent variable and the dependent variable (e.g., $b = 0$). However, researchers usually have a choice as to whether the alternative hypothesis states that the independent variable simply has some impact on the dependent variable (a two-tail test) or whether it indicates a positive or a negative impact (a one-tail test). In the evaluation of the relationship between income and the quantity demanded for pizza, our alternative hypothesis was that changes in income had an effect on the quantity demanded for pizza; it did not state whether this effect was positive or negative. If we had some a priori reason for believing that the effect of income on quantity demanded was either positive or negative, it would be reflected in the alternative hypothesis. For example, if we hypothesized that pizza is a "normal" good, the alternative hypothesis would be that changes in income have a direct relation to changes in quantity demanded. If we hypothesized that pizza is an "inferior" good, the alternative hypothesis would claim an inverse relationship between the two variables. Using the notation we have developed:

If pizza is hypothesized to be a "normal good" (i.e., the income variable's coefficient is positive), then

$$H_0 : b \leq 0$$

$$H_a : b > 0$$

If pizza is hypothesized to be an "inferior good" (i.e., the income variable's coefficient is negative), then

$$H_0 : b \geq 0$$

$$H_a : b < 0$$

If income is hypothesized simply to have an impact (either positive or negative) on the demand for pizza, then

$$H_0 : b = 0$$

$$H_a : b \neq 0$$

SUMMARY: STEPS IN CONDUCTING THE t-TEST OF THE STATISTICAL SIGNIFICANCE OF ESTIMATED REGRESSION COEFFICIENTS This has been a rather lengthy discussion of the t-test, so it might be helpful to summarize each of the steps involved in carrying out this test.

Step 1: State the hypothesis.

For example, "Pizza is a normal good." (In other words, income is hypothesized to have a direct relation to the demand for pizza.)

Step 2: Restate the hypothesis in terms suitable for statistical testing.

With respect to the preceding hypothesis about income and the pizza,

$$H_0 : b \leq 0$$

$$H_a : b > 0$$

Step 3: Establish a critical level of rejection, and find the t-value that corresponds to this level.

For example, for a one-tail test, the .05 level, and 8 degrees of freedom (the number we assumed for the pizza analysis), $t^* = 1.86$. Thus, if the t-statistic is greater than 1.86, we can reject the null hypothesis at the .05 level of significance.

Step 4: Find the t-statistic by transforming the difference between the estimated b and its hypothesized value, 0.

For example, suppose the estimated coefficient is 2.5 and the standard error of the coefficient is 1.3. Then

$$t = \frac{2.5 - 0}{1.3}$$

$$= 1.92$$

Step 5: Compare the resulting t-value with the critical value. Then decide whether or not to reject the null hypothesis.

In our example, 1.92 is greater than the critical t-value of 1.86 for a one-tail test with 8 degrees of freedom. Therefore we can reject the null hypothesis and state that income has a "statistically significant" direct impact on the demand for pizza.

Multiple Regression Analysis

Let us now turn to multiple regression analysis, which involves the use of two or more independent variables in the regression equation. The arithmetic required to estimate the coefficients of a multiple regression equation is considerably greater than that required for a simple regression equation. This explains why even the most sophisticated hand-held calculators are only programmable for simple regression analysis. However, the increasing availability of computers in industry and in academia has made it possible to use multiple regression analysis for all types of economics and business research. At present, of course, the computing power of personal computers and the burgeoning amount of "user-friendly" software makes the use of multiple regression analysis possible for all researchers.

Let us begin our explanation of multiple regression by specifying the following *linear, additive regression model* for the demand for pizza:[16]

$$Y = a + b_1X_1 + b_2X_2 + b_3X_3 + b_4X_4 \quad (5.11)$$

where Y = Quantity of pizza demanded (average number of slices per capita per month)
X_1 = Average price of a slice of pizza (in cents)
X_2 = Average annual tuition (in thousands of dollars)
X_3 = Average price of a 12-ounce can of soft drink (in cents)
X_4 = Location of campus (1 if campus is located outside of a concentrated urban area, 0 otherwise)

Assume that a regression analysis of cross-sectional data of 30 college campuses yields the following estimated relationship between the quantity demanded for pizza and our selection of independent variables:

$$\underset{(11.7)}{Y = 38.5^*} - \underset{(0.05)}{0.16X_1^*} + \underset{(3.3)}{0.02X_2} - \underset{(0.04)}{0.05X_3} + \underset{(1.8)}{2.67X_4} \quad (5.12)$$

$$\text{Adjusted } R^2 = .86 \qquad F = 38.39 \qquad n = 30$$

The asterisks indicate statistical significance at the .05 level.

In evaluating this equation, we first look at the signs of the estimated coefficients of the independent variables. (We usually ignore the intercept term, because by itself this term does not have any economic meaning.) Note that, as expected, the sign of the price variable is negative. The sign of the variable

[16]It is linear because none of the terms on the right-hand side of the equation is raised to a power greater than 1. The plus signs preceding each term explain why the model is additive.

X_2 is positive, indicating that the higher the college tuition, the more pizza is purchased by the students. The sign of X_3, the variable for the price of soft drinks, is negative, indicating that pizza and soft drinks are complementary products.

There is one variable in the equation, X_4, that may seem a bit odd. This is called a *binary* or *dummy variable*. It assumes the value of 1 if the campus is located outside of a concentrated urban area and a value of 0 otherwise. This type of variable will be explained in greater detail in a later section. However, at this point we can point out that the coefficient of this variable measures the difference in the demand for pizza by students attending colleges or universities outside of concentrated urban areas versus students in institutions located in concentrated urban areas. As you can see by the magnitude and sign of the X_4 coefficient, the former group is estimated to eat 2.67 more slices of pizza per month than the latter group.

The magnitudes of the coefficients indicate the change in the quantity of pizza demanded relative to a unit change in a particular independent variable *assuming the values of the other variables are unchanged*. This feature of multiple regression analysis is extremely useful in economic and business research because, as you can see, it follows the comparative statics approach to the analysis of problems so commonly used in economic theory. Thus, the equation tells us that, all other factors held constant, a unit (i.e., a one cent) decrease in the price of pizza will cause the quantity demanded of pizza to rise by 0.16 units. Unless one has actual experience in or prior knowledge about the retail pizza business, it is difficult to judge whether or not the magnitudes of the regression coefficients represent typical patterns of demand for pizza relative to changes in the independent variables. However, as noted earlier, one way to assess these magnitudes is to compute the elasticities of demand with respect to these independent variables. To compute these elasticities, we have to assume a certain starting point for the values of the independent variables. Let us assume the following values:

Price of pizza (X_1) $=$ \$1.75 per slice
Annual college tuition (X_2) $=$ \$15,000
Price of a soft drink (X_3) $=$ \$0.75
Location of campus (X_4) $=$ Urban area (i.e., $X_4 = 0$)

Given these values, we then compute the monthly per-capita demand for pizza to be

$$\begin{aligned} Y &= 38.5 - 0.16(175) + 0.02(15) - 0.05(75) + 2.67(0) \\ &= 7.05 \approx 7 \end{aligned} \tag{5.13}$$

Recall the general formula for point elasticity to be:

$$\frac{dY}{dX} \times \frac{X}{Y}$$

We now use this formula to compute the various demand elasticities:

Price elasticity:	$-0.16 \times \frac{175}{7}$	$= -4$
Tuition elasticity:	$0.02 \times \frac{15}{7}$	$= 0.04$
Cross-price elasticity:	$-0.05 \times \frac{75}{7}$	$= -0.53$

The equation has an adjusted R^2 of .86. This means that 86 percent of the variation in the dependent variable can be explained by variations in the independent variable. Once again, only those familiar with this type of business can really evaluate the explanatory power of this estimated equation. However, .86 is a higher R^2 than is found in most empirical studies of consumer demand that use cross-sectional data.

To conduct the t-test, we first divide the standard errors (cited in parentheses) into their respective coefficients and compare these t-ratios with the appropriate values in Table A.4 at the back of this text.[17] At the .05 level of significance, two-tail test, we see that the critical t-value for 25 degrees of freedom is 2.06. Using this critical level, we see that only X_1, the variable indicating the price of pizza, is statistically significant.

As for the policy implications of these regression findings, suppose you are an entrepreneur who is considering starting a chain of pizza parlors on college campuses across the country. The high degree of price elasticity indicated by the regression findings indicates that you might want to consider a relatively low price for your product. Moreover, the statistical significance of the coefficient of the price variable would give you a great deal of confidence that this is the correct policy to pursue. Although the tuition coefficient did not prove to be statistically significant, the relatively low "tuition elasticity of demand" might lead you to conclude that the locations of your pizza parlors should not be confined to any particular type of institution of higher education. Based on the relatively high cross-price elasticity between soft drink prices and the demand for pizza, once the pizza parlors are established you might want to consider reducing the price of beverages as a way to boost demand for pizza. However, this option has to be tempered by the fact that the soft drink coefficient did not pass the t-test. As already pointed out, location was estimated to have a relatively large impact on the demand for pizza. This being the case, you might want to consider concentrating your establishments on campuses located outside of large cities. But here again one must be careful, because the coefficient of the dummy location variable did not pass the t-test.

The F-Test

There is another test of statistical significance, called the F-test, that is commonly used in regression analysis. This test measures the statistical significance of the entire regression equation rather than of each individual coefficient (as the t-test is designed to do). Earlier, we stated that R^2 is the measure of the explanatory power of the regression model. In effect, the F-statistic is a test of the

[17]Most software programs for regression analysis automatically compute the t-ratios and list their values along with their respective estimated coefficients in the program output.

statistical significance of R^2. The null hypothesis of the F-test can be expressed as follows:

$$H_0 : b_1 = b_2 = \cdots = b_k = 0$$

where k equals the number of independent variables in the regression equation.

If the null hypothesis is true, virtually no relationship exists between the dependent variable and the k independent variables for the population, and whatever the value of R^2 (i.e., the proportion of the variation in Y explained by X), it is most probably a chance occurrence in the sampling process.

The F-value can be defined as:

$$F = \frac{\text{Explained variation}/k}{\text{Unexplained variation}/(n-k-1)}$$

where the explained variation is $\sum(\hat{Y}-\overline{Y})^2$, the unexplained variation is $\sum(Y-\hat{Y})^2$, n is the sample size, and k is the number of independent variables. It can also be expressed in terms of the value of R^2:

$$F = \frac{R^2/k}{(1-R^2)/(n-k-1)} \tag{5.14}$$

The procedure for using the F-value in the F-test is similar to the use of the t-value in the t-test. A critical value for F is established depending on the degree of statistical significance that the researcher wishes to set. Typically, the significance level is set at .05 or .01. The critical F-values corresponding to these acceptance levels are shown in Table A.3 at the back of the text. As can be seen, there are two "degrees of freedom" values that must be incorporated in the selection of the critical F-value. One value relates to the numerator of the equation for F, and the other relates to the denominator. Given this background information, we can now interpret the F-value for our multiple regression equation for pizza demand. With a sample size of 30 and four independent variables ($n = 30$ and $k = 4$), the F-table indicates that at the .05 level, the critical F-value for 4 and 25 degrees of freedom is 2.76. At the .01 level, the critical F-value is 4.18.

Because the estimated equation's F-value of 38.39 (reported in Equation 5.12) exceeds both of these critical values, we can conclude that our entire regression model accounts for a statistically significant proportion of the variation in the demand for pizzas. In general, it is fairly easy for a regression model to pass the F-test. The null hypothesis, which states that there is no relationship between the dependent variable and *all* of the independent variables, is a rather stringent statement. As long as some of the independent variables in the regression equation truly help to explain the variance in the dependent variable, the F-test will more than likely indicate a statistically significant regression model. In fact, it can be seen in Equation (5.14) that for some given sample size and set of independent variables,the higher R^2, the greater the F-value.

Another way to view the general tendency of a regression equation to pass the F-test is to recognize that regression models that *do not* pass the test must indeed be inferior. In any event, even if the F-statistic indicates the overall statistical significance of the regression model, there is still a need to subject each independent variable to individual testing. For this, we rely on the t-test.

The Use of Regression Analysis to Forecast Demand

In addition to helping researchers understand more about the determinants of demand, regression analysis can be used simply as a tool for forecasting. In the next chapter, we will discuss this topic in much greater detail. For now, let us just state that once the regression coefficients have been estimated, arriving at a forecast value of the demand for a particular good or service is simply a matter of assigning values to the independent variables. For example, suppose the regression analysis of time series data resulted in the following estimate of the demand for pizza:

$$Q = 100 - 20P + 100I + 15\text{AD} + 10P_{\text{hd}}$$

where Q = Demand for pizza (in millions of slices per year)
P = Price of pizza (in cents)
I = Per-capita income (in thousands of dollars)
AD = Advertising expenditures (in millions of dollars)
P_{hd} = Price of hot dogs (in cents)

If we assume that $P = 100$, $I = 5$, $\text{AD} = 30$, and $P_{\text{hd}} = 125$, our forecast for the quantity of pizza demanded for the coming year will be 300 (million slices). However, when regression analysis is used for forecasting, the same care that was taken in assessing the statistical significance of the individual regression coefficients must be applied. This is because the forecast is based on a sample of data. To take into account that the forecast value of 300 is based on a sample and is therefore subject to a sampling error, we use a measure called the *standard error of the estimate* (SEE). This term is also included as a regular part of the computer printout of any software regression program. As a matter of fact, it can be shown that the standard error of the coefficient ($\text{SE}_{\hat{b}}$) is actually derived from the SEE of the regression equation.

According to statistical theory, we can expect that the true (but unknown) value of Y will be within a range determined by the estimated value, plus or minus the product of the standard error of the estimate and the appropriate t-value. In notational form,

$$\hat{Y} \pm t_{n-k-1}\text{SEE}$$

For example, suppose the estimated regression equation for the pizza demand was generated from a sample size of 27 and had a SEE of 25. Given the previous values, we can say with 95 percent confidence that the actual demand for pizza is: 300 ± 2.074(25), or a range of 248.15 to 351.85.[18] Caution should be exercised when developing the forecast range for the dependent variable of the estimated regression equation. Statistical theory shows that as the given values of the independent variables (e.g. price, income, price of related products) move further away from their mean values, the forecast range widens for any given level of confidence.[19]

Additional Topics on the Specification of the Regression Model

Proxy and Dummy Variables

One of the most challenging aspects of regression analysis (or, for that matter, any type of statistical analysis) is obtaining sample data suitable for use in the analysis. For example, economic theory indicates that "tastes and preferences" is an important determinant of consumer demand. But how do we measure this factor? A researcher who cannot obtain direct information about tastes and preferences may have to use a "proxy" variable to represent this factor in the regression equation. Level of education and gender of consumers are possible proxy variables for tastes and preferences. Those with higher levels of formal schooling might have different tastes or preferences for a particular good or service. Women might have different tastes or preferences than men. Even differences in residential location might reflect differences in tastes and preferences. For example, the authors have observed that supermarkets in the northeast region of the United States carry a proportionally larger stock and variety of Italian foods than those in other parts of the country. On the other hand, the variety and quantity of Mexican food on supermarket shelves in the Midwest, the Southwest, and on the Pacific Coast are substantially greater than in the Northeast.

In certain instances, for variables such as location and gender to be used in regression analysis, they must be quantified. This can be done by creating a "dummy" or binary variable, which takes the value of 1 if the unit of observation falls into a particular category and 0 if it does not. For example, we can assign the value of one to a female consumer and zero to a male.[20] In this manner, dummy variables can be created for any nonquantitative factor.

[18] According to the t-table, the critical t-value with 22 degrees of freedom (i.e., $n - k - 1$, or $27 - 5$) is 2.074. If a greater degree of confidence were desired, the range of the expected value of the demand for pizza would obviously widen. For example, at the 99 percent confidence level, the critical t-value with 22 degrees of freedom is 2.819.

[19] For an explanation of this, see Kelejian and Oates, op. cit., pp. 123–28.

[20] The authors have observed that until recently, most studies employing dummy variables to represent gender assigned the value of one to males and zero to females. From the standpoint of statistical analysis, it does not matter which category is assigned the value of zero even though the assigned values carry with them implications that go beyond statistics.

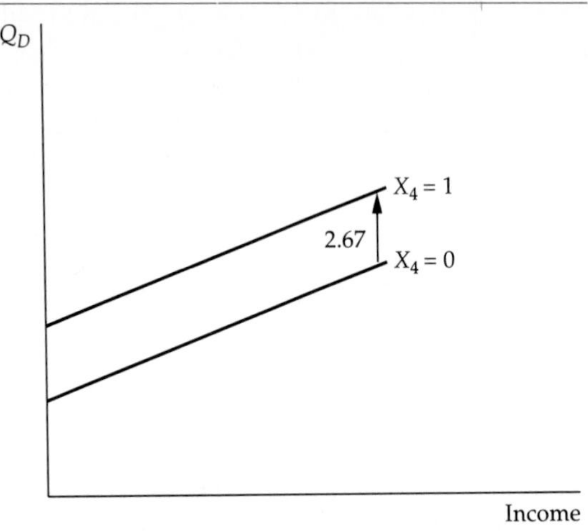

Figure 5.16 Effect of the Dummy Variable

A useful way to consider a dummy variable in a regression equation is as a "shift" factor. For example, in our regression analysis of the demand for pizza by college students, the coefficient of the dummy location variable was estimated to be 2.67. Suppose we graphed the demand equation implied by the values provided in Equation (5.13). This is shown in Figure 5.16. The original demand curve indicates the demand by those students who attend schools in concentrated urban areas (i.e., $X_4 = 0$). To determine the demand by those students who attend school outside urban areas, we simply assign the value of 1 to the X_4 variable. This gives us the second demand curve shown in Figure 5.16. In effect, the change in X_4 has caused the original curve to shift upward.

Nonlinear Relationships

The method of least squares finds the best linear relationship between the dependent and independent variables. However, in certain instances, economic theory, experience, or simple observation of the scatter plot may lead researchers to suspect that the relationship between the dependent and independent variables is nonlinear. For example, suppose data on income (I) and the demand for restaurant meals (Q_D) for a sample of households yields the scatter plot shown in Figure 5.17*a*. As you can see, the scatter implies a nonlinear relationship between income and the demand for restaurant meals. Such nonlinear representations are still suitable for estimation with the use of linear regression analysis. For example, we could specify a polynomial regression model in which the independent term, X, is raised to the second as well as to the first degree. Figure 5.17*b* illustrates this option. We could also specify our regression equation in terms of a power function. Figure 5.17*c* illustrates this possibility. In either case, the idea is to use the method of least squares to estimate the coefficients of the equations. The usual tests and statistics (e.g., t-test, F-test, R^2) are still used in evaluating the regression results.

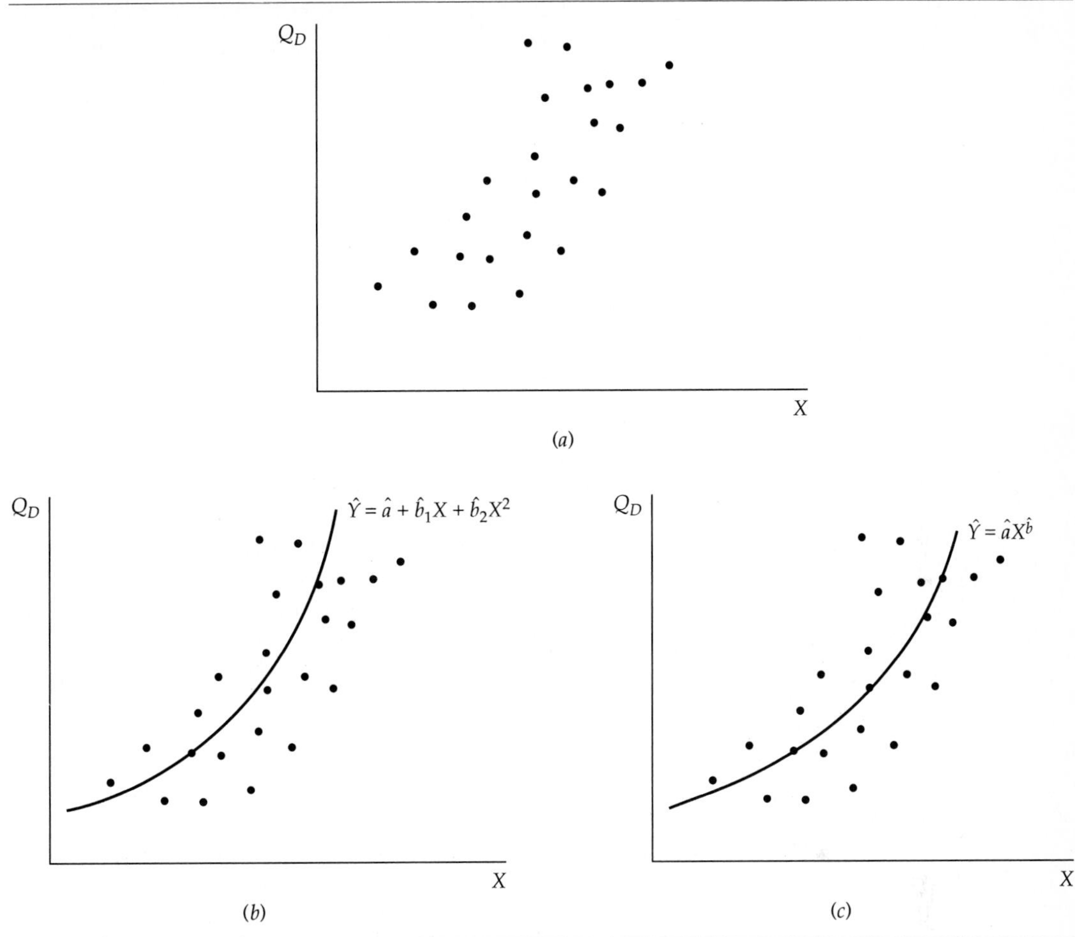

Figure 5.17 Nonlinear Relationships

When using the power function, we first apply a logarithmic transformation to the original specification. For example, let the original equation be as follows:

$$Q_D = aI^b$$

where Q_D = Demand for restaurant services (number of times a person eats in a restaurant per year)

I = Annual income

Taking the log of both sides of the equation gives us the following logarithmic transformation:

$$\log Q_D = \log a + b \log I$$

To perform a regression analysis on this type of nonlinear data, we first find the logs of each of the values of Y and X in the sample data. We then regress log Y on log X using the method of least squares. One way in which the transformed regression equation can be evaluated is to compare its R^2 with that of a simple linear equation (i.e., $Q_D = a + bI$). If the R^2 of the transformed power equation is greater than that of the simple linear expression, it would appear that the nonlinear model offers a better explanation for the variance of Q_D.

The use of a *log-linear* equation in regression analysis is particularly appealing for economists because for relatively small changes in X, the estimated coefficient of the log of X can indicate the *percentage change in Y relative to the percentage change in X*.[21] In other words, the coefficients of the transformed variables are in fact measures of the point elasticity of demand with respect to each variable. For example, if the estimated value of b in the preceding equation were 1.2, then we could immediately interpret restaurant dining as a "superior" product because its income elasticity is greater than unity.

Problems in the Use of Regression Analysis

A full discussion of the problems that may arise in regression is clearly beyond the scope of this chapter and this text. As mentioned at the outset of this chapter, entire textbooks and whole courses ranging from introductory to advanced are dedicated to the study of regression analysis. Nonetheless, we should cite and briefly explain some of these problems so that readers unfamiliar with this topic will gain an appreciation of the real challenges awaiting those who wish to apply regression analysis to business and economic research.

The Identification Problem

The identification problem presents perhaps the greatest challenge to those using regression analysis to estimate the demand for a particular good or service. To explain this problem, let us return to our pizza example. Suppose we had time series data relating the per-capita consumption of pizza with the price of pizza over a 20-year period. The scatter plot of this information is shown in Figure 5.18*a*. Notice that the scatter tends to slope upward and that a least squares regression estimate would reflect this pattern of relationship. Does this mean that the consumers of pizza behave "irrationally" and demand more pizza at higher prices? Common sense would balk at such a conclusion, but then why the positive coefficient of the price variable in the demand equation? The alert reader will state that what we have "identified" as a demand equation is probably some sort of supply equation or perhaps, the result of the movement in *both* supply and demand for pizza over the past 20 years. As can be seen in Figure 5.18*b*, if the supply remained constant over the past 20 years while demand shifted upward (because of changes in such factors as income, number of buyers, and tastes and preferences over this time period), the regression equation would really be a reflection of the supply curve S_1. If the supply

[21] For a discussion of the meaning of the coefficients in a log-linear regression equation, see the discussion of the basic mathematics of the Cobb-Douglas function in Chapter 10.

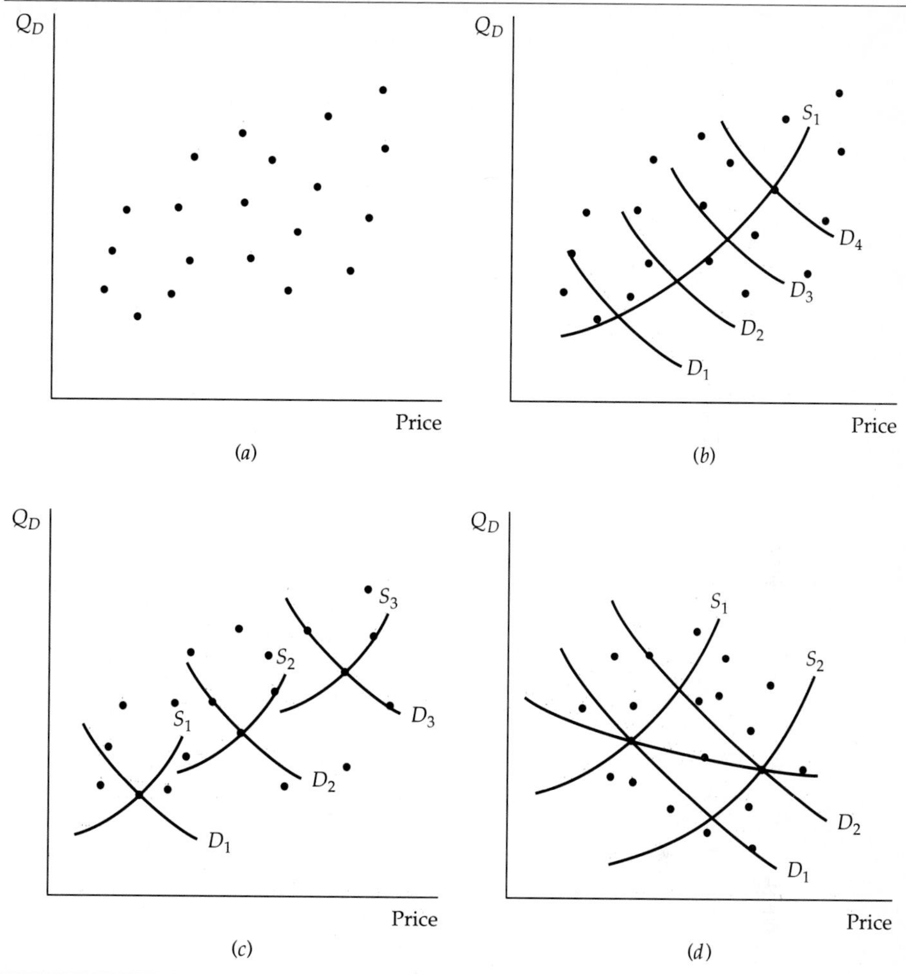

Figure 5.18 The Identification Problem

increased but demand increased more than the supply, then the regression estimate would really be a reflection of the intersection of the various S and D curves in Figure 5.18*c*. Figure 5.18*d* shows still another possibility. In this case, supply shifts more than demand, so that the estimated regression line is downward sloping and more like what we would expect of a demand curve. Nonetheless, this estimated demand curve is flatter than the "true" demand curves, which have gradually shifted to the right over the years. Thus, the regression estimate of the relationship between price and quantity demanded would be biased in the sense that it would indicate a much greater price elasticity than actually exists in the population of pizza consumers.

There are advanced estimation techniques, such as the methods of *two-stage least squares* and *indirect least squares*, that can help the researcher deal with samples in which the simultaneous shifting of demand and supply takes place. Essentially, these techniques involve the simultaneous consideration of the supply and demand equations with the use of a single regression equation. A discussion of these techniques lies outside the scope of this text. But the principal point to remember is that if the identification problem is not recognized and dealt with by the researcher, the method of ordinary least squares will result in biased estimates of the regression coefficients.

Multicollinearity

One of the key assumptions made in the construction of the multiple regression equation is that the independent variables are not related to each other in any systematic way. If this assumption is incorrect, then each of the estimated coefficients may give a distorted view of the impact of the change in each of the independent variables. For example, suppose a regression model states that the demand for luxury foreign-made automobiles depends on price, income, and education. The latter variable is included because education is a proxy for tastes and preferences, and those with higher levels of education are hypothesized to have a greater preference for luxury foreign cars. But, as you would expect, education and income are closely associated. If their values tend to move up and down together, the least squares method may arbitrarily assign a high value to the coefficient of one variable and a low coefficient value to the other. In effect, if two variables are closely associated, it becomes difficult to separate out the effect that each has on the dependent variable. The existence of such a condition in regression analysis is called *multicollinearity.*

If the regression results pass the F-test (the measure of the overall statistical significance of the regression equation) but fail the t-test for each of the individual regression coefficients, it is usually a sign that multicollinearity is present in the sample data. Multicollinearity can also be detected by examining the correlation coefficient between two variables suspected of being closely related.[22] As a rule of thumb, correlation coefficients of .7 or more provide a basis for researchers to suspect the existence of multicollinearity.[23]

If multicollinearity is a serious problem in the regression analysis, it will tend to introduce an upward bias to the standard errors of the coefficients. This will tend to reduce the t-values (which, you will recall, are computed using the standard errors of the coefficients). This makes it harder to reject the null hypothesis and, of course, to identify statistically significant independent variables in the regression model.

It should be pointed out, however, that if the researcher simply wishes to use the estimated regression coefficients as a basis for forecasting future values of the dependent variable, multicollinearity does not pose a serious problem. It is only when the researcher wishes to understand more about the underlying

---

[22] The correlation coefficient is a measure of the degree of association between two variables. This measure, denoted r, ranges from a value of -1 (perfect negative correlation) to 1 (perfect positive correlation).

[23] Douglas Downing and Jeffrey Clark, *Business Statistics*, New York: Barron's, 1985, p. 365.

structure of the demand function (i.e., what are the key determinants of demand) that this particular statistical problem should be resolved. Most software packages automatically produce a correlation coefficient matrix for the entire set of independent variables used in the regression equation. A standard remedy for multicollinearity is to drop one of the variables that is closely associated with another variable in the regression equation.

Autocorrelation

Autocorrelation is a problem that is usually encountered when time series data are used. For this reason, it is often referred to as serial correlation. Let us use the case of simple regression, involving only the dependent variable Y and one independent variable, X. Essentially, autocorrelation occurs when the Y variable relates to the X variable according to a certain pattern. For example, in Figure 5.19*a*, the scatter plot reveals that as X increases (presumably over time), the Y value deviates from the regression line in a very systematic way. In other words, the *residual term*, or the difference between the observed value of Y and the estimated value of Y given X ($\hat{Y}$) alternates between a positive and a negative value of approximately the same magnitude throughout the range of X values. In fact, if we were to plot these residuals on a separate graph, they would have the pattern shown in Figure 5.19*b*.

One possible cause of autocorrelation is that there are effects on Y not accounted for by the variables included in the regression equation. It might also be that the true relationship between Y and the independent variable(s) is nonlinear. But regardless of the reason, if autocorrelation is present in the regression analysis, it creates a problem for the validity of the t-test. Simply stated, autocorrelation tends to increase the likelihood that the null hypothesis will be rejected. This is because autocorrelation gives a downward bias to the standard

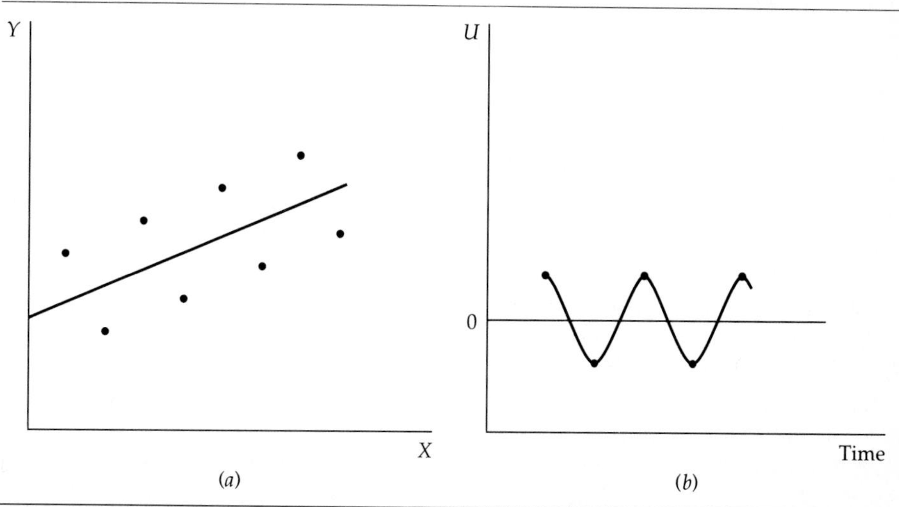

Figure 5.19 Autocorrelation

error of the estimated regression coefficient ($SE_{\hat{b}}$). Recalling that the t-value is defined as $(\hat{b} - b)/SE_{\hat{b}}$, we can see that a smaller $SE_{\hat{b}}$ would tend to increase the magnitude of the t-value, other factors held constant. Thus, in the presence of autocorrelation, researchers may well declare that certain independent variables have a statistically significant impact on the dependent variable when in fact they do not. From a policy standpoint, suppose that the estimated coefficient of the advertising variable in a regression model of demand "passed" the t-test when it really should not have. A firm might then be led to increase its advertising expenditures when in fact it should be looking at other ways to expand demand (e.g., through promotions, alternative channels of distribution, or price actions).

It may be difficult to identify autocorrelation simply by observing the pattern of the residuals of a regression equation. A standard test for identifying the presence of this problem is the *Durbin-Watson test*. The Durbin-Watson statistic (i.e., DW) is now routinely calculated in regression software packages and is presented automatically in the computer printout. As in the case of the t-test and the F-test, there is a Durbin-Watson table listing the critical values of this statistic for a given level of significance (usually the .05 level). We have included such a table in the appendix at the back of this text (see Table A.5). As a rule of thumb, if the DW statistic is around 2, there is in all probability no autocorrelation present in the data. Should the DW statistic indicate the presence of autocorrelation, there are certain things a researcher can do to correct the problem. These include transforming the data into a different order of magnitude or introducing "leading" or "lagging" data in the time series.

The Solution

As it turned out, the task of generating a statistical model was not as simple as Jennifer Harrah had anticipated. The key problem was the lack of data. The product was brand new for Global Foods, so there was no historical information that the company could provide for use as time series data in the regression analysis. She could have generated cross-sectional data by conducting a telephone survey, but there simply was not enough time. She was able to find public information on time series data from the government for such items as fruit juices, soft drinks, and beer, but these were aggregated by product type, and no other information besides average price was available. The only data set she could find within the time allowed was part of a market research study conducted in the 1950s by the *National Bottler's Gazette*. This study looked at the per-capita consumption of soft drinks by state, along with the average annual

(Continued)

temperature of the state and its per capita income. These figures are shown in Table 5.2[24] She conducted a regression analysis of these cross-sectional data using the following model:

$$Q = a + b_1\text{INC} + b_2\text{TEMP}$$

where Q = Per capita annual consumption of soft drinks

INC = Per capita annual income

TEMP = Average annual temperature

The results of the computer analysis are shown in Table 5.3. Temperature has a sizable as well as a statistically significant impact on soft drink consumption. Every additional degree of average annual temperature results in an increase in per capita soft drink consumption by 5.87 bottles. Using the "rule of 2," we can see that the t-value of 4.8 is clearly significant. The estimated coefficient for the income variable is interesting. First, its negative value indicates that a soft drink is an "inferior" product. Higher levels of income result in lower per-capita consumption, and lower income implies higher consumption. However, the t-value of 0.36 is obviously far below the critical t-value. Thus, income cannot be considered a statistically significant determinant of soft drink consumption. In addition, the magnitude of the coefficient itself (−0.8) is relatively small in comparison to the impact of temperature on soft drink consumption. The adjusted R^2 of .34 indicates that only about one third of the variation in soft drink consumption can be accounted for by the variation in per-capita income and average annual temperature. This is to be expected, considering the fact that cross-sectional data are used and that only two independent variables were incorporated into the equation. Nonetheless, the F-value of 13.369 indicates that the R^2 is statistically significant, because the critical value of F at the .05 level with 2 and 45 degrees of freedom is about 3.20.

Jennifer could have easily conducted a study of this kind with updated information. Unfortunately, as shown in Figure 5.20, data on per-capita consumption of soft drinks was available only by region of the country and not by state. This aggregate information is fairly consistent with the regression results. It indicates that in 1989 consumption in the sun belt states in the West and the South, at 637 and 663 cans, respectively, was higher than the national average of 547 cans per person. However, the states making up the west central region also were among the top consumers of soft drinks, with a per-capita average of 658 cans during that year. This might help to explain why the analysis of the historical data using dummy variables to represent the warmer states versus the colder states did not produce statistically significant results.[25]

(Continued)

[24]*Note*: The authors debated whether to use artificially created data to demonstrate all of the topics presented in this chapter or to use real data, which would limit the application of regression analysis. The latter option was chosen because in actual business situations, the lack of good data is far more limiting than either one's knowledge of statistical analysis or the computing power available to "crunch" the numbers. The soft drink consumption figures from the study by the *National Bottler's Gazette* were originally presented in a market research textbook now out of print. Unfortunately, this text did not cite the date when the figures were obtained.

[25]A dummy variable taking the value of 1 for states with annual temperatures above the average and 0 for those states below the average was included in the regression equation along with temperature and income. This did not produce statistically significant results.

Table 5.2 Soft Drink Consumption, Temperature, and Income by State

State	Consumption of Soft Drinks Per Capita	Per Capita Income (hundreds)	Mean Annual Temperature, °F
Alabama	200	$13	66
Arizona	150	17	62
Arkansas	237	11	63
California	135	25	56
Colorado	121	19	52
Connecticut	118	27	50
Delaware	217	28	52
Florida	242	18	72
Georgia	295	14	64
Idaho	85	16	46
Illinois	114	24	52
Indiana	184	20	52
Iowa	104	16	50
Kansas	143	17	56
Kentucky	230	13	56
Louisiana	269	15	69
Maine	111	16	41
Maryland	217	21	54
Massachusetts	114	22	47
Michigan	108	21	47
Minnesota	108	18	41
Mississippi	248	10	65
Missouri	203	19	57
Montana	77	19	44
Nebraska	97	16	49
Nevada	166	24	48
New Hampshire	177	18	35
New Jersey	143	24	54
New Mexico	157	15	56
New York	111	25	48
North Carolina	330	13	59
North Dakota	63	14	39
Ohio	165	22	51
Oklahoma	184	16	82
Oregon	68	19	51
Pennsylvania	121	20	50
Rhode Island	138	20	50
South Carolina	237	12	65
South Dakota	95	13	45
Tennessee	236	13	60
Texas	222	17	69
Utah	100	16	50
Vermont	64	16	44
Virginia	270	16	58
Washington	77	20	49
West Virgina	144	15	55
Wisconsin	97	19	46
Wyoming	102	19	46

Table 5.3 Computer Analysis of Soft Drink Demand

LS // Dependent Variable is QUAN
Number of observations: 48

VARIABLE	COEFFICIENT	STD. ERROR	T-STAT.	2-TAIL SIG.
C	−153.04108	87.938077	−1.7403278	0.089
INC	−0.8684284	2.4054424	−0.3610265	0.720
TEMP	5.8753198	1.2164577	4.8298594	0.000

R-squared	0.372726	Mean of dependent var	142.8958
Adjusted R-squared	0.344847	S.D. of dependent var	81.75215
S.E. of regression	66.17145	Sum of squared resid	197039.7
Durbin-Watson stat	1.019635	F-statistic	13.36947
Log likelihood	−267.7881		

Jennifer wanted to include price in her regression model. Unfortunately, no time series data were available for price. There were some cross-sectional data on the average prices in different regions of the country, but these data were not suitable for regression analysis, because the prices were basically the same for all regions. Regression analysis requires *variation* in the values of the independent variables. Otherwise, there is no scatter plot to which to fit the regression line.

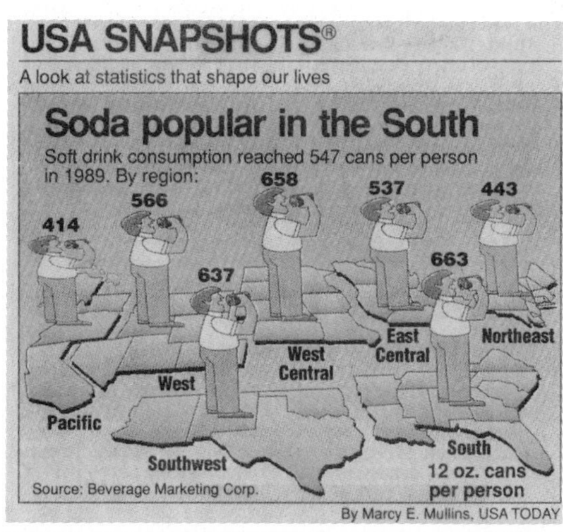

Figure 5.20 Regional Statistics on Soft Drink Consumption

Summary

This chapter has presented an introduction to regression analysis, the method most commonly utilized by economists for estimating the demand for goods and services. Actually, this chapter's material is only a small part of econometrics, which is the application of multivariate statistical analysis to economic theory. The primary importance of this chapter is as an aid in understanding how the techniques of regression analysis may be applied to businesses interested in finding out more about the quantitative aspects of the demand for their products. Readers should appreciate the challenge of applying regression analysis and other statistical techniques to business problems because of the difficulty of obtaining accurate and reliable data.

The process of applying regression analysis to the estimation of demand can be summarized in the following steps:

1. Specification of the regression model of demand
2. Collection of the relevant data
3. Estimation of the regression equation
4. Analysis and evaluation of the regression results (e.g., t-test, F-test, R^2, Durbin-Watson), and adjustment or correction for any statistical problems (e.g., multicollinearity, autocorrelation, incorrect functional form)
5. Assessment of regression findings for use in making policy decisions

In a formal econometrics course, most of the emphasis is placed on steps 1, 3, and 4 (i.e., the more technical aspects of this type of statistical analysis). In business, the most important steps are 2 and 5. Powerful computers and sophisticated software packages are available to everyone today at such a reasonable cost that it has become elementary to apply regression analysis to the estimation of demand or any other aspect of business research.[26] The real challenge is to obtain *good* data and to apply judiciously the results of the regression analysis to the managerial decision-making process. In these two areas of regression analysis, no textbook or course can take the place of actual hands-on experience.

Important Concepts

Alternative hypothesis: In regression analysis, the hypothesis that stands in contrast to the null hypothesis. It generally states that the true (but unknown) population coefficient is some value other than zero.

[26]The authors have been made very aware of this from talking to a former student who is currently the director of worldwide market research for a Fortune 100 company that manufactures fast-moving consumer goods. The data from the supermarkets are updated in the company's mainframe computer on a weekly basis. Whenever desired, the market research people down-load the data onto their PCs and then apply any type of statistical analysis they desire, including regression analysis, to the data. In fact, the research department has created an "expert system" that automatically reads and interpets the regression results (e.g., t-test, F-test, R^2, Durbin-Watson test). All that the user has to do is understand the significance of the expert system's findings and weigh these findings with respect to such policies as pricing and promotion.

Coefficient of determination (R^2): A measure indicating the percentage of the variation in the dependent variable accounted for by variations in some designated independent variable. Its value ranges from 0 to 1. Zero indicates that variations in the independent variable account for none of the variation in the dependent variable. One indicates that 100 percent of the variation in the dependent variable can be accounted for by the variations in the independent variable. In multiple regression analysis, this measure is referred to as the *multiple coefficient of determination.*

Coefficients of the regression equation: Also referred to as *parameters,* the values that indicate the quantitative impact on the dependent variable of a unit change in an independent variable. The main objective of regression analysis is to estimate the values of these coefficients from a sample of data. For this the method of ordinary least squares is often employed.

Consumer survey: The attempt to obtain data about demand directly by asking consumers about their purchasing habits through such means as face-to-face interviews, focus groups, telephone surveys, and mailed questionnaires.

Cross-sectional data: Data on a particular set of variables for a given point in time for a cross section of individual entities (e.g., persons, households, cities, states, countries).

Degrees of freedom: An adjustment factor that is required in conducting the t-test. This number is found by subtracting the number of independent variables plus 1 from the number of observations in the sample; that is, d.f. $= n - (k + 1) = n - k - 1$.

***F*-test:** A test for the statistical significance of the R^2 value. If this test is passed, a researcher can be quite confident that all of the estimated coefficients of a regression model together are not zero for the population under study.

Null hypothesis: In regression analysis, the hypothesis used in testing for the statistical significance of the estimated regression coefficient. It states that the true (but unknown) regression coefficients for the population are zero.

One-tail test: This refers to the nature of the alternative hypothesis in the t-test. If the alternative hypothesis states that the population coefficient is positive, then the upper tail of the t-distribution is used. If the alternative hypothesis states that the population coefficient is negative, then the lower tail is used. In either case, only one tail is used.

Ordinary Method of Least Squares (OLS): In simple regression analysis, a method designed to fit a line through a scatter of points indicating values of a dependent variable and an independent variable in such a way that the sum of the squared deviations of the points from the line is minimized.

Regression analysis: A statistical technique for finding the best relationship between a dependent variable and selected independent variables. If one independent variable is used, this technique is referred to as *simple regression.* If more than one independent variable is used, it is called *multiple regression.*

Rule of two: A general rule of thumb employed by economists in conducting the *t*-test. Essentially, it states that any *t*-ratio of 2 or more indicates that the estimated coefficient is statistically significant at the .05 level.

Standard error of the coefficient ($SE_{\hat{b}}$): A measure of the deviation of an estimated regression coefficient from the hypothesized value of the true (but unknown) population coefficient. In the *t*-test, the standard error of a particular estimated coefficient is divided into this coefficient, thereby indicating the *t*-value.

Standard error of the estimate (SEE): A measure of the deviation of the estimated value of the dependent variable, given the values of the independent variables. In forecasting, the standard error of the estimate is used to develop an interval that contains the true value of the dependent variable, subject to a designated degree of confidence.

***t*-table:** A numerical table indicating the different values of the *t*-ratio and the frequency of their occurrence in a *t*-distribution whose mean value is zero.

t-test: A test for the statistical significance of the estimated regression coefficients. If a coefficient passes this test, then a researcher can be quite confident that the value of the true population coefficient is not zero.

Time series data: Data for a particular set of variables that track their values over a particular period of time at regular intervals (e.g., monthly, quarterly, annually).

Two-tail test: A *t*-test in which the alternative hypothesis states that the population coefficient may be either positive or negative (i.e., it is not zero); that is, either the upper or the lower tail of the *t*-distribution may be used.

Questions

1. Explain the difference between time series data and cross-sectional data. Provide examples of each type of data.
2. Would there be any differences in the set of variables used in a regression model of the demand for consumer durable goods (e.g., automobiles, appliances, furniture) and a regression model of the demand for "fast-moving consumer goods" (e.g., food, beverages, personal care products)? Explain.
3. Explain the difference between a deterministic model and a probabilistic model of the relationship between a dependent variable and one or more independent variables.
4. Briefly explain the meaning of R^2. A time series analysis of demand tends to result in a higher R^2 than one using cross-sectional data. Why do you think this is the case?
5. Overheard at the water cooler: "My regression model of demand is better than the one that the consultant prepared for us because it has a higher R^2. Besides, my equation has three more independent variables and so is more complete than the consultant's." Comment on this statement. Would you agree with the speaker? Explain.

6. Summarize the steps involved in conducting the t-test. What is the basis for using the "rule of 2" as a convenient method of evaluating t-ratios?
7. Briefly explain the meaning of the F-test. Why do you think this test is considered to be more important in multiple regression analysis than it is in simple regression analysis?
8. What is multicollinearity? How can this problem be detected by the researcher? What is the impact of this problem on the regression estimates? What steps can be taken to deal with this problem?
9. What is the identification problem? What effect will this problem have on the regression estimates of a demand function? Explain.

Problems

1. As this textbook goes to press, the consumer electronics industry is about to unveil what it hopes will be another blockbuster product comparable to the VCR. This is a new type of compact disc player that displays sophisticated audio and video programs on a television set. The initial price of this product—which will enable users to scan programs ranging from the complete works of William Shakespeare to a cookbook with more than 450 recipes, with color photographs and voiceovers—is about $1,000.
   a. Suppose you are conducting market research for this product. Is it possible to use regression analysis for a product such as this, which has never before been on the market? If you believe so, how would you go about conducting this research?
   b. As data are accumulated on this product, suggest the type of variables that could be included in a regression analysis of the demand for this new type of CD player.
2. One of the most difficult tasks in regression analysis is to obtain the data suitable for quantitative studies of this kind. Suppose you are trying to estimate the demand for home furniture. Suggest the kinds of variables that could be used to represent the following factors, which are believed to affect the demand for any product. Be as specific as possible about how the variables are going to be measured. Do you anticipate any difficulty in securing such data? Explain.

Determinants of Demand for Furniture	*Suggested Variables to Use in Regression Analysis*
Price	
Tastes and preferences	
Price of related products	
Income	
Cost or availability of credit	
Number of buyers	
Future expectations	
Other possible factors	

3. You are the manager of a large automobile dealership who wants to learn more about the effectiveness of various discounts offered to customers over the past 14 months. Following are the average negotiated price for each month and the quantities sold of a basic model (adjusted for various options) over this period of time.
   a. Graph this information on a scatter plot. Estimate the demand equation. What do the regression results indicate about the desirability of discounting the price? Explain.

Month	*Price*	*Quantity*
Jan.	12,500	15
Feb.	12,200	17
Mar.	11,900	16
Apr.	12,000	18
May	11,800	20
June	12,500	18
July	11,700	22
Aug.	12,100	15
Sept.	11,400	22
Oct.	11,400	25
Nov.	11,200	24
Dec.	11,000	30
Jan.	10,800	25
Feb.	10,000	28

   b. What other factors besides price might be included in this equation? Do you foresee any difficulty in obtaining these additional data or incorporating them in the regression analysis?
4. The maker of a leading brand of low-calorie microwavable food estimated the following demand equation for its product using data from 26 supermarkets around the country for the month of April:

$$\begin{array}{cccccccc} Q = & -\ 5{,}200 & -\ 42P & +\ 20P_X & +\ 52I & +\ 0.20A & +\ 0.25M \\ & (2{,}002) & (17.5) & (6.2) & (25) & (0.09) & (0.21) \end{array}$$

$$R^2 = .55 \qquad n = 26 \qquad F = 4.88$$

Assume the following values for the independent variables:

Q = quantity sold per month
P (in cents) = price of the product = 500
P_X (in cents) = price of leading competitor's product = 600

I (in dollars) = per capita income of the standard metropolitan statistical area (SMSA) in which the supermarket is located = 5,500

A (in dollars) = monthly advertising expenditure = 10,000

M = number of microwave ovens sold in the SMSA in which the supermarket is located = 5,000

Using this information, answer the following questions:

a. Compute elasticities for each of the variables.

b. How concerned do you think this company would be about the impact of a recession on its sales? Explain.

c. Do you think that this firm should cut its price to increase its market share? Explain.

d. What proportion of the variation in sales is explained by the independent variables in the equations? How confident are you about this answer? Explain.

5. A manufacturer of computer workstations gathered average monthly sales figures from its 56 branch offices and dealerships across the country and estimated the following demand for its product:

$$Q = -15,000 - 2.80P + 150A + 0.3P_{\text{pc}} + 0.35P_{\text{m}} + 0.2P_c$$
$$(5,234) \quad (1.29) \quad (175) \quad (0.12) \quad (0.17) \quad (0.13)$$

$$R^2 = .68 \qquad \text{SEE} = 786 \qquad F = 21.25$$

The variables and their assumed values are:

Q = Quantity

P = Price of the basic model = 7,000

A = Advertising expenditures (in thousands) = 52

P_{pc} = Average price of a personal computer = 4,000

P_m = Average price of a minicomputer = 15,000

P_c = average price of a leading competitor's workstation = 8,000

a. Compute the elasticities for each of the variables. On this basis, discuss the relative impact that each variable has on the demand. What implications do these results have for the firm's marketing and pricing policies?

b. Conduct a t-test for the statistical significance of each variable. In each case, state whether a one-tail or two-tail test is required. What difference, if any, does it make to use a one-tail versus a two-tail test on the results? Discuss the results of the t-tests in light of the policy implications mentioned.

c. Suppose a manager evaluating these results suggests that interest rates and the performance of the computer (typically measured in millions of instructions per second, or MIPS) are important determinants of the demand for workstations and must therefore be included in the study. How would you respond to this suggestion? Elaborate.

6. Deck & Blacker is a maker of small kitchen appliances. Its economist estimates the following demand for toaster ovens using data gathered over 16 quarters from 10 major retail distributors of its product. This type of sample, which involves the use of cross-sectional and times series data, is referred to as a *pooled sample.* On the basis of this pooled sample of 160 observations, the economist estimated the following equation:

$$\begin{array}{llllll} Q = 40 & - \ 1.1P & + \ 1.5A & + \ 0.32I & + \ 0.5H & + \ 0.1P_c \\ (2.5) & (0.9) & (0.6) & (0.12) & (0.17) & (0.75) \end{array}$$

$$R^2 = .91 \qquad \text{SEE} = 2.8 \qquad F = 311.43$$

The variables and the values inserted into the equation for purposes of forecasting are as follows:

Q = Quantity demanded, in thousands
P = Price, in dollars = 55
A = Advertising expenditures, in thousands = 20
I = Average household income, in thousands = 31
H = Total number of residential sales, in thousands = 10
P_c = Price of leading competitor, in dollars = 50

a. Should this company try to market its toaster ovens in "upscale" gourmet shops? Explain.
b. How concerned should this company be about price discounts by its leading competitor? Explain.
c. How effective do you think advertising is for this company?
d. Should this company consider discounting its price in order to gain market share at the expense of its competitors? Explain.
e. Assuming the values of the variables given, indicate the 95 percent confidence interval of the forecast demand for toaster ovens.

7. You are given the following demand for European luxury automobiles:

$$Q = 1000P^{0.93}\ P_a^{0.75}\ P_j^{1.2}\ I^{1.6}$$

where P = Price of European luxury cars
P_a = Price of American luxury cars
P_j = Price of Japanese luxury cars
I = Annual income of car buyers

Assume that each of the coefficients is statistically significant (i.e., that they passed the t-test). On the basis of the information given, answer the following questions:

a. Comment on the degree of substitutability between European and American luxury cars and between European and Japanese luxury cars. Explain some possible reasons for the results in the equation.
b. Comment on the coefficient for the income variable. Is this result what you would expect? Explain.
c. Comment on the coefficient of the European car price variable. Is that what you would expect? Explain.

CHAPTER 6

Forecasting

The Situation

Frank Robinson, recently brought into Global Foods, Inc., to build a forecasting department, finds his new position to be very challenging and quite interesting. However, he also knows that forecasting, even in the relatively stable soft drink industry, can be a thankless task. From various forecast requests on his desk, he pulls out the one for the company's lemon-lime soda, Citronade, a brand recently purchased from an older, established company. He has been asked to estimate sales for the next year, and the deadline for his report is nearing. He has annual sales data for the last 11 years, and he also has sales data by quarter. In an industry where sales show considerable increases during the summer months, a forecast that estimates sales for the seasons of the year is very important.[1]

Frank first looks at the annual data, and he quickly computes year-to-year changes. These numbers are shown in Table 6.1. He notices that, although sales were up in each of the years, the percentage growth from

[1]Sales forecasts for a "real" company are made on a monthly, not a quarterly, basis. But for the purposes of this text, quarterly data will be utilized. This is done to economize on the quantity of data used. The methods employed in the analysis of the data are identical whether quarterly or monthly figures are employed.

(Continued)

year to year appears to have a declining trend. He will have to consider this phenomenon when he makes his forecast.

Quarterly data are shown in Table 6.2. As he looks over these numbers, Frank realizes that he has several busy days ahead of him.

Table 6.1 Sales of Citronade (in Thousands of Cases)

Year	*Annual Sales*	*Change*	*Percent Change*
1980	3,892		
1981	4,203	311	8.0
1982	4,477	274	6.5
1983	4,810	333	7.4
1984	5,132	322	6.7
1985	5,407	275	5.4
1986	5,726	319	5.9
1987	6,023	297	5.2
1988	6,360	337	5.6
1989	6,641	281	4.4
1990	6,954	313	4.7

Table 6.2 Quarterly Sales of Citronade, 1980–1990 (in Thousands of Cases)

Year	*First Quarter*	*Second Quarter*	*Third Quarter*	*Fourth Quarter*	*Total*
1980	842	939	1,236	875	3,892
1981	907	1,017	1,331	948	4,203
1982	953	1,103	1,406	1,015	4,477
1983	1,047	1,180	1,505	1,078	4,810
1984	1,124	1,267	1,576	1,165	5,132
1985	1,167	1,340	1,670	1,230	5,407
1986	1,255	1,403	1,766	1,302	5,726
1987	1,311	1,495	1,837	1,380	6,023
1988	1,390	1,565	1,940	1,465	6,360
1989	1,455	1,649	2,026	1,511	6,641
1990	1,536	1,714	2,103	1,601	6,954

Introduction

One of the authors remembers a poster he saw, many years ago, on the wall of the office of the director of market research of a large manufacturing corporation. It said: "Forecasting is very difficult, especially into the future." One could add: "Accurate forecasting is even more difficult." Certainly, there is a great deal of truth in this statement. Nevertheless, forecasting has become a necessity not only in business but in our daily lives. Many of us eagerly watch the weather forecasts on television, even though we know how inaccurate they tend to be. A large number of people follow the forecasts of their stock market gurus, whose track records of accuracy are probably at best mediocre.

Indeed, in a less formal sense, we all make forecasts in our everyday lives. Buying a lottery ticket or betting on a horse involves a forecast. Even a simple morning decision of whether or not to carry an umbrella to work is a forecast regarding the probability of a rainy day. Thus, forecasting is an integral part of our daily activities, and of course, it is an even more important component of the activities of organizations, whether business, government, or nonprofit institutions. Among the reasons for the growing importance of forecasting are:[2]

1. Since organizations and their environments are becoming larger and more complex, decision makers need help in weighting many factors to arrive at decisions whose results have ever-increasing impacts.
2. A rapidly changing environment requires the ability to understand changing relationships among various factors that affect a firm.
3. Systematic decision making often requires explicit justification of actions by decision makers.
4. The need to utilize existing resources efficiently and to acquire appropriate amounts of additional resources requires maximum information about the corporation's future.

One of the major roles of forecasting is to decrease the uncertainty with which a decision maker acts. But no amount of additional expense will completely remove uncertainty. Managers who use forecasts in their work "need to develop realistic expectations as to what forecasting can and cannot do."[3] "Forecasting is not a substitute for management judgment in decision making; it is simply an aid to that process."[4]

Objectives, Plans, Forecasts

Before we discuss the things that are forecast and methods of forecasting, a brief digression is needed to define and distinguish some business terms.

A business firm operates in such a way as to achieve set objectives. Plans are constructed and implemented to achieve these objectives. Forecasts are used both in setting objectives and in creating plans. Obviously, forecasts are intimately connected with objective setting and planning, but the functions are not identical.

The setting of objectives by a corporation was discussed in Chapter 2. Objectives (or goals) are usually stated in terms of revenue or profit growth, profitability or return on investment, and resource growth and deployment. In order that corporate management can set reasonable targets for its objectives, it must have available the relevant forecasts, both for the short and long terms. Thus, corporate management will consult with economists to obtain the best estimates of how the economy (e.g., gross national product) will behave over the relevant time period. In addition, management will be interested in the forecast of sales for the company's industry. These forecasts are then utilized in the process of objective setting for the corporation as a whole and for its component parts.

---

[2]The introductory sections of this chapter draw heavily on one of the leading books in the area of forecasting, Steven C. Wheelwright and Spyros Makridakis, *Forecasting Methods for Management*, 4th ed., New York: John Wiley and Sons, 1985.

[3]Ibid., p. 30

[4]Ibid., p. 35.

Both short-term and long-term objectives will be established. When these objectives are communicated from corporate headquarters to the various profit centers, the process of planning (again, short-term or long-term) begins.

Corporate planners in all areas—sales, human resources, facilities, manufacturing, finance—will utilize an array of forecasts in constructing the various portions of the plan. Actually, a forecast may show what will happen under certain conditions and assumptions. In such cases, a planner works with these forecasts but also designs actions that may counteract or revise the forecast. If, for example, a forecast shows an unfavorable trend in the sales of a particular product for the next year, the plan may recommend actions that will counteract this prediction. Then, given the new tactics or strategies incorporated into the plan, the original forecast may be superseded by a new, revised forecast, with altered conditions and assumptions.

Subjects of Forecasts

Business utilizes forecasting to obtain information about many subjects. In the final analysis, firms are interested in future sales and profits—the bottom line. But to get there, a large number of forecasts may be necessary. In this section of the chapter, we will outline the various categories of forecasts—from the most macro forecasts down to individual series.

The broadest economic forecast series is the gross national product (GNP), which describes the total production of goods and services in a country. Actually, some measures are available for the world economy (or at least the free-world economy), but these are usually composites of country forecasts. GNP forecasting is usually accomplished with highly complex econometric models that contain hundreds of variables and a huge number of calculations. Some large corporations have economic research departments that develop their own economic forecasts as a basis for corporate planning. Predominantly, however, businesses rely on forecasts made by others and sold as a service. A significant number of consulting organizations produce forecasts and tailor them to the needs of specific clients.

There are also forecasts of GNP components, for instance, consumption expenditure, producer durable equipment expenditure, or residential construction, to name just a few. Thus, a company producing heavy machinery would be interested in data on producer durable equipment and a forest products company in construction statistics. Again, such forecasts could be provided to the company by an outside organization specializing in such activities.

A step down from macro forecasting is the industry forecast. The future sales of the soft drink industry as a whole would be included here. Of course, a forecast could also relate to the automobile industry, the steel industry, or any other. In addition, concern may lie with the future sales of a particular product within an industry, such as club soda or compact automobiles.

Finally, the subject of interest may be the sales of a specific product of a specific firm, such as the diet cola of Global Foods' soft drink division.

The preceding discussion of the forecast hierarchy has concentrated on sales forecasts. But the future estimates for a given firm could be for costs and expenses (in total or for various categories), employment requirements, square feet of facilities utilized, or anything else of importance to a company.

Our major emphasis in this chapter will be with forecasting the sales of a particular product of our hypothetical soft drink manufacturer. The forecast of GNP and its constituent parts will be considered to be assumptions underlying the firm's specific product forecast.

Demand Estimating and Demand Forecasting

In the preceding chapter, regression analysis and demand estimation was discussed. Is there a difference between demand forecasting and demand estimating? There is, of course, a great deal of similarity between the two concepts. Each serves to increase the information available to decision makers. The difference lies largely in the ultimate purpose of the analysis.

The demand estimating technique will be used by a manager interested in probing the effect on the demand (or quantity demanded) of a change in one or more of the independent variables. Thus, a pricing manager may want to know the impact on the sales of the company's club soda when there is a price change, or when a competitor's price changes. Also, this manager may be interested in the effect of changes in the company's advertising expenses.

On the other hand, forecasting puts less emphasis on explaining the specific causes of demand changes and more on obtaining information regarding future levels of sales activity, given the most likely assumptions about the independent variables. Such information is then used in the construction of the company's plan. Indeed, in some cases, to be discussed later in this chapter, forecasting is achieved without the introduction of any causal factors; future sales are predicted solely by projecting the past into the future.

Prerequisites of a Good Forecast

Certain conditions should be met by any good forecast. Unfortunately, this is not always possible.

First, a particular forecast must be consistent with other parts of the business. If you forecast 10 percent growth in the shipments of your product for next year, you must make sure that your manufacturing facilities have sufficient capacity to produce this increased amount, and that the additions to the labor force necessary to produce and sell this increased amount are in the company's plan for next year.

Second, a good forecast should usually be based on adequate knowledge of the relevant past. There are, of course, exceptions to this rule. Sometimes past experience is of no help in predicting future demand. This is the case if conditions have undergone a radical change. Thus, after World War II, forecasts for automobile and appliance sales could not rely on sales data of recent years, since these items were not produced during the country's involvement in the war. Moreover, any sales patterns that held for the pre-war years could not be applied, since in 1946, when automobiles again rolled off the production line, the average age of the existing automobile stock was considerably higher than was customary, people had old cars or none at all, returning soldiers were new additions to the car market, and many people had saved up large amounts of money during the war years (when they were unable to purchase many major items) and were ready to spend.

In other instances, there may be no past on which to fall back. This could be the case for a new product or a technological breakthrough. Despite these exceptions, in most cases, past sales give a good indication of what will happen in the future. Therefore, it is usually important that the forecaster be very familiar with prior sales patterns and their variations.

Third, a forecast should take into consideration the economic and political environment. If significant changes in economic conditions or in political institutions are expected within the forecast period, these events must be accounted for, since they may have a substantial effect on the future of the business.[5]

One other prerequisite, a rather obvious one, must be added. A forecast must be timely. Sometimes accuracy may have to be sacrificed to achieve timeliness. It serves no purpose to deliver an extremely accurate forecast that is too late to be acted upon. As obvious as this point may be, it cannot be stressed strongly enough. Forecasters are often tempted to polish and improve their forecasts. Not only can such embellishment add costs that may not be worth the improvement in accuracy, it may also delay the publication of the estimate. This is particularly important at turning points in the forecast series. If the forecast is published too late to issue a warning, its great accuracy will be worthless.

Forecasting Techniques

There are many different forecasting methods. One of the challenges facing a forecaster is choosing the right technique. The appropriate method depends on the subject matter to be forecast and on the forecaster, but we can discuss some of the factors that enter into consideration.[6]

1. The item to be forecast. Is one trying to predict the continuance of a historical pattern, the continuance of a basic relationship, or a turning point?
2. The interaction of the situation with the characteristics of available forecasting methods. The manager must judge the relation between value and cost.

---

[5]Taking potential changes in political institutions into account is of importance to multinational corporations, which operate in a large number of foreign countries, probably including those whose political directions are quite unstable and whose governments may be subject to radical changes.

[6]This section relies heavily on Wheelwright and Makridakis, op. cit., pp. 33–36.

If a less expensive method can be used to achieve the desired results, it certainly should be.
3. The amount of historical data available.
4. The time allowed to prepare the forecast. Selection of a specific method may depend on the urgency of the situation.

One other point about forecasting cost and accuracy should be added here. Generally, when the requirements for forecast accuracy are high, more sophisticated and more complex methods may be used. Such methods are, as a rule, more costly. Thus, a manager will authorize greater expenditures when relatively high accuracy is warranted. However, "Empirical studies have shown that simplicity in forecasting methods is not necessarily a negative characteristic or a detriment with regard to forecasting accuracy. Therefore, the authors would advise against discarding simple methods and moving too quickly to replace them with more complex ones."[7]

Forecasting techniques can be categorized in many ways. We will use the following six categories:

1. Expert opinion
2. Opinion polls and market research
3. Surveys of spending plans
4. Economic indicators
5. Projections
6. Econometric models

As we will see in the following pages, some of the methods can be classified as qualitative, others as quantitative. Qualitative forecasting is based on judgments of individuals or groups. The results of qualitative forecasts may be in numerical form but generally are not based on series of historical data.

Quantitative forecasting, on the other hand, generally utilizes significant amounts of prior data as a basis for prediction. Quantitative techniques can be naive or causal (explanatory). Naive methods project past data into the future without explaining future trends. Of course, causal or explanatory forecasting attempts to explain the functional relationships between the variable to be estimated (the dependent variable) and the variable or variables that account for the changes (the independent variables).

Expert Opinion

Various types of techniques fit into the category of expert opinion. Only a limited number will be discussed here.

One of these methods is called the *jury of executive opinion*. As the name implies, forecasts are generated by a group of corporate executives, who may be

---

[7]Ibid., p. 277. This quote deals with the merits of relatively simple time series methods versus more complex explanatory techniques. "Thus, the evidence suggest that explanatory models do not provide significantly more accurate forecasts than time series methods, even though the former are much more complex and expensive than the latter" (ibid., p. 264).

sitting around a table discussing the particular subject to be forecast. The members of the panel are experts in the subject matter, (representing sales, finance, production, etc.). These panels can be interorganizational (i.e., from different corporations) or intraorganizational (i.e., within one corporation), depending on the breadth of the subject. This technique is used widely and is often quite successful. The major drawback of this approach is that a panel member with a forceful personality but not necessarily the greatest amount of knowledge and judgment may exercise a disproportionate amount of influence.

Another, similar technique involves the solicitation of views of individual salespeople in a company to forecast sales. This approach could have been utilized in the situation outlined at the beginning of the chapter. After all, sales representatives are expected to have a finger on the pulse of the market. The biases inherent in this type of predictive apparatus are, however, obvious. "Often sales people are poor estimators and are either overly optimistic or overly pessimistic. At other times they are unaware of the broad economic patterns that may affect demand."[8] The latter problem can be overcome to some extent by informing the respondents of general economic forecasts.

Another popular method of qualitative forecasting, utilized predominantly in predicting technological trends and changes, is the *Delphi method.* This technique was developed at the Rand Corporation in the 1960s. Delphi uses a panel of experts; however, unlike the jury of executive opinion, the participants do not meet to discuss and agree on a forecast. The entire process is carried out by a sequential series of written questions and answers. The reasons for separating the experts is to avoid the potential pitfall cited previously.

A relatively early Delphi study was that of Gordon and Helmer,[9] which asked experts to forecast six subjects as far as 50 years into the future: scientific breakthroughs, population growth, automation, space progress, probability and prevention of war, and future weapons systems. To arrive at predictions, the Delphi procedure begins by asking (e.g., by letter) the members selected to reply to a set of questions. In this study, the experts were asked to specify what advances in automation would occur over the next 50 years and to estimate the time period of occurrence. When answers were received, a list of the items was compiled and sent back to the panel for further consideration. Several iterations of this procedure were conducted until the range of choices was narrowed and specific time ranking was established. Finally, a consensus (or convergence of opinion) is obtained. But there is no need for unanimity of opinion; the forecast can include a range of opinions.

The Delphi method has been used to advantage in technological predictions and has been applied in business situations as well. A 1971 study sponsored by Corning Glass investigated trends in residential housing in the ensuing 15

---

[8]Ibid., p. 33.

[9]Gordon, T. J. and O. Helmer, *Report on a Long-Range Forecasting Study,* Rand Corporation, P-2982, September 1964. (Described in Harold Sackman, *Delphi Critique,* Lexington, Mass.: Lexington Books, 1975, pp. 37–39, 104.)

years. Included were forecasts of housing supply and demand, costs, monetary aspects, among others.[10]

Still, Delphi suffers from many drawbacks: "insufficient reliability, oversensitivity to ambiguity of questions, different results when different experts are used, difficulty in assessing the degree of expertise, and the impossibility of predicting the unexpected."[11] Given the long-term nature of Delphi predictions, these criticisms do not appear to differ greatly from those leveled against forecasts in general.

Opinion Polls and Market Research

You are probably familiar with opinion polling, since most of us have at one time or another been subjected to telephone calls or written questionnaires asking us to assess a product—or sometimes a political issue. Rather than soliciting experts, opinion polls survey a population whose activity may determine future trends. Opinion polls can be very useful since they may identify changes in trends, which, as we will see later in this chapter, may escape detection when quantitative (both naive and explanatory) methods are used.

Opinion polls are usually conducted on samples of the population. Choice of the sample is of utmost importance, since the use of an unrepresentative sample may give completely misleading results. Further, the questions must be stated simply and clearly in order that they can be easily interpreted by respondents. Often a question is repeated in a somewhat different form so that the replies can be cross-checked.

Market research is closely related to opinion polling. Thorough descriptions of this method can be found in marketing texts. Market research will indicate "not only why the consumer is or is not likely to buy, but also who the consumer is, how he or she [will use] the product, and what characteristics the consumer thinks are most important in the purchasing decision."[12] This information can then be used to estimate the market potential and possibly the market share.

Surveys of Spending Plans

The use of surveys is very similar to opinion polling and market research, and the methods of data collection are quite alike. However, the specific kinds of surveys described here merit a separate section.

Whereas opinion polling and market research usually deal with specific products and are often conducted by individual firms interested in their own markets, the the following types of surveys seek information about "macro-type" data relating to the economy. Thus, they can be a tool for businesses seeking to predict the market for products or services.

---

[10]Selwyn Enzer, *Some Prospects for Residential Housing by 1985*, Institute for the Future, R-13, January 1971. (Cited in Sackman, op. cit,. p. 99.)

[11]Wheelwright and Makridakis, op. cit,. p. 290.

[12]Ibid., p. 316.

Three major categories of surveys are capital expenditures, consumer sentiment, and inventories.

1. *Capital expenditure surveys.* Several organizations conduct and publish surveys estimating future expenditures on plant and equipment. We will describe briefly the three that are probably the most used.
   a. *U.S. Department of Commerce, Bureau of the Census.* This plant and equipment expenditure survey is published in the *Commerce News* by the Economics and Statistics Administration of the Bureau of the Census. Data are presented for a large number of manufacturing and nonmanufacturing industries. The actual quarterly data are updated, and estimates are furnished. For instance the April 1991 publication showed, among others, the following data for new plant and equipment expenditures:

Actual fourth quarter 1990	$529.02 billion
Actual year 1990	532.96
Estimates:	
First quarter 1991	540.82
Second quarter 1991	547.91
Second half 1991	548.46
Year 1991	546.41

   All of these data are shown at an annual rate. The data are in current dollars and are seasonally adusted.
   b. *McGraw-Hill/Business Week.* McGraw-Hill, a book and magazine publisher, surveys the investment plans of large and medium-sized corporations twice each year. Results are published in the November and April issues of *Business Week*.
   c. *The Conference Board.* This survey, conducted quarterly, covers capital expenditures and capital appropriations of the 1,000 largest manufacturers. Appropriations represent plans to spend in the future; thus, this measure enables one to estimate actual expenditures with a larger lead time than surveys of expenditures.
2. *Consumer intentions.* Since consumer expenditure is the largest component of the gross national product, changes in consumer attitudes and their effect on subsequent spending are a crucial variable in the forecasts and plans made by businesses. Firms producing consumer products and services are, of course, affected directly. But companies producing durable equipment will also feel the effect of any changes in this important segment of the economy. Two well-known surveys are reviewed here.
   a. *Survey of Consumers, Survey Research Center, University of Michigan.* This is probably the best known among the consumer surveys conducted. Initiated in 1946, it is conducted monthly. It contains some 40 questions covering personal finances, business cycle developments, and buying conditions. The questions can be classified into three broad categories:

Personal finance conditions—current and expected
General business conditions—in one year and in five years
Buying conditions—current

The answers to these questions are summarized into indexes (with the first quarter 1966 = 100). There is an overall index of consumer sentiment and a large number of indexes for replies to the more detailed questions.

Subscribers to this service receive analyses of the most recent surveys as well as a booklet of tables and charts showing trends.

b. *The Conference Board.* The Conference Board publishes its survey of consumer attitudes and buying plans monthly. Composite indexes are published for overall consumer confidence and for buying plans. More detailed data are shown for the appraisal of current and future business conditions, employment and income, and buying plans (within six months) for automobiles, homes, and major appliances.

3. *Inventories.* Expectations regarding sales and inventory levels are surveyed and published by the U.S. Department of Commerce, McGraw-Hill, and the National Association of Purchasing Agents. The last is based on a large sample of purchasing executives and is reported montly.

Economic Indicators

The difficult task of predicting changes in the direction of activity has been discussed previously. Some of the qualitative techniques discussed in the preceding sections are aimed at identifying such turns. The barometric technique of economic indicators is specifically designed to alert business to changes in economic conditions.

The success of the indicator approach to forecasting depends on the ability to identify one or more historical economic series whose direction not only correlates with but precedes that of the series to be predicted. Such indicators are used widely in forecasting general economic activity. Any one indicator series may not be very reliable; however, a composite of "leading" indicators can be used to predict. Such a series should exhibit a slowing (and an actual decrease) before overall economic activity turns down, and it should start to rise while the economy is still experiencing low activity.

Forecasting on the basis of indicators has been practiced in an informal fashion for many years. It is said that Andrew Carnegie used to assess the future of steel demand by counting the number of chimneys emitting smoke in Pittsburgh. Much of the work of establishing economic indicators was done at the National Bureau of Economic Research, a private organization. Today, economic indicator data are published monthly by the U.S. Department of Commerce Bureau of Economic Analysis in the *Survey of Current Business.* These monthly data are reported in the press and are widely followed.

There are three major series: leading, coincident and lagging indicators. As their names imply, the first tells us where we are going, the second where we are, and the third where we have been. Although the leading indicator series is probably the most important and is the one watched most closely, the other two are also meaningful. The coincident indicators identify peaks and troughs, and the lagging series confirms upturns and downturns in economic activity.

Many individual series are tracked monthly in the *Survey of Current Business,* but only a limited number are used in the construction of the three major indexes. The leading indicator index contains 11 series, and the coincident and lagging indicators are made up of 4 and 7 components, respectively. All the series making up the indexes are listed in Table 6.3.

It is rather evident why some of the indicators qualify as leading. They represent not present expenditures, but commitments indicating that economic activity will take place in the future. Among these are manufacturers' new orders, contracts, and orders for plant and equipment, and new private housing starts. Others are not quite as obvious. But one would expect employers to increase the hours of their work force as they increase production before committing themselves to new hiring. Stock market prices and money supply are usually thought to precede cycles.[13]

Table 6.3 Economic Indicators

Leading Indicators

1. Average weekly hours of production or nonsupervisory workers, manufacturing
2. Average weekly initial claims for unemployment insurance, state programs
3. Manufacturers' new orders in 1982 dollars, consumer goods and materials industries
4. Vendor performance, slower deliveries diffusion index
5. Contracts and orders for plant and equipment in 1982 dollars
6. Index of new private housing units authorized by local building permits
7. Change in manufacturers' unfilled orders in 1982 dollars, durable goods industries
8. Change in sensitive material prices
9. Index of stock prices, 500 common stocks
10. Money supply (M2), in 1982 dollars
11. Index of consumer expectations, University of Michigan

Coincident Indicators

1. Employees on nonagricultural payrolls
2. Index of industrial production
3. Personal income less transfer payments, in 1982 dollars
4. Manufacturing and trade sales in 1982 dollars

Lagging Indicators

1. Change in index of unit labor cost per unit of output, manufacturing
2. Ratio, manufacturing and trade inventories to sales, in 1982 dollars
3. Average duration of unemployment
4. Ratio, consumer installment credit outstanding to personal income
5. Commercial and industrial loans outstanding in 1982 dollars
6. Average prime rate charged by banks
7. Change in consumer price index for services

[13]For a more complete discussion of the economic rationale for each of the indicators, see Ronald A. Ratti, "A Descriptive Analysis of Economic Indicators," *Federal Reserve Bank of St. Louis Review,* January 1985, pp. 14–24.

Putting together the 11 series to obtain an overall index of leading indicators (as well as the other two indexes) involves a number of statistical steps. First, each individual series is standardized to avoid undue influence of the more volatile components. Each series is then assigned a weight within the composite index.[14] Then the leading and lagging indexes are adjusted to facilitate comparison with the coincident index. A trend adjustment is also made. The index has a base period of 1982 = 100.

How good a forecaster are the leading indicators? To answer this question, we must establish some criteria. First, how many months of change in the direction of the index are necessary before a turn in economic activity is expected? A general rule of thumb is that if, after a period of increases, the leading indicator index sustains three consecutive declines, a recession (or at least a slowing) will follow. On this basis, the leading indicators have predicted each recession since 1948.[15] Second, how much warning do the indicators give (i.e., by how many months do they lead) of the onset of a recession? Since 1948, the three-dip sequence has preceded the beginning of a recession by anywhere from 0 to 18 months.[16] Another way to evaluate the amount of lead time is to refer to the Survey of Current Business, which shows the number of months between the turning point in the index and the change in the direction of general economic activity:

Cycle	*Peak*	*Trough*
1953–54	5	6
1957–58	20	2
1960–61	10	10
1969–70	8	1
1973–75	8	1
1980–80	15	2
1981–82	2	10

It is obvious that the lead times vary considerably. So we can sum up by observing that leading indicators do warn us about changes in the direction of economic activity, but they really do not forecast lead times reliably. If this were the only criticism that could be leveled against this barometer of the economy, we could probably cope with it quite easily. Unfortunately, there are other, probably more severe, drawbacks:

1. In some instances, the leading indicator index has forecast a recession when none ensued. For instance, the index declined for several months in 1966. Although a decline in the growth of the economy (a growth recession)

[14] Ibid., p. 17. This article has a detailed description of how the indexes are constructed.

[15] Ibid.

[16] Ibid.

followed, there was no "official" recession.[17] A similar event occurred in 1961.

2. A decline (or a rebound after a decline) in the index, even if it forecasts correctly, does not indicate the precise size of the decline (or rise) in economic activity.
3. The data are frequently subject to revision in the ensuing months. It is not uncommon for a particular month to show a drop in the index only to have the revisions change the direction of the index one or two months later.[18] Thus, the final data may signal a different future from the one suggested by the originally published data.

The preceding criticisms of this forecasting method are certainly significant. But they indicate that this technique should be improved rather than discarded. The existing indicators are reevaluated periodically, and new ones are developed. As the structure of the economy changes, some of the indicators lose their relevance. The present index may be overly weighted toward manufacturing activities and neglects service industries, which make up a continuously increasing portion of our economy. The growing importance of international trade and capital flows suggests the inclusion in the index of a series reflecting these activities. Improved collection methods for some of the series could decrease the need for and the magnitude of revisions.[19] In the meantime, the use of leading indicators has spread to a large number of foreign countries.

In short, despite its drawbacks, the index of leading indicators (and the other two indexes as well) is a useful tool for businesspeople and will continue to be closely watched. The fact that the agencies publishing such indexes must continually strive to revise and improve their techniques does not make this forecasting method inferior to the other measurements of economic variables and the methods employed to forecast economic activity. As always, reliance on this method must be tempered by the knowledge of its imperfections.

Projections

Earlier in this chapter, we discussed several qualitative methods of forecasting. We then moved to a discussion of economic indicators, a quantitative method. To continue the presentation of quantitative techniques, we now turn to projections, which we previously identified as a naive form of forecasting. Several different methods will be discussed, but they all have a common denom-

---

[17] An "official" recession is pronounced by the National Bureau of Economic Research, which dates peaks and troughs.

[18] For instance, the November 1987 index showed a decline of 1.7 percent, reflecting the large drop in the stock market. At the same time, however, the Department of Commerce revised the October index from a 0.2 percent decline to a 0.2 percent increase and the September index from unchanged to a 0.2 percent increase.

[19] Geoffrey H. Moore, one of the prominent authorities in this area, wrote a brief article ("Those Misleading Economic Indicators," *New York Times* March 16, 1986) addressing these questions and problems.

inator: past data are projected into the future without taking into consideration reasons for the change. It is simply assumed that past trends will continue. Three projection techniques will be examined here:

1. Compound growth rate
2. Visual time series projection
3. Time series projection using the least squares method

If annual data are to be forecast, any of these three methods can be used. However, more frequent data, such as monthly or quarterly, may be necessary, as is the case in the situation presented at the beginning of the chapter. If the monthly or quarterly data exhibit no large, repetitive fluctuations, then trend analysis can still be used. But if there appear to be seasonal patterns in the data, a smoothing method must be applied. The moving-average method of smoothing will be discussed along with the least squares time series projection.

CONSTANT COMPOUND GROWTH RATE. The constant compound growth rate technique is extremely simple and is widely used in business situations. When quick estimates of the future are needed, this method has some merit. And, as we will find out, it can be quite appropriate when the variable to be predicted increases at a constant percentage (as opposed to constant absolute changes). But care must be exercised not to apply this technique when it is not warranted.

The most rudimentary application of this method is to take the first and last years of past data, and to calculate the constant growth rate necessary to go from the amount in the first period to the amount in the last. This problem is solved in the same way as if we were to calculate how much a specific sum deposited in an interest-bearing account grows in a certain number of years at a constant rate of interest that is compounded annually.[20] Suppose $1,000 is deposited at the beginning of the year and earns interest at the rate of 7 percent. How much will this deposit be worth at the end of the year? That is easy: $1,000 plus the 7 percent interest. The solution can be expressed in shorthand mathematical notation as follows:

$$E = B + Bi = B(1 + i)$$

where E = Account balance at the end of the year
B = Original deposit
i = Rate of interest

Thus,

$$1,000(1.07) = 1,070$$

Now, if this year-end amount remains in the account for another year, the entire $1,070 will earn interest, of $74.90. Thus, the balance at the end of the

[20] Presently banks compound interest on their accounts more frequently than once a year. But annual compounding will be used here to keep the procedure simple.

second year will be $1,144.90. The second-year balance could have been obtained directly by compounding two years of interest on the original deposit, as follows:

$$1,000 \times 1.07 \times 1.07$$

or

$$1,000 \times (1.07)^2$$

If the deposit is left in the account for any number of years, the ending balance can be found with the following equation:

$$E = B(1 + i)^n$$

where n represents the number of years. If n is large, the calculation can become somewhat complex. Table A.1 in the appendix to this book will make the computation much easier.[21] To find the amount to which a deposit of $1,000 will grow in 10 years at 7 percent interest, look up the factor in the table and multiply it by 1,000. The factor is 1.9672; therefore, the balance after 10 years will be $1,967.20.

Frank Robinson can use the same table to make his projection for Citronade sales. The first period and the last period amounts are known, and the missing number is the growth rate, which, of course, has the same meaning as the interest rate in the preceding example. To solve for the growth rate, the previous formula is revised as follows:

$$(1 + i)^n = E/B$$

Applying this formula to the 1980 and 1990 sales of Citronade from Table 6.1,

$$6,954/3,892 = 1.7867$$

Since there are 10 years intervening between the two sales periods, the growth rate can be found by entering the table at 10 periods and moving to the right until a number close to 1.7867 is found. At 6 percent, the factor is 1.7908. Thus, the growth rate of Citronade over the last 10 years is just under 6 percent.[22]

Can therefore, next year's sales be estimated at 7,371,000 cases, a 6 percent increase? Looking at the year to year increases in Table 6.1, Robinson noticed that the growth rate achieved in the early years (through 1984) has not been approached since. Whereas during the first four years of the available data, growth ranged between 6.5 and 8 percent, the second four years registered increases between 5 and 6 percent, and the rise in the last two years was less than 5 percent. Growth has been declining over the 10-year period.

This illustrates a major problem that is frequently encountered when the compound growth rate method of projection is employed. The only two numbers considered in determining the growth rate were the first and the last; any trends or fluctuations between the original and terminal dates are disregarded. The result obtained is merely an average of the annual growth from beginning to end.

[21]A large assortment of hand-held calculators will also perform this calculation.

[22]A more exact answer, obtained either with a calculator or through interpolation, is 5.98 percent.

Thus, when year-to-year percentage growth is not stable, any estimates based on this result can be misleading.

Figure 6.1 illustrates what may happen. The data plotted in the graphs show a strong increase in each year except for the last value, which may have been caused by an exceptional occurrence such as a severe recession or a strike. If the compound growth rate approach is used, any forecast based only on the first and last observations may be quite misleading.

One method to identify this problem is to scan the annual increases. This is what was done here. But sometimes, especially if there is a long series of numbers, the pattern may not be quite as obvious. In such cases, charting the observations on graph paper is helpful. This method will be discussed in the next section.

In summary, the compound growth rate (or CGR, as it is popularly known) method can often be useful, particularly when results are required quickly and a rough approximation is sufficient. But its drawbacks are significant and must always be considered.

VISUAL TIME SERIES PROJECTIONS. A series of numbers is often difficult to interpret. Plotting the observations on a sheet of graph paper can be very helpful since the shape of a complicated series is more easily discerned from a picture.

Frank Robinson did just that. He had two types of graph paper available to him. One was the familiar kind, with arithmetic scales on both axes, which he used to plot the annual data of Citronade sales, as shown in Figure 6.2. The observations appear to form a relatively straight line. As a matter of fact, one could easily draw a straight line just by putting a ruler through the observations, so that some points fall above and some below the line. Projecting the line to 1991 would give us a fairly good prediction—if the growth, in absolute number of cases, reflects past increases. The reason that a straight line is such a good

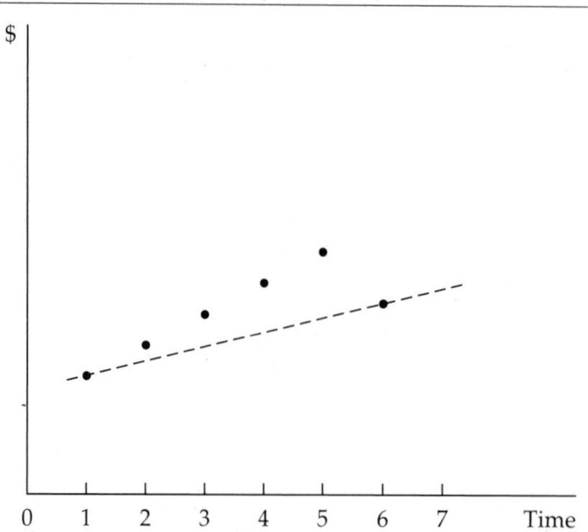

Figure 6.1 An Example in which the Constant Compound Growth Rate Approach Would Be Misleading

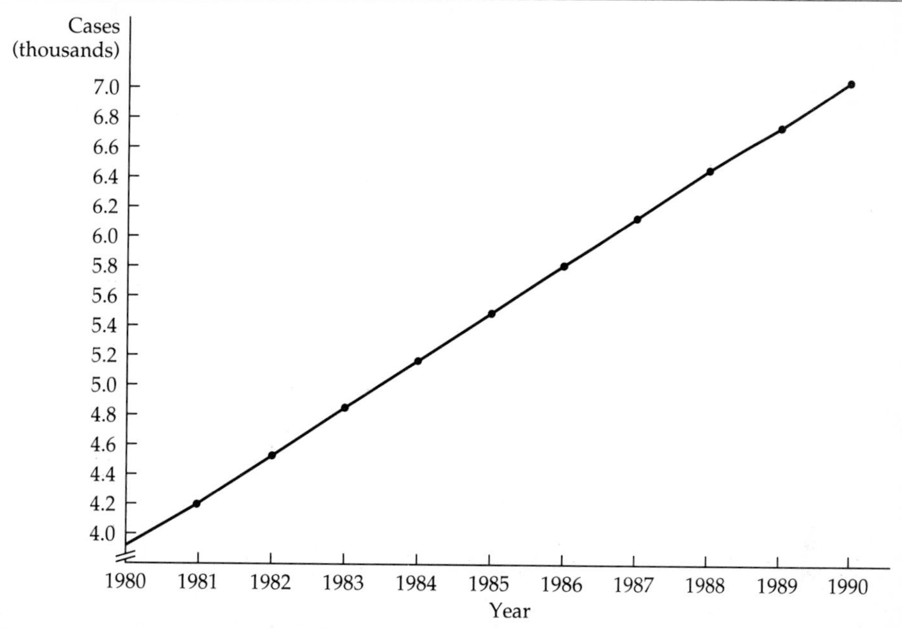

Figure 6.2 Annual Sales of Citronade (1980–1990)

fit is that the absolute annual increases in sales fluctuate around their mean of 306,000 cases without exhibiting any kind of trend (see Figure 6.3).

There is another type of graph paper often used to observe trends—semilogarithmic. This graph has an arithmetic scale along the horizontal axis, but the vertical axis transforms numbers into a logarithmic format. Equal distances between numbers on the vertical scale represent a doubling. Thus, the distance between 1 and 2 is the same as that between 2 and 4, between 4 and 8, and so on.[23] In the semi-logarithmic format, if observations that exhibit a constant growth rate are plotted, they will fall on a straight line.[24] The data for Citronade,

[23]Incidentally, the point of origin on the vertical axis is 1, not 0.

[24]A simple example will explain why a constant percentage growth rate shows up as a straight line on a logarithmic scale. Assume that the first period's quantity is 100 and that grows by 20 percent each year. Then translate each number into a common logarithm, and calculate the differences for each series:

Raw Data	*Absolute Difference*	*Logarithm*	*Difference in Logarithms*
100		2.0	
120	20	2.0792	0.0792
144	24	2.1584	0.0792
172.8	28.8	2.2375	0.0791
207.36	34.56	2.3167	0.0792

While the absolute differences increase, the differences between logarithms remain constant. Thus, if the vertical scale of a graph is shown in terms of logarithms, constant percentage differences will plot as a straight line.

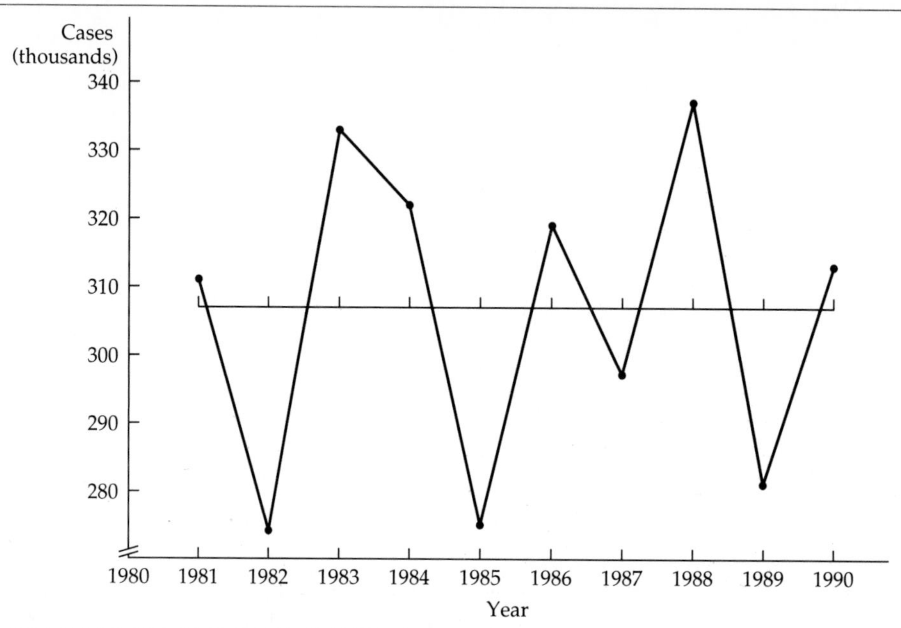

Figure 6.3 Annual Increase in Citronade Sales (1980–1990)

as was mentioned previously, appear to have a downward trend in growth. As can be seen in Figure 6.4, where the annual observations are plotted, a line drawn through the points indicates growth at a decreasing rate. Thus, if Frank

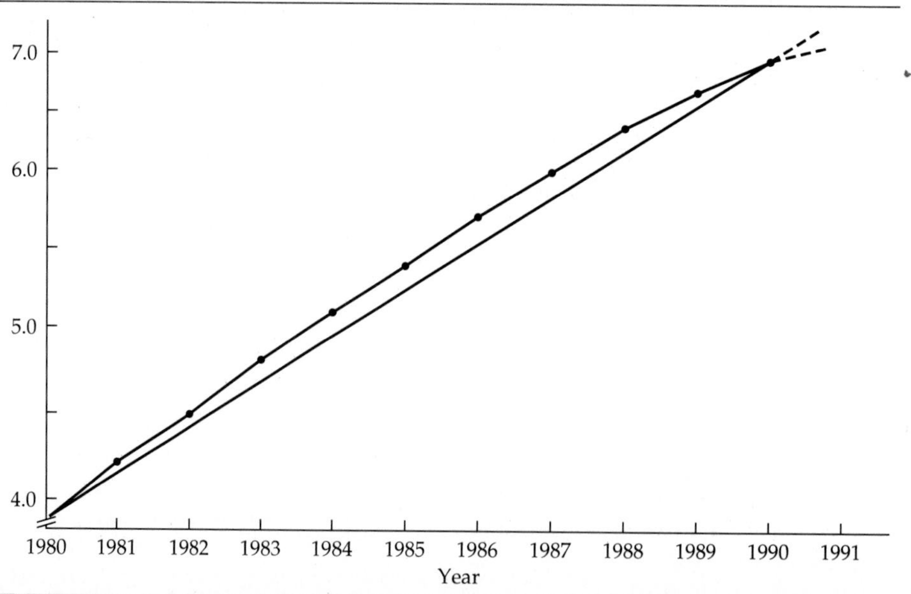

Figure 6.4 Semilogarithmic Graph of Changes in Citronade Sales

Robinson were to base his projections on this line, he would have to continue the curve on its decreasing slope.

Frank found that the compound growth rate for Citronade sales from 1980 to 1990 was 6 percent. A line representing an annual growth rate of 6 percent in Figure 6.4, is a straight line, since constant growth is assumed. The contrast between a line drawn through the observations and the 6 percent line is obvious. A projection of the straight line would result in a higher sales estimate for 1991 than if the decreasing year-to-year percentage of growth were taken into consideration.

Thus, a quick estimate of next year's sales can be made by just extending one of the lines that were drawn. If the average of the 10 years of absolute growth—306,000—were used, 1991 sales would be 7,260,000 cases, a 4.4 percent increase from the 1990 total of 6,954,000 cases. This would correspond closely to the value produced by extending the line formed by the acutal observations in Figure 6.4, which exhibits an increase at a decreasing rate. Using the compound growth rate of 6 percent—plotted as a straight line in Figure 6.4—would indicate sales of about 7,371,000 cases and would, as previously discussed, result in too high an estimate.

Although under some circumstances this type of forecast may be sufficiently accurate, most forecasters would feel that a more detailed estimate—particularly given the seasonal nature of soft drink demand—is essential. Thus, Frank will move on to perform a time series analysis using a least squares equation, and also to identify the seasonal pattern of Citronade sales.

TIME SERIES ANALYSIS. We discussed the projection of a time series visually, that is, by inspecting the past observations and continuing the line formed by them into the future. In this section we will continue to explore the time series method of projection. However, instead of visual estimation, a more precise statistical technique will be employed: the method of least squares. This method was introduced in the last chapter and was used to estimate demand. Whereas demand estimation requires the use of one or more independent variables, and the interactive relationship between these variables is of great importance, in the context of time series analysis there is only one independent variable: time. Thus, this system of forecasting is "naive," since it does not explain the reason for the changes; it merely says that the series of numbers to be projected changes as a function of time.

Despite the mechanical nature of this type of forecast, time series analysis has much to recommend it:

1. It is easy to calculate. Presently, a large number of software packages on the market will compute the least squares trend line in various ways—linear, curvilinear, or exponential.
2. It does not require much judgment or analytical skill by the analyst. It merely assumes that the pattern of prior periods will repeat into the future.
3. Unlike visual projection, it describes the line that exhibits the best possible fit for past data. In addition, it provides the analyst with information regarding the statistical errors contained in the results and gives an indication of how statistically significant the results are.

4. Finally, except when an absolute turn in the series occurs, the projection based on this method of analysis is usually reasonably reliable in the short run.

The fact that time series analysis does not take into consideration causative factors does not mean that an analyst using this method should not consider additional information about changes in the underlying forces. Any analyst using this naive method of predicition should try to fine-tune the conclusions based on information that could alter the results.[25]

When data are collected over a number of periods in the past, they usually exhibit four different characteristics:

1. *Trend.* This is the direction of movement of the data over a relatively long period of time, either upward or downward.

2. *Cyclical fluctuations.* These are deviations from the trend due to general economic conditions. For instance, if one were to observe data for the GNP over time, a long-run upward trend would be evident. Also evident in this series would be movement around that trend as the economy rises more quickly or less quickly (or actually declines). Industries may experience peculiar cycles, which may or may not coincide with fluctuations of the economy as a whole.

3. *Seasonal fluctuations.* A pattern that repeats annually is characteristic of many products. Toy sales tend to rise briefly before Christmas. Fashions have spring and fall seasons. In the soft drink industry, the expectation is for higher sales during the warmer periods of the year (i.e., June through September). Obviously, seasonal fluctuations occur more frequently than cyclical swings. Only time series in which data are more frequent than annual (monthly, quarterly) can exhibit seasonal variations.

4. *Irregular.* Departures from the norm may be caused by special events, such as strikes or catastrophes. They occur randomly and do not repeat regularly, if at all, and they certainly cannot be predicted. Actually, these random fluctuations do not have to be caused by any dramatic events. They may just represent "noise" in the series, since events never occur in a completely regular, stable manner.

Thus, time series data can be represented by the following mathematical expression:

$$Y_t = f(T_t, C_t, S_t, R_t)$$

where Y = Actual value of the data in the time series at time t
T_t = Trend component at t
C_t = Cyclical component at t
S_t = Seasonal component at t
R_t = Random component at t

[25]It is essential that all changes and alterations are well documented by the analyst so that a trail to his or her reasoning can be established.

The specific form of this equation could be additive:

$$Y_t = T_t + C_t + S_t + R_t$$

Other forms could also exist. The specification most commonly used is the multiplicative form:

$$Y_t = (T_t)(C_t)(S_t)(R_t)$$

Thus, the changes in the actual values (Y_t) are determined by four factors. The task of the analyst is to "decompose" the time series of Y into its four components.

We can now return to Frank Robinson's problem of forecasting Citronade sales not only for the entire year of 1991, but for each of the quarters. The quarterly data were given in Table 6.2. The process of decomposition starts with the identification of the seasonal factor.

Seasonality. The seasonal fluctuations of the data series are isolated using the method of moving averages. Table 6.4 lists the quarterly data of the 11 years in column 2. Column 1 simply represents all the quarters of the 11 years in the series, from 1980 to 1990, numbered sequentially.

The first step is to calculate the quarterly average for the first year (i.e., the first four quarters). The result is 973.0, so this number is placed next to quarter 3 in column 3. The next number is obtained by moving down one quarter: the first quarter is dropped, the fifth quarter is added, and the average of quarters 2, 3, 4, and 5 is calculated to be 989.3. This number is placed next to quarter 4. The same procedure is followed for the rest of the quarters, resulting in all the entries in column 3. Because of the averaging, the data for the first two quarters and the last quarter are lost.

The first moving average was placed next to the third quarter in the computation. It could have been placed next to the second quarter. Actually, the average of four quarters belongs between the second and third quarter. To solve the dilemma of where the average should be placed, another simple computation, creating a "centered" moving average, is made. An average of two adjacent numbers in column 3 is calculated and placed at the third quarter. Since 973.0 in column 3 should have appeared between quarters 2 and 3, and 989.3 should have been between quarters 3 and 4 , then the average of these two, 981.1, is correctly placed at quarter 3. These centered moving averages are shown in column 4. Now, by dividing the actual data in column 2 by the centered moving averages, we obtain ratios that are seasonal factors. In column 5, it can be seen that every fourth quarter, starting with quarter 3, has a factor greater than 1. These quarters represent the summer months (July–September), when soda consumption is at a peak. It can also be seen that the data for the second calendar quarters (i.e., quarters 6, 10, 14, etc.) are rather close to 1, and the quarters representing fall and winter are generally below 0.9. To obtain an index for each of the quarters, we average the ratios obtained by quarter. The results are shown in Table 6.5. The quarterly patterns are quite obvious.[26]

---

[26]There appears to be a minor downward trend in the third-quarter data. This will be discussed later.

Table 6.4 Citronade Quarterly Sales Analysis

(1) Quarter	(2) Actual	(3) Moving Average	(4) Centered Moving Average	(5) Ratio Actual/ CMA	(6) Adjusted Seasonal Factors	(7) Data Deseasonalized	(8) Trend	(9) Cycle and Irregular	(10) Cycle
1	842				0.889	947.1	940.2	100.74	
2	939				0.991	947.5	959.5	98.75	100.69
3	1,236	973.0	981.1	1.260	1.231	1,004.1	978.8	102.58	99.98
4	875	989.3	999.0	0.876	0.889	984.3	998.1	98.61	100.49
5	907	1,008.8	1,020.6	0.889	0.889	1,020.2	1,017.4	100.28	99.30
6	1,017	1,032.5	1,041.6	0.976	0.991	1,026.2	1,036.7	98.99	100.56
7	1,331	1,050.8	1,056.5	1.260	1.231	1,081.2	1,056.0	102.39	100.19
8	948	1,062.3	1,073.0	0.884	0.889	1,066.4	1,075.3	99.17	99.83
9	953	1,083.8	1,093.1	0.872	0.889	1,072.0	1,094.6	97.94	99.01
10	1,103	1,102.5	1,110.9	0.993	0.991	1,113.0	1,113.9	99.92	99.55
11	1,406	1,119.3	1,131.0	1.243	1.231	1,142.2	1,133.2	100.80	99.93
12	1,015	1,142.8	1,152.4	0.881	0.889	1,141.7	1,152.4	99.07	100.13
13	1,047	1,162.0	1,174.4	0.892	0.889	1,177.7	1,171.7	100.51	99.85
14	1,180	1,186.8	1,194.6	0.988	0.991	1,190.7	1,191.0	99.97	100.50
15	1,505	1,202.5	1,212.1	1.242	1.231	1,222.6	1,210.3	101.01	99.87
16	1,078	1,221.8	1,232.6	0.875	0.889	1,212.6	1,229.6	98.61	100.29
17	1,124	1,243.5	1,252.4	0.897	0.889	1,264.3	1,248.9	101.23	100.22
18	1,267	1,261.3	1,272.1	0.996	0.991	1,278.5	1,268.2	100.81	100.49
19	1,576	1,283.0	1,288.4	1.223	1.231	1,280.3	1,287.5	99.44	100.18
20	1,165	1,293.8	1,302.9	0.894	0.889	1,310.5	1,306.8	100.28	99.57
21	1,167	1,312.0	1,323.8	0.882	0.889	1,312.7	1,326.1	98.99	99.92
22	1,340	1,335.5	1,343.6	0.997	0.991	1,352.2	1,345.4	100.50	99.63
23	1,670	1,351.8	1,362.8	1.225	1.231	1,356.6	1,364.7	99.41	99.96
24	1,230	1,373.8	1,381.6	0.890	0.889	1,383.6	1,384.0	99.97	99.99
25	1,255	1,389.5	1,401.5	0.895	0.889	1,411.7	1,403.3	100.60	100.03
26	1,403	1,413.5	1,422.5	0.986	0.991	1,415.7	1,422.6	99.52	99.87
27	1,766	1,431.5	1,438.5	1.228	1.231	1,434.6	1,441.9	99.50	99.75
28	1,302	1,445.5	1,457.0	0.894	0.889	1,464.6	1,461.2	100.23	99.78
29	1,311	1,468.5	1,477.4	0.887	0.889	1,474.7	1,480.5	99.61	100.14
30	1,495	1,486.3	1,496.0	0.999	0.991	1,508.6	1,499.8	100.59	99.48
31	1,837	1,505.8	1,515.6	1.212	1.231	1,492.3	1,519.1	98.24	99.91
32	1,380	1,525.5	1,534.3	0.899	0.889	1,552.3	1,538.4	100.91	99.84
33	1,390	1,543.0	1,555.9	0.893	0.889	1,563.6	1,557.7	100.38	100.48
34	1,565	1,568.8	1,579.4	0.991	0.991	1,579.2	1,577.0	100.14	99.75
35	1,940	1,590.0	1,598.1	1.214	1.231	1,576.0	1,596.2	98.73	100.29
36	1,465	1,606.3	1,616.8	0.906	0.889	1,647.9	1,615.5	102.00	100.28
37	1,455	1,627.3	1,638.0	0.888	0.889	1,636.7	1,634.8	100.11	100.90
38	1,649	1,648.8	1,654.5	0.997	0.991	1,664.0	1,654.1	100.59	99.69
39	2,026	1,660.3	1,670.4	1.213	1.231	1,645.8	1,673.4	98.35	99.78
40	1,511	1,680.5	1,688.6	0.895	0.889	1,699.7	1,692.7	100.41	99.89
41	1,536	1,696.8	1,706.4	0.900	0.889	1,727.8	1,712.0	100.92	100.41
42	1,714	1,716.0	1,727.3	0.992	0.991	1,729.6	1,731.3	99.90	99.47
43	2,103	1,738.5			1.231	1,708.4	1,750.6	97.59	99.75
44	1,601				0.889	1,800.9	1,769.9	101.75	

Table 6.5 Averaging of Seasonal Factors

Year	*First Quarter*	*Second Quarter*	*Third Quarter*	*Fourth Quarter*	*Total*
1980			1.260	0.876	
1981	0.889	0.976	1.260	0.884	
1982	0.872	0.993	1.243	0.881	
1983	0.892	0.988	1.242	0.875	
1984	0.897	0.996	1.223	0.894	
1985	0.882	0.997	1.225	0.890	
1986	0.895	0.986	1.228	0.894	
1987	0.887	0.999	1.212	0.899	
1988	0.893	0.991	1.214	0.906	
1989	0.888	0.997	1.213	0.895	
1990	0.900	0.992			
Average	0.890	0.992	1.232	0.889	4.003
Adjusted Average	0.889	0.991	1.231	0.889	4.000

The four averages should add to 4; they do not, because of rounding. A minor adjustment must now be made. The results are then transferred to column 6 of Table 6.4. When the actual data of column 2 are divided by the seasonal factors of column 6, the deseasonalized series of numbers, in column 7, is obtained. Both the actual and the deseasonalized data have been plotted in Figure 6.5. The latter series, as should be expected, is much smoother than the former.

The first step of the decomposition procedure has now been completed:

$$(T \times C \times S \times R)/S = T \times C \times R$$

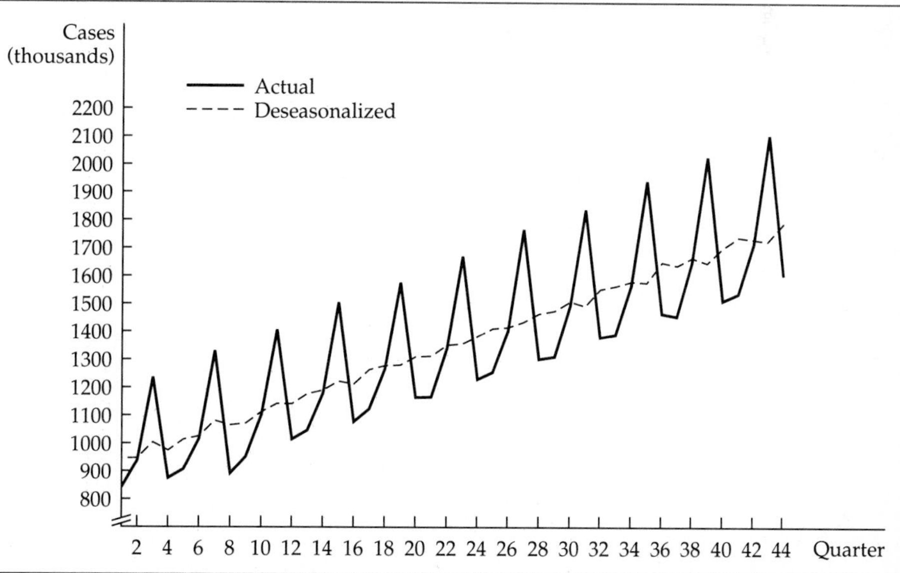

Figure 6.5 Citronade Sales Deseasonalized

The new series has eliminated the seasonality; trend, cycle, and random components still remain. The next step is to calculate the trend.

The Trend Line. Computation of the trend utilizes, as stated previously, the least squares method. The dependent variable is, of course, the deseasonalized series in column 7 of Table 6.4. The independent variable is time. Each quarter is numbered consecutively, although the initial number usually does not matter, it is easiest and most logical to start with 1. Thus, the consecutive numbers in column 1 of Table 6.4 represent the independent variable.

The form of the equation depends on the shape of the deseasonalized series. A casual observation of the deseasonalized series appears to indicate that a straight line would be most appropriate, but we actually tried three different possibilities:

Straight line: $Y = a + b(t)$
Exponential line:[27] $Y = ab^t$
Quadratic line:[28] $Y = a + b(t) + c(t)^2$

The results of the three calculations are shown in Table 6.6. The upper part of the table presents the trend series produced by each of the equations and the percentage error between the actual and the estimated numbers. The second part of the table shows the standard errors and the r^2 values. The exponential model appears to be inferior to the other two. The lower part of the table gives the equations for the three lines and the t-statistics of significance. The linear model is obviously superior for our data. The trend for this model is statistically more significant than for either of the other two. The quadratic model results show that the squared factor of the equations (which would indicate curvature) is extremely small and not statistically significant.[29]

Since the linear trend exhibits the best fit, we copy the results of the calculations in column 8 of Table 6.4. Then by dividing the data in column 7 by those in column 8, we eliminate the trend from the deseasonalized series. In terms of the fraction used previously

$$(T \times C \times R)/T = C \times R$$

Thus, only the cycle and random elements remain in column 9, which is in percentage form.

Cycle and Random Elements. At this point we could stop the analysis and do a forecast. The data in column 9 fluctuate rather irregularly within a range of about 5 percentage points. Part of this variation is due to random factors, which cannot be predicted and therefore should be ignored. However, there could be some longer business cycle wave in the data. To isolate the cycle,

---

[27] This is the equation that would best fit a straight line on a semilogarithmic chart, representing constant percentage gowth from period to period.

[28] This equation would fit a curve on a graph with arithmetic scales.

[29] A very efficient software package was used for this calculation. It came from David P. Doane, *Exploring Statistics with the IBM PC*, Reading, Mass: Addison-Wesley, 1985.

Table 6.6 Trend Calculations

Time	*Actual Y*	*Exponential Trend*	*Percent Error*	*Linear Trend*	*Percent Error*	*Quadratic Trend*	*Percent Error*
1	947.1	974.98	−2.9	940.19	0.7	941.50	0.6
2	947.5	989.24	−4.4	959.49	−1.3	960.62	−1.4
3	1,004.1	1,003.71	0.0	978.79	2.5	979.74	2.4
4	984.3	1,018.40	−3.5	998.08	−1.4	998.87	−1.5
5	1,020.2	1,033.30	−1.3	1,017.38	0.3	1,018.01	0.2
6	1,026.2	1,048.42	−2.2	1,036.67	−1.0	1,037.16	−1.1
7	1,081.2	1,063.76	1.6	1,055.97	2.3	1,056.31	2.3
8	1,066.4	1,079.32	−1.2	1,075.26	−0.8	1,075.48	−0.9
9	1,072.0	1,095.11	−2.2	1,094.56	−2.1	1,094.65	−2.1
10	1,113.0	1,111.13	0.2	1,113.86	−0.1	1,113.83	−0.1
11	1,142.2	1,127.39	1.3	1,133.15	0.8	1,133.03	0.8
12	1,141.7	1,143.88	−0.2	1,152.45	−0.9	1,152.23	−0.9
13	1,177.7	1,160.62	1.5	1,171.74	0.5	1,171.43	0.5
14	1,190.7	1,177.60	1.1	1,191.04	−0.0	1,190.65	0.0
15	1,222.6	1,194.83	2.3	1,210.33	1.0	1,209.88	1.0
16	1,212.6	1,212.31	0.0	1,229.63	−1.4	1,229.11	−1.4
17	1,264.3	1,230.05	2.7	1,248.93	1.2	1,248.36	1.3
18	1,278.5	1,248.04	2.4	1,268.22	0.8	1,267.61	0.9
19	1,280.3	1,266.30	1.1	1,287.52	−0.6	1,286.87	−0.5
20	1,310.5	1,284.83	2.0	1,306.81	0.3	1,306.14	0.3
21	1,312.7	1,303.63	0.7	1,326.11	−1.0	1,325.42	−1.0
22	1,352.2	1,322.70	2.2	1,345.40	0.5	1,344.70	0.6
23	1,356.6	1,342.05	1.1	1,364.70	−0.6	1,364.00	−0.5
24	1,383.6	1,361.69	1.6	1,384.00	−0.0	1,383.30	0.0
25	1,411.7	1,381.61	2.1	1,403.29	0.6	1,402.62	0.6
26	1,415.7	1,401.83	1.0	1,422.59	−0.5	1,421.94	−0.4
27	1,434.6	1,422.34	0.9	1,441.88	−0.5	1,441.27	−0.5
28	1,464.6	1,443.15	1.5	1,461.18	0.2	1,460.61	0.3
29	1,474.7	1,464.26	0.7	1,480.47	−0.4	1,479.96	−0.4
30	1,508.6	1,485.68	1.5	1,499.77	0.6	1,499.31	0.6
31	1,492.3	1,507.42	−1.0	1,519.07	−1.8	1,518.68	−1.8
32	1,552.3	1,529.47	1.5	1,538.36	0.9	1,538.05	0.9
33	1,563.6	1,551.85	0.8	1,557.66	0.4	1,557.44	0.4
34	1,579.2	1,574.56	0.3	1,576.95	0.1	1,576.83	0.2
35	1,576.0	1,597.59	−1.4	1,596.25	−1.3	1,596.23	−1.3
36	1,647.9	1,620.97	1.6	1,615.54	2.0	1,615.64	2.0
37	1,636.7	1,644.68	−0.5	1,634.84	0.1	1,635.05	0.1
38	1,664.0	1,668.75	−0.3	1,654.14	0.6	1,654.48	0.6
39	1,645.8	1,693.16	−2.9	1,673.43	−1.7	1,673.91	−1.7
40	1,699.7	1,717.93	−1.1	1,692.73	0.4	1,693.36	0.4
41	1,727.8	1,743.07	−0.9	1,712.02	0.9	1,712.81	0.9
42	1,729.6	1,768.57	−2.3	1,731.32	−0.1	1,732.27	−0.2
43	1,708.4	1,794.44	−5.0	1,750.61	−2.5	1,751.74	−2.5
44	1,800.9	1,820.70	−1.1	1,769.91	1.7	1,771.22	1.6

Table 6.6 (*continued*)

	Exponential Model	*Linear Model*	*Quadratic Model*
Mean absolute Percent error	1.5	0.9	0.9
Standard error	25.85077	15.69572	15.87259
R^2	.9900	.9961	.9961

Estimated Fitted Models Using Least Squares

1. Estimated exponential model (for $t = 1, 2, \ldots, 44$):

$$Y = 960.92(1.01463)^t$$

Compound growth rate: 1.5 percent
Exponential trend is very significant (t-statistic = 64.355).

2. Estimated linear model (for $t = 1, 2, \ldots, 44$):

$$Y = 920.90 + 19.2957t$$

Linear trend is very significant (t-statistic = 103.551).

3. Estimated quadratic model (for $t = 1, 2, \ldots, 44$):

$$Y = 922.40 + 19.0999t + 0.004352t^2$$

Linear trend is very significant (t-statistic = 24.786).
Quadratic trend is not significant (t-statistic = 0.262).

another smoothing operation can be performed with a moving average. The preferred length of the moving-average period cannot be determined except in each individual case. In our illustration we used three periods. If the moving average correctly eliminates the random variations remaining in column 9, then the swings that appear in column 10 should represent a cyclical index. When the index rises above 100 percent, the indication is that economic activity is strong; the opposite holds for index numbers below 100 percent. The data in column 10 fluctuate very little—less than 2 percentage points. Therefore, no great adjustment is needed here. However, if the indication is that the economy is in a downturn, which may be expected to have some influence on soft drink sales, then a minor forecast adjustment can be made. Such an adjustment can be based on current general forecasts for the economy as a whole or on the latest published leading economic indicators.

FORECASTING WITH SMOOTHING TECHNIQUES. Before we leave the section on projections, one other naive method should be mentioned. This method involves using an average of past observations to predict the future. If the forecaster feels that the future is a reflection of some average of past results, one of two forecasting methods can be applied: simple moving average or exponential smoothing.

The smoothing techniques, either moving average or exponential smoothing, work best when there is no strong trend in the series, when there are infrequent changes in the direction of the series, and when fluctuations are random rather than seasonal or cyclical. Obviously, these are very limiting conditions and greatly circumscribe the usefulness of these methods. However, if a large number of forecasts are needed quickly and if the estimates involve only one period into the future, then one of these two techniques can be employed—as long as their drawbacks are well understood by the forecaster.

Moving average. The technique of moving averages was discussed previously in connection with the smoothing of seasonal and cyclical fluctuations. Here, the average of actual past results will be used to forecast one period ahead. The equation for this construction is simply

$$E_{t+1} = (X_t + X_{t-1} + \cdots + X_{t-N+1})/N$$

where E_{t+1} = Forecast for the next period $(t + 1)$

X_t, X_{t-1} = Actual values at their respective times

N = Number of observations included in the average

The forecasts for Citronade, with their strong trend and seasonal patterns, would certainly not lend themselves well to this simple projection method. Instead, a hypothetical example will be used. Twelve observations are shown in the second column of Table 6.7.

At this point, the forecaster must decide how many observations to use in the moving average. The larger the number of observations in the average, the greater the smoothing effect. If the past data appear to contain significant randomness while the underlying pattern remains the same, then a larger number of observations will be included in the moving average. However, the analyst must remember that more historical data will be needed for the forecast if a large number of past data are to be included in the base. In Table 6.7, three

Table 6.7 Moving Average Forecasting

		Three-Month Moving Average			Four-Month Moving Average			Five-Month Moving Average		
Period	*Actual*	*Forecast*	*Absolute Error*	*Squared Error*	*Forecast*	*Absolute Error*	*Squared Error*	*Forecast*	*Absolute Error*	*Squared Error*
1	1,100									
2	800									
3	1,000									
4	1,050	967	83	6,944						
5	1,500	950	550	302,500	988	513	262,656			
6	750	1,183	433	187,778	1,088	338	113,906	1,090	340	115,600
7	700	1,100	400	160,000	1,075	375	140,625	1,020	320	102,400
8	650	983	333	111,111	1,000	350	122,500	1,000	350	122,500
9	1,400	700	700	490,000	900	500	250,000	930	470	220,900
10	1,200	917	283	80,278	875	325	105,625	1,000	200	40,000
11	900	1,083	183	33,611	988	88	7,656	940	40	1,600
12	1,000	1,167	167	27,778	1,038	38	1,406	970	30	900
13		1,033			1,125			1,030		
Total			3,133	1,400,000		2,525	1,004,375		1,750	603,900
Mean			348	155,556		316	125,547		250	86,271

Note: Some of the squared errors appear to be incorrect; this is so because decimals have been omitted.

moving averages have been computed—three, four, and five months. The resulting estimates are shown in the forecast columns. For example, the forecast of 967 units in period 4 of the three-month moving average was obtained as follows:

$$\begin{aligned} E_4 &= (X_1 + X_2 + X_3)/N \\ &= (1,100 + 800 + 1,000)/3 \\ &= 2,900/3 = 967 \end{aligned}$$

It can be seen that the three forecast columns diverge widely. These variances are shown graphically in Figure 6.6. As more observations are included in the moving average, the forecast line becomes smoother.

Which moving average should be used? One selection method is to calculate the mean error and the mean squared error of the differences between the actual data and the forecast.[30] The series with the smallest squared error would be preferred. In the example of Table 6.7, the five-month moving average minimizes the deviations.

Exponential Smoothing. The moving-average method awards equal importance to each of the observations included in the average, and gives no weight at all to observations preceding the oldest data included. However, the analyst may feel that the most recent observation is more relevant to the estimate of the next period than previous observations. In that case, it is more appropriate

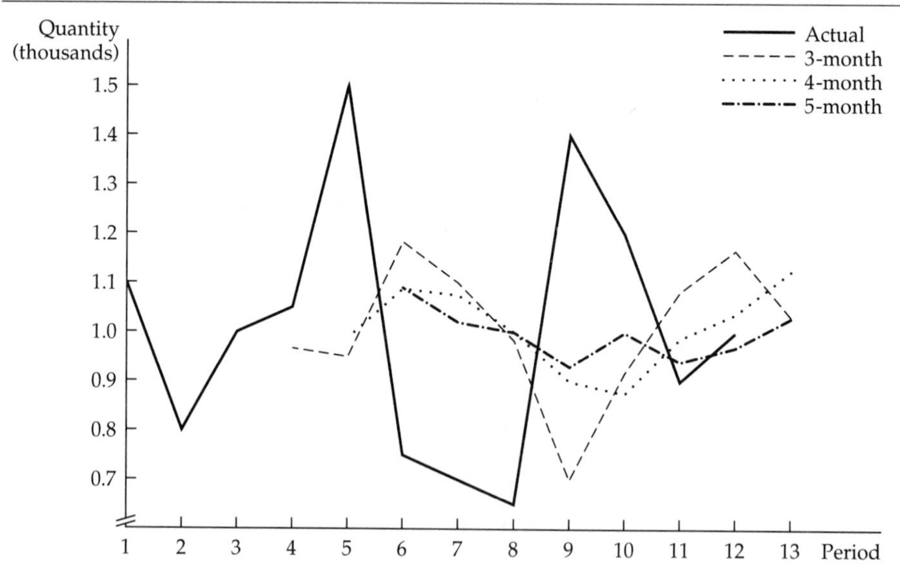

Figure 6.6 Forecasting with Moving Averages

[30]The formula for the mean squared error is

$$\sum_{n=1}^{N}(E_n - X_n)^2$$

to employ the exponential smoothing method, which allows for the decreasing importance of information in the more distant past. This is accomplished by the mathematical technique of geometric progression. Older data are assigned increasingly smaller weights; the sum of the weights, if we approached an infinitely large number of observations, would equal 1. All of the complex formulations of the geometric series can be simplified into the following expression:

$$E_{t+1} = wX_t + (1 - w)E_t$$

where w is the weight assigned to an actual observation at period t.

Thus, to make a forecast for one period into the future, all that is needed is the previous period's actual observation and the previous period's forecast. The reader should note that for exponential smoothing, the analyst does not need the extensive historical data required for the moving-average method. The most crucial decision the analyst must make is the choice of the weighting factor. The larger the w (i.e., the closer to 1), the greater will be the importance of the most recent observation. Therefore, when the series is rather volatile and when w is large, the smoothing effect may be minimal. When w is small, the smoothing effect will be considerably more pronounced. This result can be seen in Table 6.8, and Figure 6.7, where ws of .2, .4, and .8 have been used.[31] Which weights should be used? We can again calculate the mean squared error, as was done in Table 6.8. Using $w = .2$, minimizes the error, so this is the best weight for this set of data.

Table 6.8 Exponential Smoothing Forecasting

		Smoothing Factor = .2			Smoothing Factor = .4			Smoothing Factor = .8		
Period	*Actual*	*Forecast*	*Absolute Error*	*Squared Error*	*Forecast*	*Absolute Error*	*Squared Error*	*Forecast*	*Absolute Error*	*Squared Error*
1	1,100									
2	800	1,100	300	90,000	1,100	300	90,000	1,100	300	90,000
3	1,000	1,040	40	1,600	980	20	400	860	140	19,600
4	1,050	1,032	18	324	988	62	3,844	972	78	6,084
5	1,500	1,036	464	215,667	1,013	487	237,364	1,034	466	216,783
6	750	1,128	378	143,247	1,208	458	209,471	1,407	657	431,491
7	700	1,053	353	124,457	1,025	325	105,370	881	181	32,897
8	650	982	332	110,375	895	245	59,910	736	86	7,443
9	1,400	916	484	234,467	797	603	363,779	667	733	536,915
10	1,200	1,013	187	35,109	1,038	162	26,207	1,253	53	2,857
11	900	1,050	150	22,530	1,103	203	41,156	1,211	311	96,528
12	1,000	1,020	20	403	1,022	22	472	962	38	1,434
13		1,016			1,013			992		
Total			2,728	978,180		2,886	1,137,973		3,043	1,442,033
Mean			248	88,925		262	103,452		277	131,094
Factor		0.2			0.4			0.8		

Note: Some of the squared errors appear to be incorrect; this is so because decimals have been omitted.

[31]Note that the forecast for period 2 in each case is the actual observation of period 1. Since there is no forecast for period 1, a forecast must be made up. Any number could have been used, but the actual observation is probably the most logical choice.

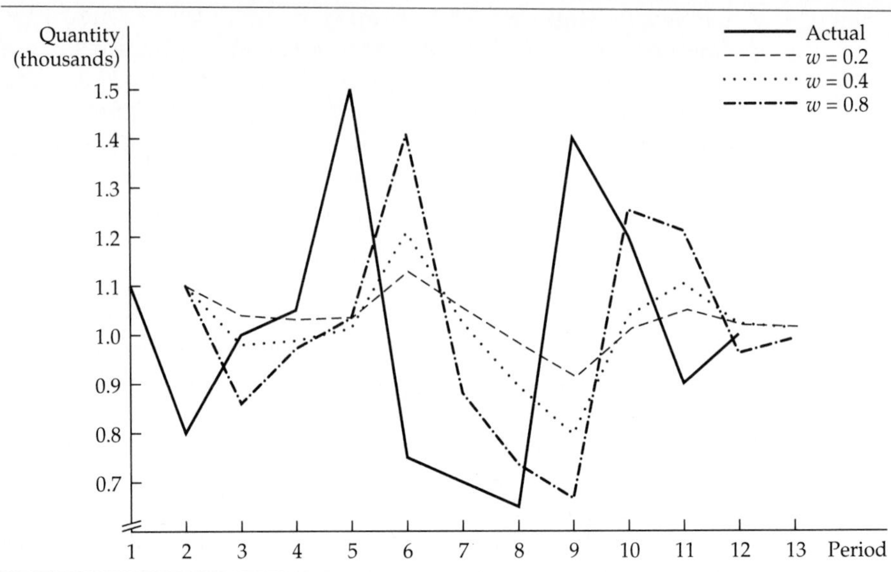

Figure 6.7 Exponential Smoothing Forecasting

Both of these naive forecasting techniques have their advantages and disadvantages. The simplicity of the methods is certainly an advantage. However, their usefulness is limited to cases where there is an underlying stability (i.e., no trend) with period-to-period random fluctuations. When a trend or a repeating pattern of fluctuations is present, the time series method with deseasonalization is a much better technique to use. In any case, the two methods just discussed should be employed only for extremely short-term estimates—preferably just one period into the future.

Econometric Models

Up to this point, all of the quantitative forecasting techniques discussed can be classified as naive. In this section of the chapter, our brief discussion will concentrate on models that are termed *causal* or *explanatory*. Some of these models were described in detail in Chapter 5.

Regression analysis is an explanatory technique. Unlike the case of a naive projection, which relies on past patterns to predict the future, the analyst performing regression analysis must select those independent (or explanatory) variables that are influential in determining the dependent variable. Although simple projection models often give adequate results, the use of explanatory variables in the analysis can enhance the accuracy as well as the credibility of the estimates. Of course, no regression equation will explain the entire variation of the dependent variable, since, in most economic relationships, there are numerous explanatory variables with complex interrelationships. As already explained Chapter 5, the person performing the analysis will have to settle for the inclusion of a limited number of variables, an equation that approximates the functional relationships, and results that explain a significant portion of but not the entire variation in the dependent variable.

The regression methods previously described employ a single equation to make estimates. Examples of both simple and multiple regressions were given. A regression equation was also calculated for the demand for soft drinks. The result of applying regression techniques yielded the following specification:

$$Q = -153 - 0.87\text{INC} + 5.88\text{TEMP}$$

where Q = per-capita annual consumption of soft drinks
INC = per-capita annual income
TEMP = Average annual temperature

Many single-equation regressions estimating demand can be found in economic literature. Just a few will be mentioned here.

Among the many studies of automobile demand, the one written by Daniel Suits[32] is quite interesting. He combined the demand equations for new cars and used cars into one, as follows:

$$\Delta R = a_0 + a_1 \Delta Y + a_2 \Delta P/M + a_3 \Delta S + a_4 \Delta X$$

where R = Retail sales, in millions of new cars
Y = Real disposable income
P = Real retail price of new cars
M = Average credit terms (number of months of the average installment contract)
S = Existing stock, in millions of cars
X = Dummy variable

All of the variables are in terms of first differences; thus, the equation estimates year-to-year changes. The years 1942 through 1948 have been excluded from the time series because of the war years, when no automobiles were produced, and the immediate postwar period, when significant distortions existed in the automobile market.

The dummy variable X takes into account the fact that not all the remaining years in the series can be treated equally. The years 1941, 1952, and 1953 were considered exceptional,[33] the first two were assigned a value of +1, the third a value of −1, and all the other years a value of 0.

Having specified the equation, Suits calculated the coefficients (the as) and tested the results by predicting 1958 new auto sales. "The demand equation predicts a level of sales of slightly less than 6.0 million. This compares favorably with a preliminary estimate of 6.1 million actual sales for the year and stands in

[32]Daniel B. Suits, "The Demand for New Automobiles in the United States, 1929–1956," *Review of Economics and Statistics*, August 1958, pp. 273–80.

[33]1941 witnessed a conversion to a wartime economy. In 1952 new automobile production was subject to government allocation and price controls and suffered from a severe steel strike. 1953 presumably was distinguished by strong recovery due to the end of the Korean War.

sharp contrast with sales forecasts of 6.5 million and over, which were common in the industry at the start of the year."[34]

Another economist studied the demand for computers.[35] He specified the following equation in terms of logarithms:

$$\log(y_t/y_{t-1}) = a_0 - a_1 \log p_t - a_2 \log y_{t-1}$$

where y_t = Stock of computers in year t

y_{t-1} = Stock of computers in year $t - 1$

p = Real price of computers

The demand in this equation is measured as the percentage change in the stock of computers from one year to the next.

A last example will be given for coffee demand in the United States.[36] Coffee demand was estimated with the following equation:

$$Q = b_0 + b_1 P_o + b_2 Y + b_3 P + \sum_{i=1}^{3} b_4 D_i + b_5 T$$

where Q = Per-capita (population over age 16) quantity of coffee

P_0 = Real retail price of coffee, per pound

Y = Real per-capita disposable income

P = Real retail price of tea, per quarter pound

D_i = Binary (dummy) variable for quarters of the year

T = Time trend

The authors found that coffee consumption is sensitive to its own price, that there had been a long-term decline in coffee consumption, and that significantly less coffee was consumed during the spring and summer months. The other coefficients did not turn out to be statistically significant. Thus, the consumption of coffee could be estimated from the time trend, from the quarterly changes, and from an assumption made regarding coffee prices.

In each of these studies, the numerical coefficients (the as and the bs) were obtained by regression analysis. To forecast using these equations, it is necessary, of course, to make estimates of each of the independent variables for the period indicated.[37] Alternative forecasts can be created by assuming different values for each of the independent variables.

An important warning is in order regarding the use of regression equations for forecasting. All the parameters (coefficients) in a regression equation are estimated using past data (whether time series or cross-sectional analysis has been employed). The forecast based on such estimates will be valid only if the

[34] Ibid., p. 273.

[35] Gregory Chow, "Technological Change and the Demand for Computers," *American Economic Review,* December 1967, pp. 1117–30.

[36] Cliff J. Huang, John J. Siegfried, and Farangis Zardoshty, "The Demand for Coffee in the United States, 1963–1977," *Quarterly Review of Economics and Business,* 20, 2 (Summer 1980), pp. 36–50.

[37] In the case of lagged variables, actual data may be available. See, for instance, y_{t-1}, the stock of computers at the end of the previous year in the equation used in Chow, op. cit.

relationships between the dependent variable and the independent variables do not change from the past into the future. Literally, a regression equation is valid only within the limits of the data used in it. When we venture outside these limits (i.e., forecast with independent variables outside the range of the past), we are treading on dangerous ground. Still, forecasting with the least squares method is a much-used technique, often employed quite successfully. But its limitations must not be forgotten by the analyst.

Although many forecasting problems can be solved with the use of single-equation regression models, there are instances when one equation is not sufficient. In such cases, economists often turn to multiple-equation systems. Extremely large models used by economists to predict the GNP and its component parts are examples of such models, which may include hundreds of variables and equations.

A single-equation model can be used when the dependent variable can be estimated using independent variables that are determined by events not part of the equation. But what happens when the determining variables are determined by other variables within the model? Then a single equation is insufficient.

In a multiple-equation system, variables are referred to as *endogenous* and *exogenous.* Endogenous variables are comparable to the dependent variable of the single-equation model; they are determined by the model. However, they can also influence other endogenous variables, so they may appear as "independent" (i.e., on the right side of the equation) variables in one or more of the equations. Exogenous variables are from outside the system and are not determined within it; they are truly independent variables.

The following is an example of an extremely simple two-equation model of the private economy:

$$C = a_0 + a_1 Y$$
$$Y = C + I$$

where C = Consumption
Y = National income
I = Investment

Here C and Y are endogenous variables. I is assumed (rather unrealistically) to be exogenous, or determined by forces outside the system of equations.

Another simple multi-equation model represents the interrelationships of activities within a firm:

$$\begin{aligned} \text{Sales} &= f(\text{GNP, Prices}) \\ \text{Cost} &= f(\text{Quantity of product, Factor prices}) \\ \text{Expenses} &= f(\text{Sales, Factor prices}) \\ \text{Product price} &= f(\text{Cost, Expenses, Profit}) \\ \text{Profit} &= \text{Sales} - \text{Cost} - \text{Expenses} \end{aligned}$$

Here there are five endogenous variables. The exogenous variables are GNP, Quantity of product, and Factor prices. These equations are given in functional form only. The specific forms of the equations would, of course, have to be specified.

Such systems of equations would then be solved to obtain all of the coefficients. The statistical methods used to solve for all the numerical values are beyond the scope of this textbook.

The Solution

Frank Robinson is now ready to make his forecast for 1991. He will do it in three steps:

1. He will project the trend for the four quarters of 1991.
2. He will apply the seasonal factors.
3. He may then make an adjustment for cyclical influences.

Since the trend equation is $Y = 920.9 + 19.2957(t)$, his trend forecasts will be as follows:

First quarter: $920.9+19.2957(45) = 1{,}789.2$
Second quarter: $920.9+19.2957(46) = 1{,}808.5$
Third quarter: $920.9+19.2957(47) = 1{,}827.8$
Fourth quarter: $920.9+19.2957(48) = 1{,}847.1$

Next, each of these results must be multiplied by the seasonal factors:

First quarter: $1{,}789.2 \times 0.889 = 1{,}590.6$
Second quarter: $1{,}808.5 \times 0.991 = 1{,}792.2$
Third quarter: $1{,}827.8 \times 1.231 = 2{,}250.0$
Fourth quarter: $1{,}847.1 \times 0.889 = 1{,}642.1$

Frank noticed, however, that the seasonal factors in Table 6.5 exhibit some trends over the 11 years. The third-quarter factor has been decreasing and the first- and fourth-quarter factors appear to be rising. To see the effect of these changes, Robinson decides to use the average of the last three observations for each quarter (and adjust to a total of 4, as was done previously). When he applies his new factors to the trend numbers, he obtains the following results:

First quarter: $1{,}789.2 \times 0.894 = 1{,}599.5$
Second quarter: $1{,}808.5 \times 0.993 = 1{,}795.8$
Third quarter: $1{,}827.8 \times 1.213 = 2{,}217.1$
Fourth quarter: $1{,}847.1 \times 0.900 = 1{,}662.4$

He decides that this last computation is more valid. The last step in his procedure is to evaluate the effect of cycles and random factors. He decides that the cycle's influence on soft drink sales will be neutral in the coming year. Although an estimate of random factors cannot be made, Frank knows that the company has plans to implement a strong advertising campaign on behalf of Citronade during the second quarter of 1991. At this point, however, he does not have sufficient information regard-

(Continued)

ing the effect of advertising on sales. He makes a note to mention that in his report as a possible plus and to try to make some quantitative estimates later.

An additional point deserves attention. We have assumed that the product whose sales Frank is forecasting has been part of a company's product line for at least 11 years. Had this been a new flavor, not previously produced, the forecast would have been much more difficult. If competing companies had been selling a similar product in the past, market information would be available in terms of very detailed statistics published by the beverage industry. Frank could then base his forecast on these data and assume some pattern of market penetration for the new brand. If, however, this is a completely new flavor not previously produced in the industry, it may be necessary to conduct market research to establish a base for a forecast. Another method would be to study the sales patterns of other soft drink products from point of introduction and to base the new product forecast on their histories.

Summary

Forecasting is an important activity in many organizations. In business, forecasting is a necessity.

This chapter has summarized and discussed a number of forecasting techniques. Six categories of forecasts were included:

1. *Expert opinion* is a qualitative technique of forecasting based on the judgment of knowledgeable people. Such forecasts can be developed by panels of experts. The Delphi method is another type of expert opinion forecast that is generally applicable in forecasting technological advances.
2. *Opinion polls and market research* are conducted among survey populations, not experts, to establish future trends or consumer responses.
3. *Surveys* of spending plans are concerened with such important economic data as capital expenditures and consumer sentiment. The forecasts are based on replies to questionnaires or interviews.
4. *Economic indicators* are indexes of a number of economic series intended to forecast the short-run movements of the economy, including changes in direction.
5. *Projections,* a quantitative method, employ historical data to project future trends. Usually, no causes for trends are identified. This chapter discussed compound growth rate projections as well as visual and least squares projection techniques.
6. *Econometric models* are explanatory or causal models in which independent variables that influence the statistic to be forecast are identified. Both single- and multiple-equation models were discussed briefly.

The chapter also examined the decomposition of least squares projections into trends, seasonal and cyclical fluctuations, and irregular movements.

One other naive forecasting method was mentioned: forecasting with smoothing techniques. Smoothing techniques fall into two major categories, moving averages and exponential smoothing, and are useful when there are no pronounced trends in the data and when fluctuations from period to period are random.

Important Concepts

Causal (explanatory) forecasting: A quantitative forecasting method that attempts to uncover functional relationships between independent variables and the dependent variable.

Compound growth rate projection: Forecasting by projecting the average growth rate of the past into the future.

Delphi method: A form of expert opinion forecasting that uses a series of written questions and answers to obtain a consensus forecast, most commonly employed in forecasting technological trends.

Econometric forecasting model: A quantitative, causal method that utilizes a number of independent variables to explain the dependent variable to be forecast. Econometric forecasting employs both single- and multiple-equation models.

Economic indicators: A barometric method of forecasting in which economic data are formed into indexes to reflect the state of the economy. Indexes of leading, coincident, and lagging indicators are used to forecast changes in economic activity.

Exponential smoothing: A smoothing method of forecasting that assigns greater importance to more recent data than to those in the more distant past.

Jury of executive opinion: A forecast generated by experts (e.g., corporate executives) in meetings. A similar method is to ask the opinion of sales representatives who are exposed to the market on a daily basis.

Moving-average method: A smoothing technique that compensates for seasonal fluctuations.

Naive forecasting: Quantitative forecasting that projects past data without explaining the reasons for future trends.

Opinion polls: A forecasting method in which sample populations are surveyed to determine consumption trends.

Qualitative forecasting: Forecasting based on the judgment of individuals or groups.

Quantitative forecasting: Forecasting that examines historical data as a basis for future trends.

Surveys of spending plans: Examination of economic trends such as capital expenditures, consumer sentiment, and inventory.

Time series forecasting: A method of forecasting from past data by using least squares statistical methods. A time series analysis usually examines trends, cyclical fluctuations, seasonal fluctuations, and irregular movements.

Trend projection: A form of naive forecasting that projects trends from past data. Trend projections usually employ compound growth rates, visual time series, or least squares time series methods.

Questions

1. Discuss the basic differences among forecasting, planning, and objective setting.
2. Despite the many inaccuracies present in the making of forecasts, forecasting is a very important activity in a large business firm. Why?
3. "The best forecasting method is the one that gives the highest proportion of correct predictions." Comment.
4. Enumerate methods of qualitative and quantitative forecasting. What are the major differences between the two?
5. Discuss the benefits and drawbacks of the following methods of forecasting:
   a. Jury of executive opinion
   b. The Delphi method
   c. Opinion polls

   Each of these methods has its uses. What are they?
6. Here are the numbers for the leading economic indicators as published in 1990:

January	145.4
February	144.1
March	145.4
April	145.2
May	146.0
June	146.2
July	146.2
August	144.4
September	143.2
October	141.5
November	139.7
December	139.5

1982 = 100

Source: U.S. Department of Commerce, Bureau of Economic Analysis, *Survey of Current Business,* March 1991, p. C-1.

What conditions do you think they forecast for 1991?

7. a. Why are contracts and orders for plant and equipment appropriate leading indicators?
   b. Why is the index of industrial production an appropriate coincident indicator?
   c. Why is the average prime rate charged by banks an appropriate lagging indicator?
8. Discuss some of the important criticisms of the forecasting ability of the leading economic indicators.
9. What is meant by "naive" forecasting methods? Describe some of the methods that fall within this category.
10. Manhattan was allegedly purchased from native Americans in 1626 for $24. If the sellers had invested this sum at a 6 percent interest rate compounded semiannually, how much would it amount to today?
11. The compound growth rate is frequently used to forecast various quantities (sales, profits, etc.). Do you believe this is a good method? Should any cautions be exercised in making such projections?
12. Explain the meaning of "semilogarithmic scale." When can it be used, and what are its advantages?
13. Describe projections that use either moving averages or exponential smoothing. Under what conditions can these techniques be used? Which of the two appears to be the more useful?
14. How do econometric models differ from "naive" projection methods? Is it always advisable to use the former in forecasting?
15. Which of the following forecasting methods are appropriate for predicting business cycles?
   a. Trend projections
   b. Leading economic indicators
   c. Lagging economic indicators
   d. Survey methods

   Explain.

Problems

1. If the sales of your company have grown from $500,000 five years ago to $1,050,150 this year, what is the compound growth rate? If you expect your sales to grow at a rate of 10 percent for the next five years, what should they be five years from now?
2. Based on past data, Mack's Pool Supply has constructed the following equation for the sales of its house brand of chlorine tablets:

$$Q = 1,000 + 100t$$

where Q is quantity and t is time (in years), with $1987 = 0$.

a. What is the sales projection for 1992?
b. The tablet sales are seasonal, with the following quarterly indexes:

Quarter 1	80%
Quarter 2	100%
Quarter 3	125%
Quarter 4	95%

What is the quarterly sales projection for 1992?

3. The sales data over the last 10 years for the Acme Hardware Store are as follows:

1981	$230,000	1986	$526,000
1982	276,000	1987	605,000
1983	328,000	1988	690,000
1984	388,000	1989	779,000
1985	453,000	1990	873,000

a. Calculate the compound growth rate for the period of 1981–1990.
b. Based on your answer to part *a*, forecast sales for both 1991 and 1992.
c. Now calculate the compound growth rate for the period of 1985–1990.
d. Based on your answer to part *c*, forecast sales for both 1991 and 1992.
e. What is the major reason for the differences in your answers to parts *b* and *d*? If you were to make your own projections, what would you forecast? (Drawing a graph will be very helpful).

4. The sales data for the Tough Steel Hardware Company for the last 12 years are as follows:

1979	$400,000	1985	$617,000
1980	440,000	1986	654,000
1981	480,000	1987	700,000
1982	518,000	1988	756,000
1983	554,000	1989	824,000
1984	587,000	1990	906,000

a. What is the 1979–1990 compound growth rate?
b. Using the result obtained in part *a*, what is your 1991 projection?
c. If you were to make your own projection, what would you forecast? (Drawing a graph will be very helpful).

5. The Miracle Corporation had the following sales durig the past 10 years (in thousands of dollars):

1981	200	1986	302
1982	215	1987	320
1983	237	1988	345
1984	260	1989	360
1985	278	1990	382

   a. Calculate a trend line, and forecast sales for 1991. How confident are you of this forecast?
   b. Use exponential smoothing with a smoothing factor $w = .7$. What is your 1991 forecast? How confident are you of this forecast?
6. You have the following data for the last 12 months' sales for the PRQ Corporation (in thousands of dollars):

January	500	July	610
February	520	August	620
March	520	September	580
April	510	October	550
May	530	November	510
June	580	December	480

   a. Calculate a three-month centered moving average.
   b. Use this moving average to forecast sales for January of next year.
   c. If you were asked to forecast January and February sales for next year, would you be confident of your forecast using the preceding moving averages? Why or why not?
7. Office Enterprises (OE) produces a line of metal office file cabinets. The company's economist, having investigated a large number of past data, has established the following equation of demand for these cabinets:

$$Q = 10,000 + 60B - 100P + 50C$$

where Q = Annual number of cabinets sold
B = Index of nonresidential construction
P = Average price per cabinet charged by OE
C = Average price per cabinet charged by OE's closest competitor

It is expected that next year's nonresidential construction index will stand at 160, OE's average price will be $40, and the competitor's average price will be $35.

   a. Forecast next year's sales.

b. What will be the effect if the competitor lowers its price to $32? If it raises its price to $36?
c. What will happen if OE reacts to the decrease mentioned in part *b* by lowering its price to $37?
d. If the index forecast was wrong, and it turns out to be only 140 next year, what will be the effect on OE's sales?

CHAPTER 7

The Theory of Production

The Situation

George Ernest, the vice president of manufacturing, had just come back to his office from an executive management committee meeting. His worst fears had been realized. The committee finally approved the firm's entry into the highly competitive soft drink market. The marketing task force assigned to evaluate the desirability of such a move had made a tremendous presentation and managed to convince the committee that the company could indeed penetrate this market sufficiently to make the venture worthwhile. Moreover, the committee members were confident that their crack new-products team could successfully battle the giants of the industry.

What was bothering George even more, however, was the fact that the marketing people did not know the first thing about what it really takes to compete on the basis of manufacturing cost in the soft drink market. In a market such as this, one has to be prepared to deal with such factors as fluctuating commodity prices, trends in packaging, and advances in manufacturing technology. A sudden rise in the price of high-fructose corn syrup, for example, could substantially erode profit margin. In the area of packaging, the switch from glass to plastic bottles was prompted primarily by the rise in oil prices during the 1970s. (The making of glass is a very energy-intensive process.) Would the recent sharp decline in oil prices suggest a switch back to glass bottles? Furthermore, the making of soft drink syrup and the bottling of the final product have become increasingly automated in recent years. How rapidly could his people adapt to the new technology?

In addition, George was concerned that the marketing case was based on the assumption that the company could penetrate the existing market with a premium product (i.e., an upscale, high-priced product). He feared that the high-priced product envisioned by the marketing people, although

(Continued)

it may provide the company with a rather comfortable profit margin per unit sold, would not generate the kind of volume needed to give his manufacturing people sufficient experience to keep up with the industry's improving cost structure. Therefore, even though the company would have a premium product, it might well be the industry's high cost producer.

George admitted to himself that all of these thoughts were mere speculation. He had a more immediate problem to deal with. The marketing task force believed that one of the ways in which Global Foods could differentiate its product was to give consumers the option of buying it in refillable bottles. This would appeal to the growing concern about the environment and at the same time enable Global's packaging to stand out from the rest. George was asked to do a production analysis of the refillable bottling process and to make a recommendation to the product manager of the new soft drinks division about whether it was economically justifiable to proceed with this form of packaging.

The Production Function

George Ernest's concerns are certainly justified. No matter how large the projected demand is for a product at a given price, if the costs of production cannot be contained, the company will have difficulty earning an acceptable profit. It is that simple. What is not as simple, however, is understanding the cost structure of a company. In economic analysis the understanding of cost begins with the production function. This is because the cost of production is measured primarily in physical units of inputs used. The production of any good or service involves a cost because it uses scarce resources that have alternative uses.

For example, suppose George has to hire a systems analyst to develop the bottling plant's production system. The monetary cost to the firm would be equal to the analyst's compensation (e.g., \$100 per hour). But the "real" cost would be its use of the analyst's services, which could have been devoted to another activity. Cost and cost estimation will be discussed in Chapters 8 and 10. This chapter serves as the foundation for the economic analysis of cost by introducing the fundamentals of production and the concept of the production function.

The production function can be defined as the relationship between productive inputs and outputs of product per unit of time. In mathematical terms,

$$Q = f(X_1, X_2, \ldots, X_k) \tag{7.1}$$

where Q = Output

$X_1, \ldots, X_k$ = Inputs used in the production process

Note that we assume that the relationship between inputs and output exists for a specific period of time. In other words, Q is not a measure of output accumulated over time. There are two other key assumptions that you should be aware of. First, we are assuming some given "state of the art" in the production technology. Any innovation in production (e.g., the use of robotics in manufacturing or a more efficient software package for financial analysis) would cause the relationship between given inputs and their output to change. Second, we are assuming that whatever inputs or input combinations are included in a particular function, the output resulting from their utilization is at the maximum level. With this in mind, we can offer a more complete definition of a production function:

> A production function defines the relationship between inputs and the maximum amount that can be produced within a given period of time with a given level of technology.

For George's company, the Xs could represent raw materials, such as carbonated water, sweeteners, and flavorings; labor, such as assembly line workers, support staff, and supervisory personnel; and fixed assets, such as plant and equipment.

For purposes of analysis, let us reduce the whole array of inputs in the production function to two, X and Y. Restating Equation (7.1) gives us

$$Q = f(X, Y) \tag{7.2}$$

where Q = Output
X = Labor
Y = Capital

Notice that although we have designated one variable as labor and the other as capital, we have elected to keep the all-purpose symbols X and Y as a reminder that any two inputs could have been selected to represent the array of inputs.

As stated earlier, in economic analysis the distinction between the short run and the long run is not related to any particular measurement of time (e.g., days, months, or years). Instead it refers to the extent to which a firm can vary the amounts of the inputs in its production process. If there is insufficient time for the firm to adjust the amounts of all inputs utilized, this represents a "short-run" time period. A sufficient amount of time to vary all of the inputs is considered the "long run," however long or short this actually is in calendar time. Perhaps this distinction can be best illustrated with a numerical example.

A hypothetical production function is displayed in Table 7.1. The numbers in the matrix indicate the amounts of output that would result from various combinations of X and Y. For example, the use of 2 units of X and 4 units of Y yields 39 units of output. Adding one more unit of X while holding constant the amount of Y yields an additional 13 units of output (Q = 52). Increasing both X and Y by 1 unit yields 58 units of output. The addition of 1 unit of X with Y unchanged is considered by definition a short-run change. An increase in both inputs by 1 unit is, of course, a long-run change.

Table 7.1 Representative Production Table

Units of Y Employed	*Output Quantity (Q)*							
8	37	60	83	96	107	117	127	128
7	42	64	78	90	101	110	119	120
6	37	52	64	73	82	90	97	104
5	31	47	58	67	75	82	89	95
4	24	39	52	60	67	73	79	85
3	17	29	41	52	58	64	69	73
2	8	18	29	39	47	52	56	52
1	4	8	14	20	27	24	21	17
	1	2	3	4	5	6	7	8
	Units of X Employed							

Tables 7.2 and 7.3 highlight the difference between the short- and long-run changes in the production function. The pattern in Table 7.2 is called *factor productivity* or *returns to a factor.* The long-run pattern shown in Table 7.3 is referred to as *returns to scale*. More will be said about these two patterns of change in later sections of this chapter.

Another way to look at the production function is by representing the input combinations and their corresponding quantities of output on a three-dimensional production surface. This is shown in Figure 7.1, where we have denoted three combinations of inputs Y and X that produce output level Q_1. Notice that we have assumed that the production function is continuous rather than discrete. (We do this partly for ease in presenting the graphical illustration, but mainly because we can then apply the concepts of calculus to discuss the details of the production function.)

Table 7.2 Short-Run Changes in Production

Units of Y Employed	*Output Quantity (Q)*							
8	37	60	83	96	107	117	127	128
7	42	64	78	90	101	110	119	120
6	37	52	64	73	82	90	97	104
5	31	47	58	67	75	82	89	95
4	(24)	(39)	(52)	(60)	(67)	(73)	(79)	(85)
3	17	29	41	52	58	64	69	73
2	8	18	29	39	47	52	56	52
1	4	8	14	20	27	24	21	17
	1	2	3	4	5	6	7	8
	Units of X Employed							

Table 7.3 Long-Run Changes in Production

Units of Y Employed	*Output Quantity (Q)*							
8	37	60	83	96	107	117	127	(128)
7	42	64	78	90	101	110	(119)	120
6	37	52	64	73	82	(90)	97	104
5	31	47	58	67	(75)	82	89	95
4	24	39	52	(60)	67	73	79	85
3	17	29	(41)	52	58	64	69	73
2	8	(18)	29	39	47	52	56	52
1	(4)	8	14	20	27	24	21	17
	1	2	3	4	5	6	7	8
	Units of X Employed							

A continuous production function assumes that the inputs are perfectly divisible. Measures of labor and capital such as amount of time worked and amount of energy used would fit such an assumption. Discrete units such as number of people employed and number of machines used would not be appropriate for a continuous function. In terms of Figure 7.1, continuity means that output level Q_1 can be produced with any combination of Y and X represented on the dotted line. In general, a continuous production function is represented by an infinite number of combinations of Y and X on the production surface of Figure 7.1 bounded by the Y and X axes. More will be said about continuous production functions in later sections of this chapter.

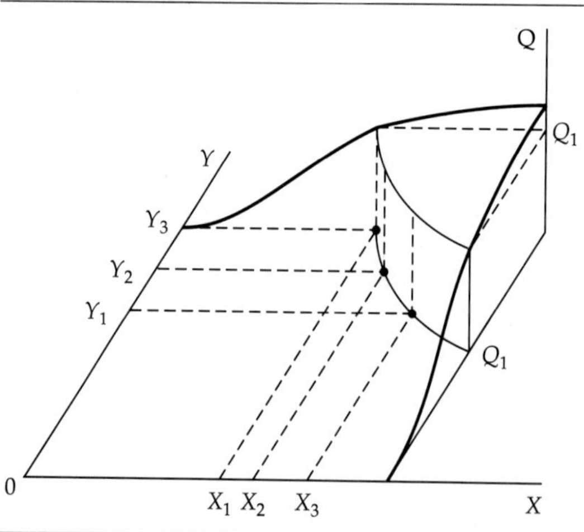

Figure 7.1 Three-Dimensional Production Function

A Short-Run Analysis of Total, Average, and Marginal Product

Before we go on to a more detailed analysis of the production function, certain key terms employed throughout this chapter should be clarified. First, economists use a number of alternative terms in reference to inputs and output:

Inputs	*Output*
Factors	Quantity *(Q)*
Factors of production	Total product *(TP)*
Resources	Product

Second, in the short-run analysis of the production function, two other terms besides the quantity of output are important measures of the outcome. They are *marginal product* (MP) and *average product* (AP). If we assume X to be the variable input, then

$$\text{Marginal product of } X = \text{MP}_X = \frac{\Delta Q}{\Delta X}, \quad \text{holding } Y \text{ constant}$$

$$\text{Average product of } X = \text{AP}_X = \frac{Q}{X}, \quad \text{holding } Y \text{ constant}^1$$

In other words, the marginal product can be defined as the change in output or total product resulting from a unit change in a variable input, and the average product can be defined as the total product per unit of input used.

To see what happens to the total product in the short run as X increases, we can go back to the data presented in Table 7.1. Assume that Y is fixed at 2 units while X increases. As illustrated in Table 7.4, total product is 8 when 1 unit of X is used, it increases to a maximum of 56 when 7 units of X are used, and it decreases to 52 units when unit 8 of the X input is added. Also notice in Table 7.4 that MP begins at 8 units, increases to a maximum of 11, and falls off to an ultimate value of -4. Average product also begins at 8, increases to a maximum of 9.67, and then drops to 6.5 units when 8 units of X are combined with the fixed amount of Y. The pattern of these changes can be seen in Figure 7.2. The total product is plotted in Figure 7.2*a*, and the average and marginal products are plotted in Figure 7.2*b*.

---

[1] In terms of calculus, MP is the partial derivative of the short-run total product function:

$$Q = f(X, Y)$$
$$\text{MP}_X = \delta Q/\delta X$$

Of course, Y would have no bearing on output because, as a constant, it would drop out of the derivation.

Table 7.4 Short-Run Production Function: Q, MP, AP

Variable Input (X)	*Total Product (Q or TP)*	*Marginal Product (MP)*	*Average Product (AP)*
0	0		
		8	
1	8		8
		10	
2	18		9
		11	
3	29		9.67
		10	
4	39		9.75
		8	
5	47		9.4
		5	
6	52		8.67
		4	
7	56		8
		−4	
8	52		6.5

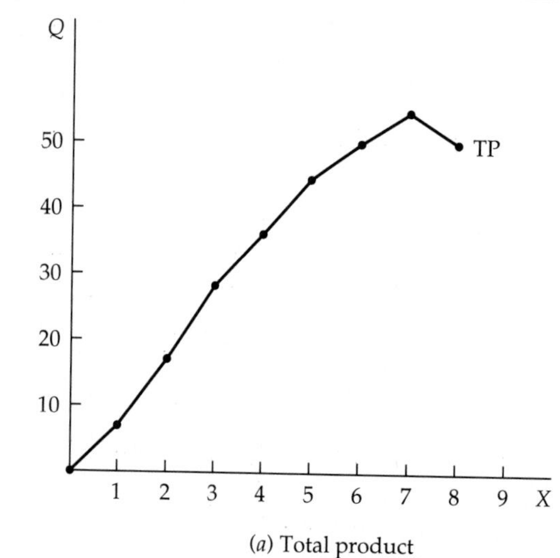

(*a*) Total product

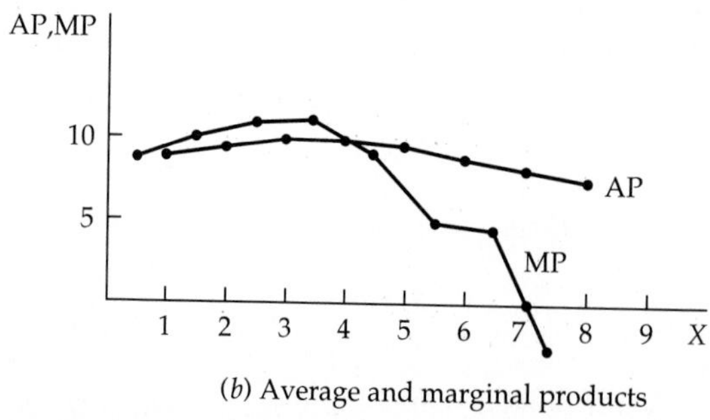

(*b*) Average and marginal products

Figure 7.2 Short-Run Production with $Y = 2$

We can observe that when Q, the quantity of the total product, reaches its maximum, MP = 0.[2] We see also that initially (as more units of X are added to the production process), MP is greater than AP, and it then becomes less than AP. Furthermore, MP = AP at AP's highest point. Because we are dealing with incremental unit changes in the input, it is difficult to see these points in Table 7.4, but they can be seen clearly in Figure 7.2. In the next section we will have more to say about the pattern of change in Q, AP, and MP and, more important, the reasons for the pattern of change.

The Law of Diminishing Returns to a Factor

The key to understanding the pattern of change in Q, AP, and MP is the phenomenon known as the *law of diminishing returns*.[3] This law states:

> As additional units of variable input are combined with a fixed input, at some point the additional output (i.e., marginal product) starts to diminish.

We will explain this law in terms of the data in Table 7.4. Judging from the MP column, the law of diminishing returns appears to take effect when more than 3 units of the X input are utilized. That is, the addition of the third unit of input increases output by 11 units, and the addition of the fourth unit increases output by 10. Up to that point, each additional unit of X employed produces increasingly more output (i.e., from 8 to 10 to 11). Up to the third unit of X, we can say that this firm experiences "increasing (marginal) returns to the X factor."

What causes the law of diminishing returns to take effect in the production process? Because this law is the basis for the short-run changes in Q, AP, and MP, we will attempt to answer this question as carefully as possible, using the case of a soft drink bottling plant as our example. To simplify the example, let us assume that there are two inputs, one fixed and the other variable. The fixed input is capital, and the variable one is labor. Now suppose the capital input consists of 25,000 feet of factory space and an automated bottling system capable of turning out 10,000 cases of bottled soft drink per hour. Suppose further that only one person is assigned to work in this plant. Thus, this person would have to do everything (e.g., order the syrup and other materials and supplies, maintain the equipment, check the quality of the bottled beverage, load the cases into the trucks, and monitor the automated system). As we can well imagine, there is no way in which this person could produce the maximum hourly output on a continuous basis. Let us say that in eight hours one person

---

[2]The relationship between the maximum Q and MP = 0 is exactly analogous to the relationship between the maximum TR and MR = 0 explained in Chapter 4.

[3]A survey conducted by an association interested in the advancement of economic education found this concept to be the one most frequently recalled by persons who studied economics. Few survey respondents could recall exactly what it meant, but many were at least familiar with the concept.

working in the plant could bottle about one-eighth of the maximum output of the production system (i.e., 1/8 × 80,000, or 10,000 cases).

Let us now add one more person to the production process. The first thing we would expect the two of them to do is divide up the tasks that have to be performed. For example, one person could monitor the input of raw materials (from the delivery of the syrup to the filling of the bottles), and the other could be responsible for the maintenance of the system and the loading of the final product onto the trucks. We may assume that the system is much too big and complex for even two persons working together to handle efficiently. However, as can be seen in Table 7.5, in an eight-hour period, the two working together can bottle 25,000 cases, or 12,500 per person. Compare this to the 10,000 cases that one person working alone was able to bottle during this same time period. We can extend the pattern of output resulting from still more additions to the work force as shown in Table 7.5. The average output continues to increase with the addition of the third person. The addition of the fourth person does not change the per-person (i.e., average) product, but the addition of the fifth person does.

The most obvious reason for the initial increase in average product is that the additional workers enabled the firm to make better use of its plant capacity. In fact, in an actual case, we can imagine that one or a few workers might not even be able to get the plant started and running. But beyond the need to have some minimum number of people simply to start up the system, it is likely that additional persons—if utilized properly—can increase the per-unit output of everyone involved in the production process, where proper utilization means the specialization of labor tasks and teamwork. This would be true for any production process in the short run.

This specialization of labor tasks also helps to explain why the average product eventually starts to decline. As additional workers are added to the production process, it becomes increasingly difficult to determine specialized tasks for each worker to perform. Indeed, once the limits to the production process are reached

Table 7.5 The Effect of Additional Labor Inputs on Production Factors

Labor Input (X)	*Total Product (Q or TP)*	*Marginal Product (MP)*	*Average Product (AP)*
0	0		
1	10,000	10,000	10,000
2	25,000	15,000	12,500
3	45,000	20,000	15,000
4	60,000	15,000	15,000
5	70,000	10,000	14,000
6	75,000	5,000	12,500
7	78,000	3,000	11,143
8	80,000	2,000	10,000

because of the firm's fixed capacity, there will be some duplication of tasks. Finally, the work force may be so large that each person actually hinders the work of the other.

However, notice that the law of diminishing returns refers to the *additional* output (i.e., marginal product) resulting from the increase in input, and not to the output per unit (i.e., average product). To track the pattern of change in marginal product and its relation to average product, let us look again at the figures in Table 7.5. For the average product to increase from 10,000 to 12,500, it was necessary for the second person to add more to the total product than the first person. In other words, for the average product to increase, the marginal product must be greater than the average product. In this case, the second person "added" 15,000 more units of output, increasing the total output to 25,000 and the average product to 12,500. (The word *added* is in quotation marks to stress the fact that the second person's marginal product was not greater than the first person's because he or she was more skilled, motivated, or efficient. If the order of assignment were reversed, with the second person put to work first, his or her marginal product would be 10,000. No matter who is assigned to the job or the order in which workers are assigned, the second person will always add more to the output than the first because specialization and teamwork enables the two of them working together to produce more than the sum of their individual efforts.[4])

In Table 7.5 we observe that when the fifth unit of input is utilized, average product falls from 15,000 to 14,000. This implies that the marginal product of the fifth person is less than the average output produced at the point when the new worker was added to the production process. In fact, the marginal product has dropped to 10,000. Thus, at some point the marginal product itself begins to decrease, and it is precisely at that point that the law of diminishing returns takes effect.[5] If still more people were added to the production process, they may disturb each other (e.g., literally bump into one another) so that the total output of the plant would start to diminish. People added at that point would lead to negative marginal products. Here again, one must be cautioned not to conclude that the negative marginal product is the result of the individual characteristics of any of the workers.

The Three Stages of Production in the Short Run

The short-run production function can be divided into three distinct stages of production. To illustrate this phenomenon, let us return to the data in Ta-

---

[4]Economists refer to this as the assumption of "homogeneous" inputs, in which units of a production system are exactly alike and perfectly interchangeable.

[5]If the marginal product of the fifth person were 15,000, then the average product would remain unchanged at 15,000. The relationship between average and marginal product is based on the general mathematical relationship between any average and marginal term. When the marginal exceeds the average, the average increases. When the marginal is less than the average, the average decreases. When the marginal is equal to the average, the average remains unchanged. More will be said about the realationship between marginal and average values in Chapter 8.

ble 7.4 and Figure 7.2. For your convenience, Figure 7.2 has been reproduced as Figure 7.3. As the figure indicates, stage I runs from zero to four units of the variable input X (i.e., to the point at which average product reaches its maximum). Stage II begins from this point and proceeds to seven units of input X (i.e., to the point at which total product is maximized). Stage III continues on from that point. According to economic theory, in the short run, "rational" firms should only be operating in stage II. It is clear why stage III is irrational: the firm would be using more of its variable input to produce less output! However, it may not be as apparent why stage I is also considered irrational. The reason is that if a firm were operating in stage I, it would be grossly underutilizing its fixed capacity. That is, it would have so much fixed capacity relative to its usage of variable inputs that it could increase the output per unit of variable input (i.e., average product) simply by adding more variable inputs to this capacity. Figure 7.4*a* summarizes the three stages of production and the reasons that the rational firm operates in stage II of the short-run production function.

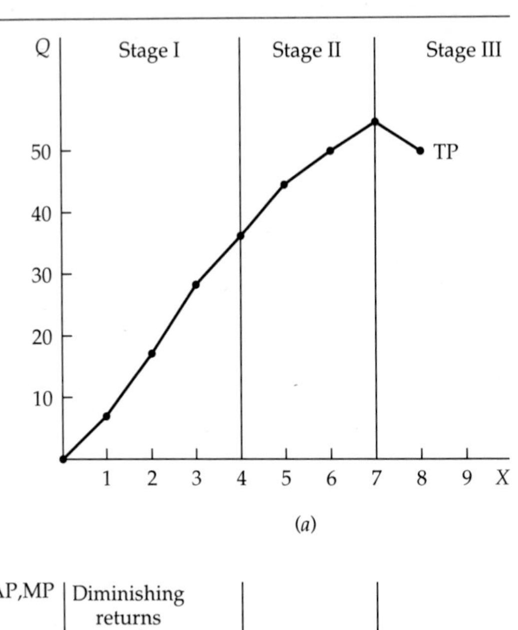

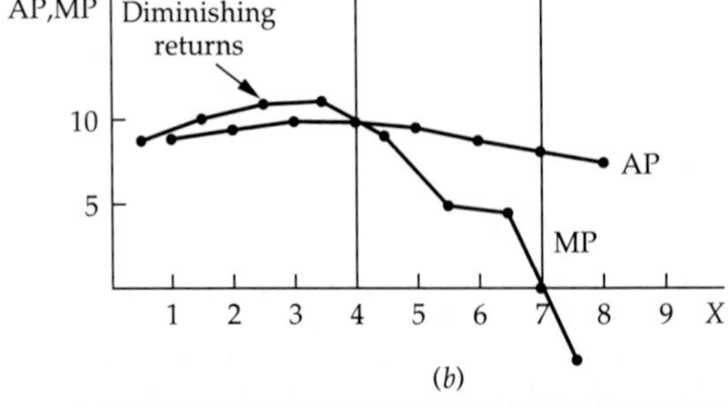

Figure 7.3 The Three Stages of Production

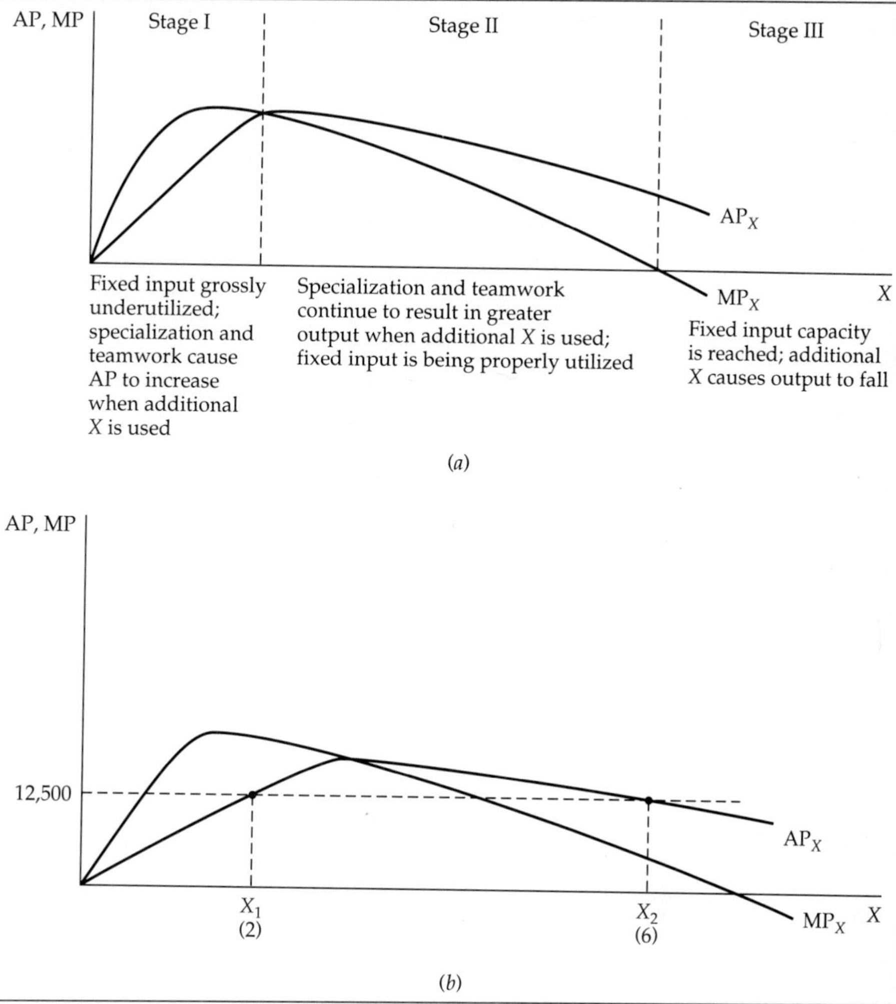

Figure 7.4 Explanation of Production Stages

If you are still not clear about the irrational nature of stage I, there is an alternative explanation. In Figure 7.4*b*, we have designated two levels of variable input usage: X_1 and X_2. Here we see that the average product is the same whether X_1 or X_2 units of the variable input are used. If output per variable input is the same regardless of which input level is used, the firm should employ X_2 because the total product will be higher. We can use the numbers in Table 7.5 to illustrate this point. Notice that the average product is 12,500 when two labor inputs are used and also when six labor inputs are used. We can also see that a level of two labor units falls in the range of stage I, whereas a level of six units falls in the range of stage II. And, of course, the total product for six units of labor (75,000) is higher than that for two units (25,000), which supports the case for a rational firm operating in stage II instead of stage I.

Derived Demand and the Optimal Level of Variable Input Usage

Given that a firm's short-run production has only one "rational" stage of production (i.e., stage II), we must still determine the level of input usage within stage II that is best for the rational, profit-maximizing firm. In Table 7.5, we see that stage II ranges from four to eight units of input. In terms of output, Stage II goes from 60,000 to 80,000. Is there any one level of input usage that we can consider optimal?

The answer to this question is based on a concept introduced in Chapter 4, derived demand. Recall that the demand for inputs is derived from the demand for their output. In other words, it would do no good for the firm to decide how many units of variable input to use without knowing how many units of output it could sell, the price of the product, and the monetary costs of employing various amounts of the X input.

To see exactly how this works, assume that a firm is operating in a perfectly competitive market for its input and its output. That is, it can sell as many units of the product as it wants as long as it does so at the going market price. Moreover, it can hire as many X inputs as it desires as long as it pays these inputs the going market price (i.e., the competitive wage rate). Building on the figures in Table 7.5, we arrive at the numbers in Table 7.6. Four new measures are used in this table:

Total revenue product (TRP): The market value of the firm's output, computed by multiplying the total product by the market price ($Q \times P$).

Marginal revenue product (MRP): The change in the firm's total revenue product resulting from a unit change in the number of inputs used (ΔTRP/ΔX). It

Table 7.6 Combining Marginal Revenue Product (MRP) with Marginal Labor Cost (MLC)

Labor Unit (X)	*Total Product (Q or TP)*	*Average Product (AP)*	*Marginal Product (MP)*	*Total Revenue Product (TRP)*	*Marginal Revenue Product (MRP)*	*Total Labor Cost (TLC)*	*Marginal Labor Cost (MLC)*	*TRP − TLC*	*MRP − MLC*
0	0		0	0		0		0	0
1	10,000	10,000	10,000	20,000	20,000	10,000	10,000	10,000	10,000
2	25,000	12,500	15,000	50,000	30,000	20,000	10,000	30,000	20,000
3	45,000	15,000	20,000	90,000	40,000	30,000	10,000	60,000	30,000
4	60,000	15,000	15,000	120,000	30,000	40,000	10,000	80,000	20,000
5	70,000	14,000	10,000	140,000	20,000	50,000	10,000	90,000	10,000
6	75,000	12,500	5,000	150,000	10,000	60,000	10,000	90,000	0
7	78,000	11,143	3,000	156,000	6,000	70,000	10,000	86,000	−4,000
8	80,000	10,000	2,000	160,000	4,000	80,000	10,000	80,000	−6,000

Note: P = Product price = \$2
W = Cost per unit of labor = \$10,000
MRP = MP × P
TLC = $X \times W$
MLC = ΔTLC/ΔX

can also be computed by multiplying the marginal product by the product price (MP × P).

Total labor cost (TLC): The total cost of using the variable input, labor, computed by multiplying the wage rate (which we assume to be some given and constant dollar amount) by the number of variable inputs employed (Wage rate × X).

Marginal labor cost (MLC): The change in total labor cost resulting from a unit change in the number of variable inputs used. Because the wage rate is assumed to be constant regardless of the number of inputs used, the MLC is the same as the wage rate.[6]

In deriving the figures in Table 7.6 from Table 7.5, we have assumed a product price of $2 and a wage rate of $10,000 per unit. Given these figures, you can see that a rational firm would want to hire 6 units of labor. Up to that point it pays for the firm to add more labor because the additional cost to the firm (MLC) to do so is more than made up for by the additional revenue (MRP) brought in by the sale of the increased output. Beyond that point the firm would pay more in additional labor cost than it would receive in additional revenue.

Can you discern how the demand for the output is incorporated into this analysis, that is, how the demand for the input X is actually derived from the demand for the output? Suppose the market demand increased and drove the market price up to $4. This would increase the market value of the labor input's efforts. In other words, the market value of each additional labor unit's contribution to the total product would double. This increase in the labor input's MRP would then justify the firm's use of a seventh unit of labor. Thus, an increase in the market demand for the output leads to an increase in the demand by the firm for labor input, all other factors held constant. The original figures from Table 7.6 as well as the case in which market price is assumed to increase to $4 are illustrated in Figure 7.5.

We can summarize this relationship between the demand for the output and the demand for the input in terms of the following optimal decision rule:

> A profit-maximizing firm operating in perfectly competitive output and input markets will be using the optimal amount of an input at the point at which the monetary value of the input's marginal product is equal to the additional cost of using that input—in other words, when MRP = MLC.

---

[6]This term is also referred to as *marginal resource cost* (MRC) and *marginal factor cost* (MFC). By assuming that the firm hires workers in a perfectly competitive labor market, we also assume that it can hire as many workers as it chooses at some going market wage rate determined by the supply and demand for this particular type of worker. This would not be the case if the firm were operating in an imperfectly competitive market. We will not consider the imperfectly competitive case in this text. Interested readers should consult any economics principles or intermediate microeconomics text for a full discussion on this type of labor market and its impact on the input decisions of the firm.

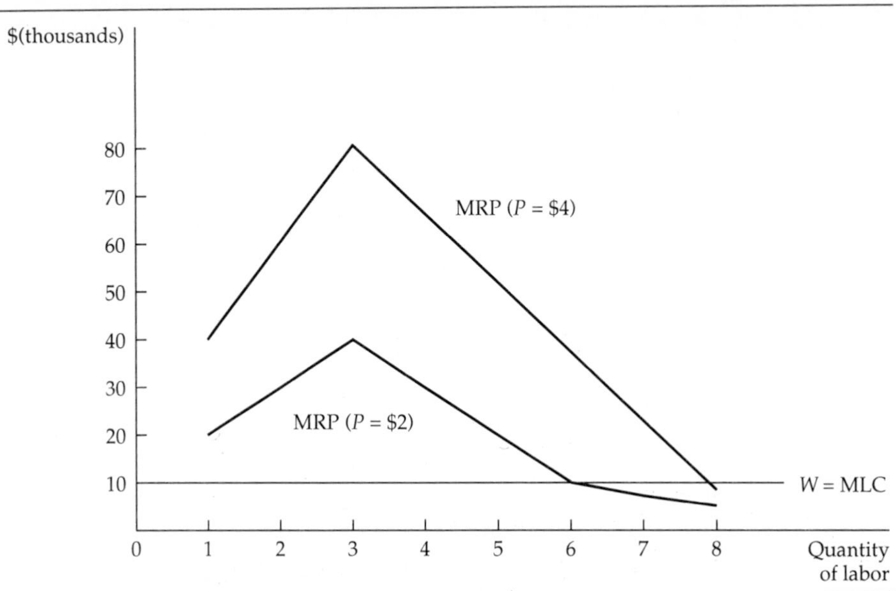

Figure 7.5 The Effect of Increased Market Price on the Demand for Labor

The Multiple-Input Case

We now turn to the more general case in which a firm seeks the optimal combination of inputs, rather than simply the optimal level of one particular input. For explanatory purposes, we will address the problem of determining the optimal combination of inputs using the two-input case presented earlier in this chapter. Mathematically, there is no problem in considering any number of inputs, but we will use two inputs for ease of graphical illustration. Nonetheless, it should be noted that the decision rule for determining the optimal combination of inputs is the same whether two inputs or more than two are used in the production process.

From the standpoint of economic theory, the two-input case can be considered either a short-run or a long-run analysis, depending on what assumption is made about the nature of the firm's inputs. If we assume that the firm has only two inputs (or, more realistically, that all of its inputs can be divided into two basic categories), then the two-input case must be considered a long-run analysis because, in effect, all of the firm's inputs are allowed to vary. However, if the firm is assumed to have other inputs that are being held constant while the two inputs are being evaluated, then the analysis must be considered short-run. Readers should be able to discern from the context of our discussion which case applies for our examples.

To illustrate the two-input case, we will use the data in Table 7.1, reproduced as Table 7.7. Suppose the firm produces 52 units of output ($Q = 52$). According

Table 7.7 Representative Production Table Illustrating Isoquants

Units of Y Employed	*Output Quantity (Q)*							
8	37	60	83	96	107	117	127	128
7	42	64	78	90	101	110	119	120
6	37	(52)	64	(73)	82	90	97	104
5	31	47	58	67	75	82	89	95
4	24	39	(52)	60	67	(73)	79	85
3	17	(29)	41	(52)	58	64	69	(73)
2	8	18	(29)	39	47	(52)	56	(52)
1	4	8	14	20	27	24	21	17
	1	2	3	4	5	6	7	8
	Units of X Employed							

to the table, the firm can employ the following combinations of inputs Y and X respectively: 6 and 2, 4 and 3, 3 and 4, 2 and 6, and 2 and 8. Together, they form the isoquant shown in Table 7.7. An isoquant is a curve representing the various combinations of two inputs that produce the same amount of output. Notice that isoquants for $Q = 29$ and $Q = 73$ are also shown in Table 7.7. The isoquant for $Q = 52$ is plotted in Figure 7.6.

A continuous production function, in which inputs are assumed to be perfectly divisible, is illustrated in Figure 7.7. Here the isoquant appears as a smoothed out version of that depicted in Figure 7.6. Notice that both the discrete and continuous isoquants are downward sloping and convex to the origin.

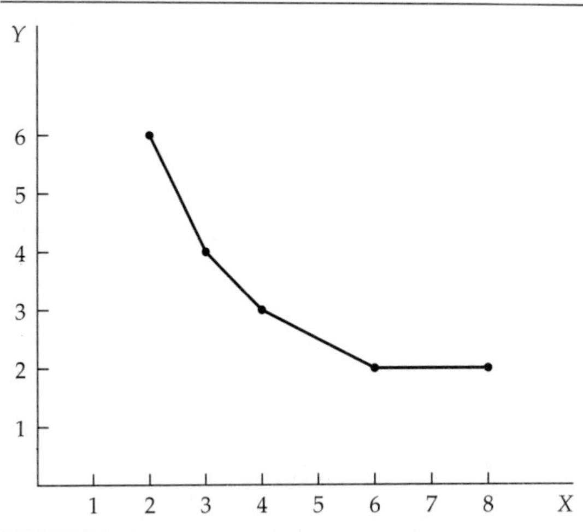

Figure 7.6 Graph of Isoquant $Q = 52$

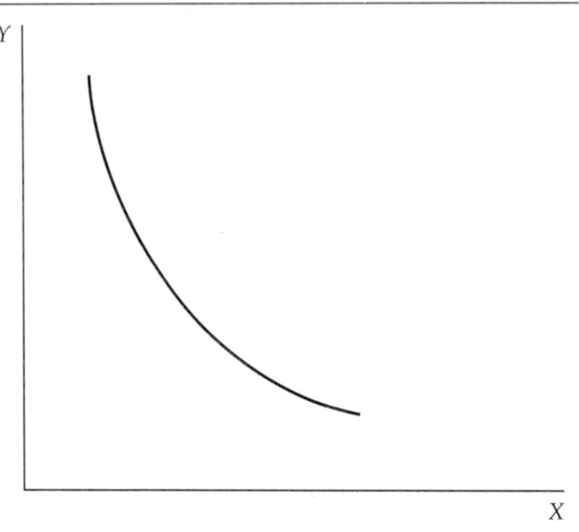

Figure 7.7 Isoquant for Continuous Production Function

The latter characteristic means that the slope of the isoquant becomes less steep as one moves downward and to the right. These characteristics pertain to the degree to which the two inputs can be substituted for one another.

SUBSTITUTING INPUT FACTORS The degree of substitutability of two inputs is a measure of the ease with which one input can be used in place of the other in producing a given amount of output. To explain this further, let us use the example of the making of soft drinks. Consider the ingredients listed on the label of a typical soft drink:

> Carbonated water, sugar and/or corn syrup, citric acid, natural flavoring, sodium benzoate as a preservative, and caramel coloring.

Notice that the sweetening component of the recipe is listed as "sugar and/or corn syrup." This implies that the two ingredients are *perfect substitutes* for each other. The linear isoquant shown in Figure 7.8*a* depicts the perfect substitutability between the two ingredients. The hypothetical numbers on the *X* and *Y* axes serve to caution you not to assume that perfect substitutability means the two inputs must be substitutable at a ratio of 1 to 1. In this illustration, the substitution ratio is 2 to 1. That is, 2 grams of sugar can always be substituted for 1 gram of corn syrup, no matter how much sugar or corn syrup is used.

If we divide a soft drink into two components, "natural flavoring" and "all other ingredients," we can illustrate the relationship between these two inputs with the isoquant shown in Figure 7.8*b*. Presumably, what gives the soft drink its special flavor is the unique ratio of the flavoring to the rest of the components. The hypothetical numbers in Figure 7.8*b* indicate that adding one more part of flavoring without increasing the other contents by five parts will not yield more output. Thus, we see that natural flavoring and the other ingredients are what economists term *perfect complements* to each other, because they must always be used together in some fixed proportion (i.e., one part of flavoring and five parts of the other ingredients).

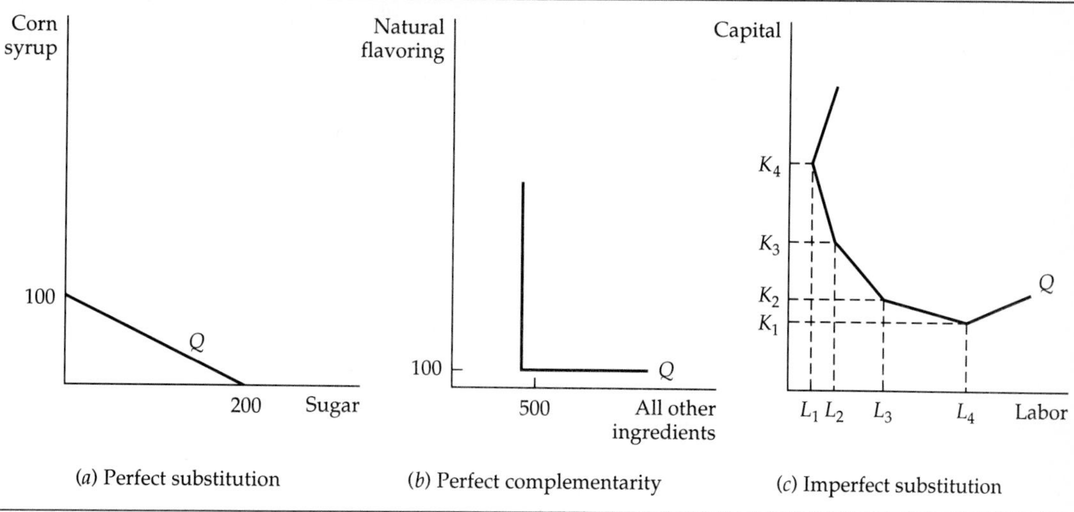

Figure 7.8 Substitutability of Two Inputs in a Production Function

Between the extremes of perfect substitutability and perfect complementarity lies the case illustrated in Figure 7.8*c*. Here labor and capital are *imperfect substitutes* for each other. That is, one can be substituted for the other, but only up to a limit. (As shown in the figure, any addition of labor beyond L_4 units requires more capital rather than less to maintain the level of output at Q.) Furthermore, as more of one input is used in place of the other, it becomes increasingly difficult to substitute. As can be seen in Figure 7.8*c*, when the firm is employing L_1 units of labor and K_4 units of capital,[7] it can substitute a relatively small amount of labor for capital and still maintain the same level of output. However, when it is using L_2 units of labor and K_3 units of capital, it must substitute a larger amount of labor to maintain the same level of output. More will be said about imperfect substitution in the next section.

In terms of selecting the optimal combination of inputs, it is clear that the case of imperfect substitutability represents the greatest challenge to the firm. Perfectly complementary inputs must be used together in some fixed proportion. The case of perfectly substitutable inputs is equally trivial. If one input can always be substituted in some fixed amount for another (no matter how much of each input is being used), the only determinant of the optimal combination is input price.[8]

---

[7]Economists generally use the letter K to represent the capital input because they do not want to confuse it with cost, for which the letter C is generally reserved.

[8]For example, in the United States corn syrup is used much more than sugar to sweeten soft drinks "naturally." On the other hand, in Europe sugar is used almost exclusively as the natural sweetener. The agricultural policy of the European Community is to subsidize heavily the sugar beet farmers. Consequently, sugar is substantially less expensive than corn syrup in Europe. In the United States, restrictive import quotas on sugar make it more expensive than corn syrup.

In the case of imperfectly substitutable inputs, the optimal combination depends both on the degree of substitutability and on their relative prices. For example, suppose labor costs much less than capital. Does this automatically mean that the firm should use more labor relative to capital, (i.e., a labor-intensive production process)? No, because the relative productivities of the two inputs also have to be considered. If capital is much more productive than labor, it will benefit a firm to use more capital relative to labor if the difference in productivity more than compensates for the difference in cost. One brief example should help to reinforce this point.

In recent years, a growing number of American companies have shifted their production overseas, particularly to countries in the Asia-Pacific region. The press has referred to companies heavily engaged in this practice as "hollow corporations."[9] Cheap labor is the usual explanation offered by the popular press. To a large extent, this is true. However, if the workers in these Asian countries were not very productive, it would not necessarily pay for the American companies to shift production to them, especially since transportation costs must be considered. Put another way, there are countries outside of the Asia-Pacific region that have even lower wages. Why have the American companies not shifted all of their production to these places?

Before we explain how economists determine the optimal combination of two inputs that are imperfect substitutes, we should explain how the degree of imperfection is measured. The measurement itself is called the *marginal rate of technical substitution* (MRTS). We will consider an example in which we gradually substitute more of the X input for the Y input. Algebraically, the marginal rate of technical substitution of X for Y can be expressed as:

$$\text{MRTS } (X \text{ for } Y) = \frac{\Delta Y}{\Delta X} \tag{7.3}$$

Notice that the numerator shows the amount of Y that is removed from the production process, and the denominator indicates the amount of X needed to substitute for Y to maintain the same amount of output. Graphically, the MRTS can be represented by moving downward and to the right along any isoquant (see Figure 7.9). Indeed, if we look back at the algebraic expression of MRTS (X for Y), we see that it is the measure of the slope of the isoquant.

To see exactly how MRTS is measured along the isoquant, let us use the discrete case illustrated in Table 7.7. The different input combinations that can be used to produce 52 units of output are summarized in Table 7.8. The changes in Y and X as one moves from combination A to E are shown in Figure 7.10. Moving from combination A to E, we measure the marginal rate of substitution of X for Y as follows:

---

[9] *Business Week*, March 3, 1986, pp. 57–59.

Movement	*MRTS (X for Y)* = $\Delta Y/\Delta X$
A to B	$\frac{-2}{1}$
B to C	$\frac{-1}{1}$
C to D	$\frac{-1}{2}$
D to E	$\frac{0}{2}$

Notice that because the isoquant is downward sloping, $\Delta Y/\Delta X$, or the MRTS, will always have a negative value. However, in discussing the economic significance of MRTS, it is easier to treat it as a positive value. Therefore, let us for the moment simply drop the negative sign. Thus, for example, the MRTS between A and B becomes: MRTS = $\frac{2}{1}$. Between B and C and between C and D, the MRTS values are 1 and $\frac{1}{2}$, respectively. Expressed as a positive value, MRTS can be clearly seen to diminish as we move from combination A to combination E. Economists refer to this phenomenon as the *law of diminishing marginal rate of technical substitution.* As you might expect, this relates to the law of diminishing returns.

When we move from A to B, we substitute one unit of *X* for two units of *Y*. In other words, the loss in output resulting from the use of two fewer units of *Y* can be made up for by adding one unit of *X*. When we move from B to C,

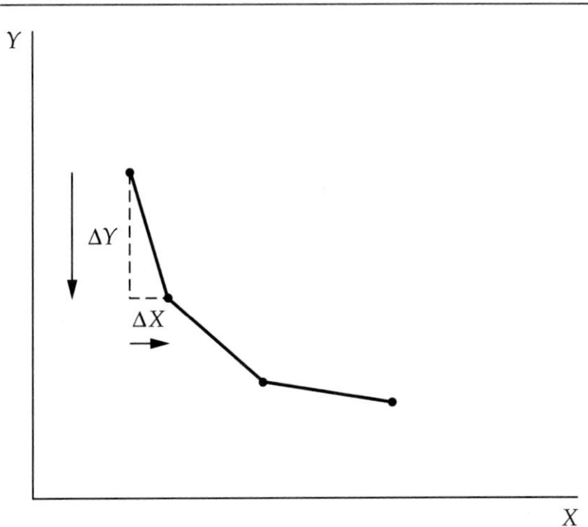

Figure 7.9 MRTS (*X* for *Y*)

Table 7.8 Input Combinations for Isoquant $Q = 52$

Combination	Y	X
A	6	2
B	4	3
C	3	4
D	2	6
E	2	8

the loss in output resulting from the use of one fewer unit of Y must be made up for by adding one unit of X. From C to D we see that the loss in output resulting from the use of one fewer unit of Y must be made up for by adding two units of X. Finally, when we move from D to E, we find that rather than substituting X for Y, we must add more units of X to maintain the output level at 52.

Apparently, as we move from A to D, increasingly more X must be added relative to the amount of Y taken out of the production process to maintain the same amount of output. We started out by having to add only one unit of X to replace two units of Y and ended up having to add two units of X to replace one unit of Y. In other words, as more X is used relative to Y in the production process, the productivity of X diminishes relative to Y. This is a result of none other than the law of diminishing returns. Recall that this law states that as additional units of a variable factor are added to a fixed factor, at some point the additional output starts to diminish. If this holds true when one of the inputs is fixed, it must certainly hold when this same input is reduced.

To understand fully why increasingly more of input X is needed to compensate for the loss of a given amount of input Y to maintain the same output, we need to incorporate the concept of marginal product into our analysis. Looking

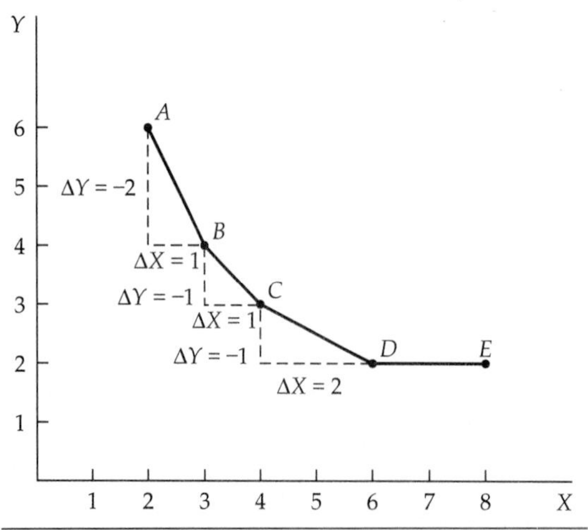

Figure 7.10 Measuring MRTS along an Isoquant

Table 7.9 Representative Production Table

Units of Y Employed	*Output Quantity (Q)*							
8	37	60	83	96	107	117	127	128
7	42	64	78	90	101	110	119	120
6	37	(52)	64	73	82	90	97	104
5	31	47	58	67	75	82	89	95
4	24	39→	(52)	60	67	73	79	85
3	17	29	41	(52)	58	64	69	73
2	8	18	29	39	47	(52)	56	(52)
1	4	8	14	20	27	24	21	17
	1	2	3	4	5	6	7	8
	Units of X Employed							

back at Table 7.1 (reproduced as Table 7.9 for your convenience), we observe that the movement from A to B actually involves two distinct steps. First, input Y is reduced by 2 units (from 6 to 4), resulting in a reduction in output by 13 units (from 52 to 39). This is indicated by the downward-pointing arrow in Table 7.9. Next input X is added to the production process to compensate for the reduction in Y. As can be seen in the table, an additional unit of X is required to restore the output to its original level of 52. This is indicated by the right-pointing arrow in the table.

Recall from an earlier discussion that the marginal product is defined as the change in output relative to the change in some given input. In this case, the movement from A to B in two separate steps reveals that the marginal product of input Y is

$$\frac{\Delta Q}{\Delta Y} = \frac{-13}{-2} = 6.5$$

The marginal product of input X is

$$\frac{\Delta Q}{\Delta X} = \frac{13}{1} = 13$$

Proceeding next to combination C and then on to D using the same two-step process gives us the following ratios of the marginal products of $X$and Y: between B and C, $MP_X/MP_Y = 1$; between C and D, $MP_X/MP_Y = 1/2$.

In reviewing the ratios of the marginal products of X and Y along the isoquant $Q = 52$, you probably have spotted a very important link between the MRTS, the slope of the isoquant, and these ratios. Indeed, they are all equal. More specifically,

$$\text{MRTS} = \frac{\Delta Y}{\Delta X} = -\frac{MP_X}{MP_Y} \tag{7.4}$$

This equation is illustrated in Table 7.10.

Table 7.10 MP_X/MP_Y in Relation to MRTS (*X* for *Y*)

Combination	*Q*	*Y*	MP_x	*X*	MP_y	*MRTS (X for Y)*	MP_X/MP_Y
A	52	6		2			
			13		6.5	2	2
B	52	4		3			
			11		11	1	1
C	52	3		4			
			6.5		13	1/2	1/2
D	52	2		6			

Because Equation (7.4) will play an important part in a later section of this chapter, let us briefly explain its derivation. Consider once again the movement along an isoquant between two given points. As illustrated using specific numbers in the previous pages, this movement involves two distinct steps: the reduction in one input (e.g., input *Y*) and the increase in the other input (e.g., input *X*). The decrease in the output resulting from a decrease in input *Y* can be stated as

$$\frac{MP_Y}{\Delta Y}$$

The increase in output resulting from an increase in input *X* can be stated as

$$\frac{MP_X}{\Delta X}$$

Along the isoquant, the output level must be maintained at a constant level. Thus,

$$\frac{MP_Y}{\Delta Y} = \frac{MP_X}{\Delta X}$$

Rearranging the terms in this equation and remembering that $\text{MRTS} = \Delta Y / \Delta X$ gives us

$$\text{MRTS} = \frac{\Delta Y}{\Delta X} = -\frac{MP_X}{MP_Y}$$

THE OPTIMAL COMBINATION OF MULTIPLE INPUTS Earlier we stated that the determination of the optimal combination of imperfectly substitutable inputs depends on both their relative prices and on the degree to which they can be substituted for one another. In the previous section, you learned that the degree to which one input can be substituted for another is actually a reflection of the relationship between their marginal products. Therefore, the optimal combination of inputs depends on the relationship between the inputs' relative marginal products and their relative prices. In the case of two inputs, we can state this relationship mathematically as

$$\frac{MP_X}{MP_Y} = \frac{P_X}{P_Y} \tag{7.5}$$

To demonstrate this relationship we will use *isocost curves*[10] and combine them with the isoquant curves developed in the previous section. First we will rearrange Equation (7.5) in the following way:

$$\frac{MP_X}{P_X} = \frac{MP_Y}{P_Y} \tag{7.6}$$

In other words, two inputs are combined in the best possible way when the marginal product of the last unit of one input in relation to its price is just equal to the marginal product of the last unit of the other input in relation to its price.

This statement may be a bit confusing, so let us use our earlier example about companies shifting production overseas to illustrate the point. Suppose that the HiTek Corporation, a major producer of home computer peripherals based in Silicon Valley, finds that, at its current levels of production and input usage in California and Hong Kong, the following data apply:

Marginal product of labor in Hong Kong (MP_{HK}) = 9
Marginal product of labor in California (MP_{CA}) = 12
Wage rate in Hong Kong (W_{HK}) = \$3/hr
Wage rate in California (W_{CA}) = \$6/hr

If you were the president of the company, what would you conclude from these figures? First, we can see that labor is cheaper in Hong Kong than in California but is less productive. From Equation (7.5),

$$\frac{MP_{HK}}{MP_{CA}} = \frac{9}{12} > \frac{W_{HK}}{W_{CA}} = \frac{3}{6} \tag{7.7}$$

Using Equation (7.6) gives us

$$\frac{MP_{HK}}{W_{HK}} = \frac{9}{3} > \frac{MP_{CA}}{W_{CA}} = \frac{12}{6} \tag{7.8}$$

From Equation (7.8) we see that the additional output (marginal product) per last dollar spent on labor in Hong Kong (9/\$3 = 3) is greater than the additional output per last dollar spent on labor in California (12/\$6 = 2). In short, HiTek can obtain more additional output per dollar by producing more in Hong Kong and less in California. Put another way, "at the margin," one dollar less in California reduces output by two units, and transferring that labor dollar to Hong Kong increases output by three. Therefore, rearranging input combinations so that more labor is used in Hong Kong and less is used in California enables the firm to increase its total output without increasing its total expenditure on labor.

As a test of your understanding of marginal analysis, consider this question: In the short run, should HiTek shift all of its production to Hong Kong? Remember, as more labor is used in Hong Kong, we can expect that the marginal

[10] Just as an isoquant represents input combinations that produce the same quantity, the isocost line represents input combinations that cost the same.

product of labor there will eventually diminish (according to the law of diminishing returns). Moreover, if many other companies have the same idea, their combined demand for labor in the Hong Kong market could drive wage rates up. In terms of Equation (7.8), we could then see that MP_{HK} will fall and W_{HK} will rise. At some point the inequality expressed in Equation (7.8) would no longer hold, and the two sides of the equation will be equalized. That is,

$$\frac{MP_{HK}}{W_{HK}} = \frac{MP_{CA}}{W_{CA}}$$

It is at that point that the firm would stop shifting labor tasks from California to Hong Kong.

Let us now return to the more formal economic analysis of optimal input combinations by explaining the optimality rule with the use of isoquants and isocost curves. Suppose $P_X = \$100$ and $P_Y = \$200$. Suppose further that a firm has a budget of $1,000 to spend on inputs X and Y. At these prices and this expenditure limit, any of the combinations of X and Y in Table 7.11 could be purchased.

Algebraically, the budget can be expressed as follows:

$$E = P_X \times X + P_Y \times Y \tag{7.9}$$

where E = Total budget allotment for inputs X and Y
P_X = Price of X
P_Y = Price of Y
X = Quantity of input X
Y = Quantity of input Y

In other words, the amount spent for X and Y is equal to the number of units of X multiplied by its price plus the number of units of Y multiplied by its price. In this case,

$$\$1,000 = \$100X + \$200Y \tag{7.10}$$

Using this equation to plot the numbers in Table 7.11, we obtain the isocost curve shown in Figure 7.11.

Table 7.11 Input Combinations for $1,000 Budget

Combination	*X*	*Y*
A	0	5
B	2	4
C	4	3
D	6	2
E	8	1
G	10	0

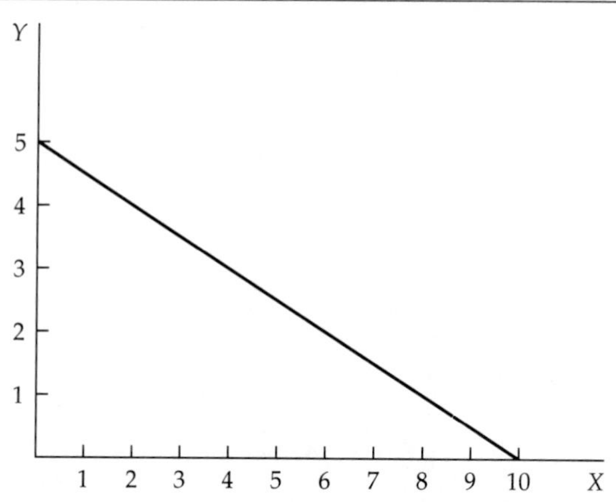

Figure 7.11 Isocost Curve for Inputs X and Y

Note that the isocost curve is linear because the prices of the inputs are constant. A few algebraic manipulations of Equation (7.9) will indicate that the prices of the inputs in relation to each other (i.e., P_X/P_Y) are represented by the slope of the isocost line:[11]

$$E = P_X \times X + P_Y \times Y$$
$$P_Y \times Y = E - P_X \times X$$
$$Y = \frac{E}{P_Y} - \frac{P_X}{P_Y} \times X \qquad (7.11)$$

Figure 7.12 combines the isocost curve shown in Figure 7.11 and the isoquant shown in Figure 7.10. Note that the isocost line and the isoquant are tangent to each other between points (4,3) and (6,2). This means that between these two points the slopes of the two curves are identical. Therefore, if the slope of the isocost line is $-P_X/P_Y$ and the slope of the isoquant is $-\text{MP}_X/\text{MP}_Y$, then between these two points

$$-\frac{\text{MP}_X}{\text{MP}_Y} = -\frac{P_X}{P_Y}$$

If we cancel the negative signs on both sides of the equation, we arrive at the optimality rule first stated in Equation (7.5). Given a budget of \$1,000 and the input combinations represented by the isoquant in Figure 7.12, the firm would employ the optimal combination of inputs if it used either four units of X and three of Y or six units of X and two of Y.

We are not able to find a unique combination of inputs because we have used a discrete set of input combinations. Graphically, we can show quite easily how the use of a continuous production function enables us to find one optimal

[11]The coefficient of X, $-P_X/P_Y$, represents the b coefficient of the common expression of the linear function, $Y = a + bX$. The Y intercept is E/P_Y.

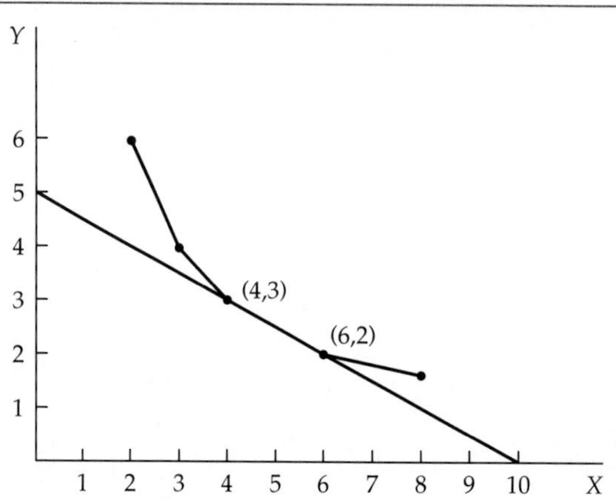

Figure 7.12 Optimal Combinations of Inputs X and Y

input combination. In Figure 7.13, we have combined the isocost curve with a series of smoothed or continuous production isoquants. Point B represents the firm's optimal combination of inputs. Let us explain why.

To begin with, point D must be ruled out because at that point the firm would not be spending the full amount of its budget allotment. On the other hand, point E represents a combination beyond the limits set by the budget. This leaves points $A, B,$ and C, each representing a combination that can be purchased with the budget allotment. Of these three points, point B represents the best combination because the firm would be producing the maximum amount given its budget limitation.

In terms of the marginal analysis developed previously, we can see that point B is the only one that fulfills the optimality condition expressed in Equations (7.5) and (7.6). That is, at point B, the slope of the isocost curve and the slope of the isoquant are identical. (Recall that the slope of a continuous isoquant is measured by the slope of the line tangent to the curve at a particular point.) Therefore, at point B, $\text{MP}_X/\text{MP}_Y = P_X/P_Y$.[12]

THE OPTIMAL LEVELS OF MULTIPLE INPUTS. By following the optimality condition first presented in Equation (7.5) and (7.6), a firm ensures that it will be producing in the least costly way, regardless of the level of output. Therefore, Equation (7.5) could be more specifically called the condition for cost minimiza-

[12]The same line of reasoning indicates that at point A

$$\frac{\text{MP}_X}{\text{MP}_Y} > \frac{P_X}{P_Y} \quad \text{or} \quad \frac{\text{MP}_X}{P_X} > \frac{\text{MP}_Y}{P_Y}$$

and at point C

$$\frac{\text{MP}_X}{\text{MP}_Y} < \frac{P_X}{P_Y} \quad \text{or} \quad \frac{\text{MP}_X}{P_X} < \frac{\text{MP}_Y}{P_Y}$$

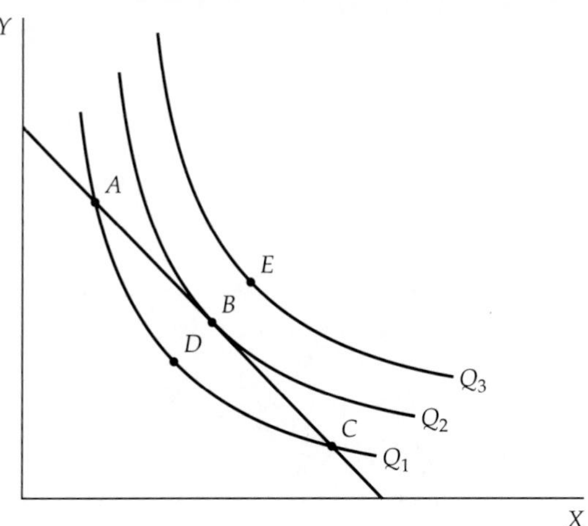

$$A:\quad \frac{MP_X}{MP_Y} > \frac{P_X}{P_Y} \quad \text{or} \quad \frac{MP_X}{P_X} > \frac{MP_Y}{P_Y}$$

$$B:\quad \frac{MP_X}{MP_Y} = \frac{P_X}{P_Y} \quad \text{or} \quad \frac{MP_X}{P_X} = \frac{MP_Y}{P_Y}$$

$$C:\quad \frac{MP_X}{MP_Y} < \frac{P_X}{P_Y} \quad \text{or} \quad \frac{MP_X}{P_X} < \frac{MP_Y}{P_Y}$$

Figure 7.13 Selecting the Optimal Input Combination for a Continuous Production Function

tion. But how much output should the firm be producing? The answer to the question, as was the case for a single input, depends on the demand for the product.

As you recall, the decision regarding the number of units of a single input to use was based on the condition $P_X = \text{MLC} = \text{MRP}_X$. That is, the firm should use the X input up to the point at which its cost (i.e., P_X) just equals the market price of the additional input's efforts (i.e., MRP_X). By the same token, the decision rule for two or more inputs requires that the firm use each input up to the point

$$P_i = \text{MRP}_i \tag{7.12}$$

where P_i = *Price of input i*
MRP_i = Marginal revenue product of input i

If the firm is utilizing two inputs (X and Y), its optimality condition is

$$P_X = \text{MRP}_X \quad \text{and} \quad P_Y = \text{MRP}_Y \tag{7.13}$$

We can explain the rationale for the optimality condition with two or more inputs simply by saying that what applies in the case of one input must apply to more than one input. However, there is a more formal explanation in microeconomic theory using several terms and concepts that will not be presented in detail until Chapter 11. Nonetheless, following is a brief version of this theoretical explanation.

According to economic theory, the firm that wishes to maximize its profit will always try to operate at the point where the extra revenue received from the sale of the last unit of output produced is just equal to the additional cost of producing this output. In other words, its optimal level of production is at the point where marginal revenue (MR) is equal to marginal cost (MC). In Chapter 11, you will learn in much greater detail about the rationale and application of the "MR = MC rule." For now, let us simply explain the justification for the rule governing the optimal use of more than one input.

Marginal cost, or MC, is the cost of producing an additional unit of output. Using the terms developed in previous examples in this chapter,

$$\mathrm{MC} = \frac{P_i}{\mathrm{MP}_i} \tag{7.14}$$

where MC = Marginal cost of production
Pi = Price of the input i (i.e., the cost to the firm of using an additional unit of the input i)
$\mathrm{MP_i}$ = Marginal product of the input i

For example, suppose the input used is labor (measured in hourly units), and the price of labor is the wage rate given to the firm under perfectly competitive labor market conditions. Assume a wage rate of $10 per hour. Assume also that a particular hour of labor has a marginal product of 20 units of output. On a per-unit basis, these additional 20 units will cost the firm $0.50 (i.e., $10/20) to produce. In other words, at this point the marginal cost is $0.50.

Let us assume that the firm is operating at the profit-maximizing level of output—in other words, at the point where

$$\mathrm{MR} = \mathrm{MC} \tag{7.15}$$

Let us also assume that the firm employs two inputs, X and Y. Substituting Equation (7.14) into (7.15) gives

$$\mathrm{MR} = \frac{P_x}{\mathrm{MP_X}} \quad \text{for the X input}$$

$$\mathrm{MR} = \frac{P_Y}{\mathrm{MP_Y}} \quad \text{for the Y input} \tag{7.16}$$

Rearranging terms gives us

$$P_X = \mathrm{MR} \times \mathrm{MP_X} \quad \text{and} \quad P_Y = \mathrm{MR} \times \mathrm{MP_Y} \tag{7.17}$$

Since $\mathrm{MR} \times \mathrm{MP}_i = \mathrm{MRP}_i$, the firm will be satisfying the optimality condition with that combination of X and Y at which

$$P_X = \mathrm{MRP_X} \quad \text{and} \quad P_Y = \mathrm{MRP_Y} \tag{7.18}$$

In short, the optimal level of multiple inputs occurs when the additional revenue that each input accounts for is just equal to the additional cost to the firm of using each of the inputs. Another way to view this optimality condition is to remember that it is actually derived from the assumption that the firm is already producing at the profit-maximizing level of output (i.e., where MR = MC). This, in turn, implies that the firm is combining its inputs in an optimal fashion. If not, then it could not possibly be maximizing its profit.

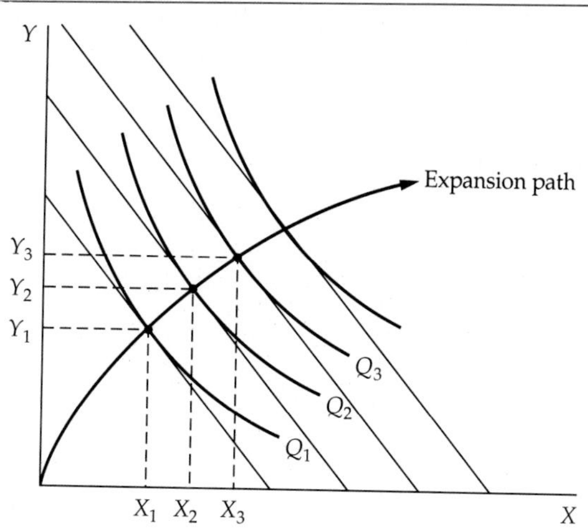

Figure 7.14 Cost-Minimizing and Profit-Maximizing Input Combinations

Figure 7.14 illustrates the difference between the cost-minimizing and the profit-maximizing combinations of inputs. You can see that any one of the points along the "expansion path" represents the cost-minimizing combination of inputs X and Y. However, suppose that the MR = MC rule for profit maximization dictates that a firm produce Q_3 units for sale in the competitive marketplace. As you can see, this implies that only one combination of inputs (X_3 and Y_3) should be used. All the other combinations of inputs will be cost-efficient but will not enable the firm to maximize its profits.

Returns to Scale

Earlier in this chapter we explained the difference between the short-run production function and the long-run production function in terms of the flexibility a firm has in varying the amounts of inputs. In the simple case of two inputs, the short run allows a firm time enough to vary only one of the inputs, whereas the long run enables it to vary both of them. In the short run, as the firm increases its variable input, it will presumably experience the law of diminishing returns and the three stages of production. In this section, we discuss a phenomenon believed to occur in the long run: *returns to scale*. This phenomenon can be defined as follows:

> Returns to scale represents the additional output resulting from an increase in *all* of a firm's inputs by some proportion.

Tables 7.2 and 7.3 were used to illustrate the difference between the short run and the long run. Table 7.3 also illustrates returns to scale. For your convenience, we have reproduced it here as Table 7.12. This table shows what

Table 7.12 Returns to Scale

Units of Y Employed	*Output Quantity*							
8	37	60	83	96	107	117	127	(128)
7	42	64	78	90	101	110	(119)	120
6	37	52	64	73	82	(90)	97	104
5	31	47	58	67	(75)	82	89	95
4	24	39	52	(60)	67	73	79	85
3	17	29	(41)	52	58	64	69	73
2	8	(18)	29	39	47	52	56	52
1	(4)	8	14	20	27	24	21	17
	1	2	3	4	5	6	7	8
	Units of X Employed							

happens to output as a firm increases both inputs, X and Y, by some proportion. For example, if it uses 1 unit of X and 1 unit of Y, it will produce 4 units of output. If the firm doubles its inputs (i.e., 2 units of X and 2 units of Y), it will produce 18 units of output. Thus, a doubling of inputs has produced more than a fourfold increase in output. Proceeding further, we notice that an additional doubling of inputs (i.e., 4 units of X and 4 units of Y) results in more than a threefold increase in output, from 18 to 60. What we are observing in this table is *increasing returns to scale.*

According to economic theory, if an increase in a firm's inputs by some proportion results in an increase in output by a greater proportion, the firm experiences *increasing returns to scale.* If output increases by the same proportion as the inputs increase, the firm experiences *constant returns to scale.* A less-than-proportional increase in output is called *decreasing returns to scale.*

You might simply assume that firms generally experience constant returns to scale. For example, if a firm has a factory of a particular size, then doubling its size along with a doubling of workers and machinery should lead to a doubling of output. Why should it result in a greater-than-proportional or, for that matter, a smaller-than-proportional increase? For one thing, a larger scale of production might enable a firm to divide up tasks into more specialized activities, thereby increasing labor productivity. Also, a larger scale of operation might enable a company to justify the purchase of more sophisticated (hence, more productive) machinery. These factors help to explain why a firm can experience increasing returns to scale. On the other hand, operating on a larger scale might create certain managerial inefficiencies (e.g., communications problems, bureaucratic red tape) and hence cause decreasing returns to scale. More will be said about the factors that can cause increasing or decreasing returns to scale in the next chapter, when we discuss the related concepts of economies and diseconomies of scale.

One way to measure returns to scale is to use a coefficient of output elasticity:

$$E_Q = \frac{\text{Percentage change in Q}}{\text{Percentage change in all inputs}}$$

Thus,

If $E > 1$, we have increasing returns to scale (IRTS).
If $E = 1$, we have constant returns to scale (CRTS).
If $E < 1$, we have decreasing returns to scale (DRTS).

Another way of looking at the concept of returns to scale is based on an equation that was first presented at the outset of this chapter:

$$Q = f(X, Y) \tag{7.19}$$

Recall in the original specification of this equation that it may include as many input variables as necessary to describe the production process (i.e., i variables). For ease of discussion, we will limit this number to two: X and Y. Now suppose that we increase the amount of each input by some proportion k. For example, if we increase the inputs by 10 percent, $k = 1.10$. If we double the inputs, $k = 2.0$. Of course, Q is expected to increase by some proportion as a result of the increase in the inputs. Let h represent the magnitude of this increase. Expressed in terms of Equation (7.19),

$$hQ = f(kX, kY) \tag{7.20}$$

Using this notation, we can summarize returns to scale in the following way:

If $h > k$, the firm experiences increasing returns to scale ($E_Q > 1$).
If $h = k$, the firm experiences constant returns to scale ($E_Q = 1$).
If $h < k$, the firm experiences decreasing returns to scale ($E_Q < 1$).

We will illustrate returns to scale with several numerical examples. Suppose we have the following production function:

$$Q_1 = 5X + 7Y$$

If we use 10 units of each input, the output will be

$$\begin{aligned} Q_1 &= 5(10) + 7(10) \\ &= 50 + 70 = 120 \text{ units} \end{aligned}$$

Now let us increase each input by 25 percent (i.e., $k = 1.25$). This will give us

$$\begin{aligned} Q_2 &= 5(12.5) + 7(12.5) \\ &= 62.5 + 87.5 = 150 \end{aligned}$$

The 25 percent increase in X and Y has led to a proportional increase in output (i.e., 150 is 25 percent more than 120).

We can also illustrate the concept of returns to scale graphically. Figure 7.15 shows the three possible types of returns to scale. In each case, we assume

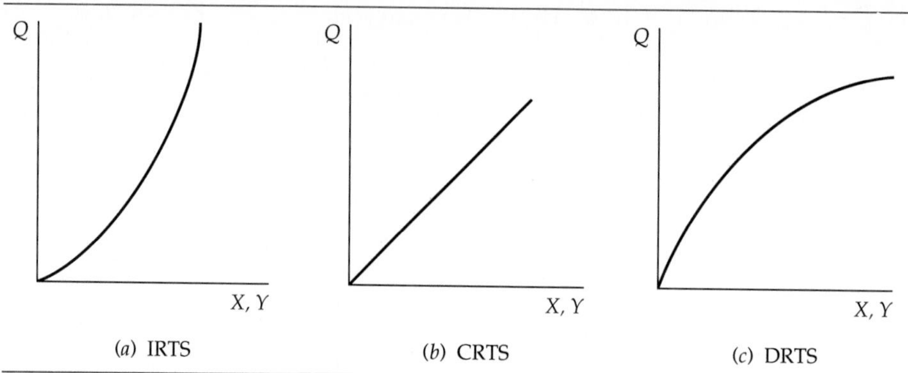

(*a*) IRTS (*b*) CRTS (*c*) DRTS

Figure 7.15 Graphic Representations of Returns to Scale

that the inputs (X and Y) are increased by the same proportion; thus, they are both included on the horizontal axis. Obviously, these graphs are idealized representations of returns to scale. In reality, we would not expect the changes in output relative to the changes in inputs to behave in such a smooth and orderly fashion.

Incidentally, when returns to scale are measured, economists always assume that the firm is operating with the optimal combination of inputs. In Figure 7.16, we view returns to scale "from above" rather than "from the side" as we did in Figure 7.15. In this figure the different levels of output resulting from increases in input are found on a ray from the origin. (This ray is actually the locus of points indicating the optimal combination of inputs for different levels of budgetary constraint.) As implied by the hypothetical numbers assigned to the isoquants, the values of these isoquants in relation to the values of the op-

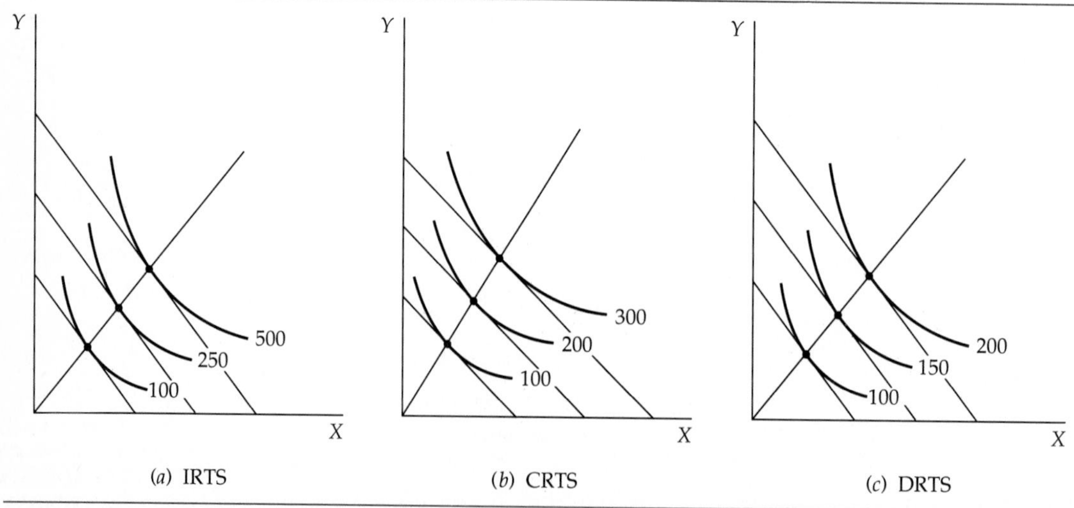

(*a*) IRTS (*b*) CRTS (*c*) DRTS

Figure 7.16 Optimal Input Combinations and Returns to Scale timal input combinations indicate whether the firm is experiencing increasing, constant, or decreasing returns to scale.

More will be said about returns to scale in Chapter 10, when the empirical estimation of production and cost functions is discussed. There are also several exercises at the end of this chapter that will give you some practice in computing different types of returns to scale. But rather than delve further into the mathematical nature of production functions, we will conclude this rather theoretical chapter with the important implications of production functions for managerial decision makers.

The Importance of Production Functions in Managerial Decision Making

As stated in the introductory section of this chapter, the production function is an important part of the economic analysis of the firm because it serves as the foundation for the analysis of cost. You will see this in the next chapter. But for managers, an understanding of the basic concepts discussed in this chapter also provides a solid conceptual framework for decisions involving the allocation of a firm's resources both in the short run and in the long run. Discussed next are two key management principles illustrated in the economic theory of production.

Careful Planning Can Help a Firm to Use Its Resources in a Rational Manner

In our discussion of the short run, we stated that a firm is expected to have three stages of production. Stage I represents the underutilization of a firm's fixed inputs relative to its variable ones. Stage III represents an overutilization of its fixed inputs relative to its variable ones. Indeed, firms operating in this stage would find their total output *decreasing* as they increased their variable input. The only stage for a rational firm to be in is stage II. Assuming that this information is well known to managers, why would a firm find itself in stage I or III? The answer is, of course, that production levels do not depend on how much a company wants to produce, but on *how much its customers want to buy.*

Suppose we consider the short-run production function shown in Figure 7.17. As we can see, stage II applies to production levels between $Q_1 = 200$ and $Q_2 = 275$. If people want to buy less than 200 units or more than 275 units, for example, then in the short run the firm would be forced to operate in either stage I or stage III.[13]

[13]You may wonder why a firm would ever want to operate in stage III, since it would mean declining output with increasing input. This could easily happen in situations where managers do not have the information (which is so nicely provided in textbook examples such as this) that will enable them to see on a marginal basis what happens to output as additional units of inputs are added. More than likely, managers must simply make decisions on the basis of their present levels of operations. Thus, a manager could well be in stage III (or, for that matter, in stage I) without even realizing it. Only after marginal changes in input and output levels are made will the stage of production in which the firm is operating be recognized.

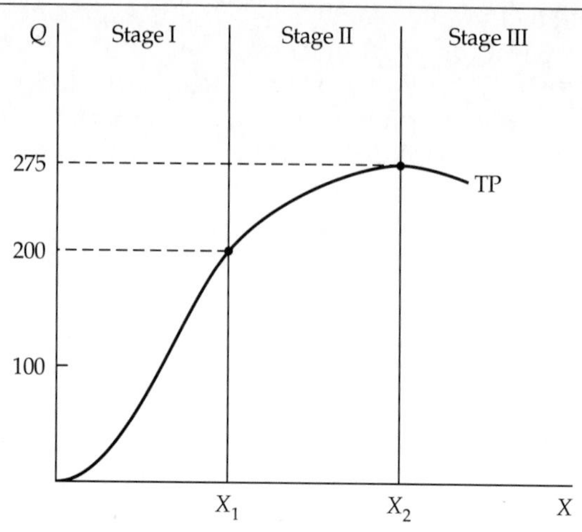

Figure 7.17 Production Stages and Capacity Planning

The information in Figure 7.17 implies that for a firm to avoid having to operate in either stage I or stage III, there must be careful planning regarding the amount of fixed inputs that will be used along with the variable ones. In business, this is often referred to as *capacity planning*. For example, if the firm anticipated that the demand for its product would be in the range of 200 to 275, then the capacity implied in Figure 7.17 is perfect for its needs. However, if a firm forecasts the demand to be greater than 275, it would have to consider increasing its capacity so that stage II would include the higher level of output. By the same token, if the firm forecasts a demand less than 200, it would have to consider decreasing its capacity. These alternative capacity levels are illustrated in Figure 7.18.

Good capacity planning requires two basic elements: (1) accurate forecasts of demand and (2) effective communication between the production and marketing functions (particularly in large organizations, where these functions are often handled by separate work groups). The first element is rather obvious but, as you have seen in Chapters 5 and 6, not very easy to achieve. The second element may not be so obvious, especially for those who have not had work experience in large organizations. It is not uncommon for manufacturing people to proceed merrily with their production plans on a purely technical basis (i.e., from a strictly engineering point of view) without fully incorporating the marketing plans of those whose main responsibility is to sell the products. It is also quite possible for marketing people to try to sell as many units of the product as possible (as marketing people are supposed to do) without consulting the production people as to whether the firm has the capacity to meet the increase in demand. A full discussion of these problems of management and organization is beyond the scope of this book. However, they are mentioned to underscore the importance for managers of understanding production theory.

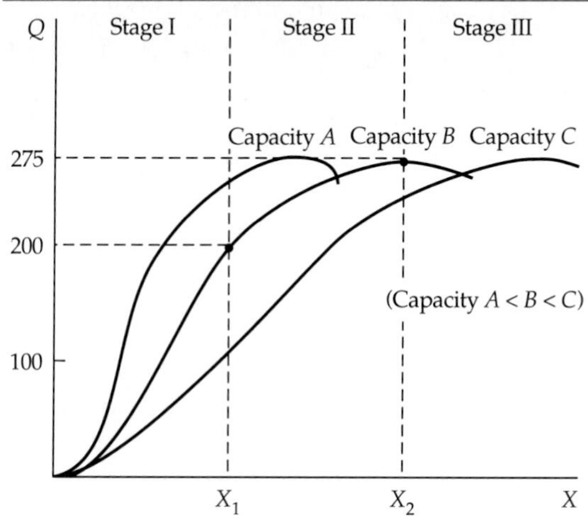

Figure 7.18 Adjusting Capacity Based on Demand

Managers Must Understand the Marginal Benefits and Costs of Each Decision Involving the Allocation of Scarce Resources

One of the most difficult subjects to learn is the use of isoquants and isocosts in production theory. This is not so much because the material is complex as because it appears so far removed from the reality of the "real world" of business. However, the essence of this model, is a vital part of the everyday decision making of a business manager. Basically, what this model should tell managers is that in the allocation of scarce resources, certain trade-offs in terms of benefits and costs are involved. The smart manager will understand the nature of these trade-offs and make decisions in which the marginal benefits outweigh the marginal costs. It is that simple.

However, in the real-world analysis of production, the data on the marginal products of each input may not be known. Consequently, a manager may be unable to find the optimal combination of inputs.[14] Nonetheless, managers can utilize the concept of trade-offs in their decision making regardless of whether detailed quantitative information exists. Let us cite a few examples:

The capital-labor trade-off. Suppose a company is considering the installation of a new voice-messaging system (e.g., phone mail, automated menu-driven responses through touch-tone phones, or call or message forwarding). This would greatly reduce the need for receptionists, operators, and secretaries.

[14]When the data are available, there are quantitative techniques such as linear programming to help managers find the optimal combinations of inputs. See Chapter 9.

The question is whether the cost of installing such a system is outweighed by the cost savings resulting from the elimination of certain support personnel.

The labor-labor trade-off. A company may have a sales team consisting of marketing representatives and technical and administrative support. Can the "output" (i.e., the volume of sales) be increased by varying the combination of sales, technical, and administrative personnel? If so, then the MP of one of these functional types relative to their compensation must be greater than the ratios of MP to compensation for the other types.

The labor–raw materials trade-off. As mentioned earlier in this chapter, high-fructose corn syrup and sugar are perfect substitutes for each other. The only factor that presumably determines how much of each is used in the production of soft drinks is relative price. However, in certain developing countries, sugar is the predominant sweetener. This is mainly because the labor required to transport the sugar is cheaper than in developed countries which reduces the overall relative cost of using sugar versus HFCS. (Remember that sugar is much heavier and bulkier than HFCS.)

The capital-capital trade-off. Many information systems managers are considering much more decentralized forms of computing, using workstations and personal computers tied together in networks rather than terminals hooked into one large computer. The cost of using more decentralized forms of data processing is rapidly declining, making this approach much more attractive. However, there are still questions of security and reliability that must be taken into account when switching from mainframe computing to workstation/network computing. In other words, output (more specifically, the reliability of output) must be considered in addition to cost.

These are only a few of the many types of decisions managers must make involving the trading off of benefits and costs. As a final example, the following anecdote was shared by the owner-operater of one of the most successful Chinese restaurants in the New York metropolitan area.[15] One day a regular customer decided to give him some friendly advice about the running of his restaurant. "I notice that you always serve such a generous portion of duck sauce," said the customer. "You must waste quite a bit of it. Why don't you save money by serving less?" The restaurant owner (who, incidentally, has an MBA), smiled and thanked the customer for his advice. Later, when he recounted this incident to the authors, he said that this advice was given by someone who clearly did not understand the restaurant business. "If I served smaller portions of duck sauce, my customers would be constantly asking my waiters for refills. This takes up their valuable time. The few cents that I might save in duck sauce would be clearly offset by the time wasted by my waiters." In the opinion of the authors, whether or not the restaurant owner remembered his isoquant and isocost curves, he surely captured the essence of production analysis in this little story.

---

[15]This restaurant has consistently maintained a four-star rating from the *New York Times*.

The Solution

To: Product Manager, Soft Drinks Division
From: George Ernest, Vice President of Manufacturing
Re: The Economic Feasibility of Refillable Glass Bottles

I do not recommend the use of refillable glass bottles for our new soft drink products. Instead, we should use either aluminum or plastic. Following is a summary of my reasons for this recommendation.

To begin with, glass is a more expensive material than either plastic or aluminum. Furthermore, because it is heavier and more fragile than these other materials, higher costs will be incurred due to: (1) increased back injuries to employees, (2) the need for special handling care (e.g., bottle carriers, protective cardboard), (3) breakage, and (4) higher fuel costs for tansportation. Another consideration is that existing machinery enables us to fill cans much faster than bottles. It is also obvious that the use of plastic bottles or aluminum cans eliminates the need for expensive bottle-washing and sorting equipment and the labor that accompanies the cleaning process. Finally, an increasing number of states and localities are mandating or encouraging the recycling of plastic, aluminum, and glass containers. Thus, the reusable glass bottles can no longer be said to be superior to other materials insofar as the environment is concerned.

Let me tell you a few things about the process of using refillable bottles. There are three basic ways to sort and clean the returned bottles: (1) totally automatic sorting system, (2) totally manual sorting system, and (3) hybrid system. The choice of system depends primarily on the anticipated volume of returned bottles. As a secondary consideration, the plant may be located in a low-wage area, making it more difficult to justify the significant investment in automated sorting equipment.

When a manual sorting system is used (either exclusively or in combination with an automated sorter), production managers must be aware of the impact on production of a phenomenon referred to in economics as "the law of diminishing returns." A typical manual sorting area is about 30 feet long and there is usually no room in a plant for expansion. Each sorter requires about 3 feet of space. The conveyor runs along a wall, so sorters can only work from one side of the conveyor. The standard productivity measure used in the plant is "cases sorted per person-hour." If only one person is sorting bottles, he or she will not be able to keep up with the flow. The bottles tend to back up, and the system has to stop while the sorter tries to catch up. Experience shows that the optimal number of sorters is two per flavor. Thus, if five flavors need to be sorted, 10 people shold be used. These sorters will take up the maximum length of the sorting area (30 feet) if the recommended 3 feet per person is allocated. If more than 10 sorters are used, productivity tends to decrease; the sorters have less

(Continued)

than 3 feet of space to work in and tend to get in each other's way. Table A illustrates what we have found to occur when more sorters are added to the line.[16] The maximum output per person is reached when 10 persons are used. Beyond this number, the output starts to decline. The law of diminishing return takes effect when the extra output resulting from an additional person on the sorting line starts to decrease. As you can see from Table A, this occurs when the sixth person is added. Shortly afterward, the law of diminishing returns starts to affect average output, causing it to decrease as sorters are added. In Table A, this occurs when seven persons are used in the sorting process.

Table A also points out that when an eleventh person is added to the sorting line, the marginal product goes negative. That is, the total number of cases sorted per hour decreases. When this occurs, it is definitely time to consider adding an automated sorter to the line. The main point of this example is that if a manual process is used, a careful forecast of the demand for the sorters' services must be made so as not to push the sorting process beyond its short-run limits.

To reiterate my recommendation, I believe that the economics of the refillable bottle simply makes it too costly for us to use. However, I am not aware of the demand side of this issue. If the marketing people believe that this type of packaging will give a substantial boost to sales by clearly differentiating our products from those of competitors, we should definitely consider its use.

Table A Productivity of Manual Sorting

Number of Sorters	*Total Product (cases per hour)*	*Marginal Product*	*Average Product*
0	0		0
1	10	10	10
2	30	20	15
3	60	30	20
4	100	40	25
5	140	40	28
6	170	30	28.3
7	190	20	27.1
8	200	10	25
9	205	5	22.8
10	208	3	20.8
11	204	−4	18.5

[16]The description of the sorting process is based on the actual experience of a bottling plant. Plant managers have indeed found that operating a conveyor at maximum speed to sort five flavors, two persons per flavor result in the maximum number of cases sorted per person-hour. For purposes of illustration, we have added hypothetical numbers to this actual statistic to produce a set of numbers that resembles the idealized short-run production function shown earlier in this chapter (see, for example, Table 7.4).

Summary

The topics in this chapter represent the foundation for the economic analysis of supply. After all, people may be very willing to purchase a firm's product at a certain price, but will the firm be willing to supply the product at this price? The answer to this question begins with the relationship between the firm's inputs and the resulting output, that is, the firm's production function. In the short run, where at least one of the firm's inputs is fixed, we have learned that the firm is subject to the law of diminishing returns and the three stages of production. This means that as additional inputs are added to the fixed input, at some point the additional output (i.e., marginal product) resulting from the additional input will start to diminish. Once this level of production is exceeded, the output per unit of variable input (i.e., average product) will reach a maximum and then start to diminish. The point of maximum average product marks the end of stage I and the beginning of stage II, the stage in which the rational firm should be operating. The use of still more units of variable inputs will eventually cause the total output to decline (i.e., cause MP to assume negative values). By assigning monetary values to both the variable input and the output along with the use of marginal analysis, we were able to determine precisely where in Stage II the firm should be operating. A similar analysis was used to derive the conditions for the optimal use of more than one input.

The long-run function, in which a firm is able to vary all of its inputs, was also considered in this chapter. When a firm is able to vary its entire scale of production, it may experience varying returns to scale. That is, the increase in output may be proportional, less than proportional, or greater than proportional to the increase in all of its inputs.

In the next chapter, we present an analysis of a firm's cost function. We will then see how a solid background in the economic analysis of production will provide a better understanding of the cost structure of a firm, in both the short and the long runs.

Important Concepts

Average product (AP): The total product divided by the number of units of a particular input employed by the firm.

Inputs: The resources used in the production process. Examples in economic analysis generally involve the inputs *capital* (representing the fixed input) and *labor* (representing the variable input). Other terms used in reference to these resources are *factors* and *factors of production*.

Isocost: A line representing different combinations of two inputs that a firm can purchase with the same amount of money. In production analysis, the isocost indicates a firm's budget constraint.

Isoquant: A curve representing different combinations of two inputs that produce the same level of output.

Law of diminishing returns: A law stating that as additional units of a variable input are added to a fixed input, at some point the additional output (i.e., the marginal product) will start to diminish. Because at least one input is required to be fixed for this law to take effect, this law is considered a short-run phenomenon.

Long-run production function: The maximum quantity of a good or service that can be produced by a set of inputs, assuming that the firm is free to vary the amount of *all* inputs being used.

Marginal labor cost (MLC): The addtional cost to the firm of using an additional unit of labor. This is also referred to as *marginal factor cost* (MFC) or *marginal resource cost* (MRC). Labor is used in this term because it is the most commonly used variable input in the economic analysis of production.

Marginal product (MP): The change in output resulting from a unit change in one of the firm's variable inputs.

Marginal rate of technical substitution (MRTS): Given two inputs X and Y, the marginal rate of technical substitution of X for Y represents the reduction in Y relative to the amount of X that a firm must add to replace Y to maintain the same amount of output. Mathematically speaking, it is represented by the slope of some given isoquant or $\Delta Y / \Delta X$ ($\delta y / \delta x$ for continuous isoquants).

Marginal revenue product (MRP): The additional amount of revenue resulting from the use of an additional unit of a variable input. It can be calculated by taking an input's marginal product and multiplying it by the market price of the product. For example, given some input i, that $\text{MRP}_i = \text{MP}_i \times P$.

MRP = MLC rule: A rule that guides a firm in its decision about how many units of a variable input it should use relative to its fixed input. The rule states that the firm should employ a particular input up to the point at which the revenue contribution of the additional input is equal to the cost incurred by the firm to employ this particular input. In the case of more than one input, this condition applies separately for every input used by the firm.

Production function: The maximum quantity of a good or service that can be produced by a set of inputs. Production functions are divided into two types: short-run and long-run.

Returns to scale: The increase in output that results from an increase in all of a firm's inputs by some proportion. If the output increases by a *greater* proportion than the increase in inputs, the firm is experiencing increasing returns to scale. If the output increases by the *same* proportion as the inputs, the firm is experiencing constant returns to scale. Finally, if the output increases by a *smaller* proportion than the increase in inputs, the firm is experiencing decreasing returns to scale.

Short-run production function: The maximum quantity of a good or service that can be produced by a set of inputs, assuming that the amount of *at least one* of the inputs used remains unchanged as output varies.

Stages of production: In a short-run production function, there are three stages of production. Stage I starts at zero and ends at the point where the firm has reached the maximum level of *average* product. Stage II continues from this point on to the point at which the firm has reached the maximum level of *total* product. Stage III continues from this point on. Economic theory suggests that the rational firm will try to produce in the short run in stage II. In stage I the firm would be underutilizing its fixed inputs, and in stage III it would be overutilizing its fixed inputs.

Total product (TP): The firm's output for a given level of input usage, also referred to as *quantity*, or simply Q.

Questions

1. Explain the difference between a short-run and long-run production function. Cite one example of this difference in a business siuation.
2. Define the law of diminishing returns. Why is this law considered a short-run phenomenon?
3. What are the key points in a short-run production function that delineate the three stages of production? Explain the relationship between the law of diminishing returns and the three stages of production.
4. Explain why a firm's adherence to the MRP = MLC rule enables it to find the optimal number of units of a variable input to use in the short-run production process.
5. Define returns to scale. Why is this considered a long-run phenomenon?
6. According to the rule for optimal input usage, a firm should hire a person as long as his or her marginal revenue product is greater than his or her marginal cost to the company. It is well known that many companies have management training programs in which new trainees are paid relatively high starting salaries and are not expected to make substantial contributions to the company until after the program is over (programs may run between 6 to 18 months). In offering such training programs, is a company violating the optimality rule? Explain.
7. Show what will happen to the following diagram as a result of the changes listed.

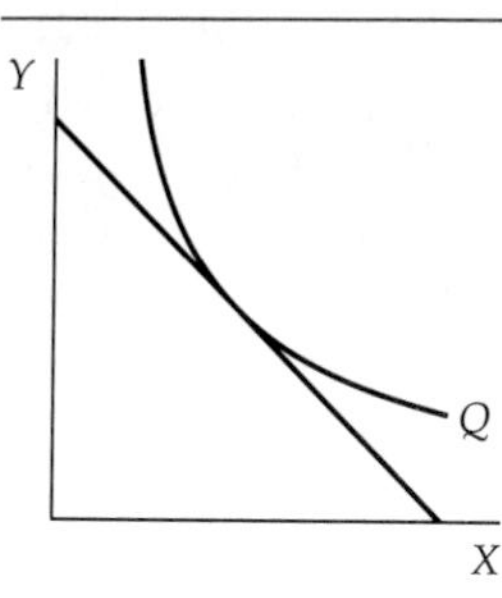

   a. The firm's budget increases.
   b. The price of Y decreases.
   c. The price of X decreases.
   d. Y becomes more expensive, and X becomes less expensive.
   e. Technology makes the Y input more productive.
   f. Technology increases the productivity of both inputs by the same proportion.
8. Cite and discuss possible reasons a firm may actually find itself operating in stage I or stage III of the short-run production function.
9. Discuss the problems of measuring productivity in actual work situations. How might productivity be measured for each of the following industries?

a. Education (e.g., elementary and secondary education, higher education—undergraduate and graduate)
b. Government (e.g., the Social Security Office, the Internal Revenue Service)
c. Manufacturing (e.g., soap and toothpaste, computers, heavy machinery)
d. Finance and insurance (e.g., banks, insurance companies, brokerage houses)

10. For those of you currently or previously employed, how is (was) productivity measured in your organization?

Problems

1. Indicate whether each of the following statements is true or false. Explain why.
   a. When the law of diminishing returns takes effect, a firm's average product will start to decrease.
   b. Decreasing returns to scale occurs when a firm has to increase all of its inputs at an increasing rate in order to maintain a constant rate of increase in its output.
   c. A linear short-run production function implies that the law of diminishing returns does not take effect over the range of output being considered.
   d. Stage I of the production process ends at the point where the law of diminishing returns occurs.
2. The Oceanic Pacific fleet has just decided to use a pole-and-line method of fishing instead of gill netting to catch tuna. The latter method involves the use of miles of nets strung out across the ocean and therefore entraps other sea creatures besides tuna (e.g., porpoises and sea turtles). Concern for endangered species was one reason for this decision, but perhaps more important was the fact that the major tuna canneries in the United States will no longer accept tuna caught by gill netting.

   Oceanic Pacific decided to conduct a series of experiments to determine the amount of tuna that could be caught with different crew sizes. The results of these experiments follow.

Number of Fishermen	*Daily Tuna Catch (lb.)*
3	300
4	450
5	590
6	665
7	700
8	725
9	710

a. Determine the point at which diminishing returns occurs.
b. Indicate the points that delineate the three stages of production.
c. Suppose the market price of tuna is \$3.50/pound. How many fishermen should the company use if the daily wage rate is \$100?
d. Suppose a glut in the market for tuna causes the price to fall to \$2.75/pound. What effect would this have on the number of fishermen used per boat? Suppose the price rose to \$5.00/pound. What effect would this have on its hiring decision?
e. Suppose the firm realizes that to keep up with the demand for tuna caught by the more humane pole-and-line method of fishing, each of its boats must catch at least 1,000 pounds of fish per day. Given the preceding data, what should it consider doing? Explain.

3. Suppose you are given the following production function:

$$Q = 100K^{0.5}L^{0.5}$$

a. Use this function to generate the data for the following table:

K									
8									
6									
5									
4									
3									
2									
1									
0	1	2	3	4	5	6	7	8	L

b. Identify as many isoquants as you can.
c. Comment on the returns to scale exhibited in this figure. (*Suggestion:* Start by assuming one unit of L and one unit of K are used. Then systematically increase both inputs by some given proportion.)

4. Following are different algebraic expressions of the production function. Decide whether each one has constant, increasing, or decreasing returns to scale.

a. $Q = 75L^{0.25}K^{0.75}$
b. $Q = 75A^{0.15}B^{0.40}C^{0.45}$
c. $Q = 75L^{0.60}K^{0.70}$
d. $Q = 100 + 50L + 50K$
e. $Q = 50L + 50K + 50LK$
f. $Q = 50L^2 + 50K^2$
g. (Optional) Based on the answers for the preceding equations, can you make any generalizations about the functional form of a production equation, the relative magnitudes of the coefficients, and the nature of the returns to scale? Explain. (Refer to Appendix 7A.)

5. Use the production matrix presented to answer the following questions.

Y									
	8	31	67	101	133	161	184	202	213
	7	30	62	93	122	147	168	184	193
	6	27	54	82	108	130	149	168	163
	5	23	45	69	91	108	126	137	142
	4	17	34	54	72	89	101	108	111
	3	12	25	38	54	65	74	79	79
	2	6	14	24	33	44	54	47	43
	1	3	7	11	17	27	19	16	8
		1	2	3	4	5	6	7	8	X

a. Determine the returns to scale for this matrix. (Start with one unit of *X* and one unit of *Y*.)

b. Suppose the firm has a budget of \$100 and that the price of *Y* is \$20 and the price of *X* is \$10. What is the optimal combination of inputs *X* and *Y* for this firm?

c. Suppose the prices of *Y* and *X* are now \$10 and \$20, respectively. What effect will this have on the firm's optimal input combination?

d. Illustrate the answers to the preceding questions with the use of an isoquant/isocost diagram.

6. A firm has the following short-run production function:

$$Q = 50L + 6L^2 - 0.5L^3$$

where Q = Quantity of output per week
L = Labor (number of workers)

a. When does the law of diminishing returns take effect?

b. Calculate the range of values for labor over which stages I, II, and III occur.

c. Assume each worker is paid \$10 per hour and works a 40-hour week. How many workers should the firm hire if the price of the output is \$10? Suppose the price of the output falls to \$7.50. What do you think would be the short-run impact on the firm's production? The long-run impact?

7. The owner of a small car rental service is trying to decide on the appropriate numbers of vehicles and mechanics to use in the business for the current level of operations. He recognizes that his choice represents a trade-off between the two resources. His past experience indicates that this trade-off is as follows:

Vehicles	*Mechanics*
100	2.5 (includes one part-timer)
70	5
50	10
40	15
35	25
32	35

a. Assume the annual (leasing) cost per vehicle is $6,000 and the annual salary per mechanic is $25,000. What combination of vehicles and mechanics should he employ?
b. Illustrate this problem with the use of an isoquant/isocost diagram. Indicate graphically the optimal combination of resources.

8. An American company that sells consumer electronics products has manufacturing facilities in Mexico, Taiwan, and Canada. The average hourly wage, output, and annual overhead cost for each site are as follows.

	Mexico	*Taiwan*	*Canada*
Hourly wage rate	$1.50	$3.00	$6.00
Output per person	10	18	20
Fixed overhead cost	$150,000	$90,000	$110,000

a. Given these figures, is the firm currently allocating its production resources optimally? If not, what should it do? (Consider output per person as a proxy for marginal product.)
b. Suppose the firm wants to consolidate all of its manufacturing into one facility. Where should it locate? Explain.

9. A branch office of a large computer company has two basic types of marketing personnel: (1) the people who sell computer hardware and (2) software consultants. The branch manager is trying to decide whether she has the right mix of salespeople and consultants for her office. Salespeople are paid a base salary plus a commission of 10 percent on products they sell. Consultants are simply paid a salary. She estimates the average compensation for each type of job and the administrative expenses incurred to support each job:

Sales Personnel		*Consultants*	
Salary:	$50,000	Salary:	$60,000
Commission:	40,000		
(Based on average sales of $400,000			
Annual costs of administrative support associated with sales activity: $300,000		Annual costs of administrative support associated with consulting activity: $210,000	

a. Using the above data, determine whether she is currently using the optimal mix of salespersons and consultants. Assume annual revenue per salesperson to be $400,000 and annual revenue per consultant to be $250,000.
b. Suppose increasing competition in the hardware business reduces the average sales to 350,000, and increasing demand in the consulting business

increases consulting revenues to $350,000 per year. Demonstrate why this should lead her to increase the number of consultants and decrease the number of salespeople.

c. Suppose she decides to move salespeople into consulting jobs. What *practical* problems might she encounter in implementing such a move? Would you expect similar problems in shifting people from consulting to sales jobs? Explain.

10. The owner of a car wash is trying to decide on the number of people to employ based on the following short-run production function:

$$Q = 6L - 0.5L^2$$

where Q = Number of car washes per hour
L = Number of workers

a. Generate a schedule showing total product, average product, and marginal product. Plot this schedule on a graph.
b. Suppose the price of a basic car wash (no undercoating, no wax treatment, etc.) in his area of business is $5. How many people should he hire if he pays each worker $6/hour?
c. Suppose he considers hiring students on a part-time basis for $4/hour. Do you think he should hire more workers at this lower rate? Explain.

APPENDIX 7A
Expressing the Production Function with the Use of Calculus

In this chapter, we have relied primarily on tables and graphs to illustrate our analysis of the production function. This appendix shows you how calculus can be used in the analysis.

A Brief Review of the Production Function

The production function expresses the relationship between the output and one or more inputs. The output is referred to either as *total product* (TP) or Q (quantity). We began our analysis of the production function by presenting the relationship between different combinations of two inputs (i.e., labor and capital) and output in a numerical table (see Table 7.1). As already explained, the production function takes the general form:

$$Q = f(L, K) \tag{7A.1}$$

Table 7A.1 Cobb-Douglas Production Function

K	Output Quantity							
8	282	400	488	564	628	688	744	(800)
7	264	373	456	528	588	644	(700)	744
6	244	345	422	488	544	(600)	644	688
5	223	315	385	446	(500)	544	588	628
4	200	282	346	(400)	446	488	528	564
3	173	244	(300)	346	385	422	456	488
2	191	(200)	244	282	315	345	373	400
1	(100)	141	173	200	223	244	264	282
	1	2	3	4	5	6	7	8
				L				

where Q = Quantity of output
L = Labor (i.e., the variable input)
K = Capital (i.e., the fixed input)

By stating this general functional form in more specific terms, we have an equation that can be used to generate a tabular model of the production function.

One popular form is the *Cobb-Douglas* production function.[17] It can be stated as follows:

$$Q = AL^aK^b \tag{7A.2}$$

Q, L, and K have the same definitions as in Equation (7A.1). The values for A, a, and b determine the actual values in the production table. For example, suppose $A = 100$, $a = 0.5$, and $b = 0.5$. The production function would be

$$Q = 100L^{0.5}K^{0.5} \tag{7A.3}$$

This equation can be used to generate the numbers in Table 7A.1.

Marginal Product: The First Derivative of the Total Product Function

As shown in the discussion of isoquants, the marginal product expressed in terms of calculus is the partial derivative of the total product function. We can use the Cobb-Douglas form of the production function shown in Equation (7A.3) to illustrate how the derivative is used to find this marginal product.

[17]The Cobb-Douglas production function is also presented in Chapter 10, where particular attention is paid to the estimation of various types of production functions. In addition, some of the material discussed in this appendix is reinforced in that chapter.

Suppose we want to find the marginal product of the fourth unit of labor added to the production process, assuming that we are currently using four units of capital. We simply take the partial derivative of the equation with respect to L, set $L = 4$ and $K = 4$, and find the resulting value of total product:

$$\begin{aligned}\frac{\partial Q}{\partial L} &= 100(0.5)L^{-0.5}K^{0.5} \\ &= 100(0.5)4^{-0.5}4^{0.5} \\ &= 50 \qquad (7A.4)\end{aligned}$$

In Table 7A.1 we note that the marginal product of the fourth unit of labor assuming 4 units of capital is 54 (i.e., 400 − 346). The two values differ because the use of calculus actually enables us to compute marginal product right at the point at which four units of labor are being used, rather than that amount of output resulting from the addition of the fourth unit.[18]

The Long-Run Production Function

The Cobb-Douglas production function can also be used in the analysis of the long-run production function and returns to scale. Recall that the long-run production function is the case in which a firm is able to change all of its inputs. The change in the output resulting from this long-run change in all of a firm's inputs is called *returns to scale.*

Let us use the general expression of the Cobb-Douglas production function presented in Equation (7A.2):

$$Q = AK^aL^b$$

Suppose we double the capital and labor inputs. This should result in Q increasing by some proportion, which we shall denote by h:

$$hQ = A(2K)^a(2L)^b \qquad (7A.5)$$

Factoring out the 2s on the right side of the equation and rewriting the exponential terms gives

$$\begin{aligned}hQ &= 2^a2^b(AK^aL^b) \\ &= 2^{a+b}(AK^aL^b) \qquad (7A.6)\end{aligned}$$

[18] Note that upon the addition of the fifth unit of labor, Table 7A.1 indicates a marginal product of 46 (i.e., 446 − 400). The average of the marginal products between three and four units of labor and between four and five units of labor is 50 (i.e., [54 + 46]/2), which is what we calculated the marginal product to be right at four units of labor.

Since $Q = AK^aL^b$, we can cancel out Q on the left side of Equation (7A.6) and AK^aL^b on the right side. This will leave us with the following relationship:

$$h = 2^{a+b} \tag{7A.7}$$

If $a + b = 1$, $h = 2$. This means that a doubling of each of the inputs results in a doubling of the total product. Actually, if a and b sum to unity, then an increase in the inputs by any proportion will result in an increase in the output by the same proportion. Readers should recognize this condition as one of constant returns to scale. Of course, if $a + b > 1$, then the long-run production function exhibits increasing returns to scale. If $a + b < 1$, this would indicate decreasing returns to scale.

If we refer back to Table 7A.1, it is clear that the numbers generated from this form of the production function (i.e., $Q = 100L^{0.5}K^{0.5}$) indicate constant returns to scale. For example, starting with one unit each of labor and capital and then increasing them by some proportion will result in an increase in total product by the same proportion. This is highlighted for you in the table.

The Optimal Combination of Two Inputs

In the main body of this chapter, we showed that if a firm is producing a level of output that maximizes its profit, then it must be using its inputs in such a way that the marginal revenue product of every input used is equal to its price (or cost). In other words, if a firm uses k inputs, then

$$\begin{aligned} \text{MRP}_1 &= \text{Cost of input 1} \\ \text{MRP}_2 &= \text{Cost of input 2} \\ &\vdots \\ \text{MRP}_k &= \text{Cost of input } k \end{aligned}$$

Earlier we showed why a rational firm would be using its inputs in the most cost-efficient manner if it combined them in such a way that the ratio of each input's marginal product relative to its price is equal for all inputs used:

$$\frac{\text{MP}_1}{P_1} = \frac{\text{MP}_2}{P_2} = \cdots = \frac{\text{MP}_k}{P_k}$$

In this section, we employ calculus to demonstrate mathematically why this is so.

We begin by stating the profit function in the following manner:

$$\pi = \text{TR} - \text{TC} \tag{7A.8}$$

where π = Total profit
TR = Total revenue
TC = Total cost

By definition, total revenue is equal to price times quantity:

$$\text{TR} = P \times Q \tag{7A.9}$$

where P = Price of the output
Q = Quantity of output sold

Total cost is equal to the amounts of the inputs used multiplied by their respective prices. Let us assume that the firm is using two inputs, labor and capital, and that their prices are the wage rate and some rental cost of using the capital. Thus, we can say that

$$\text{TC} = wL + rK \tag{7A.10}$$

where L = Labor
K = Capital
w = Wage rate of labor
r = Rental cost of using capital

Substituting Equations (7A.10) and (7A.9) into Equation (7A.8) gives us

$$\begin{aligned} \pi &= PQ - (wL + rK) \\ &= PQ - wL - rK \end{aligned} \tag{7A.11}$$

As you know, the production function can be stated in general terms as

$$Q = f(L, K) \tag{7A.12}$$

Substituting this equation into Equation (7A.11) gives us

$$\pi = Pf(L, K) - wL - rK \tag{7A.13}$$

To find the level of input that will maximize the firm's profit, we can take the partial derivative of the profit function with respect to each of the inputs, L and K, while holding the other one constant and set each equal to zero:[19]

$$\frac{\partial \pi}{\partial L} = PfL - w = 0 \tag{7A.14}$$

$$\frac{\partial \pi}{\partial K} = Pf_K - r = 0 \tag{7A.15}$$

[19] A common notation used in calculus to represent the derivative of the function with respect to a particular variable such as K is f_K.

If we express Equations (7A.14) and (7A.15) in terms of the prices of the inputs, we obtain

$$w = Pf_L \tag{7A.16}$$

$$r = Pf_K \tag{7A.17}$$

Recall that the definition of the marginal product of a particular input is the change in output with respect to a change in that input. In other words

$$\text{MP}_L = f_L \tag{7A.18}$$

$$\text{MP}_K = f_K \tag{7A.19}$$

Recall further that the definition of the marginal revenue product (MRP) is the MP of a particular input multiplied by product price. Thus, Equations (7A.16) and (7A.17) are nothing more than a restatement of the conditions necessary for the optimal use of inputs discussed earlier in the main body of this chapter. That is,

$$Pf_L = \text{MRP}_L = w \tag{7A.20}$$

$$Pf_K = \text{MRP}_K = r \tag{7A.21}$$

Now that we have established the relationship, we can easily use the same equations and notations to show how the condition necessary for the most cost-efficient combination of inputs is derived. If we divide equation (7A.16) by Equation (7A.17). we obtain

$$\frac{w}{r} = \frac{Pf_L}{Pf_K}$$

The Ps in the denominator and the numerator on the right-hand side cancel out, giving

$$\frac{w}{r} = \frac{fL}{fK}$$

Using the definitions of marginal product stated in Equations (7A.18) and (7A.19) and rearranging the terms gives the condition for the most efficient combination of input usage:

$$\frac{\text{MP}_L}{w} = \frac{\text{MP}_K}{r} \tag{7A.22}$$

APPENDIX 7B
A Computer Application

The following computer application is designed to reinforce your understanding of how the optimal short-run level of variable input usage is determined. Table 7B.1 shows the Lotus l-2-3 workspace. Fill in the blanks in columns A and B with any labor input and total product figures that you desire. For column E, choose a product price (enter at C18), and multiply that price by the corresponding total product number in column B. For column G, choose a cost per unit of labor (enter at H18), and multiply it by the corresponding labor input in column A.

Using the same data for labor input, total product, product price, and labor cost as in Table 7.5, we arrive at the results shown in Table 7B.2. Also shown in this table are the cell formulas used to produce the results. A graph of the variables used to determine the optimal input level is exhibited in Figure 7B.1. As can be seen, the optimal quantity of labor is determined at the point of intersection between the MRP and MLC lines.

Table 7B.1 Revenue Product and Labor Cost

	A	B	C	D	E	F	G	H
1				REVENUE PRODUCT AND LABOR COST				
2								
3					TOTAL	MARGINAL	TOTAL	MARGINAL
4	LABOR	TOTAL	AVERAGE	MARGINAL	REVENUE	REVENUE	LABOR	LABOR
5	INPUT	PRODUCT	PRODUCT	PRODUCT	PRODUCT	PRODUCT	COST	COST
6	X	TP	AP	MP	TRP	MRP	TLC	MLC
7								
8				0	0		0	
9			ERR	0	0	0	0	0
10			ERR	0	0	0	0	0
11			ERR	0	0	0	0	0
12			ERR	0	0	0	0	0
13			ERR	0	0	0	0	0
14			ERR	0	0	0	0	0
15			ERR	0	0	0	0	0
16			ERR	0	0	0	0	0
17								
18	Product Price				Factor cost/unit			
19			________					________
20								

	I	J	K	L	M	N	O	P
1								
2								
3								
4	TRP	MRP						
5	MINUS	MINUS						
6	TLC	MLC						
7								
8	0	0						
9	0	0						
10	0	0						
11	0	0						
12	0	0						
13	0	0						
14	0	0						
15	0	0						
16	0	0						
17								
18								
19								
20								

Table 7B.2 Revenue Product and Labor Cost

LABOR INPUT X	TOTAL PRODUCT Q or TP	AVERAGE PRODUCT AP	MARGINAL PRODUCT MP	TOTAL REVENUE PRODUCT TRP	MARGINAL REVENUE PRODUCT MRP	TOTAL LABOR COST TLC	MARGINAL LABOR COST MLC	TRP MINUS MLC	MRP MINUS MLC
0	0		0			0		0	0
1	10000	10000	10000	20000	20000	10000	10000	10000	10000
2	25000	12500	15000	50000	30000	20000	10000	30000	20000
3	45000	15000	20000	90000	40000	30000	10000	60000	30000
4	60000	15000	15000	120000	30000	40000	10000	80000	20000
5	70000	14000	10000	140000	20000	50000	10000	90000	10000
6	75000	12500	5000	150000	10000	60000	10000	90000	0
7	78000	11143	3000	156000	6000	70000	10000	86000	-4000
8	80000	10000	2000	160000	4000	80000	10000	80000	-6000

Product Price 2.00 Factor cost/unit 10000.00

```
A8: U 0
B8: U 0
D8: +B8-B7
E8: +$C$18*B8
G8: +$H$18*A8
I8: +E8-G8
J8: +F8-H8
A9: U 1
B9: U 10000
C9: (F0) +B9/A9
D9: +B9-B7
E9: +$C$18*B9
F9: +E9-E8
G9: +$H$18*A9
H9: +G9-G8
I9: +E9-G9
J9: +F9-H9
A10: U 2
B10: U 25000
C10: (F0) +B10/A10
D10: +B10-B9
E10: +$C$18*B10
F10: +E10-E9
G10: +$H$18*A10
H10: +G10-G9
I10: +E10-G10
J10: +F10-H10
A11: U 3
B11: U 45000
C11: (F0) +B11/A11
D11: +B11-B10
E11: +$C$18*B11
F11: +E11-E10
G11: +$H$18*A11
H11: +G11-G10
I11: +E11-G11
J11: +F11-H11
A12: U 4
B12: U 60000
C12: (F0) +B12/A12
D12: +B12-B11
E12: +$C$18*B12
F12: +E12-E11
G12: +$H$18*A12
H12: +G12-G11
I12: +E12-G12
J12: +F12-H12
A13: U 5
B13: U 70000
C13: (F0) +B13/A13
D13: +B13-B12
E13: +$C$18*B13
F13: +E13-E12
G13: +$H$18*A13
H13: +G13-G12
I13: +E13-G13
J13: +F13-H13
A14: U 6
B14: U 75000
C14: (F0) +B14/A14
D14: +B14-B13
E14: +$C$18*B14
F14: +E14-E13
G14: +$H$18*A14
H14: +G14-G13
I14: +E14-G14
J14: +F14-H14

A15: U 7
B15: U 78000
C15: (F0) +B15/A15
D15: +B15-B14
E15: +$H$18*B15
F15: +E15-E14
G15: +$H$18*A15
H15: +G15-G14
I15: +E15-G15
J15: +F15-H15
A16: U 8
B16: U 80000
C16: (F0) +B16/A16
D16: +B16-B15
E16: +$C$18*B16
F16: +E16-E15
G16: +$H$18*A16
H16: +G16-G15
I16: +E16-G16
J16: +F16-H16
A18: 'Product price
C18: (F2) U 2
E18: 'Factor cost/unit
H18: (F2) U 100000
C19: /-
H19: /-
```

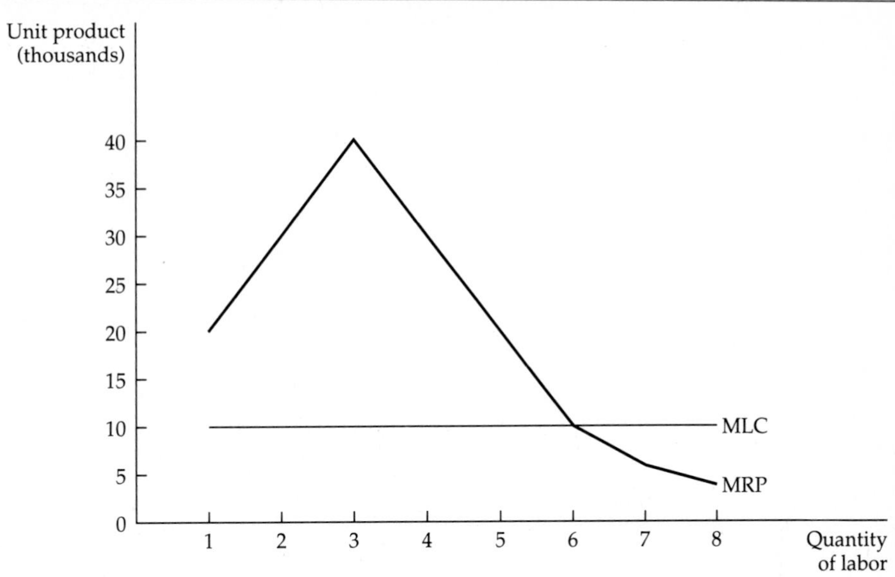

Figure 7B.1 Optimal Short-Run Level of Variable Input

CHAPTER 8

Cost

The Situation

Marie Jacobs could not have dreamed up a more challenging first assignment. As a newly hired MBA, her task was to analyze the cost of producing the company's highly touted new cola product. "You're going to report to George Ernest first thing Monday morning," said her manager. "Consider yourself an internal consultant. What I want are a fresh perspective, objectivity, and a careful analysis. Listen to what everyone has to say, from the man who drives the forklift all the way to the vice-president of manafacturing, George himself. But don't let anyone sway your views. What we want to know is: Do we have the ability to be among the lowest-cost producers in the industry? How can we improve our cost structure in the short run? And, over the long run, what can we do to become even more cost-efficient?"

The Importance of Cost in Managerial Decision Making

Cost stands out among the different factors that are considered in making business decisions because it is the variable that a firm can most directly influence. In its pursuit of profit, a firm may try to increase demand through such means as advertising and promotion. But at best this has only an indirect effect on one of the determinants of demand, namely, tastes and preferences. Furthermore, increasing advertising and promotion involves increasing costs. A firm may also try to increase the quantity demanded of its products by reducing price, but the desirability of this action depends on the extra revenue from these price cuts (i.e., the price elasticity of demand) relative to the additional costs incurred.

On the other hand, there are a number of direct ways to reduce the cost of doing business. For example, corporations may try to reduce costs rather quickly by cutting down on such discretionary expenses as travel and entertainment allowances. Further cost reduction can be achieved by laying workers off or by offering early retirement incentives, but these measures take longer to implement. Given even more time, firms can resort to such cost-cutting measures as relocating facilities to less expensive quarters or shutting down selected production sites.

To be sure, control of certain costs may be completely beyond the power of the firm. For example, interest expenses increased drastically for American firms during the late 1970s and the early 1980s. Moreover, American companies that use a considerable amount of foreign-produced components faced higher costs of goods sold as the dollar fell against other major currencies starting in 1985. In a similar fashion, Japanese companies were forced to adjust to a change in the yen/dollar rate beginning in the mid-1980s. In 1985 a dollar could buy 260 yen. By the early 1990s, the dollar had fallen so far against the yen (i.e., the yen had strengthened so much against the dollar) that it could only buy about half as much. This "yen shock" drastically increased the cost of Japanese exports and forced the Japanese companies to resort to a number of cost-cutting measures to offset the rising value of their currency.

It should also be noted that the consideration of cost in business decisions often evokes mixed feelings among managers. This is because efforts to reduce costs may involve the "downsizing" of staff, the layoff of workers, reductions in discretionary expenses (such as training and attendance at professional conferences), or the elimination of executive perquisites (such as corporate jets, first-class air travel, chauffeured limousines, or front-row seats at the U.S. Open tennis championship). On the other hand, efforts to increase revenues involve growth and all of the activities that accompany it (such as new hires, better equipment, new offices, and increases in discretionary expenditures and perquisites).[1] Yet, from an objective standpoint, it is obvious that a dollar saved, given some level of output and revenue, adds as much to profit as an additional dollar of revenue, given some level of output and cost.

In any event, let us now turn to the formal analysis of cost with an eye toward learning the extent to which Marie Jacobs can draw from economic theory to help her evaluate and improve her company's cost competitiveness.

The Definition and Use of Cost in Economics

In the typical business organization, cost is generally considered the domain of the accounting department. As such, the definitions and appropriate uses

[1]Jokes about those who try to save the company money (e.g., cost accountants and controllers) generally play on the stereotypical image of the "bean counters" or "the guys with the green eyeshades." This stands in contrast to the typical office humor about the marketing people. These stories usually celebrate (or at least good-naturedly forgive) the excesses of those who do whatever it takes to "bring in the business."

of various cost concepts are bound by the conventional practices of those in this functional area. Economists often draw on the data gathered by a firm's accountants to do their own analysis of business decisions. But as a result, their use of the data on cost is based on one key question: How *relevant* is the cost to the decision being considered? By confining their analysis only to relevant cost, economists sometimes use or interpret the cost data differently than accountants do. This section clarifies the particular ways in which economists use and define various measures of cost.[2]

Simply stated, a cost is considered to be relevant if its incurrence has an impact on the alternatives being considered in a business decision. In deciding whether a cost actually has an impact on the options available to the decision maker, the following distinctions should be kept in mind.

Historical versus Replacement Cost

Suppose a manufacturer of personal computers has an inventory of $750,000 worth of 256k random-access memory (RAM) chips left over from its discontinued line of home computers. Strong protectionist measures by Congress have created a shortage of these chips, driving their market value up to $1,000,000. Meanwhile, the firm decides to reenter the home computer market. (This time, it will manufacture the product in Mexico and Taiwan and will begin production with the leftover inventory of chips.) How much will it cost the firm to use this inventory? Although the historical value is $750,000, the replacement value is $1,000,000. According to the principle of relevant cost, the firm should use the latter figure in computing its cost of reentering the home computer market.[3] Let us see why this is so.

If the firm were to decide not to proceed with project but instead to sell its inventory of 256K chips in the open market, it could receive the full market value of $1,000,000. Therefore, by using the chips, it is forgoing the opportunity to receive $1,000,000 for their sale in the open market. Moreover, if it decided to buy chips rather than use its inventory, it would have to pay $1,000,000 for the same quantity that it holds in inventory. The $1,000,000 is the relevant sum because it is the amount that has an impact on the alternatives being considered. If you still have doubts about this rationale, consider another important distinction that economists make about cost.

---

[2] Accountants also often use the various cost concepts discussed in this section, as any cost or managerial accountant will verify. It is with the *financial* accountants that economists sometimes differ in their use of cost terminology.

[3] The recording of the cost of an asset for purposes of financial reporting is subject to generally accepted accounting principles (GAAP), which state that assets and liabilities should be recorded in financial statements at historical cost. Inventories may be reported at historical cost or current market value, whichever is lower. But regardless of the rule set for external reporting, economists and cost accountants (as opposed to financial accountants) recommend that a firm use current market value for internal management decisions.

Opportunity Cost versus Out-of-Pocket Cost

Previous discussions pointed out that opportunity cost is one of the most important and useful concepts in economic analysis because it highlights the consequences of making choices under conditions of scarcity. We can now use this term in a more specific way to help explain the concept of relevant cost. Opportunity cost, as you recall, is the amount or subjective value that is forgone in choosing one activity over the next best alternative. This type of cost can be contrasted with "out-of-pocket cost." On occasion, economists refer to opportunity cost as *indirect cost*[4] or *implicit cost,* whereas out-of-pocket cost is referred to as *direct cost* or *explicit cost.*

In the case of the company with the inventory of computer chips, we can clearly see that the opportunity cost of using the inventory in its second attempt to penetrate the home computer market involves the cost of not being able to resell the inventory for $1,000,000. Seen in this way, this sum is the firm's "relevant opportunity cost." The $750,000 is not relevant because it is not the opportunity cost of going ahead with the project. Incidentally, the firm's out-of-pocket cost of using chips would be the cost of buying additional chips for the production process. For example, if the firm decides that it needs $1,500,000 worth of chips (at current market prices) in the first year of the project's operation, we can infer that this figure consists of $1,000,000 in opportunity cost and $500,000 in additional out-of-pocket cost.

Sunk versus Incremental Cost

Let us evaluate the cost to the firm of using its inventory of chips with a reversal in market conditions. Instead of the firm's inventory increasing in value, suppose something happens to cause its value to fall to $550,000. For example, no trade barriers are erected, and a flood of chips from Japan and Korea drives down the market price of the product. Under these circumstances, how much will it cost the firm to use the inventory for which it originally paid $750,000? To answer this question, we employ the distinction that economists make between *incremental* and *sunk* costs. *Incremental cost* is the cost that varies with the range of options available in a decision. *Sunk cost* is the cost that does not vary in accordance with the decision alternatives. Our computer manufacturer has already paid $750,000 for the chips and can really do nothing about the fact that changes in market conditions have driven the value of the chips down to $550,000. If the firm decides to sell the inventory, it will receive at the most only $550,000. If it decides to go ahead with the project, the incremental cost (i.e., the part of its cost that is affected by the decision) of using the inventory of chips will be $550,000 and not $750,000. And, as you have probably already concluded, the $200,000 difference between these two sums must be considered a sunk cost to

---

[4]We will avoid using the term *indirect cost* in reference to opportunity cost because some readers may confuse it with another definition. In manufacturing, *indirect cost* usually refers to the cost of using labor not directly involved in the making of a product (e.g., finance, personnel, research and development, and other support or staff functions).

the firm. As it turns out, the $550,000 can also be considered the opportunity cost of using the chips instead of selling them. Therefore, in summary, the firm should consider $550,000 to be the relevant cost of using its inventory of chips, because it is an *incremental opportunity cost.*

An extreme but instructive example of the use of incremental and opportunity costs to determine relevant cost is the case of a new technology suddenly rendering the entire inventory of chips obsolete. In this event, no one would want to buy the chips at any price, and the value of this inventory would be reduced to zero. The entire $750,000 investment in inventory would be considered a sunk cost to the firm. Furthermore, since the resale value of the inventory is zero, the firm's use of the chips in its project would not incur an opportunity cost.[5] In economic terms, the chips would represent a "free resource" because there would be no amount forgone with their use in the project. Would the firm be tempted to use the chips simply because of this? Would you want to build a new computer product with obsolete chips? Obviously, if people will not buy the product, there would indeed be a high opportunity cost in terms of forgone sales.

The Relationship Between Production and Cost

The economic analysis of cost is tightly bound to the economic analysis of production discussed in the previous chapter. As a matter of fact, one can say that the cost function used in economic analysis is simply the production function expressed in monetary rather than physical units. Furthermore, all the limiting assumptions used in specifying the short-run production function apply to the short-run cost function. The only additional assumption needed to determine the short-run economic cost function pertains to the prices of the inputs used in the production process. Here we assume that the firm acts as a "price taker" in the input market; that is, it can hire or use as many or as few inputs as it desires, as long as it pays the going market price for them.

Table 8.1 presents an example of the numerical relationship between production and cost in the short run. The cost of using the variable input is determined by multiplying the number of units by the unit price. In this case, each unit of labor is assumed to be the equivalent of a 40-hour work week. The weekly wage rate is $500. As indicated in the table, when the total product (Q) increases at an *increasing* rate, total variable cost (TVC) increases at a *decreasing* rate. When Q increases at a *decreasing* rate, TVC increases at an *increasing* rate. Plotting these numbers on a graph makes it quite apparent that total variable cost is a "mirror image" of total product (see Figure 8.1.)

In the previous chapter, the marginal product was defined as the change in total product divided by the change in the amount of the variable input used

[5]It should be noted that if a firm decides to write off the obsolete inventory, there could be a tax benefit (decreased taxes due to the loss); therefore, some opportunity cost could be involved.

Table 8.1 Relationship between Production and Cost, Short Run

Total Input (L)	*Q*	*TVC* ($L \times \$500$)	*MC* ($\Delta TVC/\Delta Q$)	*Reference Point in Figure 8.1*
0	0	0		
			0.50	
1	1,000	500		A (*A′*)
			0.25	
2	3,000	1,000		B (*B′*)
			0.16	
3	6,000	1,500		C (*C′*)
			0.25	
4	8,000	2,000		D (*D′*)
			0.50	
5	9,000	2,500		E (*E′*)
			1.00	
6	9,500	3,000		F (*F′*)
			1.42	
7	9,850	3,500		G (*G′*)
			3.33	
8	10,000	4,000		H (*H′*)
			−3.33	
9	9,850	4,500		

in the production process. Similarly, the rate of change in total variable cost is called *marginal cost*. Expressed in symbols,

$$MC = \Delta TVC/\Delta Q \qquad \text{or} \qquad MC = \Delta TC/\Delta Q$$

Note that marginal cost is either the change in total variable cost or the change in total cost with respect to the change in output. This is because the fixed cost component of total cost never changes as output increases. Using marginal cost and marginal product, we can restate the relationship shown in Figure 8.1 in

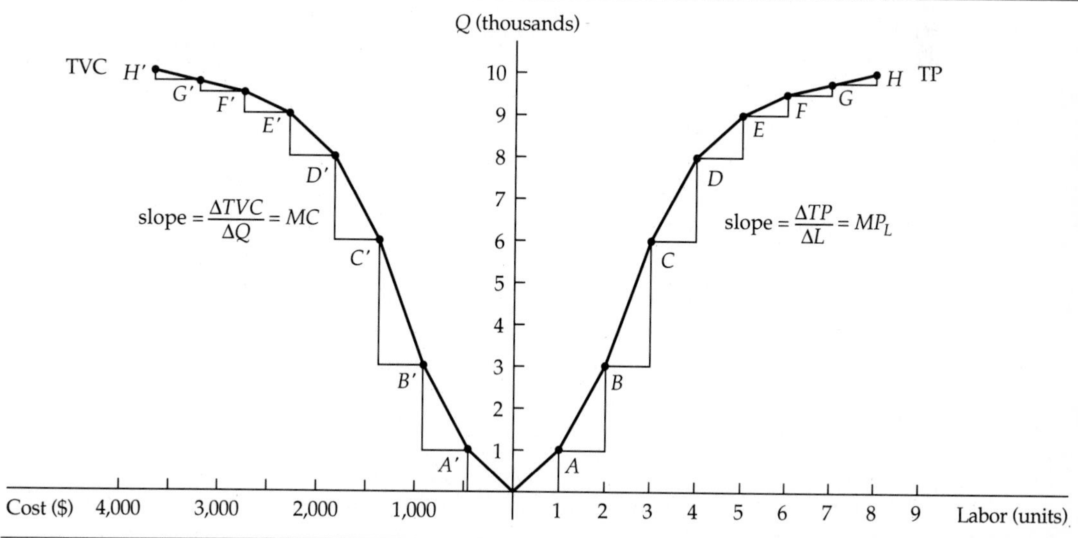

Figure 8.1 Short-Run Production and Cost

this way: When the firm's marginal product is increasing, its marginal cost of production is decreasing; when its marginal product is decreasing (i.e., *when the law of diminishing returns takes effect*), its marginal cost is increasing.

The relationship between diminishing returns and increasing marginal cost can also be illustrated algebraically. First, assume that the variable input is labor (L), and its unit cost is some given wage rate (W). Now let us start by defining marginal cost as:

$$\text{MC} = \frac{\Delta\text{TVC}}{\Delta Q} \tag{8.1}$$

Since TVC $= L \times W$, we can say that

$$\Delta\text{TVC} = \Delta L \times W \tag{8.2}$$

Substituting Equation (8.2) into equation (8.1) gives us

$$\text{MC} = \frac{\Delta L \times W}{\Delta Q} = \frac{\Delta L}{\Delta Q} \times W \tag{8.3}$$

Recalling the definition of MP, we know that $\text{MP}_L = \Delta Q/\Delta L$. Incorporating this observation into Equation (8.3) gives us

$$\text{MC} = \frac{1}{\text{MP}} \times W = \frac{W}{\text{MP}} \tag{8.4}$$

Clearly, Equation (8.4) tells us that, assuming a constant wage rate, MC will decrease when MP increases and will increase when MP decreases (i.e., when the law of diminishing returns takes effect).

In economic theory, the relationship between diminishing returns and marginal cost represents a key link between a firm's short-run production function and its short-run cost function, because it is the law of diminishing returns that gives the short-run cost function its peculiar nonlinear form. Consequently, as will be seen in ensuing sections of this chapter, the firm's total cost, total variable cost, average cost, average variable cost, and marginal cost functions are all constructed in accordance with this nonlinearity.

The Short-Run Cost Function

This section deals with the focal point of this chapter: the firm's short-run cost function. A numerical model of the behavior of the firm's short-run cost is shown in Table 8.2. Before commenting on each of the columns in the table, let us review all of the assumptions that economists make in specifying a model of this kind.

1. The firm employs two inputs, labor and capital.
2. The firm operates in a short-run production period. Labor is its variable input, and capital is its fixed input.
3. The firm uses the inputs to make a single product.

Table 8.2 Total and Per-Unit Short-Run Cost

Quantity (Q)	*Total Fixed Cost (TFC)*	*Total Variable Cost (TVC)*	*Total Cost (TC)*	*Average Fixed Cost (AFC)*	*Average Variable Cost (AVC)*	*Average Total Cost (AC)*	*Marginal Cost (MC)*
0	100	0.00	100.00				
1	100	55.70	155.70	100.00	55.70	155.70	55.70
2	100	105.60	205.60	50.00	52.80	102.80	49.90
3	100	153.90	253.90	33.33	51.30	84.63	48.30
4	100	204.80	304.80	25.00	51.20	76.20	50.90
5	100	262.50	362.50	20.00	52.50	72.50	57.70
6	100	331.20	431.20	16.67	55.20	71.87	68.70
7	100	415.10	515.10	14.29	59.30	73.59	83.90
8	100	518.40	618.40	12.50	64.80	77.30	103.30
9	100	645.30	745.30	11.11	71.70	82.81	126.90
10	100	800.00	900.00	10.00	80.00	90.00	154.70
11	100	986.70	1,086.70	9.09	89.70	98.79	186.70
12	100	1,209.60	1,309.60	8.33	100.80	109.13	222.90

4. In producing the output, the firm operates at a given level of technology. (Recall that in our discussion on the short-run production function, we assumed that the firm uses state-of-the-art technology in the production process. The same holds when we talk about short-run cost.)
5. The firm operates at every level of output in the most efficient way.
6. The firm operates in perfectly competitive input markets and must therefore pay for its inputs at some given market rate. In other words, it is a price taker in the input markets.
7. The firm's underlying short-run production function is affected by the law of diminishing returns.

As we proceed in this chapter, you will see why these assumptions are crucial to the understanding of the short-run cost function.

The variables listed in Table 8.2 are defined as follows:

Quantity (*Q*): The amount of output that a firm can produce in the short run. (*total product* is also used in reference to this amount.)

Total fixed cost (TFC): The total cost of using the fixed input *K*

Total variable cost (TVC): The total cost of using the variable input *L*

Total cost (TC): The total cost of using all of the firm's inputs (in this case, *L* and *K*)

Average fixed cost (AFC): The average or per-unit cost of using the fixed input *K*

Average variable cost (AVC): The average or per-unit cost of using the variable input *L*

Average total cost (AC): The average or per-unit cost of using all of the firm's inputs

Marginal Cost (MC): The change in a firm's total cost (or, for that matter, its total variable cost) resulting from a unit change in output

The important relationships among these various measures of cost can be summarized as follows:

$$\begin{aligned} TC &= TFC + TVC \\ AC &= AFC + AVC \quad (\textit{or } TC/Q) \\ MC &= \Delta TC/\Delta Q \quad (\textit{or } \Delta TVC/\Delta Q) \\ AFC &= TFC/Q \\ AVC &= TVC/Q \end{aligned}$$

In evaluating the schedule of numbers in Table 8.2, note that as a matter of convenience, we have considered unit changes in output over the range of production being considered. Since ΔQ will always be equal to 1, we can quickly figure the marginal cost as output increases. For example, the marginal cost of the second unit of output is simply the change in the firm's total cost (or total variable cost) between one unit and two units of production. In Table 8.2, we observe that this amount is \$49.90.

As output increases from 0 to 12, observe what happens to the various measures of cost. Total fixed cost, as expected, remains constant at \$100 over the range of output. Total variable cost increases at a decreasing rate, but when the fourth unit of output is produced, it starts to increase at an increasing rate. The same is true for total cost. When the numbers are plotted on a graph (see Figure 8.2*a*), the rate of change in total cost can be seen as the slope of the TC curve. The constancy of fixed cost is depicted by the horizontal line emanating from the corresponding point on the Y-axis.

As for the per-unit cost measures, we see that average fixed cost declines steadily over the range of production. This is to be expected, because a constant sum of \$100 is being divided by the larger amounts of output. Average variable cost declines, reaches a minimum at four units of output, and then starts to increase. Average total cost behaves in a similar fashion but reaches its minimum point at six units of output. Marginal cost declines and then starts to increase once the third unit of output is produced.

Notice in Table 8.2 that the values for marginal cost are placed between the output intervals, indicating that this measure of cost shows how total cost changes as a result of a unit change in quantity. For this same reason, marginal cost data are also plotted on a diagram between the output intervals. This particular way of showing marginal cost graphically can be seen in Figure 8.2, along with the average total cost and average variable cost curves.

Figure 8.2 shows a particular relationship between marginal cost and the two other per-unit cost measures that is not as evident in Table 8.2. Notice that when marginal cost is equal to average variable cost, the latter measure is at its minimum point. (This occurs at four units of output.) When marginal cost is equal to average cost, average cost is at its minimum point. (This occurs at six units of output.) Another way to describe these relationships is to state that as long as marginal cost is below average variable cost, average variable

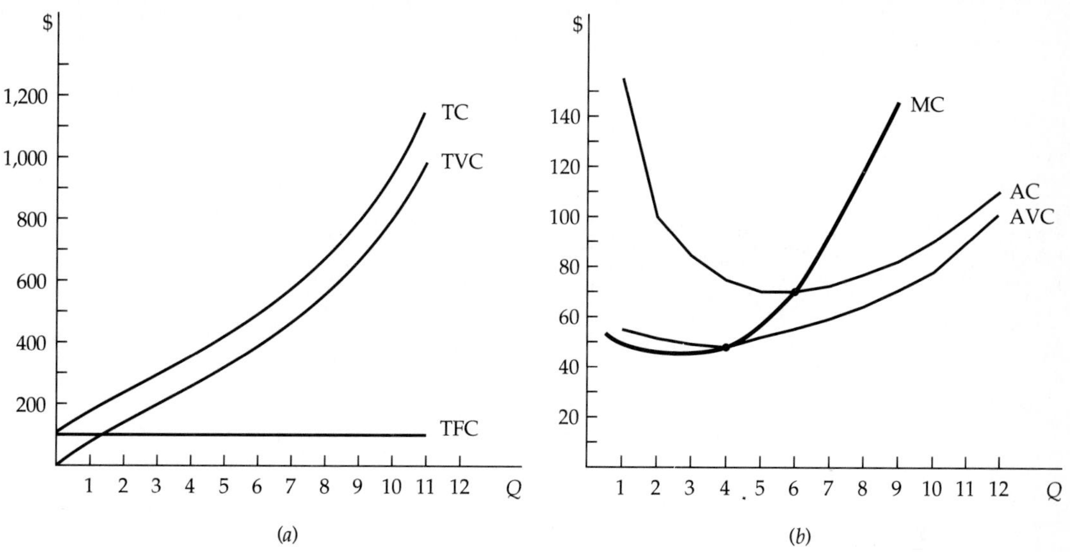

Figure 8.2 Total Cost, Total Variable Cost, Total Fixed Cost, Average Cost, Average Variable Cost, and Marginal Cost

cost declines as output increases. However, when marginal cost exceeds average variable cost, average variable cost starts to increase. The same relationship holds between marginal cost and average total cost. The economic significance of these relationships will be explained in Chapter 11. But for now, it is important at least to note these relationships among the different per-unit measures of cost. Summarizing these relationships in abbreviated form:

When MC < AVC, AVC is falling.
When MC > AVC, AVC is rising.
When MC = AVC, AVC is at its minimum point.

To summarize the relationship between marginal cost and average cost, simply substitute AC for AVC.

It is important to understand how the concept of relevant cost can be incorporated into the analysis of short-run cost. Suppose a firm is currently producing six units of output per period and is considering increasing this amount to seven. In deciding whether to produce the seventh unit of output, the relevant cost is the marginal cost. In other words, it is the *change* in total cost and not the total cost itself that must be considered. This is because whether the firm produces six or seven units of output per time period, it still must pay the same amount of fixed cost. By evaluating the change in total cost, the firm automatically excludes fixed cost from consideration.

Increasing Cost Efficiency in the Short Run

As will be seen in Chapters 11 and 13, the short-run cost function plays a central part in the economic analysis of production and pricing. For now, we can

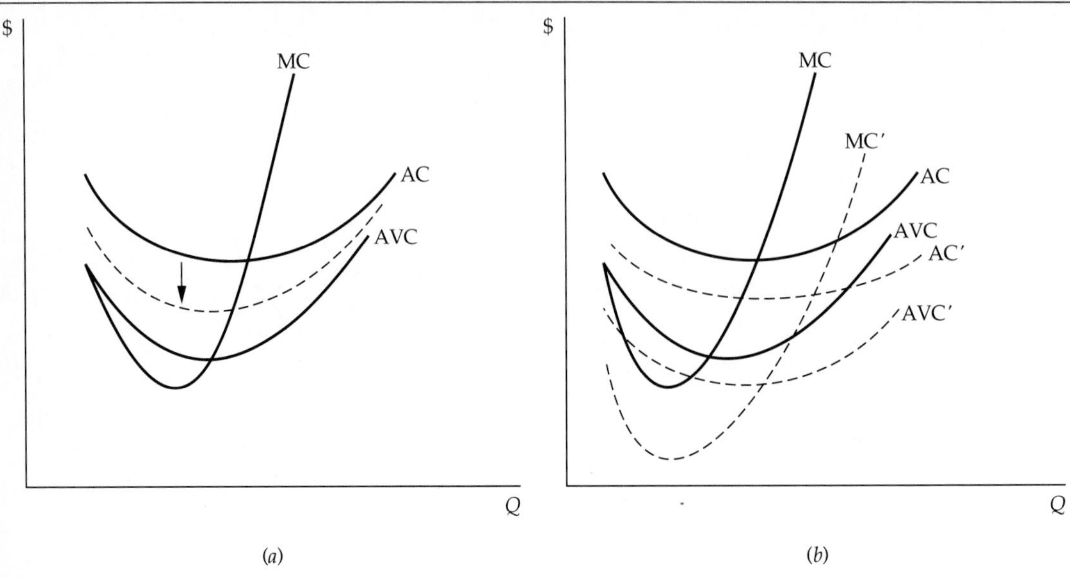

Figure 8.3 Effects on Short-Run Cost Structure of Price Changes in Variable and Fixed Inputs

appreciate the value of this model by considering the ways in which a company might attempt to become more economically efficient. The assumptions listed when the model was specified provide a convenient guide.

To start with, the model assumes that the firm is already operating as efficiently as possible. If we assume that the firm is in fact operating as best it can with state-of-the-art technology, then the only possibility to reduce cost in the short run is for the inputs to decrease in price. If this were to happen, there would be a downward shift in the firm's short-run cost curves. This effect is shown in Figure 8.3*a* and *b*. Notice that a reduction in the firm's fixed cost (e.g., a reduction in rental payments) would simply cause the average cost line to shift downward, whereas a reduction in the firm's variable cost (e.g., a reduction in wage rates or raw materials costs) would cause all three cost lines—AC, AVC, and MC—to shift. MC actually shifts downward and to the right.

The purchase of capital equipment was not considered in the discussion because we assumed it to be our model's fixed input. Actually, the addition of capital equipment could be considered a short-run change *if we assume labor to be the fixed input*. For example, a work force of a certain size might be given additional machinery with which to work. The point is that in the short run analysis of cost, at least one of the inputs must be held constant.

Alternative Specifications of the Total Cost Function

In economic analysis, the most common form of the short-run cost function is the one that has been used thus far in this chapter. That is, the total cost function is specified as a cubic relationship between total cost and output. As output increases, total cost first increases at a decreasing rate, and then at some point it increases at an increasing rate. By now you should be well aware that this is due to the underlying relationship between the firm's variable input and the resulting output. Total cost increases at a decreasing rate because the firm is experiencing increasing returns to its variable input. When the law of diminishing returns takes effect, the firm begins to experience decreasing returns to its variable factor, thereby causing its total cost to begin increasing at an increasing rate.

In addition to this cubic form of the cost function, two other important functional relationships between total cost and output are considered in economic analysis. One is a quadratic relationship, and the other is a linear one. These relationships along with the cubic cost function are shown in Figure 8.4. This figure also shows the general algebraic expressions for the three forms of total cost. These variations can be explained once again by the underlying relationship between the firm's variable input and the resulting output. In Figure 8.4*c* we can see that the quadratic total cost function increases at an increasing rate from the outset of production. This implies that the law of diminishing returns takes effect as soon as the firm starts to produce. On the other hand, the linear cost function, shown in Figure 8.4*e*, indicates that total cost increases at a constant rate. Think about this for a moment. What does this mean in terms of the underlying relationship between the firm's variable input and its output? It means that the firm is experiencing neither increasing nor diminishing returns as its variable input is added to its fixed input. Each additional unit of variable input adds the *same* amount of additional output (marginal product) throughout the short-run range of production. Therefore, the change in the total cost relative to the change in output (which, as you recall, is indicated by the slope of the total cost line) is the same throughout the range of output considered.

Rather than discuss the different specifications of the firm's short-run cost function in terms of total cost, it might be easier and more meaningful to discuss the alternative forms in terms of unit costs, both average and marginal. Thus, instead of referring to total cost "increasing at an increasing rate," we can simply say that the firm's marginal cost is increasing. An increase in total cost at a constant rate means a constant marginal cost. We can also use Figure 8.4 to illustrate this point.

In Figure 8.4*b*, we see the familiar set of short-run cost curves depicted earlier. As output increases, marginal cost falls, reaches a minimum, and then starts to increase (as the law of diminishing returns takes effect). As it increases, marginal cost intersects with average variable cost and average total cost at their respective minimum points, for reasons explained earlier. In Figure 8.4*d*, we see that marginal cost increases as soon as production begins, just as we noted when evaluating the slope of the total cost function. As in the case of Figure 8.4*b*, marginal cost intersects average variable cost and average cost at their minimum points.

In the case of the linear total cost function, shown in Figure 8.4*f*, the horizontal marginal cost line denotes that marginal cost remains constant as output increases. But also witness that marginal cost is equal to average variable cost, unlike the cases in Figure 8.4*b* and *d*. To illustrate this relationship, consider the following numerical example. Suppose you are given the following cost function:

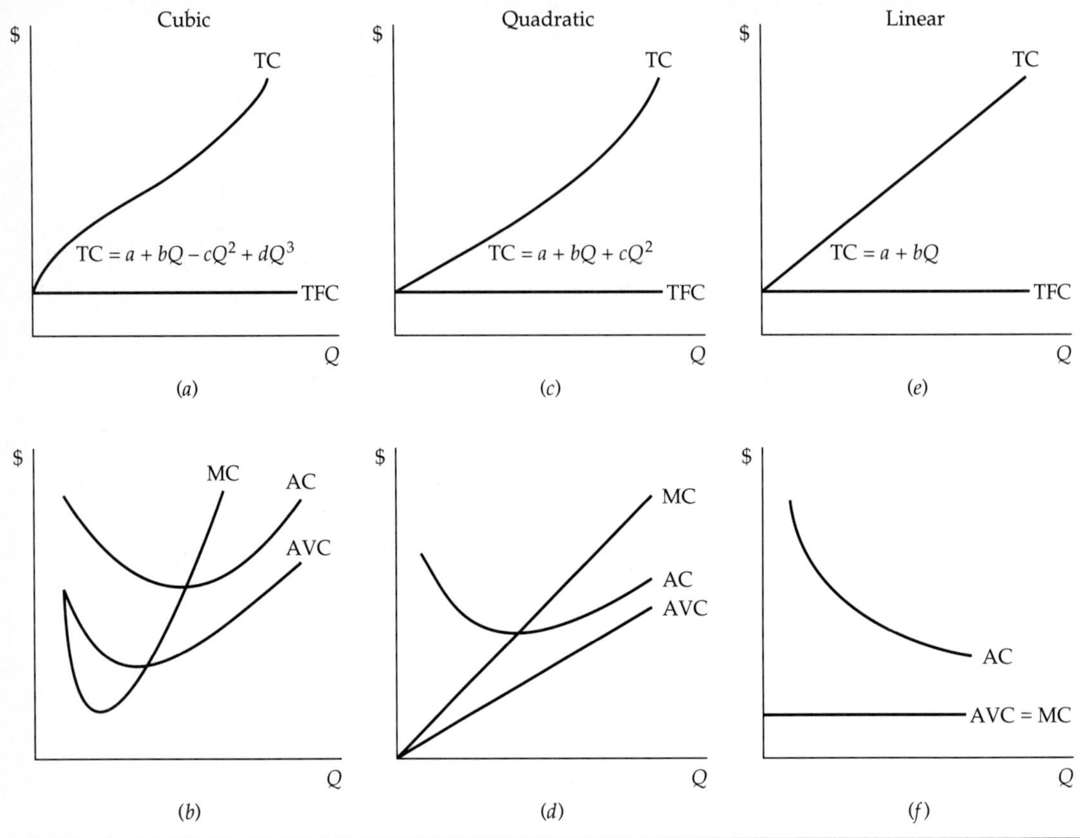

Figure 8.4 Alternative Representations of Total, Average, and Marginal Costs

$$TC = 100 + 0.50Q \tag{8.5}$$

Assuming the intercept and slope coefficients represent dollar units, this function tells us that the firm's total fixed cost is \$100 and its marginal cost is \$0.50. That is, each additional unit of production adds \$0.50 to the firm's total cost. Omitting the fixed cost component of the equation gives us

$$TVC = 0.50Q \tag{8.6}$$

Recall by definition that AVC = TVC/Q. Dividing Equation (8.6) by Q gives an AVC of \$0.50, which is the same as the marginal cost.

The mathematics of the this example may seem rather trivial. Nonetheless, it is important to elaborate on this relationship between average variable cost and marginal cost because these two measures of cost are often used interchangeably in the business world. For example, when cost accountants use the term *standard variable cost*, they are usually referring to *both* marginal cost and average variable cost. In so doing, they are assuming that the total cost function is linear, that the firm experiences neither increasing nor diminishing returns in the short run. The importance of these assumptions as well as the role of the linear total cost function in economic analysis will be discussed further in Chapters 10 and 12.

The Long-Run Cost Function

The Relationship Between Long-Run Production and Long-Run Cost

In the long run, all inputs to a firm's production function may be changed. Because there are no fixed inputs, there are no fixed costs. Consequently, all costs of production are variable in the long run. In most work situations, managers of firms make decisions about production and cost that economic theory would consider short-run in nature. For example, they might have to decide how many labor hours are required for a particular project or whether or not the existing work force requires more machinery to meet increased demand.[6] But from time to time, managers must make long-run production decisions. That is, they must consider possible changes in *all* of the firm's inputs and, hence, changes in all of the firm's cost of operation. Decisions of this kind are considered by economists to be part of a manager's planning horizon.

In explaining the nature of the long-run cost function, we begin with a schedule of numbers showing a firm's long-run cost function in relation to its long-run production function. Unlike the case of short-run cost presented in Table 8.2, the hypothetical numbers in Table 8.3 are based on the assumption that greater amounts of output are the result of increases in *all* of the firm's inputs. Consistent with this assumption, this table implies that the firm would incur no cost if it chose not to produce any output, because in the long run there is no fixed cost.

As output increases, observe that total cost increases, but not at a constant rate. As with the short-run function, the rate of change of the long-run total cost function is called the marginal cost (long-run marginal cost, to be more precise). In

Table 8.3 Long-Run Cost Function

Scale of Production (capacity level)	*Total Product (output/mo.)*	*Long-Run Total Cost (LRTC)*	*Long-Run Marginal Cost (LRMC)*	*Long-Run Average Cost (LRAC)*
A	10,000	$ 50,000	$5.00	$5.00
B	20,000	90,000	4.00	4.50
C	30,000	120,000	3.00	4.00
D	40,000	150,000	3.00	3.75
E	50,000	200,000	5.00	4.00
F	60,000	260,000	6.00	4.33

[6]Recall that we stated earlier that the "short run" in economic theory requires only that at least one of the inputs in the production function be held constant. Thus, we can treat the addition of capital equipment as a short-run change if the amount of factory space or the amount of labor, for example, remains unchanged.

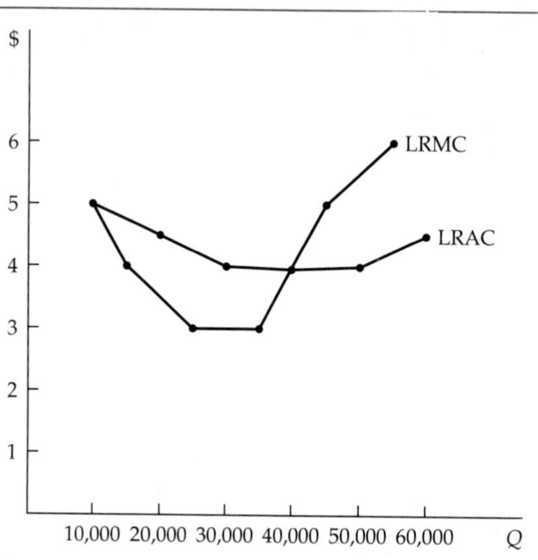

Figure 8.5 Long-Run Average and Marginal Cost

looking at the long-run marginal cost column in Table 8.3, we see that this measure at first decreases, then is constant, and finally increases over the range of the output. The numbers in Table 8.3 are plotted on a graph in Figure 8.5. The rate of change in the long-run total cost can be seen by observing the slope of this curve as well as by observing the behavior of the long-run marginal cost curve.

The reason for this particular behavior of the firm's long-run marginal cost (or the rate of change in its long-run total cost) pertains to returns to scale. As explained in the previous chapter, economists hypothesize that a firm's long-run production function may at first exhibit increasing returns, then constant returns, and finally decreasing returns to scale. This being the case, we would expect a firm's long-run cost to change in a reciprocal fashion.

When a firm experiences increasing returns to scale, an increase in all of its inputs by some proportion results in an increase in its output by some *greater* proportion. Assuming constant input prices over time, this means that if the firm's output increases by some percentage, its total cost of production increases by some *lesser* percentage. The graphs in Figure 8.6 illustrate the reciprocal behavior of long-run cost and long-run production.

It is important to stress that although the long-run cost function appears to exhibit the same pattern of behavior as the short-run cost function, the reasons for their respective patterns are entirely unrelated. The short-run cost function is affected by increasing and diminishing returns, a phenomenon that is assumed to take effect when at least one of the inputs is held constant, and the long-run function is affected by increasing and decreasing returns to scale, a phenomenon assumed to take effect when all of the firm's inputs are allowed to vary. Figure 8.7 serves as a reminder of this distinction.

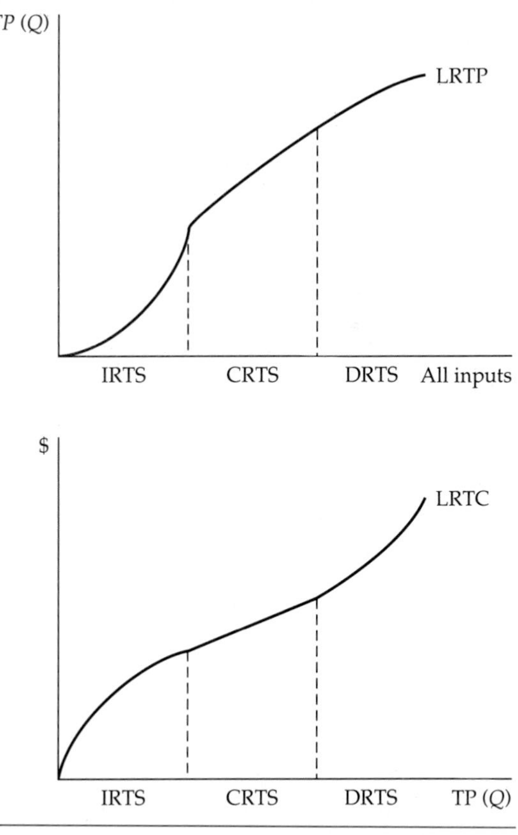

Figure 8.6 Returns to Scale for Long-Run Total Cost and Long-Run Total Production

Economies of Scale

One of the measures of cost in Table 8.3 has yet to be discussed: long-run average cost. This variable is the key indicator of a phenomenon called *economies of scale*. If a firm's long-run average cost declines as output increases, the firm is said to be experiencing economies of scale. If long-run average cost increases, economists consider this to be a sign of *diseconomies of scale*. There is no special term to describe the situation in which a firm's long-run average cost remains constant as output increases or decreases. We shall simply say that such a firm experiences neither economies nor diseconomies of scale. Figure 8.8 illustrates a typical U-shaped average cost curve reflecting the different types of scale economies that a firm might experience in the long run.

The primary reason for long-run scale economies is the underlying pattern of returns to scale in the firm's long-run production function. Further evaluation of Table 8.3 indicates that as long as marginal cost is falling, it is less than long-run average cost and in effect pulls the average down—a sure sign of economies of scale. However, once the firm starts to experience decreasing returns to scale, its long-run marginal cost begins to rise. Eventually it becomes greater than

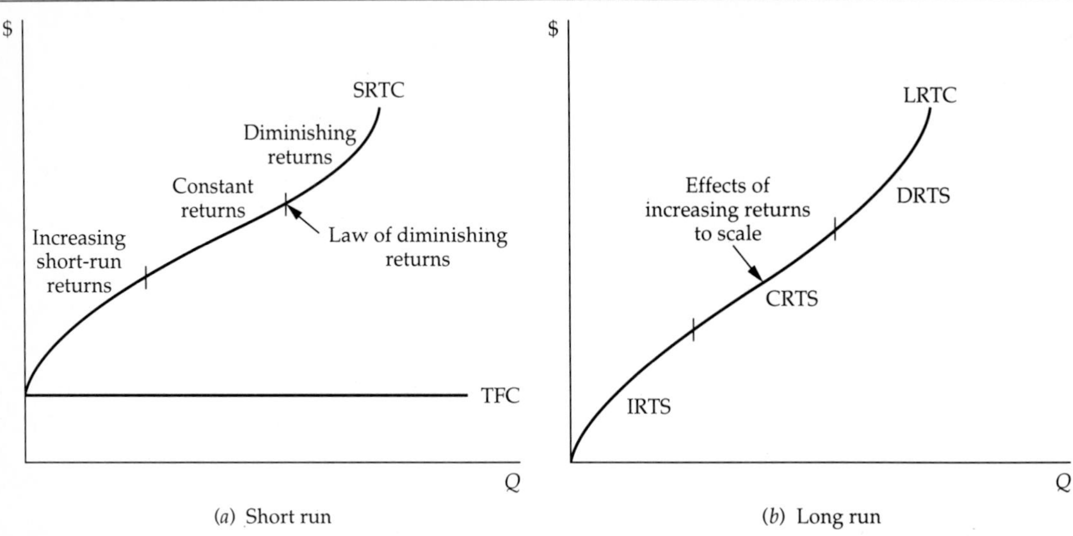

(*a*) Short run (*b*) Long run

Figure 8.7 Long-Run versus Short-Run Cost Function

long-run average cost, causing LRAC to rise and signifying diseconomies of scale.[7]

Scale economies and diseconomies may result from factors besides those relating to returns to scale. These other factors pertain primarily to the prices of the firm's inputs. For example, as the firm's scale of production increases, it may be able to exert some market power over its suppliers and thus receive volume discounts for bulk purchases of raw materials and component parts.[8] Another example involves a firm's use of capital equipment with better *price-performance ratios*. As the firm increases its scale of production, it may be worthwhile to buy more cost-effective machinery whose price and capacity could not be justified at smaller scales of production. Only a few years ago, a typical illustration cited by economists of this type of scale economy was the computer. But with the advent of personal and midsize computers, there are now machines with prices and levels of computing power that are appropriate for firms of all sizes. Furthermore, with the tremendous advances in technology and software, the prices of the machines relative to their computing power (i.e., their price-performance ratios) do not differ much among the various sizes of computers.[9]

---

[7]You should recognize the relationship between LRMC and LRAC to be the same mathematically as the relationship between SRMC and SRAC. That is, regardless of whether a short- or a long-run time period is assumed, when the marginal is below the average, it brings the average down. When the marginal is above the average, it pulls the average up.

[8]In this case, economists would say that the firm is exercising *monopsonistic power* in the input market. Recall that *monopoly* means one seller. *Monopsony* means one buyer. Firms with monopsonistic power are able to influence the market price for inputs in the same way that firms with monopolistic power can influence the price of outputs.

[9]One of the authors recalls attending a conference on computer technology in which a speaker asked the audience, "What is the difference between a mainframe computer and a personal computer?" Answer: "18 months!"

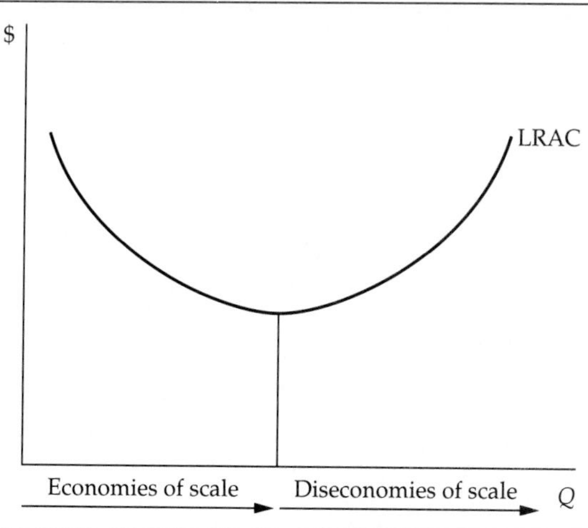

Figure 8.8 Long-Run Average Cost Curve

We should briefly mention two other factors contributing to economies of scale. First, larger firms may be able to raise funds in capital markets at a lower cost than smaller ones. For instance, a large company may be able to secure short-term funds in the commercial paper market and long-term funds in the corporate bond market, whereas a small company may be able to secure borrowed funds only from a bank. Generally, the interest rates that firms must pay for funds in money and capital markets are less than for bank loans with comparable maturities. Second, a large firm may be able to take advantage of economies resulting from the spreading out of promotional costs. If a firm expands its scale of production, it may not have to expand its advertising budget by the same proportion, if at all. The same can be said about research-and-development expenditures.

As far as diseconomies of scale are concerned, if the firm's scale of production becomes so large that it begins to affect substantially the total market demand for its inputs, it may start to increase the price of these inputs. A typical case is the expansion of a major employer in a local area with a relatively fixed supply of labor. If the firm's higher scale of production sufficiently increases its demand for labor, it could begin to drive up local wage rates.

Another factor not related to the long-run production function that could cause diseconomies of scale is a firm's transportation costs. As a firm increases the production capacity of a particular manufacturing facility, per-unit transportation cost tends to rise rather than to fall. This is largely because transportation costs involve more than just the delivery of goods from one point to another. In addition, there are handling expenses, insurance and security expenses, and inventory costs (as goods await shipment). Increases in these types of expenses help to increase the total transportation cost to the extent that average transportation cost increases as well. Furthermore, basic delivery expenses may rise at a faster rate than other kinds of cost if the firm has to ship the additional output to farther destinations. Economists hypothesize that eventually the increase in unit transportation cost will more than offset the fall

Table 8.4 Factors Affecting Economies and Diseconomies of Scale

Possible Reasons for Economies of Scale
Specialization in the use of labor and capital*
Indivisible nature of many types of capital equipment*
Productive capacity of capital equipment rises faster than purchase price
Economies in maintaining inventory of replacement parts and maintenance personnel*
Discounts from bulk purchases
Lower cost of raising capital funds
Spreading of promotional and research-and-development costs
Management efficiencies (line and staff)*
Possible Reasons for Diseconomies of Scale
Disproportionate rise in transportation costs
Input market imperfections (e.g., wage rates driven up)
Management coordination and control problems*
Disproportionate rise in staff and indirect labor*

*Indicates reason related directly to economies or diseconomies of scale in the long-run production function

in unit cost due to economies of scale. If this happens, then diseconomies of scale (i.e., rising average total cost) will result. Table 8.4 summarizes the key reasons for economies and diseconomies of scale. Factors that primarily relate to returns to scale are noted with an asterisk.

The Long-Run Average Cost Curve as the Envelope of Short-Run Average Cost

Up to now, we have been discussing long-run average cost as part of the firm's planning horizon. That is, the firm is assumed to be free to choose any level of capacity that it wants, because in our theoretical long-run time period, all inputs may vary. However, once a firm commits itself to a certain level of capacity, it must consider at least one of the inputs fixed as it varies the rest. In terms of production cost, this means that once a capacity level is decided on, the firm must work with a short-run cost function. We can illustrate this by returning to the example in Table 8.3.

Suppose that the capacity levels shown in the table represent plants of increasing size. Figure 8.9 shows these capacity levels in relation to each plant's short-run average cost curve. The points labeled *a* through *f* represent the levels of output and average cost shown in Table 8.3. The dotted lines passing through the points indicate the short-run average cost curves that we imagine to exist once the firm has locked into one of the plant sizes represented by the labeled points.

As expected, short-run average cost (SRAC) curves for the larger plants are positioned to the right of the curves for smaller ones, indicating greater produc-

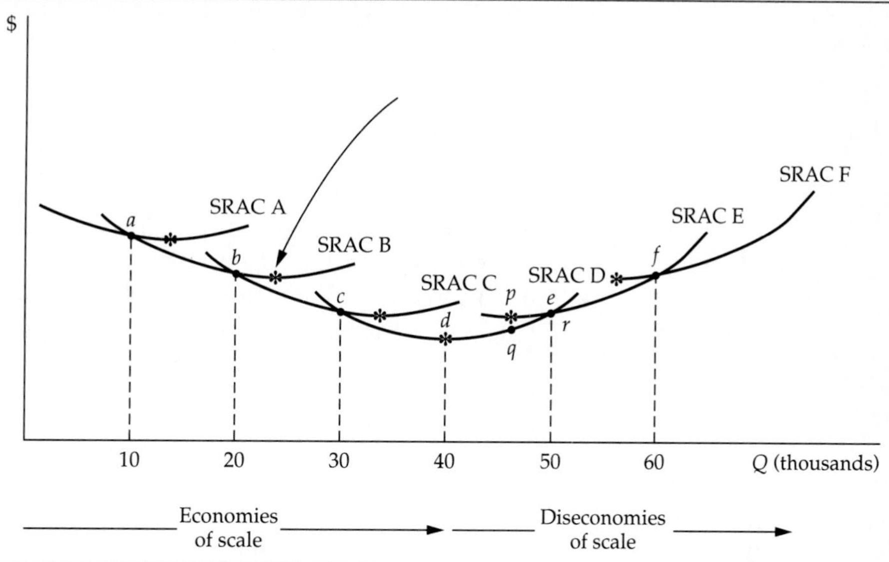

Figure 8.9 Capacity Level and Short-Run Average Cost

tion capacity. For example, SRAC B is to the right of SRAC A, because plant B is larger than plant A. But, as noted in Figure 8.9, plants with larger capacities are greatly influenced by economies and diseconomies of scale. Because of the impact of economies of scale, plant B's SRAC curve is positioned below as well as to the right of plant A's, so that the minimum point of B's SRAC curve is *lower* than that for A. The same can be said for plant C's minimum SRAC in relation to plant B's and for D's in relation to C's. However, because of the impact of diseconomies of scale, plant E's SRAC curve is positioned above and to the right of D's, and plant F's is above and to the right of E's. That is, the SRAC curves of plants larger than plant D have progressively higher minimum average cost points. For reference, the minimum SRAC points for all of the plants are marked in Figure 8.9 with asterisks.[10]

[10]Readers may wish to consider the following illustration, in which there are neither economies nor diseconomies of scale as production capacity grows.

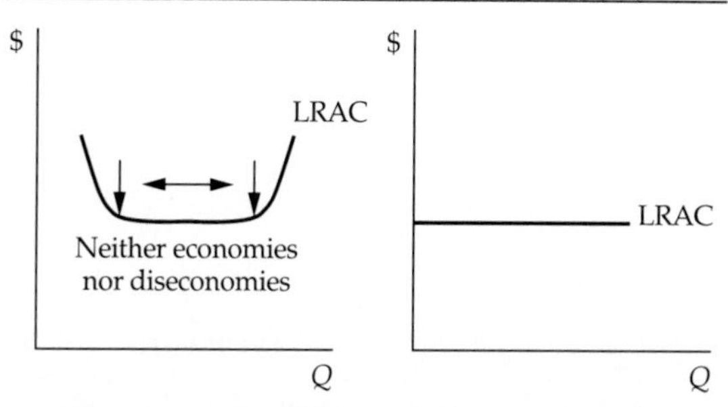

Another important aspect of Figure 8.9 is that none of the labeled dots is at the lowest point of its respective short-run average cost curve *except for the dot representing plant D*. For example, the asterisk marking plant B's minimum short-run average cost depicts a level above the average cost that would be incurred by plant C in the short run for a comparable level of production (see arrow in Figure 8.9). A logical extension of this illustration is the observation that if a firm wants to produce between 20,000 and 30,000 units of output per month, it would be better off utilizing the manufacturing capacity provided by plant C than to try to increase the usage of the smaller plant B. To understand the full economic implication of this observation, it is necessary to take a slight detour in our discussion to explain the particular way in which economists represent plant capacity with the use of short-run average cost curves.

You will recall that the typical short-run average cost curve (based on a cubic total cost function) declines, reaches a minimum point, and then rises as the firm produces more with some fixed amount of input. By definition, economists consider the lowest point of the short-run average cost curve to represent the firm's maximum capacity. Although "maximum capacity" usually denotes the physical limit of production (i.e., a plant simply cannot produce any more output), Figure 8.9 shows that a firm is clearly capable of producing beyond the output level at which average cost is at its lowest point. Rather than try to figure out the reason for this particular use of the term, just remember that for economists, "maximum plant capacity" coincides with a level of output that costs a firm the least amount per unit to produce in the short run.[11]

Thus, Figure 8.9 shows that over certain ranges of output, a firm is better off operating a larger plant at less-than-maximum capacity than a smaller plant at maximum capacity. The average cost of production in the larger plant is lower than the lowest possible average cost of production in the smaller plant. What causes this to happen? Economies of scale, of course. Because of this phenomenon, we can expect that over certain ranges of output, the reduction in average cost resulting from the economies of using a larger plant will be greater than the reduction in average cost resulting from operating a smaller plant at its most efficient (the economic "maximum") level of capacity!

As a cautionary note, we should add that once diseconomies of scale take effect, it is better for a firm to operate a plant of a given size beyond its "maximum capacity" than to build a plant of a larger size. We leave it to you to work through a detailed explanation of this observation. Suffice to say that the reasoning is very similar to the explanation regarding the impact of economies of scale. (If you need help, refer to Figure 8.9, points p, q, and r.)

Looking at Figure 8.9 from another perspective, we can see that the firm's long-run average cost curve is actually the envelope of the various short-run average cost curves. As such, the long-run curve outlines the lowest per-unit costs that the firm will incur over the range of output considered, given the

[11] Actually, a more accurate label for the output level corresponding to the minimum per-unit cost is "maximum (output) level of production efficiency" rather than maximum (output) level of production capacity. However, the latter term was originally designated in microeconomic theory.

possibility of using plant sizes A through F. Figure 8.10*a* illustrates this point. As the number of choices of plant size approaches infinity, the envelope becomes a continuous version of the graph; this version is shown in Figure 8.10*b*. You should recognize it as the long-run average cost curve first shown in Figure 8.8.

Using Long-Run Average Cost as a Decision-Making Tool: The Importance of Coordinating Production Plans with Market Forecasts

In planning for its long-run capacity, which plant size should a firm choose? Using the schedule of numbers in Table 8.3, we can see that if a firm decides to build plant A, then the lowest per-unit cost of production it can expect is $5. But if it decides to build a plant with greater capacity—for instance, plant C—the potential for reducing per-unit cost is considerable because of economies of scale. Using plant C, the firm could produce its output for as little as $4 per unit. Indeed, this is where accurate forecasts of product demand are needed to help the firm plan for the best plant size. There would be no sense in investing in plant C, for example, if monthly demand is only 20,000. In this case, the smaller plant B would be more suitable. Actually, given the plant size options shown in Table 8.3 and Figure 8.9, we see that it is not necessary for a firm to forecast a specific amount of demand, but it should at least have a good idea of what the range of demand will be in the future. Table 8.5 presents a schedule showing the most appropriate plant size for different ranges of demand and production.

You should recognize that because diseconomies of scale take effect when plant D is used, plant C is appropriate for a wider range of production than the other plants. The penalty for selecting the inappropriate level of capacity is the incurrence of unnecessary cost, whether the actual demand turns out to

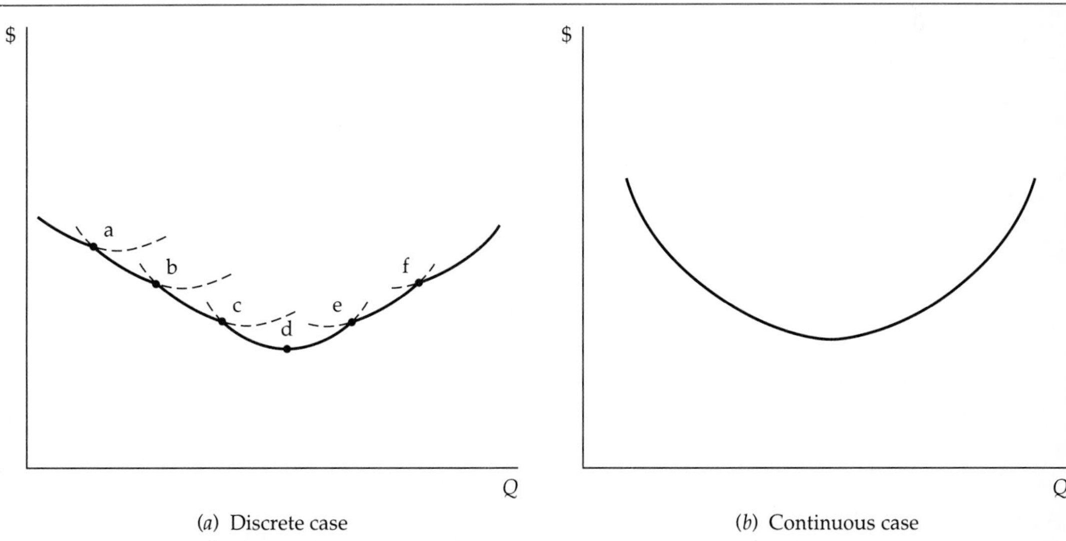

Figure 8.10 Forming LRAC Curve from SRAC Curves

Table 8.5 Optimal Plant Size According to Expected Demand

Units of Output Produced, Based on Expected Demand	*Appropriate Plant Size*
0 to 10,000	A
10,000 to 20,000	B
20,000 to 30,000	C
30,000 to 50,000	D
50,000 to 60,000	E
60,000 to 70,000 (not shown on graph)	F

be above or below the range used as a basis for the firm's decision on long-run production capacity. In Figure 8.11, we can see that if the firm had decided to build plant B and the demand turned out to be 25,000, it would lose on a per-unit basis the amount depicted by the arrow. If demand were such that it required the firm to produce only 5,000 units per month, the firm would suffer a similar type of loss.[12]

As a final comment on long-run cost, it is very easy to put the onus for picking the best level of long-run capacity on the market forecasters. After all, their estimates of future demand should be the main guide for the decision makers who plan production capacity. Nevertheless, the production people in a business could become carried away with considerations of production capacity

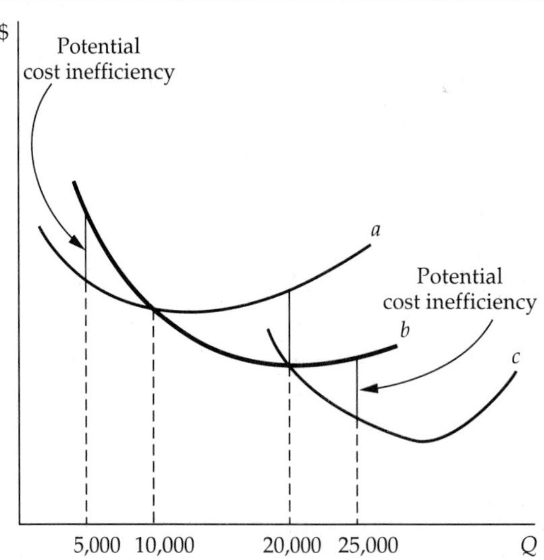

Figure 8.11 Unnecessary Costs Due to Inappropriate Plant Size

[12]Readers should recognize this "loss" as a form of opportunity cost. By choosing the wrong plant size, the firm would be forgoing an opportunity to produce the output at a lower per-unit cost.

and efficiency for their own sake (e.g., "let us build a plant of the size that will enable us to benefit substantially from economies of scale") and convince the management to overbuild the company's long-run capacity. Certainly, optimal long-run production decisions require a balanced contribution from both the engineers and the marketing people.

The Learning Curve

The *learning curve* is a line showing the relationship between labor cost and additional units of output. Its downward slope indicates that this additional cost per unit declines as the level of output increases because workers improve with practice. The reduction in cost from this particular source of improvement is often referred to as the *learning curve effect.*

Specifically, a learning curve is measured in terms of the percentage decrease in additional labor cost each time output doubles. Table 8.6 presents data for an "80 percent" learning curve. Each time the output doubles, the cost of producing the next increment of output decreases to 80 percent of the previous level (i.e., declines by 20 percent). As you can see in this table, the first unit costs $100,000; the second unit costs 80 percent of this amount, or $80,000; the fourth unit costs 80 percent of this amount, or $64,000; and so on. Notice that the percentage reduction is actually with respect to labor hours. However, given some wage rate (in this case, $10/hour), the labor cost decreases by the same percentage. The data in Table 8.6 are plotted in Figure 8.12.

There is a mathematical formula for determining the pattern of reduction in labor cost based on a selected percentage decline. This formula is

$$Y_x = Kx^n$$

where Y_x = Units of factor (labor hours) or cost to produce xth unit
K = Factor units or cost to produce kth (usually first) unit
x = Product unit (the xth unit)

Table 8.6 Numerical Example of the Learning Curve

Unit Number	*Unit Labor Hours*	*Cumulative Labor Hours*	*Cumulative Average Labor Hours*	*Unit Labor Cost*	*Cumulative Average Labor Cost*
1	10,000	10,000.0	10,000	$100,000	$100,000
2	8,000	18,000.0	9,000	80,000	90,000
4	6,400	31,421.0	7,855.3	64,000	78,553
8	5,120	53,459.1	6,682.4	51,200	66,824
16	4,096	89,201.4	5,575.1	40,960	55,751
32	3,276.8	146,786.2	4,587.1	32,768	45,871
64	2,621.4	239,245.3	3,738.2	26,214	37,382
128	2,097.2	387,439.5	3,026.9	20,972	30,269
256	1,677.7	624,731.8	2,404.6	16,777	24,046

Wage rate = $10/hr.

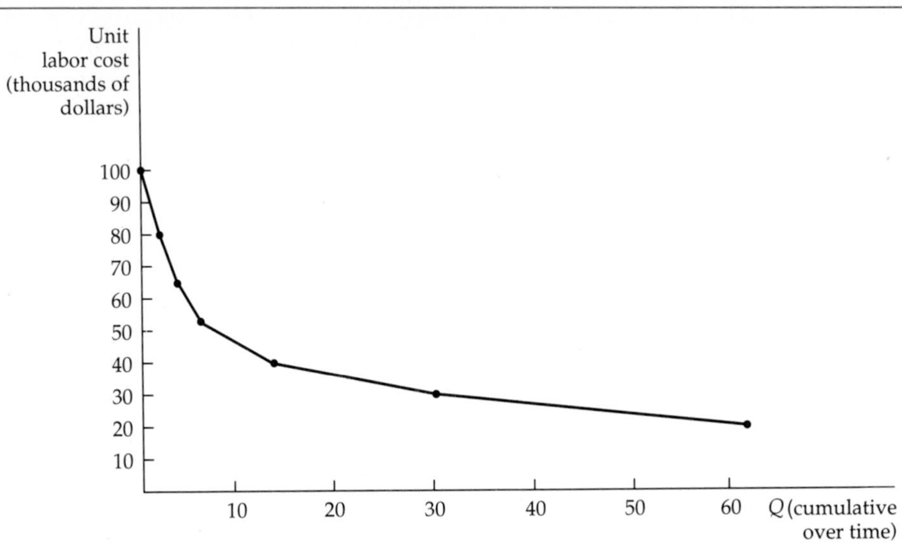

Figure 8.12 An 80 Percent Learning Curve

$$\text{where } n = \log S / \log 2$$
$$S = \text{Slope parameter}$$

For an 80 percent learning curve, the number of direct labor hours required to produce the eighth unit of output is

$$S = .8$$
$$Y_8 = 100,000(8)^{\log .8/\log 2}$$
$$= 100,000(8)^{-.322}$$
$$= \frac{100,000}{8^{.322}}$$
$$= \frac{100,000}{1.9535} = 51,200$$

This answer conforms to Table 8.6 and Figure 8.12. You may want to try constructing other learning curves based on different percentages.[13]

Although the learning curve is expressed in terms of the marginal cost of production, the impact of improving with practice can also be seen in terms of the decline in average cost. Table 8.6 also shows the cumulative labor cost and the cumulative average labor cost of producing various levels of output. As can be seen, the average labor cost also decreases, although not as sharply as the marginal labor cost. In any case, the learning curve effect clearly has an impact

[13]For those interested, learning curves or "progress functions," as they are often referred to by engineers, are already computed for many different proportional declines or slopes. They can be found in tables in engineering or operations research texts.

on the short-run cost presented earlier. In particular, the learning curve effect causes the short-run average cost curve to shift downward.[14] This is shown in Figure 8.13.

The Japanese have been frequently cited in academic studies and in the popular press for their use of the learning curve in driving down costs. This is most dramatically shown in their production of computer chips and consumer electronics. Their particular use of the learning curve involves accelerating production experience through aggressive price-cutting measures. The price cuts enhance sales and give them production experience more rapidly. This in turn helps to drive down costs of production faster. The tactic of learning curve pricing is illustrated in Figure 8.14.

In concluding this section on the learning curve effect, we should note that this phenomenon was first observed in the production of aircraft more than 50 years ago. The reason cited for the learning curve effect was the repetition of tasks performed by workers actually manufacturing the product (e.g., direct labor). Later on, the experience gained from repetition by those indirectly related to the production process (e.g., engineers and researchers) was also included in this phenomenon. Thus, such factors as the development of new process and engineering methods, the substitution of lower-cost materials or processes, and product redesign were also considered as factors causing unit costs to decrease as production levels increased. The recognition of these additional factors prompted the use of the broader term *experience curve*. Today, *experience curve* and *learning curve* are generally used interchangeably. However, some business managers and consultants still prefer to make a distinction between the two terms.[15]

Economies of Scope

Before summarizing this chapter, we should introduce briefly a concept often used in business but that does not quite fit into the conventional economic theory of cost, namely, *economies of scope*. This term can be defined as

> the reduction of a firm's unit cost by producing two or more goods or services jointly rather than separately.

The effort by our hypothetical firm Global Foods, Inc., to increase its profits by expanding into the soft drink industry offers a good example of a company seeking to take advantage of economies of scope. The company already has the knowledge, experience, and skills to produce and distribute processed food

[14]For a detailed analysis of the link between the learning curve and the short-run cost function, see Jack Hirshleifer, "The Firm's Cost Function: A Successful Reconstruction?" *Journal of Business*, July 1962, pp. 235–55.

[15]For example, see Bruce D. Henderson, "The Application and Misapplication of the Experience Curve," *Journal of Business Strategy* 4 (Winter 1984), pp. 3–9.

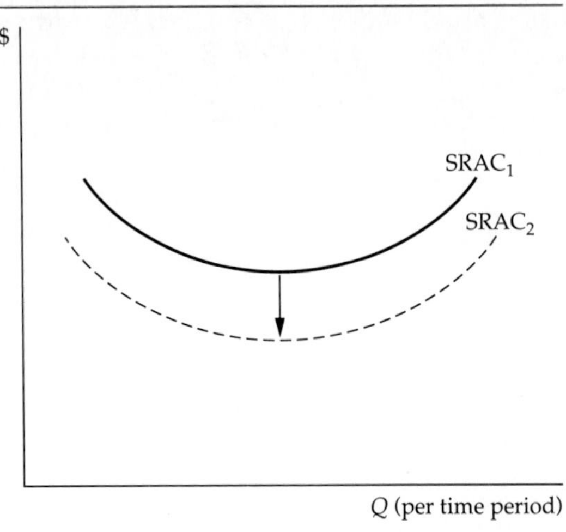

Figure 8.13 Impact of Learning Curve Effect on Short-Run Average Cost per Time Period

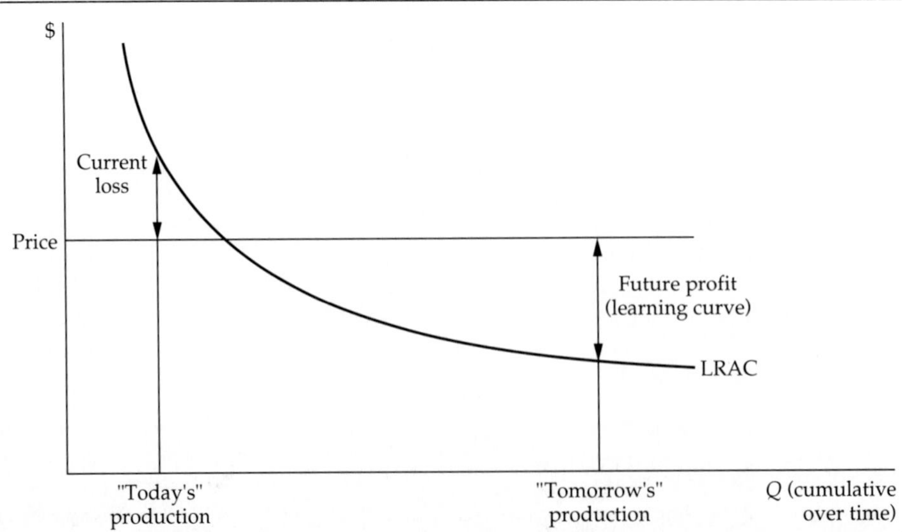

Figure 8.14 Pricing Based on Learning or Experience Curve

items and hopes to use these attributes in the production and distribution of soft drinks.[16]

In a sense, the concept of economies of scope is closely related to economies of scale. Engaging in more than one line of business may require a firm to have a certain minimum scale of operation. Another way to view this relationship between scale and scope is to consider that a company's expansion into different lines of business naturally increases its scale of operation.

The Importance of Cost Functions in Managerial Decision Making

Focus on relevant cost when making economic decisions. One of the most important lessons that managers can learn in the economic analysis of cost is the importance of using relevant cost in decision making. This chapter defined relevant cost and provided examples of how one can distinguish relevant cost from "irrelevant cost." The actual use of one type of relevant cost (i.e., marginal cost) in the making of economic decisions on output and pricing must await a later chapter. (See Chapter 11.)

Recognize the possibility of diminishing returns in the short-run production process, and be aware that this will cause marginal cost to increase as output increases. It is often a matter of convenience to assume that the production of additional units of a product will cost the same extra amount (i.e., constant marginal cost). Indeed, cost accountants often speak of some "standard variable cost" in reference to the cost of producing additional units of a good or service. Managers should recognize that the law of diminishing returns will cause marginal cost to increase. Thus, even though a firm is able to sell more at the same price, additional profit from the sale of these additional units may begin to decline if marginal cost begins to increase.

Be aware that economies of scale, the learning curve effect, and economies of scope may enable a firm to reduce its unit cost of production as it increases its entire scale of operation. In the long run, economic theory suggests that firms may be able to reduce their unit costs due to the impact of economies of scale, the learning curve effect, and possibly economies of scope. Managers should recognize this possibility and observe whether indeed the unit costs of production decrease as a firm increases the size of a particular site (e.g., sales branch office, manufacturing facility, warehouse operation) or its scale of operation for the entire firm.

Be aware that increasing the entire scale of operation does not automatically lead to a reduction in per unit cost. Two factors may prevent the firm from experiencing a reduction in unit cost as its scale of operation increases. One is the simple

---

[16]In recent years, PepsiCo has exemplified the opposite situation by diversifying into the food business. See "Pepsi Is Going Better with Its Fast Foods and Frito Lay Snacks," *Wall Street Journal*, June 13, 1991.

fact that the *demand* for the product may be inadequate to enable a firm to take advantage of the larger scale of operation. At lower levels of demand, it may be beneficial to operate at a lower level of capacity at maximum efficiency than to operate at a higher level of capacity at less-than-maximum efficiency. This point is very similar to one made in the previous chapter, on production. There is often a temptation for manufacturing people to push for a large scale of production in order to take advantage of economies of scale or "increasing returns to scale" regardless of whether the demand will be high enough to justify the larger scale of operation.

Managers should also bear in mind that an increase in the scale of operation could just as easily lead to an *increase* in unit costs as to a decrease. This is because of diseconomies of scale, a phenomenon caused mainly by inefficiencies related to a large bureacracy and the tendency for the number of staff positions to grow at a disproportionate rate relative to line jobs as the firm expands in size.

The Solution

Initially, Marie Jacobs considered the reduction of cost in five areas of operation, which are listed here along with some of her remarks about their cost-cutting potential.

1. *Wage rates:* Unfortunately, there is no room for improvement in this area. The company is already paying the going market wage rate for semiskilled labor.
2. *Labor productivity:* Here again, there is little opportunity to reduce costs. On the average, workers have been at their jobs for seven years and know their jobs very well. Thus, further training or experience would not really help them to be more efficient.
3. *Raw material costs:* If costs are to be reduced here, it would have to be because of circumstances beyond the company's control. Global Foods is, to a large extent, a price taker in the raw materials markets. It is still relatively small compared to the two giants in the soft drink industry, so it cannot extract any volume-pricing agreements with the raw materials suppliers.
4. *"Make versus buy" in packaging:* Perhaps some savings could be had by making plastic one- and two-liter bottles rather than purchasing them from a vendor. The bottle-making facility could be set up right next to the bottling plant, resulting in additional savings in transportation and storage costs. This, in fact, would be a perfect way to implement "just-in-time" inventory control.
5. *Single versus multiple plant operations:* Because the company plans eventually to distribute its product nationwide, it is not too early to consider whether it

(Continued)

should operate one plant (or perhaps several large plants) or many small plants situated all over the country. Large plants would provide cost savings in terms of economies of scale, but small plants would help to reduce the transportation costs of the incoming raw materials as well as the outgoing final product.

Items 4 and 5 had potential, but they would require a considerable investment in time and money before the cost savings would begin to materialize. Just as Marie was beginning to feel a trifle discouraged about finding any substantial ways to reduce the costs of bottling, she recalled something that she had observed in one of her tours of a bottling plant. Toward the end of the bottling process, she noticed that each can on the conveyor belt passed a measuring device called a "fill height detector" that checked if there were at least 12 ounces of liquid in the container. Those with less were discarded. This measuring device shot a gamma beam about 1/4 inch below the top of the can's lid. Because it was not necessary for the product to be filled to the very top of the can, there might be an opportunity for raw materials savings. What if the lid were made smaller? It would certainly not affect the volume of liquid. Figure 8.15 illustrates this. The cost savings from the reduction in the aluminum content of the can would be considerable, given the volume of production involved.

In addition to reducing a can's lid size, another idea occurred to her. In reviewing the monthly reports, she noticed that there were substantial periods of time when a plant was not operating at full capacity. She therefore concluded that there was a significant opportunity for Global Foods to perform some contract bottling for other companies during these slack periods. Marie considered that Global Foods, in effect, would be reducing the opportunity cost of its excess capacity by using it to bottle the products of other firms.

Marie's manager liked her cost-saving ideas as well as her analysis of the cost structure of the bottling plant. He had only one reservation. "Soon everyone will be using a smaller lid size," he cautioned. "But that's competition. If we don't act now,

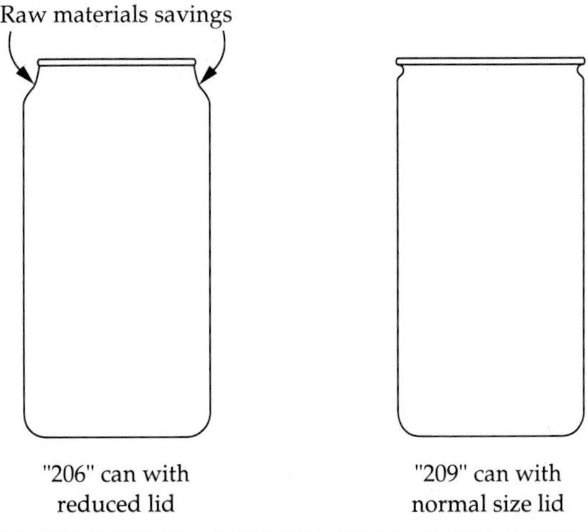

Figure 8.15 Using Reduced-Lid Can to Achieve Raw Materials Savings

someone else will probably think of it anyway and beat us to the punch. In any event, even a slight lead in this area of production will give our marketing people time to generate a solid nationwide demand for our product. Furthermore, your suggestions to reduce costs over the long run are very good. You have even got me thinking about the value of using better equipment to help our workers do their jobs more effectively. By coincidence, just the other day, someone came in to see me about a new depalletizing machine." (More will be said about this sales call to Marie's manager in Chapter 14.)

Summary

This chapter has been devoted to the analysis of the cost structure of the firm, both in the short run and the long run. In the short-run analysis, it is important to keep in mind that "behind the scenes," the law of diminishing returns causes the firm's marginal cost to increase, and that this increase in turn affects the pattern of behavior of the firm's average variable cost and average total cost. In the long-run analysis, it is important to recognize that certain factors may cause the firm's unit costs to decrease as its scale of operation increases. However, certain other factors may actually cause the unit cost to increase if the scale of operations becomes too large. In addition, other factors such as the learning curve effect and economies of scope must be taken into account in the long-run analysis of cost.

The material that has been covered in this chapter may seem rather mundane because of the great emphasis placed on defining the various cost terms used in economic analysis. However, your patience and thoroughness in reading this chapter will be rewarded when you arrive at Chapter 11. There you will find that the material in this chapter, together with the analysis of demand presented in Chapters 3 and 4, forms the core of the economic analysis of the firm. As that chapter explains, all the decisions involving the production and pricing of goods or services—and, in a much broader sense, the very desirability for a firm to be in a particular line of business—depend on the demand for the particular product, the cost at which the firm is able to provide this product, and the competitive structure of the market in which it is operating.

Important Concepts

Average fixed cost (AFC): The fixed cost per unit of output.

Average total cost (AC or ATC): The total cost per unit of output.

Average variable cost (AVC): The variable cost per unit of output.

Diseconomies of scale: The increase in the unit cost of production as the firm increases its capacity. Like economies of scale, this is considered to be a long-run phenomenon. Among the more important reasons a firm may experience rising unit costs as its scale of production increases are (1) management coordination and control problems and (2) a disproportionate increase in staff in relation to indirect labor.

Economies of scale: The reduction in the unit cost of production as the firm increases its capacity (i.e., increases all of its inputs). It is considered a long-run phenomenon. Among the reasons a firm experiences economies as its scale of production increases are: (1) the ability to exact volume discounts from vendors, (2) the ability to utilize more fully specialization and division of labor, (3) the ability to justify the use of certain types of capital equipment or technology appropriate only for very large scales of production, and (4) management efficiencies resulting from an increased span of control at all levels of management.

Economies of scope: The reduction in cost resulting from the joint production of two or more goods or services.

Experience curve: The relationship between the unit cost of labor and all inputs associated with the production process (i.e., both direct labor, such as factory workers, and indirect labor, such as design engineers).

Functional form of total cost: Economic analysis considers three basic functional forms of total cost: cubic, quadratic, and linear. The microeconomic theory of the firm relies almost entirely on the cubic function, and break-even analysis generally uses the linear form.

Historical cost: The cost incurred in a past activity (e.g., the purchase price of an asset or the cost of a project incurred up to the point at which a decision is to be made).

Incremental cost: The total cost associated with a particular decision (e.g., the cost of building an additional wing to an office building, the cost of going into the soft drink business). If incremental cost is considered on a per-unit basis, it becomes marginal cost. For example, incremental cost can be considered the change in total variable cost, whereas marginal cost can be considered the change in total variable cost divided by the change in output.

Learning curve: The relationship between the unit cost of labor and the total amount of output produced by labor that is directly associated with the production process (.i.e., "direct labor"). Essentially, this concept is based on the principle that one improves with practice. The resulting productivity gains lead to a reduction in the direct labor cost of producing a unit of output.

Marginal cost (MC): The cost to a firm of producing an additional unit of an output.

Opportunity cost: The amount or subjective value forgone in choosing one activity over the next best alternative.

Relevant costs: Costs that are affected by a current decision alternative and that must therefore be taken into account in the decision. Variable costs and incremental costs are considered to be relevant costs.

Sunk cost: A cost incurred in the past that is not affected by a current decision. If a resource has no opportunity cost (i.e., it has no market value in an alternative use), it is considered to be sunk. A sunk cost is irrelevant to a current decision.

Total cost (TC): The total cost of production, including both total variable and total fixed costs.

Total fixed cost (TFC): A cost that remains constant as the level of output varies. In a short-run analysis, fixed cost is incurred even if the firm produces no output.

Total variable cost (TVC): The total cost associated with the level of output. This can also be considered the total cost to a firm of using its variable inputs.

Questions

1. Define and compare the following types of cost:
   a. Sunk cost versus incremental cost
   b. Fixed cost versus variable cost
   c. Incremental cost versus marginal cost
   d. Opportunity cost versus out-of-pocket cost
2. Point out which costs in the preceding question are considered "relevant" and which are considered "irrelevant" to a business decision. Explain why.
3. Explain the relationship between a firm's short-run production function and its short-run cost function. Focus on the marginal product of an input and the marginal cost of production.
4. "If it were not for the law of diminishing returns, a firm's average cost and average variable cost would not increase in the short run." Do you agree with this statement? Explain.
5. Explain the distinction made in economic analysis between the short run and the long run.
6. Define economies of scale. How does this relate to returns to scale? Cite and briefly discuss the main determinants of economies of scale.
7. Define diseconomies of scale. Cite and briefly discuss the main determinants of this phenomenon.
8. Define economies of scope. Is this concept related to economies of scale? Explain.
9. Explain the relationship between the learning curve and a firm's cost function. Would economists consider the learning curve a short-run or a long-run phenomenon?
10. Define the experience curve. Compare its impact on a firm's cost function with that of the learning curve.
11. "Because of economies of scale, it is sometimes more cost-effective for a firm to operate a large plant at less-than-maximum efficiency than a small plant at maximum efficiency." Do you agree with this statement? Explain.

12. Overheard at the water cooler: "I think our company should take advantage of economies of scale by increasing our output, thereby spreading out our overhead costs." Would you agree with this statement (assuming this person is not your boss)? Explain.

Problems

1. Based on your knowledge of the definition of the various measures of short run cost, complete the table below.

Q	*TC*	*TFC*	*TVC*	*AC*	*AFC*	*AVC*	*MC*
0	120	___	___	x	x	x	x
1	___	___	___	265	___	___	___
2	___	___	264	___	___	___	___
3	___	___	___	161	___	___	___
4	___	___	___	___	___	___	85
5	___	___	525	___	___	___	___
6	___	___	___	120	___	___	___
7	___	___	___	___	___	97	___
8	___	___	768	___	___	___	___
9	___	___	___	___	___	97	___
10	___	___	___	___	___	___	127

2. Mr. Lee operates a green grocery in a building he owns in one of the outer boroughs of New York City. Recently, a large chemical firm offered him a position as a senior engineer designing plants for its Asian operations. (Mr. Lee has a masters degree in chemical engineering.) His salary plus benefits would be $95,000 per year. A recent annual financial statement of his store's operations indicates the following:

Revenue	$625,000
Cost of goods sold	325,000
Wages of workers	75,000
Taxes, insurance, maintenance, and depreciation on building	30,000
Interest on business loan (10%)	5,000
Other miscellaneous expenses	15,000
Profit before taxes	$175,000

If Mr. Lee decides to take the job, he knows that he can sell store for $350,000 because of the goodwill built with a steady clientele of neighborhood customers and the excellent location of the building. He would still hold on to the building, however, and he knows he could earn a rent of $50,000 on this asset. If he did sell the business, assume that he would use some of the proceeds from the sale to pay off his business loan of $50,000. He could then invest the difference of $300,000 (i.e., $350,000 − $50,000) and expect to receive an annual return of 9 percent. Should Mr. Lee sell his business and go to work for the chemical company?

In answering this question, also consider the following information:

a. In his own business, Mr. Lee works between 16 and 18 hours a day, six days a week. He can expect to work between 10 and 12 hours a day, five days a week, in the chemical company.
b. Currently, Mr. Lee is assisted by his wife and his brother, both of whom receive no salary but share in the profits of the business.
c. Mr. Lee expects his salary and the profits of his business to increase at roughly the same rate over the next five years.

3. Joe enjoys fishing and goes out about 20 times per year with three of his friends. One day, his wife Sarah told him that fishing is simply too expensive a hobby. "I think that you should stop going fishing," she exclaimed. "I did a little calculation, and I figured that it costs us about $28.75 for every fish that you catch, because you usually catch about 20 fish per trip. Besides, I always end up having to clean them. We would be much better off buying ready-to-cook fish from the local fish market."

Comment on Sarah's remarks. Do you agree with her argument? Explain. (Following below are her cost estimates.)

Boat (cost = $30,000, usable for 10 years, 20 outings per year)	$150
Boat fuel	45
Dock fees and insurance for the boat (average per trip)	130
Travel expenses to and from the lake (100 miles @ $0.25 per mile: gas, oil and tires, $0.18, and depreciation and insurance, $0.07)	25
New fishing equipment purchased this year (prorated over 20 trips)	25
Annual fishing license	35
Bait and miscellaneous expenses	50
Food	40
Beverages	35
Traffic fine received on the way to the lake	40
Total cost per trip	$575

4. You are given the following cost functions:

$$TC = 100 + 60Q - 3Q^2 + 0.1Q^3$$
$$TC = 100 + 60Q + 3Q^2$$
$$TC = 100 + 60Q$$

   a. Compute the average variable cost, average cost, and marginal cost for each function. Plot them on a graph.
   b. In each case, indicate the point at which diminishing returns occur. Also indicate the point of maximum cost efficiency (i.e., the point of minimum average cost).
   c. For each function, discuss the relationship between marginal cost and average variable cost and between marginal cost and average cost. Also discuss the relationship between average variable cost and average cost.
5. A manufacturer of furniture bought a shipment of teakwood from Thailand for $500,000 to make office furniture. As a result of the recession, it had to suspend operations of its office furniture division. A year later, when the economy recovered, it resumed operations. By then, Thai teakwood had become more expensive because of efforts by the Thai government to conserve its forests. That same shipment held in the company's inventory was now worth $750,000 in the open market. The head of the company's home furniture division wanted the company to allow it to use the wood because the profit margin was higher in home furniture than in office furniture. The head of the office furniture division argued that his division should be allowed to use the inventory. He argued that the operating profit of his division would be higher because he had already bought the inventory at the lower price. Comment on his argument. What would you do if you were the president of the company? (Note: If you believe that there is insufficient information to answer this question, what additional data would be helpful in making this decision?)
6. Decide whether the following statements are true or false and explain why.
   a. A decision maker must always use the historical cost of raw materials in making an economic decision.
   b. The marginal cost curve always intersects the average cost curve at the average cost's lowest point.
   c. The portion of the long-run cost curve that is horizontal indicates that the firm is experiencing neither economies nor diseconomies of scale.
   d. Marginal cost is relevant only in the short-run analysis of the firm.
   e. The rational firm will try to operate most efficiently by producing at the point where its average cost is minimized.
7. Indicate the effect that each of the following conditions will have on a firm's average variable cost curve and its average cost curve.
   a. The movement of a brokerage firm's administrative offices from New York City to New Jersey, where the average rental cost is lower
   b. The use of two shifts instead of three shifts in a manufacturing facility

c. An agreement reached with the labor union in which wage increases are tied to productivity increases
d. The elimination of sugar quotas (as it pertains to those firms that use a lot of sugar, such as bakeries and soft drink bottlers)
e. Imposition of stricter environmental protection laws

8. You are given the following *long-run* cost function:

$$TC = 160Q - 20Q^2 + 1.2Q^3$$

a. Calculate the long-run average cost and marginal cost. Plot these costs on a graph.
b. Describe the nature of this function's scale economies. Over what range of output does economies of scale exist? Diseconomies of scale? Show this on the graph.

APPENDIX 8A
A Mathematical Restatement of the Short-Run Cost Function

The general form of the short-run cost function is

$$TC = f(Q) \tag{8A.1}$$

where TC = Total cost
Q = Output

As stated in this chapter, three specific forms of this function are used in economic analysis: the cubic, the quadratic, and the linear. Microeconomic theory relies primarily on the cubic equation because it encompasses the possibility of increasing returns to a factor as well as diminishing returns. The quadratic form of the total cost function implies that only the law of diminishing returns affects the short-run relationship between a firm's output and its variable input. The linear form indicates that neither increasing nor diminishing returns to a factor take place in the short run as the firm uses additional units of its variable input. In this appendix, we use calculus to state the cubic equation, the one most frequently used in economic theory.

Consider the following equation (which, incidentally is the one used to generate the cost data in Table 8.2 and Figure 8.2):

$$TC = 100 + 60Q - 5Q^2 + 0.7Q^3 \tag{8A.2}$$

The total fixed-cost component of this equation is simply the constant term, 100. The balance of the right-hand side gives us total variable cost. The average and marginal costs can be derived from Equation (8A.2) using the definitions provided in the chapter, which are restated in the following equations:

$$\text{Average fixed cost (AFC)} = \frac{\text{TFC}}{Q} = \frac{100}{Q} \tag{8A.3}$$

$$\text{Average total cost (AC)} = \frac{\text{TC}}{Q} = \frac{100}{Q} + 60 - 5Q + 0.7Q^2 \tag{8A.4}$$

$$\text{Average variable cost (AVC)} = \frac{\text{TVC}}{Q} = 60 - 5Q + 0.7Q^2 \tag{8A.5}$$

$$\text{Marginal cost (MC)} = d\text{TC}/dQ = 60 - 10Q + 2.1Q^2 \tag{8A.6}$$

Notice that to find marginal cost, we simply took the first derivative of the total cost function stated in Equation (8A.2).

CHAPTER 9

Linear Programming

The Situation

At the Wednesday morning meeting of the management committee of Global Foods, Inc., the vice president of marketing concluded her presentation with the following statement: "Given our forecast of sales for the next 12 months, I think that our present distribution system is totally inadequate. We need to act *now* to remedy this situation. To be sure, we need eventually to build or buy new bottling plants in key locations throughout the country. But right now, I believe that we should at least set up new warehouses in each distribution region so that we can meet the demands of our customers more effectively."

"Just what do you mean by 'effective,' Sarah?" asked Jim Benson, distribution manager of the beverage division. "Don't you simply mean 'faster'? After all, building new warehouses will cost us money. Can we really justify this added cost?"

At this point Ed Wong, the newly appointed head of the beverage division, entered the discussion. "Well, Jim, why can't we have both? After all, given our present distribution network, additional warehouses in each region might cut down on transportation costs enough to offset the added warehousing cost. You could do a thorough cost analysis of our distribution system and come back with a recommendation for next week's meeting."

When Jim returned to his office that afternoon, he realized that a thorough study of the distribution system was certainly needed. Sales had indeed grown since the company entered the soft drink business last year. He had been so busy getting the system up and running that he had not had time to figure out whether it was the best possible system to use. He called in his staff assistant, Earl Jones, a young man just brought in from the field for an 18-month staff assignment.

"Earl, as you know, in many regions our product is shipped directly to the points of sale from our bottling plants as well as from our warehouses. The marketing peo-

(Continued)

ple want us to build new warehouses in all our regions to get the product to these points of sale more quickly. I have a gut feeling that this is going to end up costing us more than our present way of doing things. The trouble is, I don't know how to prove it. We've been in this business for almost a year now, so our accounting department must have enough data on our distribution costs. I want you to help me analyze the data and come up with a recommendation.

Incidentally, I know you were a management science major in college and that you are familiar with quantitative techniques to find the so-called optimal solution. However, I need the results by next week, and I need to present them in a way everyone can understand. Therefore, we should keep the analysis simple. Perhaps we can focus on the region where we have just one plant, only a few warehouses, and a relatively small number of points of sale. Of course, we'll analyze all the regions, but we'll keep these results in our back pocket just in case people ask for them."

Earl went back to his office. "Jim thinks this is a complex task," he thought. "But this is exactly the kind of problem that linear programming can help to solve. Actually, the most time-consuming part of this project is to work with the accounting people to obtain exactly the right kind of data. It's a good thing that I play tennis with one of the cost accountants. With his help, I'm sure that I'll get the numbers by Friday. In the meantime, I'll find the region most appropriate for this task and set up the structure of the LP problem."

Introduction

The material on production presented in Chapter 7 is firmly rooted in the microeconomic theory of the firm. An understanding of the concepts and principles of production theory (e.g., marginal product, diminishing returns, economies of scale, stages of production, short- and long-run time periods) can help business decision makers structure and analyze production problems more clearly. Moreover, as illustrated in Chapter 8, a thorough understanding of the theoretical production function is a prerequisite for understanding the economic analysis of cost.

Unfortunately, it is rather difficult to apply production theory directly to everyday business problems. A major limitation of the application of production theory is that perfectly continuous substitutions among inputs (as is assumed in the construction of isoquants) is not realistic in today's economy. Historically, the marginal analysis of production was intended for the more simple production processes found in agriculture. Production processes today are much more complex and less flexible than marginal analysis assumes. They also involve the production of services more than the production of goods. Therefore, instead of finding the best combination of inputs among a continuous range of choices, today's production decisions involve the selection of a particular production process accompanied by a relatively inflexible combination of labor, land, and capital. (e.g., specialized labor working with specialized machines).[1]

As a supplement to the more general analysis of production theory in managerial decision making, economists utilize linear programming. This approach to allocating a firm's scarce resources stresses the technical side of the problem. Moreover, instead of assuming a continuous combination of inputs, the linear programming (LP) approach assumes that only a limited number of technical processes are available to the firm. The goal is to select the process that best achieves some objective, subject to certain constraints. The objectives can be—and very often are—the same as those inherent in microeconomic theory, such as the maximization of profit or the minimization of cost. Moreover, the LP approach can be used for a host of other problems involving the allocation of scarce resources. Numerous applications have been developed in other areas of business decision making, such as marketing, accounting, banking, and finance.[2] The transportation problem faced by Jim Benson is perfectly suited for LP analysis.

Our discussion of this topic is intended only as a brief introduction for those unfamiliar with this technique or as a general review for those who have already studied it. Any coverage beyond that contained in this chapter is beyond the scope of this text. Because this is only an overview of the topic, we will consider the case of only two inputs. This will enable you to see analogies to the two-input case used in Chapter 7. Everything said about two inputs will apply to cases with more than two inputs. Moreover, you will be given an opportunity to deal with cases involving more than two inputs in the questions and problems. Finally, students interested in pursuing this topic further are encouraged to take courses in operations research, management science, or advanced economics topics.[3]

One aspect of linear programming that is covered in courses such as those just noted is the simplex method, the principal method for finding the solution to the LP problem. But there is really no need to delve into this aspect of linear programming in this text, because the ready accessibility of software packages enables both students and businesspeople to arrive at solutions to LP problems with ease. For this presentation, we use a popular software package called LINDO.[4] We will focus on a general understanding of the nature of the LP problem and the interpretation of the results obtained via the simplex method. We will also discuss the economic assumptions that lie behind the LP problem. Such assumptions limit the applicability of linear programming to certain business problems.

---

[1]Economists have long recognized the practical limitations of production theory. See, for example, R. G. D. Allen, *Mathematical Economics*, London: Macmillan, 1960, pp. 618–21.

[2]For example, in advertising, the most effective combination of media (e.g., radio, newspapers, television) can be found with the help of linear programming. This technique can also help portfolio managers find the optimal combination of financial instruments to invest in.

[3]For an excellent management science text, see F. J. Gould, G. D. Eppen, and C. P. Schmidt, *Introductory Management Science*, Englewood Cliffs, N.J.: Prentice-Hall, 1987.

[4]LINDO is a registered trademark for the software.

The Basic Elements of Linear Programming

Linear programming is a mathematical technique that enables a decision maker to arrive at the optimal solution to problems involving the allocation of scarce resources. The goal of this approach is to maximize or minimize a particular linear function (called the objective function) subject to a set of conditions (called constraints), which are also expressed in linear terms. In effect, every linear programming problem must have three basic elements: the objective function, the variables, and the constraints. To use linear programming, a decision maker must be able to state the problem in terms of these three elements and obtain the necessary information to provide quantitative values for them. To explain this further, we will use a simple example of a hypothetical firm called A-1 Clone.

A-1 Clone is a manufacturer of IBM-compatible PCs and dot-matrix printers. Essentially, this company's activities consist of buying the components of the PCs and printers, assembling and packaging these components, and distributing the final product to retail distribution outlets.[5] It also ships the product directly to customers via an 800 number and mail-order operation. For purposes of analysis, we will divide A-1's business into two activities: assembly and packaging. The assembly activity is self-explanatory. The packaging activity includes the packaging, storage, order taking, and shipping of the finished product. The two activities are conducted in separate areas of the manufacturing site, which we will label "site 1" and "site 2." Table 9.1 summarizes the time involved in the completion of each of these activities.

To simplify this problem, we assume that A-1 has only two inputs in the production process: assembly labor and packaging labor. Given the amounts of these two types of labor available to the firm and the amounts required to produce a unit of PCs and a unit of printers, the management of the company wants to know what combination of PCs and printers will maximize total profit.

In linear programming, "total profit" is defined as total revenue minus total variable cost. On a unit basis, this would be price (the revenue per unit) minus average variable cost. To avoid confusing this type of profit with net profit, we

Table 9.1 Production Data for the Making of PCs and Printers by A-1 Clone

	Assembly time per unit (hr.) (site 1)	*Packaging time per unit (hr.) (site 2)*	*Number of items to be made*	*Profit per unit*
PCs	5	3	X	$50
Printers	2	2	Y	$30
Labor available for production	220 hours	180 hours		

[5]This example is adapted from a linear programming problem originally presented in William J. Adams, *Finite Mathematics for Business and Social Science*, Lexington: Xerox, 1974, pp. 3–45.

will refer to it as *gross profit* or *profit contribution*. The term GP (for *gross profit*) will be used in equations to represent this variable. Recall from Chapter 8 that economists include only relevant cost in their analysis. Since fixed cost does not change as the level of production changes, it is not relevant to the LP problem. Thus, we subtract only variable (i.e., relevant) cost from revenue to determine the profit earned in the production of PCs and printers.[6]

A preliminary inspection of the data in the table might lead you to conclude that the firm should produce only PCs, because the gross profit per unit for this product ($50) is more than that earned from the sale of printers ($30). But obviously, if it were this simple, there would be no need to set up the linear programming program. The key is the fact that the firm does not have unlimited use of resources to produce its output and it must use its labor resources in a certain fixed proportion.

Suppose the firm decides simply to produce as many PCs as it can until it runs out of resources. With 220 hours of assembly time at its disposal, the firm can produce 44 PCs (220 hr./5 hr.). These 44 PCs would require 132 hours of packaging time (3 hr. × 44 PCs). But since the firm has 180 hours of packaging time available, 48 hours of time would be unused. In any case, 44 PCs multiplied by a gross profit per unit of $50 would earn the firm a total of $2,200.

Could the firm do better by shifting some of its assembly time to the making of printers in order to utilize the packaging labor more fully? If so, this means that the firm's gross profit from shifting some of its resources to the production of printers would exceed the forgone gross profit from the PC sales.[7] In this simple example, it is possible to consider all combinations of quantities of PCs and printers that a firm could produce given the resource constraints and to find the combination that would maximize gross profit. But the use of linear programming offers a much more systematic approach to finding the solution and, of course, enables decision makers to handle far more involved problems.

Let us return to the main line of discussion by viewing the production data in terms of the three basic elements of a linear programming problem. We see that the objective function involves finding the profit-maximizing combination of output. The variables involved are the output of PCs and the output of printers. The constraints are the work times required for the assembly and packaging of the PCs and printers and the number of labor hours available for each activity. This problem can be stated more concisely using the following set of mathematical equations.

Maximize: $$\text{GP} = 50X + 30Y \tag{9.1}$$

subject to: $$5X + 2Y \leq 220 \tag{9.2}$$

$$3X + 2Y \leq 180 \tag{9.3}$$

$$X \geq 0 \tag{9.4}$$

$$Y \geq 0 \tag{9.5}$$

[6]In terms of economic theory, we can see that the linear programming approach provides a short-run solution to the production problem.

[7]Notice the similarity of this kind of analysis with the construction of isoquants and isocost curves.

where GP = Gross profit or profit contribution
X = Number of PCs produced in one day
Y = Number of printers produced in one day

Equation (9.1) is the objective function, and equations (9.2) through (9.5) are the constraints. Equations (9.4) and (9.5) are usually referred to as the nonnegativity constraints. They state that because it is impossible for a firm to produce a negative amount of output, the solution to the problem cannot involve negative values for either X or Y. Equations (9.2) and (9.3) are the constraints imposed by the availability of assembly and packaging labor.

Once the linear problem has been specified in this manner, the use of LINDO or similar software packages enables us to find the optimal combination of PCs and printers. As it turns out, A-1 should produce 20 PCs and 60 printers daily to maximize its profit from these operations. For your reference, the relevant section of LINDO's computer printout of this problem is shown in Figure 9.1.

Slack Variables

Notice that the computer printout in Figure 9.1 also presents separate columns labeled "Slack or Surplus" and "Dual Prices." Dual prices will be explained in a later section. Slack variables are needed to solve the linear programming problem using the simplex method, a topic that, as stated earlier, will not be covered

```
MAX      50 X + 30 Y
SUBJECT TO
        2)   5 X + 2 Y <=   220
        3)   3 X + 2 Y <=   180
        4)   X >=   0
        5)   Y >=   0


    LP OPTIMUM FOUND  AT STEP      2

         OBJECTIVE FUNCTION VALUE

 1)          2800.00000

VARIABLE          VALUE            REDUCED COST
        X       20.000000              .000000
        Y       60.000000              .000000

   ROW       SLACK OR SURPLUS      DUAL PRICES
        2)          .000000           2.500000
        3)          .000000          12.500000
        4)        20.000000            .000000
        5)        60.000000            .000000

NO. ITERATIONS=        2
```

Figure 9.1 Sample of LINDO Computer Printout for A-1 Clone in this text. Nonetheless, it is important for readers to understand what slack variables represent in the computer output and how to interpret their values.

Slack variables can be explained in terms of the constraint equations used in an LP problem. Recall that the constraint equations are expressed as nonnegativities (notice the $\leq$ signs in equations 2 and 3 at the top of Figure 9.1). In linear programming, the insertion of slack variables in nonnegativity constraints changes them into equalities. Letting S_A represent the slack variable for the assembly constraint and S_P the one for the packaging constraint, we can express the constraints in the LP problem as

$$5X + 2Y + S_A = 220$$

$$3X + 2Y + S_P = 180$$

Thus, if the LP solution calls for a less-than-complete use of the available inputs, the slack variable(s) will be equal to some positive amount. In other words, the slack variable is a measure of the optimizing firm's excess capacity. In this particular case, all 220 hours of assembly labor and 180 hours of packaging labor are required by the solution. Thus, both slack variables equal zero. This is indicated in Figure 9.1 in rows 2 and 3 of the "Slack or Surplus" column.

A Graphical Analysis of the Linear Programming Problem

As pointed out earlier, software packages such as LINDO employ the simplex method for finding the solution to LP problems. The computational power of a computer and the sophistication of the simplex method are required when a linear program involves many variables and constraints. However, in the simple case we have chosen for discussion, there are only two variables and two constraints.[8] Thus, this problem can be readily illustrated on a graph and in fact can be solved with the use of this graph.

Figure 9.2 shows the numbers of PCs and printers that A-1 is considering producing. The objective function of the problem, $GP = 50X + 30Y$, can be plotted as a series of lines called *isoprofit* curves.[9] Curves farther from the origin represent higher levels of gross profit. Obviously, the firm would like its isoprofit curve to be as far out and to the right as possible, but it must also consider the constraints. Figure 9.3a, shows a plot of the linear equation $5X + 2Y = 220$, which represents the constraint resulting from the limited amount of labor that the firm is able to use to produce PCs. The shaded area to the left of the line is called the *feasible region* because the firm is free to use any number of

[8]We have chosen two variables and two constraints primarily for simplicity. Actually, more than two constraints can be shown on a two-dimensional graph. Three variables can be handled on a three-dimensional graph, but more than three are difficult to illustrate.

[9]Once again, notice the similarity between linear programming and the isocost/isoquant analysis of production theory.

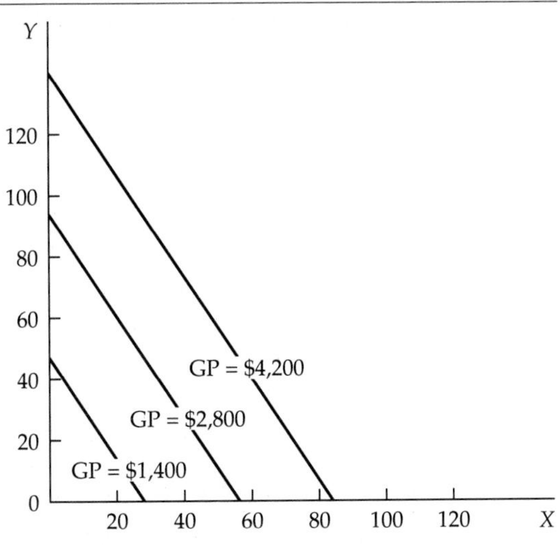

Figure 9.2 Isoprofit curves for A-1 Clone.

hours up to its available amount of assembly labor to produce its two outputs. (The shaded area reflects the use of the ≤ sign in the formal statement of the LP problem.) Clearly, any labor combination on the constraint line indicates that the firm is using up all its available assembly labor to produce PCs and printers. Of course, the firm has an additional constraint due to the limited amount of packaging labor available. This constraint is illustrated graphically in Figure 9.3*b*. The same interpretation used in Figure 9.3*a* applies to this line. Figure 9.3*c* combines the two constraint lines and shows the feasible region that results from considering both resource constraints simultaneously.

The graphical solution to the linear programming problem can be obtained by combining the isoprofit curves shown in Figure 9.2 with the constraints and feasible region shown in Figure 9.3*c*. This is presented in Figure 9.4. As can be seen, the highest profit that can be earned subject to the resource constraints is determined by the point at which the feasible region is tangent to the isoprofit line representing $2,800. In linear programming terms, this is called a *corner solution.*

It is possible for the isoprofit curve, representing the objective function, to coincide with one of the boundaries of the feasible region. This is illustrated in Figure 9.5. If this is the case, then in theory an infinite number of combinations of output could produce a maximum amount of profit.

The Economic Significance of Linearity and Other Assumptions Used in Linear Programming

Once the solution is arrived at, this does not necessarily mean that the company should then go ahead and produce the recommended combination of outputs. There are certain limitations to the ability of linear programming to

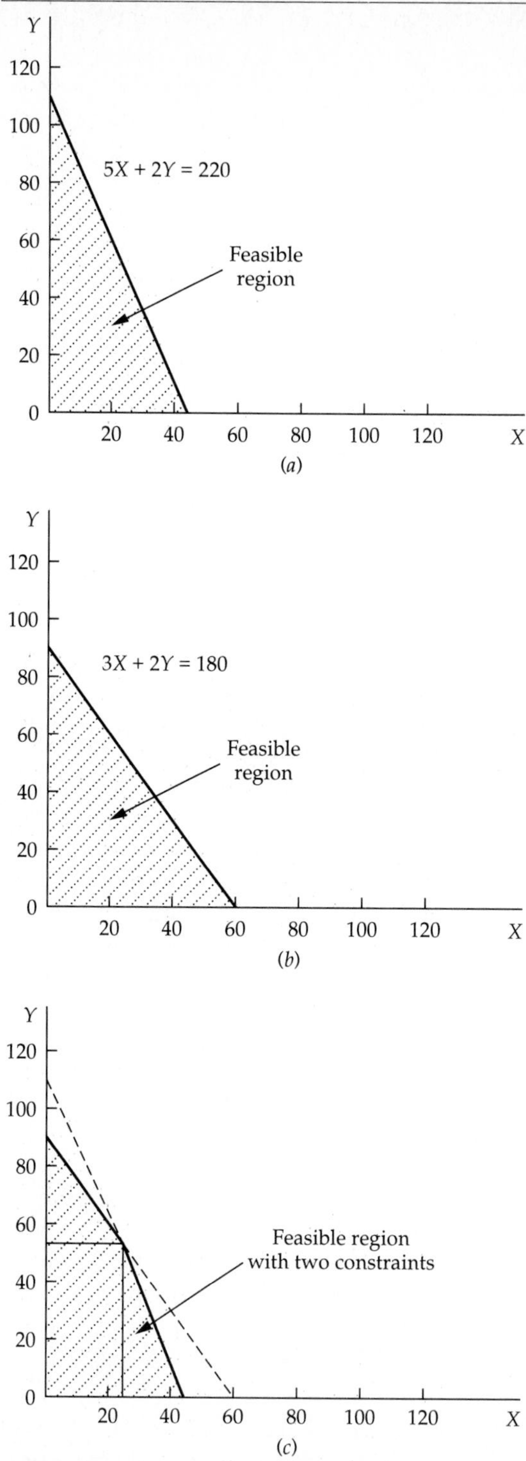

Figure 9.3 Plotting of constraints for A-1 Clone Problem

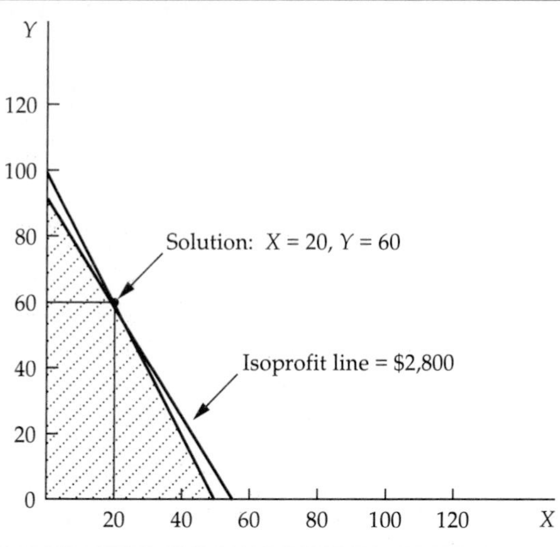

Figure 9.4 Optimal Solution

optimize the use of a firm's scarce resources. To be sure, linear programming offers managers a more practical approach to the resource allocation problem than does the microeconomic theory of the production function. Nonetheless, linear programming entails certain simplifying assumptions, just as economic theory does. Consequently, any manager who wishes to implement the LP solution must recognize that the effectiveness of this action will be only as good as the validity of the assumptions made in the construction of the model.

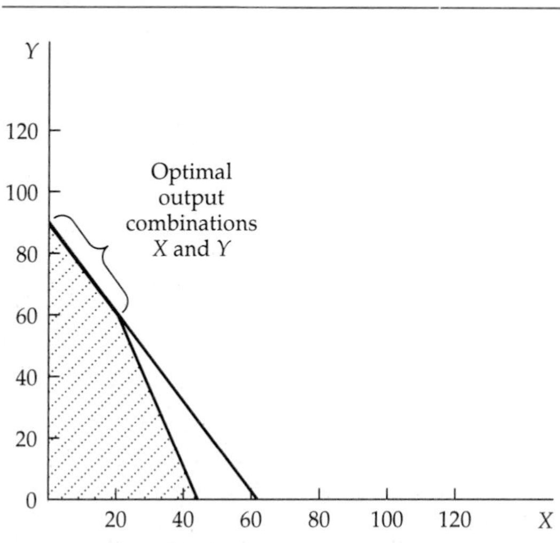

Figure 9.5 Isoprofit curve coinciding with Feasible Region Boundary

Perhaps the most important assumption made in linear programming is that the objective function and the constraints are linear. When the objective function is gross profit and the constraints are available resources, this assumption has considerable implications regarding the economic environment in which the firm is operating and the nature of the production function underlying its cost structure.

In the profit-maximizing production problem, a linear objective function means that a constant rate of gross profit per unit is earned as output increases. A linear resource constraint implies that a constant combination of inputs must be used in the production process. A-1's objective function, for example, states that it will earn a constant rate of gross profit from the sale of its two products: $50 profit for each PC sold and $30 profit for each printer sold. Recall that we defined unit profit as price minus average variable cost (P – AVC). In order for gross profit per unit to remain constant as additional units of output are produced and sold, selling price and average variable cost must also be constant. If these two factors vary as output increases, then so will the per-unit gross profit. For example, if A-1 had to reduce its price to sell more PCs, its additional gross profit per unit would also decrease. A constant price, however, means that A-1 can sell as many as it wants at some given market price. In other words, a constant rate of gross profit per unit means that A-1 is assumed to act as a price taker in the market for PCs (and printers).

A constant gross profit per unit implies a constant average variable cost. Constant average variable cost means that the law of diminishing returns does not influence the firm's production process. Otherwise, increasing the level of production would cause the firm's marginal cost to increase. And, as explained in Chapter 8, this would eventually cause the firm's average variable cost to increase. A constant average variable cost also means that a firm is able to acquire additional units of its resources at constant prices. If it had to pay more for additional units, the average variable cost would increase as output increased. The main implications of the linearity assumption are summarized in Figure 9.6.

The economic significance of linearity in the constraints is related to the long-run nature of a firm's production function. More specifically, the linear resource constraint equation assumes that the firm experiences constant returns to scale. Looking at A-1's constraints, we see that it uses 5 hours of assembly and 3 hours of packaging for each PC produced. It also uses 2 hours of assembly and 2 hours of packaging to produce the printers. The LP solution tells us that the optimal utilization of the 220 hours of assembly and 180 hours of packaging results in the production of 20 PCs and 60 printers. If, for example, A-1 had twice as much labor available as it currently has (i.e., 440 hours of assembly and 360 hours of packaging), it stands to reason that the LP solution would indicate a production level of twice as many units of output (i.e., 40 PCs and 120 printers). This is because the linearity of the constraint equations means that the labor resources are used in a fixed proportion to produce the output. From Chapter 7, you should recognize this doubling of output resulting from a doubling of inputs as an indication of constant returns to scale in the long-run production function.

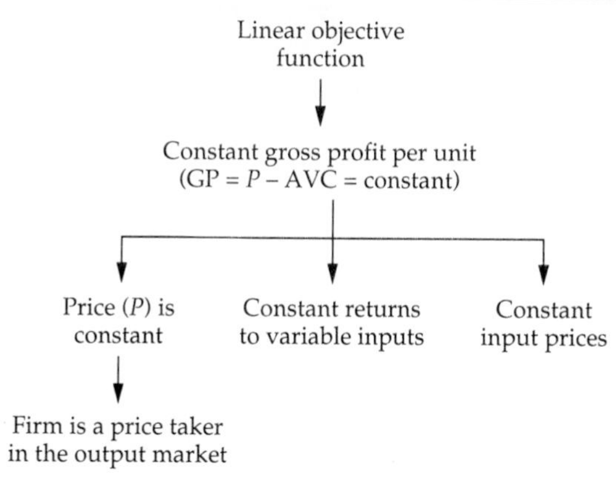

Figure 9.6 Summary of the Economic Interpretation of the Linearity Assumption in Linear Programming (Profit-Maximizing Objective Function)

A Closer Look at the Inputs in the Profit-Maximizing Problem: An Introduction to the Dual in Linear Programming

In linear programming, the solution for the profit-maximizing combination of outputs automatically determines the input amounts that must be used in the production process. We can see this by returning to the original data for the problem. Table 9.1 indicates that it takes 5 hours of assembly and 3 hours of packaging to produce one PC, and that it takes 2 hours of assembly and 2 hours of packaging to produce one printer. Based on these fixed technical requirements, we can say that the production of 20 PCs and 60 printers will require a total of 220 hours of assembly time (100 hours of assembly for the PCs and 120 hours of assembly for the printers) and a total of 180 hours of packaging time (60 hours for the PCs and 120 for the printers). Equations (9.4) and (9.5) indicate the maximum amount of labor hours the firm has available for the assembly and packaging: 220 hours and 180 hours, respectively. Thus, adhering to the output combination called for in the LP solution requires that the firm use up all the labor hours available for assembly and for packaging.

In linear programming terminology, the utilization of all available inputs indicates that the constraints are *binding*. Under these conditions, any reduction in the use of the inputs will reduce the firm's profits. By the same token, any increase in the availability of the labor inputs will increase the firm's profits. The amount by which profit is reduced or increased for a unit change in a particular input can be considered the firm's *marginal opportunity cost* of using that input. It is a "marginal" cost because we are considering a unit change relative to an already established level of total input usage. It is an "opportunity cost" because some amount of profit would be forgone by reducing the input by one unit. Another way to say this is that by *not* increasing the input by one unit, the firm forgoes a certain amount of profit.[10] The important point is that this way of determining the cost of using a firm's input is completely distinct from the acquisition cost of an input. The latter type involves the firm's out-of-pocket cost for additional units of inputs (e.g., the hourly wage rate). Indeed, if a firm determines that the opportunity cost of an input is greater than its acquisition cost, then it will try to exceed the input constraints and expand production capacity. But before we can make this comparison, we must first determine what these opportunity costs are for the firm.

Fortunately, every linear programming problem has an associated problem whose solution provides us with the values of the opportunity costs of input usage. The original problem is called the *primal problem*, and the associated problem is called the *dual problem*. If the objective function of the primal problem is profit maximization subject to resource constraints, then the objective function of its dual is cost minimization subject to certain profit requirements. For A-1 Clone, the dual problem takes the following form:

Minimize: $$C = 220a + 180p \tag{9.6}$$

subject to: $$5a + 3p \geq 50 \tag{9.7}$$

$$2a + 2p \geq 30 \tag{9.8}$$

$$a \geq 0 \tag{9.9}$$

$$p \geq 0 \tag{9.10}$$

where C = Total opportunity cost of using inputs in the production of PCs and printers

a = Opportunity cost of using an additional unit of labor for the assembly of PCs and printers

p = Opportunity cost of using an additional unit of labor for the packaging of PCs and printers.

You can see from the preceding set of equations that the numbers are very similar to those in the primal problem. In fact, looking back at Table 9.1, you can see that the values of the dual problem are found by going across each row, and the values of the primal are found by going down each column.

To understand the dual in linear programming and its economic significance to decision makers, suppose that A-1 Clone also owns and operates another factory that produces typewriters and small copying machines. The tasks involved are the same as in the PC and printer plant: assembly and packaging. Because of changing market conditions, A-1's management decides to concentrate all efforts in the manufacturing of typewriters and copiers. It wants to shift the labor in the PC and printer plant to the typewriter and copier plant. Because

[10] Recall that opportunity cost is defined as the amount forgone or sacrificed in choosing one activity over the next best alternative. Opportunity cost is opportunity lost. In dealing with opportunity cost at the margin, it generally does not matter whether the alternatives involve a reduction or an increase in the input, because the change is very small (i.e., one unit).

this represents an internal transfer of human resources, it might be assumed that the use of this additional labor in the typewriter and copier plant does not entail an additional cost to the firm. But, of course, from an economic standpoint (as opposed to an accounting standpoint), there is indeed an additional cost to the firm in the form of the forgone profits from the PC/printer operation. In other words, the transfer of resources from the PC/printer operation to the typewriter/copier plant involves an opportunity cost. If the objective function of the primal LP problem is the maximization of profit, then the dual of this primal is the minimization of the opportunity cost.

Thus, the total opportunity cost of using the labor resources in the typewriter/copier plant instead of in the PC/printer plant is:

$$C = 220a + 180p$$

The terms a and p represent the cost per hour of using the assembly and packaging labor, respectively. You may consider this equation to be somewhat trivial. After all, is not the total cost of the resources simply the hourly wage rate times the number of hours? However, remember that C refers to the total opportunity cost and not the total accounting or out-of-pocket cost to the firm. Thus, a and p refer to the *opportunity cost* of using an hour of labor for assembly and for packaging, respectively. Other terms that are used for these variables are *imputed cost* and *shadow price*. The objective of the dual problem is to find the values of a and p that minimize the total opportunity cost of using the labor resources in the typewriter/copier plant instead of the PC/printer plant. In so doing, we will have found the minimum shadow prices for each type of labor resource.

Recall that it takes 5 hours of assembly and 3 hours of packaging to produce one PC, and the sale of one PC results in a $50 profit contribution. It takes 2 hours of assembly and 2 hours of packaging to produce one printer and the sale of one printer results in a $30 profit contribution. Equation (9.7) states that the imputed cost of using these 5 hours of assembly labor and 3 hours of packaging labor must be *at least* as great as the profit they helped to earn for producing PCs. The same applies to equation (9.8) and the shifting of resources away from the making of printers.

Using the simplex method to solve for the primal of the LP problem automatically provides the solution to the dual problem. Turning to the LINDO printout in Figure 9.1, we see that the optimal values of a and p are found in rows 2 and 3 in the column labeled "Dual Prices." They are $2.50 and $12.50, respectively. In the following equation, note that the insertion of these values into the objective function gives us a total minimum opportunity cost of $2,800, the same as the maximum total profit found for the primal problem!

$$220(\$2.50) + 180(\$12.50) = \$2,800$$

It can be proved mathematically that as long as the primal has a solution, the objective function of the primal and its dual always have the same optimal values.[11] However, let us try to explain this in a simpler fashion. As-

[11]The proof is called the "Duality Theorem," developed by the famous mathematician John Von Neumann.

sume that the firm is using its scarce resources in some activity (e.g., the making of PCs and printers) in a way that maximizes its profit. In shifting its resources from this original activity to another (e.g., the making of typewriters and copiers), the firm must be prepared to give up the most that it could earn in profits (e.g., \$2,800) by keeping the resources where they are. It could not reduce this "opportunity cost" below this amount, for this would imply that the firm is not maximizing its profits in the original activity. Furthermore, it does not have to give up any more than this amount (e.g., \$2,800), because this is the maximum profit that the resources can earn in the original activity.

The imputed costs of each type of labor resource used in the production process, a and p, are also based on the concept of opportunity cost—more particularly, on the concept of *marginal* opportunity cost. Recall that marginal analysis involves the consideration of small changes around some given point. Suppose the firm decreased by one unit the amount of assembly labor available to the production process (i.e., it decided to use 219 hours of assembly labor). Since the solution to the dual problem tells us that the minimum imputed value for this type of labor is \$2.50, this means that the firm would have to forgo a profit contribution of \$2.50. In other words, at the margin, a unit decrease in assembly labor involves a \$2.50 opportunity cost. In a similar fashion, if the firm increased its assembly labor by one unit, it would be gaining \$2.50. In terms of opportunity cost, this means that if the firm *does not* increase the amount of assembly labor by one unit (i.e., it just maintains the optimal level of 220 hours), it is giving up the opportunity to earn an additional \$2.50.

At this point in the discussion, you may be a bit puzzled by the consideration of opportunity cost with respect to increases in the amount of the firm's resources, because the linear programming solution calls for the use of all available assembly and packaging hours. In other words, why would a firm consider the use of the 221st unit of assembly labor when it only has 220 hours available? The obvious answer is that the increases can be achieved by relaxing the constraints of the primal problem. But given this allowance for additional resource capacity, a further question is whether it would be worthwhile for the firm to proceed with this increase. In answering this question, the real importance of the dual in linear programming to decision makers can be understood.

The restatement of the primal problem in its dual form enables decision makers to quantify the true economic value of each unit of resource used. By comparing this value to what an additional unit of resource would actually cost the firm, a decision maker can determine whether it is worthwhile to expand the firm's resource constraints. For example, if assembly labor is paid \$2.00 an hour, it would be economically justifiable to hire an additional unit of this type of labor, because its profit contribution to the firm, \$2.50, exceeds the out-of-pocket cost. However, if the hourly wage rate exceeds \$2.50, then it would not be desirable because the additional unit would cost more than its imputed value to the firm.

As it turns out, the solution to A-1 Clone's resource allocation problem called for the use of all of its available resources of assembly labor and packaging labor. In linear programming terminology, we would say that both of its constraints are binding. However, if a primal solution indicates that a resource should not be entirely utilized in the production process, then the imputed cost of the resource is zero.

A Useful Application of Linear Programming: The Transportation Problem

A key way in which linear programming can be used by a firm is to help find the least costly way of distributing its product to customers. As an example, let us consider the problem of transporting soft drinks from a bottling plant to points of sale (e.g., supermarkets, restaurants, convenience stores). Suppose a company (such as Global Foods) has one bottling plant, one warehouse, and five points of sale. The location of each site is shown in Figure 9.7. In transportation analysis, each of the sites is usually referred to as a *node,* and they are labeled in some numerical order. As the arrows indicate, shipments from the plant (node 1) to the points of sale (nodes 3 to 7) can be made directly, as well as indirectly via the warehouse (node 2). Suppose further that each point of sale has a fixed amount of demand. Given this information, we see that the challenge for this firm is to devise a shipment plan that satisfies the demand by the five points of sale in the least costly way. In linear programming terminology, the objective function is the minimization of (transportation) cost, subject to the demand constraints of each of the points of sale.

The cost that the firm seeks to minimize is the cost that is relevant to the decision.[12] By this we mean only the cost that is actually affected by the shipment of goods from one point to another. For example, during the time period being considered (e.g., one month), whether one thousand cases or no cases of soft drinks are shipped from the plant to the warehouse or a selling point, the firm would still incur certain fixed costs, such as rent, utility and insurance payments, and certain labor compensation. These costs would be irrelevant to the decision and are therefore not included in the objective function. Examples or relevant costs are wages for drivers and fuel and maintenance costs for their vehicles. These variable costs are the ones included in the objective function.[13]

With these preliminary remarks about the nature of the transportation problem, let us proceed to a formal statement of the linear programming problem. Assume that the bottling plant has a production capacity of 150,000 cases of product per month and that the monthly demand for the product by each point of sale (nodes 3 to 7) is 20,000, 30,000, 10,000, 40,000, and 20,000, respectively. Given this information, the linear programming problem is as follows:

---

[12]The concept of "relevant cost" is discussed in detail in the prior chapter.

[13]Readers should note that the rationale for including only variable costs in the objective function of the cost minimization problem is similar to the reason that total "gross profit" or profit contribution rather than total "net profit" is included in the objective function of the profit maximization problem.

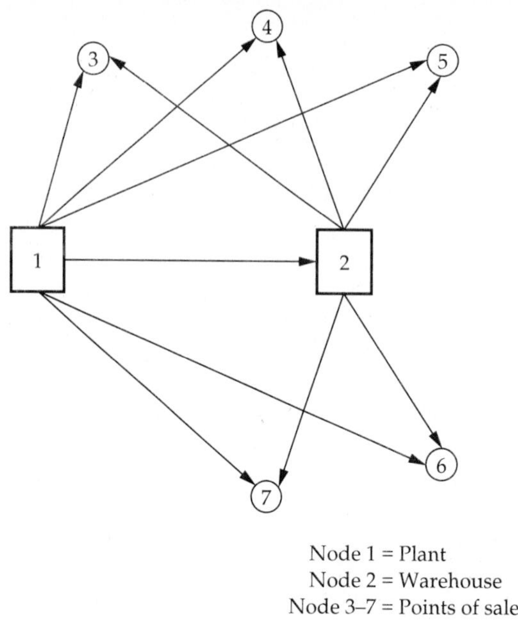

Figure 9.7 Location of plant, warehouse and points of sale, Global Foods beverage division region III.

$$\text{Minimize:} \quad TC = \Sigma C_{ij} X_{ij}$$
$$= C_{12}X_{12} + C_{13}X_{13} + C_{14}X_{14} + \cdots + C_{17}X_{17} + C_{23}X_{23} + C_{24}X_{24} + \cdots + C_{27}X_{27}$$

subject to: $X_{12} < 60$ (Up to 60,000 cases/mo. can be shipped from plant to warehouse.)

$-X_{12} + X_{23} + X_{24} + \cdots + X_{27} = 0$ (Total inflow from plant to warehouse must be equal to total outflow from warehouse to selling points.)

$$X_{13} + X_{23} > 20$$
$$X_{14} + X_{24} > 30$$
$$X_{15} + X_{25} > 10$$
$$X_{16} + X_{26} > 40$$
$$X_{17} + X_{27} > 20$$

(Total shipments from plant and warehouse must at least meet the monthly demand by each selling point.)

Note in this statement that C_{ij} represents the unit cost of transportation from node i to node j, and X_{ij} represents the total number of units of the product shipped from node i to node j. Thus, the total cost of shipping X units from note i to node j is $C_{ij}X_{ij}$, and the total shipping cost for the entire distribution network is $\Sigma C_{ij}X_{ij}$. For your convenience, an elaboration of the meaning of the constraints is included in the parenthetical statements to the right of the statement of the LP problem.

The data on the cost of transporting the product are shown in Table 9.2. The values in this table are inserted into the objective function, and LINDO is then

Table 9.2 Unit Costs of Transportation between Nodes

From Plant to Warehouse and Selling Points	*From Warehouse to Selling Points*
C_{12} = $ 400	C_{23} = $400
C_{13} = $ 300	C_{24} = $300
C_{14} = $ 800	C_{25} = $200
C_{15} = $ 900	C_{26} = $300
C_{16} = $1,000	C_{27} = $300
C_{17} = $ 400	

used to solve the primal of the cost minimization problem. LINDO provides us with the following solution:

$$\text{Minimum cost} = \$71,000$$

$$\begin{array}{lll} X_{12} = 60 & X_{16} = 0 & X_{25} = 10 \\ X_{13} = 20 & X_{17} = 20 & X_{26} = 40 \\ X_{14} = 20 & X_{23} = 0 & X_{27} = 0 \\ X_{15} = 0 & X_{24} = 10 & \end{array}$$

The results indicate that the firm can minimize its monthly shipping cost (i.e., pay $71,000/month) by adhering to this pattern of transportation. The value of each of the X variables represents the amount of product that is shipped from one node to another in thousands of cases. For example, the value $X_{13} = 20$ indicates that the optimal solution calls for a shipment of 20,000 cases of product from the plant (represented by the subscript 1) to selling point 3. The value $X_{24} = 10$ tells us that the firm should ship 10,000 cases of product from the warehouse (represented by the subscript 2) to selling point 4. Based on all of the assumptions and information used to set up the linear programming problem, we must conclude that there is no more efficient way for the firm to distribute its product.

The Solution[14]

Earl identified a region in which one bottling plant was serving five selling points directly as well as via one warehouse, at a total variable cost of $85,000 per month. He obtained data on the production capacity of the plant, the storage capacity

(Continued)

of the warehouse, the demand for product by each selling point, and the variable costs of transporting product between nodes in the distribution network. He established the linear programming problem as one of minimizing the total variable cost of transportation, subject to the constraints of bottling and storage capacity and demand.

The most difficult part of Earl's task was securing the required data. Once he did, it was simply a matter of using an available software package to find the solution. In fact, he found that by using the distribution network suggested by the linear programming solution, the company would be able to meet its current demand at a variable cost of $71,000 per month, thus saving about $168,000 per year!

After conducting this analysis, Earl decided to demonstrate some initiative by checking with the company's real estate department to see if there was any unused warehouse space from the firm's food operations that could be used for the soft drink's distribution system. As luck would have it, there was a company-owned warehouse located between nodes 3, 4, and 5 that was completely empty. According to the real estate people, this warehouse could probably hold about 60,000 cases, the same as the one currently in use. By restating the cost minimization problem to include the additional warehouse (designated in the linear programming problem as node 8), Earl arrived at the following solution:

$$\text{Minimum total (variable) cost} = \$70,000$$

$$\begin{aligned} &X_{12} = 60 && X_{26} = 40 \\ &X_{13} = 20 && X_{18} = 10 \\ &X_{14} = 10 && X_{85} = 10 \\ &X_{17} = 10 && X_{15}, X_{16}, X_{16}, X_{23}, X_{25}, X_{27}, X_{83}, \\ &X_{24} = 20 && X_{84}, X_{86}, X_{87} = 0 \end{aligned}$$

Thus, Earl found that an additional $1,000 per month could be saved by adding another warehouse to the distribution network. Moreover, as can be seen in the figures given, the optimal solution still allowed for considerable excess capacity for the second warehouse. That is, X_{18} indicates that 10,000 cases should be shipped from the plant to the second warehouse, and X_{85} indicates that these 10,000 cases should in turn be shipped to the point of sale designated as node 5. This excess capacity of 50,000 (shown as a slack variable in his computer printout) could then be used when the demand by the points of sale increased, as predicted by the marketing people. Earl was indeed excited about his findings and looked forward to sharing them with his manager.

[14]For convenience, we are using the transportation problem presented in the previous section as the basis for our solution to the situation.

Summary

The economic theory of production deals with the optimal use of a firm's scarce resources. Unfortunately, the theory is limited in its application because of the assumptions concerning the continuous nature of the theoretical production function. Linear programming is a mathematical technique that helps decision makers apply the concepts introduced in economic theory. Although linear programming is also subject to certain assumptions that may limit its applicability to actual business problems, it is one of the most practical techniques available for managers to help deal with resource allocation problems.

Because of the availability of computer power and software, it is rather simple to solve most linear programming problems in business. The real challenge for a manager is to understand the nature of the problem and to decide whether the linear programming approach will be helpful in arriving at a solution. The manager must then obtain the data necessary to state the problem in terms of a formal linear programming structure (i.e., objective function, variables, and constraints). Once this is accomplished, the manager should be able to interpret the solutions to both the primal and the dual problems. Finally, once the solution is obtained and understood, it must be implemented.

Important Concepts

Constraints: The limits within which one seeks to find the optimal solution to a linear programming problem. (Constraints presume the existence of scarce resources, exemplifying the basic economic problem of allocating resources under conditions of scarcity.)

Duality problem: The opposite of the primal linear programming problem (e.g., cost minimization is the dual of the profit maximization problem).

Duality theorem: A mathematical theorem stating that as long as the primal of a linear programming problem has a solution, its dual will have the same optimal values.

Feasible region: The area that covers all possible solutions for a linear programming problem, given the problem's constraints.

Linear programming: A mathematical technique enabling one to arrive at the optimal solution to problems involving the allocation of scarce resources.

Nonnegativity constraint: A requirement in the linear programming problem that the optimal solution cannot contain a variable that has a negative value. (The nonnegativity constraint is used in economic analysis because it would be nonsensical to include negative values for the output and the inputs in the production process.)

Objective function: The function to be optimized in linear programming analysis.

Optimal solution: The best solution for the objective function, given the constraints with which the firm must contend. The optimal solution can either be a maximum (e.g., in the case of profit-maximizing problems) or a minimum (e.g., in the case of cost-minimizing problems).

Primal problem: The statement of the original function to be optimized given the constraints of the linear programming problem.

Shadow price: The marginal value "imputed" to the use of an additional input in the production process. It is not the market price of the input, but rather the opportunity cost inherent in using the input in the activity under consideration instead of in an alternative activity (also referred to as the *imputed cost*).

Simplex method: A mathematical technique used to solve the linear programming problem. Software packages such as LINDO rely on this method of finding the optimal values for the objective function.

Slack variable: An input used in the production process which the optimal linear programming solution does not require to be fully utilized. A positive slack variable in the solution indicates excess capacity; a zero slack variable indicates a fully utilized resource.

Questions

1. Discuss how linear programming might be used to help solve the following problems. In each case, suggest a linear programming model (i.e., the LP equation and the constraints).
   a. The allocation a company's advertising budget to various media (e.g., radio, TV, magazines, and newspapers).
   b. The allocation of cash into various financial investments (e.g., stocks, bonds, U.S. Treasury bills).
   c. The combination of steel, aluminum, and plastic in the making of an automobile.
   d. The assignment of sales personnel among the various branch offices across the nation.
2. Discuss the importance of the following assumptions in the construction of the linear programming model.
   a. The firm's long-run production function exhibits constant returns to scale.
   b. The firm operates as a price taker in the market for its product.
   c. The firm operates as a price taker in the market for its inputs.
3. Explain the meaning of *feasible region*. What prevents a firm from operating outside of this region?
4. Define the *inputed cost* or *shadow price* of an input. Explain how the concept of opportunity cost helps to define this term. How is the shadow price related to the actual market price that a firm pays for the input?
5. (For those with current or previous work experience.) Discuss some ways in which linear programming might be used to help solve certain problems in your particular business.
6. Define *slack variable*. Explain why the shadow price of an input is zero when its slack variable is positive.
7. Discuss the relationship between the linear programming model in this chapter and the microeconomic theory of the production function discussed in Chapter 7. In particular, compare and contrast the isoquant-isocost diagram used in Chapter 7 with the diagram shown in Figure 9.4.
8. Explain the relationship between the primal problem and the dual problem in linear programming.

Problems

1. The following equations define a linear programming problem.

$$\begin{aligned} \text{Maximize:} \quad & 3X + 9Y \\ \text{subject to:} \quad & 15X + 10Y \leq 150 \\ & 11X + 14Y \leq 154 \\ & 2Y \geq 6 \\ & X, Y \geq 0 \end{aligned}$$

   a. Use the graphical method to determine the optimal solution.
   b. (Optional) Check your answer with the use of a software package.

2. Maximize: $4X + 6Y$

$$\begin{aligned} \text{subject to:} \quad & X + 2Y \leq 16 \\ & 3X + Y \leq 21 \\ & X \leq 6 \\ & X, Y \geq 0 \end{aligned}$$

   a. Use the graphical method to determine the optimal solution.
   b. (Optional) Check your answer with the use of a software package.

   Note: Use a linear programming software package (e.g., LINDO) to solve the remaining problems.

3. Maximize: $10X + 8Y$

$$\begin{aligned} \text{subject to:} \quad & 2X + 4Y \leq 48 \\ & 6X + 3Y \leq 60 \\ & 2X \geq 8 \\ & 5X - 3Y \leq 45 \\ & X, Y \geq 0 \end{aligned}$$

   Find the optimal solution and the optimal value of the objective function.

4. A particular brand of cat food is produced in two varieties, based on the mix of two types of soybeans used in their production. The data for the two varieties are shown in the following table. It is decided that each can should contain at least 6 ounces of protein and 2 ounces of fat. What is the minimum-cost combination of output that should be used? In other words, how many units of product 1 and product 2 should be produced?

Variety	*Cost/oz. ($)*	*Protein (%)*	*Fat (%)*
1	0.06	45	20
2	0.03	20	25

5. The Franklin toy company produces two popular toys, helicopters and jet planes. Demand is expected to be at least 500 helicopters and 600 planes per month. Their production capacity is 1,500 helicopters and 1,600 planes per month. The requirements for labor and materials are:

	Labor (hr.)	*Materials (oz.)*
Helicopters	1	5
Planes	1	6

There are a total of 2,200 labor hours and 7,000 oz. of materials available each month. Each helicopter contributes \$0.75 to total profit, and each plane contributes \$0.80.

a. Formulate a profit-maximizing linear program for the company.
b. Solve the problem.
c. Interpret the dual prices provided in the computer output.

6. Suppose three different fuel types have the weights, energy contents, and costs given by the following table

	1	*2*	*3*
Weight per unit volume	20	15	25
Energy per unit volume	35	30	50
Cost per unit volume	1	0.8	1.5

These fuel types can be mixed in any proportion, and the weight and energy content of the mixture are the sum of the weights and energy contents of the component fuel types. Assume that the firm wants to obtain, at minimum possible cost, a mixture of 20 units of volume whose total weight is no more than 180 units and whose total energy is at least 350 units.

a. Formulate this problem as a linear programming problem.
b. What volume of fuels would minimize cost?
c. If the energy content is increased to 351, what would happen to cost?

7. A small company produces three products A, B, and C. Each product has to go through two production stages, machining and assembling. Total sales of the products are limited to 50 units due to the limited sales force available to market these items. Also, management has decided to produce at least 10 units each of products A and B. The profit margins of A, B, and C are \$1, \$2, and \$3, respectively. The per-unit usage (in hours) of the fixed resources, namely, time in the machine shop and assembly area, along with the total amount of time available, are as follows:

	A	*B*	*C*	*Maximum Hours Available*
Per-unit usage of machine shop (hr.)	6	3	4	180
Per-unit usage of assembly shop (hr.)	5	2	3	150

a. Formulate this as a linear programming problem and determine the maximum profit.

b. What quantities of products would maximize profit?
c. What resources, if any, are not fully utilized?

8. The chief financial officer of an investment company has to determine the optimal investment policy for her company. She has available funds of $5 million for year 1 and $4 million for year 2. Each project can be undertaken as a fraction up to 100 percent. Her investment possibilities include the following (with amounts in thousands of dollars).

	Investment		
Project	*Year 1*	*Year 2*	*Return at End of Year 2*
Shopping center	800	800	2,000
Motel	100	70	310
Office buildings	2,200	2,000	5,300
Condominium	1,500	1,200	3,800

Funds not invested can be put into a money market account paying 11 percent. She wants to maximize funds at the end of year 2. Formulate and solve a linear programming model for this problem.

9. Jack and Jane have opened a cookie store in New York City. They make three types of cookies. The selling price and variable cost for each type of cookie are listed below. Fixed costs are $11,000 per month. At least 60 percent of the cookies are to be French cookies. Also, they received an order from a restaurant chain for at least 400 chocolate chip cookies for the month. Formulate a cost-minimizing linear programming model and compute the amounts of each type of cookie needed for them to break even.

Cookie	*Variable Cost ($)*	*Selling Price ($)*
Chocolate chip	0.40	1.17
Lemon	0.34	1.04
French	1.04	2.50

CHAPTER 10

The Estimation of Production and Cost Functions

The Situation

The director of manufacturing of Global Foods' soft drink division, Donald Aiken, was speaking with Jillian Corey, a new hiree from one of the major business schools in the country. "We generate a large amount of data on our production costs each month. We know how much we produce in our plants; we break down our unit costs into labor, materials, and overhead; and we also keep track of our production of canned versus bottled beverages. Then we make monthly and annual comparisons for each of our bottling plants, and we try to analyze the reasons for the change in unit costs from one period to the next. We attempt to rank our plant managers on the basis of the improvement in costs they have shown over time, and also on the basis of absolute unit costs they achieve."

"But I know that things are not quite as simple as we think they are. I still remember the introductory economics course I took when I was a college sophomore. I recall that the professor talked about an optimal level of production—number of units produced per period—at which units costs were minimized. He said that, according to economic theory, as a plant increases its periodic production, its unit costs will be relatively high at low quantities, then they will decrease to some minimum, and then they will start rising again. This increase in unit costs does not necessarily occur only when a plant reaches its capacity. The professor referred to this as a *U-shaped average cost curve.*"

"Our bottling plants vary in size from relatively small ones to very large ones. I would like to find out if, in our company, there is such a thing as an optimal-size plant. If we could determine the plant size that would show lowest unit costs,

(Continued)

we could accomplish at least two things. First, we could rate our managers against a benchmark, which would be a much fairer system. But even more important, in our long-range planning, we could design our plants to conform to this optimal size. We could make decisions on locating these plants in areas where sales could approximately match the most efficient rate of production. Over time, the accrued benefits could make us much more competitive vis-á-vis our big rivals. Jillian, take these reports and whatever other data you can find in the files, and try your hand at investigating the production costs of our plants."

Introduction

In Chapter 5, following our examination of the theory of demand and demand elasticity, we discussed the estimation of demand curves. Now, having analyzed the theory of production and cost functions, we will look for tools that will enable us to estimate them as well.

We will encounter difficulties similar to those noted previously. In economics, it is usually not possible to perform controlled laboratory experiments as is done in the physical and biological sciences. Instead, it is usually necessary to collect actual operating data and with the use of statistical procedures arrive at inferences regarding the behavior of production and costs.

The collection of data for use in the estimation of production and cost functions can be even more difficult than it is in the case of demand. For production functions, it may be relatively easy to calculate the use of labor in production (i.e., number of workers or labor hours). But the task of calculating the usage of capital (i.e., machinery and plants) is often formidable. And the problems continue in the estimation of costs. Most cost data are obtained from accounting records, and thus they do not necessarily conform to costs as defined by the economist. And how about the assumption that technology is constant for a given production or cost function? Obviously, these are some serious hurdles to overcome in arriving at plausible estimates of output and cost. The various methods used by economists to cope with these obstacles will be discussed in this chapter.

The chapter begins with a discussion of production function estimates. The most common method used by economists in this area is the Cobb-Douglas function, named for the two men who developed it in the late 1920s.[1] In the second half of the chapter, we will turn to the empirical estimation of short- and long-run cost functions.

[1]One of the developers of this function, Professor Paul H. Douglas of the University of Chicago, later served for several terms as a senator from the state of Illinois.

Production Functions: A Review of Theory

In Chapter 7 we discussed both short-run and long-run production functions. Recall that in economic analysis, the short run is characterized by the existence of one or more fixed factors (inputs). In the simple model used to illustrate the short-run production function, only two productive factors were employed, one fixed and one variable. The fixed factor was (as is usual) represented by capital, and the variable input was labor. To obtain a short-run production function, all that is necessary is to relate the changes in the variable factor to changes in total quantity produced, as shown in the following equation:[2]

$$Q = f(V)_K$$

where quantity of output, Q, is determined by the quantity of the variable factor, V, with the fixed factor, K, given.

In the long run, all factors can change, and if they change in the same proportion, the function conforms to the law of returns to scale. In the long run, with a two-variable model, our equation becomes

$$Q = f(V, K)$$

Let us first look at the short-run production function, of the form $Q = f(V)_K$. The shape of this function can be linear or nonlinear. If it is linear, the specific form of the equation is

$$Q = a + bV$$

This is very simple, but it tells us nothing about the important economic concept of the law of diminishing returns. If quantity is a linear function of the variable factor, marginal product will be constant.[3] The total product curve will be a straight line with slope b. Of course, a straight-line production function may actually hold in some real situations, but given the existence of a fixed factor, constant marginal product should not be expected to prevail over wide changes in quantities produced. Therefore, the next step is to investigate a quadratic production function. The form of such an equation is

$$Q = a + bV - cV^2$$

and the total product line will show a bend as in Figure 10.1*a*.

---

[2]In Chapter 7, the letters x and y were utilized to designate inputs. This stressed the generality of the production function. In this chapter, in a two-factor analysis, we will use the letter v for the variable factor, and we will use k for the factor that is fixed in the short run but is variable in the long run.

[3]Marginal product, as previously explained, is the first derivative of quantity. If $Q = a + bV$, then $dQ/dV = b$. The average product under these circumstances is $AP = a/Q + b$, which indicates that average product should decline as quantity increases. In reality, the intercept is often omitted, and average product and marginal product are equal.

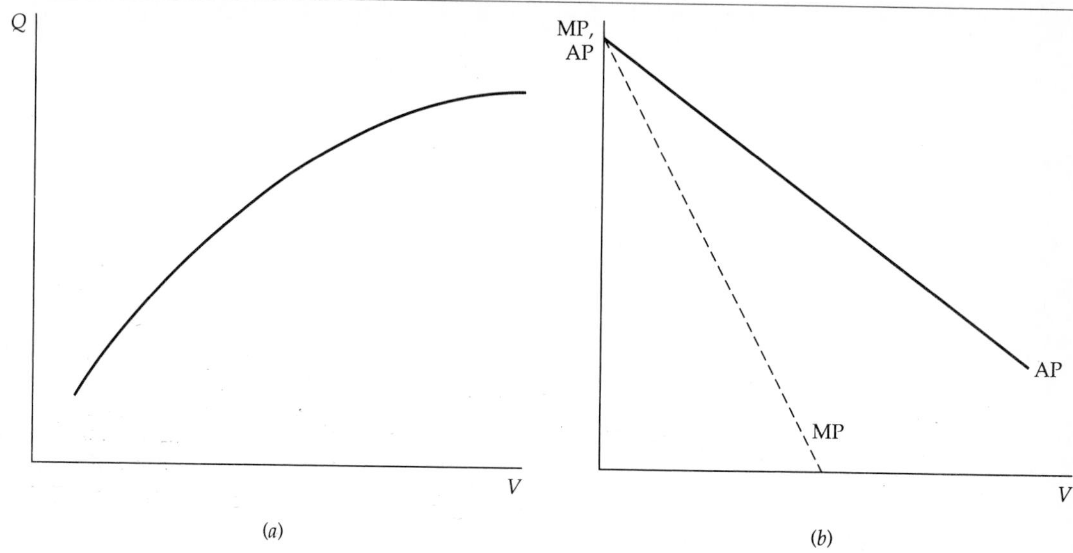

Figure 10.1 Quadratic Production Function

Obviously, the concept of diminishing marginal product is utilized in this equation, as shown in Figure 10.1*b*.[4] If such an equation is used there will be no stage I, in which marginal product initially rises. A cubic function will take care of this problem, if necessary. The form of such an equation is

$$Q = a + bV + cV^2 - dV^3.$$

The total product line based on this equation has two turns in it, as shown in Figure 10.2*a*, and thus it corresponds to the short-run production function discussed in Chapter 7. Here all three stages of production can be found. In Figure 10.2*b*, an interval exhibiting increasing marginal product (stage I) is seen at the extreme left side of the graph.[5]

Another form of the production function is the power function, which takes the following form:

$$Q = aV^b$$

The shape of this production function depends on the exponent b. As shown in Figure 10.3, quantity will increase at an increasing rate if $b > 1$, at a decreasing rate if $b < 1$, and at a constant rate if $b = 1$.

A major advantage of the power function is that it can be transformed into a linear function when it is expressed in logarithmic terms, making it amenable to linear regression analysis:

---

[4]The marginal product in this case is $MP = b - 2cV$—a straight line, as shown in Figure 10.1*b*. The average product is $a/Q + b - cV$; if the intercept is omitted, then the average product is also a straight line.

[5]The formula for marginal product in this case is $MP = b + 2cV - 3dV^2$.

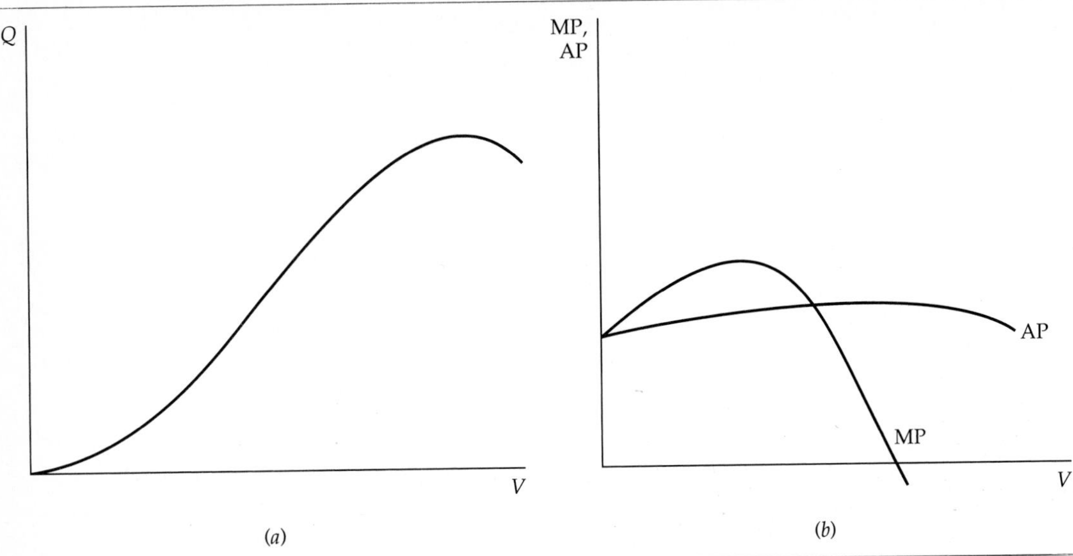

Figure 10.2 Cubic Production Function

$$\log Q = \log a + b \log V$$

Further, this function permits the slope of the line to exhibit increasing, constant, or diminishing marginal product.[6] It cannot, however, exhibit two directions for marginal product on the same function, as was possible with the

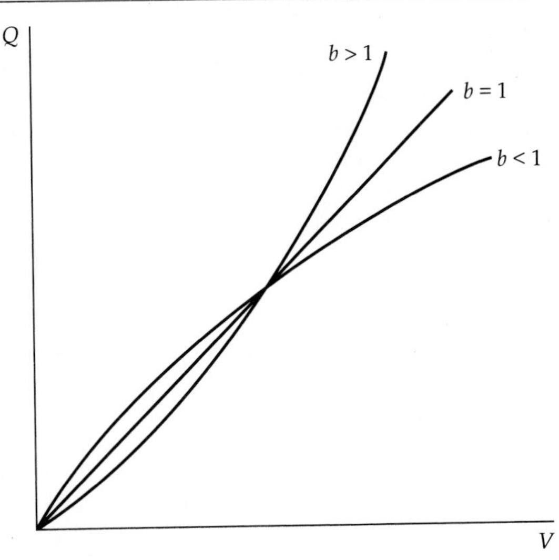

Figure 10.3 Power Production Function

[6]The direction of marginal product depends on the size of the exponent b. If $b > 1$, marginal product is increasing; if $b = 1$, it is constant; and if $b < 1$, it is decreasing.

cubic equation form. Despite this shortcoming, it is the type of function used most frequently in empirical work. One reason for its popularity is that it can be readily transformed into a function with two or more independent variables:

$$Q = aV_1^b V_2^c \ldots\ldots V_n^m$$

Using more than one independent variable in a production function is certainly more realistic than limiting the analysis to only one, and when it is assumed that all inputs are variable, we have then moved from short-run analysis to the long run. Indeed, this function can be employed in both analyses. In a simple two-variable model (e.g., labor and capital), the power function permits the estimation of marginal product (e.g., when labor changes and capital remains the same) and of returns to scale (when both variables change). This method of estimating production functions was developed and popularized by the mathematician Charles W. Cobb and the economist Paul H. Douglas. We now turn to a more thorough description of the Cobb-Douglas model.

The Cobb-Douglas Production Function

The Cobb-Douglas production function was introduced in 1928,[7] and it is still a common functional form in economic studies today. It was originally constructed for all of the manufacturing output in the United States for the years 1899 to 1922. The two inputs used by the authors were number of manual workers and fixed capital. The formula for the production function, which was suggested by Cobb, was of the following form:

$$Q = aL^b K^{1-b}$$

where Q = Total production
L = Quantity of labor
K = Quantity of capital
a, b = Constants

What properties of this function have kept it popular over the last 60 years?

First, to make this equation useful, both inputs must exist for Q to be a positive number. This makes sense, since total product is a result of combining two or more factors.[8]

Second, in the original form of their function, Cobb and Douglas assumed that returns to scale are constant. The function is constructed in such a way that the sum of the exponents is equal to 1: $b + 1 - b = 1$. (Some of the mathematical properties of this function are somewhat complicated. For those interested in

[7] C. W. Cobb and P. H. Douglas, "A Theory of Production," *American Economic Review*, 8, 1 (March 1928, suppl.), pp.139–65.

[8] If an additive function, such as the straight-line

$$Q = a + bL + cK$$

were employed, output would still be positive even if one of the two inputs were zero.

some of the basic mathematics of the Cobb-Douglas function, a brief description follows this section of the chapter.) However, since a specific production function may not have constant returns, and since in estimating a long-run production function it is precisely the nature of returns to scale we may be investigating, in later studies Cobb and Douglas (as well as other researchers) relaxed this requirement and rewrote the equation as follows:

$$Q = aL^bK^c$$

where $b + c$ could equal 1, more than 1, or less than 1. The properties of this power function are that if $b + c = 1$, the production function exhibits constant returns to scale. If $b + c > 1$, returns are increasing. If $b + c < 1$, returns are decreasing.

The third important characteristic of the Cobb-Douglas function is that it permits us to investigate the marginal product for any factor while holding all others constant. Thus, it is also useful in the analysis of short-run relationships. In the two-factor model discussed here, the marginal product of labor turns out to be $MP_L = bQ/L$, and the marginal product of capital is $MP_K = cQ/K$. The two coefficients, b and c, will usually be less than 1. Since the law of diminishing marginal returns requires that the coefficients be less than 1, an estimate of the marginal product will place the results in stage II—which, as we concluded in Chapter 7, is the relevant area of production. Coefficients b and c would have to be negative to place the results in stage III, and greater than 1 to put them in stage I.

Another important concept discussed in Chapter 7 is the elasticity of production, defined as the percent change in output for a given percent change in one input, holding all other inputs constant. The elasticities turn out to be equal to the exponents (coefficients) b and c. Thus the elasticities of labor and capital inputs are constant.

As can be seen from the preceding exposition, the Cobb-Douglas function has a number of advantages for the calculation of production functions, but it also has some shortcomings. Let us summarize both. Among the most important strengths are the following:

1. It gives a nonlinear increasing function for output, given increases in one of the inputs. That is, the marginal product decreases when an input is added while all other inputs remain the same. This situation prevails as long as the input's exponent is less than 1.
2. It makes it possible to investigate whether long-run returns to scale are increasing, constant, or decreasing.
3. Since a power function can be converted to a linear function by using logarithms, the Cobb-Douglas function is convenient and lends itself to relatively easy calculation with any software package.
4. Although we have limited our discussion to just two input variables (L and K), Cobb-Douglas can accommodate any number of independent variables. Thus, the production function could be of the following general form:

$$Q = aX_1^b X_2^c X_3^d \ldots X_n^m$$

5. A theoretical production function assumes that technology is constant. However, the data fitted by the researcher may span a period over which technology has progressed. One of the independent variables in the general equation just given could represent technological change (a time series) and thus adjust the function to take technology into consideration.

The Cobb-Douglas function has the following shortcomings:

1. Although the function can be solved for diminishing marginal product (or, in exceptional cases, for increasing or constant marginal product), it cannot accommodate all three possibilities in one specification. Thus, the function cannot show the marginal product of, say, labor to go through increasing, decreasing, and negative stages. (A cubic function, as discussed earlier, would be necessary to achieve this.)
2. Similarly, Cobb-Douglas can be solved to show increasing, constant, or decreasing returns to scale, but it cannot show a unit (or industry) to move through all three stages.
3. There are also important problems with the specification of data to be utilized in empirical estimates. These problems will be discussed later.

THE BASIC MATHEMATICS OF THE COBB-DOUGLAS FUNCTION[9]

1. The Cobb-Douglas function is nonlinear; it is an exponential function. However, it can be converted into a linear function in terms of logarithms:

$$Q = aL^bK^c$$
$$\log Q = \log a + b \log L + c \log K$$

2. The original form of the function was

$$Q = aL^bK^{1-b}$$

This model assumes constant returns to scale. In other words, if both labor and capital inputs are changed by a certain proportion s, Q will also change by s:

$$\begin{aligned} Q &= a(sL)^b(sK)^{1-b} \\ &= a[s^bL^b][s^{1-b}K^{1-b}] \\ &= (s^bs^{1-b})(aL^bK^{1-b}) \\ &= (s^{b+1-b})(Q) \\ &= s^1Q \end{aligned}$$

Thus, the new quantity, Q, will equal the old quantity times s—the proportion by which both L and K changed.

The later version of the function relaxed the requirement of constant returns since it permitted $b + c$ to be less than, equal to, or greater than 1. In this case, the results would be as follows:

[9]This section can be omitted without loss of continuity.

$$\begin{aligned} Q' &= a(sL)^b(sK)^c \\ &= a(s^bL^b)(s^cK^c) \\ &= a(s^{b+c})(L^bK^c) \\ &= (s^{b+c})(Q) \end{aligned}$$

If $b + c > 1$, then for an input change s, Q will increase by more than s (i.e., increasing returns). If $b + c < 1$, the increase in Q will be less than s (i.e., decreasing returns).

3. The marginal product of a factor is the partial derivative of quantity of output with respect to the factor:

$$\begin{aligned} MP_L &= \partial Q/\partial L \\ &= abL^{b-1}K^{1-b} \\ &= abL^bL^{-1}K^{1-b} \\ &= bL^{-1}Q \\ &= bQ/L \end{aligned}$$

Similarly, the marginal product of capital, MP_K, equals cQ/K or $(l - b)Q/K$.

4. The elasticity of production measures the sensitivity of total product to a change in an input in percentage terms:

$$E_Q = \frac{\text{Change in } Q(\%)}{\text{Change in input } (\%)}$$

or, in the case of labor,

$$\Delta Q/Q \div \Delta L/L = \Delta Q/Q \times L/\Delta L = \Delta Q/\Delta L \times L/Q = \Delta Q/\Delta L \div Q/L$$

$\Delta Q/\Delta L$ is, of course, the marginal product of labor; Q/L is the average product of labor (with capital held constant). Thus, the elasticity of production is equal to the marginal product divided by the average product. It was shown that the marginal product of labor is bQ/L and, as we have just pointed out, the average product of labor is Q/L. Dividing MP_L by AP_L,

$$MP_L/AP_L = bQ/L \div Q/L = bQ/L \times L/Q = b$$

Thus, the elasticity of production for labor is b (and for capital, it is c). These are the original constant exponents of the Cobb-Douglas function. For any percentage increase (or decrease) in the quantity of a factor, holding quantity of the other factor or factors the same, the increase (or decrease) in total product will be a constant percentage. And since the exponents are less than 1, the percent increase in total product is less than the increase in the quantity of the factor.

The Estimation of Production Functions

In this section we will discuss the types of business entities for which production functions can be estimated and the types of data usually employed in this estimation.

The theoretical production function discussed in Chapter 7 dealt with the relationship between inputs and outputs for an individual plant or firm. Data to construct an estimate would therefore typically come from company records—accounting, employment, purchasing, output, and others.

When a plant produces just one product, establishing Q, the total output, is relatively easy.[10] As expected in a production function, Q is specified in terms of physical units (e.g., number, tons, gallons). However, if a plant produces a number of different products, and it is not possible to segregate properly the inputs and outputs of the products, estimation becomes considerably more difficult. In such a case, the investigator probably must settle for some measure of value, assigning weights to products depending on the value (in terms of cost or selling price) produced. There are some obvious problems with this procedure. First of all, over time the data will have to be deflated to account for price or cost changes. Second, the price or cost of a product may not be an exact reflection of the inputs combined in the total value. However, until better measurement methods are found, such valuing methods will have to suffice.

Measuring inputs also can be relatively easy or quite difficult. Inputs should be measured as "flow" rather than "stock" variables, and this is not always possible.[11]

Usually, the most important productive input is labor. Hours of labor input are probably the best measure for our purposes. Data for direct labor hours are ordinarily available from company records. If they are not, then number of direct workers is the next best choice. However, it must be remembered that number of workers is a stock variable and does not necessarily represent the amount of labor expended in production. If indirect labor is also a desired input, then number of workers is most likely the appropriate measure. For materials, a physical measure is again best. In some cases, such data are readily available (weight of materials consumed, for instance). If different materials are consumed in production, there may be a choice of measurements. Of course, since we do not wish to proliferate the number of independent variables, choosing only the most important raw material may be indicated. Alternatively, a combination (by weight or value) may prove to be a viable option. Utilities (electricity, gas, etc.) may also be included; in this case, physical quantities should be fairly easily obtained.

The most difficult input variable is the all-important capital input. How can one measure the use of plant, machinery, and other facilities or equipment in production? Since different components of plant and equipment are of varying durability and different input intensity, usage per period is very hard to establish. In some cases, periodic depreciation may be an indicator of the capital use. However, depreciation as recorded in the company's books is often based

---

[10]We say "relatively" since even if just one product is produced, its form, content, packaging, and other features can change over time.

[11]Flows measure the usage of services consumed in producing a product, whereas stocks represent the amounts of factors present and available for productive use.

on accounting convention or legal requirement. Further, the projected depreciation life of a piece of equipment tends to depend on tax rules, since the firm wishes to take advantage of the fastest write-off permitted for tax purposes. Some capital items, such as land, are not depreciated at all. Unless some rather consistent measurement of capital usage can be designed by the researcher (and this is certainly a formidable—if not impossible—task), the common method of measuring capital by the use of a stock variable (e.g., fixed assets) is probably indicated. Obviously, this is not a perfect solution, since the price of plant and machinery is a function of when the assets were acquired. Thus, the asset figure must be adjusted by a price index. Should gross fixed assets (i.e., the original cost of all plant and equipment) be used, or net fixed assets (gross assets minus accumulated depreciation)? Again, this is a difficult question. There is no specific answer. The method used must be determined by the investigator as that which is most reasonable (and available) for each specific case.

The estimating method must also be determined. If regression is used, then the choice is between time series and cross-sectional analysis.[12] Which of the two techniques is utilized depends on the data available and on the purpose of the investigation. If the data have been collected for one plant over a period of time, the method to apply is the time series. If the data are given for the same time period for a number of similar plants, then cross-sectional analysis is appropriate. Both methods have their advantages and disadvantages.

For the time series method:

1. If any of the data used in the calculation are in monetary terms (e.g., a weighted measure of output of different products, as described previously), an inflation adjustment is necessary.
2. Technology may have changed over time; therefore, the input-output relationship of the early periods may not be directly comparable to the later periods.[13]
3. The production function assumes that production always takes place where the input combination is the most efficient. This may not be the case.

For the cross-sectional method:

1. Although we overcome the problem of technological change over time, which is present in the time series analysis, we introduce a new problem: the assumption that all of the plants in the investigation are of the same technological quality.
2. If some of the data in the analysis are in monetary terms, an adjustment for differentials in wage or price levels across different geographical areas must be made.

[12]Time series and cross-sectional regression analyses were discussed in Chapter 5.

[13]A time adjustment may have to be used to account for technological change. At other times, a dummy variable may be useful.

3. Again, there is no assurance that each of the plants in the analysis operates at the most efficient input combination for the period examined.

Thus, as in all cases, there is no perfect way to measure and analyze the data. It is the responsibility of the investigator to make the appropriate choices.

Before we turn to a discussion of aggregate production functions, a numerical illustration of an individual firm's production function will summarize the material just covered. Also, two published studies will be discussed.

A NUMERICAL EXAMPLE OF A COBB-DOUGLAS PRODUCTION FUNCTION. A cross-sectional sample of 20 soft drink bottling plants has been selected. The data are given for a specific month in 1988. Only two independent variables are used: (1) number of direct workers and (2) plant size. (Rather than determining the amount of capital by some accounting measure, the plants have been sorted by size, from 1 to 1.75. This size measure was devised by engineers and is based on square footage, number of production lines, etc.)

Production, the dependent variable, is stated in terms of gallons of product shipped during the period. Table 10.1 contains the data for both the dependent and independent variables and the results of the analysis.

The Cobb-Douglas function of the form $Q = aL^bK^c$ was applied to the numbers. The regression output[14] in the table shows the results. The regression equation is as follows:

$$Q = 1.18L^{0.66}K^{0.32}$$

R^2 (the coefficient of determination) is quite high, showing that 98 percent of the deviations are explained. The two coefficients are significantly different from zero since they both pass the t-test.[15] The sum of the two coefficients is 0.985. This tells us that these 20 plants exhibit almost constant returns to scale. True, the coefficient is less than 1, but it is so close that no one could seriously assert that decreasing returns are the rule. Since each of the coefficients is also less than 1, both inputs exhibit decreasing marginal returns.

TWO STUDIES OF INDIVIDUAL PRODUCTION FUNCTIONS. In 1967, a study of the production function of the Pacific halibut industry was published. A Cobb-Douglas function appeared to give good results and showed that constant returns are probably the rule in this industry. A "good captain" variable was added—a confidential rating of the management abilities of the captains of the 32 boats in the sample. It was found that good captains made a difference.[16]

A very recent study included management in the production function equation. This study dealt with a sample of plants of a multinational consumer

---

[14]The results were calculated using the Lotus (Version 2) regression analysis program. The raw data were transformed into logarithms, and a straight-line regression in logarithms was computed.

[15]Labor's t-test is significant at the 1 percent level, and capital's is significant at the 5 percent level.

[16]Salvatore Comitimi and David S. Huang, "A Study of Production and Factor Shares in the Halibut Fishing Industry," *Journal of Political Economy*, August 1967, pp. 366–72.

Table 10.1 Production Function: Soft Drink Bottling Plants

TOTAL PRODUCT	LABOR	CAPITAL
97	15	1.00
98	17	1.00
104	20	1.00
120	22	1.00
136	22	1.25
129	25	1.25
145	30	1.25
170	32	1.25
181	35	1.25
166	30	1.50
175	35	1.50
190	38	1.50
212	42	1.50
220	44	1.50
207	45	1.50
228	44	1.75
226	47	1.75
240	52	1.75
270	55	1.75
280	58	1.75

Regression Output:

Constant		1.180015
Std Err of Y Est		0.020818
R Squared		0.980965
No. of Observations		20
Degrees of Freedom		17
X Coefficient(s)	0.664370	0.321471
Std Err of Coef.	0.075371	0.147006

goods manufacturer. Time series and cross-sectional data were combined to obtain 127 observations over eight years (1975–1982). Management was measured as a performance ranking of each plant in terms of three criteria—output goal attainment, cost over- or underfulfillment, and quality level of output. The results showed that the management variable was statistically significant. Another feature of this study was the conclusion that increasing returns existed up to a certain plant size and that decreasing returns resulted at larger sizes.[17]

Aggregate Production Functions

A large proportion of the studies performed using the Cobb-Douglas function did not deal with data for individual firms, but rather with aggregations of industries or even the economy as a whole. Although much of this work has

[17] Robert N. Mefford, "Introducing Management into the Production Function," *Review of Economics and Statistics*, February 1986, pp. 96–104.

proved to be quite fruitful in describing production functions, the interpretation of the results may not be quite as meaningful as for individual production functions. When data for the economy as a whole are used, the model must accommodate different technologies and different processes and thus does not represent a specific technological process of a given firm. When the aggregation is done at the level of an industry rather than the overall economy, the assumption of similar technology is more appropriate, but even in such a case many dissimilarities may occur.

Gathering data for such aggregate functions would be extremely difficult. To facilitate the process, economists have generally used indexes of aggregate data. Thus, for the economy as a whole, gross national product—in real terms—could be used to measure output. For specific industries, data from the Census of Manufactures or the production index published by the Federal Reserve Board can be employed. Data for investment and depreciation by industry are also available for the construction of appropriate indexes for the capital variable. The Bureau of Labor Statistics publishes a great deal of data on employment and work hours.

As already mentioned, Cobb and Douglas performed their earliest study on U.S. manufacturing in the form of a time-series regression for the years 1899–1922. Using the original version of their formula, which restricted results to constant returns to scale, they obtained the following result:

$$Q = 1.01L^{0.75}K^{0.25}$$

Other studies used the same technique with similar results.

In 1937, David Durand suggested that the equation should not necessarily limit the results to constant returns to scale.[18] After Durand's article, it was accepted that the exponents in the equation no longer had to equal 1. Douglas corrected the original study to follow Durand's suggestion, and he found that the coefficient of labor was reduced to about two-thirds, whereas capital's exponent rose to about one-third. But the sum of the two exponents still summed to about 1, and thus constant returns to scale appeared to prevail.[19]

At about the same time, cross-sectional analysis, rather than time series, came into use, and most of the studies done since then have utilized this technique. The observations were now individual industries in a particular year. Many other studies were conducted on data from the United States, Australia, Canada, and New Zealand. In a majority of these investigations, the sum of the exponents turned out to be very close to 1.

Another interesting analysis was published in 1967. The author performed a cross-sectional study of 18 industries using data from the 1957 Census of

[18]David Durand, "Some Thoughts on Marginal Productivity with Special Reference to Professor Douglas," *Journal of Political Economy*, 45, 6 (December 1937) pp.740–58.

[19]The history of the Cobb-Douglas function and the major studies were summarized by Douglas himself in his article "The Cobb-Douglas Production Function Once Again: Its History, Its Testing, and Some New Empirical Values," *Journal of Political Economy*, 84, 5 (October 1976), pp. 903–15.

Manufactures.[20] The observation units were individual states. (Thus, a different number of observations was used for each industry, depending on the number of states in which such industries were located.) Three independent variables were used:

1. Production worker hours
2. Nonproduction worker years
3. Gross book value of depreciable and depletable assets

The dependent variable, Q, was represented by the value added in each industry.

The results showed that the sums of the three exponents in the 18 industries ranged from about 0.95 to 1.11, indicating a span from decreasing to increasing returns. Tests of significance showed than in only 5 of the 18 industries was the sum of the coefficients significantly different from 1. Thus, again, in the majority of cases, constant returns to scale appeared to dominate.

Cost Estimating

The literature of empirical economic inquiry deals heavily with estimation of cost curves. This work has its origins with Joel Dean, who wrote the first textbook on managerial economics. Many of the studies he conducted date back to the 1930s.

As in the case of production functions, we are interested in estimating cost functions both in the short run and in the long run. The purposes of the estimation differ between the two functions. The short-run function helps to define short-run marginal costs and thus assists the manager in determining output and prices. In the long run, the decision that a firm faces involves building the most efficient size of plant. That determination will depend on the existence of scale economies and diseconomies.

Short-run cost functions (like short-run production functions) assume that at least one factor is fixed. Thus, cost is influenced by the quantity produced as changes occur in the variable factor. To estimate such a short-run function, we must find data in which quantity and costs change while certain factors change and others remain fixed. As in the section on production functions, we can make the simplifying assumption that in a two-input model, labor changes while capital remains fixed.

In investigating short-run cost functions using regression analysis, researchers have most frequently employed the time series technique with data for a specific plant or firm over time. It is important that when time series data are collected, the period over which observations are taken is limited to a relatively short span. A major reason is that the size of the plant or firm should not change significantly during the time interval used in a short-run cost function. Also, there must not have been any significant changes in technology, since a cost

[20]John R. Moroney, "Cobb-Douglas Production Functions and Returns to Scale in U.S. Manufacturing," *Western Economic Journal*, 6, 1 (December 1967), pp. 39–51.

function is constructed for a given state of the art. To conduct a meaningful analysis, there must be a sufficient number of observations, and there must be variations in production from observation period to observation period.[21] Thus, each observation period, where possible, should be limited to a month, and sometimes even a shorter period (a week or two weeks). If months are used, 36 observations can be obtained over a 3-year period, an interval that may be short enough to preclude significant changes in the size or technology of the plant.

Long-run cost functions—the planning functions—allow for changes in all inputs. Thus, size of plant (or, in general, capital investment) can change along with all the other factors. Time series regression analysis can be employed if changes in plant size occurred during the period over which the observations were collected, but here we probably need a long period of time for our model. In addition, plant size changes are not likely to be continuous in nature, but to occur at specified intervals. Thus, even given a relatively long time span, we probably could identify no more than one or two significant changes in the size of the plant. For this reason, much of the empirical work done to estimate long-run cost functions has used cross-sectional analysis. Here observations are recorded in a particular time period for a number of plants, each of which will have a different set of inputs and outputs. Neither of the two methods (time series for the short run, cross-sectional for the long run) is free of cost specification and estimation problems.

Our discussion will proceed as follows: Short-run and long-run analyses will be examined separately. For each, the problems of data specification and collection will be addressed, and where possible, solutions to these problems and data adjustments used in published studies will be reviewed. Then we will present the models of cost-output relationships and describe one or two studies performed by economists with a general conclusion about the shape of the cost functions empirically estimated.

The Estimation of Short-Run Cost Functions

Problems and Adjustments

Economic versus Accounting Costs. Most empirical studies of cost functions have utilized accounting data that record the actual costs and expenses on a historical basis. However, decision-making data—economic data—should also include opportunity costs. No amount of adjustment will ever completely reconcile these concepts, but certain corrections can be made.

- Changes in prices of labor, materials and other inputs must be adjusted so that current prices are used.[22]

---

[21]Ideally, these changes in quantities produced should occur under relatively normal circumstances rather than due to some abnormal upheaval. Thus, production cuts because of plant damage or a strike, for instance, may not produce valid data.

[22]Since different inputs may incur different relative price changes, some factor substitution may result over time. It can only be hoped that such effects will not be significant, since they are extremely difficult, if not impossible, to remove.

- It is important that only those costs that could affect production and pricing decisions be included. Thus, costs that are not a function of output should be exempted. Since we are dealing with short-run cost functions, fixed costs should not have an influence on pricing or output decisions. Many analysts try to isolate only the direct costs of production, omitting fixed overhead expenses. But care must be taken to include all expenses that vary with output in the cost calculations.
- Closely allied to the previous point is the question of depreciation. Accountants usually record depreciation on a time-related basis, and, as mentioned previously, depreciation is often not related to actual usage but follows accounting convention as adapted to tax rules. If "use" depreciation can be isolated from the accounting data, only that portion should be included in costs. But it must be kept in mind that recorded depreciation is based on the original cost of the equipment, whereas economic depreciation should be based on replacement value.

The problems that arise because of differences between accounting and economic costs are the most difficult to solve. In most cases, some type of compromise is necessary. No definitive advice can be given here to prospective researchers. We can only point out the significant issues and suggest some possibly appropriate adjustments. What is done in the final analysis depends on the data available and the ability of the investigator to make the corrections.

Rate Changes. In addition to inflationary changes in the prices of various inputs, costs can also change due to variations in tax rates, Social Security contributions, labor insurance costs (unemployment insurance or worker's compensation rates), and various benefit coverages that affect costs. Additional types of cost changes could be enumerated. Since most of these rate changes are not based on quantity produced, they should be excluded.

Output Homogeneity. The problems encountered in cost estimation are similar to those discussed for the production function. The analysis is easiest when output is relatively homogeneous. If only one product is produced in the plant, the quantity produced (or shipped) can be handled in a rather uncomplicated manner. But if there are several products moving through the plant simultaneously, some weighting apparatus must be employed to obtain the quantity produced.[23]

Timing of Costs. In many cases, costs and the service performed to create these costs do not occur at the same time. For instance, a machine that is in use continuously may be scheduled for maintenance periodically. In the airline industry, for example, major maintenance on engines is performed after a given

[23]If a weighting scheme involving costs or direct inputs for each of the products is utilized, then, in a way, we are employing costs to determine output and then measuring costs as a function of this output. In other words, we are introducing a dependency into the relationship between costs and output, when we are really trying to determine the relationship between the two. This presents a serious problem. But, given the state of the art of cost estimating, as long as accounting and production records of a firm are employed, there is no easy way out of this dilemma.

number of flight hours. When such timing differences occur, care must be taken to spread the maintenance costs over the period of machine usage.

Accounting Changes. When a time series analysis using accounting data is performed, it is very important that the researcher ascertain whether changes in accounting methods and procedures have occurred during the period included in the study. For instance, there may have been changes in depreciation methods or in the timing of the recording of development expenses. Such changes must be scrupulously adjusted to reflect uniformity in the measurements over time.

Given all the warnings about the problems that can be encountered in empirical cost estimation, you may have been persuaded that no useful conclusions can be obtained from such studies. Actually, such difficulties have not turned away many economists. Starting with Dean in the 1930s and continuing until today, economic journals contain many articles investigating statistical cost functions. The studies have also been summarized in articles as well as books.

THE SHAPES OF SHORT-RUN COST FUNCTIONS In Chapter 8, Figure 8.4, three different specifications of cost functions are shown. Each represents a possible shape of the cost curves. The economist, after collecting and adjusting the data, will use one of these specifications to measure the relationship between cost and output. Other statistical functions could be employed (such as the Cobb-Douglas power function), but the shapes introduced in Chapter 8 are the ones most frequently encountered in statistical studies. For your convenience, these diagrams have been reproduced in this section.

Figure 10.4 represents the normal theoretical function, which exhibits both decreasing marginal and average costs and increasing marginal and average costs. The curves can be drawn in terms of total costs or unit costs. Figure 10.4*a* shows total costs.[24] The mathematical function that describes such a curve is a polynomial function of the third degree, that is, a cubic function:

$$TC = a + bQ - cQ^2 + dQ^3$$

where TC = Total cost
Q = Total output

The negative sign preceding the quadratic term of the equation causes the total cost first to increase at a decreasing rate (decreasing marginal costs). Then the cubic term causes it to increase at an increasing rate (increasing marginal costs). The average and marginal costs shown in Figure 10.4*b* exhibit the usual U-shape, and their expressions can be written as follows:[25]

---

[24]If only variable costs are estimated, this curve would be the variable cost curve. Theoretically, it should begin at the origin since there are no variable costs when production is zero. However, when the curves are statistically estimated, even if only variable costs are included, the line will most likely intercept the Y-axis at a point other than zero. From the investigator's viewpoint, this is not terribly important, since most of the observations included in the statistical estimate will not be anywhere near zero production. The intercept thus turns out to be meaningless.

[25]The average cost curve is obtained by dividing TC by Q. To obtain the marginal cost, some elementary calculus is needed. The marginal cost is the first derivative of the total cost function with respect to Q.

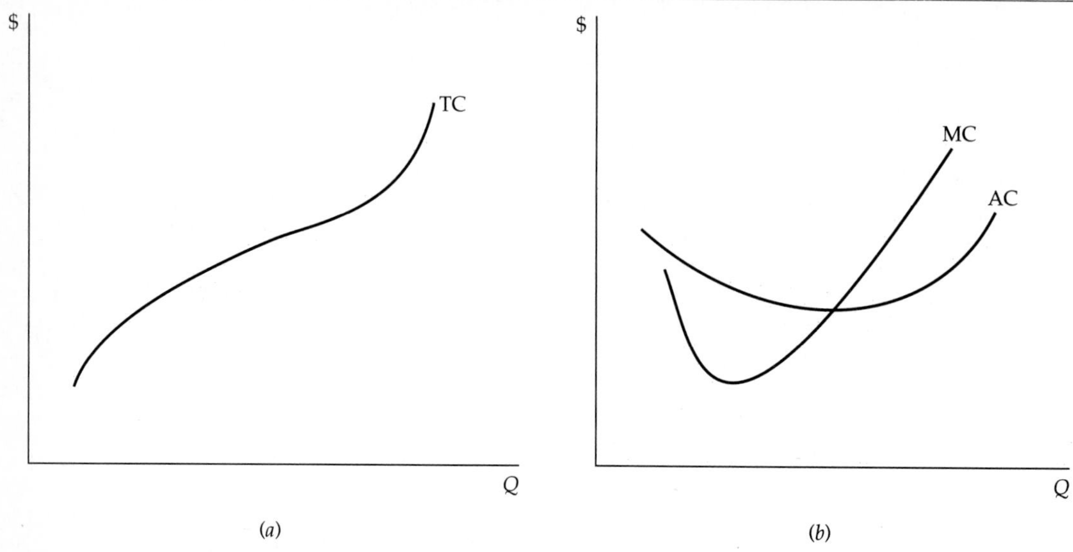

Figure 10.4 Cubic Cost Function

$$AC = a/Q + b - cQ + dQ^2$$
$$MC = b - 2cQ + 3dQ^2$$

If the data do not quite fit the cubic function, the quadratic function can be tested. The three equations in this case are as follows:

$$TC = a + bQ + cQ^2$$
$$AC = a/Q + b + cQ$$
$$MC = b + 2cQ$$

As can be seen in Figure 10.5, the shapes of these functions exhibit characteristics that differ substantially from the cubic function. The total cost curve consists of only that section that increases at an increasing rate. Thus, there are no decreasing marginal costs (increasing marginal product) in this construction.[26] This can be seen in Figure 10.5*b*, where the MC curve is a straight line increasing at all points (i.e., not U-shaped).

A linear total cost function can also be fitted.[27] The three equations take the following form:

$$TC = a + bQ$$
$$AC = a/Q + b$$
$$MC = b$$

[26] Earlier in this chapter a similar illustration was shown for a production function that did not go through stage I.

[27] In Chapter 12, on break-even analysis, we use this function exclusively.

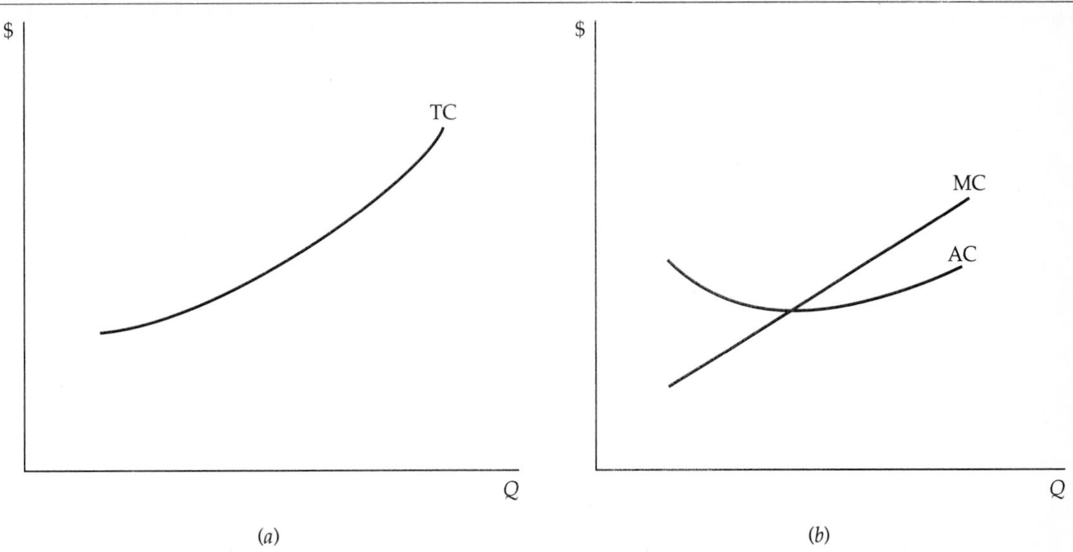

Figure 10.5 Quadratic Cost Function

Figure 10.6*a* and *b* shows the curves based on the linear form.[28] Note that the "law of diminishing marginal returns" has been eliminated. Each additional unit's cost is the constant, b. Thus, this specification of the cost curve exhibits strictly constant marginal costs. This type of analysis does not appeal intuitively to an economist, who knows that if units of a variable factor are continually added to a fixed factor (plant), somewhere at higher producion levels unit costs must rise.

These three specifications can fit various types of cost data. But even when a really good set of data is available to the investigator, chances are that the range of observations will be rather limited and will tend to cluster around a midpoint. Very seldom will we have data corresponding to near-zero production,[29] and very seldom will data be given for production equaling or exceeding theoretical capacity. Thus, the statistical results economists obtain may not reflect the behavior of costs at the two extremes of the curve. In the following discussion of some of the empirical work that has been performed in the past, we find that this is precisely the case.

[28]The average total cost curve in this case declines continuously and approaches the marginal cost curve asymptotically. The reason for this, in the formula, is that the first term a/Q, decreases as Q increases and the second term, b, is a constant. If we were dealing exclusively with variable costs, where the a term does not exist (because costs are zero when production is zero), then $AVC = b$ and the marginal and average variable costs equal each other. This, of course, must be true, since if each additional (marginal) unit costs the same, then the average variable cost of each unit does not change and must equal the marginal cost.

[29]We may have such data in case the plant burns down or a strike occurs; but such occurrences are not normal and probably should not be included in the study. In terms of statistics, such data are called *outliers* and are usually ignored.

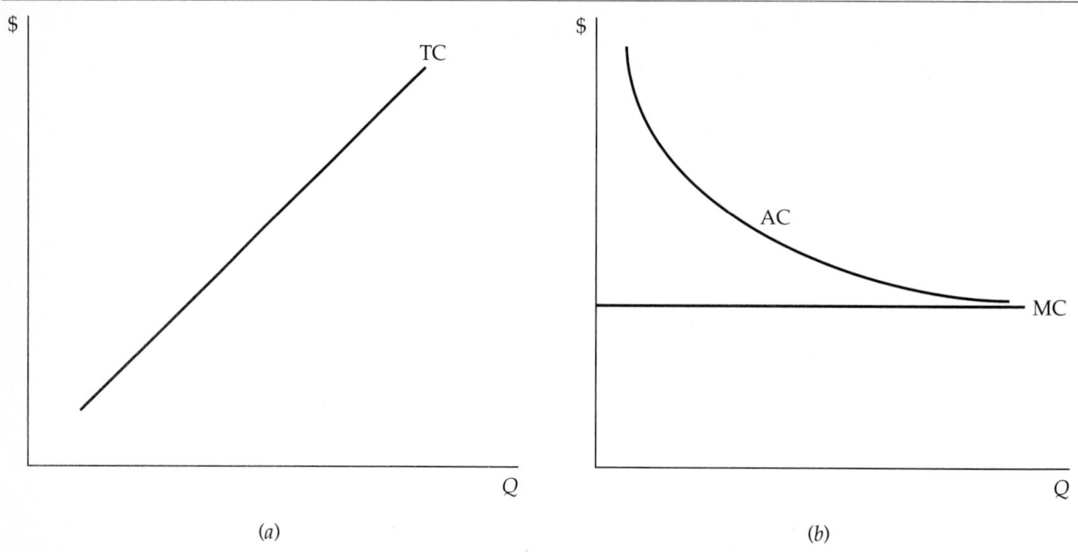

Figure 10.6 Linear Cost Function

A SAMPLING OF SHORT-RUN COST STUDIES. There is a large number of cost studies from which we could choose for purposes of illustration. We have selected three studies covering different industries and different time periods. Although some of the estimating procedures have become somewhat more sophisticated over time, the studies all used time series regression analysis.

The Hosiery Mill. One of several studies conducted by Joel Dean in the 1930s and 1940s focused on a mill of a large hosiery manufacturer.[30] Its equipment was highly mechanized and its labor skilled.

Data for 54 months from 1935 to 1939 were employed. During this period, the size of the plant did not change, and the equipment remained approximately the same. Production during these months varied from zero to near physical capacity. Direct labor, indirect labor, and overhead costs were included.[31] These costs were adjusted by factor price indexes. Output was a weighted index of individual products, and the weights were based on relative labor costs. The result, using a linear regression form, was

$$TC = 2,935.59 + 1.998Q$$

where TC = Total cost,
Q = Output, in pairs of hosiery.

[30]Joel Dean, *Statistical Cost Functions of a Hosiery Mill*, Studies in Business Administration, vol. 11, no. 4, Chicago: University of Chicago Press, 1941. This study and others have been reprinted in a volume of Dean's work, *Statistical Cost Estimation*, Bloomington: Indiana University Press, 1976.

[31]Separate calculations were made for each of the three cost components, but the combined cost and direct labor cost regressions were the only ones that were statistically meaningful.

The results were statistically significant, and the correlation coefficient was .973 (and, therefore, the coefficient of determination, R^2, was .947).

Dean also tried to fit quadratic and cubic equations to the data. The results, however, were not meaningful. The slope coefficients were not statistically significant, and the signs of the equations turned out to be the opposite from those expected based on economic theory. Thus Dean's analysis appeared to point to the existence of a straight-line total cost curve, a decreasing average total cost curve, and constant marginal costs.

Road Passenger Transport. In the United Kingdom J. Johnston collected data from one of the larger transportation companies, with a fleet of some 1,300 vehicles, that operated some 45 million car miles per year.[32] The data were grouped into four-week periods over three years, 1949–1952; thus, there were some 39 observations. Production exhibited a marked seasonal pattern, so varying production amounts per period could be observed.

Several categories of costs were included. Sixty-two percent of the costs and expenses were accounted for by vehicle operations, which included wages, clothing, gasoline, oil, and tires. All of these costs varied with output. Maintenance and depreciation made up about 20 percent of total costs. Vehicle maintenance varied with mileage, and depreciation was charged on a strict mileage basis. Another 10 percent of the costs went for traffic staff, bus cleaning, toll costs, and other expenses that were mostly mileage-related. The remaining 8 percent of expenses were not directly related to the amount of traffic, but since they were such a small proportion of the total, they were included in the cost analysis. Output was measured in car miles during the period. The data were adjusted by individual price indexes where price changes had occurred.

Again, a straight-line total cost function provided the best fit:

$$TC = 0.65558 + 0.4433Q$$

where Q represents car miles, in millions. The correlation coefficient was .95. So, as in Dean's study, the total cost curve was a straight line with constant marginal costs.

Plastic Containers. In a study conducted for 10 different products moving through a plant at the same time, 21 monthly observations were taken during the period of January 1966 to September 1967.[33] During this period plant capacity was fixed, and all input prices were also fixed by contract. Only direct costs of labor, machinery, and materials were included, so no allocation problems for overhead items had to be handled. The firm reported wide production fluctuations during the period, with several observations being somewhat above 90 percent of capacity level.

Each of the three function forms (straight-line, quadratic, and cubic) were calculated using time series regression analysis. The results showed that the linear

---

[32] J. Johnston, *Statistical Cost Analysis,* New York: McGraw-Hill 1960, pp. 74–86.

[33] Ronald S. Coot and David A. Walker, "Short-run Cost Functions of a Multi-product Firm;" *Journal of Industrial Economics,* April 1970, pp. 118–28.

cost function gave the best fit for each of the 10 products. Some testing also was done to investigate whether the results for each product were influenced by the level of output for other products. The conclusion was that such cost interrelationships did not exist. The squared and cubed terms in the quadratic and cubic regressions did not add anything to the results and, in fact, were in most cases not significant statistically.

The authors also tested for the firm's aggregate cost-output relationship. The total physical output was obtained by weighting each product by its base-period price. Again, the best results were given by a straight-line equation,

$$TC = 56,393 + 3.368Q$$

with the t-test significant at the 1 percent level and the R^2 a respectable .89.

MARGINAL COST: U-SHAPED OR CONSTANT? Each of the three studies just cited seemed to conclude that in the short run, the total cost curve is a linear function of production and that the marginal cost is constant.[34] Quite a few other empirical studies of costs have come to the same conclusion. In addition to the hosiery mill, Dean also studied a furniture factory and a leather belt shop. Johnston conducted investigations into a food-processing firm and coal mining, among others. Studies of the steel industry, cement industry, and electric power were also done. Most of these came to conclusions similar to those of the three studies we described briefly. Actually, some of the researchers found decreasing marginal costs to be the rule.

Does that mean that economists should revise their thinking about U-shaped average and marginal cost curves? Although these findings should cause economists to pause and do some additional thinking, the results of these studies—even over the relatively long period of 50 or more years—can easily be reconciled with the traditional shapes of cost curves:

1. The data employed in most of the studies concentrated on output levels that were limited in range. Thus, even though in some cases production may have taken place at about 90 percent of capacity, it is quite possible that plants are built and equipped in such a way that over a fairly long range of outputs, unit costs are relatively constant. The theoretical curves that economists draw show very distinct minimum points to make the important point quite obvious to students of elementary economics. But in reality, the "'bottom" of the curve can represent a fairly large interval, and unit costs may rise (quite steeply) only when physical capacity is reached. Management should know at which production point unit costs could start rising steeply and will, whenever possible, avoid reaching such a stage. Figure 10.7 shows an average cost curve (A) that most students have seen on blackboards in elementary microeconomics courses. But curve B, which still conforms to the economist's valid thinking about rising unit costs, may be the one that is more

[34] And, as mentioned before, the average variable cost is a constant, and the average total cost—given the existence of fixed costs in the short run—is downward sloping.

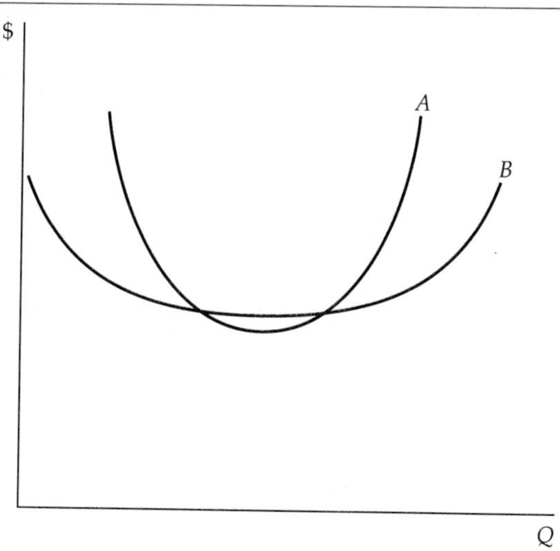

Figure 10.7 Theoretical versus Realistic Average Cost Curve

true to life. The minimum point of this curve is not as low as that on curve *A*, but there is a relatively wide range of outputs on curve *B* where costs remain low—lower than for curve *A*. Since production tends to fluctuate from period to period, output is more likely to take place on the relatively constant unit cost segment on curve *B* than at curve *A*'s narrowly defined minimum.

2. Many economists explain straight-line cost curves by pointing out that although theory requires capital inputs to be fixed in the short run, they really are not. For instance, when production increases, a firm can easily set up an additional assembly line to keep the fixed/variable input ratio constant. Thus, since the fixed factor is utilized in a fixed proportion with the variable factor, increasing marginal cost will not necessarily occur.
3. Regression analysis is not a perfect tool. If, as we said in the first point, most of the production observations fall into an intermediate output range, there may just not be a sufficient number of observations at the extremes to convert a linear fit to a curvilinear one.

Thus, although economists would certainly feel more gratified if empirical work were to confirm their theories, the evidence of the studies is not so overwhelming that an immediate reevaluation of microeconomic theory is necessary. Further, real-life data seem to be consistent with the existence of upward-sloping marginal cost curves. We learned earlier that the upward-sloping short-run supply curve of a firm or industry is based on the existence of an upward-sloping marginal cost curve. The fact that rising demand for a product raises the price and causes an increase in quantity supplied in the short run is evidence of the existence of an upward-sloping supply curve that is theoretically explained by the existence of an upward-sloping marginal cost curve. Thus, despite some of the empirical findings, it appears that corporate managers act as if they were confronted by a marginal cost curve of the kind described by economic theory.

The Estimation of Long-Run Cost Functions

The estimation of long-run cost curves, although conceptually similar to the estimation of short-run costs, presents some new challenges. As you will recall, in the economic long run, all cost are variable. That means that capital (plant and equipment), which is ordinarily held fixed in the short run, is now permitted to change. As a matter of fact, it is precisely the goal of long-run cost analysis to trace unit costs for different sizes of plant and different amounts of equipment capacity. Our interest in long-run costs is to investigate the existence of returns to scale. Is production susceptible to decreasing costs as plant capacity increases, or is there some plant size that will afford minimum costs and where unit costs will increase as the capacity rises beyond this minimum point? Another possibility, of course, is that costs will be constant, displaying no economies or diseconomies of scale.

The question of costs in relation to size is important not only for planning decisions regarding plant or firm expansion. Firms must also consider costs when deciding on potential mergers. Will the synergy of the new units indicate a potential decrease in unit costs as a function of size?

When we speak of the long run, we may imagine that such research requires data for a given plant or firm over a considerable interval of time, so that changes in capacity can be observed. Since such changes do not occur continuously, the period of observation should enable several capacity increases to be traced. However, even if such data were available and could be handled through price adjustments, a new, serious obstacle arises. Given a longer period of time, the one important parameter that must be kept constant—the state of art, or technology—will certainly not stand still. It is almost if not totally impossible to find firms that have not changed their production methods or installed improved equipment over an interval of several years. Chances are that firms that have not made such technological changes have gone out of existence, and studying them would be an exercise in futility.

So, although some long-run statistical cost studies have employed time series regression analysis, most investigators have turned to the use of cross-sectional regression. This method of analysis has some obvious advantages for long-run cost estimation. However, it introduces some new problems that must be considered and that will require adjustments to be designed, if possible.

Among the strengths of cross-sectional analysis are the following:

1. Observations are recorded for different plants (or firms) at a given point of time. Since different plants generally come in different sizes, the independent variable, quantity of output, can vary over relatively large ranges.

2. Since all observations are taken at a given point in time (e.g., one year), the technology is known and does not change. This does not necessarily mean that all plants will be using the same technology. Under ideal circumstances, each plant will utilize that level of technology, within the known state of the art, that is most efficient for that specific plant. Unfortunately, this ideal is usually not reached. (We will encounter the question of technology again when we look at some of the drawbacks of cross-sectional analysis.)

3. Adjusting the various costs for inflation or other price changes is not necessary under cross-sectional analysis. If annual observations are used for the sample of plants, an average figure for costs (e.g., per labor hour or ton of material) will be satisfactory. Only under conditions of very severe inflation—hyperinflation—would the averaging of annual costs become a significant problem, but any studies undertaken under such conditions would surely be of dubious quality in any case.

These are the major advantages of fitting a cross-sectional regression to the data. But, as always, not everything can be rosy in economic analysis, especially in empirical estimating. The use of the cross-sectional technique also creates some difficulties of which the researcher must be well aware. Just a few of these are the following:

1. Inflationary problems may be avoided by abandoning the time series method, but a new problem is introduced. Since the observations are taken from plants (or firms) in different geographical areas, we may encounter interregional cost differences in labor rates, utility bills, material costs, or transportation costs, for example. Adjustments to some common base must be made. And again, if such adjustments are made, there is a chance that an important phenomenon is being swept under the rug. Not only can the level of input prices vary from geographical area to area; there is also a good possibility that relative prices of inputs differ and that the combination of inputs in a particular location is a function of these relative differences. By adjusting prices to a specific benchmark, we may be obliterating the conscious choice made by management in a particular location based on relative prices of different inputs.

2. Although the known state of the art for each firm is the same, it is not necessarily true that all plants are, at a given point of time, operating at the optimal level of technology. In terms of economics, the assumption that each plant is operating most efficiently for its production level does not necessarily hold. This can be illustrated by drawing an envelope curve, which became a familiar tool of analysis in Chapter 8. In Figure 10.8 an envelope curve, *ABC*, is drawn. This long-run average cost curve represents all the optimal points of production. Point *B* is the minimum cost point, which represents the most efficient plant size. If, however, the plants in the sample do not operate at optimal points for any level of production, we may end up with observations along curve *DF*, which will tend to be above the optimal curve, *ABC*, and which indicates not only a level but also a slope quite different from the optimal cost curve. There really is no way to correct for this potential error completely. The researcher must endeavor to choose plants that are as homogeneous as possible, without trivializing the estimates by choosing a small number of plants that exhibit almost identical characteristics.

3. If accounting data are used to make the estimates, it is very important that the economist verify that there are no significant differences in the way costs are recorded on the firms' books of account. Although different depreciation

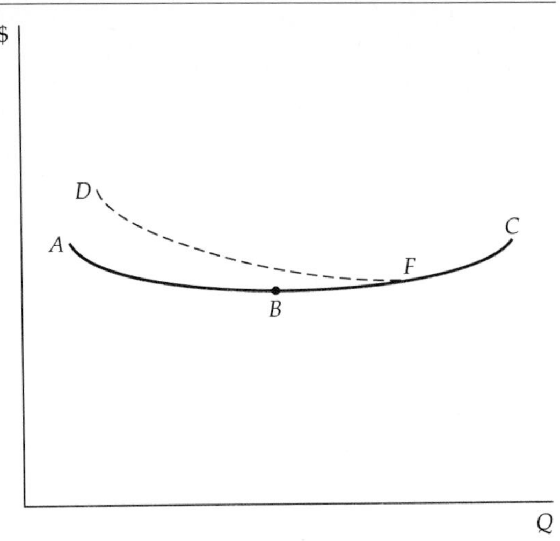

Figure 10.8 Optimal and Suboptimal Cost Curves

procedures are the most important cause of discrepancies, varying inventory valuation methods and amortization of other expenses can also lead to substantial distortions. The best possible adjustments must always be made.

4. One other possible danger must be considered. Different companies may pay their cost factors differently. This is most important in the case of labor costs. Total labor costs can comprise varying fractions of wages and benefits (such as vacation time, holidays, and medical care). In some cases, employees may receive part of their income in stock, or stock may be sold to them at a discounted price. The estimator must be certain to include all relevant costs.

Once the economist is satisfied that all possible sources of error have been minimized, the task of making the cost estimates begins. In the following section, we discuss a small sample of studies that have been performed and published.

SAMPLING OF LONG-RUN COST STUDIES. As in the case of short-run costs, a large number of inquiries into the properties of long-run costs have been conducted over the last 50 years or so. A small number of these will be mentioned here to provide a flavor of method and results.

Shoe Store Chain. In one of the early studies conducted by Joel Dean, the sample comprised 55 shoe stores owned by one firm.[35] All were located in metropolitan areas. "Such units possess the important advantage of being

[35]Joel Dean and R. Warren James, *The Long-Run Behavior of Costs in a Chain of Shoe Stores: A Statistical Analysis*, Studies in Business Administration, vol. 12, no. 3, University of Chicago Press, 1942, reprinted in Joel Dean, op. cit., pp. 324–60.

almost identical with respect to records, merchandise, layout, personnel and management methods."[36] Pairs of shoes were the output. Costs were mainly composed of selling expenses (including wages), handling expenses, and building expenses. Corporate allocations were omitted. The study was based on annual data for 1937 and 1938. Quadratic total cost curves gave the best fit for both years, indicating a U-shaped average cost curve and a rising marginal cost curve.

Building Societies. In the United Kingdom, building societies are roughly equivalent to savings and loan associations in the United States. Johnston studied 217 such enterprises in the year 1953.[37] The companies were grouped into six size categories based on total annual revenue.

Johnston found that a U-shaped long-run cost curve existed for these enterprises. Cost in this study was measured as a ratio of management expenses to revenue. Middle-size societies were found to have the lowest ratio. However, when Johnston segregated the 217 observations into 149 societies with no branches and 68 with branches, somewhat different results appeared. Most of the firms in the former group were concentrated in the four lower size categories and most firms in the latter group were in the top four. When the nonbranch societies and the branch societies were analyzed separately, the former firms appeared to have a declining cost ratio whereas the companies with branches had a constant ratio. Thus, the appearance of a U-shaped average cost curve and, therefore, economies of scale at the low end and diseconomies of scale at the high end, were the result of two separate underlying patterns.

Electric Utilities. The electric utility industry has been a frequent target of economists studying cost curves. Output is fairly easily defined (electricity produced), and the United States has a large number of independently owned utilities of many different sizes. Since these companies must regularly deal with state regulatory commissions in rate cases, they collect large volumes of data pertaining to costs and revenues. Utilities have also been observed to have constant productivity improvements and technological progress. The study summarized here was performed using 1971 data for 74 utilities.[38] The companies included in the sample sold to residential, commercial, and industrial customers; had fossil steam capacity representing at least 80 percent of their total power; and generated at least 80 percent of their own power. Since the data are for 1971, this study rules out any effects of pollution control equipment on costs.

The authors studied different types of costs, but most important was the cost of electricity production. Although many independent variables were used to adjust for differences, the major costs were best described by a quadratic function, which lead to a U-shaped average cost curve. The cost coefficients were statistically highly significant. The authors identified the intervals for which

---

[36]Ibid., p. 325.

[37]J. Johnston, op. cit., pp. 103–5.

[38]David A. Huettner and John H. Landon, "Electric Utilities: Scale Economies and Diseconomies," *Southern Economic Journal*, April 1978, pp. 883–912.

economies of scale existed and the appropriate minimum cost point. They found that diseconomies of scale appeared beyond moderate firm size. Many earlier studies of utilities found economies of scale throughout the range of observations. This study, as well as another one for the year 1970,[39] found the possibility of scale diseconomies in firms of larger size.

Financial Institutions. A recent article reviewed some 13 studies that attempted to estimate economies of scale and economies of scope for credit unions, savings and loan associations, and commercial banks.[40] Economies of scale are defined as those associated with firm size, whereas economies of scope relate to the joint production of two or more products. "Economies of scale exist if per unit or average production costs decline as output rises. Economies of scope arise if two or more products can be jointly produced at a lower cost than is incurred in their independent production."[41] Each of the studies used a logarithmic function and employed similar measures of economies. The author summarized the results of these 13 studies as follows:

- Overall economies of scale appear to exist only at low levels of output, with diseconomies at larger output levels.
- There is no consistent evidence of global economies of scope.
- There is some evidence of cost complementarities (product-specific economies of scope).
- The results appear to exist generally across the three types of institutions studied as well as across different data sets and product and cost definitions.

Empirical Long-Run Cost Studies: Summary of Findings. Some of the studies just summarized show the possible existence of diseconomies of scale for larger firm and plant size. However, a majority of the empirically estimated functions suggest the existence of scale economies up to a point. As output increases to a substantial size, these economies rapidly disappear and are replaced by constant returns for long intervals of output. Most studies have not found the existence of declining average costs at very large quantities. And findings of diseconomies of scale for high rates of production are rather rare.

TWO OTHER METHODS OF LONG-RUN COST ESTIMATING. The use of regression analysis in long-run (as well as short-run) cost estimating involves the use of accounting data. At the beginning of the discussion of cost estimating, we issued a warning that accounting magnitudes may not correspond to economic measures. However, all the analyses just reviewed employed accounting data

---

[39] L. R. Christensen and W. H. Greene, "Economies of Scale in U.S. Electric Power Generation," *Journal of Political Economy,* 84, 4 (August 1976), pp. 655-76.

[40] Jeffrey A. Clark, "Economies of Scale and Scope at Depository Financial Institutions: A Review of the Literature," *Economic Review,* Federal Reserve Bank of Kansas City, September/October 1988, pp. 16–33.

[41] Ibid., p. 17.

and, through various adjustment procedures, attempted to make the numbers correspond more closely to the cost concepts meaningful to the economist. In addition, economists have tried to use methods that are not dependent on numbers drawn from companies' accounting records. Two techniques of analysis will be discussed briefly: the engineering cost method and the survivor technique.

Engineering Cost Estimates. Engineering costs are based on a thorough understanding of inputs and outputs and their relationships. Knowledgeable professionals will calculate the quantity of inputs needed to produce any quantity of outputs. These calculations are based on optimal assumptions (i.e., the largest output for a given combination of inputs). This is really a production function. From here it is a relatively easy step to apply monetary quantities to the inputs to arrive at costs.

The advantages of such a method are quite obvious. Technology is held constant. There are no problems of inflation. Problems of changing output mix are eliminated. As a matter of fact, such calculations are often made by corporations planning to introduce a new product. While the market research and product forecasting departments concentrate on preparing estimates of sales at different prices, cost estimators in a corporation (engineers and others) prepare estimates of costs for different levels of output.[42] Then members of the pricing department take all the available data and calculate profitability at different prices and levels of output. It is through this process that product prices are obtained.

Although the engineering cost estimating technique avoids some of the pitfalls of regression analysis, it suffers from some problems of its own. First of all, it arrives at cost estimates that are, for all intents and purposes, of a normative nature. The estimates represent what engineers and cost estimators believe cost should be, not necessarily what they actually will be. Since they are really forecasts, calculations may omit certain components that contribute to costs.[43] Further, most of the time, only direct output costs are estimated. Other costs that may be directly associated with the product (such as some portion of overhead and direct selling expenses) are not included, or if they are, it is through some rather arbitrary allocation. Often such estimates are made on the basis of pilot plant operations and do not consider actual production, which may be attended by bottlenecks and other problems, causing costs to differ from those estimated.

Generally, engineering cost estimates will show declining unit costs up to a point and substantially flat unit costs at higher production quantities. The possible existence of diseconomies of scale is usually ignored.

It is quite possible for a study to combine engineering cost estimates for some segments of costs with utilization of accounting data for others. Such an analysis was performed some years ago, when a group of economists at the Transporta-

---

[42]Care must be exercised here since these estimates often reflect the learning curve concept rather than the effect on costs of different rates of production per period.

[43]Engineers are at times somewhat optimistic about the costs they estimate.

tion Center at Northwestern University published a forecast of aircraft prices.[44] One important step in arriving at the forecast was the calculation of aircraft operating costs. These were computed for a large number of different types of aircraft and utilized both actual data and engineering estimates. Crew salaries were calculated from a number of union contracts and compared with historical data to arrive at an average. Maintenance costs were calculated from a formula supplied by the Air Transport Association. Fuel consumption was obtained from engineering curves produced by aircraft manufacturers and airlines, and reconciled with some actual published data. Other costs (employee benefits, landing fees, liability and property damage insurance) were estimated in similar ways. The resulting curves reflected direct operating costs per aircraft mile for a series of different stage length categories ranging from 0–200 miles to 2,500 miles and over. The resulting cost curves generally exhibited a downward slope up to the limit of the stage length that each of the aircraft could fly nonstop.

Survivorship Principle. A prominent American economist and Nobel Prize winner, George J. Stigler, developed an intriguing method for estimating long-run costs.[45] Stigler felt that the use of accounting data, with all their distortions and subsequent need for adjustments, made the validity of cost estimation based on such data questionable. His method was to observe an industry over time, categorize the firms in the industry by size (measured as a percent of total industry capacity or output), and then arrive at a conclusion regarding cost efficiency based on the relative growth or decline of these size categories. His results for the steel industry (using data for 1930, 1938, and 1951) showed that medium-size firms (defined as between 2.5 percent and 25 percent of industry capacity) appeared to have gained in share of total industry output over the 21-year period, from 35 percent to 46 percent of total, whereas small firms (less than 2.5 percent of capacity) and large firms (actually just one firm, with over 25 percent of capacity) lost market share. Stigler concluded the existence of a U-shaped long-run average cost curve whose path first showed net economies of scale, then constant returns, and finally diseconomies of scale. Figure 10.9 illustrates Stigler's conclusions.

This approach is intuitively appealing due to its simplicity and avoidance of unreliable data. However, it also suffers some serious limitations. It is of no help in measuring costs for planning purposes. The survivor technique merely tells us which company size appears to be more efficient; it says nothing about relative costs. Further, it implicitly assumes that the industry is highly competitive, so that survival and prosperity are solely a function of efficient use of resources and not of market power or the erection of barriers to entry. Changing technology and inflation over a long span can also cause distortions. As time passes, the structure of an industry can change in such a way that firms of certain size are favored over others.

[44]Stephen P. Sobotka, Paul G. Keat, Constance Schnabel, and Margaret Wiesenfelder, *Prices of Used Commercial Aircraft, 1959–1965,* Evanston, Ill.: Transportation Center at Northwestern University, 1959.

[45]George J. Stigler, "The Economies of Scale," *Journal of Law and Economics,* 1, 1 (October 1958), pp. 54–81.

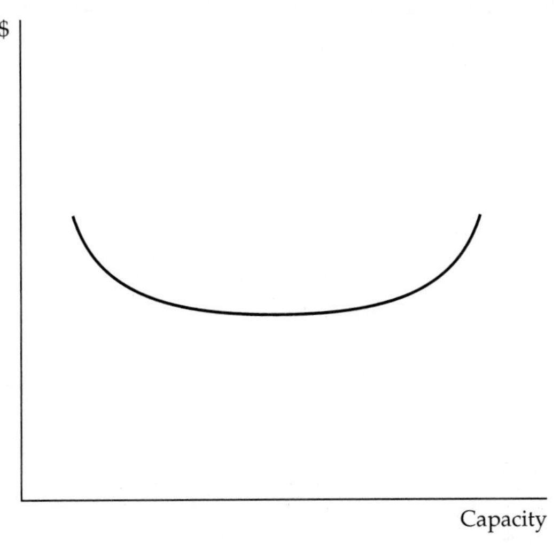

Figure 10.9 Average Cost Curve for Steel Industry

Although Stigler's analysis of the steel industry showed a U-shaped cost curve, he could not obtain similar results for the automobile industry, where the survivor cost curve showed declining and constant portions but there was no evidence of diseconomies of scale at high production quantities.

The Solution

Jillian Corey returned to her office after her meeting with Donald Aiken and started looking at the plant reports he had given her. The data were for a period in 1989 for some 36 plants. She thought that she could obtain information for other periods and construct a time series regression for several plants, but then she decided against this method. First of all, the number of periods available differed from plant to plant. Also, a large number of plants had undergone modernization rather recently, so the data may not be comparable over time. And, most important, Aiken was interested in the "optimal-size plant" and a planning- type cost curve. This indicated that she should conduct her analysis on a cross-sectional basis. She decided to use the data for one period for all the plants in the report. Thus, she would obtain a long-run cost curve for different plants of different sizes at the same point in time.

Her first calculation was to perform a simple straight-line regression of the form:

$$TC = a + bQ$$

(Continued)

After all, many economic studies had shown a relatively straight-line relationship with no existence of diminishing returns (increasing costs). Very quickly she obtained her first results:[46]

$$R^2 = .624$$
$$a = 0.879$$
$$b = 0.276$$
$$t = 7.51$$

These were good results. Emboldened, Jillian decided to test whether a cubic function would give her better results than the straight-line function. The new equation was:

$$TC = a + bQ + cQ^2 + dQ^3$$

Her results were really quite satisfactory:

$R^2 = .700$
F-statistic = 24.87

	a	b	c	d
Estimate	0.078	0.891	−0.096	0.004
t-test		3.653	−2.240	1.910

The coefficient of determination had increased, the F-statistic was quite significant, and t-test (except for the d coeffecient) did not look bad either. There was one other important characteristic Jillian did not fail to notice. The c coefficient was negative, whereas b and d were positive. This indicated that the total cost curve would first increase at a decreasing rate, and then at an increasing rate—a picture of the economist's theoretical cost curve and a U-shaped unit cost curve.

But Jillian had learned that it costs less to produce canned sodas than bottled sodas. Since she knew the percent of cans to total production for each of the plants, she decided to include this percentage as another independent variable, with the following results:

$R^2 = .828$
F-statistic = 37.45

	a	b	c	d	e
Estimate	−0.177	1.316	−0.146	0.006	−1.575
t-test		6.358	−4.229	3.597	−4.823

This was another substantial improvement. The increase in R^2 was dramatic, and so was the improvement in the t-statistics. The coefficient signs were correct, including the e coefficient, representing percentage of cans, which indicated that production costs would decrease as the proportion of canned soda production increased. Therefore, she felt fully justified to include the percentage of can production in her analysis.

This certainly represented a good day's work, Jillian concluded. She planned to incorporate additional factors and adjustments the next day to ascertain whether she could further improve the results. Then she would draw graphs based on her results and identify for Donald Aiken the approximate optimal size for a plant.

[46]The results in this solution were obtained using numbers furnished in confidence by a large company.

Summary

Developing theories of production functions and cost functions is an important skill for any economist. However, before these theories can be accepted (or rejected), economists must subject their ideas and hypotheses to empirical testing.

Production and cost studies exist in abundance in economic literature. We summarized a number of these studies in this chapter, and we discussed the advantages and drawbacks of various methods of analysis. With some exceptions, economists have generally utilized the regression method to perform their empirical inquiries.

Production Functions

Most studies of production functions have used an exponential expression that results in a monotonically increasing output as inputs are added. This model was introduced by Cobb and Douglas in the 1920s. The original studies utilized the time series method of analysis, but researchers soon switched to cross-sectional regression, which they found more useful. The Cobb-Douglas function permits the investigation of both marginal product in short-run situations (with the presence of a fixed factor) and returns to scale in the long run. It is difficult to summarize the large number of studies conducted over the years, but the results generally indicate that constant returns to scale are the rule in manufacturing industries in the United States as well as in other countries.

Cost Functions

Accounting data have generally been used to investigate short-run and long-run cost functions. These data present the researcher with a host of problems since the economic and accounting definitions of costs can differ substantially. Also, depending on how the data are collected, adjustments for price changes, geographical differentials, and other variations must be made.

Time series analysis has largely been used to estimate short-run costs, whereas the cross-sectional regression technique appears more suited for long-run cost estimation.

A large majority of these studies have concluded that marginal cost in the short run is relatively constant. In the long run economies of scale predominate at the low end of production, and at higher output, constant returns to scale appear to exist.

The upward-sloping—U-shaped—average and marginal cost curves postulated by economic theory tend to be the exception in empirical findings. Although such results should make economists pause and reexamine some of their theoretical conclusions, the studies have generally been conducted in such a way that the possibility of eventually rising marginal costs and diseconomies of scale cannot be discounted.

Some economists prefer not to use accounting data in their inquiries. Thus, two other methods of cost estimation were briefly described in the chapter. Engineering cost analysis is based on the expert knowledge of the relationship between inputs and outputs and standard costs. It avoids the use of accounting information and does not run into the problem of adjusting for changing technology and inflation. The survivorship method bases its findings on the change in the proportion of total industry output produced by firms of different size categories. It concludes that the more efficient firms will gain share of production at the expense of less efficient ones.

Important Concepts

Cobb-Douglas production function: A power function in which total quantity produced is the result of the product of inputs raised to some power (e.g., $Q = aL^bK^c$).

Engineering cost estimating: A method of estimating long-run costs. Professionals familiar with production facilities calculate optimal combinations of inputs needed to produce given quantities of output. Monetary values are then assigned to obtain cost.

Estimation of long-run cost functions: Analysis that assumes that all factors, especially capital, are variable. Cross-sectional regression analysis is customarily employed in the estimation.

Estimation of short-run cost functions: An analysis in which certain factors are assumed to be fixed during the period analyzed. Time series regression analysis is customarily employed in the estimation.

Power function: A mathematical function of the form $Y = X^n$, where the index n is a fixed number and X takes positive values continuously.

Survivorship technique: A method for estimating long-run cost curves. The proportion of total industry output by firms of different sizes is observed over a period of time. That size segment of the industry that gains in proportion of industry output over time is deemed most efficient (lowest-cost).

Questions

1. Write a production function equation that expresses the existence of diminishing marginal returns. How will this equation differ from one that shows both increasing and decreasing marginal returns?
2. In a power function $Q = aV^b$ how can you tell whether diminishing marginal returns are present?
3. Discuss the properties of the Cobb-Douglas function, $Q = aL^bK^{1-b}$. What conceptual change occurs when the equation is changed to $Q = aL^bK^c$?
4. What are the two statistical methods most frequently used to estimate production functions? What are the advantages and disadvantages of each of these two methods? Is each method more applicable under different circumstances?
5. Why is it frequently assumed in the calculation of long-run production functions that returns to scale are constant?
6. Design a study of a production function for a steel mill. Which variables would you use, and what statistical method would you select?
7. When a Cobb-Douglas function with at least two inputs shows the existence of constant returns to scale, it implies that the marginal product of each input is diminishing. Ture or false? Explain.

8. Discuss the estimation of short-run cost functions. Which regression method is most frequently used, and what are some of the problems a researcher will encounter? What adjustment factors may have to be employed?
9. Discuss the estimation of long-run cost functions. Which regression method is most frequently used, and what are some of the problems a researcher will encounter? What adjustment factors may have to be employed?
10. Discuss the potential shapes of cost functions.
11. A majority of short-run cost studies have found the existence of straight-line total cost curves and constant (or even decreasing) marginal costs. Do these results necessarily invalidate economic theory, which postulates the existence of increasing marginal costs?
12. Distinguish economies of scale and economies of scope.
13. Comment briefly on the following methods of cost estimation.
    a. Engineering costs
    b. Survivorship principle

    Discuss the strengths and shortcomings of these methods and the circumstances under which each can be applied.

Problems

1. The economist for the ABC Truck Manufacturing Corporation has calculated a production function for the manufacture of their medium-size trucks as follows:

$$Q = 1.3L^{0.75}K^{0.3}$$

where Q is number of trucks produced per week, L is number of labor hours per day, and K is the daily usage of capital investment.

a. Does the equation exhibit increasing, constant, or decreasing returns to scale? Why?
b. How many trucks will be produced per week with the following amounts of labor and capital?

Labor	*Capital*
100	50
120	60
150	75
200	100
300	150

c. If capital and labor both are increased by 10 percent, what will be the percentage increase in quantity produced?
d. Assume that only labor increases by 10 percent. What will be the percentage increase in production? What does this result imply about marginal product?
e. Assume that only capital increases by 10 percent. What will be the percentage increase in production?

f. How would your answers change if the production function were $Q = 1.3L^{0.7}K^{0.3}$ instead? What are the implications of this production function?

2. The Noble Widget Corporation produces just one product, widgets. The company's new economist has calculated a short-run production function as follows:

$$Q = 7V + 0.6V^2 - 0.1V^3$$

where Q is number of widgets produced per day and V is number of production workers working an eight-hour day.

a. Develop a production schedule with V equaling 1 to 10.
b. Calculate average and marginal products.
c. Draw a graph.

3. Suppose Noble's production function (see problem 2) is as follows:

$$Q = 7V - 0.5V^2$$

where Q is number of widgets produced per day and V is number of production workers working an eight-hour day.

a. Develop a production schedule with V equaling 1 to 10.
b. Calculate average and marginal products.
c. Draw a graph.
d. Discuss the difference between the form of the production function in this problem and the form in problem 2. Discuss, among other things, the implications for the three stages of production.

4. The International Calculator Company of Hong Kong produces hand-held calculators in its plant. It tries to keep the number of workers in the plant constant, so that the only variable factor that can be measured is materials. Over the last seven monthly periods, the data for materials and quantity produced were the following:

Materials	*Quantity*
70	450
60	430
80	460
95	490
77	465
100	550
85	490

a. Calculate a Cobb-Douglas production function of the form $Q = aM^b$.
b. Discuss the important properties of your results.
c. What is the marginal product of materials?

5. The Brady Corporation has 11 plants located around the world. In a recent year, the data for each plant gave the number of labor hours (in thousands), capital (total net plant assets, in millions), and total quantity produced:

Capital	*Labor*	*Quantity*
30	250	245
34	270	240
44	300	300
50	320	320
70	350	390
76	400	440
84	440	520
86	440	520
104	450	580
110	460	600
116	460	600

The plants all operate at a similar level of technology, so that a production function can be derived from the data.

a. Use a Cobb-Douglas production function to calculate a regression, and discuss the important characteristics of your results, such as the form of the equation, R^2, and the statistical significance of the coefficients.
b. Calculate the estimated production for each plant.
c. Does the result indicate constant, decreasing, or increasing returns to scale?
d. What are the elasticities of production of labor and of capital? What is the meaning of the elasticities?
e. Is the marginal product of labor decreasing?

6. Over the last 50 years or so, many studies of cost curves have been published. The results of two of these are summarized here. In each case, interpret the equation and discuss the shapes of the total cost curve, the marginal cost curve, and the average cost curve.
   a. A study of a light plant over a six-month period resulted in the following regression equation:

$$Y = 16.68 + 0.125X + 0.00439X^2$$

where Y = Total fuel cost
X = Output

   b. One of the original cost studies was an analysis of the steel industry by Theodore Yntema. The results were based on annual data for 12 years:

$$Y = 182{,}100{,}000 + 55.73X$$

where Y = Total cost
X = Weighted output, in tons

A time series analysis usually indicates a short-run cost study. Do you believe that a 12-year period is too long? Explain.[47]

[47]See J. Johnston, op. cit., Chapter 5.

7. You have been presented with the following cost data and asked to fit a statistical cost function:

Quantity	*Total Cost*
10	104.0
20	107.0
30	109.0
40	111.5
50	114.5
60	118.0
70	123.0
80	128.5
90	137.0
100	150.0

   a. Plot the data on a graph, and a draw a freehand curve that best fits the data.
   b. Fit three possible statistical cost functions to the data. Use straight-line, quadratic, and cubic formulas. Do the results confirm the curve you drew in *a*?
   c. Discuss the statistical results you obtained in *b*. Include in your discussion R^2, the coefficients, and the statistical significance of the coefficients.
   d. If the data represent 10 months of production for one plant of a specific company, would you consider this to be a short-run analysis?
   e. How would your answer to part *d* change if you were told that the data represent 10 different plants during a particular month of the year?
8. The economist for the Grand Corporation has estimated the company's cost function, using time series data, to be

$$TC = 50 + 16Q - 2Q^2 + 0.2Q^3$$

where TC = Total cost
Q = Quantity produced per period

   a. Plot this curve for quantities 1 to 10.
   b. Calculate the average total cost, average variable cost, and marginal cost for these quantities, and plot them on another graph.
   c. Discuss your results in terms of decreasing, constant, and increasing marginal costs. Does Grand's cost function illustrate all of these?
9. Discuss the following three cost functions:

$$TC = 20 + 4Q$$

$$TC = 20 + 2Q + 0.5Q^2$$

$$TC = 20 + 4Q - 0.1Q^2$$

a. Calculate all cost curves:

- Total cost
- Total fixed cost
- Total variable cost
- Average total cost
- Average fixed cost
- Average variable cost
- Marginal cost

b. Plot these curves on graphs.

c. Compare the shapes of these curves and discuss their characteristics. (Particularly interesting should be the last cost function, whose shape is often found in engineering cost studies.)

CHAPTER 11

Market Structure and Output and Pricing Decisions

The Situation

For the job of product manager for the new soft drink, Joan Faranda, the senior vice president of CPD (Consumer Products Division), did not want a new MBA fresh out of the company's management training program. There was simply too much at stake to entrust the job to a rookie. She firmly believed that the job of bringing the new product to market should be given to a seasoned manager with a proven record of accomplishments. Finding a person with the necessary qualifications from within the company was not Going to be easy, because all successful product managers were rapidly promoted to higher management positions. Joan could have used a "headhunter" firm to find an outside person, but she preferred to give someone within the company a chance to make the project work.

"I've got just the person for you," the executive vice president exclaimed at lunch one day. "There is a real sharp manager over in market research. I think he was the one who did the background study on the soft drink market. It would be nice to give him a chance to put his ideas into practice."

The person recommended for this critical job was none other than Frank Robinson, the head of the forecasting department. (See Chapter 6.) In his first meeting with Joan after being hired, Frank was briefed on the job. "Because this new product is so important to the growth strategy of our firm," Joan said, "and because of your experience and accomplishments, we decided that we wanted you rather than one of the outside people who were considered for the job.

"One of the first tasks you should pursue is an analysis of the optimal price of this beverage. Tell us what price we should charge to maximize our profit in this new venture. The CEO told us the other day that the Wall Street analysts were questioning our judgment in getting into such

(Continued)

a crowded and highly competitive market. We need to prove as fast as possible that we made the right decision, so we want to maximize our profit in this venture in as short a time as possible.

"As always, the management committee has the final say on the price of the new beverage, just as for all our products and services. But don't get discouraged. As I know from the other products that I've managed, pricing is a very useful exercise, because it forces one to bring together all the different elements of the business. The market research that you have already done on this product will provide you with a quantitative estimate of the demand as well as a general competitive analysis of the entire beverage industry. Our production people and cost accountants will give you the cost estimates. It will be up to you to put everything together to arrive at a suitable price for the new beverage."

Introduction

In every pricing and output decision, there are three basic factors to consider: cost, demand, and market structure.[1] We have already examined cost in Chapter 8 and demand in Chapters 3 and 4. Now we are ready to combine these two elements with the third, market structure, into a complete model of economic decision making concerning the price and output levels for the profit-maximizing firm. We will begin with an analysis of market structure, of which there are four basic types: perfect competition, monopoly, monopolistic competition, and oligopoly. After the characteristics of each have been examined, we will proceed to analyze the pricing and output decisions that a firm must make in each of these types of markets, using the economic theory of cost and demand. We will conclude this chapter with the key implications that economic theory has to offer managers such as Frank Robinson in their decisions regarding the pricing and output levels of their products.

Market Structure

Figure 11.1 formally outlines the ways in which economists divide up the different types of competition in the marketplace. The most important distinction is the degree to which firms in these markets exercise control over the price of their products. In the market labeled *perfect competition*, for example, it is virtually impossible for a firm to set the price of its product. There are so many firms in the market that buyers do not need to rely on any one firm to meet their demand. In other words, if a single firm decided to restrict its supply in order to extract a higher price, customers would simply turn to other sellers, who would gladly sell them the product at the going market price.

[1]Marketing people sometimes refer to these factors as the "three *C*s of pricing": cost, customers, and competition.

You might be thinking that a seller could exercise control over price by adding some sort of perceived value to the product. For instance, special packaging, added service, or simply "service with a smile" might make customers willing to pay more. But in a perfectly competitive market all products are standardized. That is, there is no way in which a firm can distinguish its products from those of all the other firms in the market.

How many times have you bought an item at a store only to find out the next day that you could have bought it for less at another store? Your first reaction might have been anger at the first store for charging you more. But a store can do this if there are people like you who do not have complete information about the selling prices of the item at various stores. As long as it is possible for you to check the prices at all stores, you really cannot blame the first store. This is why economists include the third characteristic of perfect competition cited in Figure 11.1.[2] "Complete information" among consumers would make it impossible for

Perfect Competition

1. Large number of sellers and buyers
2. Standardized product
3. Complete information about market prices
4. Complete freedom of entry into and exit out of markets

Monopoly

1. One-firm industry
2. Unique product (no close substitutes)
3. Absolute control over supply within a price range
4. Entry into industry restricted by law or very difficult in practice

Monopolistic Competition

1. Large number of sellers acting independently
2. Product differentiation
3. Partial (and limited) control over product price
4. Entry and exit relatively easy

Oligopoly

1. Relatively few sellers
2. Either standardized or differentiated products
3. Control over price closely circumscribed by the interdependence of the competing firms
4. Relatively difficult to enter

Figure 11.1 The Four Basic Market Structures

[2]To be sure, you might have decided against shopping around for prices at different stores all over town. In this case, economists would say that, as a rational consumer, you had decided not to incur the "opportunity cost" of comparison shopping. Indeed, if the opportunity cost of the time spent going from store to store is added to the "lowest price in town," you could actually end up paying a much higher economic price for the product. If gasoline, parking fees, and other transportation costs are added, the price would be still higher.

this situation to occur. Buyers simply would know what everyone was selling the product for, and everyone would end up selling it for the same—or a very similar—price.

The fourth characteristic of a perfectly competitive market is "free entry and exit." This means that in a perfectly competitive market there are no legal or practical barriers to keep firms from entering or leaving the market. A patent is an example of a legal barrier to entry. Another is the monopoly rights granted by the government to a public utility. Import restrictions are also a form of market barrier to entry—in this case, against foreign sellers.

Examples of practical barriers to entry can be found in such markets as the American automobile manufacturing and breakfast food industries. High start-up capital requirements and strong brand identification by the general public have made it difficult for a firm to enter the American automobile industry—although foreign competition, particularly the Japanese, have certainly proved that it can be done. Strong brand identification and entrenched market distribution channels (e.g., supermarket shelf space garnered by food brokers) have made it difficult for any manufacturer of processed food to come into the breakfast foods market. In a related example, consider the millions of dollars that Procter & Gamble had to spend in advertising and promotion to bring its orange juice Citrus Hill into the market to do battle with the established brands Tropicana and Minute Maid.[3] In a perfectly competitive market, none of these barriers would exist.

"Free exit" may at first seem a rather strange characteristic of a perfectly competitive market. But consider some recent government efforts to keep firms from going into bankruptcy. The bailout of the Continental Illinois Bank by the Federal Reserve and the Federal Deposit Insurance Corporation is one example. The guaranteeing of bank loans to the Chrysler Corporation is another. "Perfect competition" gives firms the chance to earn profits but implies that firms that cannot make any profit must face the possibility of going out of business.

In the other three market types—monopoly, monopolistic competition, and oligopoly—sellers can exercise varying degrees of control over the prices of their products. A closer look at the characteristics of these markets in Figure 11.1 will indicate why it is possible for these firms to enjoy what economists call "market power," or the power that a firm has to set its own price.

In the case of a *monopoly* market, there is only "one game in town." The single seller in the market has no competitor offering a close substitute for its product. Public utilities such as electric and water companies immediately come to mind. But the only jewelry store in a shopping center or a "last chance" gas station at the edge of the Nevada desert also enjoys a monopoly status.

Monopolistic competition is a hybrid market. It is considered competitive because there are many sellers and because it is relatively easy to enter this market. But it is monopolistic because sellers try to differentiate their products as much as possible from those of their competitors. The best examples of this

---

[3]The press has reported that Procter & Gamble may leave this market. See "P&G May Soon Peddle Something New: Its Food and Beverage Division," *Wall Street Journal*, June 11, 1991.

kind of market can be found in small businesses. Small retail stores (e.g., boutiques, luggage stores, shoe stores, stationery shops), restaurants, repair shops, laundries, and beauty parlors all compete in this type of market. One Chinese restaurant may attempt to differentiate itself by offering a cuisine from a relatively unknown region of China. A repair shop may try to distinguish itself from its competitors by opening seven days a week. If consumers perceive these differences to be important enough, these retail establishments may be able to charge a higher price than their competitors.

Oligopoly markets have relatively few sellers who are large in size (as measured by such indicators as market share, assets, and number of employees). A large part of the manufacturing sector in the United States is structured in this way. The makers of processed foods, appliances, computers, chemicals, cars, steel, personal care products, soft drinks, and airlines with national routes all compete in oligopolistic markets. These firms may either sell standardized products (e.g., aluminum, plastics, chemicals) or differentiated ones (e.g., cars, soap, breakfast cereals). Therefore, the key factor that gives rise to their market power is size.

Pricing and Output Decisions in Perfect Competition

The Basic Business Decision

Imagine a firm that is considering entry into a perfectly competitive market. Given the existing market price, the firm must decide on whether it is desirable to enter this market. This decision can be divided into a series of questions.

1. Given the market price, how much should we produce?
2. In producing such an amount, how much of a profit will we earn (or how much of a loss will we incur)?
3. Should we be in this market at the present time? What are the long-run prospects for competing in this market?

Perhaps even the output decision may seem superfluous. After all, is not the firm so small that it can sell as much as it wants without affecting the market price? Yes, but although the market price does not vary with an individual firm's level of output, the *unit cost* of production most certainly does. Think back to our discussion in Chapter 8 about the cost of additional units of output. If we assume that marginal cost rises as output increases (thanks to the law of diminishing returns), then it seems reasonable to expect that eventually the extra cost per unit will exceed the selling price of the product. At this point, it no longer would make sense for a profit-maximizing firm to produce, because each additional unit sold would cost the firm more to produce than the price at which it could sell the product. Much more will be said about this shortly. But the point to emphasize here is that there is indeed a limit as to how much a perfectly competitive firm should produce in the short run. It is up to the firm to determine what this limit is.

Because the perfectly competitive firm must operate in a market in which it has no control over selling price, there may be times when the price does not fully cover the unit cost of production (i.e., average cost). Thus, a firm must assess the extent of its losses in relation to the alternative of discontinuing production. In the long run, a firm that continues to incur losses must eventually leave the market. But in the short run, it may be economically justifiable to remain in the market, with the expectation of better times ahead. This is because in the short run, certain costs must be borne regardless of whether the firm operates. These fixed costs must be weighed against the losses incurred by remaining in business. It is reasonable to expect that a firm will remain in business if its losses are less than its fixed costs—at least in the short run.

Key Assumptions of the Perfectly Competitive Market

As you are well aware, it is critical to know the assumptions made in the development of an economic model. Let us summarize the key assumptions made in analyzing the firm's output decision in perfect competition.

1. The firm operates in a perfectly competitive market and therefore is a price taker.
2. The firm makes the distinction between the short run and the long run.
3. The firm's objective is to maximize its profit in the short run. If it cannot earn a profit, then it seeks to minimize its loss. (See Chapter 2 for a review of the goals of a firm.)
4. The firm includes its opportunity cost of operating in a particular market as part of its total cost of production.

All four assumptions have been discussed earlier, some in greater detail than others. But it might be useful to review certain aspects of these assumptions before proceeding to numerical and graphical examples.

For the economic analysis of a firm's output and pricing decisions to have a unique solution, the firm must establish a single, clear-cut objective. This objective is the maximization of profit in the short run. If the firm has other objectives, such as the maximization of revenue in the short run, the output that it would select would differ from the one based on this model. (This point will be illustrated in a later section of this chapter.)

The consideration of opportunity cost in the cost structure of the firm is vital to this decision-making model. The firm must check whether the going market price enables it to earn a revenue that covers not only its out-of-pocket costs, but also the costs incurred by forgoing alternative activities. A brief numerical example should help to convey this point.

Suppose the manager of a "stop and shop" convenience store wants to own and operate a store of her own. She knows she will have to leave her job and use $50,000 of her savings (currently earning 10 percent interest). A statement of the projected cost of operating in the first year follows.

Cost of goods sold	$300,000
General and administrative expenses	150,000
Total accounting cost	$450,000
Forgone salary for being a store manager	45,000
Forgone interest earnings from savings (at 10% interest)	5,000
Total opportunity cost	$50,000
Total economic cost (total accounting cost plus total opportunity cost)	$500,000

To keep this example as simple as possible, we did not include depreciation and taxes.

Suppose this budding entrepreneur forecasts revenue to be $500,000 in the first year of operation. From an accounting standpoint, her profit would be $50,000 ($500,000 − $450,000). But from an economic standpoint, her profit would be zero, since the revenue would just equal her total economic cost. Certainly, there would be nothing wrong with "breaking even" in the economic sense of the term, because this indicates that the firm's revenue is sufficient to cover both its out-of-pocket expense and its opportunity cost. Another way to view this situation is to note that when a firm "breaks even" in the economic sense, it is actually earning an accounting profit equal to its opportunity cost. In other words, if this entrepreneur's annual revenue is $500,000, she will earn an accounting profit that offsets the opportunity cost of going into business for herself. It is clear why we refer to this situation in economic analysis as one in which the firm is earning "normal" profit.

The logical extension of this use of the term *normal* can be seen in situations in which the entrepreneur's revenue is higher or lower than $500,000. Suppose her revenue is $550,000. In this case, she will earn a profit of $50,000 ($550,000 − $500,000). We refer to this sum as "above normal," "pure," or "economic" profit because it represents an amount in excess of the out-of-pocket cost plus the opportunity cost of running the business.

In the case where revenue is less than economic cost, clearly a loss is incurred. However, this economic loss might well coincide with a firm's actually earning an accounting profit. For example, suppose our entrepreneur's revenue is $480,000. The economic loss would be $20,000 ($480,000 − $500,000), but the accounting profit would be $30,000 ($480,000 − $450,000). Figure 11.2 summarizes the three scenarios discussed above.

With these assumptions in mind, we are now ready to discuss the decision-making process. Suppose that in determining whether to operate in a particular market at some level of output, the firm is faced with the short-run total cost structure presented in Table 11.1. (For convenience, the cost data are the same as those first presented in Table 8.2.)

Let us assume that the market price is $110. Given this price, the firm is free to produce as much as or as little as it desires. The demand, total revenue, marginal revenue, and average revenue schedules for this firm are shown in Table 11.2. Notice that because the price to the firm remains unchanged regardless

	Normal Profit	*Economic Profit*	*Economic Loss*
Revenue	$500,000	$550,000	$480,000
Accounting cost	450,000	450,000	450,000
Opportunity cost	50,000	50,000	50,000
Profit	–0–	$50,000	($20,000)
	Note: Accounting profit of $50,000 equals the opportunity cost of $50,000	Accounting profit of $100,000 exceeds the opportunity cost of $50,000	Accounting profit of $30,000 is less than the opportunity cost of $50,000

Figure 11.2 Normal Profit, Economic Profit, and Economic Loss

of its output level, the total, marginal, and average revenue schedules do not resemble the schedules analyzed in Chapter 4. As a price taker, the firm faces a demand curve that is "perfectly elastic." That is, customers are willing to buy as much as the firm is willing to sell *at the going market price*. This special type of demand curve can be seen in Figure 11.3. Moreover, the firm receives the same marginal revenue from the sale of each additional unit of product. This marginal revenue is, of course, simply the price of the product. Recall that the price is tantamount to average or per-unit revenue. Hence, a perfectly competitive firm's demand is also its marginal and its average revenue over the

Table 11.1 Total and Per-Unit Short-Run Cost

Quantity (Q)	*Total Fixed Cost (TFC)*	*Total Variable Cost (TVC)*	*Total Cost (TC)*	*Average Fixed Cost (AFC)*	*Average Variable Cost (AVC)*	*Average Total Cost (AC)*	*Marginal Cost (MC)*
0	100	0.00	100.00				
							55.70
1	100	55.70	155.70	100.00	55.70	155.70	
							49.90
2	100	105.60	205.60	50.00	52.80	102.80	
							48.30
3	100	153.90	253.90	33.33	51.30	84.63	
							50.90
4	100	204.80	304.80	25.00	51.20	76.20	
							57.70
5	100	262.50	362.50	20.00	52.50	72.50	
							68.70
6	100	331.20	431.20	16.67	55.20	71.87	
							83.90
7	100	415.10	515.10	14.29	59.30	73.59	
							103.30
8	100	518.40	618.40	12.50	64.80	77.30	
							126.90
9	100	645.30	745.30	11.11	71.70	82.81	
							154.70
10	100	800.00	900.00	10.00	80.00	90.00	
							186.70
11	100	986.70	1086.70	9.09	89.70	98.79	
							222.90
12	100	1209.60	1309.60	8.33	100.80	109.13	

Table 11.2 Revenue Schedules

Quantity	*Price (AR)*	*TR*	*MR*
0	110	0	
1	110	110	110
2	110	220	110
3	110	330	110
4	110	440	110
5	110	550	110
6	110	660	110
7	110	770	110
8	110	880	110
9	110	990	110
10	110	1,100	110
11	110	1,210	110
12	110	1,320	110

range of output being considered. Note in Figure 11.3 that the demand curve is also labeled "AR" and "MR."

Figure 11.4 compares the perfectly elastic demand curve with the typical downward-sloping linear demand curve used in Chapter 4. It also shows the total revenue curves in relation to the two types of demand curves. As is the case with perfect elasticity, a downward-sloping demand curve is the same as the average revenue curve, because P by definition is equal to AR. However, recall that a linear, downward-sloping demand curve is associated with a marginal revenue curve that is twice as steep. In addition, this type of demand results in

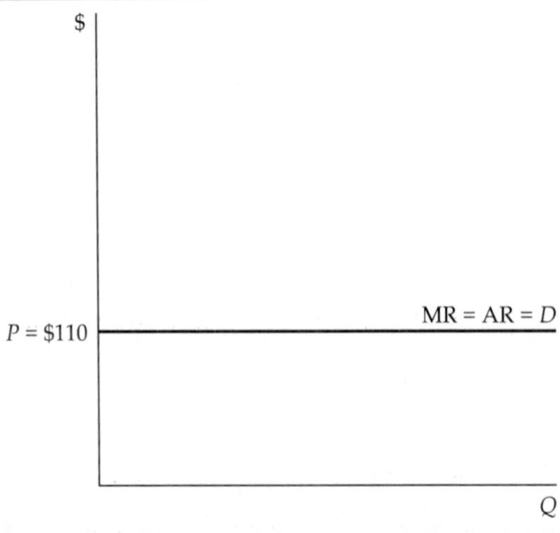

Figure 11.3 Perfectly Elastic Demand Curve

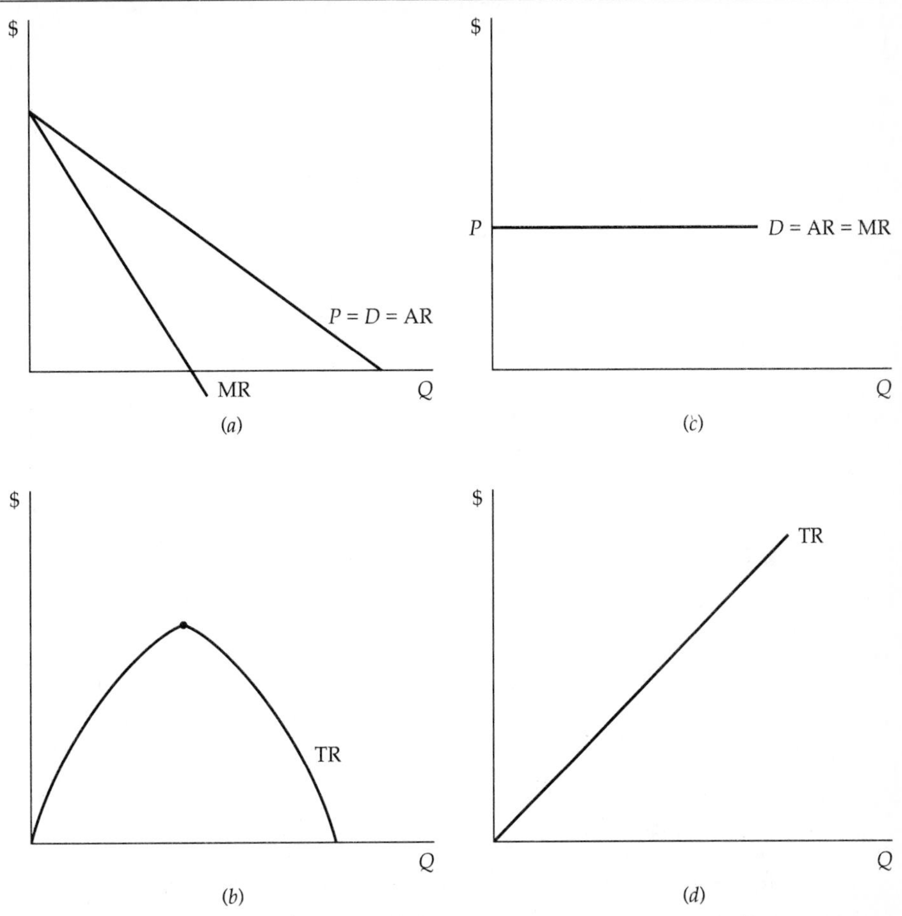

Figure 11.4 Different Types of Demand Curves and Associated Total Revenue Curves

a nonlinear total revenue curve that reaches a maximum at the point at which marginal revenue equals zero (see Figure 11.4*b*). In contrast, as shown in Figure 11.4*d*, there is no limit to the amount of total revenue that firms can garner in a perfectly competitive market. The more a firm produces, the more revenue it will obtain. The limit to its output is based on revenue in relation to the firm's cost of production, that is, the profit earned at various levels of output.

Armed with its cost and revenue schedules, all that a firm needs to do is to combine the sets of information to find the level of output that maximizes its profit (or minimizes its loss). We will see how this is done in the next section.

The Total Revenue–Total Cost Approach to Selecting the Optimal Output Level

The most logical approach to selecting the optimal level of output is to compare the total revenue with the total cost schedules and find that level of output that either maximizes the firm's profit or minimizes its loss. This is shown in

Table 11.3 Cost and Revenue Schedules Used to Determine Optimal Level of Output

Quantity (Q)	*Price (P)*	*Total Revenue (TR)*	*Total Fixed Cost (TFC)*	*Total Variable Cost (TVC)*	*Total Cost (TC)*	*Total Profit (π)*
0	110	0	100	0.00	100.00	−100.00
1	110	110	100	55.70	155.70	−45.70
2	110	220	100	105.60	205.60	14.40
3	110	330	100	153.90	253.90	76.10
4	110	440	100	204.80	304.80	135.20
5	110	550	100	262.50	362.50	187.50
6	110	660	100	331.20	431.20	228.80
7	110	770	100	415.10	515.10	254.90
8	**110**	**880**	**100**	**518.40**	**618.40**	**261.60**
9	110	990	100	645.30	745.30	244.70
10	110	1100	100	800.00	900.00	200.00
11	110	1210	100	986.70	1086.70	123.30
12	110	1320	100	1209.60	1309.60	10.40

Table 11.3 and Figure 11.5. As can be seen in the table and the figure, this output level is 8, at which the firm would be earning a maximum profit of $261.60. Graphically, this output level can be seen as the one that maximizes the distance between the total revenue curve and the total cost curve. By convention, this point has been labled Q^*.

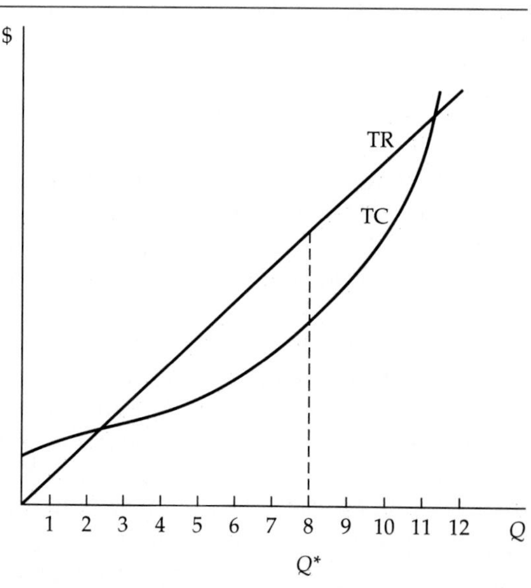

Figure 11.5 Determining Optimal Output from Cost and Revenue Curves—Perfect Competition

The Marginal Revenue–Marginal Cost Approach to Finding the Optimal Output Level

Marginal analysis is at the heart of the economic analysis of the firm. Indeed, once we explain how marginal analysis is used by the firm to determine its optimal level of output, we will rely primarily on this type of analysis throughout the rest of this chapter.

Table 11.4 presents the cost and revenue data on a per-unit basis. The marginal revenue and marginal cost columns contain the key numbers the firm must use to decide on its optimal level of output. Let us examine the marginal revenue and the marginal cost associated with additional units of output, starting with zero units. As you can see in Table 11.4, the first unit would result in additional revenue of $110 and cost the firm an additional $55.70 to make. The second unit would add another $110 to revenue and would add $49.90 to the firm's total cost. Continuing on in this manner, we observe that it would be worth-while for the firm to produce more as long as the added benefit of each unit produced and sold (i.e., the marginal revenue) exceeds the added cost (i.e., the marginal cost). Because the marginal revenue is equal to the existing market price, it does not change as output increases. However, because of the law of diminishing returns, the firm's marginal cost begins to increase with the fourth unit of output. From that point on, each additional unit of output costs *increasingly more* to produce. Between zero and eight units of output, we observe that marginal revenue exceeds marginal cost. However, production of the ninth unit of output will cost the firm more than the revenue that it would add (MC = $126.90 and MR = $110). In Table 11.4, MR = MC actually occurs between eight and nine units of output, but we use eight as the approximate level of optimal output.

Using the relationship between marginal revenue and marginal cost to decide on the optimal level of output is referred to in economics as the *profit-maximizing* (or *loss-minimizing*) rule. The rule is stated as follows:

> A firm that desires to maximize its profit (or minimize its loss) should produce a level of output at which the additional revenue received from the last unit is equal to the additional cost of producing that unit. In short, MR = MC.

Table 11.4 shows that by following the MR = MC rule and producing eight units of output, the firm would earn a profit of $261.60 [8(AR - AC)], which is what we already learned by following the total revenue–total cost approach. Hence, the rule apparently works. Another way to think about MR and MC is in terms of marginal (i.e., additional) profit. If TR–TC is equal to total profit, then MR–MC must be equal to marginal profit. The last column in Table 11.4 indicates the amount of additional profit that would be earned by the firm in producing additional units of output. As you can see, this column is merely the difference between the MR column and the MC column. When MR is equal to MC, marginal profit must be zero. When marginal profit is equal to zero, it indicates that the firm can make no more *additional* profit and therefore should not produce at a higher level of output.

Of course, there is nothing to prevent the firm from producing more or less than eight units of output. As you can see in the last column of Table 11.3, it

Table 11.4 Using Marginal Revenue (or Price) and Marginal Cost to Determine Optimal Output: ***The Case of Economic Profit***

Quantity (Q)	*Marginal Revenue (MR = P = AR)*	*Average Fixed Cost (AFC)*	*Average Variable Cost (AVC)*	*Average Total Cost (AC)*	*Marginal Cost (MC)*	*Marginal Profit (Mπ)*
0	110					
1	110	100.00	55.70	155.70	55.70	54.30
2	110	50.00	52.80	102.80	49.90	60.10
3	110	33.33	51.30	84.63	48.30	61.70
4	110	25.00	51.20	76.20	50.90	59.10
5	110	20.00	52.50	72.50	57.70	52.30
6	110	16.67	55.20	71.87	68.70	41.30
7	110	14.29	59.30	73.59	83.90	26.10
8	**110**	**12.50**	**64.80**	**77.30**	**103.30**	6.70
9	110	11.11	71.70	82.81	126.90	−16.90
10	110	10.00	80.00	90.00	154.70	−44.70
11	110	9.09	89.70	98.79	186.70	−76.70
12	110	8.33	100.80	109.13	222.90	−112.90

still earns a profit if it produced at any of the output levels 2 to 12, but none of these amounts except 8 is the *maximum* that it could earn. Remember that we are not referring to *total revenue* and *total cost*. If the firm were to produce at the level where these two measures are equal, then clearly all it would be doing is earning a "normal" profit.

Although the optimal output level can be found just as easily by using the TR–TC approach, economists rely much more on the MR–MC approach in analyzing the firm's output decision. Essentially, this approach is an extension of the basic analytical technique of "marginal analysis" that was introduced in earlier chapters on demand, production, and cost. Furthermore, the practical implications of this approach are similar to those discussed in these earlier chapters. Very often firms do not have the benefit of complete columns of numbers depicting cost and revenue. Instead, they must rely on actual cost and revenue data at a particular level of output and then conduct sensitivity analysis involving relatively small incremental changes around that level. As will be illustrated in the ensuing sections, "marginal analysis" is much better suited to this situation than "total analysis."

THE MR–MC APPROACH IN GRAPHS. A graphical analysis using the MR–MC approach employs the data in Table 11.4 and is shown in Figure 11.6. Also shown is the firm's demand curve, a horizontal line intersecting the vertical axis at the level of the given market price of $110. Thus, the demand curve of this price-taking firm is "perfectly elastic." The optimal output level is clearly seen as the level at which the firm's MC line and its MR line (demand line) intersect. The amount of profit earned is represented by the shaded rectangle *ABCD*. Because these graphs will be utilized in this way throughout the rest of the chapter, it is crucial that you clearly understand their interpretation.

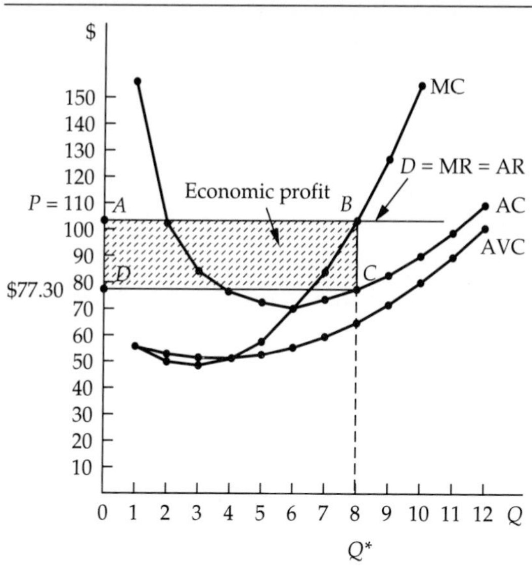

Figure 11.6 Graphical MR–MC Approach Indicating the Earning of Economic Profit

Any point on each of the unit cost curves indicates the dollar value of the cost at different levels of output. Therefore, at output level Q^*, the average cost is represented by the distance between point C and the horizontal axis (i.e., CQ^*). It follows that since total cost is average cost multiplied by the quantity of output, it is shown as the area of the rectangle determined by OQ^* and CQ^* (rectangle $ODCQ^*$). In the same manner, we can show that total revenue can be displayed as the rectangle determined by OQ^* and BQ^* (rectangle $OABQ^*$). Therefore, profit (i.e., the shaded rectangle *DABC*) can be represented by the difference between the larger rectangle, depicting total revenue, and the smaller one, showing total cost.

Economic Profit, Normal Profit, Loss, and Shutdown

The preceding example assumed that the market price was high enough for the firm to earn an economic profit by following the MR = MC rule. But because the firm is just one of many price-taking sellers in this market, there is no reason to expect that market price will always be this beneficial for the firm. Indeed, given the vagaries of supply and demand, it is just as likely that a firm will be faced with prices that result in only normal profit,—or worse, in operating losses. Tables 11.5 and 11.6 and Figure 11.7 demonstrate these possibilities. To focus on the marginal-revenue–marginal cost approach, we include only the per-unit cost data in the tables and figure.

The situation depicted in Table 11.6 and Figure 11.7*b* indicates a loss for the firm. Does this mean that the firm should not be in this market? As you know, in the short run, the firm must bear certain fixed costs regardless of the level of its output. Using the data in Table 11.6, if the firm were to shut down its

Table 11.5 Using Marginal Revenue (or Price) and Marginal Cost to Determine Optimal Output: ***The Case of Normal Profit***

Quantity (Q)	*Marginal Revenue (MR = P = AR)*	*Average Fixed Cost (AFC)*	*Average Variable Cost (AVC)*	*Average Total Cost (AC)*	*Marginal Cost (MC)*	*Marginal Profit (Mπ)*	*Total Profit or Loss (Q[P − AC])*
0	71.87						−100[a]
					55.70	16.17	
1	71.87	100.00	55.70	155.70			−83.83
					49.90	21.97	
2	71.87	50.00	52.80	102.80			−61.86
					48.30	23.57	
3	71.87	33.33	51.30	84.63			−38.28
					50.90	20.97	
4	71.87	25.00	51.20	76.20			−17.32
					57.70	14.17	
5	71.87	20.00	52.50	72.50			−3.15
					68.70	**3.17**	
6	**71.87**	**16.67**	**55.20**	**71.87**			0
					83.90	−12.03	
7	71.87	14.29	59.30	73.59			−12.04
					103.30	−31.43	
8	71.87	12.50	64.80	77.30			−43.44
					126.90	−55.03	
9	71.87	11.11	71.70	82.81			−98.46
					154.70	−82.83	
10	71.87	10.00	80.00	90.00			−181.30
					186.70	−114.83	
11	71.87	9.09	89.70	98.79			−296.12
					222.90	−151.03	
12	71.87	8.33	100.80	109.13			−447.12

[a] If $Q = 0$, firm still incurs a total fixed cost of $100 in the short run.

Table 11.6 Using Marginal Revenue (or Price) and Marginal Cost to Determine Optimal Output: ***The Case of Economic Loss***

Quantity (Q)	*Marginal Revenue (MR = P = AR)*	*Average Fixed Cost (AFC)*	*Average Variable Cost (AVC)*	*Average Total Cost (AC)*	*Marginal Cost (MC)*	*Marginal Profit (Mπ)*	*Total Profit or Loss (Q[P-AC])*
0	58						−100
					55.70	2.30	
1	58	100.00	55.70	155.70			−97.70
					49.90	8.10	
2	58	50.00	52.80	102.80			−89.60
					48.30	9.70	
3	58	33.33	51.30	84.63			−79.89
					50.90	7.10	
4	58	25.00	51.20	76.20			−72.80
					57.70	**.30**	
5	**58**	**20.00**	**52.50**	**72.50**			**−72.50**
					68.70	−10.70	
6	58	16.67	55.20	71.87			−83.22
					83.90	−25.90	
7	58	14.29	59.30	73.59			−109.13
					103.30	−45.30	
8	58	12.50	64.80	77.30			−154.44
					126.90	−68.90	
9	58	11.11	71.70	82.81			−223.29
					154.70	−96.70	
10	58	10.00	80.00	90.00			−320.00
					186.70	−128.70	
11	58	9.09	89.70	98.79			−448.69
					222.90	−164.90	
12	58	8.33	100.80	109.13			−613.56

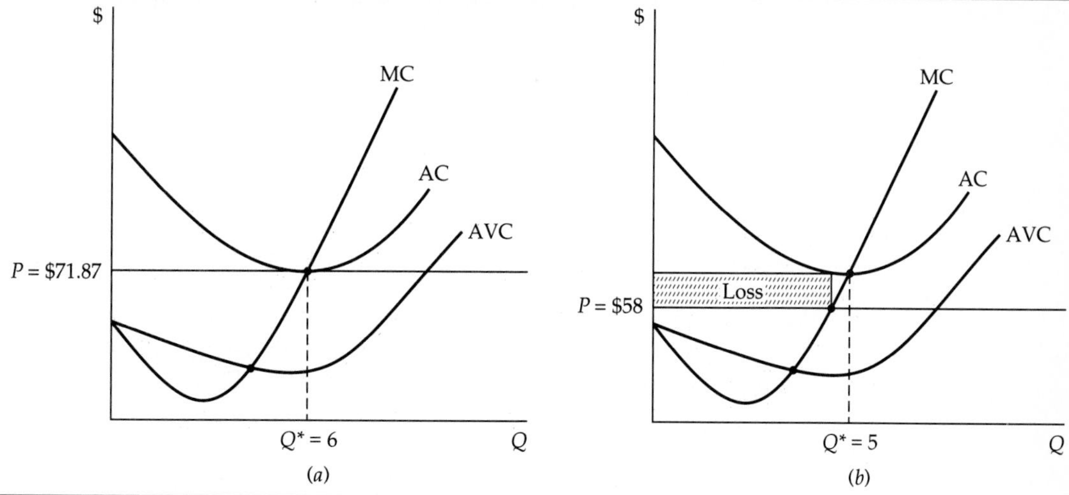

Figure 11.7 (*a*) Normal Profit and (*b*) Economic Loss

operations (i.e., if $Q = 0$), it would still have a fixed cost of $100. Given the market price of $58, we know that the best that a firm can do is to follow the MR = MC rule, produce 5 units of output, and lose $72.50. But if the firm were to shut down, it would lose $100 because this is the amount of fixed cost that it would incur, whether or not it operates in the short run. Therefore, with a market price of $58, *it would be better for a firm to operate at a loss than to cease its activities in this market*. This is illustrated in Figure 11.8*a*.

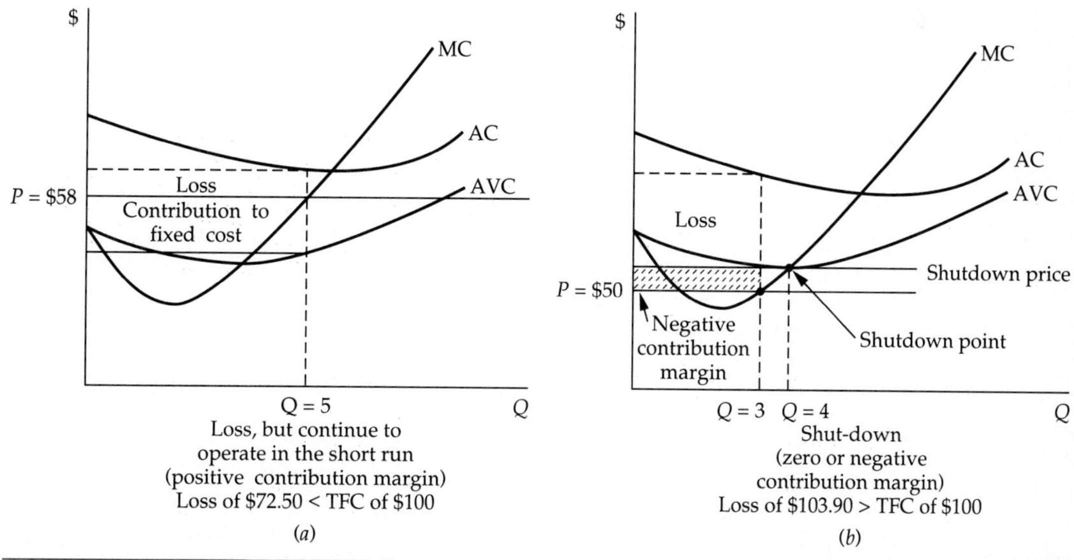

Figure 11.8 Contribution Margin

Another way to understand this rationale is to compare the firm's total revenue at the $58 price with its total variable cost, assuming a production level of five units. The total revenue is $290 ($P \times Q$), and the total variable cost is $262.50 ($Q \times$ AVC). Clearly, this revenue is sufficient to cover the firm's total variable cost. Moreover, the amount left over ($27.50) can be used to pay for a part of its fixed cost. Hence, we can also conclude that as long as a firm's total revenue is greater than its total variable cost (or on a per-unit basis, as long as the market price exceeds average variable cost), it is better to operate than to shut down because at least part of its fixed cost will be defrayed. We refer to the amount by which total revenue exceeds total variable cost as the *contribution margin.* (See Figure 11.8*a*.) You should also recognize that the portion of fixed cost that is *not* covered by the contribution margin is in fact the amount of the firm's loss (i.e., $27.50 − $100 = -$72.50.

It is not always advisable to operate in the short run at a loss. Suppose the market price fell to $50. In this case, even if the firm followed the MR = MC rule, it would still incur a loss greater than it would have to bear by shutting down. This situation is not shown in a separate table but will be discussed in relation to the figures in Table 11.6. By literally following the MR = MC rule, the firm would be led to produce three units of output. But we can see that at this level, the total revenue of $150 ($50 × 3) would not even be enough to cover the firm's total variable cost of $153.90 ($51.30 × 3), resulting in a negative contribution margin of $3.90. Looking at this situation in terms of the firm's loss versus its fixed cost, we can see that its total loss of $103.90 is clearly greater than the fixed cost of $100 that it would incur if it decided to shut down its operations. (As you can see, the firm's loss is the combination of its fixed cost and negative contribution margin.) Thus, given the market price of $50, the firm would be better off by shutting down its operations. This is illustrated in Figure 11.8*b*.

Also shown in this figure is what economists refer to as the *shutdown point.* At this point, the market price is at a level in which a firm following the MR = MC rule would lose an amount just equal to its fixed cost of production. Expressed in another way, this price would result in a zero contribution margin. At the shutdown point, we assume that a firm would be indifferent about operating versus shutting down. However, it would certainly give strong consideration to ceasing to operate in the short run. As you can see, the shutdown point coincides with the point at which the firm's average variable cost is at its minimum.

The Competitive Market in the Long Run

Regardless of whether the market price in the short run results in economic profit, normal profit, or a loss for competing firms, economic theory states that in the long run, the market price will settle at the point where these firms earn a normal profit. This is because over a long period of time, prices that enable firms to earn above-normal profit would induce other firms to enter the market, and prices below the normal level would cause firms to leave the market. We just completed a discussion of the rationale for a firm's operating at a loss in the short run. However, in the long run, we assume that firms that are losing money would have to seriously consider leaving the market even if they have positive contribution margins. Recall that in the long run, firms have the time to vary their fixed factors of production. This means that they would have sufficient time to liquidate the fixed assets that account for their fixed costs.

We discussed the long-run adjustment process of entering and exiting firms in Chapter 3. The entry of firms shifts the supply curve to the right, driving down market price. The exiting of firms shifts the supply curve to the left, placing upward pressure on market price. A firm's motivation to go into or get out of the market can now be examined in greater detail. There is only one price at which firms neither enter nor leave the market. This, of course, is the price that results in normal profits. The long-run process of entering and exiting firms is illustrated in Figure 11.9.

Figure 11.9*a* shows a hypothetical short-run situation in which the price (determined by supply and demand) is high enough to enable a typical firm competing in this market to earn economic profit. (In other words, given the market price, the firm's cost structure is low enough to enable it to earn economic profit.) Over time, new firms would enter the market, and the original firms would expand their fixed capacity in response to the incentive of economic profit. This would have the effect of increasing the market supply (shifting the supply curve to the right) and reducing the market price. At the point where firms earn only normal profit, this adjustment process would cease. Figure 11.9*b* shows the opposite case, in which a short-run loss incurred by firms in the market causes firms in the long run to leave the market. This causes price to rise toward the level in which the remaining firms would earn a normal profit.

The concept of a long-run "resting point" may seem a bit far-fetched to readers wishing for actual business examples. Has there ever been an instance when the long-run equilibrium point was reached? As much as we try to use real-world examples to support the theory of managerial economics, it is extremely difficult, if not impossible, to find examples of this principle in action. For one thing, in actual market situations, demand does not remain constant while supply adjusts toward the normal price. Tastes and preferences, the number of buyers, incomes, and prices of related goods are constantly changing. For another, the economic notion of the long run is a theoretical construct, not a period that can be measured in calendar time. If the market price has not reached the normal level, economists can say that the market is still adjusting toward long-run equilibrium. But herein lies the principal relevance of this concept to the real world of business. For business decision makers, the process of adjustment toward equilibrium is far more important than the equilibrium price itself.

An understanding of the conditions motivating market entry or exit over the long run should lead the firms to consider the following points:

1. The earlier the firm enters a market, the better its chances of earning above-normal profit (assuming a strong demand in this market).
2. As new firms enter the market, firms that want to survive and perhaps thrive must find ways to produce at the lowest possible cost, or at least at cost levels below those of their competitors.

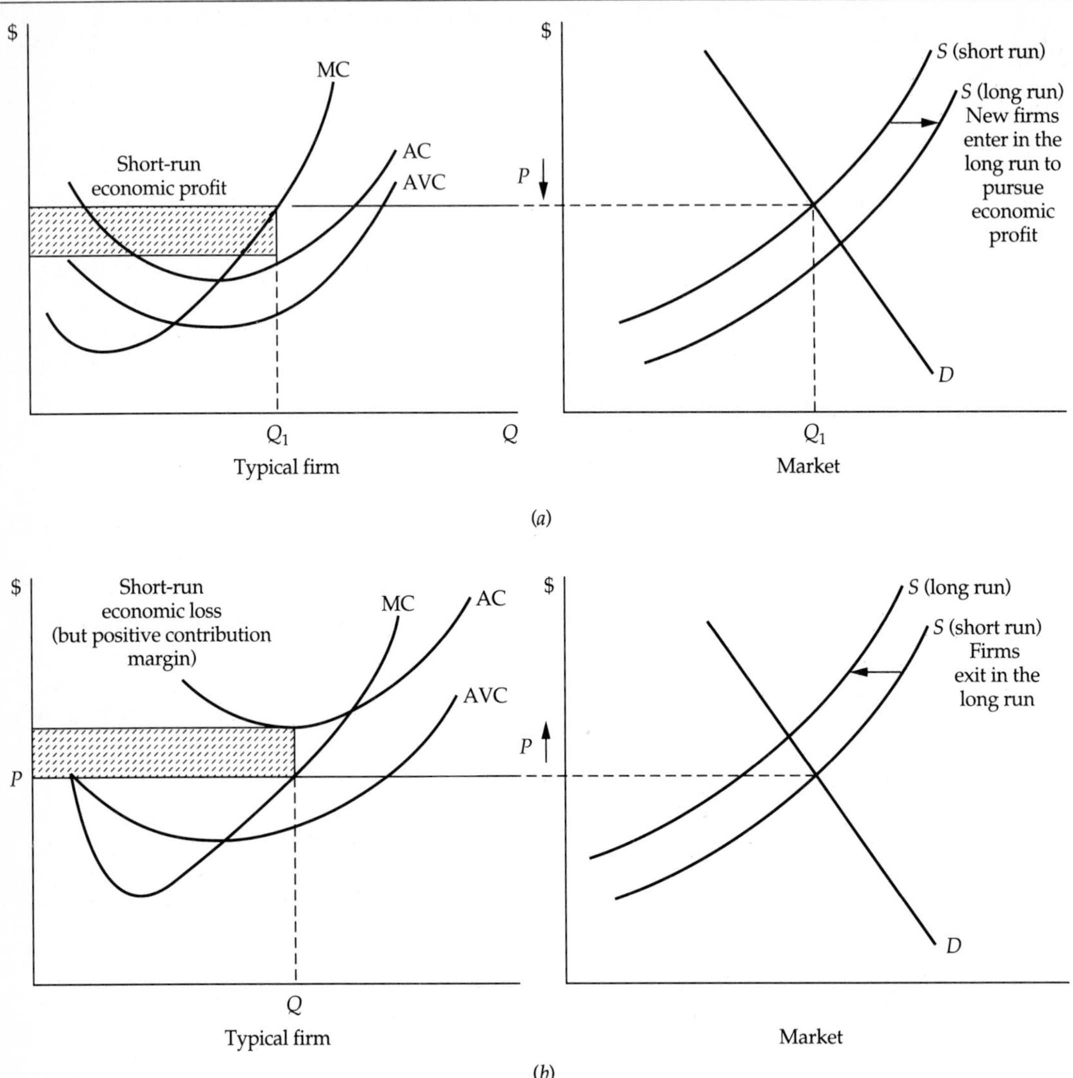

Figure 11.9 Long-Run Effect of Firm's Entering and Exiting the Market

3. Firms that find themselves unable to compete on the basis of cost might want to try competing on the basis of product differentiation instead.

The importance of Statements 1 and 2 should be apparent. Above-normal profit might be considered a reward to those firms willing to take the risk of being among the first to enter a market. Cost cutting may involve economies of scale or the reduction of fixed or variable costs. Statement 3 suggests that a firm might try to get away from being simply a price taker in the market. Instead it might seek to exercise some control over its price by making its product to stand out from the rest. With this statement in mind, it is time to move on to markets in which firms do have some control over their prices.

Pricing and Output Decisions in Monopoly Markets

A monopoly market consists of one firm. The firm *is* the market. Examples are gas and electric utilities and firms selling products under protection of U.S. patent laws. Prior to its breakup in 1984, AT&T was considered one of the largest monopolies in the world. The seven regional companies that were formed after divestiture still represent monopolies in many of the local calling areas within their respective regions. Most monopolies cited above are closely regulated by government or government-appointed agencies. (A notable exception are companies selling patented products.) Because this regulation severely constrains their ability to choose price and output levels, regulated monopolies are analyzed as a separate group of firms in Chapter 16.

In the absence of regulatory constraints, the monopoly stands as the counterpoint to the perfectly competitive firm. Firms in perfectly competitive markets have no power to set their prices; the monopoly firm has the power to establish any price that it wishes. If you were responsible for setting the price of a product that you alone were selling in the market, how much would you charge? The lay-person's answer to this questions is usually "as much as I can" or "whatever the market will bear." On the surface, this answer seems reasonable enough. Unfortunately, it is too simplistic to be of much help to the monopolist. In 1948, when Polaroid first offered its camera, it could have charged any price that it wanted. The original price was $85 (which was a considerable sum at that time), but it could just as well have been $850 or $8,500. The market could have borne those prices because some people probably would have been willing to buy the camera at higher levels. The question is *how many* people would have bought the cameras and *when*. As it turned out, Polaroid offered five cameras for sale on the first day and sold them all in several hours. Who knows how long it would have taken them to sell the five units at $8,500?

The key point is that a monopoly firm's ability to set its price is limited by the demand curve for its product and, in particular, the price elasticity of demand for its product. Recall that according to the law of demand, people will buy more as price falls and vice versa. The price elasticity of demand indicates how much more or less people are willing to buy in relation to price decreases or increases. If we assume that the firm's downward-sloping demand curve is linear, we know that as the price of the product falls, the marginal revenue from the sale of additional units falls, reaches zero, and then becomes negative. For purposes of illustration, let us also assume that the firm's marginal cost is constant in the short run. The linear, downward-sloping demand curve, the marginal revenue curve, and the constant marginal cost curve for such a firm are shown in Figure 11.10. Notice that if the firm charges too high a price (e.g., P_1), its marginal revenue will exceed its marginal cost; hence, it will be forgoing some amount of marginal profit (shown by the lighter shade). If the firm sets its price at too low a level, its marginal cost will exceed its marginal revenue, and and the firm will experience a marginal loss (shown by the darker shade).

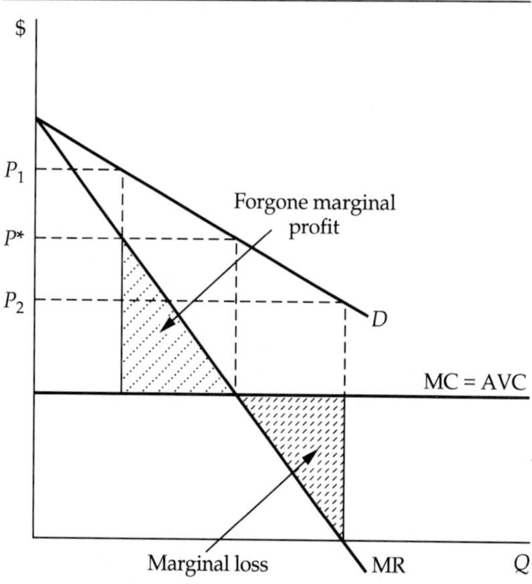

Figure 11.10 Demand, MR, and MC Curves for a Monopoly

The ability of a monopoly to set its price is further limited by the possibility of rising marginal costs of production. If this is the case, then surely at some point the increasing cost of producing additional units of output will exceed the decreasing marginal revenue received from the sale of additional units. This begins at Q', shown in Figure 11.11.

In conclusion, the firm that exercises a monopoly power over its price should not set its price at the highest possible level. Instead, it should set it at the *right* level. And what is this "right" level? It is the level that results in MR = MC.

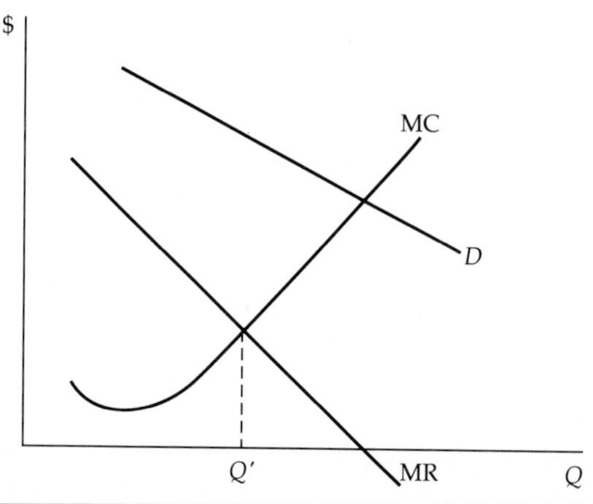

Figure 11.11 Increasing Marginal Costs in Relation to Decreasing Marginal Revenue

Table 11.7 Using Marginal Revenue and Marginal Cost to Determine Optimal Price and Output: The Case of Monopoly

Quantity (Q)	*Price (P)*	*Total Revenue (TR)*	*Marginal Revenue (MR)*	*Average Total Cost (AC)*	*Total Cost (TC)*	*Marginal Cost (MC)*	*Total Profit (π)*
0	180	0			100.00		−100.00
			170			55.70	
1	170	170		155.70	155.70		14.30
			150			49.90	
2	160	320		102.80	205.60		114.40
			130			48.30	
3	150	450		84.63	253.90		196.10
			110			50.90	
4	140	560		76.20	304.80		255.20
			90			57.70	
5	130	650		72.50	362.50		287.50
			70			**68.70**	
6	**120**	**720**		**71.87**	**431.20**		**288.80**
			50			83.90	
7	110	770		73.59	515.10		254.90
			30			103.30	
8	100	800		77.30	618.40		181.60
			10			126.90	
9	90	810		82.81	745.30		64.70
			−10			154.70	
10	80	800		90.00	900.00		−100.00
			−30			186.70	
11	70	770		98.79	1086.70		−316.70
			−50			222.90	
12	60	720		109.13	1309.60		−589.60

To see how the MR = MC rule applies to the monopolist as well as to the perfect competitor, see Table 11.7. Note that the table presents only the cost data relevant to this example. For purposes of comparison, the same cost figures used in the previous section for the perfectly competitive firm have been selected.[4] But in this case, we assume that the firm is the "only game in town." Note that the price is not equal to the marginal revenue, because the firm is a price setter and not a price taker. Its demand schedule consists of columns 1 and 2, and the total revenue and marginal revenue schedules are those that normally accompany a downward-sloping demand curve.

Starting from the zero output level, let us consider the price, output, marginal revenue, marginal cost, and marginal profit as additional units of output are produced. You can see that as output increases, the marginal revenue associated with each unit exceeds the marginal cost up to six units. Beyond this level, the firm actually incurs a marginal loss. As the firm moves beyond this level, total profit is still positive, but it is not at its maximum. In other words, by following the MR = MC rule, a profit-maximizing firm would want to produce 6 units of output per time period. To do so, it would have to set a price of $120.

---

[4]By maintaining consistency in the cost data, we realize that we are sacrificing some realism because a monopoly would obviously produce more than a perfectly competitive firm. However, this shortcoming can be rectified by simply assuming that each unit of output is the equivalent of a larger number of units (e.g., $Q = 1 = 1,000$).

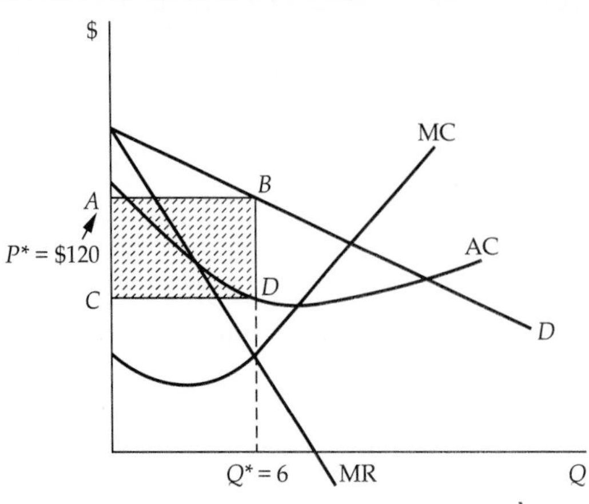

Figure 11.12 Graphical Depiction of MR = MC Rule for a Monopoly

The way in which the MR = MC rule underlies the monopoly price can perhaps be more clearly seen in a graph. In Figure 11.12, we see that the firm would select P^* because, given the particular demand for the product, this is the price that would prompt customers to buy Q^*. And Q^* is the quantity that the firm would want to produce per time period because this is the amount at which the revenue received from the last unit produced is just equal to its cost (i.e., marginal revenue = marginal cost). With the same graphical references to total revenue and total cost as used in the analysis of perfect competition, we arrive at the measure of total profit as the shaded area $ABCD$.

In a perfectly competitive market, the short-run economic profit enjoyed by the monopoly firm in this example would be vulnerable in the long run to the entry of other firms wishing to earn similar amounts of profit. But because we assume it is a monopoly, this firm would not be subject to such threats in the long run. Nonetheless, the preceding illustration is not meant to give the impression that a monopoly automatically earns economic profit in either the short or the long run. Whether or not it does depends on the demand for its product. For example, a company may have a monopoly on a toy for children that is in great demand and consequently enables it to earn the kind of economic profit illustrated in Figure 11.12. But as the market demand is filled or as children begin to tire of the product, the demand could decline (e.g., the demand curve shifts to the left) to the extent that the firm earns only a normal profit or perhaps even incurs a loss. This holds true for any product in a mature market.[5]

[5]An obvious example is the Cabbage Patch dolls phenomenon of the 1980s. Who knows what will become of the Teenage Mutant Ninja Turtles? Incidentally, Coleco, the company that produced the Cabbage Patch dolls, filed for bankruptcy in 1989.

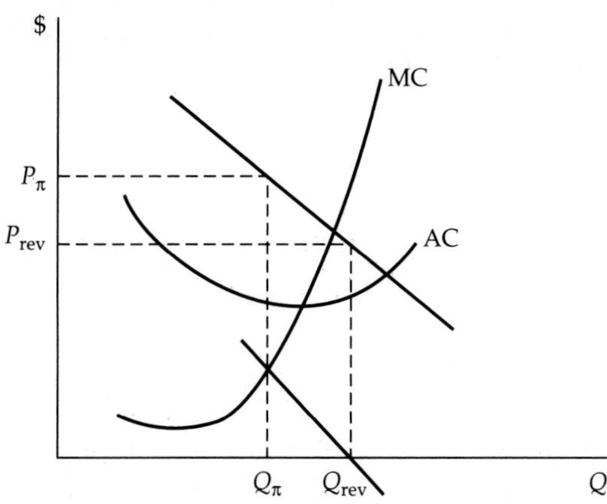

Figure 11.13 Relationship between the Profit-Maximizing and Revenue-Maximizing Price and Quantity

Suppose a price-setting firm does not wish to maximize its short-run profit but instead wants to maximize its revenue. Let us explore this possibility using the data in Table 11.7. The price that maximizes the total revenue can be determined simply by observation. As you can see, by charging $90 for its product, the firm will receive the maximum total revenue of $810. You can also see that this revenue-maximizing price is lower than the one that maximizes the firm's total profit (i.e., $90 < $120). This is to be expected because of the relationship between a price that equates marginal revenue with marginal cost and one that equates marginal revenue to zero.[6] This relationship is illustrated in Figure 11.13. This dichotomy between the price that maximize profit and the one that maximize revenue will be discussed in greater detail in Chapter 13.

Monopolistic Competition

Monopolistic competition is a market in which there are many firms and relatively easy entry. However, it is also one in which firms exercise some control over their prices. The main characteristic of monopolistic competition that

[6]Readers should recall in our discussion of price elasticity in Chapter 4 that the price at which a firm maximizes its revenue is determined at the point where its marginal revenue is equal to zero.

enables firms to be more than just price takers is product differentiation. However, just as in a perfectly competitive market, the ease of entry means that when firms in the market earn above-normal profits, there is the threat of increased competition from newcomers or the expansion of capacity by firms already in the market.

On the surface, a numerical or graphical illustration of monopolistic competition is identical to the case of a monopoly. As a matter of fact, the numbers and the graph shown in Table 11.7 and Figure 11.12 can be relabeled "monopolistic competition."[7] Accordingly, we illustrate the monopolistically competitive firm by reproducing Figure 11.12 as Figure 11.14*a*. As in the cases of perfect competition and monopoly, we have assumed the monopolistic competitor to be a short-run profit maximizer. Therefore, its price and output decisions are based on the MR = MC rule. The difference between monopolistic competition and monopoly can be seen in the *long-run* analysis of this market.

If the firm is in the situation depicted in Figure 11.14*a*, that is, if it is earning above-normal profit, then we can expect newcomers to be attracted to this market. The effect of this added competition on the monopolistic competitor can be seen in Figure 11.14*b*. Notice that the entry of new firms causes the original firm's demand curve to shift downward and to the left. If you are confused by this movement and the movement of the supply curve in the perfectly competitive market, remember that we are talking about this change from the point of view of the *individual firm,* not of the entire market. From an individual firm's perspective, the entry of additional firms in the market would decrease its market share by reducing the demand for its product. The leftward shift in the demand curve serves to illustrate this decline in market share. To be sure, this case assumes that the total market demand remains unchanged while the new firms are entering the market. If the total market demand were increasing while newcomers entered the market, the direction and extent of the shift in demand would be uncertain.

In the long run, economists hypothesize that the same situation would exist for monopolistic competition as for perfect competition: firms would be earning normal profit. If firms either earned above-normal profit or incurred losses, then the entry or exit of firms, along with the adjustment of fixed capacity by existing firms, would cause each individual firm's demand curve either to increase or decrease until firms in the market earned only normal profit.

As pointed out earlier in this chapter, the best examples of monopolistic competition can be found in the small businesses. Restaurants, grocery stores, dry cleaners, stationery stores, florists, hardware stores, pharmacies, and video rental stores are all markets in which entry is fairly easy and the number of sellers is relatively large. However, firms within each of these markets try to differentiate themselves from the competition, using such factors as location,

---

[7] Actually, economists prefer to show a flatter demand curve for monopolistic competition than the one used for a monopoly. This indicates a relatively greater price elasticity because consumers have more than one seller to buy from.

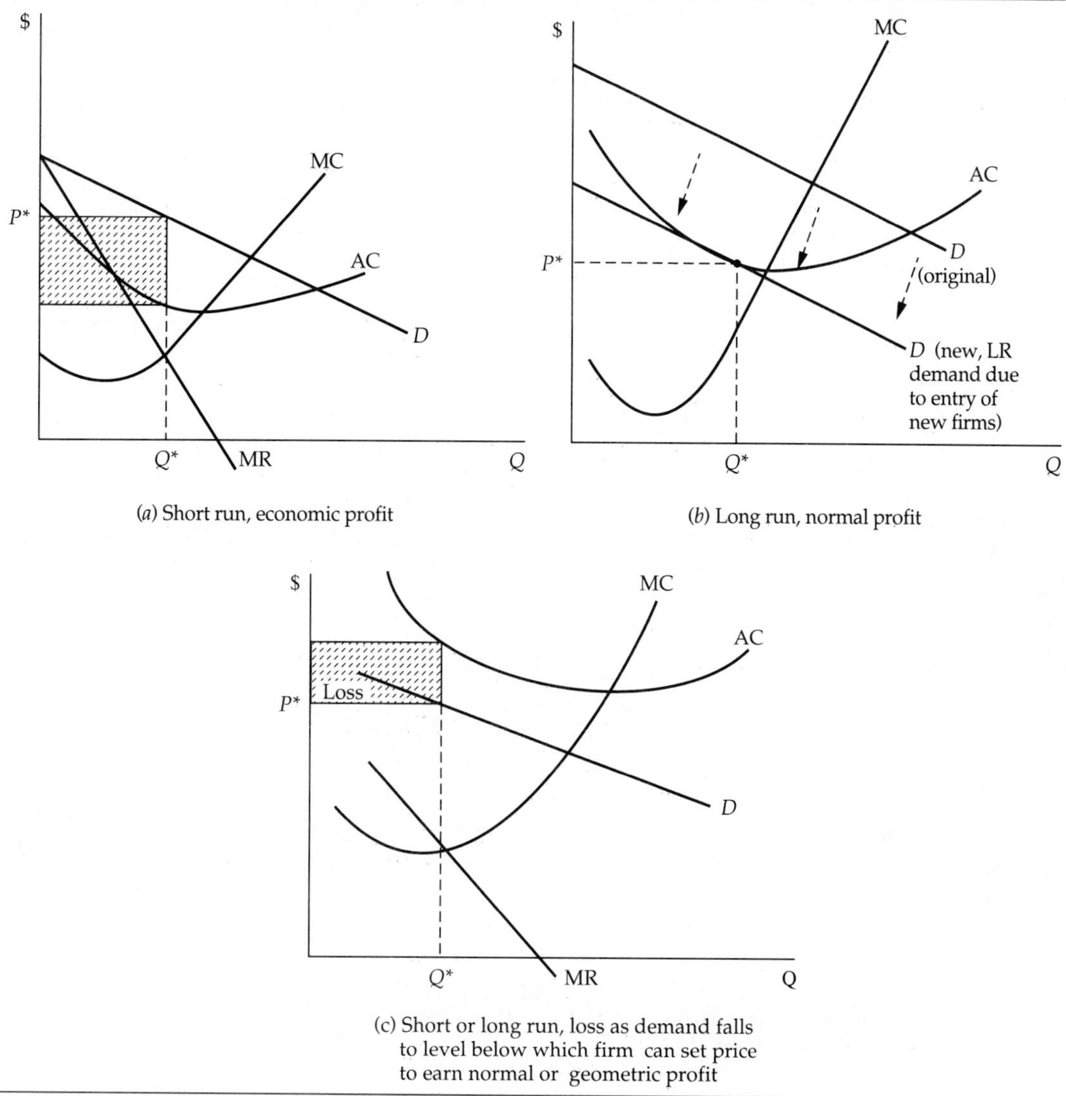

Figure 11.14 Monopolistic Competition

type of service (i.e., "service with a smile"), or ambiance (e.g., candelight and tablecloths vs. plain formica tables in a restaurant). In effect, the extent to which a retail firm can exercise control over its price depends on the extent to which it can differentiate itself from its competitors on the basis of nonprice factors. The first Chinese restaurant to offer "Mongolian-style barbecue beef" may be able to charge more for its offerings than its competitors. However over time more and more Chinese restaurants can be expected to offer this particular style of cooking.

The next time you visit your local shopping area or mall, observe how each of the retail establishments tries to differentiate itself from the rest. Also observe how easy it is for newcomers to begin selling a product or service that has been profitable for businesses already in the market. Six or seven years ago, how many video rental stores were operating in your neighborhood? How many are there today? How many do you think will be in business three or four years from now? Why do you rent tapes from a particular store? Is it friendly and efficient service? Location? Variety of tapes available? Availability of the latest and most popular tapes? It is probably a combination of all these things.

As far as prices are concerned, you will probably notice that competitors tend to charge very similar amounts for their products. This is not so much a contradiction of the theory as a reflection of the intensity of competition in the market. As soon as one store tries to differentiate itself in some way, others copy it. For example, if one video store charges a membership fee of $25 a year for the privilege of renting tapes at a discount, other stores will begin to offer the same membership policy. This would then make it very difficult for any one seller, including the one who originated this service, to charge a higher price. Moreover, in pricing the product, the monopolistic competitor may already be thinking about the pricing policy of its competitors. To understand this particular aspect of pricing, we turn to the fourth market type, oligopoly.

Oligopoly

Oligopoly is a market dominated by a few relatively large firms. The products they sell may be either standardized or differentiated. Part of the control that oligopolists exercise over price and output stems from their ability to differentiate their products. But regardless of this ability market power stems mainly from the sheer size and dominance of the largest firms in this type of market.

The best examples of oligopoly in the U.S. economy are found in the manufacturing sector. Automobiles, appliances, mainframe computers, many types of processed foods (e.g., breakfast cereals and peanut butter), and beverages such as soft drinks and beer are all markets usually cited in introductory textbooks as examples of an oligopoly.[8] Do not be misled by the number of brands in each of the markets. Although it is common knowledge that the U.S. automakers produce different makes and models, the general public is not as aware that the breakfast cereal industry consists essentially of four large food manufacturing concerns, notwithstanding the myriad of brand names and cereal types found on supermarket shelves. Examples of oligopolies that produce standardized products can be found in industries that produce raw materials such as steel, aluminum, copper, and various kinds of chemicals.

You have probably noticed that the phrase "relatively small number of large firms" is not a precise definition of oligopoly. There are no specific quantitative measures of number and size needed for a market to qualify as an oligopoly.

[8]In recent years, the onslaught from foreign companies, particularly the Japanese, has changed the nature of competition in the U.S. automobile industry. Indeed, some might argue that this market is more like monopolistic competition than oligopoly.

Existing government data have been used to measure the degree to which market power is concentrated in the hands of a small number of firms. Table 11.8 presents the *concentration ratios* of a selected number of industries. These ratios measure the percentage of market share held by each industry's top four and top eight firms. The higher the concentration ratio, the more likely it is that the pricing of products is controlled by the top firms. As a rule of thumb, industries with "four-firm concentration ratios" of 80 and above are considered highly concentrated and most likely to be oligopolistic.

The reason for the wording "most likely to be oligopolistic" is that the primary trait distinguishing oligopoly from the other market types is more behavioral than quantitative. It does not matter whether there are only 2 firms in the market or 10. What makes a market an oligopoly is whether each of its firms determines its price and output while contemplating the action or reaction of its competitors. If this type of interdependence in pricing exists, we can safely say that this market is an oligopoly. You can see, then, the limitation of using data such as those in Table 11.8, which only provide a numerical description of each industry, with no indication of the way in which firms in these industries price their products. Of course, it is reasonable to assume the existence of interdependence in highly concentrated industries. Hence, the concentration ratio is actually a proxy indicator for the presence of interdependence, the real indicator of an oligopoly market.

Table 11.8 A Representative Sample of Four-Digit Census Industries, 1982

Standard Industrial Classification (SIC) Code	*Description*	*Number of Firms*	*Industry Sales (millions of dollars)*	Market Share (percent)	
				Top Four Firms	*Top Eight Firms*
2011	Meat packing plants	1,658	$ 5,824.6	29	43
2043	Cereal breakfast foods	32	4,131.9	86	[a]
2047	Dog, cat, and other pet food	222	4,402.2	52	71
2067	Chewing gum	9	915.3	95	[a]
2095	Roasted coffee	118	5,826.9	65	76
2371	Fur goods	503	419.3	12	19
2387	Apparel belts	317	556.5	19	30
2621	Paper mills	135	20,994.6	22	40
2711	Newspapers	7,520	21,276.3	22	34
3425	Handsaws and saw blades	119	487.3	47	65
3711	Motor vehicles and car bodies	284	70,739.7	92	97
3721	Aircraft	139	28,024.3	64	81
3732	Boat building and repairing	1,834	2,369.2	14	22
3995	Burial caskets	270	682.1	52	60

Note: [a] indicates an industry with so few competitors that the Census Bureau withholds data to avoid disclosing individual company information.

Source: U.S Census data presented in James L. Pappas and Mark Hirschey, *Managerial Economics*, Hinsdale, Ill: Dryden Press, 1987, p. 400.

The question you may now be asking is: If each oligopolist tries to anticipate competitors' responses to a price action, then who actually sets the price? Furthermore, if they all watch each other, would it not seem likely that they all end up charging the same price for their products? From your experience as a consumer, you probably know the answers to these questions. Think about instances when you had to choose among a small number of competing brands of the same product. If they were all sold in the same store, and if the store was not sponsoring pricing specials on selected brands (which are often supported by the manufacturers of these brands), it is likely that the prices of these competing brands were the same. This is even true for competing products in the industrial market for steel, aluminum, and chemicals.

For example, put yourself in the position of a manager in a chemical company who is responsible for the pricing of hydrochloric acid. If you set a price that is higher than those of your competition, you will lose sales because customers can buy the same product from other firms at a lower price. If you set a lower price, you might gain some sales at the expense of your competitors, but you also risk a retaliatory price cut or a price war among all firms in the market.

Referring to Figure 11.15, consider the following example. Suppose all firms in the market are charging P_1 per unit for hydrochloric acid. Also suppose that the demand for your firm's output is such that at this price, you could expect sales per time period to be Q_1. Now say you consider lowering your price to P_2 to woo customers away from your competitors. This means that you have assumed your demand between P_1 and P_2 to be elastic. If not, a price reduction would enable you to sell more units (according to the law of demand), but your total revenue would actually fall (because when demand is price-inelastic, total

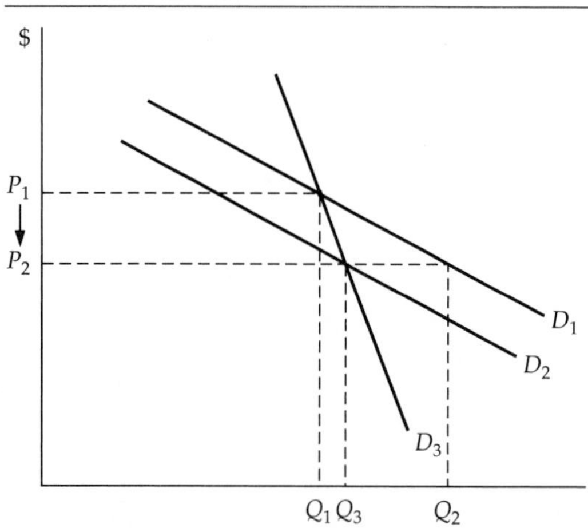

Figure 11.15 Pricing and Demand in an Oligopoly

revenue decreases with a price reduction). The implementation of this price action is shown by the arrow in Figure 11.15.

Now suppose you have explicitly considered the reactions of your competitors to this move. Knowing that they do not want to lose market share, you assume that your price cut will be followed by theirs. The effect of their price cut would be a reduction in the demand for your product as the customers that you tried to take from them return to their original sources of product. This can be depicted by a leftward shift in your demand curve (D_1 to D_2 in Figure 11.15). Remember from Chapter 3 that a change in the price of a substitute product—in this case, a competitor's product—causes a decrease in the demand for the product in question—in this case, your product. When the smoke from all this activity clears, you would have a demand curve similar to D_3 in Figure 11.15. As you can see, this demand curve connects the point determined by P_1 and the corresponding quantity on the original demand curve, D_1, with the point determined by P_2 and the quantity on the lower demand curve, D_2. What is important to observe about this composite demand curve D_3 is that it is *inelastic* over the range of prices P_1 and P_2. On the basis of this scenario, you would conclude that it is not worthwhile to lower your price because the response by your competitors would render your demand curve inelastic. And it does not pay for a firm to reduce its price in the face of inelastic demand.

Now consider an increase in your firm's price, and suppose you expect that your competition will not follow suit. This would lead to a downward shift in your demand curve because customers would find your competitors' price to be lower. Anticipation of this response to your price increase by your competitors would lead you to the same conclusion: it is not worth doing.

If every firm anticipated the behavior of other firms in this way, the whole market would be paralyzed. One firm or a group of firms has to seize the initiative and set a price that everyone else can follow. In oligopolistic markets in the United States, the role of the "price leader" is usually assumed by the company with the largest share of the market. For example, General Motors is often the first to announce price increases for the next year's line of cars and trucks. IBM often sets the pace for the rest of the industry in large, mainframe computers. Different companies in the industry may take the leader role in setting prices for different products. Sometimes companies take turns in setting the price. In one instance, Coca-Cola may set the price of its product; in others Pepsi-Cola may take the lead. This rotation in the leadership position indicates that it is not always the largest company that is the first to raise or lower the price. When the prime rate is changed in the banking industry, for example, Citicorp, the largest bank in the United States, is seldom the first bank to do so.

Price leadership is a necessary accompaniment to interdependence. Without leadership, there would be no mechanism for oligopolistic firms to set or change their prices—at least no legal way. Throughout this discussion of oligopoly pricing, it might have occurred to you that an easy solution to this quandary would be for all the firms to get together and set the price that they feel is in their best interest. This is considered "collusion" and is illegal under existing U.S. laws of commerce.[9] The only kind of "price fixing" possible in an oligopoly is in international markets. A group of sellers that operate internationally with a formal agreement on price and output levels for their products is called a *cartel.* The OPEC cartel is probably the best known of these groups. But international cartels also exist for such products as coffee and tin, although they have not been as effective as OPEC once was in maintaining their desired levels of price.[10]

The Importance of the Economic Theory of Output and Pricing in Managerial Decision Making

In essence, economic theory states that there are "three Cs" managers must consider when making decisions about the pricing of a product: cost, customers, and competition. "Cost" includes both the short-run and the long-run cost structure. "Customers" refers to the demand function and, in particular, the price elasticity of the product being offered in the market. "Competition" refers to the nature of the market in which the firm is competing (perfect competition, monopoly, monopolistic competition, or oligopoly). Of course, in the perfectly competitive market, in which all firms are price takers, only cost needs to be considered in relation to the market price in deciding how much output to produce.

The economic theory of optimal output and pricing decisions provides a solid conceptual framework that firms can use to integrate cost, customers, and competition. However, the extent to which the MR = MC rule can be applied depends primarily on the amount of information that a firm has at its disposal. Large firms that have the resources to obtain data on their cost, structure, and the pricing decisions and product offerings of its competition, and the demand function and forecasts, will of course be able to make extensive use of the MR = MC rule.[11] Companies with fewer resources may have to experiment with different pricing structures. However, an understanding of the economic theory will be most helpful in evaluating the outcomes. As a simple example of this, suppose a firm does not know the demand equation for its product. If it drops its price and then finds that its revenue increases, it can conclude that its demand is price-elastic. This increase in revenue can then be compared to the increase in cost (i.e., only those costs associated with the higher volume of sales, not all costs) to determine whether the price reduction was indeed profitable.

To be sure, there are a number of complicating features of the pricing and output decision that the basic economic theory presented in this chapter does

---

[9] In the agricultural sector, cartels have often been formed with the support of the federal government. For example, in many states or regions of the country, dairy associations have been formed to control the production levels and, hence, the price of milk.

[10] A number of topics discussed in this section, such as price leadership and cartels, are presented in greater detail in Chapter 13.

[11] One of the authors was involved for a number of years in the pricing function of the IBM Corporation. The pricing of computers relies very heavily on all of the elements discussed in this chapter: cost, demand, and the anticipated response by the other competitors in the industry.

not cover. For example, firms may have other objectives besides the short-run maximization of profit. Also, pricing of more than one product at a time may have to be considered. Firms may want to consider charging different prices for a given product in different segments of the market. In the absence of a price leader or a clear-cut pattern of action and reaction among the firms in an oligopolistic market, a firm may have a difficult time pricing its product. Many of these issues will be covered in Chapter 13.

The Solution[12]

Armed with all the available figures on the estimated cost and demand for the new soft drink, Frank spent the next week trying to come up with an optimal price for the product. The weekly demand for the firm's product was estimated to be:

$$Q_D = 2,000 - 1,000P \qquad (11.1)$$

Where Q_D = Quantity of 12 oz. containers (in thousands)

P = Price per container

Based on estimates provided by the bottling plant, Frank expressed the cost function as:

$$\text{TC} = 150 + 0.25Q \qquad (11.2)$$

where TC = Total cost per week (in thousands of dollars)

Q = Output of 12 oz. containers (in thousands)

To find the optimal price on the basis of the MR = MC rule, Frank first found the total revenue and marginal revenue functions based on the data in Equation (11.1). Expressing this equation in terms of price,

$$P = 2 - 0.001Q \qquad (11.3)$$

and substituting this into the equation for total revenue (i.e., TR = $P \times Q$), he found total revenue to be

$$\text{TR} = 2Q - 0.001Q^2 \qquad (11.4)$$

To find marginal revenue, he took the first derivative of this equation and set it equal to the firm's marginal cost. (Based on Equation (11.2), he knew that the firm incurred a constant marginal cost of \$0.25 per unit of the product.) He then solved for the quantity (Q^*) that satisfied the equality. He then found the optimal price by substituting the value of this optimal quantity into Equation (11.3).

$$\text{MR} = \frac{d\text{TR}}{dQ} = 2 - 0.002Q$$

$$2 - 0.002Q = 0.25 \qquad (11.5)$$

$$Q^* = 875 \quad (875,000 \text{ units per week})$$

(Continued)

[12]You may wish to consult the appendix to this chapter before going over this solution.

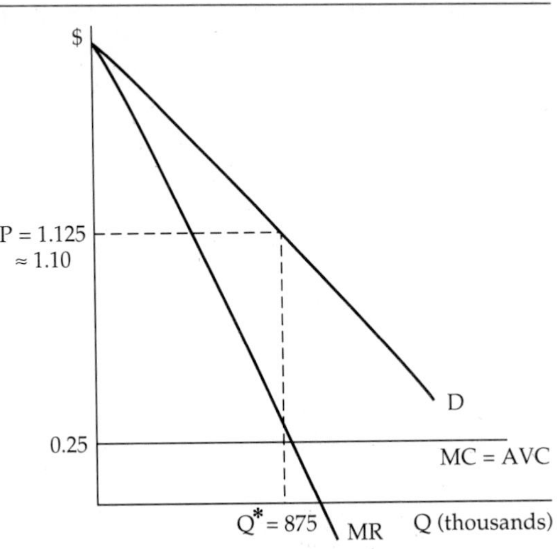

Figure 11.16 Frank's Result for the Optimal Pricing Problem

$$P = 2 - 0.001(875)$$
$$P^* = 1.125 \qquad (11.6)$$
$$= \$1.10 \text{ (rounding to the nearest 10 cents)}$$

Figure 11.16 shows Frank's solution on a per-unit basis.

Frank assumed that the main distributors of the soft drink would be small retail food establishments, which generally mark up the wholesale price of a soft drink by about 100 percent. Therefore, Frank determined the wholesale price that Global Foods could charge the retail stores by simply taking 50 percent of the optimal price of $1.10. For every unit sold, the company would receive $0.55.

Frank then estimated the company's weekly profit from the production and sale of soft drinks.

$$\text{TR} = \$0.55 \times 875$$
$$= 481.25, \text{ or } \$481,250$$
$$\text{TC} = 150 + 0.25(875)$$
$$= 368.75, \text{ or } \$368,750$$
$$\text{Total profit} = \$481,250 - \$368,750$$
$$= \$112,500$$

It was all there in black and white: the profit-maximizing retail price for this product was $1.10, and the profit-maximizing wholesale price was $0.55 (based on the assumption that the retailers would use a 100 percent markup). The only thing left to do was to prepare for the big presentation to the management committee.

Summary

This chapter has presented a view of the pricing and output decisions facing firms under four distinct market conditions. We demonstrated that firms that wish to maximize their short-run profit (or minimize their short-run loss) should establish their price and output levels in accordance with the MR = MC rule. For those firms in perfectly competitive markets, MR is in fact equal to the price that has already been established for them by the forces of supply and demand. For these "price-taking" firms, the only task is to decide what output quantity results in the matching of the market price (i.e., marginal revenue) and the marginal cost of producing the last unit of output. For those firms with the power to establish their own price (i.e., monopolists, monopolistic competitors, and oligopolists who act as price leaders), following the MR = MC rule involves pricing the product at the level whereby the quantity that people purchase is the amount needed to bring MR in line with MC. Variations of the MR = MC rule along with further applications of the economic theory of demand and cost and market structure will be presented in the next two chapters.

Important Concepts

Contribution margin: The amount of revenue that a firm earns above its total variable cost. According to economic analysis, a firm experiencing a loss may continue operating in the short run if it has a positive contribution margin. A firm experiencing a negative contribution margin must shut down its operations because its revenue cannot even cover its variable costs of operations.

Economic cost: All cost incurred to attract resources into a company's employ. Such cost includes explicit cost usualy recognized on accounting records as well as opportunity cost.

Economic loss: A situation that exists when a firm's revenues cannot cover its accounting cost as well as its opportunity cost of production.

Economic profit: Total revenue minus total economic cost. An amount of profit earned in a particular endeavor above the amount of profit that the firm could be earning in its next best alternative activity. Also referred to as *abnormal profit* or *above-normal* profit.

Long-run market analysis: Firms are expected to enter a market in which sellers are earning economic profit. They are expected to leave a market in which sellers are incurring economic losses.

Market power: The power to establish the market price.

Market structure: The number and relative sizes of the buyers and sellers in a particular market. A "competitive" market structure implies that the number of buyers and sellers in a market is large enough that it is difficult, if not impossible, for any one buyer or seller to determine the market price.

Monopolistic competition: A market distinguished from perfect competition in that each seller attempts to differentiate its product from those of its competitors (e.g., in terms of location, efficiency of service, advertising, or promotion). Good examples of this type of market can be found in small businesses, particularly those in the retail trade.

Monopoly: A market in which there is only one seller for a particular good or service. There may be legal barriers to entry into this type of market (e.g., regulated utilities, patent protection).

MR = MC rule: A rule stating that if a firm desires to maximize its economic profit, it must produce an amount of output whereby the marginal revenue received at this particular level is equal to its marginal cost. This implies that those firms with market power must set a price that prompts buyers to purchase this particular level of output.

Mutual interdependence: A situation in which each firm in the market sets a price based on its costs, price elasticity, *and* anticipated reaction of its competitors. This type of pricing situation prevails in oligopolistic markets.

Normal profit: An amount of profit earned in a particular endeavor that is just equal to the profit that could be earned in a firm's next best alternative activity. When a firm earns normal profit, its revenue is just enough to cover both its accounting cost and its opportunity cost. It can also be considered as the return to capital and management necessary to keep resources engaged in a particular activity.

Oligopoly: A market in which there is a small number of relatively large sellers. Pricing in this type of market is characterized by mutual interdependence among the sellers. Products may either be standardized or differentiated.

P = MC rule: A variation of the MR = MC rule for those firms operating in perfectly competitive markets. In such markets, firms are price takers. Thus, the price they must deal with (which has been determined by the forces of supply and demand) is in fact the same as a firm's marginal revenue. Firms using this rule must also be careful that the price is greater than average variable cost as well as equal to marginal cost (i.e., $\text{AVC} < P = \text{MC}$). If a firm cannot operate at the production level where this condition holds, it should shut down its operations.

Perfect competition: A market with four main characteristics: (1) a very large number of relatively small buyers and sellers, (2) a standardized product, (3) easy entry and exit, and (4) complete information by all market participants about the market price. Firms in this type of market have absolutely no control over the price and must compete on the basis of the market price established by the forces of supply and demand.

Price leadership: One company in an oligopolistic industry establishes the price, and the other companies follow. Two types of price leadership, barometric and dominant, are discussed in Chapter 13.

Price takers: Firms that operate in perfectly competitive markets.

Pricing for profit: The method of pricing that follows the MR = MC rule.

Pricing for revenue: The pricing of a product in order to maximize a firm's revenue. In this case, the firm would try to price its product to sell an amount of output whereby the revenue earned from the last unit sold would be equal to zero (i.e., MR = 0). Assuming that the firm faces a linear demand curve, the price it establishes to maximize revenue would be lower than the price that would maximize its profit.

Shutdown point: The point at which the firm must consider ceasing its production activity because the short-run loss suffered by operating would be equal to the short-run loss suffered by not operating (i.e., the operating loss = total fixed cost). In a perfectly competitive situation, this point is found at the lowest point of a firm's average variable cost curve. If the market price falls to this point, the firm should consider shutting down its operations. Any price lower than this would dictate that the firm should cease its operations.

Total fixed cost (TFC): A cost that remains constant as the level of output varies. In a short-run analysis, fixed cost is incurred even if the firm produces no output. Also referred to simply as *fixed cost.*

Total variable cost (TVC): The total cost associated with the level of output. This can also be considered the total cost to a firm of using its variable inputs. Also referred to simply as *variable cost.*

Questions

1. What are the main characteristics of a perfectly competitive market that cause buyers and sellers to be price takers? Explain.
2. Explain the importance of free entry and exit in the perfectly competitive market. That is, if free entry and exit did not exist, what impact would this have on the allocation of resources and on the ability of firms to earn above-normal profits over time?
3. "The perfectly competitive model is not very useful for managers because very few markets in the U. S. economy are perfectly competitive." Do you agree with this statement? Explain. Regardless of whether or not you agree, what lessons can managers learn by studying perfectly competitive markets?
4. Explain the key difference between perfect competition and monopolistic competition.
5. Assume that firms in the short run are earning above-normal profits. Explain what will happen to these profits in the long run for the following markets.
   a. Pure monopoly
   b. Oligopoly
   c. Monopolistic competition
6. Explain why the demand curve facing a perfectly competitive firm is assumed to be perfectly elastic (i.e., horizontal at the going market price.)
7. Explain why the demand curve facing a monopolist is less elastic than one facing a firm that operates in a monopolistically competitive market (all other factors held constant).
8. In certain industries, firms buy their most important inputs in markets that are close to perfectly competitive and sell their output in imperfectly competitive markets. Cite as many examples as you can of these types of businesses.

Explain why the profits of such firms tend to increase when there is an excess supply of the inputs they use in their production process.

9. "In the short run, firms that seek to maximize their market share will tend to charge a lower price for their products than firms that seek to maximize their profit." Do you agree with this statement? Explain.
10. Explain why it is sometimes difficult to apply the MR = MC rule in actual business situations.
11. Define interdependence. Why is the price leader so important in markets where this arrangement prevails?

Problems

(For certain questions, consult Appendix 11A.)

1. Following is the graphical representation of a short-run situation faced by a perfectly competitive firm. Is this a good market for this firm to be in? Explain. What do you expect will happen in the long run? Explain.

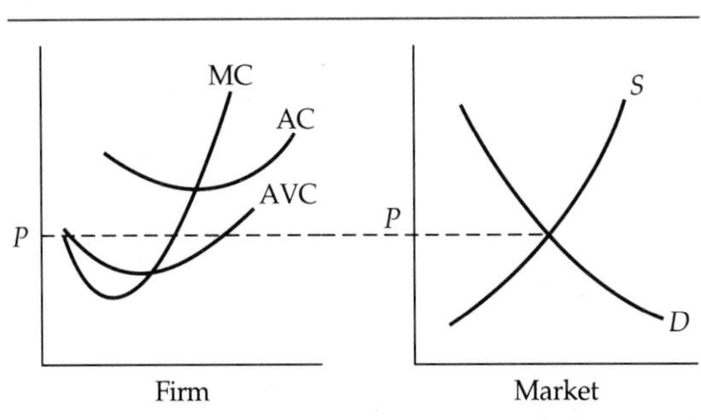

2. Indicate whether each of the following statements is true or false and explain why.
   a. A competitive firm that is incurring a loss should immediately cease operations.
   b. A pure monopoly does not have to worry about suffering losses because it has the power to set its prices at any level it desires.
   c. In the long run, firms operating in perfect competition and monopolistic competition will tend to earn normal profits.
   d. Assuming a linear demand curve, a firm that wishes to maximize its revenue will charge a lower price than a firm that wishes to maximize its profits.
   e. In an oligopoly, the firm that has the largest market share will also be the price leader.
   f. The demand curve facing a firm in a monopolistically competitive market is more elastic than one facing a pure monopoly.
3. Kelson Electronics, a manufacturer of VCRs, estimates the following relation between its marginal cost of production and monthly output:

$$\text{MC} = \$150 + 0.005Q$$

a. What does this function imply about the effect of the law of diminishing returns on Kelson's short-run cost function?
b. Calculate the marginal cost of production at 1,500, 2,000, and 3,500 units of output.
c. Assume Kelson operates as a price taker in a competitive market. What is this firm's profit-maximizing level of output if the market price is $175?
d. Compute Kelson's short-run supply curve for its product.

4. The trucking market is dominated by four large firms that currently account for 50 percent of the industry's total revenue. The largest of these firms wants to reduce the average price it charges per pound from $1.50 to $1.25 in an attempt to increase its market share. Its marginal cost of transporting a package is about $0.95. Do you think that it would be wise for this firm to cut its price? Explain.
5. A manufacturer of electronics products is considering entering the telephone equipment business. It estimates that if it were to begin making telephones, its short-run cost function would be as follows:

Q (thousands)	*AVC*	*AC*	*MC*
9	41.10	52.21	30.70
10	40.00	50.00	30.10
11	39.10	48.19	30.10
12	38.40	46.73	30.70
13	37.90	45.59	31.90
14	37.60	44.74	33.70
15	37.50	44.17	36.10
16	37.60	43.85	39.10
17	37.90	43.78	42.70
18	38.40	43.96	46.90
19	39.10	44.36	51.70
20	40.00	45.00	57.10

a. Plot the average cost, average variable cost, marginal cost, and price on a graph.
b. Suppose the average wholesale price of a telephone set is currently $50. Do you think this company should enter the market? Explain. Indicate on the graph the amount of profit (or loss) earned by the firm at the optimal level of production.
c. Suppose the firm does enter the market and that over time increasing competition causes the price of telephones to fall to $35. What impact will this have on the firm's production levels and profit? Explain. What would you advise this firm to do?

6. This same manufacturer of electronics products has just developed a handheld computer. Following is the cost schedule for producing these computers on a monthly basis. Also included is a schedule of prices and quantities that the firm believes it will be able to sell (based on some previous market research).

Q (thousands)	*Price*	*MR*	*AVC*	*AC*	*MC*
0	1,650				
1	1,570	1,570	1,281	2,281	1,281
2	1,490	1,410	1,134	1,634	987
3	1,410	1,250	1,009	1,342.33	759
4	1,330	1,090	906	1,156	597
5	1,250	930	825	1,025	501
6	1,170	770	766	932.67	471
7	1,090	610	729	871.86	507
8	1,010	450	714	839	609
9	930	290	721	832.11	777
10	850	130	750	850	1,011

a. What price should the firm charge if it wants to maximize its profits in the short run?
b. What arguments can be made for charging a price *higher* than this price? If a higher price is indeed established, what amount would you recommend? Explain.
c. What arguments can be made for charging a *lower* than the profit-maximizing level? If a lower price is indeed established, what amount would you recommend? Explain.

7. A group of five students have decided to form a company to publish a guide to eating establishments located in the vicinity of all major college and university campuses in the state. In planning for an initial publication of 6,000 copies, they estimated the cost of producing this book to be as follows:

Paper	$12,000
Research	2,000
Graphics	5,000
Reproduction services	8,000
Miscellaneous	5,000
Personal computer	4,000
Desktop publishing software	500
Overhead	3,500
Binding	3,000
Shipping	2,000

By engaging in this business, the students realized that they would have to give up their summer jobs. Each student made an average of $4,000 per summer. However, they felt that they could keep expenses down by doing much of the research for the book by themselves with no immediate compensation.

They decided to set the retail price of the book at \$12.50 per copy. Allowing for the 20 percent discount that retail stores in their state generally required, the students anticipated a per-unit revenue of about \$10.00. The director of the campus bookstore advised them that their retail price was far too high, and that a price of about \$8.75 would be more reasonable for a publication of this kind.

One of the students, who was a math and statistics major, asked the bookstore manager to provide her with historical data on sales and prices of similar books. From these data, she estimated the demand for books of this kind to be

$$Q = 18,500 - 1,000P$$

where Q = Number of books sold per year
P = Retail price of the books

a. Construct a numerical table for the retail demand curve, and plot the numbers on a graph. Calculate the elasticity of demand for the interval between \$12.50 and \$8.00.
b. Do you think the students should follow the store manager's advice and price their book at \$8.75? Explain. If you do not agree with this price, what would be the optimal price of the book? Explain.
c. Assuming that the students decide to charge the optimal price, do you think that they should proceed with this venture? Explain.
d. Assuming that the student's demand equation is accurate, offer some possible reasons why the bookstore manager would want to sell the book at the lower price of \$8.75.

8. The manufacturer of high-quality fax machines is trying to decide what price to set for its product. The costs of production and the demand for the product are assumed to be as follows:

$$\text{TC} = 500,000 + 0.85Q + 0.015Q^2$$
$$Q = 14,166 - 16.6P$$

a. Determine the short-run profit-maximizing price.
b. Plot this information on a graph showing AC, AVC, MC, P, and MR.

9. The demand and cost function for a company are estimated to be as follows:

$$P = 100 - 8Q$$
$$\text{TC} = 50 + 80Q - 10Q^2 + 0.6Q^3$$

a. What price should the company charge if it wishes to maximize its profit in the short run?
b. What price should it charge if it wishes to maximize its revenue in the short run?
c. Suppose the company lacks confidence in the accuracy of cost estimates expressed in a cubic equation and simply wants to use a linear approxi-

mation. Suggest a linear representation of this cubic equation. What difference would it have on the recommended profit-maximizing and revenue-maximizing prices?

10. Overheard at the water cooler: "The demand and cost estimates that were provided at the meeting are very useful [$Q = 90 - 6.5P$ and $\text{TC} = 150 + 3.5Q$]. Unfortunately, what we didn't realize at the time was that our fixed costs were underestimated by at least 30 percent. This means that we'll have to adjust upward our price by at least 30 percent to cover the added fixed cost. In any case, there is no way in the world that we can survive by charging less than $9 for our product."
    a. Comment on this statement. Do you agree with the speaker? Explain. Illustrate your answer with the use a graph indicating the firm's short-run cost structure.
    b. What price do you think this firm should charge if it wants to maximize its short-run profit?

APPENDIX 11A
The Use of Calculus in Pricing and Output Decisions

Thus far, we have discussed the firm's pricing and output decisions with the use of tabular and graphical examples. Using both the "total" approach and the "marginal" approach, we arrived at the MR = MC rule for determining the optimal level of output and price for those firms able to exercise market power. As a supplement, we now explain the MR = MC rule with the use of calculus.

To simplify our illustrations, we assume that the firm has a quadratic total cost function, rather than the cubic function used throughout the examples in the previous sections of this chapter.

Perfect Competition

Suppose that you are the owner and operator of a perfectly competitive firm with the following total cost function:

$$\text{TC} = 2{,}000 + 10Q + 0.02Q^2 \tag{11A.1}$$

Suppose further that the current market price is $25. By definition, $\text{TR} = P \times Q$, so your total revenue function can be stated as:

$$\text{TR} = 25Q \tag{11A.2}$$

Profit (π) is defined as TR−TC. Therefore, using Equations (11A.1) and (11A.2), your firm's profit function can be expressed as:

$$\begin{aligned} \pi &= 25Q - (2{,}000 + 10Q + 0.02Q^2) \\ &= 25Q - 2{,}000 - 10Q - 0.02Q^2 \\ &= -2{,}000 + 15Q - 0.02Q^2 \end{aligned} \tag{11A.3}$$

The optimal output level (Q^*) can be found at the point where your firm's marginal profit is equal to zero. In other words, additional units of output should be produced as long as your firm earns additional profit from their sale. Using calculus, the marginal profit can be expressed as the first derivative of the profit function:

$$\frac{d\pi}{dQ} = 15 - 0.04Q \tag{11A.4}$$

Setting Equation (11A.4) equal to zero and solving for the optimal level of output (Q^*),

$$\begin{aligned} 15 - 0.04Q &= 0 \\ Q^* &= 375 \end{aligned} \tag{11A.5}$$

Returning to the total profit function presented in Equation (11A.3) and substituting Q^* for Q results in the following profit:

$$\begin{aligned} \pi &= -2,000 + 15(375) - 0.02(375)^2 \\ &= \$812.50 \end{aligned} \tag{11A.6}$$

We conclude that at the price of \$25, the firm will earn maximum economic profit by producing 375 units of output per time period.

An alternative way of finding P^* and Q^* is to set the firm's marginal revenue function equal to its marginal cost function and then solve for Q^*. We already know that MR $= P$. The marginal cost function is the first derivative of the total cost function:

$$\text{MC} = \frac{d\text{TC}}{dQ} = 10 + 0.04Q \tag{11A.7}$$

Setting MR equal to Equation (11A.7) and solving for Q^* gives us

$$\begin{aligned} 25 &= 10 + 0.04Q \\ 15 &= 0.04Q \\ Q^* &= 375 \end{aligned} \tag{11A.8}$$

Comparison of Equations (11A.8) and (11A.5) provides a useful and concise explanation of the MR = MC rule. As you can see, using this rule is the mathematical equivalent of finding the level of output that maximizes the total profit function.

Monopoly

As the manager of a product that only your company sells (e.g., a patent-protected product), suppose you are given the following information:

$$\text{TC} = 10,000 + 100Q + 0.02Q^2 \tag{11A.9}$$

$$Q_D = 20,000 - 100P \tag{11A.10}$$

You can use the same procedure employed in the case of perfect competition to find Q^* and P^*.

First, determine your marginal revenue function. Because you are a price setter and not a price taker, you cannot assume that MR $= P$. Instead, you must derive the marginal revenue function from your firm's demand function, shown in equation (11A.10). Because your objective is to find the level of output that will maximize your profit (i.e., Q^*), you must rearrange the terms in the equation so that price depends on the level of output:

$$P = 200 - 0.01Q \tag{11A.11}$$

By definition, TR $= P \times Q$. So by substitution,

$$\begin{aligned} \text{TR} &= (200 - 0.01Q)Q \\ &= 200Q - 0.01Q^2 \end{aligned} \tag{11A.12}$$

The marginal revenue function is the first derivative of the total revenue function:

$$\text{MR} = \frac{d\text{TR}}{dQ} = 200 - 0.02Q \tag{11A.13}$$

From the example of perfect competition, we know that the first derivative of the total cost function is the marginal cost function:

$$\text{MC} = \frac{d\text{TC}}{dQ} = 100 + 0.04Q \tag{11A.14}$$

Thus, the MR $=$ MC rule is adhered to by setting Equation (11A.13) equal to Equation (11A.14) and solving for Q^*:

$$\begin{aligned} 200 - 0.02Q &= 100 + 0.04Q \\ 0.06Q &= 100 \\ Q^* &= 1,667 \text{(rounded to the nearest whole number)} \end{aligned} \tag{11A.15}$$

To find P^* we return to Equation (11A.11) and substitute Q^* for Q.

$$\begin{aligned} P &= 200 - 0.01(1,667) \\ P^* &= \$183.33, \text{ or } \$183 \end{aligned} \tag{11A.16}$$

At the rounded price of $183, your firm can expect to sell 1,667 units of output per time period and earn an economic profit of $73,333 (rounded to the nearest dollar). From the example on perfect competition, you should be aware of how the profit figure was determined.

* * *

As you can see from the preceding examples, the use of calculus offers a very concise way of explaining the output decision for price-taking firms in perfectly competitive markets and the pricing/output decision for monopoly firms. The same procedures could be applied for those firms in monopolistic competition and even for oligopolistic firms that have clear-cut roles as price leaders in their markets. However, tables and graphs similar to those used in previous sections of this chapter provide the same answers as the calculus method. Our intention is for this appendix to serve as a supplement rather than an advanced treatment of the pricing/output decision.

CHAPTER 12

Break-Even Analysis (Volume-Cost-Profit)

The Situation

October and November of each year are extremely busy months for the department of financial planning at Global Foods, Inc. It is during this period that the financial plan for the next two years is prepared. As is customary in business, greater emphasis is always placed on the first of the two years. Planning data are collected from all departments—covering projected sales, costs, and expenses. After checking as much as possible to ensure reasonability and accuracy, the department consolidates the numbers to obtain a planned income and expense statement. The plans are prepared along profit center lines, usually by specific flavors of the products.

Suzanne Prescott is the senior analyst responsible for the diet cola line plan. She and her assistant have worked on this project for two weeks and have completed the profit plan, which she will present to the manager of the financial planning department.

The first page of the presentation shows the income statement for the diet cola profit center (see Table 12.1.) The first column of numbers shows the proposed plan amounts for the year 199X + 1.[1] The next column presents the percent change from the outlook for year 199X. Since the plan is being prepared late in the year 199X, the final figures are not yet available. Therefore, an outlook has been used, which includes the actual results through October and estimates for the last two months.

Suzanne has kept her manager, Dorothy Simon, informed regarding the progress of the plan. As is quite common during a corporate planning cycle, their final discussion has been delayed several times due to late data, changed numbers, and

[1]Assume that 199X represents the current year; thus, next year is 199X + 1.

(Continued)

missed schedules. Thus, Suzanne and Dorothy are meeting just one day before the results are to be presented to the company's controller. Dorothy agrees with the method with which the plan has been put together and with the results Suzanne has presented. But she expects that the controller will require additional information. She asks Suzanne whether she has performed a sensitivity analysis calculating profit results if sales were to be 10 percent lower or 10 percent higher than planned. She is also interested in the level of sales at which profit would be zero, to establish the "worst case." Suzanne admits that this analysis is incomplete due to lack of time. Since the presentation must be ready the next day, there is not enough time to rework the complete plan to obtain the alternative results. Suzanne will therefore have to devise a method by which she can obtain some good estimates for the "what if" cases, estimates sufficiently reliable to show the controller. She remembers that in graduate school, she learned a method called break-even or volume-cost-profit analysis. Fortunately, she happens to have a few old textbooks in her office.

Table 12.1 Income Statement for Diet Cola Profit Center

	Plan for 199X + 1($000)	*Percent Change from 199X*
Sales	$50,000	5.0
Cost of sales:		
Materials	8,000	4.5
Labor	10,000	5.5
Overhead	9,500	4.0
Total cost of sales	27,500	4.7
Gross profit	22,500	5.4
Selling and administrative expenses	11,500	5.8
Research and development expenses	3,000	3.4
Total expenses	14,500	5.3
Net earnings before taxes	$ 8,000	5.6

Introduction

The analysis to be described in this chapter is derived from price/output decision making in the short run, which was discussed in the previous chapter.

The graph illustrating the firm's decision-making mechanism with some form of imperfect competition[2] in the short run is presented in Figure 12.1*a*. The total

[2]Either monopoly or monopolistic competition.

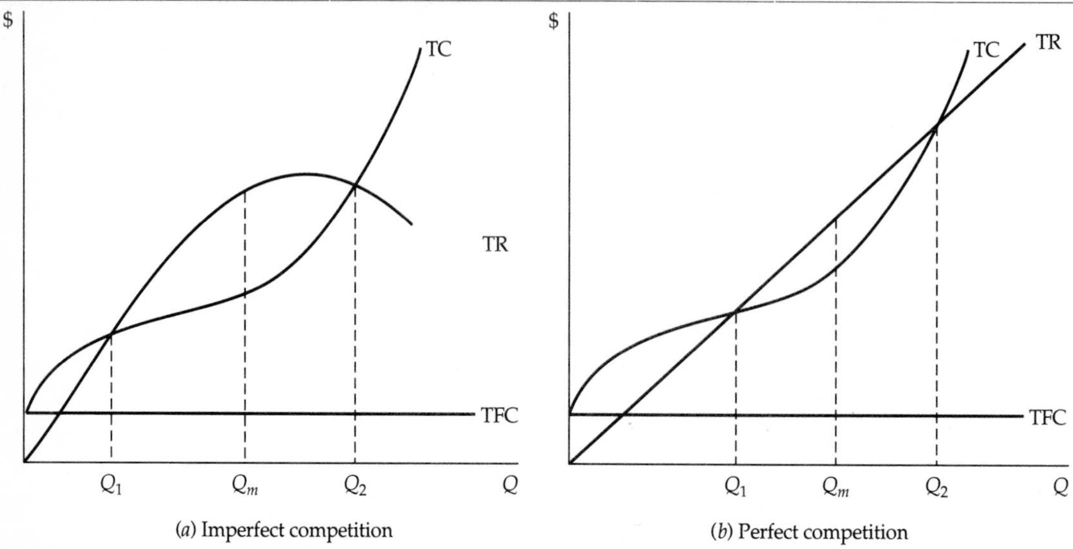

Figure 12.1 Total Revenue and Cost Functions

revenue function rises at a decreasing rate and finally drops absolutely because the price of the product decreases as more of it is sold. The costs are composed of fixed and variable portions. The fixed cost remains the same regardless of quantity produced. The variable cost at first exhibits increasing marginal product (or decreasing marginal costs), but as quantity rises, decreasing marginal returns begin. Profit is achieved at quantities between Q_1 and Q_2, and there is a unique maximum profit point at Q_m, where the vertical distance between TR and TC is the largest.[3]

The TC curve in Figure 12.1*b* is the same as in Figure 12.1*a*, but the TR curve is a straight line. This represents the case of perfect competition under which the firm is able to sell any number of units it produces at a given price. As in the imperfectly competitive case, profit is present between quantities Q_1 and Q_2 and is maximized at Q_m.

Both of these cases should be quite familiar. In this chapter, we will simplify these two situations even further in the discussion of what is commonly referred to as *break-even* or *volume-cost-profit* analysis.

The concept of fixed costs will be retained, as will the straight-line total revenue curve. The change arises in the treatment of variable costs, which in both the competitive and monopoly cases assumed the presence of first increasing and then decreasing marginal product (or first decreasing and then increasing marginal cost). For the present analysis, constant marginal product (or constant marginal cost) will be assumed. Consequently, the variable cost curve (again added to the fixed cost line) will be a straight line, since if marginal cost is constant, so is average variable cost. This construction is presented in Figure 12.2.

[3]This is, of course, the point at which marginal cost and marginal revenue are equal.

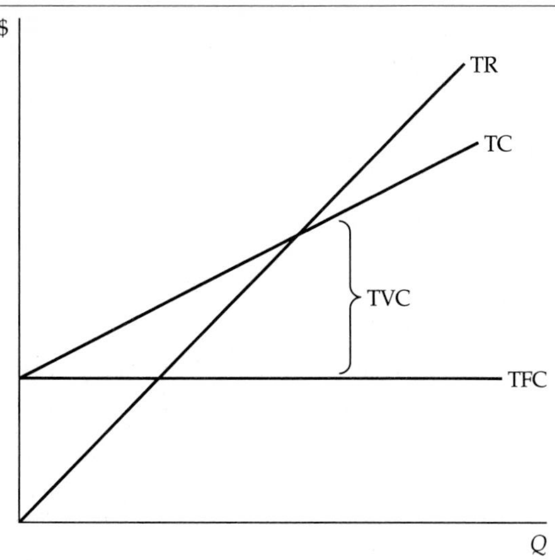

Figure 12.2 Total Revenue and Cost Curves (Constant Average Variable Cost)

Thus, break-even analysis can be seen as a simplification of the usual short-run analysis in economics:

1. It assumes that in the short run there is a distinction between variable and fixed costs.

2. It assumes linearity (i.e., straight-line curves) throughout the entire analysis.

3. It implicitly assumes the presence of perfect competition since the price is considered to be the same regardless of quantity. (This procedure is followed, however, more for convenience than for theoretical reasons and can be changed.[4])

4. The straight-line cost curve implies that marginal product is neither increasing nor decreasing, and that the entire range of the graph exhibits constant returns (constant marginal product) and, therefore, constant average and marginal costs. However, as with the straight-line total revenue curve, the presence of constant returns for the entire range is not essential (see footnote 4). With the relevant range of decision making limited to some reasonable interval

[4]It also must be understood that the horizontal (quantity) axis on graphs used in economics tends to measure very large quantity intervals. To claim that exact relationships hold over these long intervals is rather unrealistic. It is done for convenience and ease of exposition. But a firm will generally not consider such wide-ranging alternatives. It is much more likely that a company, given a particular level of production, will try to analyze some limited deviations from that level to, say, 5–10 percent higher or 5–10 percent lower. In such a limited interval, it is quited possible that a significant price change may not be necessary. Thus, even if the particular firm is not in a perfectly competitive market, a straight-line total revenue curve (i.e., no price change) in the relevant range may be close to reality.

on the horizontal (quantity) axis, it is quite conceivable that the variable cost per unit will not change significantly. So, the ultimate presence of diminishing marginal returns need not be denied in this analysis. Even if some change were to occur, it may not be large enough to affect the final results seriously. Figure 12.3 illustrates this point. The vertical distance between the two lines in the delineated interval is not great, nor is the difference in slope. Thus, the marginal costs specified by the two curves will not exhibit extreme differences.

Furthermore, as mentioned in the discussion of empirical cost estimates, the existence of constant unit variable costs in industry over a considerable range of quantities is a distinct possibility.

There are, however, some important differences between customary economic analysis and the break-even method that should not be overlooked.

1. The short-run economic chart shows two points where economic profits are zero, and maximum profit is identified somewhere between these two points. In break-even analysis, there is only one no-profit (break-even) point. As quantities rise beyond this point, profit increases continuously until, presumably, capacity is reached,[5] and no additional quantities of product can be achieved. At this point, costs become infinitely high, and the total cost line would thus cross the total revenue line.

2. There is also a major difference between the objectives of the two analyses. In Chapter 11, interest focused on the question of resource allocation—the

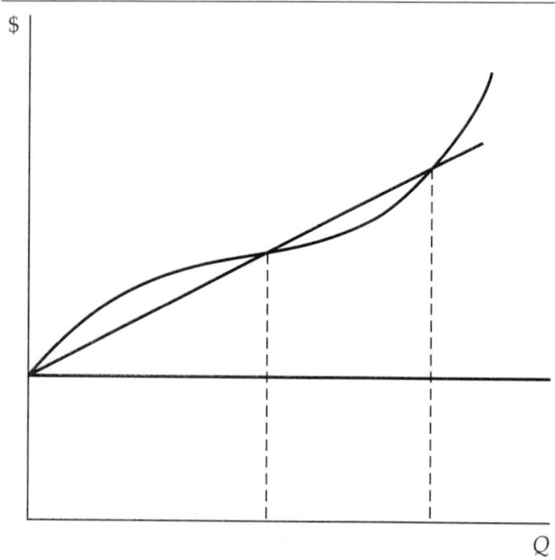

Figure 12.3 The Implicit Assumption of Constant Returns

[5]Since break-even analysis deals with the short run only, capacity does not change.

effect of a price change or a cost change on the quantity produced. In break-even analysis, the question is: What impact does a change in quantity have on variable costs and profit?

3. The third difference lies in the use of the cost concept. Economic costs, as previously discussed, are based on replacement costs and include imputed costs and normal profit. Break-even analysis, as practiced in business, usually relies on accounting costs (often standard costs as used in cost accounting), which include explicit costs only and represent historical data. However, in this case, careful treatment of data could convert accounting data into economic cost data. For instance, as will be shown later, a "required" minimum profit, which can represent the normal profit, can be included in the calculation.

In the following sections of this chapter, we will outline formulas utilized in the calculation of break-even analysis.

The Break-Even Point

The first of the calculations we will examine identifies the quantity at which the company will just break even—no profit, no loss. It is, of course, this point that gives the analysis its name. But this is not the point where company executives wish the firm to be. The break-even point merely sets the stage to investigate the relationship between quantity of the product, the cost to produce this quantity, and the profit—hence the name *volume-cost-profit* analysis.

The same abbreviations used in previous chapters will be utilized here:

P = Price	TC = Total cost
TVC = Total variable cost	Q = Quantity produced
AVC = Average variable cost	TR = Total revenue
TFC = Total fixed cost	π = Profit

The very simple equation for profit is:

$$\begin{aligned} \pi &= \text{TR} - \text{TC} \\ &= \text{TR} - \text{TVC} - \text{TFC} \\ &= (P \times Q) - (\text{AVC} \times Q) - \text{TFC} \\ &= Q(P - \text{AVC}) - \text{TFC} \end{aligned}$$

To obtain the no-profit—break-even—point, total revenue is set equal to total cost:

$$\begin{aligned} \text{TR} &= \text{TVC} + \text{TFC} \\ (P \times Q) &= (\text{AVC} \times \text{Q}) + \text{TFC} \\ (P \times Q) - (\text{AVC} \times \text{Q}) &= \text{TFC} \\ Q(P - \text{AVC}) &= \text{TFC} \end{aligned}$$

Thus, the break-even quantity is

$$Q = \text{TFC}/(P - \text{AVC})$$

For example, if P = \$5, AVC = \$3, and TFC = \$20,000,

$$Q = 20{,}000/(5 - 3) = 20{,}000/2 = 10{,}000$$

This result can be checked as follows:

Total revenue (10,000 × 5)	50,000
Total variable cost (10,000 × 3)	30,000
Total fixed cost	20,000
Total cost	50,000
Profit	0

If the quantity produced is larger than 10,000 units, a profit will result. If quantity drops below 10,000, the company will incur a loss.

A simple Lotus program has been written to facilitate computation of the results. The three variables are entered, and the break-even quantity and revenue are calculated. At the same time, a table is created showing the revenues, costs, and profits for different quantities of product. The results are shown in Table 12.2. From this table, a graph (Figure 12.4) is generated, which shows clearly the break-even point and, to the right of this point, the ever-increasing size of the profit.

What happens to the break-even point when one or more of the variables change? A rise in average variable costs will increase the slope of the total cost line and will raise the break-even point. If total fixed costs increase, the curve will rise (parallel to the previously drawn total cost curve), and so will the break-even point. Similarly, a decrease in price will raise the break-even point. Movements in the opposite direction (a cost decrease or a price increase) will lower the break-even point.

Figure 12.5*a* and *b* illustrates two such changes. In Figure 12.5*a*, price has been increased to \$5.50. The break-even point is now

Table 12.2 Break-Even Analysis

Variables	
Price per unit	5.00
Variable cost per unit	3.00
Total fixed cost	20000
Break–even quantity	10000
Break–even revenue	50000

UNITS	FIXED COST	VARIABLE COST	TOTAL COST	REVENUE	PROFIT
0	20000	0	20000	0	−20000
5000	20000	15000	35000	25000	−10000
10000	20000	30000	50000	50000	0
15000	20000	45000	65000	75000	10000
20000	20000	60000	80000	100000	20000
25000	20000	75000	95000	125000	30000
30000	20000	90000	110000	150000	40000
35000	20000	105000	125000	175000	50000
40000	20000	120000	140000	200000	60000

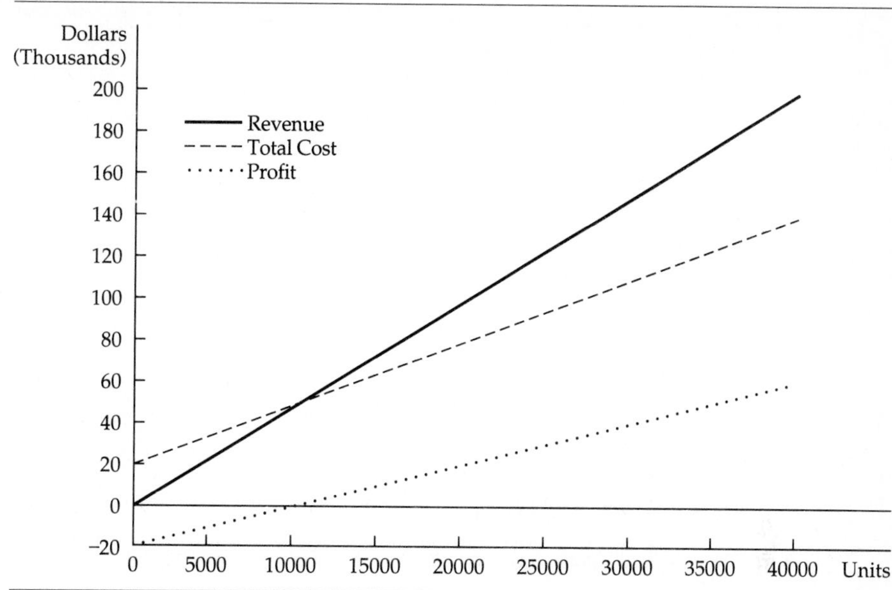

Figure 12.4 Break-Even Analysis

$$20{,}000/(5.50 - 3) = 20{,}000/2.50 = 8{,}000$$

Raising the price by 10 percent has resulted in a 20 percent decrease in the break-even point.

Figure 12.5*b* illustrates an increase in variable cost to \$3.33, with price remaining at \$5 per unit. The result here will, of course, be opposite from that shown in Figure 12.5*a*. More will have to be produced for the firm to break even, and profits will start at this higher quantity. The new calculation will be as follows:

$$20{,}000/(5 - 3.33) = 20{,}000/1.67 = 12{,}000$$

If fixed cost were to increase to \$25,000 (with price and average variable cost remaining at \$5 and \$3, respectively), the break-even point would rise to 12,500. Students can easily calculate and graph this or any other result.

Break-Even Revenue

Under certain circumstances, the product price and the unit variable costs may not be available. This will happen—frequently—when more than one product is produced in a plant. Since each of the different products being manufactured side by side has a different price and a different unit variable cost, it is difficult to utilize the formula of the previous section to establish the break-even point of the plant.

One way out of this dilemma is to calculate a weighted average price and unit cost for the products.[6]

[6]This, of course, presupposes that the proportions of the various products in the total product quantity remains the same.

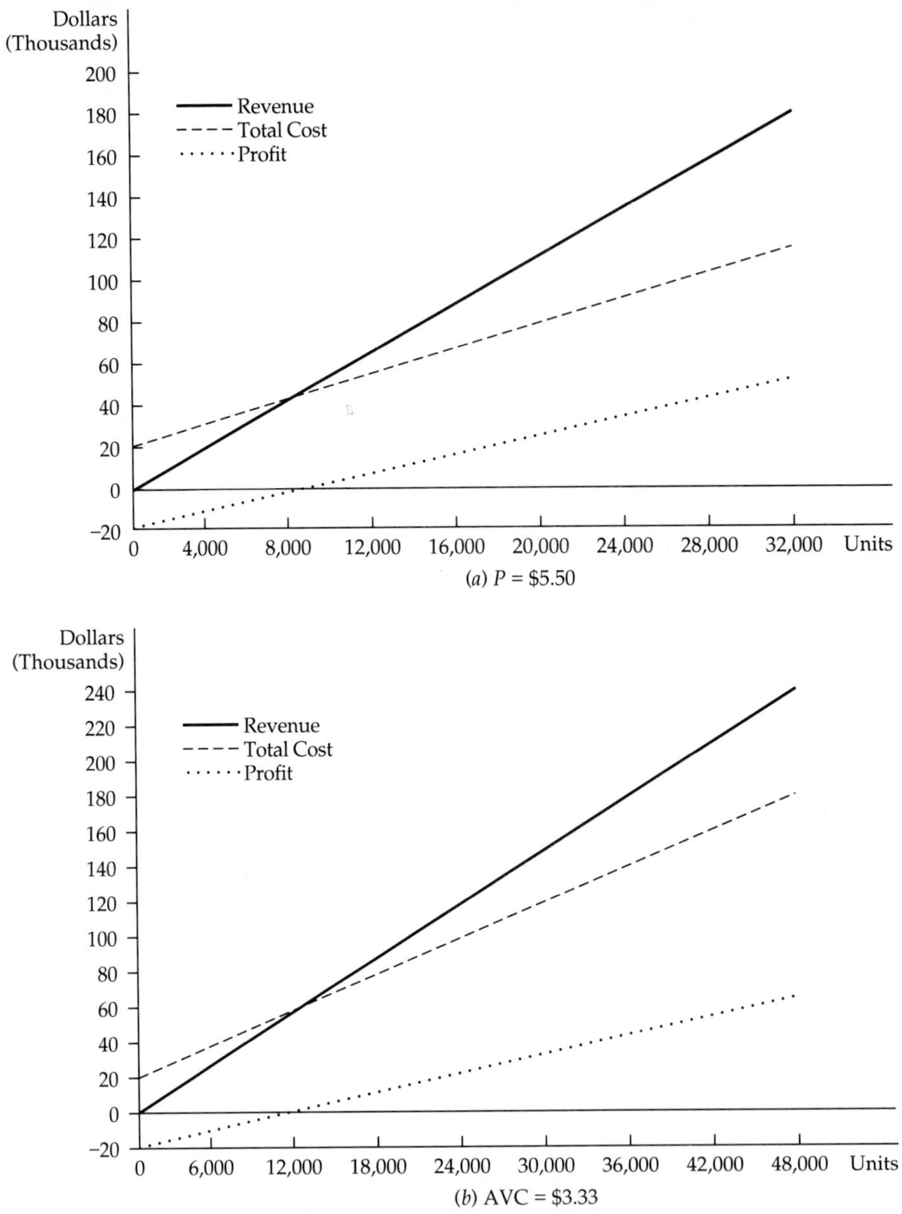

Figure 12.5 Effect of Variable Change on Break-Even Analysis

Another method is to calculate a break-even revenue figure directly. In this case, however, a simplifying assumption is necessary: Total variable cost must be a constant percentage of total revenue. Actually, this condition is no different from assuming a constant price and a constant average variable cost, as we did in the previous section. If the products' average variable costs represent different percentages of each product's price, then, for the total variable costs to bear a constant relationship to total revenue as total revenue changes, the proportion of each product's revenue to the total must remain the same; in other words, the quantities of the products will change in the same proportion. Again, making such an assumption does not appear to be unrealistic for relatively small changes in total revenue.

Starting with the equation that shows revenue at break-even,

$$\text{TR} = \text{TVC} + \text{TFC}$$

we now convert TVC into a constant fraction of total revenue.

If $a = \text{TVC}/\text{TR}$, then $\text{TVC} = a \times \text{TR}$, where a is a constant less than 1. Then

$$\begin{aligned} \text{TR} &= (a \times \text{TR}) + \text{TFC} \\ \text{TR} - (a \times \text{TR}) &= \text{TFC} \\ \text{TR}(1 - a) &= \text{TFC} \end{aligned}$$

and break-even total revenue is

$$\text{TR} = \text{TFC}/(1 - a)$$

For example, if $\text{TFC} = 20{,}000$ and $a = .6$, then break-even TR is

$$\text{TR} = 20{,}000/(1 - .6) = 20{,}000/.4 = 50{,}000$$

which is the same result as obtained previously, since if $P = 5$, and $\text{AVC} = 3$, $a = .6$ expresses the same relationship.

Required Profit

If the only objective of this analysis were to find the point at which a plant or a company breaks even, not much would be accomplished. We have already shown a table of quantities and profits that can be generated. In this section and the next, additional formulas will be constructed to answer more interesting questions. A required profit level is included in the equation in this section. Subsequently, the sensitivity of profits to quantity will be investigated.

For a company to prosper, it must earn profits, not just break even. If a firm has a particular dollar profit objective per period, a small adjustment of the break-even equation will provide the appropriate output measure. A specific, fixed dollar amount of required profit can be handled as an addition to fixed cost; it also does not change as a function of quantity.

Continuing the illustration that has been used throughout this chapter, if the owners of the firm require a \$10,000 profit, the equation is altered as follows:

$$\begin{aligned} Q_{\pi'} &= (\text{TFC} + \text{Profit requirement})/(\text{P} - \text{AVC}) \\ &= (20{,}000 + 10{,}000)/(5 - 3) \\ &= 30{,}000/2 = 15{,}000 \end{aligned}$$

where Q_{π} stands for break-even with profit requirement. These results can be checked readily:

Total revenue ($15,000 × $5)	$75,000
Total fixed cost	20,000
Total variable cost ($15,000 × $3)	45,000
Total cost	65,000
Profit	$10,000

If a specific profit per unit of product is required, this unit profit must be added to the average variable cost. For instance, suppose the company's objective is 40 cents profit per unit. Then AVC is changed to $3.40, and

$$Q = 20{,}000/1.60 = 12{,}500$$

Checking results, we obtain,

Total revenue (12,500 × 5)	$62,500
Total fixed cost	20,000
Total variable cost (12,500 × 3)	37,500
Total cost	57,500
Total profit	$5,000
Profit per unit (5,000/12,500)	$0.40

Earlier in this chapter it was stated that the calculation of cost in volume-cost-profit analysis usually involves the use of accounting data. However, the "required profit" concept can easily be interpreted to represent the implied or opportunity costs that economists find crucial to the analysis of the firm. Thus, the profit measure, whether total or per unit, can be the normal profit, which is the minimum amount necessary to cause the owner to continue operating this business.

Degree of Operating Leverage

Since volume-cost-profit analysis is concerned with the effect of a change in quantity of product on the profits of a firm, we must develop a method to quantify this effect. Such a method, called *degree of operating leverage* (DOL), is, in fact, a type of elasticity formula. The calculation result is a coefficient that measures the effect a percentage change in quantity has on the percentage change in profit.

$$\text{DOL} = \frac{\%\Delta\pi}{\%\Delta Q}$$

The percent change in profit can be written as follows:

$$\%\Delta\pi = \frac{\Delta\pi}{\pi} = \frac{\Delta Q(P - \text{AVC})}{Q(P - \text{AVC}) - \text{TFC}}$$

The percent change in quantity equals $\Delta Q/Q$. Putting these two expressions together:

$$\frac{\Delta Q(P - \text{AVC})}{Q(P - \text{AVC}) - \text{TFC}} \div \frac{\Delta Q}{Q} = \frac{\Delta Q(P - \text{AVC})}{Q(P - \text{AVC}) - \text{TFC}} \times \frac{Q}{\Delta Q} = \frac{Q(P - \text{AVC})}{Q(P - \text{AVC}) - \text{TFC}}$$

Thus,

$$\text{DOL} = \frac{Q(P - \text{AVC})}{Q(P - \text{AVC}) - \text{TFC}}$$

To better explain the meaning of DOL, let us use the example of the preceding section. At a production of 15,000 units, profit was $10,000. DOL can now be measured at the 15,000 quantity:

$$\text{DOL} = \frac{15{,}000(5 - 3)}{15{,}000(5 - 3) - 20{,}000} = \frac{30{,}000}{10{,}000} = 3$$

DOL = 3 means that, at $Q = 15{,}000$, a 1 percent change in quantity will result in a 3 percent change in profit (and a 10 percent change in Q will lead to a 30 percent change in profit. Also, a 15 percent change will bring about a 45 percent change, etc.). The DOL effect can be seen in terms of an income statement at quantities of 13,500 and 16,500 (a 10 percent decrease and a 10 percent increase):

	Q = 13,500	Q = 15,000	Q = 16,5000
Total revenue	$67,500	$75,000	$82,500
Total fixed cost	20,000	20,000	20,000
Total variable cost	40,500	45,000	49,500
Total cost	60,500	65,000	69,500
Profit	$ 7,000	$10,000	$13,000

At a quantity of 13,500, profit is $7,000, or 30 percent less than at a quantity of 15,000 units. Conversely, at a quantity of 16,500 units, the profit is $13,000, or 30 percent larger.[7]

The importance of the degree of operating leverage is that it reveals to management the effect on profits of a small change in quantity. This construction will hold only, of course, as long as all variables remain the same (i.e., price, average variable cost, and total fixed cost).

The relative sizes of fixed and variable costs influence the level of the DOL coefficient. A plant with high fixed costs and low variable costs will have a higher DOL than a plant with lower fixed costs and higher variable costs. The former plant will also have a higher break-even point. The significance of this relationship is that a firm with high fixed costs—a capital-intensive firm—will usually achieve break-even at a higher quantity, but since it has a higher DOL,

[7]The degree of operating leverage can be calculated at any point in the profit or loss area. However, it cannot be calculated at the break-even quantity, since a percentage change in profit from zero does not make sense. (The denominator of the DOL formula is zero at break-even quantity.)

its profits will grow at a relatively high rate when production rises above break-even. Its profits will also decline more quickly during downturns in economic activity, and the firm will become unprofitable at a relatively high point of production (since its break-even quantity will be high). On the other hand, a plant with lower fixed costs and higher variable costs—a labor-intensive plant, perhaps somewhat obsolete—will break even at lower quantities, and its profits will tend to rise or fall less quickly when quantity produced moves up or down.

Thus, the break-even quantity and the DOL can have a very significant influence on a firm deciding whether or not to convert from an old—labor-intensive—manufacturing facility to a more modern, automated (i.e., capital-intensive) plant. For example, using income statement from the diet cola profit center presented at the beginning of this chapter, let us assume that the average variable costs per unit are $2.75 and total fixed costs are $14,500. [8] The break-even point for a $5 price, is easily calculated as 6,444 units (rounded to the nearest integer).

Now suppose that additional, more up-to-date machinery were installed in the plant, increasing annual fixed costs to $20,000 and driving average variable cost down to $2.25. The break-even point for the modernized plant will be at a production of 7,273 units. Thus, given these new conditions, the minimum quantity needed to break even has risen by 829 units. Why, then, should the company invest in the new machinery? Since the newly equipped plant enjoys a higher degree of operating leverage, its profits will rise more quickly with increases in production. At some quantity, the modernized plant and the old one will achieve equal profits. In this case, the point of equality is 11,000 units, at which both plants will show a profit of $10,250. [9]

At the production level of 11,000 units, the DOL values for the old and modernized plants are 2.41 and 2.95, respectively. Thus, if more than 11,000 cases of diet cola to be produced annually in the future, the profit from the modernized plant will be greater. If, however, the quantity is expected to remain at 10,000 cases per year, as in the company's plan, modernization would not be advisable at this time. Another, simple Lotus program has been written to compare two plants with different costs. The data for the present example are shown in Table 12.3.[10] Tables 12.4 and 12.5 and Figures 12.6 and 12.7 present the resulting numbers and graphs for the two situations, showing the effects of the different DOLs.

---

[8]These are the numbers Suzanne Prescott will arrive at later in this chapter.

[9]This point is calculated as follows:.

$$Q(P - AVC_a) - TFC_a = Q(P - AVC_b) - TFC_b$$

where the subscripts a and b denote the old plant and the modernized plant, respectively.

$$\begin{aligned} Q(2.25) - 14{,}500 &= Q(2.75) - 20{,}000 \\ 0.5Q &= 5{,}500 \\ Q &= 11{,}000 \end{aligned}$$

The profit for a quantity of 11,000 units is $10,250 for each plant.

[10]Three variables (P, AVC, TFC) must be entered for each of the plants.

Table 12.3 Break-Even and DOL Data for Old versus Modernized Plants

	Old Plant	Modern Plant
Price per unit	5.00	5.00
Variable Cost per unit	2.75	2.25
Total fixed cost	14,500	20,000
Break-even quantity	6,444	7,273
Break-even revenue	32,222	36,364
Equal profit		
Quantity	11,000	11,000
Profit	10,250	10,250
Degree of operating leverage at equal-profit quantity	2.41	2.95

Table 12.4 Cost and Revenue Data for Old Plant

UNITS	FIXED COST	VARIABLE COST	TOTAL COST	REVENUE	PROFIT
0	14,500	0	14,500	0	-14,500
3,222	14,500	8,861	23,361	16,111	-7,250
6,444	14,500	17,722	32,222	32,222	0
9,667	14,500	26,583	41,083	48,333	7,250
12,889	14,500	35,444	49,944	64,444	14,500
16,111	14,500	44,306	58,806	80,556	21,750
19,333	14,500	53,167	67,667	96,667	29,000
22,556	14,500	62,028	76,528	112,778	36,250
25,778	14,500	70,889	85,389	128,889	43,500

Table 12.5 Cost and Revenue Data for Modern Plant

UNITS	FIXED COST	VARIABLE COST	TOTAL COST	REVENUE	PROFIT
0	20,000	0	20,000	0	-20,000
3,636	20,000	8,182	28,182	18,182	-10,000
7,273	20,000	16,364	36,364	36,364	0
10,909	20,000	24,545	44,545	54,545	10,000
14,545	20,000	32,727	52,727	72,727	20,000
18,182	20,000	40,909	60,909	90,909	30,000
21,818	20,000	49,091	69,091	109,091	40,000
25,455	20,000	57,273	77,273	127,273	50,000
29,091	20,000	65,455	85,455	145,455	60,000

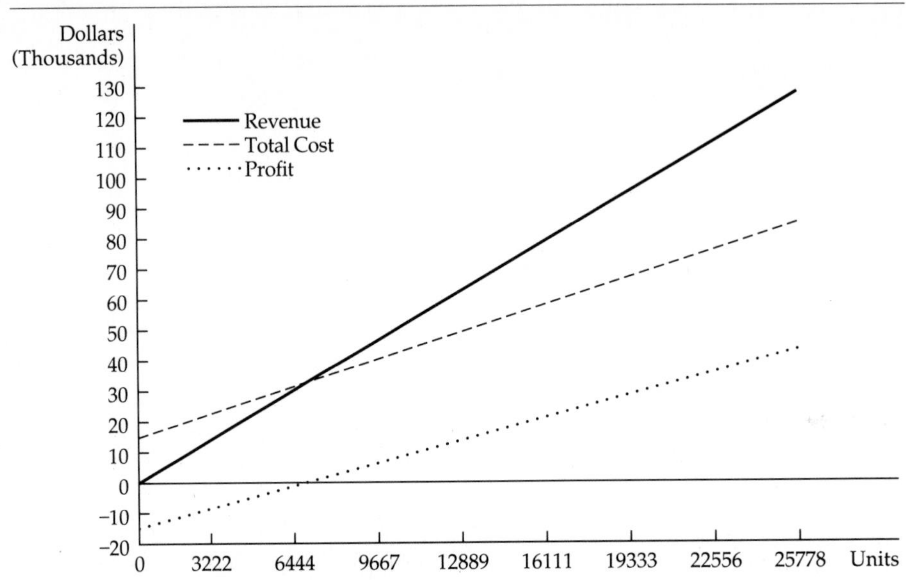

Figure 12.6 Plot of Data from Table 12.4

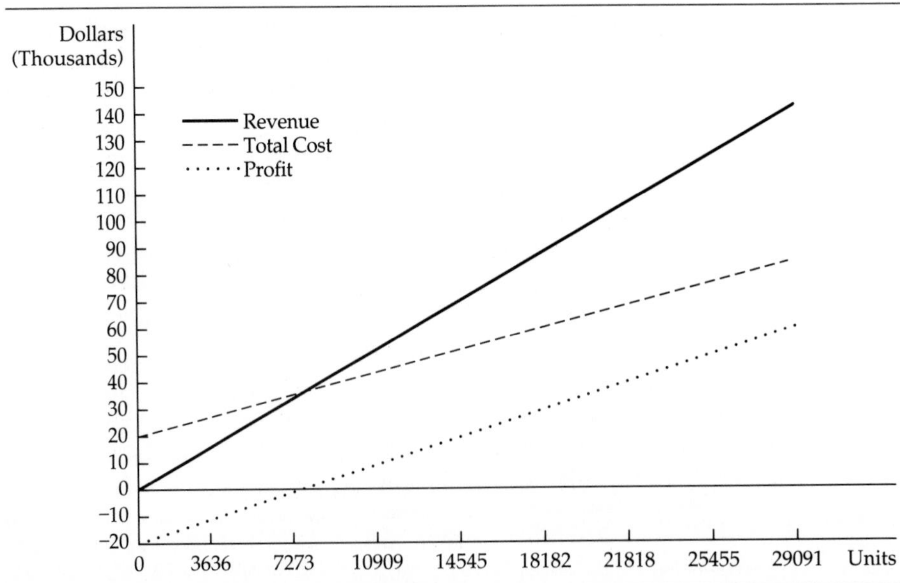

Figure 12.7 Plot of Data from Table 12.5

The Uses and Limitations of Volume-Cost-Profit Analysis

Volume-cost-profit analysis is a very useful tool under certain circumstances, but its limitations must be understood. Some past economics and finance textbooks have included this material in the chapter on financial or profit planning.

When a corporation prepares its financial plan for the next year or even the next two years, it usually engages in what is referred to as "bottom-up" planning, a process that is not only time-consuming but extremely detailed. Many parts of the corporate organization contribute data on sales forecasts, prices, manufacturing costs, administrative and marketing expenses, and other measures. Data may be generated from every department in the corporation. Consolidating these data and making various changes in them before bringing a final plan up to top management for approval is a mammoth undertaking. A corporation would not use volume-cost-profit analysis for this type of planning.

However, since a large number of pages have been devoted to this subject here, it must be of some importance. The main use of this analysis lies in calculating alternative cases in a restricted period of time. It can also be used to make small, relatively quick corrections. In addition, during early stages of the plan, when detailed data are not yet available, estimates using variable and fixed costs can be used to establish some rough benchmarks for the eventual detailed plan.

However, despite its usefulness, break-even analysis has some important limitations, some of which have already been mentioned.

1. It assumes the existence of linear relationships, constant prices, and average variable costs. These simplifying assumptions can, of course, be changed. Different prices and variable costs can be substituted and new results computed; linear relationships are still preserved. If, however, the prices are permitted to change over the range of quantities, and/or variable costs include the notion of diminishing marginal returns, the analysis then becomes more complex and resembles price/output determination, discussed in Chapter 11. The use of linear construction, although limiting, serves the intended purpose for this analysis. When the effects of relatively small changes in quantity are measured, linear revenues and variable costs are certainly good approximations of reality.

2. It is assumed that costs (and expenses) are either variable or fixed. Such an assumption is not completely realistic, but again, within a limited range of quantities it can be accepted. The existence of fixed costs limits this analysis to the short run. Changes in capacity are ordinarily not considered.

3. For break-even analysis to be used, only a single product must be produced in a plant or, if there are several products, their mix must remain constant.

4. The analysis does not result in identification of an optimal point; it focuses on evaluating the effect of changes in quantity on cost and profits.

Although these limitations are surely important, the simplicity of the break-even (volume-cost-analysis) technique and its possible wide range of applications makes it a useful tool of economic analysis.

The Solution

To calculate results for sales of 10 percent more and 10 percent less, Suzanne Prescott needs to make estimates of price per unit, average variable cost, and total fixed cost. She had the production figure and price per case of $5. Breaking up the cost and expense numbers into fixed and variable components was a much more difficult task. Working with her assistant, she arrived at the following estimated breakdown:

Cost of sales	
Variable materials and labor	$18,000
Variable overhead	5,000
Fixed overhead	4,500
Expenses	
Variable selling and administrative	4,500
Fixed selling and administrative	7,000
Fixed research and development	3,000

Thus, total fixed costs were found to be $14,500, and total variable cost $27,500, or $2.75 per unit.

She calculated the break-even point as follows:

$$\frac{14{,}500}{5 - 2.75} = 6{,}444$$

For the + 10 percent and − 10 percent she used the DOL equation:

$$\frac{10{,}000(5 - 2.75)}{10{,}000(5 - 2.75) - 14{,}500} = \frac{22{,}500}{8{,}000} = 2.8125$$

For every 1 percent change in quantity, profit will change by 2.8125 percent. Thus, if quantity changes by 1,000 units (i.e., 10 percent), profit will change by 28.125 percent, from its $8,000 level down to $5,750 or up to $10,250.

Suzanne proceeded to prepare the presentation chart showing the planned figures, the two 10 percent variations, and the worst case. Table 12.6 illustrates the results. She is now ready for the next day's meeting with the controller.

Table 12.6 Alternative Plans for Year 199X+1

	Best Estimate	*+10 Percent*	*−10 Percent*	*Worst Case*
Quantity	10,000	11,000	9,000	6,444
Sales	$50,000	$55,000	$45,000	$32,222
Cost of sales				
Variable mat. and labor	18,000	19,800	16,200	11,600
Variable overhead	5,000	5,500	4,500	3,222
Fixed overhead	4,500	4,500	4,500	4,500
Total cost of sales	27,500	29,800	25,200	19,322
Gross profit	22,500	25,200	19,800	12,900
Expenses				
Variable sell. and admin.	4,500	4,950	4,050	2,900
Fixed sell. and admin.	7,000	7,000	7,000	7,000
Fixed research and dev.	3,000	3,000	3,000	3,000
Total expenses	14,500	14,950	14,050	12,900
Net earnings before taxes	8,000	10,250	5,750	0

Summary

Break-even (volume-cost-profit) analysis is a simplification of the economic analysis of the firm. It involves several limiting assumptions, such as constant prices and constant average variable costs. Since fixed costs are an essential component of this technique, it is strictly a short-run tool. Yet, despite these simplifications—and possibly because of them—break-even analysis is a very useful aid to an economic or financial analyst. It is, however, necessary to be aware of the method's limitations.

Several specific tools were discussed. The first was the break-even formula itself stated in terms of quantities of production units. If a single product cannot be identified, then a break-even formula for total revenue can be used.

Since the firm's objective is certainly not to break even but to achieve profitability, an equation was developed to identify the required quantity of production, given a lump-sum profit requirement or a profit-per-unit requirement.

To measure the effect of change in quantity on profits, the concept of degree of operating leverage was introduced. This elasticity-like formula measures the relation between a percentage change in quantity sold and a percentage change in profit. This equation was also shown to be useful in comparing two plants employing differing technologies (and therefore having different relationships between fixed and variable costs) or in making decisions on modernizing a plant.

The usefulness of break-even analysis in evaluating alternatives and in making quick corrections was discussed. The limitations in the application of this technique were also pointed out.

Important Concepts

Break-even analysis: Also called *volume-cost-profit analysis,* a simplification of the economic analysis of the firm that measures the effect of a change in quantity of a product on the profits of the firm.

Break-even point: The level of output at which the firm realizes no profit and no loss.

Break-even revenue: The amount of revenue at which the firm realizes no profit and no loss.

Degree of operating leverage: An elasticity-like formula that measures the percentage change in profit resulting from a percentage change in quantity produced or revenue.

Total fixed cost (TFC): A cost that remains constant as the level of output varies. In a short-run analysis, fixed cost is incurred even if the firm produces no output. Also referred to simply as *fixed cost.*

Total variable cost (TVC): The total cost associated with the level of output. This can also be considered the total cost to a firm of using its variable inputs. Also referred to simply as *variable cost*.

Required profit: Profit that can represent the opportunity cost or the normal profit and that can be incorporated in the break-even formula. A fixed dollar amount of required profit can be handled as an addition to fixed cost; a specific profit per unit of product can be added to the average variable cost.

Questions

1. Although volume-cost-profit analysis uses graphs similar to those used by economists, the analysis differs in content. Discuss these differences.
2. Does the volume-cost-profit method analyze short-run or long-run situations?
3. What is the difference between fixed costs and constant costs?
4. How realistic is the assumption of constant variable unit costs in volume-cost-profit analysis? Does it detract a great deal from the value of this analysis?
5. What is the effect on break-even quantity of
   a. A decrease in unit price?
   b. A decrease in average variable cost?
   c. A decrease in fixed cost?

   Assume some numbers and illustrate the effect by drawing graphs showing the break-even point.
6. Business risk is usually defined in terms of variations of return (or profit) to a firm due to changes in activity resulting from changes in general economic activity. Can the degree of operating leverage therefore be described as a measure of business risk? Why?
7. Would you expect a company whose production is rather stable from period to period and growing slowly from year to year to have relatively high fixed costs?
8. How would you account for required profit in the break-even formula when
   a. Profit is set as a requirement for a time period (e.g., a year)?
   b. Profit is set as a specific monetary amount per unit?
9. Can the degree of operating leverage be measured at the break-even quantity point? Why or why not?
10. Is volume-cost-profit analysis a good planning tool?
11. What are some useful applications of volume-cost-profit analysis?

Problems

1. The Automotive Supply Company has a small plant that produces speedometers exclusively. Its annual fixed costs are $30,000, and its variable costs are $10 per unit. It can sell a speedometer for $25.

a. How many speedometers must the company sell to break even?
b. What is the break-even revenue?
c. The company sold 3,000 units last year. What was its profits?
d. Next year's fixed costs are expected to rise to $37,500. What will be the break-even quantity?
e. If the company will sell the number of units obtained in part *d* and wants to maintain the same profit as last year, what will its new price have to be?

2. Writers' Pleasure, Inc., produces gold-plated pen and pencil sets. Its plant has a fixed annual cost of $50,000, and the variable unit cost is $20. It expects to sell 5,000 sets next year.
   a. In order to just break even, how much will the company have to charge for each set?
   b. Based on its plant investment, the company requires an annual profit of $30,000. How much will it have to charge per set to obtain this profit? (Quantity sold will still be 5,000 sets).
   c. If the company wants to earn a markup of 50 percent on its variable costs, how many sets will it have to sell at the price obtained in part *b*?
3. Bikes-for-Two, Inc., produces tandem bicycles. Its costs have been analyzed as follows:

Variable costs	
Materials	$30/unit
Manufacturing labor	3 hours/unit ($8/hour)
Assembly labor	1 hour/unit ($8/hour)
Packing materials	$3/unit
Packing labor	20 minutes/unit ($6/hour)
Shipping cost	$10/unit
Fixed costs	
Overhead labor	$50,000/year
Utilities	$5,000/year
Plant operation	$65,000/year
Selling price	$100/unit

   a. Calculate the break-even quantity.
   b. Calculate the break-even revenue.
   c. Develop a chart to show profits at quantities of 2,000, 4,000, 6,000, 8,000, and 10,000.
4. Music Makers Company, a wholesale distributor, is considering discontinuance of its long-playing record line due to stiff competition from tapes, CDs,

and other new, technologically advanced recordings. The variable cost of its tapes last year was about 40 percent of its tape revenue, and the allocated fixed cost equaled $100,000 per year. Last year's sales were $250,000, but it is expected that in the future, annual revenue will drop by 20 percent and variable costs will rise to 50 percent of revenue (because of price reductions). Will tapes still be profitable for the company?

5. The ABC company sells widgets at $9 each; variable unit cost is $6, and fixed cost is $60,000 per year.
   a. What is the break-even quantity point?
   b. How many units must the company sell per year to achieve a profit of $15,000?
   c. What will be the degree of operating leverage at the quantity sold in part *a*? In part *b*?
   d. What will be the degree of operating leverage if 30,000 units are sold per year?
6. Two companies, Perfect Lawn Co. and Ideal Grass Co., are competing in the manufacture and sale of lawnmowers. Perfect has a somewhat older plant and requires a variable cost of $150 per lawnmower; its fixed costs are $200,000 per year. Ideal's plant is more automated and thus has lower unit variable costs of $100; its fixed cost is $400,000. Since the two companies are close competitors, they both sell their product at $250 per unit.
   a. What is the break-even quantity for each?
   b. At which quantity would the two companies have equal profits?
   c. At the quantity obtained in part *b*, what is each company's degree of operating leverage?
   d. If sales of each company were to reach 4,500 units per year, which company would be more profitable? Why?
7. Elgar Toaster Co. is contemplating a modernization of its antiquated plant. It now sells its toasters for $20 each; the variable cost per unit is $8, and fixed costs are $840,000 per year.
   a. Calculate the break-even quantity.
   b. If the proposed modernization is carried out, the new plant would have fixed costs of $1,200,000 per year, but its variable costs would decrease to $5 per unit.
      (1) What will be the break-even point now?
      (2) If the company wanted to break even at the same quantity as with the old plant, what price would it have to charge for a toaster?
   c. If the new plant is built, the company would want to decrease its price to $19 to improve its competitive position.
      (1) At which quantity would profits of the old and the new plants be equal (assuming the price of a toaster is $20 for the old plant but $19 for the new)? How much would the profit be at this quantity?

(2) Calculate the degree of operating leverage for each plant at the quantity obtained in part (1).
(3) If sales are projected to reach 150,000 units per year in the near future, would you recommend construction of the new plant? Why or why not? (Assume that both plants have the capacity to produce this quantity.)

CHAPTER 13

Special Pricing Practices

The Situation

One of the most difficult challenges in the food and beverage industries is the establishment of effective channels of distribution. Many food-processing and beverage companies rely on food brokers to sell their products to retail outlets such as supermarkets and grocery stores. In the case of soft drinks, the product is shipped from the bottling plants to the individual retail establishments. Obviously, there must first be a willingness on the part of these retail businesses to carry a particular product line.

The task of establishing the relationship between Global Foods, Inc., and the retail stores was given to Rebecca James, assistant vice president of marketing of the beverage division. Since the product was so new, she found considerable resistance among the major supermarket chains to carrying Global's line of soft drinks. Thus far, she had been able to sell relatively small volumes to smaller grocery stores, convenience stores, delicatessens, and sandwich shops. Then she learned that a major catering company that provided food service in major airports all across the country wanted to carry an additional line of soft drinks. This firm had put out a request for bids to all the major beverage companies and also to Global Foods. After all, Global had an established reputation in the food business.

Rebecca was eager to land this major account. But she also realized that her bid would have to be considerably lower than that offered to her present customers. However, this lower price would be more than made up by the potential volume of sales, as well as by the creation of a base from which to further penetrate the market for soft drinks. But she was not quite sure how to decide on the price she should recommend. She decided to consult with Philip Olds, an executive in the company's foods service division. Philip had considerable experience in preparing bids on large customer contracts.

Introduction

In previous chapters we discussed output and pricing decisions under different market arrangements. We will now continue this discussion and apply our knowledge to pricing decisions made in specific situations. Some of these situations are derivatives of the general cases we encountered previously; others may seem to be special cases, although they may not be. We will also be confronted by some complications: whereas we have previously assumed that a firm produces only one product, we will now have to allow for the pricing of several products simultaneously.

Pricing under conditions of perfect competition is rather straightforward and was explained thoroughly in Chapter 11. However, when competition is less than perfect and the demand curve facing a company has a downward slope, pricing decisions may become much more complex. The situations we will encounter in this chapter usually occur under imperfectly competitive conditions.

The Kinked Demand Curve

The kinked demand curve appears to be an oligopoly phenomenon. In other words, it applies only when a company expects its competitor or competitors to react to its price action. Since this potential reaction may be damaging to the company, no price action may be taken. The outcome is that, under oligopolistic market conditions, prices may remain relatively rigid. The kinked demand curve model was developed by Paul Sweezy in the late 1930s,[1] and it was accorded some popularity for a time. The basic assumption of this model is that a competitor (or competitors) will follow a price decrease but will not make a change in reaction to a price increase. Thus, the firm contemplating a price change may refrain from doing so for fear that quantities sold will be affected in such a way as to decrease profits.

If our firm lowers its price, this may have an immediate impact on the competition. Our firm takes its action to increase sales by drawing customers away from the higher-priced competitors, but when competitors realize what is happening (i.e., their sales are declining), they will quickly follow the price cut to maintain their market share. If our firm undertakes the opposite action—a price increase—assuming incorrectly that competitors will follow suit, its sales will drop markedly if competitors fail to do so.

It is easy to demonstrate the "kink" in such a demand curve with the simple graph in Figure 13.1. Let us assume that the original price and quantity are found at point A. If the firm lowers its price, expecting that quantity demanded will move along the more elastic demand curve D_f, then, if this result materializes, it will gain a relatively large quantity of additional sales for a relatively small decrease in price. If it lowers its price from P to P_1, it will expect to

[1]Paul Sweezy, "Demand Under Conditions of Oligopoly," *Journal of Political Economy,* 47 (1939), pp. 568–73.

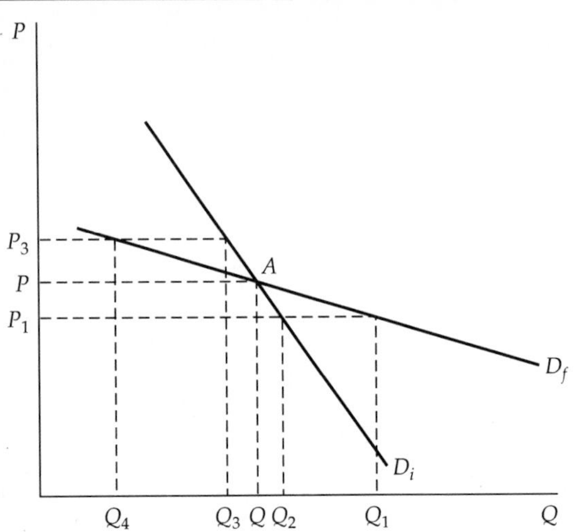

Figure 13.1 Demand Curves for an Oligopoly Considering a Price Increase/Decrease

increase its sales from Q to Q_1. This is the relevant demand curve for the firm if other companies do not retaliate. Our firm would thus gain customers at the expense of competition. However, if competitors do react and match the price cut, our company will increase its sales only to Q_2, along demand curve D_i; this is the relevant demand curve when all companies in the industry decrease their price equally. There will be a relatively small increase in sales, since all prices in the industry are lower, but not nearly as much as the company expected when it reduced its price.

On the other hand, suppose our company decides to raise its price, anticipating that competitors will follow the increase. It thus expects to move along D_i to Q_3 when it boosts its price to P_3. It would thus sustain some loss in sales while benefiting from a significantly higher price. However, suppose its competitors refuse to play along and keep their prices unchanged. The company's situation now becomes more precarious, since its quantity sold drops to Q_4: the demand curve for the firm alone is much more elastic than if all firms raise their prices in unison.[2]

The prospect of being stung by such action will make the company much more loath to change its price from P. From that vantage point, it will appear to the company that the appropriate demand curve is D_i if price is lowered and D_f if the price is increased. Thus, in Figure 13.2, we show the company's perception of its demand curve—a curve with a kink in it.

Now that we have developed a demand curve for this oligopolist, we can derive a marginal revenue curve as well. This marginal revenue curve will be

[2]A company can announce that a price increase is to take place some time (say, 30 days) in the future in order to "test the waters." If other firms do not follow, then the increase can be rescinded. More about this will be said in the section on barometric leadership.

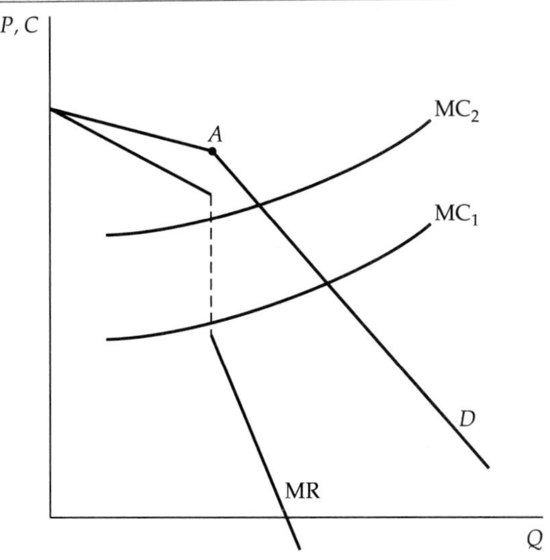

Figure 13.2 The Kinked Demand Curve

discontinuous: there will be a gap at the point where the kink occurs. As we know, a company will maximize its profits at the point where marginal cost equals marginal revenue. The two marginal cost curves drawn in Figure 13.2 both imply the same price and quantity, at point *A*. Thus, a significant change in costs could occur for our firm, but it will not react by changing its price. Actually, the price may remain unchanged even if the demand curve moves to the right or left, as long as the kink remains at the same price level. Hence, it can be concluded that under the circumstances described, a kinked demand curve will result in price rigidities despite changes in demand and cost.

However, like any newly proposed hypothesis, the kinked demand curve was challenged by other economists. In particular, Nobel Prize laureate George Stigler investigated several oligopolistic industries and found little empirical support for Sweezy's model. Stigler found that in these industries, price increases were followed as quickly as were price decreases.[3] Such findings, of course, contradict the existence of the kink. Further, the model does not explain how the price was originally set at the kink. Was it originally set where marginal revenue equaled marginal cost, or was it by some other means, such as tradition? Despite its shortcomings, there still is the possibility that the model of the kinked demand curve has some validity.

However, if firms in an oligopolistic industry are fearful of the reaction of their competitors, one way out is for the firms to cooperate on price and market share

[3] George J. Stigler, "The Kinky Oligopoly Demand Curve and Rigid Prices," *Journal of Political Economy*, October 1947, pp. 432–39. Similarly, see Julian J. Simon, "A Further Test of the Kinky Oligopoly Demand Curve," *American Economic Review*, December 1969, pp. 971–75.

setting. Such an arrangement, commonly referred to as a *cartel*, is the subject of the next section.

Cartel Arrangements

Competition is a very tough taskmaster. To survive in competition in the long run, a company must operate at its most efficient (minimum) cost point, and it will earn no more than a normal return. Thus, there is always an incentive for a company to try to become more powerful than its competitors—in the extreme, to become a monopolist. In an oligopolistic type of industry, where there are several powerful firms, it would probably be impossible for one firm to eliminate all the others. So, in order to reap the benefits of a monopoly (i.e., higher profits, stable market shares and prices, and the general creation of a more certain and less competitive environment), it may be advisable for companies in the industry to act together as if they were a monopoly. In other words, they all agree to cooperate with one another; they form a cartel. Cartel arrangements may be tacit, but in most cases some sort of formal agreement is reached. The motives for cartelization have been recognized for many years. Indeed, an early recognition can be found in a passage in Adam Smith's famous book: "People of the same trade seldom meet together, even for merriment and diversion, but the conversation ends in a conspiracy against the public, or in some contrivance to raise prices."[4]

Cartels were made illegal in the United States with the passage of the Sherman Anti-Trust Act of 1890. Thus, most "official" cartels are found in countries other than the U.S. Probably the most famous cartel in existence today is the Organization of Petroleum Exporting Countries (OPEC). But there are others, such as the IATA (International Air Transport Association), to which U.S. airlines can belong. Collusive agreements have existed in the United States as well. One of the most famous cases of price and market share fixing was in the electrical industry and involved General Electric, Westinghouse, and other large corporations. The case was tried and concluded in 1961 and resulted in prison sentences for several executives and large fines. Although this case is not really recent, it is a classic example of collusion and will be described briefly following a discussion of the characteristics and effects of cartels.

Cartels may not flourish in all oligopolistic markets. Following are some of the conditions that influence the formation of cartels.

1. The existence of a small number of large firms facilitates the policing of a collusive agreement.
2. Geographical proximity of the firms is favorable.
3. Homogeneity of the product makes it impossible for cartel participants to cheat on one another by emphasizing product differences.

---

[4] Adam Smith, *An Inquiry into the Nature and Causes of the Wealth of Nations*, New York: Modern Library, 1937, p. 128.

4. The role of general business conditions, that is, whether prosperity or depression fosters the formation of cartels, presents somewhat contradictory arguments. Cartels are often established during depressed industry conditions, when companies attempt to forestall what they consider to be ruinous price cutting. However, it also appears that cartels disintegrate as demand for the product falls, and each member thinks it can do better outside the cartel. The cartel may then reestablish itself during the recovery period. Thus, cartels can form or fall apart during either phase of the business cycle.[5]
5. Entry into the industry must be difficult. The case of OPEC is a good example. It is impossible for countries that do not possess the basic resource to begin petroleum production and compete for monopoly profits.
6. If cost conditions for the cartel members are similar and profitability thus will not differ greatly among members, cartels will be easier to maintain. Product homogeneity, mentioned earlier, will contribute to cost uniformity.

The ideal cartel will be powerful enough to establish monopoly prices and earn maximum monopoly profits for all the members combined. This situation is illustrated in Figure 13.3. For simplicity, assume that there are only two firms in this oligopolistic industry. The total industry demand curve is shown in Figure 13.3*c*. The marginal revenue curve is constructed for this demand curve in the usual manner. Each of the two competitors (illustrated in Figure 13.3*a* and *b*) have their respective average total cost and marginal cost curves, which can differ.

The two individual marginal cost curves are then added horizontally, and the result is plotted on the industry graph (MC_T). Industry output will take place where MC_T equals the industry marginal revenue, and the price charged will be found by drawing a vertical line to the demand curve (point A). This is, of course, the classical monopoly situation, and monopoly profits will be maximized at this point.

The next step is to establish how much each of the two companies will sell at this price. In order that the entire industry output be sold, each company will sell that output corresponding to the point at which a horizontal line drawn from the MC = MR intersection on the industry graph crosses the marginal cost curve of each of the two firms. It can be seen that each of the two firms will produce different quantities and achieve different profits depending on the level of the average total cost curve at the point of production. Generally, the lower-cost company will be the more profitable one. This result, although maximizing combined profits, may also be one of the reasons for the subversion of cartels. A very efficient company with low average costs, and most likely with excess capacity under cartel conditions, may find it profitable to cheat by offering its product at a lower price and capturing a larger share of the total business.

[5]A very cogent description of this phenomenon can be found in George J. Stigler, *The Theory of Price*, New York: Macmillan, 1949, pp. 274–75. Stigler also puts forward the idea that, regardless of the level of business activity, government action in support of such collusion is an important factor in a cartel's success. An important example is the U.S. National Recovery Act (NRA) of the 1930s, later declared unconstitutional by the Supreme Court.

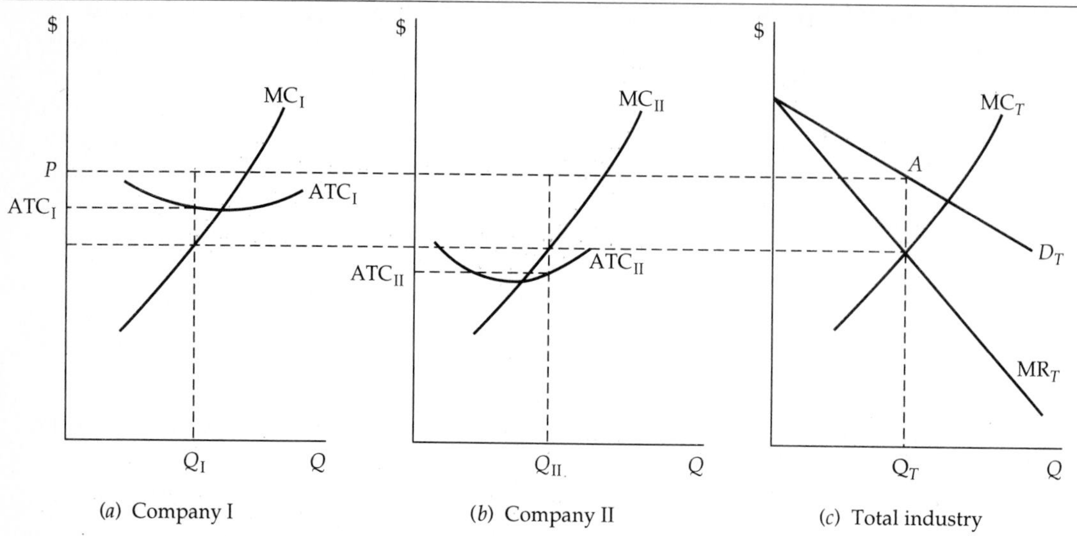

Figure 13.3 The Ideal Cartel

Such a cartel may be unstable. Unless strictly enforced, cartels will have a tendency to break down. Secret price cuts may be extremely profitable since (if the product is undifferentiated) the demand curve for an individual firm in a cartel will be quite elastic. Cartel subversion often occurs during slumps in demand, since individual members will be looking to increase their share to avoid significant quantity decreases.

Cartels often have agreements specifying the market share of each participant. Such allotments may be based on history, or they can be arranged to give each member a certain geographical area. Collusion can also exist in much more informal ways. Thus, physicians within a geographical area coincidentally charge similar fees for their services. Trade associations are often suspected of collecting and conveying information that will lead to the fixing of prices. Recently, the U.S. Department of Justice charged eight Ivy League schools and the Massachusetts Institute of Technology with illegally fixing the amounts of financial aid given to prospective students. All of the schools, with the exception of MIT, arranged to settle the charges by agreeing not to collude in the future. Additional schools were still under investigation when this settlement was announced.[6]

The Electrical Conspiracy

On February 6, 1961, in a Philadelphia federal court, 7 executives of General Electric, Westinghouse, and other companies were sent to prison and fined; 23 others were given suspended sentences and fined; and 29 companies were

[6]"U.S. Charges 8 Ivy League Universities, MIT with Illegally Fixing Financial Aid," *Wall Street Journal*, May 23, 1991.

fined a total of about $2 million. This was the result of a price-fixing and market-sharing conspiracy that began shortly after the end of World War II and continued through the 1950s. The conspiracy involved a number of heavy electrical equipment products, such as switching gear, circuit breakers, transformers, and turbine engines.

The story of these collusive practices reads like a mystery story.[7] There were meetings in hotel rooms during conventions of the National Electric Manufacturers Association. There were hotel meetings at various locations in which the participants did not register under their company affiliations and recorded trips to other locations in their expense accounts. There were code numbers given to each company. There were telephone calls at the participants' homes and even a conspiratorial round of golf.

The conspiracies did not always work smoothly; there appeared to be a great deal of "chiseling." When it had been agreed that one company would make the low bid, another participant would renege on the deal. In some cases outright price wars resulted, and the cartel would break up for some period of time. Then, as overcapacity in the industry built up, the cartel would be reestablished. However, even if one cartel was inoperative for a time, several others, in other products, would continue.

Disagreements also existed regarding market share distribution. For instance, in 1958 General Electric, Westinghouse, and Allis-Chalmers, after hours of heated debate at the Traymore Hotel in Atlantic City, N.J., agreed to cut their shares (General Electric from 45 percent to 40.3 percent, Westinghouse from 35 percent to 31.3 percent, and Allis-Chalmers from 10 percent to 8.8 percent) of the circuit breaker market to permit Federal Pacific to increase its share (from 10 percent to 15.6 percent), and to permit an industry newcomer, I-T-E Circuit Breaker, to obtain a part of the market (4 percent).

The companies involved pleaded guilty and "no contest" to the federal indictments, resulting in the judgments imposed early in 1961.

Price Leadership

When collusive arrangements are not easily achieved, another type of pricing practice may occur under oligopolistic market conditions. This is the practice of price leadership, in which there is no formal or tacit agreement among the oligopolists to keep prices at the same level or change them by the same amount. However, when a price movement is initiated by one of the firms, others will follow. Examples of such practices abound. You may have observed that at two or more gasoline stations at the same intersection, prices for each grade of gasoline are either identical or almost the same most of the time.[8] Another

---

[7]The description of this case has been obtained from two articles in *Fortune* (April 1961, pp. 132–37+, and May 1961, pp. 161–64+), and from the *Wall Street Journal*, January 10 and 12, 1962.

[8]In some cases, there will be a pervasive difference of 1 or 2 cents among stations located close to one another. When one changes its price, the others soon follow to reestablish the differential.

example is automobile companies, which in recent years have come up with rebate programs. Surely you have seen advertisements offering "$1,000 cash or 3.9 percent financing." One company is usually the first to announce such a program; the others follow in short order. Another case is IBM. For many years, in the 1950s and 1960s, IBM was considered to be the price leader in the computer industry. In fact, IBM's prices were considered to form an "umbrella" for industry pricing. It was said that IBM would establish a price, and since it was the most powerful and preferred manufacturer and thus could command a higher price (an umbrella over the others), its competitors would tend to set their prices at some slightly lower level for similar equipment.

We have just described two major variants of the price leadership phenomenon: barometric and dominant price leadership.

Barometric Price Leadership

There may not be a firm that dominates all the others and sets the price each time. One firm in the industry—and it does not always have to be the same one—will initiate a price change in response to economic conditions, and the other firms may or may not follow the leader. If the leader has misjudged the economic forces, the other companies may not change their prices or may effect changes of a different, possibly lesser, magnitude. If the firm has correctly gauged the sentiment of the industry, all of the firms will settle in comfortably at the new price level. But if this does not happen, the price leader may have to retract the price change; or a series of iterations may be set in motion until a new price level, agreeable to all, is reached. Such a pattern of price changes has been observed in many industries, including automobile, steel, and paper.

The airline industry furnishes a good recent example of barometric leadership that was not followed. American Airlines announced a fare increase of 23 percent in April 1990. When other major airlines did not follow with similar price actions, American withdrew the fare increase. Apparently, American Airlines overestimated the improvement in air traffic that would have justified the increase.[9]

Dominant Price Leadership

When an industry contains one company distinguished by its size and economic power relative to other firms, the dominant price leadership model emerges. The dominant company may well be the most efficient (i.e., lowest-cost) firm. It could, under certain circumstance, force its smaller competitors out of business by undercutting their prices, or it could buy them out on favorable terms. But such action could lead to an investigation and eventual suit by the U.S. Department of Justice under the Sherman Anti-Trust Act. To avoid such difficulties, the dominant company will actually act as a monopolist, setting its

---

[9]This item was reported in the *Wall Street Journal*, April 17, 1990.

price at the point where it will maximize its profits, and it will permit the smaller companies to continue to exist and sell as much as they wish at the price set by the leader. The theoretical explanation of the dominant price leadership model is quite straightforward and is presented in all microeconomics textbooks. We will follow its development in Figure 13.4.

The demand curve for the entire industry is D_T. The marginal cost curve of the dominant firm is MC_D, and the sum of all the marginal cost curves of the follower firms is represented by MC_R. The demand curve for the leader, D_D, is derived by subtracting at each point the marginal cost curve of the followers from the total demand curve, D_T. The reason is that if the small firms supply the product along their combined marginal cost curve, MC_R, then the dominant firm will be left with product demand shown along D_D. When the leader's marginal revenue curve, MR_D, is drawn in the usual manner, the leader can establish its profit-maximizing quantity at point A, and price at point B. This price is then accepted by the smaller firms in the industry, which will supply the rest of the market at this price. The followers are thus actually faced by a horizontal demand curve at price P.

Such an arrangement is satisfactory to the dominant firm. It maximizes profits and at the same time permits the small firms to exist, thus possibly avoiding legal action. On the other hand, the followers will be able to assure themselves of a piece of the market without inviting the possibility of a price war, which they would most likely lose.

As in the case of cartels, dominant price leadership arrangements tend to break down. As markets grow, new firms enter the industry and decrease the interdependence among the firms. Technological changes may bring changes in pricing, and in the long run the leadership of the dominant firm is likely to erode.

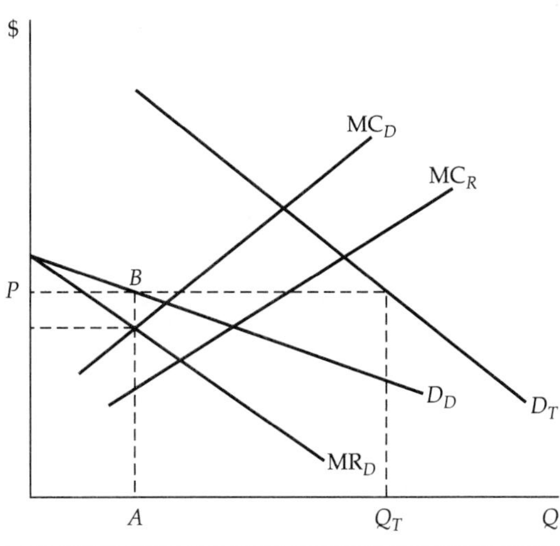

Figure 13.4 Dominant Price Leadership

Revenue Maximization

Another model of oligopolistic behavior was developed some years ago by the American economist William Baumol.[10] Ignoring interdependence, Baumol suggests that a firm's primary objective, rather than profit maximization, can be the maximization of revenue, subject to satisfying a specific level of profits. He gives several reasons for this objective, among them (1) a firm will be more competitive when it achieves large size (in terms of revenue) and (2) management remuneration may be more closely related to revenue than to profits.

This situation is depicted in Figure 13.5. The figure shows three solid curves. The total revenue curve is the usual one for a firm in imperfect competition, with revenue increasing at a decreasing rate because the firm is faced by a downward-sloping demand curve.[11] The total cost curve also is no surprise; it indicates first decreasing and then, at higher production levels, increasing marginal cost. The third line represents profits. It is simply the vertical difference between the revenue and cost lines.

If the firm were a profit maximizer (the traditional economic objective), production would take place at point Q_P, where the profit line hits its peak. On the other hand, should the firm be a pure revenue maximizer, equilibrium would occur at output Q_S, where the total revenue curve reaches its peak. This point, as we learned earlier, occurs where demand elasticity is unity (i.e., marginal revenue equals zero).

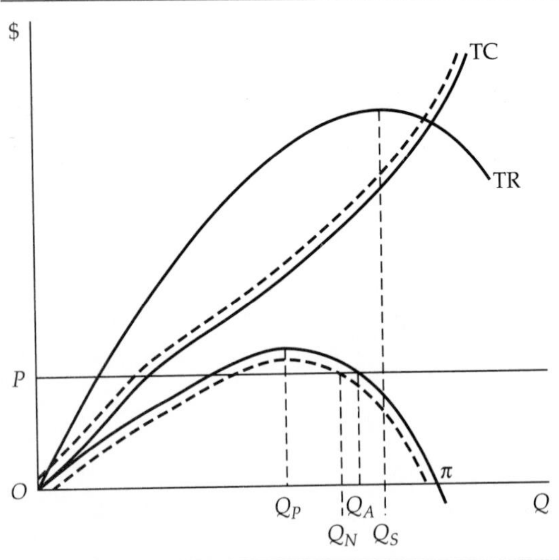

Figure 13.5 Revenue versus Profit Maximization

[10]William J. Baumol, *Economic Theory and Operations Analysis*, 3d ed., Englewood Cliffs, N.J.: Prentice-Hall International Editions, 1972, Chapter 13.

[11]Thus, each quantity represents a different price.

However, revenue maximization is subject to the constraint that an acceptable profit level exists. This profit will tend to be at a lower level than the maximum achievable. Assuming that this acceptable level is at OP, output will settle at Q_A. This will achieve the highest possible revenue while satisfying the profit requirement. Thus, total revenue will be higher than would have been attained under conditions of profit maximization, but lower than if pure revenue maximization (without a minimum profit constraint) had been pursued.

An interesting implication of this model is the effect of a change in fixed costs. Recall that under conditions of profit maximization, a change in fixed costs will have no effect on price or quantity, since neither marginal revenue nor marginal cost is impacted, and thus the maximizing requirement of MR = MC will remain the same. However, in the Baumol model, a rise in fixed costs will raise the cost curve and decrease the profit line. Both new lines will be parallel to the old ones. The two broken lines in Figure 13.5 represent this shift. As can be seen, the existence of the profit constraint will cause output to decrease to Q_N. At this lower output, price will be higher.

Baumol's model is an interesting attempt to present an alternative to the traditional maximization hypothesis. Since his model has not been extensively tested, it is difficult to assess its validity. There have been some empirical studies investigating the relationship between executive pay and revenue (as opposed to profits), but no definitive verdict has been obtained. Some of the studies found a more solid relationship between executive pay and revenue, and others appeared to favor a relationship with profits. Still others arrived at ambiguous answers. One important question remains: Are corporate owners (stockholders) more concerned—and thus determine the market value of a corporation—with revenue or profitability? In the long run, the most likely answer is the latter. Thus, it is doubtful that Baumol's model, although possibly applicable to some corporate behavior in the short run, will ever replace the traditional profit-maximizing objective.

Price Discrimination

Up to this point, we have assumed that a firm will sell identical products at the same price in all markets. (When the term *identical* is used in this context, it implies that the costs of producing and delivering the product are the same.) But such is not always the case. When a company sells identical products in two or more markets, it may charge different prices in the markets. Such a practice is usually referred to as *price discrimination*. The word *discrimination* here is not used in a normative sense; there is no judgment being made about whether this practice is good or bad. It merely expresses a situation where customers in one market are charged a price different from customers in another market. (The term *differential pricing*, could be used instead, but the former term has become part of the everyday language of the economist.)

Price discrimination means one of the following:

1. Products with identical costs are sold in different markets at different prices.
2. The ratio of price to marginal cost differs for similar products.

The practice of price discrimination is not an isolated event. It occurs in many familiar situations. Later in this section we will cite a number of common examples. Here we will mention just two, to illustrate each general instance just listed. In the first case, price discrimination exists when an adult and a child are charged different prices for tickets (of the same quality and at the same time) at a movie theater. The latter can be illustrated by the selling of cosmetic items, identical except for names on the labels and the quality of packaging, for vastly different prices at department or specialty stores on the one hand and variety ("five-and-dime") stores on the other.

Such discriminating price differentials cannot exist under all circumstances. In fact, two conditions are necessary for such a market arrangement:

1. The two or more markets in which the product is sold must be capable of being separated. Specifically, this includes the requirement that there can be no transfer or resale of the product (or service) from one market to the other. That is, there is no leakage among the markets. Only if the markets are sealed off from one another (by natural or contrived means) will the buyers in the various markets be unable to trade the products among these markets. And only in such a case will the seller be able to charge different prices without the price differential being nullified through competition.

2. The demand curves in the segmented markets must have different elasticities at given prices. Without this condition, price discrimination would be futile.

The reason that companies attempt to engage in price discrimination is that it can enhance profits. From the viewpoint of the consumers of the product, those in the lower-price market may benefit compared to situations where a uniform price is charged. However, consumers in the higher-price market are at a disadvantage.

Economists normally identify three degrees of discrimination. First-degree discrimination is the most profitable for the seller, but it can be enforced only infrequently. Third-degree discrimination, which is not as profitable, is the most commonly observed.

1. First-degree discrimination exists when the seller can identify where each buyer lies on the demand curve and can charge each buyer the price he or she is willing to pay. Thus, the demand curve actually becomes the marginal revenue curve as faced by the seller. Of course, for the seller—a monopolist—to achieve this advantageous position, it must have considerable information on where each of the buyers can be found on the demand curve, admittedly a herculean amount of market knowledge rarely attained. It is probably almost impossible to find such a pure case in real life, but let us attempt an example. A consumer purchasing a new automobile will generally bargain with the salesperson until they finally agree on a price. If the automobile dealer were clever enough to figure out the highest price that each individual was willing to pay, he or she could then conclude a deal with each customer at the maximum price (but only if no other dealer offered a lower price). Thus, each price the dealer obtains is on the buyers' demand curve. In reality, auto-

mobile dealers (and we must surely be thankful for this) are usually not endowed with such omniscience. We could stretch this example to apply to certain personal services such as medical or legal, where different customers (i.e., patients and clients) could be charged different fees based, for example, on their incomes.

2. Second-degree discrimination, although encountered somewhat more frequently than first-degree, also is not commonplace in real life. It involves differential prices charged by blocks of services. An example is the way some public utilities price. They will charge the highest unit price (e.g., per kilowatt of electricity) for small quantities (at the top of the demand curve) and lower prices as the rate of consumption per period increases.[12] Thus, again, only if the monopolist seller has a great deal of information about the demand curve will it be able to roughly "skim" the curve and exact higher revenues from its customer set. To be able to engage in second-degree discrimination, a firm must be able to meter the services consumed by the buyers.

3. Third-degree discrimination is by far the most frequently encountered. In this case, the monopolist segregates the customers into different markets and charges different prices in each. Such market segmentation can be based on geography, age, sex, product use, or income, for example.

Third-Degree Discrimination

If the firm can segment markets successfully, it can increase its profits above what they would be if a single price were charged. We will show the pricing results with graphs, and subsequently we will show a numerical example comparing the profitability of differential pricing versus uniform pricing. As shown in Figure 13.6, the company operates in two markets, A and B. In Figure 13.6*a* and *b*, it can be seen that A's demand curve is less elastic than B's. Figure 13.6*c* shows the horizontal summation of both demand and marginal revenue curves to represent the company's total market.

Since we assume that the products sold in the two markets are homogeneous, we can draw a marginal cost curve for the firm as a whole, as shown in Figure 13.6*c*. Output will take place at the point where MR = MC. Had a uniform price been charged, it would have been at point C on the aggregate demand curve. However, the firm can increase its profit by differentiating prices between the two markets. By drawing a horizontal line from the MR = MC intersection across the graphs for the two separate markets, we can allocate total production to the two markets. For each market, this will be the point where the horizontal line intersects the marginal revenue curve. Marginal revenue is thus the same for both markets. The price charged in each market can be found by drawing a vertical line at the corresponding quantity to the demand curve. Price will be considerably higher in market A, whose demand elasticity is lower.

[12]The price differential here is not related to pricing at peak versus off-peak periods. Such pricing may be related to the cost of producing the service and therefore does not represent discrimination.

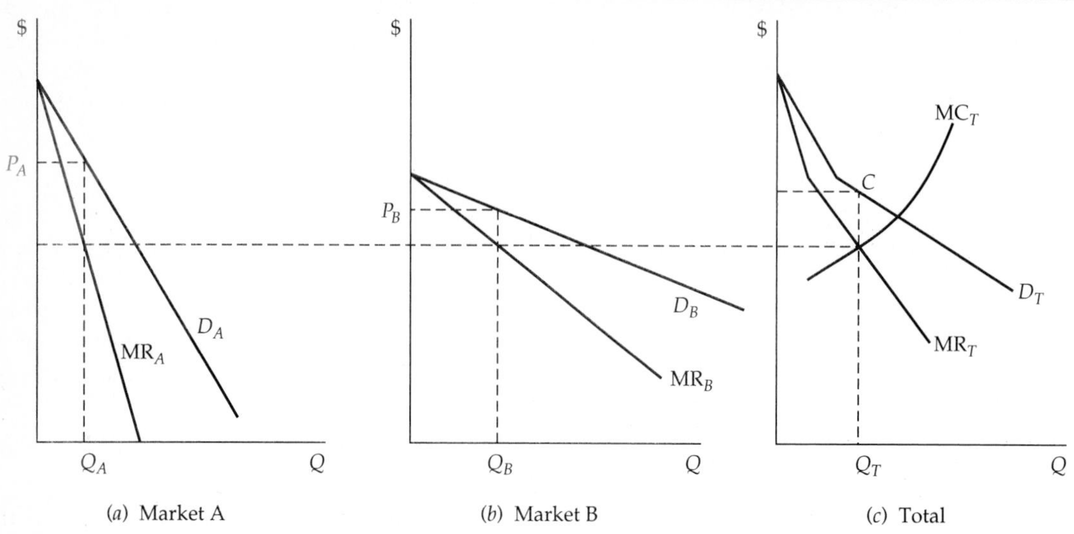

Figure 13.6 Third-Degree Price Discrimination

A numerical example will illustrate third-degree discrimination.[13] Section A of Table 13.1 presents the demand schedule for two markets as well as the combined schedule for the entire market. Assume that fixed costs are $12,000 per period, and that the average variable cost is constant (and consequently so is marginal cost) at $3 per unit.

If the company were to sell at a uniform price in both markets, it would maximize its profits at a price of $18. At that point, its profit would be $10,500. This can be seen in section B of Table 13.1. But if our company can separate the two markets, it can increase its total profit, as shown in sections C and D of the table. If it charges $24 per unit in market A and $12 per unit in market B, its profits will be $12,900 and $300, respectively. Thus, it will be able to increase its profit by $2,700.[14]

Had the company been able to carry out first-degree discrimination and sold to all potential customers at the prices they were willing to pay (with the exception of the last 500 units, which would not have been produced), its profits would have risen to $25,500, as shown in Table 13.2.

[13]We have chosen to show a numerical example of price discrimination rather than a mathematical proof. The latter would have been more precise. However, the simpler numerical illustration should be more useful. A brief outline of a mathematical solution is presented in the next section.

[14]We have arbitrarily divided the fixed costs equally between the two markets. But this has no effect on the total profits of the company or on the levels of sales in the two markets that will lead to profit maximization. Indeed, we could have omitted the fixed costs altogether, and there would have been no impact, except that the profits would have been $12,000 higher in both cases. Also, it should be noted that the quantity sold in this case is somewhat higher than in the one-price case. This is an inaccuracy caused by using discrete numbers in our demand schedule. Had this case been solved mathematically, using calculus, this inaccuracy would not have arisen.

Table 13.1 Numerical Example of Third-Degree Discrimination

A. Demand Schedules

Price	Market A Quantity	Market B Quantity	Total Quantity
36	0	0	0
30	475	25	500
24	900	100	1,000
18	1,100	400	1,500
12	1,300	700	2,000
6	1,450	1,050	2,500
0	1,500	1,500	3,000

B. Total Market

Price	Quantity	Total Revenue	Marginal Revenue	Fixed Cost	Average and Marginal Costs	Total Cost	Profit
36	0			12,000		12,000	−12,000
30	500	15,000	30	12,000	3	13,500	1,500
24	1,000	24,000	18	12,000	3	15,000	9,000
18	1,500	27,000	6	12,000	3	16,500	10,500
12	2,000	24,000	−6	12,000	3	18,000	6,000
6	2,500	15,000	−18	12,000	3	19,500	−4,500
0	3,000	0	−30	12,000	3	21,000	−21,000

C. Market A

Price	Quantity	Total Revenue	Marginal Revenue	Fixed Cost	Average and Marginal Costs	Total Cost	Profit
36	0			6,000		6,000	−6,000
30	475	14,250	30	6,000	3	7,425	6,825
24	900	21,600	17	6,000	3	8,700	12,900
18	1,100	19,800	−9	6,000	3	9,300	10,500
12	1,300	15,600	−21	6,000	3	9,900	5,700
6	1,450	8,700	−46	6,000	3	10,350	−1,650
0	1,500	0	−174	6,000	3	10,500	−10,500

D. Market B

Price	Quantity	Total Revenue	Marginal Revenue	Fixed Cost	Average and Marginal Costs	Total Cost	Profit
36	0			6,000		6,000	−6,000
30	25	750	30	6,000	3	6,075	−5,325
24	100	2,400	22	6,000	3	6,300	−3,900
18	400	7,200	16	6,000	3	7,200	0
12	700	8,400	4	6,000	3	8,100	300
6	1,050	6,300	−6	6,000	3	9,150	−2,850
0	1,500	0	−14	6,000	3	10,500	−10,500

Table 13.2 Profits from First-Degree Discrimination

Price	*Quantity*		*Revenue*
$30	500		$15,000
24	500		12,000
18	500		9,000
12	500		6,000
6	500		3,000
Total revenue			$45,000
Fixed cost		$12,000	
Variable cost (2,500 × $3)		7,500	
Total cost			19,500
Profit			$25,500

A MATHEMATICAL SOLUTION FOR THIRD-DEGREE DISCRIMINATION We will discuss briefly a simple method to solve for prices and quantities in the presence of third-degree discrimination.

1. Assume that there are two markets, A and B, and the demand curves are straight lines, that is,

$$Q_A = a_A - b_A P_A \quad \text{and} \quad Q_B = a_B - b_B P_B$$

2. Reverse these equations so that P is the dependent variable:

$$P_A = \frac{a_A}{b_A} - \frac{Q_A}{b_A} \quad \text{and} \quad P_B = \frac{a_B}{b_B} - \frac{Q_B}{b_B}$$

3. Now calculate total revenue by multiplying by Q:

$$\text{TR}_A = \frac{a_A Q_A}{b_A} - \frac{Q_A^2}{b_A} \quad \text{and} \quad \text{TR}_A = \frac{a_B Q_B}{b_B} - \frac{Q_B^2}{b_B}$$

4. Calculate the first derivative of total revenue to obtain marginal revenue:

$$\text{MR}_A = \frac{a_A}{b_A} - \frac{2Q_A}{b_A} \quad \text{and} \quad \text{MR}_B = \frac{a_B}{b_B} - \frac{2Q_B}{b_B}$$

5. Now set the marginal revenue equal to the company's marginal cost, which we will assume to be a constant:

$$\text{MR}_A = \text{MC} \quad \text{and} \quad \text{MR}_B = \text{MC}$$

6. Substituting for MR_A and MR_B and solving the two equations give the quantity sold in each market.
7. From here it is easy to find the contribution profit for the two markets and for the combination of the two. Remember that since MC is a constant, average variable cost is constant also, so that total variable cost can be calculated simply by multiplying AVC (= MC) by quantity. Fixed cost, if any, can then be subtracted.

8. If we wish to find out what the price would be if a uniform price were charged, we first add the two demand functions found in step 1. We then reverse the resulting equation in terms of price, as in step 2, and obtain marginal revenue. Marginal revenue is then equated to MC, and the price, quantity, and contribution profit are obtained in the same manner as in steps 3 to 7. The quantity sold will be the same as if discrimination existed, but the profit will be lower.

EXAMPLES OF PRICE DISCRIMINATION Price discrimination is an extremely common practice encountered in all types of situations. It should be remembered that a difference in price elasticities among different markets is a necessary condition. From prior discussions of the elasticities of demand curves, you will recall that the more intense the competition, the more elastic will be the demand curve facing the firm. A number of rather common examples follow:

1. In the past, physicians often set their fees in accordance with patient income. In a way, it could be argued that such a fee arrangement was quite equitable: those who can afford to pay higher prices will do so. However, as stated before, we are not concerned here with the normative aspects of differential pricing. The result of such a practice will still be an increase in the physician's income.

Presently, medical price discrimination exists in a somewhat different guise. Physicians frequently charge a patient who has health insurance more for the same services than they charge a patient who does not. The difference cannot be explained by the cost incurred by the physician in filing insurance documents. However, the two conditions necessary for differential pricing exist. The elasticities in the two markets (uninsured and insured) are certainly different, and the markets are sealed from each other (either the patient has insurance or does not have it).

2. Very often, products going into the export market will be priced lower than those sold domestically. A major reason for the differential is that international competition is stronger than that faced by the firm in its (frequently sheltered) domestic markets. Japanese electronics and French wines are just two examples of such discrimination.

3. Many pubs and bars have "ladies' hours," and in the past, major league baseball parks had ladies' days on Wednesdays. In both cases, the price for women is lower than that charged their male counterparts.

4. Theaters, cinemas, and sports events often charge lower prices for children occupying equal accommodations as adults. The same arrangement is frequently offered to senior citizens.

5. Public transportation systems commonly offer reduced fares to senior citizens.

6. State universities charge higher tuition fees to out-of-state students, although there is no cost differential to the university between in-state and out-of-state students.

7. Public utilities (electric, gas, telephone) customarily charge higher rates to business customers than to residential customers.

8. University bookstores offer 10–15 percent discounts to faculty while charging full prices to students.

9. Individuals can order publications from publishers at lower prices than those charged to libraries and other institutions. Most professional journals are priced in this way.

We leave it to you to think of additional examples. In all of these instances, different prices are charged at a single time. A senior citizen and a person 40 years of age traveling in the subway together will pay different fares. Differential utility charges to business and residential customers are in effect at the same time during the day.

However, there are also price differences that depend on when products or services are consumed:

1. Theaters charge different ticket prices for matinees and evening performances.
2. Theaters charge higher ticket prices on weekends than on weekdays.
3. Daytime telephone rates are higher than nighttime rates.
4. Hotels catering mostly to business travelers charge lower room rates during weekends.

Are these also examples of price discrimination? Many economics texts subscribe to this notion. (Of course, where a firm's costs differ at different times, no price discrimination would be claimed.) However, if these are types of discrimination they do not really belong with the original examples given. After all, movements of a demand curve over time will change the prices of many products without the presence of price discrimination. What appears to be the case here is that weekend theater ticket demand, for example, is considerably higher than demand on a Tuesday or a Wednesday, while the supply curve is essentially vertical. And prices change as demand changes. Whether this qualifies as price discrimination is questionable.

Nonmarginal Pricing

Throughout this text we appear to have blithely assumed that all businesspeople calculate demand and cost schedules, obtain marginal revenue and marginal cost curves, equate marginal revenue with marginal cost, and thus determine their profit-maximizing selling price and production quantity. But how many business owners or managers actually know how to make these calculations? (How many have had or remember their course in microeconomics?) And even if they have the knowledge, how many have the time and, even more important, sufficient information to make such calculations?

In fact, it is often claimed (as discussed in Chapter 2) that businesses are really not profit maximizers, that they have other objectives. It has been said that management will seek only satisfactory levels of profit for the owners. The term *satisficing* has been used in this context.[15] Other corporate goals may also be important, such as the achievement of a desired market share, a target profit margin (i.e., percent of profits to revenue), or a target rate of return on assets (profit divided by assets) or on equity (profit divided by stockholder equity).

It also appears that one of the most popular pricing methods, believed to be pervasive throughout industry is the cost-plus or full-cost method, which at first glance seems not to employ the marginal pricing principle at all. It is this subject that will be discussed next.

Cost-Plus Pricing

A researcher questioning a sample of businesspeople on their pricing methods, would probably be told by a majority that they simply calculate the variable cost of the product, add to it an allocation for fixed costs, and then add a profit percentage or markup on top of these total costs to arrive at price.[16] Thus, for instance, if the direct (variable) cost of a product is \$8, its allocated overhead is \$6, and the desired mark-up is 25 percent, the price of the product will be \$17.50 $(8 + 6 + 0.25 \times 14)$.[17]

Such a calculation appears to be extremely simple,[18] and the whole method is often described as naive. But this apparent simplicity hides some fairly difficult calculations and assumptions:

1. How are average variable costs calculated?
2. How are fixed costs allocated? And why are fixed costs included in the price calculation? Economic theory tells us that fixed costs do not affect price.[19]
3. How is the size of the markup determined? Usually, it is said that the markup should guarantee the seller a "fair profit," or some target profit margin or target rate of return. If this is the case, are demand conditions taken into consideration at all?

We will discuss these problems, and as we go through this analysis we may find that cost-plus pricing and marginal pricing have a lot in common.

In cost-plus pricing, costs, both variable and fixed overheads, are usually calculated at some standard or normal quantity, as done by the accountants.

---

[15]See Herbert Simon, "Theories of Decision Making in Economics and Behavioral Science," *American Economic Review*, 49 (June 1959), pp. 253–83. This condition usually prevails in large corporations, where professional managers may not act in conformance with the wishes of stockholders. In the textbooks on corporate finance, considerable attention is accorded this subject, which has been named "agency theory." It is based on a famous article by Michael C. Jensen and William H. Meckling, "Theory of the Firm: Managerial Behavior, Agency Costs, and Ownership Structure," *Journal of Financial Economics*, October 1976, pp. 305–60.

[16]One of the original studies was R. L. Hall and C. J. Hitch, "Price Theory and Business Behavior," *Oxford Economic Papers*, 2 (May 1939), pp. 12–45.

[17]Markup is ordinarily calculated as a percentage of cost. Profit margin is commonly computed as a percentage of price. Thus, a 25 percentage markup is equivalent to a 20 percent profit margin.

[18]It is said that restaurants usually mark up the food cost four times to arrive at the price of a menu item—a very simple calculation indeed.

[19]Only in the Baumol revenue maximization model does fixed cost enter into price determination.

These are historical costs and do not appear to include an opportunity cost. But economic theory tells us that unit costs tend to vary with quantity, and the expected quantities may not correspond to those that result.[20] Also, as mentioned, fixed costs should not be used in the determination of prices.

However, if we take these criticisms in turn, the shortcomings of cost-plus pricing may not be as serious as they appear. There is no real reason why accounting costs cannot include some measure of opportunity cost. And even if it is not incorporated, a normal profit (another name for opportunity cost) certainly could easily be included in the markup. Now, it is often said that cost-plus pricing is a long-term concept. If that is the case, then, according to economic theory, all costs are variable; a cost allocation is then an estimate of the additional variable costs in the long run. Further, although economists like to draw nice U-shaped cost curves, it is quite possible that in the longer run the bottom portion of the average cost curve is quite shallow (saucer-shaped) and that over some production range it may appear to be almost horizontal.[21] In that case, as long as a firm is producing in the range at which standard costs are calculated, the problem of costs varying with quantity is obviated. Also, if the curve is relatively horizontal, marginal cost will be identical or almost identical to the average cost in that interval, and pricing on basis of average cost will thus be substantially similar to marginal cost pricing. In addition, economic theory tells us that, under perfect competition, in the long run all but normal profits will disappear. The markup, then, must certainly represent normal profit. It is more likely, however, that competition in the real world is not quite perfect, and the firm will therefore be faced by a downward-sloping demand curve.

This brings us to the question of the demand curve. If a markup is applied to obtain a "fair" profit, the implication is that demand conditions are not taken into consideration. But that would indicate almost complete inflexibility regarding the size of the markup. However, it has been observed in innumerable cases that markup percentages differ among different product lines of the same firm. The fact that a company accepts a lower markup for some products than others indicates that demand conditions and the competitive environment are included

[20] The accountant's cost for a normal quantity can be shown as one point on the economist's average cost curve:

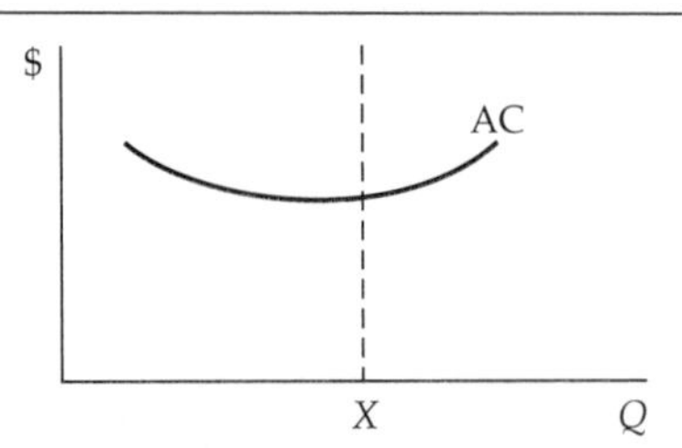

Point X is the "normal" quantity, at which costs would be calculated. But other quantities would be produced at different costs.

[21] This situation is consistent with constant returns to scale.

in the price decision making. As will be shown, the markup percentage tends to vary inversely with demand elasticity. This makes obvious sense: when a firm is faced by very strong competition, the demand curve facing it will tend to be nearly or completely horizontal: under those circumstances, the firm will not be able to afford a very large markup.

One other important point must be made. Not only will different markups be applied for different product lines of a given firm, but the markup will probably change on a given product from time to time. Such changes could be caused by changing demand or changing cost conditions. When this occurs, a firm will adjust its markup and, thus, its price to meet the new circumstances. Its purpose for such action is most probably to increase or protect its profits. And as long as a firm changes its prices to "do better," (i.e., increase its profit or minimize its loss), it is acting as if it has knowledge of its demand and costs curves: that is, it is acting consistently with marginal pricing.

It is certainly true that businesspeople do not have sufficient knowledge to estimate marginal revenue and marginal costs curves with any degree of accuracy. Thus, cost-plus pricing can be a substitute for marginal pricing in the absence of sufficient knowledge. But given the proclivity for firms to adjust their markups in response to demand and cost conditions in such a way as to improve profitability, profit maximization and cost-plus pricing can be quite compatible.

AN ARITHMETIC RECONCILIATION OF COST-PLUS AND MARGINAL PRICING It can be shown mathematically that under certain circumstances, cost-plus pricing can be consistent with profit maximization (i.e., MR = MC).

Most microeconomics textbooks show the mathematical relationship among price, marginal revenue, and demand elasticity as follows:[22]

$$\text{MR} = P\left(1 + \frac{1}{E_P}\right)$$

Since profit is maximized when MR = MC, we can rewrite the equation as

$$\text{MC} = P\left(1 + \frac{1}{E_P}\right)$$

Further, under certain conditions, marginal cost will equal average cost. Thus, our equation becomes

---

[22]The equation is derived in the following way: Total revenue (TR) equals price times quantity $(P \times Q)$. To obtain marginal revenue, total revenue must be differentiated with respect to quantity:

$$\text{MR} = \frac{d\text{TR}}{dQ} = \frac{d(P \times Q)}{dQ} = P \times \frac{dQ}{dQ} + Q \times \frac{dP}{dQ} = P \times 1 + Q \times \frac{dP}{dQ} = P\left(1 + \frac{Q}{P} \times \frac{dP}{dQ}\right)$$

Note that the product inside the parentheses is the reciprocal of elasticity; hence,

$$\text{MR} = P\left(1 + \frac{1}{E_P}\right)$$

Remember that demand elasticity has a negative sign.

$$AC = P\left(1 + \frac{1}{E_P}\right)$$

and can then be rewritten as

$$AC = P\left(\frac{E_P + 1}{E_P}\right)$$

To show how price is based on average cost, we can rearrange the equation as

$$P = AC\left(\frac{E_P}{E_P + 1}\right)$$

Under conditions of cost-plus pricing,

$$P = AC(1 + M)$$

where M stands for the markup percentage. If the two previous equations are comparable, then

$$(1 + M) = \frac{E_P}{E_P + 1}$$

It can be shown that there is an inverse relationship between markup and demand elasticity. For example, if $E_P = -2$, then $(1+M) = -2/-1 = 2$ and M is therefore 100 percent. If, however, $E_P = -5$, then $(1+M) = -5/-4 = 1.25$, and markup is only 25 percent. This result is quite reasonable; it indicates that the less elastic the demand curve, the larger will be the markup.

Thus, under the not infrequent conditions where the average cost curve is constant in the relevant range of production, cost-plus pricing may give results identical to those that would be obtained if managers were pursuing profit maximization.

Multiproduct Pricing

In economics much of the analysis makes use of simplifying assumptions. Thus, some aspects of the analysis may seem rather unrealistic. For example, we know that very few products in our economy are produced under conditions of perfect competition. Nevertheless, a large portion of our text—and all other economics texts—is devoted to its discussion. There are good reasons for this practice. First, perfect competition is the simplest of the economic models and is thus a good starting point for the discussion of derivative, more complex systems, such as monopoly, monopolistic competition, and oligopoly. Second, many markets, although not perfectly competitive (i.e., firms are faced by downward-sloping demand curves), can be analyzed as such because their behavior resembles perfect competition closely enough. Any predictions based on this analysis will be sufficiently accurate to obviate the need for more complex models.[23]

Another simplification frequently made in economic theory is assuming that a firm or a plant produces a single product. Up to this point, we have done so in this text. Actually, we first assumed that single products were sold in single markets. Then we discussed price discrimination and extended our analysis to operations in more than one market. Now we will provide a brief treatment of cases in which a plant or a firm produces two or more products, which are, of course, the norm rather than the exception.

The various products produced by a firm can be independent of one another. This means that neither the demand for nor the cost of one product is affected by the demand for or cost of another product. In such a case, each product will be produced, as usual, at the level where its marginal revenue equals its marginal cost. The analysis can then proceed as if only one good were produced.

In most cases, however, there is some relationship among products produced by one firm. The relationships can exist either on the demand side or the cost side—or both. We can distinguish (at least) four different interrelationships:

1. Products are complements in terms of demand. One company may produce both personal computers and software, or a fast-food restaurant may sell both hamburgers and soft drinks.
2. Products are substitutes in terms of demand: A company may produce different models of a personal computer, or a soft drink company may bottle both cola and lemon-lime soda.
3. Products are joined in production. The extreme case of joint production occurs when two products are produced in fixed (or almost fixed) proportions, such as cattle production, which involves one skin and one carcass per steer.
4. Products compete for resources. If a company making different products that compete for the available resources produces more of one product, it will have to do so at the expense of producing the other product or products. The production of different models of the same computer is an example.

Let us now discuss each of these cases.

Products Complementary in Demand

When two products are complementary, an increase in the quantity sold of one will bring about an increase in the quantity sold of the other. This may be due to an increase in the demand for product A or a price decrease for product A (bringing about an increase in the quantity demanded). Products may be so closely related that they are bought in fixed proportions. An example is kitchen knives, each of which must be made of one wooden handle

[23]It is the accuracy of the prediction provided by a model that is important to scientists, not the reasonability or realism of the assumptions. This point has been successfully argued by Milton Friedman in "The Methodology of Positive Economics," contained in his *Essays in Positive Economics*, Chicago: University of Chicago Press, 1953, pp. 3–43.

and one metal blade. Other complementary products are a personal computer and a keyboard, and still another example is an automobile body and a set of four wheels. Somewhat less fixed in proportion but still closely related products are razors and razor blades, tennis rackets and tennis balls, and computers and software. There are also more remotely related products where the demand for one can easily have a beneficial effect on the demand for the other. For instance, a popular textbook in economics published by a particular company may enhance the sales of a finance textbook by the same publisher.

The important point is that the demand for a product is affected not only by its price, by income, and by tastes, for example, but also very strongly by the prices of related commodities. This subject was discussed in Chapter 3, where we defined the determinants of the demand curve in general. Here we will concentrate on the effects of complementary commodities on the revenues of one firm. Thus, if products A and B are complementary, a change in revenue from A will entail a change in the revenue from B. In both cases, profit maximization will occur at the familiar point where the marginal revenue of each product equals its marginal costs. Since each of the demand equations will include the prices of both products, the pricing problem will require the solution of simultaneous equations.

If managers had nice, neat demand and cost functions available for each of these products, they could arrive at the combined profit maximization positions using relatively simple mathematical formulas.[24] However, since in real life the decision maker would most likely not have sufficient data on hand, the maximization process would proceed along a trial-and-error course, where markups (and thus prices) for the products would be adjusted until the optimal combination is reached. Such results could easily be reached at some point where the unit profit (as well as total profits) for one of the products is considerably less than for the other product. Actually, the process would be even more complex in reality, since it is not only the complementary relationship between the firm's two products that has an important influence on the firm's revenue (and profit); competitors' products that are substitutes for our firm's products must also be considered in the process of price setting.

There is another instance in which a company must consider these interrelationships. It is not necessary that a firm produce two related products simultaneously. It may just produce one and be in the process of deciding whether or not to embark on the production of a complementary product. In calculating the profitability of such expansion, the company must include the increase in sales

[24]For a two-product situation, a manager could calculate the marginal revenue for each of the interrelated products. Since

$$Q_A = f(P_A, P_B) \quad \text{and} \quad Q_B = f(P_B, P_A)$$

then

$$\text{MR}_A = \frac{d\,\text{TR}_A}{d\,Q_A} + \frac{d\,\text{TR}_B}{d\,Q_A} \quad \text{and} \quad \text{MR}_B = \frac{d\,\text{TR}_B}{d\,Q_B} + \frac{d\,\text{TR}_A}{d\,Q_B}$$

Each of the marginal revenues would be equated to their respective marginal costs simultaneously:

$$\text{MR}_A = \text{MC}_A \quad \text{and} \quad \text{MR}_B = \text{MC}_B$$

of and profit earned on the earlier product. If it omitted this positive effect, it would be understating the benefits of the new product. It may decide against the product's introduction when in fact the total profits of the company would increase if the new product were brought to market. As an example, suppose a successful producer of television sets is considering whether or not to introduce a new line of VCRs. In calculating the potential profitability of producing VCRs, the producer must include the possibility of enhanced sales (and profits) from its television line.

Products Substitutable in Demand

A brief treatment of substitutability and pricing will suffice, since this case is extremely similar to that of complements. For substitutes, the effect to be considered is the decrease (increase) in revenue and profits of a second product if quantities bought, either because of changes in demand or changes in price of the first product, rise (fall). Examples of such cases abound. Two different sizes of personal computers certainly are substitutes for one another. The different automobile models produced by one manufacturer (sedans vs. convertibles, Ford Escorts vs. Ford Tempos, Chevrolets vs. Pontiacs, etc.) are relatively close substitutes, so it is necessary to price them jointly. Another example is Global Foods' soft drink division, which produces cola-type and non-cola type sodas simultaneously.

Just as in the case of complementary products, substitution can occur when a new product is introduced. Thus, a computer manufacturer developing a new generation of computers must consider the impact that the introduction will have on similar but less advanced products now being marketed.

The analysis of these cases is basically the same as for complementary commodities. The marginal revenue of one product will be a function of the quantities sold of both commodities, and the prices of the two will be found by solving simultaneous equations. However, in this case, the sale of one product will have a negative impact on the sales of the other. Again, in the actual world of business, such price setting tends to be done by trial and error with sequential adjustments made until the optimal profit is reached.[25] Thus, the marginal principles of pricing will again be fulfilled.

Joint Products with Fixed Proportions

Certain products will be produced together from one set of inputs. In some instances, the two products will be produced in fixed proportions to one another. Although precisely fixed proportions may not occur often in the real world, relative fixity is commonly encountered, particularly in the short run. The example given earlier involved the products a beef carcass and a hide (only one of each can be obtained from one steer). Other examples are soybean meal

[25] A producer of computers will announce the introduction of a new line and set prices. In some cases, it may immediately change the price of its already-available computers. In other cases, price changes in the new line or old line may occur after some time elapses subsequent to the announcement of the new line.

and soybean oil, and coconut milk and coconut meat. In many cases, there is a principal product and one or more by-products. Even though the case of fixed proportions in production is relatively rare, it is a useful analytical abstraction, and we will discuss it here briefly.

Assume that products A and B are produced jointly in fixed proportions. Only one cost curve can be constructed in this case. However, the demand curves for the two products are independent (e.g., the demand for coconut meat is not related to the demand for its milk). Thus, the two demand curves and their respective marginal revenue curves can be added vertically to obtain a total demand curve and a total marginal revenue curve. Observe, however, that when one of the separate marginal revenue curves goes negative, it becomes irrelevant to the solution of the problem, since no business would produce at a point where marginal revenue is negative. To the right of this point, the total marginal revenue curve will be coincident with the marginal revenue of the product, which is still in the positive range. Production will take place (using our usual maximization rule) where total marginal revenue equals marginal cost. The prices of the two separate products can be found at the quantity indicated on their respective demand curves. Figure 13.7 shows the results. D_A, D_B, MR_A, and MR_B are the demand and marginal revenue curves for the two products, and MR_S represents the vertical summation of the two individual marginal revenue curves. (The summed demand curve is actually irrelevant to the solution of the problem and need not be shown.) As can be seen, MR_S becomes identical with MR_B to the right of the point where MR_A becomes negative.

The curve MC represents the marginal cost of the joint product. Production will take place where marginal cost is equal to MR_S, which is at quantity Q on the graph. The prices charged for the two products will be found on their

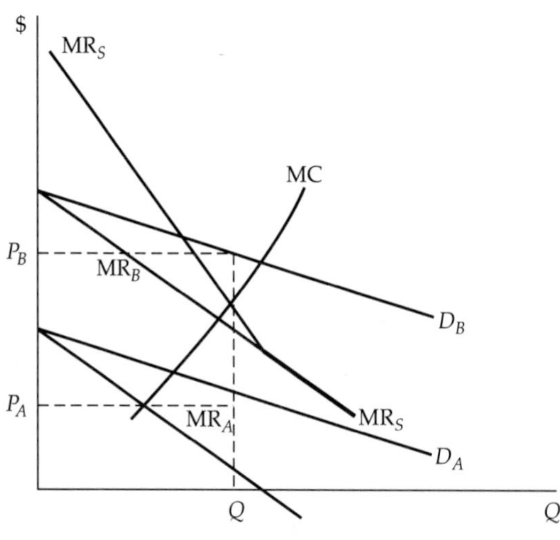

Figure 13.7 Price Determination for Joint Products Made in Fixed Proportions

respective demand curves at P_A and P_B. An interesting aspect of this type of construction is that if the optimal production quantity were to the right (i.e., at higher quantities) of the point where one of the marginal revenue curves (in our case, that for product A) becomes negative, it would become profitable for the company to produce this total amount but not to sell quantities of product A beyond the point where its marginal revenue becomes zero.

Another important point is the effect of the change in the demand for one of the two jointly produced products. If the demand for product B rises and the price of B thus increases, there will be a decrease in the price of A (since it will be produced at a lower point on its demand curve).

Joint Products in Variable Proportions

When we relax the limitation of fixed proportions, we have the usual case of joint production. Indeed, when two products are produced from similar resources in variable proportions (i.e., if we produce more of one product we must produce less of the other) the situation is not dissimilar to the general case of production of different products with limited resources. We are essentially describing the "guns or butter" situation. Under short-run conditions, there is a given amount of resources with which the two products can be produced.

Figure 13.8 illustrates this situation. Curve I_1 is an isocost curve; the total cost of production is the same at each point. An essential requisite is that the curve be concave to the origin: as more of one product is produced, progressively larger quantities of the other must be given up. The isocost curve shows the alternative quantities of product A and B that can be produced. If the prices of the two products are constant regardless of quantity (i.e., we are implicitly operating under conditions of perfect competition), then a straight-line isorevenue curve can be drawn. At each point on R_1 in Figure 13.8, identical revenue

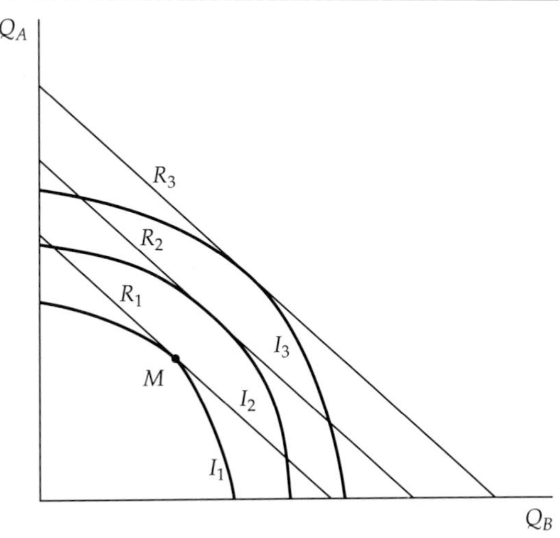

Figure 13.8 Joint Production Using Variable Proportions

is obtained. To optimize, the company will produce at the point of tangency between the isorevenue and isocost curves (Point M in the figure). This represents the highest revenue that the company can attain for a given total cost. If revenue at this point is greater than cost, economic profit will result.

The company could also move from one isocost curve to another (e.g., from I_1 to I_2 to I_3), and consequently from one isorevenue curve to another, representing the use of additional variable resources. Production would take place at the tangency point that results in the largest difference between total revenue and total cost. This point signifies the maximum economic profit the company can achieve. In the long run, these isocost curves would include changes in all resources, including those (such as plant and equipment) that are fixed in the short run. Under conditions of perfect competition, the optimal tangency would occur where total revenue just equals total cost, with no economic profit. At all other points, economic losses would be sustained.

We have limited our discussion to a simple model, utilizing only two products and assuming perfect competition. Much more complex models could be developed, involving more than two products, noncompetitive conditions, and demand interrelationships, for example. The results would be more difficult to obtain, and relatively complicated mathematical models would have to be introduced, but the principles of economic maximization would still apply. Whenever a company takes action in introducing a new product, producing more of one at the expense of another or eliminating a certain commodity from its product line, and when such action is taken to improve its short-run or long-run profitability, the company is guided by the basic principle of equating marginal cost with marginal revenue.

Other Pricing Practices

Several special applications of pricing theory have been discussed in this chapter. Although we have dealt with a number of important topics, economic and marketing literature abounds with descriptions of other pricing practices. A brief review of some of these will complete the material of this chapter.

Transfer Pricing

In today's complex industrial world, many companies have subdivided their operations into several groups or divisions. As a product moves from its early stages to the point where it is ready to be sold to consumers, it is passed from one operating division of the company to another. In the automobile industry, for example, various auto parts may be produced in different plants and then assembled into the finished product in yet another plant. Computer and peripheral equipment components may be produced in one plant and assembled into different products at other plants. Then, to sell the products, the marketing arm of the company may have to assemble the various individual machines into complete systems.

To continue this analysis, it is necessary to address the notion of *profit center*, a frequently used term that refers to a situation prevalent in large corporations.

The management of each division is charged with a profit objective. Thus, each stage of production must measure its costs and then establish a price at which it will "transfer" its product to the next stage. However, if each intermediate profit center were to set its price to maximize its own profit, the price of the final product may not maximize the profit of the company as a whole, which is the appropriate objective. The price set by the division transferring the intermediate product becomes the cost of the division receiving this product. If that price is set too high, this may start a chain reaction resulting in the final product price being higher than the price which would maximize the company's profit. The pricing mechanism must be geared toward maximizing total company profit; therefore, the final pricing policy may be dictated centrally from the top of the corporation.

Such processes can be extremely complicated, particularly if there are more than two steps in the transfer process. Further, the intermediate products may be only for internal usage. On the other hand, the producing division may also be selling its product in an external market, and the receiving division may be free to purchase the intermediate product from a competitor, if that would improve the company's profit situation. Let us discuss each of these cases in turn. To simplify matters, we will assume the existence of just two divisions, one that manufactures components (division C), and another that assembles them into the final product and sells it (division A).

NO EXTERNAL MARKETS If there is no possibility for division A to buy components from a competing firm and no possibility for division C to sell components to other companies, then the two divisions must deal with equal quantities; division C will produce exactly the number of components that will be utilized by division A for assembly and sales. The company will be faced by a demand curve for the final product and two marginal cost curves. The two MC curves, one for each division, will be summed vertically to obtain total marginal cost, and the company will maximize its total profit by equating the total marginal cost with marginal revenue. Production will take place at that intersection, and the price for the final product will be the corresponding price on the demand curve.

EXTERNAL MARKETS It may be possible for division C to sell its (intermediate) product in a competitive market and for division A to purchase division C's product (an identical product) in a competitive market. In that case, the pricing of the product will proceed as follows:

1. Division C will produce at the point where its marginal cost equals the market price. (Since we are assuming the existence of a competitive market, the demand curve is horizontal, resulting in a uniform price regardless of quantity.)
2. The cost of the intermediate product to division A is the market price. This will be added to division A's marginal cost curve to obtain the total marginal cost for the final product.
3. Production will take place at the quantity where the total marginal cost equals the marginal revenue for the final product.

4. If the final product quantity is less than the quantity of the intermediate product produced by C, then C will sell the surplus in the competitive external market. If the output of C is less than A wishes to buy, A will turn to the external market for the additional units of the intermediate product it needs to maximize company profit.

Of course, should division C for some reason attempt to price the intermediate product in excess of the market price, then A would buy all of the intermediate product in the external market.

Price Skimming and Penetration Pricing

Price skimming can be practiced by a firm that is the first to introduce a product. During the time when competitors are trying to catch up, the firm may have a virtual monopoly. It can therefore try to price along the demand curve, a practice similar to first-degree discrimination, discussed earlier. However, the different prices will be charged at different times. The customers willing to pay the highest price will buy first; then the firm will lower its price to attract the next group of customers. To practice price skimming efficiently, the firm will require a great deal of information about its demand curve.

Penetration pricing may be done by a company entering a new market and endeavoring to secure a certain share of the market. The company will charge a lower price in order to gain a foothold in the industry.

Prestige Pricing

For some products, it is believed that demand will be higher at a higher price because of the prestige that ownership will bestow on the buyer. An example is the luxury automobile market, where the high price gives the appearance of higher quality, even though other makes of automobiles of similar quality are sold at a lower price. Actually, buyers are perceiving the two makes of automobiles to be different products. The basis for this seeming contradiction is either that customers are not well informed about the quality of the various products or that the producer has succeeded in creating a special snob appeal for its product.

Psychological Pricing

A demand curve for a particular product may be quite inelastic over a certain range of prices but become rather elastic at one specific higher or lower price. Such a demand curve has the appearance of step function. Another type of pricing is illustrated by stores that sell products at $19.95 or $9.99, because these prices are preferred considerably to $20 and $10, respectively. The change in the first digit appears to create the illusion on the part of customers that this is a rather significant price difference. This may be a temporary phenomenon with some consumers, and over an extended period of time such pricing would appear to have limited application.

The Solution

Rebecca James went to see Philip Olds of the food division to solicit his advice on the bid she intended to make for the soft drink supply contract with the large airport catering company.

"One thing is certain," he said. "You have to bid at a price considerably lower than the price at which you sell to small retail stores. These stores have a leeway in how much they can charge their customers, since they are really selling convenience. A small variance in price is not going to change their sales significantly, so they will not stop buying from us as long as our price is not out of line. The other suppliers of soft drinks know that also and will tend to keep their prices relatively high.

"However, your potential new customer intends to give a contract to only one additional supplier, and 10 cents per case will make a large difference when hundreds of thousands of cases are involved. Thus, you will have to shave your markup as much as possible. It may turn out that the profit you will make on this contract, if you get it, will cover little more than your variable cost plus some allocation of your plant's fixed cost."

Philip was telling Rebecca that the demand price elasticity of the large caterer was quite different from that of the small retailers. As a result, Global Foods could sell to these two markets at different prices.

Rebecca is thus confronted with a case of price discrimination. The demand elasticities in the two markets are probably quite different; thus, higher prices can be charged in the market displaying lower elasticity. And the separation of the two markets, (i.e., no cross-selling) represents the second important condition for the existence of price discrimination.

She decides that she will have to propose a significantly lower price to the caterer than she is used to obtaining from the small retailers, and she must now determine the differential. She assumes that the average cost per case of soft drinks for the two customers is the same. Although this is certainly not quite accurate (the large shipments the company will make to the new customer if the bid is won will probably create some cost savings), the unit cost differences probably will not be significant, so her analysis will lose little if she assumes equality.

She estimates the company 's usual markup to be about 50 percent. After some additional consideration, and a review of some data for the industry that she obtained, she feels that a 20 percent markup would put the company in a good competitive position. She decides this is the number she will recommend to her boss.

The decision that she has made has some rather important implications for the estimate of demand elasticities for the two classes of customers. The lower the demand elasticity, the higher will be the markup that a company can obtain. Following the equation developed previously,

(Continued)

$$(1 + M) = \frac{E_P}{E_P + 1}$$

(where demand elasticity is a negative number), an elasticity of 3 conforms to a markup of 50 percent, whereas an elasticity of 6 corresponds to a 20 percent markup. Of course, these numbers are approximations, but such an estimate could be of great help to Rebecca in her attempt to set the proper price.

Summary

This chapter has built upon the foundation laid in Chapter 11 by applying the principles of pricing and output to specific pricing situations, most under conditions of imperfect competition. Briefly, we learned the following:

1. The kinked demand curve is an attempt to explain potential price rigidities in oligopolistic markets.
2. Cartels are formed to avoid the uncertainties of a possible reaction by one competitor to price and production actions by another. The firms in the industry agree on unified pricing and production actions to maximize profits. However, as history shows, such arrangements are not always stable.
3. Price leadership exists when one company establishes a price and others follow. Two types of price leadership were discussed: barometric and dominant.
4. Baumol's model describes the actions of a company whose objective is to maximize revenue (rather than profits) subject to a minimum profit constraint.
5. Price discrimination (or differential pricing) exists when a product is sold in different markets at different prices. Third-degree price discrimination is the most common. By charging different prices in separate markets that have demand curves with different price elasticities, a firm can increase its profits over what they would be if a uniform price were charged.
6. Cost-plus pricing appears to be a very common method. However, such pricing does not necessarily imply that marginal principles and demand curve effects are not taken into consideration.
7. Since most firms and plants produce more than one product at the same time, multiproduct pricing was examined. Multiple products produced by one firm can be complements or substitutes, both on the demand side and the supply side. Four possible cases were discussed, and it was shown how application of the marginal principle brings about profit maximization.
8. Several other pricing practices were summarized. One was transfer pricing, which is used to determine the price of a product that progresses through several stages of production within a firm.

Important Concepts

Barometric price leadership: In an oligopolistic industry, a situation in which one firm, perceiving that demand and supply conditions warrant it, announces a price change, expecting that other firms will follow.

Baumol model: A model hypothesizing that firms seek to maximize their revenue subject to some minimum profit requirement (i.e., the profit constraint).

Cartel: A collusive arrangement in oligopolistic markets. Producers agree on unified pricing and production actions to maximize profits and to eliminate the rigors of competition.

Cost-plus pricing: Also called *full-cost pricing*, a practice in which prices are calculated by adding a markup to total cost.

Dominant price leadership: In an oligopolistic industry, a firm, usually the largest in the industry, sets a price at which it will maximize its profits, allowing other firms to sell as much as they wish at that price.

Kinked demand curve: A theoretical construction that attempts to explain price rigidities in oligopolistic markets.

Multiproduct pricing: Pricing that reflects the interrelationship among multiple products of a firm that are substitutes or complements.

Penetration pricing: A company charges a lower price than indicated by economic analysis in order to gain a foothold in market.

Prestige pricing: A perception that charging a higher price will increase quantity sold because of the prestige obtained by the buyer.

Price discrimination: A situation in which an identical product is sold in different markets at different prices.

Price leadership: One company in an oligopolistic industry establishes the price, and the other companies follow. Two types of price leadership are common: barometric and dominant.

Price skimming: The practice of charging a higher price than indicated by economic analysis when a company introduces a new product and competition is weak.

Psychological pricing: The practice of charging, for example, $9.95 rather than $10 for a product in the belief that such pricing will create the illusion of significantly lower price to the consumer.

Transfer pricing: A method to correctly price a product as it is transferred from one stage of production to the next.

Questions

1. "If a company sets its prices on basis of a cost-plus calculation, it cannot possibly suffer a loss on its products." True or False? Comment.
2. Price discrimination is often defended on the basis of equity. What is meant by this statement? Comment on its validity.

3. Which products in each pair would tend to have higher markups in a supermarket?
   a. Cigarettes versus tomatoes
   b. Potatoes versus orange juice
4. Many years ago, a neighborhood lunch counter charged 15 cents for a cup of coffee and 15 cents for a buttered hard roll. One day, a customer ordered the two items and was told that the total price was 35 cents. When the customer asked which of the two items had been raised by 5 cents, the owner's condescending reply was, " Which do you think? " In your opinion, which of the two items was affected and why?
5. Why does the theory of the kinked demand curve lead to expectations of price rigidity?
6. Differentiate barometric price leadership and dominant price leadership.
7. Is there a similarity between cartel pricing and monopoly pricing?
8. What conditions are favorable to the formation and maintenance of a cartel?
9. Can government be a potent force in the establishment and maintenance of monopolistic conditions? Name and describe such occurrences.
10. Describe the properties of the Baumol revenue maximization model. Do you consider this to be a good alternative to the profit maximization model?
11. Telephone companies charge different rates for calls during the day, in the evening, and at night or weekends. Do you consider this to be price discrimination?
12. Is cost-plus pricing necessarily inconsistent with marginal pricing?
13. Airline ticket prices may differ with respect to when the ticket is bought, how long a passenger remains on the trip (e.g., over a weekend) and other variables. Are these differences a case of price discrimination?
14. Does cost-plus pricing necessarily ignore the demand curve?
15. Define and describe (giving examples):
    a. Transfer pricing
    b. Psychological pricing
    c. Price skimming
    d. Penetration pricing

Problems

1. A firm in an oligopolistic industry has identified two sets of demand curves. If the firm is the only one that changes prices (i.e., other firms do not follow), its demand curve takes the form $Q = 82 - 8P$. If, however, it is expected that competitors will follow the price actions of the firm, then the demand curve is of the form $Q = 44 - 3P$.
   a. Develop demand schedules for each alternative and draw them on a graph.
   b. Calculate marginal revenue curves for each.
   c. If the present price and quantity position for our firm is located at the intersection of the two demand curves, and competitors follow any price

decrease but do not follow a price increase, show the demand curve relevant to our firm.

d. Draw the appropriate marginal revenue curve.

e. Show the range over which a marginal cost curve could rise or fall without affecting the price our firm charges.

2. An amusement park, whose customer set is made up of two markets, adults and children, has developed demand schedules as follows:

	Quantity	
Price ($)	*Adults*	*Children*
5	15	20
6	14	18
7	13	16
8	12	14
9	11	12
10	10	10
11	9	8
12	8	6
13	7	4
14	6	2

The marginal operating cost of each unit of quantity is $5. (*Hint:* Since marginal cost is a constant, so is average variable cost. Ignore fixed cost.) The owners of the amusement park wish to maximize profits.

a. Calculate the price, quantity, and profit if:

(1) The amusement park charges a different price in each market.

(2) The amusement park charges the same price in the two markets combined.

(3) Explain the difference in the profit realized under the two situations.

b. (Mathematical solution) The demand schedules presented in problem 2 can be expressed in equation form as follows (where subscript *A* refers to the adult market, subscript *C* to the market for children, and subscript *T* to the two markets combined):

$$Q_A = 20 - 1P_A$$
$$Q_C = 30 - 2P_C$$
$$Q_T = 50 - 3P_T$$

Solve these equations for the maximum profit that the amusement park will attain when it charges different prices in the two markets and when it charges a single price for the combined market.

3. The Bramwell Corporation has estimated its demand function and total cost function to be as follows:

$$Q = 25 - 0.05P$$
$$\text{TC} = 700 + 200Q$$

Answer the following questions either by developing demand and cost schedules (*Hint:* Use quantities from 1 to 14) or by solving the equations.

a. What will be the price and quantity if Bramwell wants to:
   (1) Maximize profits?
   (2) Maximize revenue?
   (3) Maximize revenue but require the profit to be a minimum of \$300?
b. Now assume that the cost function is TC = 780 + 200Q while the demand function remains the same. What will the price and quantity be if Bramwell wants to:
   (1) Maximize profits?
   (2) Maximize revenue?
   (3) Maximize revenue but require the profit to be a minimum of \$300?
c. Why are the answers the same in $a(1)$ and $b(1)$ but different in $a(3)$ and $b(3)$?

4. The Great Southern Paper Company has the following marginal cost schedule for producing pulp:

Quantity (tons)	*Marginal Cost*
1	\$18
2	20
3	25
4	33
5	43

Pulp can be bought in the open market for \$25 per ton. The marginal cost of converting pulp into paper is MC = 5 + 5Q, and the demand for paper is P = 135 − 15Q. Calculate the marginal cost of paper if the company produces its own pulp. What is the profit-maximizing quantity? Should the company purchase pulp from the outside or produce it in-house?

5. The purchase price of Fancy Shoes, sold by Bradbury Footwear Stores, is \$30 per pair. The company's economist has estimated the point price elasticity to be −1.8. What price should the company charge if it wants to maximize its profits?
6. An airplane manufacturer has annual fixed costs of \$50 million. Its variable costs are expected to be \$2 million per plane. If the manufacturer wants to earn a 10 percent rate of return on its investment of \$400 million and expects to produce 100 aircraft this year, what will its markup on total cost have to be? If it expects to produce 150 aircraft, what will its markup have to be?
7. Schultz's Orchard grows only two types of fruit—apples and peaches—and over the years it has been able to chart two production levels and the resulting total cost. The figures are shown in the following table, where quantity produced is given in bushels.

Apples	*Peaches*	*Apples*	*Peaches*
900	0	1400	0
800	200	1200	300
600	400	900	600
400	500	700	700
250	550	300	850
0	600	0	900
Total cost: $15,000		Total cost: $25,000	

This year it is expected that the price of apples will be $30 per bushel and that of peaches will be $45 per bushel.

What is the best production level at each cost? How much is the profit at each level?

8. The Prestige Office Equipment Company produces and sells different types of office furniture. One of the important items it sells is a high-quality desk. During the past year, Prestige sold 5,000 of these at a price of $500 each. The contribution profit for this line of furniture last year was $700,000.

   A consultant suggests that Prestige decrease the price of each desk by $30. In his opinion, another 500 desks could then be sold, and the total profit would be maintained. A trade publication that employs an economist has estimated price elasticity of office furniture (including desks) to be about −1.8.

   Assume that the variable unit cost per desk in the coming year will remain the same. Evaluate the consultant's proposal. Be sure to include in your answer the price elasticity assumed by the consultant, as well as the published elasticity estimate.

CHAPTER 14

Capital Budgeting

The Situation

George Kline is the manager of Global Foods' capital planning department. He is responsible for analyzing projects that require extensive expenditures and whose payoffs occur over a significantly long period of time—capital budgeting projects. When the analysis is completed, George and his staff of five make presentations up the company hierarchy—to the treasurer (George's boss) and the vice president of finance. If the proposal is large enough, it may finally have to be approved by the Corporate Management Committee (a group composed of top executives).

George has in front of him two new project proposals that require extensive analysis by his staff. The first is the proposed expansion of company activities into a new geographical region. Global is investigating the possibility of entering a new region where its soft drink products have not been marketed previously. Annual sales for this area have been estimated at 100,000,000 cases. A 4 percent annual increase in total consumption is forecast. The market research people have estimated that, given an extensive advertising campaign, the first year's market share could reach 1 percent, and it may grow to some 5 percent four years later.

For the company to compete in this new area, it must establish a plant. An unused, somewhat obsolete bottling plant is available in the area for $5 million. The total costs of rebuilding and renovating the plant and purchasing and installing the new equipment, are expected to amount to $2 million. During the first year, the company will incur expenses of recruiting a new work force. Just before production starts in year two, there will be an extensive advertising and promotion campaign. These expenses are estimated at $750,000.

If Global Foods actually achieves a 1 percent share of the market, it will sell 1 million cases. Each case sells for $5. Production costs will be $2.50 per case. General and administrative expenses will be $650,000 during the first year. Of this amount, $500,000 is fixed; the remainder is a function of quantity. Distribution and selling expenses will

(Continued)

be 60 cents per case. Advertising expenses will be 5 percent of sales.

The cost of rebuilding and renovating the plant will be depreciated over 31 1/2 years. The remainder, $1 million (for new machinery, etc.), will be depreciated over seven years using double-declining balance depreciation. The purchase cost of the plant is to be allocated as follows: 10 percent for land, 50 percent for building, and 40 percent for equipment. The same methods of depreciation will be used. (Land is not depreciable.)

Global also expects that it will have to increase the size of its working capital by $750,000, to cover the additional inventory, accounts receivable, and cash for transactions.

The analysis will span seven years, including the first year of expenditures and six years of operations. This is a relatively conservative assumption—if the company cannot make a viable business of this plant over a seven-year time period, it would consider the operation too risky to undertake. Two other important pieces of information needed to complete the analysis are:

The company's marginal income tax rate (federal, state, and local) is 40 percent.

The cost of capital for this project will be 15 percent.

The second project George must consider is replacing an old depalletizing machine, which, although still in good working condition, is relatively slow and expensive to operate. A new machine will increase revenue and decrease operating and maintenance expenses. The total annual benefit from this will amount to $18,000.

A new machine will cost $100,000 and is conservatively expected to last 10 years. The old machine has a present book value of $10,000. If properly maintained, it can be made to last another 10 years. At that point it will have no market value. If sold today (there is a market for used depalletizers), it would have a cash value of $12,000.

The remaining depreciation life of the old machine is two years; it is being depreciated on a straight-line basis. The new machine will be depreciated over seven years, also using the straight-line method.

The company's income tax rate is 40 percent. The required rate of return (cost of capital), since this project is less risky than the expansion project, is 12 percent.

Introduction

In Chapter 2, we discussed the question of profit maximization as an objective of the firm. In all the chapters that followed we explicitly assumed that firms were actively pursuing this objective. We dealt with a firm's action during a specified period of time, such as a year, a month, or a day.[1] For example, a demand curve and revenues flowing to the firm were defined in terms of quantities per year; costs were stated in term of quantities produced for the same period. Even when we discussed long-term relationships, such as the

[1]The only exception was the discussion of the learning curve, which was defined over a given production run, regardless of the time involved.

long-run cost curve (the envelope curve), where each point on the horizontal (quantity) axis represented a plant of a different size, we did not concentrate on how the firm changed from a smaller to a larger plant. It was merely accepted that at each point on the horizontal axis, different quantities were produced by plants of different capacities.

To increase production over time, a firm must invest in new capacity. Even for a firm to maintain level capacity, it must replace worn-out equipment and plant. Such action also involves investment of resources.

A definition of the word *investment* may be in order at this point. In economics, *investment* means the building and/or acquisition of productive capacity, such as plant and machinery. In everyday language, this term is used more broadly. For example, people say that they make an investment when they buy shares of stock in the stock market. In this case, however, only an exchange of financial instruments has occurred; there is no increase in productive capacity. If new stock is issued by a company so that it can finance the construction of a new plant, then investment takes place, in economic terms, when resources are expended on the erection of the new facility.

In short, a company's decision to commit funds in order to obtain revenues not only in the current period, but also in future periods, has not yet been analyzed. A brief reference regarding the consideration of expenditures to obtain payoffs over a considerable period of time in the future was made in Chapter 2, in the section on maximizing the wealth of stockholders. We are now prepared to discuss decisions leading to this maximization criterion.

The subject of capital budgeting is generally taught in courses in finance. Large portions of basic and more advanced courses are devoted to this topic, and in some schools the finance curriculum includes a one-semester course in capital budgeting. However, the principles of capital budgeting are properly a part of microeconomic theory extended to multiperiod problems. The application of incremental and marginal analysis will be encountered in this chapter just as in all the previous ones. Thus, it is not only desirable to include a chapter on this subject, but it is essential to make this book a complete treatment of managerial economics.

The Capital Budgeting Decision

Capital budgeting describes decisions where expenditures and receipts for a particular undertaking will continue over a period of time. These decisions usually involve outflows of funds (expenditures) in the early periods (sometimes just one expenditure will be made at the beginning of a project, as for the purchase of a new machine), and the inflows (revenues) start somewhat later and (it is hoped) continue for a significant number of periods.[2]

[2]Note that the term *flows*, meaning inflows or outflows, is being used in this chapter. In capital budgeting decisions, the quantities considered are the actual expenditures and receipts of cash, not quantities adjusted by accounting conventions, such as accruals. Cash flows are quite objective—either cash goes out or it comes in—and there are no allowances made for when revenues and expenses are recognized in the company's books of account.

The following figure is a simple illustration of the components to be considered in making capital budgeting decisions. The figure shows one outflow at the beginning of the project and five inflows in subsequent periods. This model could represent the purchase of a new machine that will last five years and provide new revenues (or savings, if it decreases the cost of production) during that time.[3] We could have shown an example with outflows occurring during, say, the first three years. Such outflows could represent a company's decision to build a new plant and equip it with new machines. Such a large investment could easily occur over a period of three years, and revenues would not start until the fourth year or even later.[4]

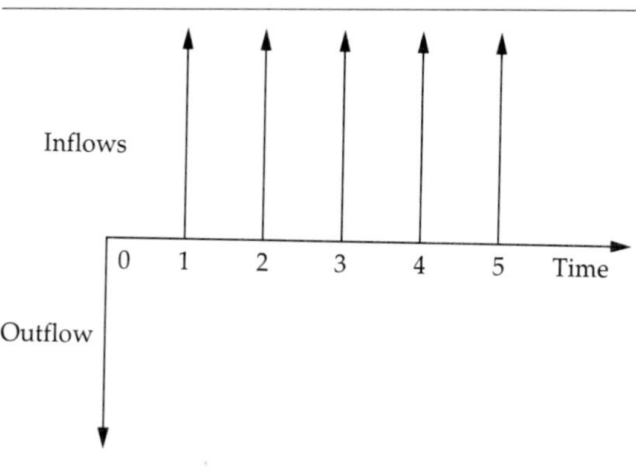

Types of Capital Budgeting Decisions

Now that we have described the general characteristics of a capital budgeting decision, we can list types of projects that fit this category.

Expansion of facilities. Growing demand for a company's products leads to consideration of a new or additional plant. Planning for other new facilities, such as sales offices or warehouses, would also be included here. George Kline's first project is an expansion proposal.

New or improved products. Additional investment may be necessary to bring a new or changed product to the market.

Replacement. Replacement decisions can be of at least two types: (1) replacement of worn-out plant and equipment or (2) replacement with more efficient machines of equipment that is still operating but is obsolete. George's second proposal falls in this group.

[3]The depalletizer proposal could be represented by this figure, but it would be extended to show 10 years of cash inflows.

[4]The expansion proposal on George Kline's desk resembles this case, except that expenditures will occur now and in year 1, and cash inflows will begin in year 2.

Lease or buy. A company may need to decide whether to make a sizable investment in buying a piece of equipment or to pay rental for a considerable time period.

Make or buy. A company may be faced with deciding whether to make a significant investment to produce components for its product or whether to forgo such investment and contract for the components with a vendor.

Other. The preceding list is certainly not complete, since a capital budgeting problem exists whenever initial cash outflows and subsequent cash inflows are involved. For instance, a bond refunding decision would lend itself to the same method of analysis.

Safety or environmental protection equipment. Such investments may be mandated by law and therefore are not necessarily governed by economic decision making. However, if there are alternate solutions, capital budgeting analysis may be helpful in identifying the most cost-efficient alternative.

Time Value of Money

If a capital budgeting problem simply involved the subtraction of outflows from inflows, the mechanics of obtaining a solution would be extremely easy. However, since the various flows occur at disparate times in the future, we must adjust these numbers to make them equivalent. Differences in the values of the flows are based on the *time value of money.*

All this term really means is that a dollar today is worth more than a dollar tomorrow. For example, if you were offered a choice between a gift of $100 today and the same amount one year from now (the receipt of both amounts being certain), you would most likely select the first alternative. If you were to take the $100 today and put it in a bank paying 5 percent interest, you would have $105 a year from now; thus, the $100 today would be equivalent to $105 a year later. As long as you have an opportunity to earn a positive return on your funds over the one-year period, a dollar today and a dollar a year from now are not equivalent. Some people would conclude that this phenomenon is due to the presence of inflation, that is, a decrease in the value of the purchasing power of money over time. But inflation is not a necessary condition. Certainly, during a period of rising prices, nominal interest rates will be higher than during times of price stability. However, even when inflation is absent, funds that are saved and invested will earn interest for their owner.

Thus, to put cash flows originating at different times on an equal basis, we must apply an interest rate to each of the flows so that they are expressed in terms of the same point in time. For instance, if you borrow $5,000 today and must pay the amount back one year from now with 10 percent interest, you will pay $5,500. That is easy. But suppose the period involved is longer than a year. Generally, interest has to be compounded.[5] If interest is compounded annually,

[5]Compounding can occur more frequently than once a year, as discussed in Appendix 14A. Here we will assume annual compounding.

then after one year the first period's interest is added to the principal, and it also earns interest. If you borrow $5,000 for two years with interest compounded annually, then at the end of the second year you would owe $6,050. The interest for the first year is $500, and for the second year it is $550 (10 percent of $5,500, the original $5,000 loan plus $500 of interest).

In capital budgeting calculations, cash flows are usually brought back from various points in the future to the beginning of the project—time zero. It is then said that all cash flows are discounted to the present to obtain a present value. This is a useful convention, although we could discount or compound the flows to any date.

Those of you who have had previous exposure to the mechanics of compounding and discounting will be able to move immediately into the discussion of the solution of capital budgeting problems, which follows. However, those of you who are unfamiliar with the calculations or whose memory on this subject is somewhat hazy will benefit from reading Appendix 14A.

Methods of Capital Project Evaluation

Various methods are used to make capital budgeting decisions, that is, to evaluate the worth of investment projects. Two of these, the payback method and the accounting rate of return, have been around for a long time. Although still employed quite frequently, they both appear to be inadequate because they do not include the criterion of the time value of money in their computations.

The two methods that do discount cash flows to a present value are *net present value* (NPV) and *internal rate of return* (IRR).[6] Both of these techniques satisfy the two major criteria required for the correct evaluation of capital projects: use of cash flows and use of the time value of money.

An Example

To illustrate each of the techniques just listed above, we will use a specific numerical example.

A proposal requires one initial investment of $100. It has a life of five years, and annual after-tax profits will be $5, $15, $20, $20, and $10, in that order. To convert these numbers to cash flows, depreciation must be added back. Assuming five-year straight-line depreciation, or $20 each year, the annual cash flows will become $25, $35, $40, $40, and $30.[7]

---

[6] A third calculation method using discounted cash flows is called the *profitability index* or *index of present value*. This is a derivative of the other two methods and will not be discussed in this text. You should refer to any of the leading textbooks in managerial finance.

[7] Cash flows will be discussed in greater detail later. Here suffice it to say that this definition follows the one usually employed by accountants:

$$\text{Operating cash flow} = \text{Profit after taxes} + \text{Depreciation}$$

PAYBACK The payback method is still used by businesspeople. It is a rather crude way of calculating the acceptability of a project, but it does tell management how long it will take for the original investment to be paid back.

The simplest definition for payback is

Original investment/Annual cash flow

If a machine costs $100, has a five-year life, and will have five uniform annual cash inflows of $40 each, the payback will be

$$100/40 = 2.5$$

In other words, the investment will be repaid in two and one-half years. Using the numbers given, which are not uniform from year to year, we add successive annual cash flows until they equal the initial outlay:

$$25 + 35 + 40 = 100$$

Payback is in three years.

A short payback period will be required by management of a risk-averse company. After all, if the entire investment is repaid in two or three years, the company will not be going too far out on a limb (i.e., counting on cash flows far into the future).

What are the major drawbacks of this technique?

Any cash flows after the payback are not counted. Thus, for our sample project, with a payback of three years, the last two years of cash flows have no impact on the result. A project with only a three-year life returning cash flows of $25, $35, and $40 would be considered equal to the proposal in the example. However, the five-year project is certainly more desirable, with a potential of two additional years of cash inflows, but this difference is not recognized in the payback calculation.

The time value of money is not considered. Each year's cash flow is merely added to the next, with no consideration that later payments are more severely discounted than earlier cash flows.[8]

THE ACCOUNTING RATE OF RETURN ON INVESTMENT As indicated by its name, the accounting rate of return method has long been utilized by accountants and also by financial analysts. It employs data obtained from the company's books of account. It is applied as often to the measurement of overall company data as to the evaluation of specific programs.

There are several ways of calculating the rate of return on investment (ROI), but probably the most accepted is

$$\text{ROI} = \frac{\text{Average annual profit}}{\text{Average investment}}$$

[8]If an alternative technique, *discounted payback,* is used, this objection is eliminated. In that case, cash flows will be discounted at an appropriate discount rate. However, the first drawback of the payback method still is not overcome.

For the example put forth earlier, the average annual profit is \$14 [i.e., (5 + 15 + 20 + 20 + 10)/5]. The average amount of investment over the five years is \$50.[9] Thus, ROI = 28 percent.

The calculation is simple, and the result is given as a percentage, a form often favored by management. But as a measure of investment value, the accounting ROI is deficient. Why?

As with the payback measure, the time value of money is not considered.

An average annual profit is calculated. This procedure makes it impossible to identify annual incomes. Obviously, the shape of the stream of earnings from period to period is important.

The numerator of the fraction is profit. However, it is cash flow—a strictly objective measure—that is the important variable in a capital budgeting decision. In arriving at profit, accountants make ajdustments for accrued expenses, income received but not earned, and other items. It could be said that profit is what the accountants make it. By the same token, the denominator—investment—does not represent the actual cash outflow at the beginning, but an average that can be affected by depreciation methods.[10]

NET PRESENT VALUE The net present value of a project is calculated by discounting all flows to the present and subtracting the present value of all outflows from the present value of all inflows. In simple mathematical terms,

$$\text{NPV} = \sum_{t=1}^{n} \frac{R_t}{(1+k)^t} - \sum_{t=0}^{n} \frac{O_t}{(1+k)^t}$$

where t = Time period (e.g., year)
n = Last period of project
R_t = Cash inflow in period t
O_t = Cash outflow in period t
k = Discount rate (cost of capital)

Some of these terms must be explained further. Inflows are shown from period 1 to period n; however, inflows may not occur in all periods. Should

[9]The initial investment of \$100 is depreciated annually by \$20. Thus, at the end of the first year, the book value of the investment will be \$80, at the end of two years \$60, and so on. Therefore, the first year's average investment is \$90, the second year's is \$70, and so on. If all these averages are averaged, the result is \$50. A more straightforward way of computing this number, given straight-line depreciation, is to add the initial investment and final book value, and divide by 2: $(100 + 0)/2 = 50$.

[10]An alternative definition of ROI could be

$$\frac{\text{Profit before depreciation}}{\text{Original investment}}$$

This definition appears to be more closely related to the concept of cash flows, but it still suffers from the other shortcomings of the ROI measure.

the project under consideration be the construction of a plant, the time elapsed before the first shipment of product, and thus the first inflow, may not occur until period 3, for example. Remember that in George Kline's expansion project, inflows will not begin until the second period.

Outflows are shown starting in period 0 (i.e., at the very beginning of the project). Indeed, the only outflow may occur in period 0 if the proposal being evaluated is the purchase of a machine that will begin to produce cash inflows upon installation. The depalletizing machine is a case in point. On the other hand, the expansion proposal considered by Kline will have outflows in periods 0 and 1.

Thus, the two terms have been generalized to allow for inflows and outflows throughout the life of the project, even though flows of one kind or the other may not occur in all periods.

The discount rate, k, is the interest rate used to evaluate the project. This rate represents the cost of the funds employed and is often called the *cost of capital.* It can also be referred to as the *hurdle rate,* the *cut off rate,* or the *minimum required rate of return.*[11]

The same numerical example used previously will also be used here to illustrate the NPV method. The cost of capital is assumed to be 14 percent. The relevant amounts are as follows:

Inflows		
Year 1	25 × .8772	$ 21.93
2	35 × .7695	26.93
3	40 × .6750	27.00
4	40 × .5921	23.68
5	30 × .5194	15.58
		$115.12
Outflow, year 0		$100.00
Net present value		$ 15.12

All the estimated cash inflows have been brought back (discounted) to the present at the 14 percent cost of capital and then added. (The factors by which each of the cash flows is multiplied have been obtained from Table A.1*c* in the appendix at the end of this text.) The total present value of cash outflows is deducted. In this case, there is only one outflow occurring at period 0 (now);

[11]The term *cost of capital* often applies to the overall average cost of funds for a corporation. This cost may differ from the rate used for a specific division of the company or for a particular capital budgeting proposal. One of the major reasons for the difference is risk (both business and financial risk). Thus, the corporation's cost of capital represents an average for the whole entity, but specific areas of the business may be more or less risky than the average and thus require higher or lower discount rates. Thus, the discount rate may differ from area to area or project to project within the same company.

thus, no discounting is necessary. The net present value equals $15.12. Should this proposal be accepted?

The answer is yes. The net present value for this program is positive. Stated somewhat differently, if we add all the cash inflows discounted at the cost of capital and deduct the cash outflow, we still have something left over. We expect to earn more than the cost of capital (i.e., the cost of financing this project). The proposal earns what the suppliers of capital require plus an additional amount.

We have arrived at the NPV rule for evaluating capital budgeting programs. If the NPV is positive, the project is financially acceptable. If NPV is negative, rejection is indicated. If NPV is exactly zero, this proposal is just earning the cost of capital; we are on the boderline. However, since the return just equals the required rate of return, the project appears to be acceptable.[12]

THE INTERNAL RATE OF RETURN IRR is the second of the two methods we will discuss that discounts cash flows. However, rather than looking for an absolute amount of present-value dollars, as in the NPV analysis, we solve for the interest rate that equates the present value of inflows and outflows:

$$\sum_{t=1}^{n} \frac{R_t}{(1+r)^t} = \sum_{t=0}^{n} \frac{O_t}{(1+r)^t}$$

or

$$\sum_{t=1}^{n} \frac{R_t}{(1+r)^t} - \sum_{t=0}^{n} \frac{O_t}{(1+r)^t} = 0$$

The r term in the equations is the internal rate of return—the unknown variable for which we solve. Actually, the IRR solution is only a special case of the NPV technique; the internal rate of return of a project is the discount rate that causes NPV to equal zero (which occurs when the project is just earning the cost of capital).

The calculation of the IRR is often cumbersome. Unless all cash inflows are uniform and there is only one outflow (in which case we can simply employ the annuity formula), it is necessary to find the answer by trial and error.[13] One must first choose an applicable interest rate—and this may be no more than an educated guess—and then iterate until the correct answer is obtained.

Turn again to the example used before. Since we found in the NPV analysis that, with a 14 percent cost of capital, net present value is positive ($15.12),

---

[12]This case is similar to one encountered previously, in Chapter 11. Production takes place at the point where marginal cost equals marginal revenue. If discrete quantities are involved, the cost of the "last" unit produced is the same as the revenue received from it; it earns no economic but only normal profit. In capital budgeting, the situation is really the same: the "last" proposal that would be accepted is the one that just earns the rate required by the suppliers of capital.

[13]Of course, many computer programs calculate IRR, and many hand-held electronic calculators have features that provide IRR solutions. But if only tables are available, the iterative procedure is the only alternative.

the internal rate of return must be greater than 14 percent. We will first try 18 percent (again using the factors in TableA.1c):

Inflows		
Year 1	25 × .8475	$ 21.19
2	35 × .7182	25.14
3	40 × .6086	24.34
4	40 × .5158	20.63
5	30 × .4371	13.11
		$104.41
Outflow, year 0		$100.00
Net present value		$ 4.41

Since the result is still positive, we will choose a higher discount rate, 20 percent:

Inflows		
Year 1	25 × .8333	$ 20.83
2	35 × .6944	24.30
3	40 × .5787	23.15
4	40 × .4823	19.29
5	30 × .4019	12.06
		$ 99.63
Outflow, year 0		$100.00
Net present value		$ −0.37

Since NPV is now negative, 20 percent is too high. Thus, the result lies somewhere between 18 percent and 20 percent. It is readily seen that the IRR is much closer to 20 percent than to 18 percent, because $ − 0.37 is much nearer to 0 than is $4.41. A more precise answer can be obtained using linear interpolation; this would result in an internal rate of return of about 19.8 percent.

The accept/reject criterion for the internal rate of return is based on a comparison of the IRR with the cost of capital of the project. Although the cost of capital is not used in the calculation of the IRR, it is still an all-important component of decision making. If the internal rate of return is larger than the cost of capital—the required rate of return—of the proposal, it signals acceptance. If IRR$< k$, the proposed project should be rejected. If IRR $= k$, although it could be said that decision makers would be indifferent on whether or not to undertake the project, an argument can be made that the project is earning its cost of capital and therefore should be accepted at the margin.

NPV versus IRR

Two methods have just been described that conform to the criteria specified for a valid capital budgeting decision. Is one preferred over the other, or are the two equally valid?

In a large majority of cases, either NPV or IRR can be used with confidence. These two tests of investment worth give consistent accept/reject indicators. In other words, when

$\text{NPV} > 0, \text{IRR} > k$

$\text{NPV} = 0, \text{IRR} = k$

$\text{NPV} < 0, \text{IRR} < k$

Thus, either of the two measures gives the correct answer. In some cases, however problems may arise. We will give only a brief description of these to show the caution that must be exercised in capital budgeting analysis. This subject is usually treated at great length in managerial finance textbooks, and those who are interested in further study should consult one of these.

When independent projects are being analyzed, both IRR and NPV criteria give consistent results. "Independent" implies that if a company is considering several projects at the same time, they can all be implemented simultaneously as long as they pass the NPV or IRR tests, and as long as funds are not limited.[14] The adoption of one independent project will have no effect on the cash flow of another. For example, the two proposals on George Kline's desk are independent. Global Foods can expand into a new territory and replace the depalletizing machine at the same time. The acceptance of one proposal does not preclude executing the other.

However, proposals may be mutually exclusive. This occurs when two solutions for a particular proposal are offered, only one of which can be accepted. Suppose Global decides to acquire a new depalletizer. At this point, sales representatives from two manufacturers of these machines descend upon the company, and each offers a new version. But the company needs only one depalletizer. If both NPV and IRR are calculated, inconsistent recommendations can result. NPV analysis may suggest purchase of machine A while IRR indicates machine B. Such disparate signals can occur if one or both of the following conditions are present:

1. The initial costs of the two proposals differ.
2. The shapes of the subsequent cash inflow streams differ; for instance, one alternative may have large early inflows with the other exhibiting increasing inflows over time.[15]

The reason for the differences between IRR and NPV results is the implicit reinvestment assumption. In the NPV calculation, as inflows occur, they are automatically assumed to be reinvested at the cost of capital (the project's k). The IRR solution assumes reinvestment at the internal rate of return (the project's r).

Conflicting accept/reject signals may not occur frequently in capital project analysis, but they do occur and they may cause the analyst some anxious moments.

Another problem that may occur concerns the case of nonconventional cash flows. Conventional cash flows occur when cash outflows are followed by a

[14]The case of limited funds, ordinarily referred to as *capital rationing* is discussed briefly in Appendix 14.B, at the end of this chapter.

[15]Examples of these two conditions are discussed further in Appendix 14.B. Those who desire additional explanations of these cases should refer to any standard textbook in corporate finance.

series of cash inflows for the remainder of the project's life. In other words, over time, there is only one change from negative flows (outflows) to positive (inflows). But suppose there are two or more changes, as in the following example.

A company leases land from the local government for 10 years to build and operate an amusement park. The company also contracts to restore the land to its original condition at the end of the lease term. Thus, the company will make an original investment in equipment and installation (a cash outflow). It will then (it is hoped) enjoy 10 years of cash inflows. Finally, in the eleventh year, it will expend cash to restore the property. This project involves a starting negative flow, then a series of positive flows, and a final cash outflow. If the IRR technique is used to evaluate this proposal, the result will be two different rates of return. Such an answer is obviously not satisfactory. If NPV analysis is used, a single answer will be obtained.

Writers of financial and economic literature almost unanimously recommend NPV as the theoretically more correct measure. The explanation of the reasons for this choice would be quite long. For the purpose of our limited exposition of this subject, let us mention just briefly two arguments:

1. The financial objective of the firm is the maximization of stockholder wealth, and the NPV method is more applicable to this end. Projects with the largest NPVs will add up to the highest present value for the business.
2. The NPV reinvestment assumption, at k, appears to be more realistic in most cases than reinvestment at r of a particular project.[16]

Although NPV is recommended by theorists and textbook writers, in actual business practice, IRR is by far the more frequently used.[17] Why? Business people—especially nonfinancial managers—are much more comfortable making their judgments by looking at percentages. The NPV number, a dollar figure, is not readily recognizable. (Incidentally, the second most popular technique cited in the Gitman and Forrester article was the accounting rate of return, also expressed as a percentage. NPV came in third but was also frequently mentioned as the second choice). Only in the case of mutually exclusive projects may IRR fail to give the correct signal. However, in many evaluations—probably a majority—even where mutual exclusivity exists, the IRR and NPV methods will lead to consistent answers.

The fact that large corporations use one or the other of the evaluation methods incorporating the time value of money is important. Such was not the case 20

---

[16]There is a method that has been gaining favor and that corrects some of the problems encountered with the internal rate of return. It is called the *modified internal rate of return* (MIRR) and is calculated by discounting, at the cost of capital, all cash outflows to year zero and compounding all inflows to the end of the project. The discount rate that equates the sum of the ending values to the sum of the beginning values is the MIRR. Using this method reinvests the cash flows at the cost of capital. Also, the possibility of obtaining more than one solution (nonconventional cash flows) is eliminated. However, accept/reject signal conflicts with NPV can still occur. For a longer explanation, see Eugene F. Brigham and Louis C. Gapenski, *Intermediate Financial Management*, 3d ed., Hinsdale, Ill.: Dryden, 1990, pp. 282–284.

[17]Lawrence J. Gitman and John R. Forrester, Jr., "A Survey of Capital Budgeting Techniques Used by Major U.S. Firms," *Financial Management*, Fall 1977, pp. 66–71.

years ago. Only in the recent past have the more "scientific" ways of project assessment assumed prominence.

Cash Flows

Up to this point the discussion has concentrated on the methods and mechanics of the capital budgeting process. Cash flows were assumed and put into the appropriate formulas for processing. The term *cash flow* has been used in abundance but has not been explained thoroughly.

When confronted with a capital budgeting proposal, the analyst's most difficult task is to enter the best estimates of cash flows into the analysis. Since all of the inflows and outflows are in the future, their amounts and timing are uncertain. Some of them can be assessed with relative certainty. For instance, if a replacement proposal is being considered, the cost of the new machine has probably been established. But as the analyst tries to assess future annual benefits and costs, the amount of uncertainty increases.

In most cases, the capital budgeting analyst does not generate the inputs for the model. He or she obtains the estimates from other parts of the organization, such as market research, marketing, manufacturing, engineering, or service. There will be market forecasts, price estimates, and cost and expense forecasts. These data have to be examined for potential bias. Market forecasts may be too high, since the people who prepare them are interested parties. Costs often are underestimated. In general, estimated cash flows tend to be optimistic and must be adjusted to make them more realistic.[18]

The person organizing the data must understand the following points:

1. All revenues and costs must be stated in terms of cash flows.

2. All cash flows should be incremental. Only those flows that will change if the proposal is accepted should be recorded. A reallocation of present (fixed) costs, for example, will not affect the project. This is not as easy as it sounds. Suppose a proposal to expand production will utilize a part of the plant that is now standing idle. Should the cost of this presently vacant floor be included? It depends on the circumstances. Is there another potential project waiting in the wings that could use the vacant space, now or in the near future? Could this part of the plant possibly be leased to a tenant? All possibilities must be considered before the analyst can give a definite answer.

3. Any effect on other parts of the operation must be taken into account. If the introduction of a new diet soda will have an adverse impact on sales of current soft drinks, this amount must be subtracted from the cash flows planned for the new product. On the other hand, impact may be positive. For example, if the company also sells alcoholic beverages, the introduction of a "light" tonic could enhance sales of the company's gin. These are, of course, examples of the familiar cases of substitutes and complements. Some idea of the size of cross-

[18]Stephen W. Pruitt and Lawrence J. Gitman, "Capital Budgeting Forecast Biases: Evidence from the Fortune 500," *Financial Management*, Spring 1987, pp. 46–51.

elasticities of demand is needed to estimate these impacts. Cost impacts must also be considered.

4. Generally, in capital budgeting analysis, interest paid on debt is not considered. Since interest is included in the discount rate, showing it as a cash outflow would amount to double-counting.

Types of Cash Flows

Cash flows come in many varieties. Some of the most common and important types are discussed next.

INITIAL CASH OUTFLOWS Cash flows occur at the inception of the project. If a new machine is installed, this represents a one-time outflow. But initial outflows can also be spread over a period of time. As mentioned previously, if an expansion proposal involves buying land, building a plant, and purchasing and installing new equipment, outflows can extend over two or three years.

OPERATING CASH FLOWS When a new project goes on line, it begins to generate cash inflows (revenues). Of course, it also generates cash outflows (costs and expenses), which must be subtracted from the inflows. In the early years of operations, outflows can exceed inflows; thus, the annual net outflow can continue even after the initial investment stage.

So far this exposition is relatively simple. But one of the expenses that accountants record in the income statement of a company is depreciation (and amortization). Obviously, this is not a cash flow; it is a bookkeeping entry to show that the value of the plant and equipment is declining. The actual cash flow occurred when the plant was built and the machinery purchased, and it was recorded as such in the capital investment analysis. If we were living in that ideal society with no income tax, we would simply ignore depreciation in calculating cash flows.

But because income taxes are a fact of life, they must be considered in the treatment of depreciation. The after-tax profit reflects the deduction of depreciation. But since depreciation did not result in a cash outflow, it has to be added back to the after-tax profit to obtain net cash flow.

An example will illustrate this procedure. If cash sales during a period are $100, cash costs and expenses are $50, depreciation of buildings and equipment is $20, and the income tax rate is 40 percent, then net cash flow for the period will be $38:

Sales	$100
Costs and expenses	50
Depreciation	20
Total costs and expense	$ 70
Net profit before tax	30
Income tax	12
Net profit after tax	$ 18
Depreciation	20
Net cash flow	$ 38

For each of the periods (years), operating cash flows have to be calculated and the results discounted to the present.

ADDITIONAL WORKING CAPITAL In the case of an expansion proposal, in addition to new plant and equipment, increased working capital may be required. Inventories may be larger, accounts receivable may grow, and more cash may be needed to finance the transactions engendered by the growth in operations. Investing in working capital is a cash outflow that is similar in nature to an investment in brick and iron. We must account for it. However, there may not be a periodic write-down (i.e., depreciation) for such investments in the plan. When the proposed project comes to the end of its life, inventories will be used up, accounts receivable will be collected, and the additional cash will no longer be needed. So the same amount that was expended at the beginning of the program may be returned at the end—with one big difference: The cash outflow occurs at or near the beginning of the operations, whereas the inflow of the same amount occurs at the end and must be discounted to the present.

The ending amount of working capital may actually be less than the original investment since some accounts receivable may turn out to be uncollectible and some inventory may become obsolete. The actual loss on this decrease in working capital can be deducted from the cash flows for a tax benefit.

SALVAGE OR RESALE VALUES At the end of the project's life, a machine that has been completely depreciated (i.e., has an accounting book value of zero) may turn out to have a residual resale value or some scrap value. If cash can be obtained for it, a cash inflow will result.

But care must be exercised in including this cash flow. If the market value is greater than the book value, a profit will result, with inevitable tax consequences. Thus, if a fully depreciated piece of equipment is expected to bring in \$5,000 in resale value at the end of the project life, and if the tax rate is 40 percent, then the actual cash flow will be only \$3,000, since \$2,000 must be paid in taxes. The formula for computing the cash flow in such a case is:

$$\text{SV} - (\text{SV} - \text{BV})T$$

where SV = Salvage or resale value
BV = Book value
T = Tax rate

NONCASH INVESTMENT Sometimes a new project involves an investment that does not require a cash flow. For instance, suppose an old, fully depreciated machine is standing on the factory floor. This machine is not needed for present production requirements. But then a new expansion proposal is accepted, allowing this old machine to be utilized. Does it represent a cash outflow? Yes, if the machine has a salvage value; no, if it has no market value at all. Thus, as in all cases of capital budgeting decisions, the alternatives have to be considered.

Cost of Capital

In each of the capital budgeting decision described, a certain cost of capital was assumed. Its derivation has not been explained. Much space is usually devoted to this subject in finance textbooks—an entire chapter or more. Such an exposition is beyond the scope of this text. However, a brief explanation of this important concept is essential.

To invest in capital projects, a company must obtain financing. Financing, of course, comes from different sources. There is debt, either short-term or long-term. Then there is equity. A company may retain earnings, which then become part of its equity, or it can issue new shares. Each type of financing must be paid for; each has its cost. It is these costs that establish a company's cost of capital. When each of the costs has been identified they are combined to arrive at an average cost of capital for a given debt/equity mix.[19]

Debt

The cost of debt is the easier to explain. It is simply the interest rate that must be paid on the debt. But since interest expense is tax-deductible, the actual cost of the debt to the company is the after-tax cost. The expression for the cost of debt is

$$\text{Interest rate} \times (1 - \text{Tax rate})$$

Which interest rate should be used? If a company already has debt outstanding, it pays a certain rate. But the rate being paid on past debt is not relevant. What is important to the company in measuring its cost of capital is the interest it would have to pay if it were to borrow today. Thus, the present rate being charged in the market for the kind of debt the company would issue (e.g., life to maturity, risk category) determines the company's cost of debt.

Equity

The cost of equity is more difficult to obtain. A large body of literature exists on this subject, and there are different methods to arrive at this cost. Two of these will be described here.

THE DIVIDEND GROWTH MODEL The cost of equity is determined by the population of stockholders. Since the stockholder expects to receive dividends (D) plus a selling price (P_n) for the shares in the future, the price he or she is willing to pay for the stock today (P_0) is determined by discounting the future cash flows to the present at the rate of return (k_e) the stockholder requires in order

[19] Admittedly, there are other financial instruments with which a company obtains funds, such as preferred stocks or convertible bonds. However, this short description will limit itself to debt and common equity.

to buy the stock:

$$P_0 = \sum_{t=1}^{n} \frac{D_t}{(1 + k_e)^t} + \frac{P_n}{(1 + k_e)^t}$$

The stockholder will sell the shares at time n to a new stockholder, who again may hold the stock for a limited period before selling it to a third stockholder, and so on. Since the buying and selling of the stock merely represent an exchange and thus cancel out, the net cash flow from this stock is the dividend, which will continue over an infinite period of time if it is assumed that the corporation will live in perpetuity. The equation showing an infinite stream of dividends can be written as

$$P_0 = \sum_{t=1}^{\infty} \frac{D_t}{(1 + k_e)^t}$$

The dividend does not have to be the same in each period. An assumption is often made that the dividend will grow at a constant rate (g) forever. The equation then converts to

$$P_0 = \frac{D_0(1 + g)}{(1 + k_e)} + \frac{D_0(1 + g)^2}{(1 + k_e)} + \cdots + \frac{D_0(1 + g)^n}{(1 + k_e)^n}$$

which can be simplified to

$$P_0 = \frac{D_1}{k_e - g}$$

Since it is the cost of capital that we seek, the equation can be written in terms of k_e as

$$k_e = \frac{D_1}{P_0} + g$$

Thus, this construction states that the cost of equity capital (k_e) equals the dividend in year 1 divided by today's stock price—the dividend yield—plus the expected growth rate in the dividend. This formula is often referred to as the Gordon model, so named for Myron J. Gordon, an economist who has done a great amount of work in this area and who is credited with a major role in developing this model.[20]

The dividend growth model just presented is generally applicable when a company reinvests the earnings that have not been paid out as dividends. If a company issues new stock in the financial markets, it incurs an additional cost. The proceeds from the sale of the stock will be less than the current market price, P_0. The cost of underwriting the issue must be taken into consideration. If these costs, often referred to as *flotation costs*, f, are expressed as percentage

---

[20]See, for instance, Myron J. Gordon, *The Investment, Financing, and Valuation of the Corporation*, Homewood, Ill.; Irwin, 1962.

of P_0, the Gordon model converts to

$$k_0 = \frac{D_1}{P_0(1-f)} + g$$

Obviously, the cost of equity capital will be higher for newly issued stock than for retained earnings.

The assumption of a constant growth rate may, of course, not always be realistic. For a variable growth rate, period growth in dividends must be estimated and the entire equation solved for k_e.[21] Such a model is useful for estimating the equity cost for companies experiencing rapid growth but whose annual increases cannot be expected to continue at the high rate forever.

While the Gordon model formula appears rather simple, it requires a forecast of growth. Forecasts, as we have found out, are always tenuous. Thus, the calculation of the cost of capital can be only as good as the estimates entered into it.

THE CAPITAL ASSET PRICING MODEL (CAPM) The capital asset pricing approach also had its birth in the 1960s.[22] It is based on the principle that there is a relationship between risk and return. The more risky the investment, the higher will be the required return. Only a brief description of this model will be given here.

An important conclusion of this model is that the required rate of return[23] on a stock is a function of the volatility (market risk) of its returns relative to the return on a total stock market portfolio. This volatility is referred to as *beta*, and is calculated by regression analysis. The variability of the individual stock's return is the dependent variable, and the variability of the market return is the independent variable. The higher the volatility of the individual stock's return compared to the market return, the higher the beta. A beta of 1.0 signifies that

---

[21] In the case of a company that expects rapid growth at first, then a slowdown, and finally some "normal" constant growth, the equation becomes somewhat complicated:

$$P_0 = \sum_{t=1}^{n} \frac{D_0(1+g_t)^t}{(1+k_e)^t} + \frac{D_{n+1}}{k_e - g}\left[\frac{1}{1+k_e}\right]$$

where n = Number of years of nonconstant growth

g_t = Expected annual growth rate during nonconstant growth period

g = Expected annual growth rate during the constant growth period

D_{n+1} = Dividend in first period of constant growth

D_0 = Dividend paid in period 0

For additional information on this construction, see any finance textbook, for instance: Eugene F. Brigham and Louis C. Gapenski, op. cit.

[22] See, for instance, William F. Sharpe, "Capital Asset Prices: A Theory of Market Equilibrium under Conditions of Risk," *Journal of Finance*, 19 (September 1964), pp. 425–42.

[23] Return is defined as dividend plus or minus the change in stock value.

the stock's return is as volatile as the market's. If the beta is greater than 1.0, the stock's return is more variable, and, therefore, the stock is more risky; the reverse situation holds when beta is less than 1.0.

One other item is included in this model, the riskless interest rate. The riskless rate is usually represented by interest paid on U.S. Treasury securities. The beta coefficient is used to arrive at the risk of the individual stock relative to the difference between the average return for the market portfolio and the riskless rate.

The required rate of return on an individual stock is calculated as follows:

$$k_j = R_f + \beta(k_m - R_f)$$

where k_j = Required rate of return on stock j
R_f = Risk-free rate
k_m = Rate of return on the market portfolio

This model has experienced immense popularity—and also criticism. Although it provides a logical explanation of maximizing behavior under conditions of risk, it suffers, as does the Gordon model, from difficulties of obtaining the relevant data. Probably one of the most serious objections is that the model tries to predict the present and future costs of equity capital with past data. It assumes, therefore, that the past relationship between stock return and market return will continue into the future. This, of course, is a shortcoming of all forecasts made using regression analysis.

Another criticism of CAPM lies in the fact that betas are not always stable. They vary depending on the time period used in making the analysis, and they are affected by the specific statistical method used. Thus, again, the cost-of-capital estimate is only as good as the data used in the computation and he method used. It is obvious that there is much work yet to be done to improve the estimates of the equity cost of capital.

The Weighted Cost of Capital

Despite the fact that the measurements of the components of capital costs are not entirely satisfactory, they are the best available at the present, and they are used in obtaining an overall cost of capital of the firm. This is achieved by weighting the various costs by the relative proportion of each component's value in the total capital structure.

A question arises at this point. Should the weights be based on book values (i.e., the numbers on the balance sheet) or market values? The answer is market values, since they reflect the actual values of the various components today, and the prices the securities would command if new financing is needed.

If debt makes up 20 percent and equity 80 percent of a company's financial structure, and their respective costs are 6 percent and 14 percent, the weighted cost of capital is

$$.2(.06) + .8(.14) = .012 + .112 = .124 = 12.4 \text{ percent}$$

Since that the cost of debt capital is usually thought of as being lower than that of equity, this formula would indicate that a company can decrease its cost of capital (and thus increase the value of the firm) by increasing the ratio of debt to equity. This is misleading, however. As the proportion of debt increases (i.e.., as leverage rises), the financial community will view the company as more risky. Consequently, the cost of both components, debt as well as equity, will rise, causing the weighted average to rise also. There is probably some point where the combination of components is optimal, and where the weighted cost of capital of a particular firm is at a minimum.

The Capital Budgeting Model

In the arena of corporate decision making, capital budgeting is an application of the marginal revenue–marginal cost principle. Figure 14.1 illustrates this principle.

Assume that a company is faced with a menu of seven capital budgeting proposals. The capital planning department has analyzed each of them and has calculated the internal rate of return, which is the evaluation technique the company uses. In Figure 14.1, the projects have been ranked by IRR from highest to lowest. Each proposal is represented by a bar; its height represent the IRR, and the width indicates the size of the investment. If a line were drawn connecting the tops of the bars and then smoothed, it would resemble a marginal reve-

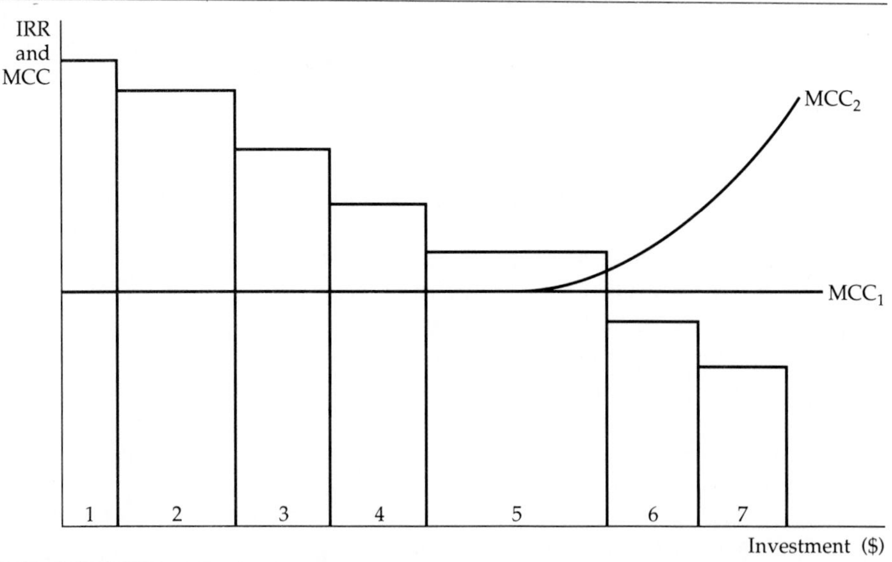

Figure 14.1 The Capital Budgeting Decision

nue curve. In this case, it would be a curve representing the internal rate of return on successive doses of investment—a marginal investment opportunity curve.

The marginal cost curve is based on the cost of capital. In Figure 14.1, two possible constructions of the cost of capital curve are shown. The first, a horizontal line (MCC_1), implies that a company can obtain the funds it needs at a set cost. Such a situation is possible, but it is not very probable.

In the more likely case, as a company requires additional funds (i.e., moves from left to right on the graph), it will be forced to pay higher costs. We have already said that obtaining new equity carries a higher cost of capital than retained earnings. If a company has large requirements for investment funds, and after using up its retained earnings it must look to the outside equity market for additional financing, the marginal cost of capital will rise at that point. If the company's debt–equity ratio is considered optimal, the company will increase its debt proportionally in order to maintain it. As the company increases its borrowing, it will most likely be required to pay increasing interest rates for additional amounts of debt capital.

Thus, as the costs of both debt and equity rise, the marginal weighted cost of capital will show an increase as the corporation increases its demand for capital funds. Hence, it is considerably more realistic to draw the weighted marginal cost of capital as a rising curve (MCC_2), particularly after the capital budget of a certain size is reached.

The company will reach the optimal investment budget at the point where the marginal investment opportunity curve and marginal cost of capital curve intersect. This is, of course, the principle that was applied in the one-period case. In the example shown in Figure 14.1, the conclusion is that projects 1 through 5 should be accepted, and those with lower IRRs (projects 6 and 7) should be rejected.

The illustration shown here is a great simplification. A menu of projects will not usually be put on the table at one time. Projects typically arrive at the capital planning department at various times, and the proposals have to be evaluated one at a time. However, this simplification should be sufficient to show that capital budgeting is indeed an application of the marginal principle.

The marginal rule indicates that the company should invest in every project whose IRR exceeds the marginal cost of capital. However, some corporations impose a limit on capital spending during a particular interval, and not all projects that pass the IRR test will be accepted. This situation, referred to as capital rationing, occurs when management is not willing to obtain external financing. There are various reason for such a practice. For instance, there may be a reluctance to incur increasing levels of debt. Alternatively, management may not wish to add to equity in fear of diluting control. Although such corporate behavior is not value-maximizing, it occurs frequently.

In the presence of capital rationing, more complex methods of analysis, including mathematical programming, must often be employed. A brief discussion of a simple model of capital rationing is included in Appendix 14B.

The Solution

Project 1: Expansion Proposal

George Kline is now ready to put some numbers together. He ascertains that the market forecast of 100 million cases pertains to Global's first year of production, and the 4 percent assumed growth rate will apply thereafter. Since the market research people expect, rather optimistically, that market share will grow to 5 percent after four years, George sets market share at 2, 3, and 4 percent respectively, for the interim years. He calculates the seven-year double-declining balance depreciation for the equipment using the midyear convention as required by the 1986 tax law. (Generally, under this law, only one-half of the first year's depreciation can be taken in the first year and one-half at the end. Thus, if a piece of equipment is depreciated on a seven-year basis, it will actually be depreciated over eight years. The depreciation percentages used in this example are 14 percent, 24 percent, 17 percent, 13 percent, 10 percent, 9 percent, 9 percent, and 3 percent.) Depreciation will start in year 2; thus, the equipment will not be fully depreciated at the end of six years; nor will the buildings. He assumes that the remaining book values will represent the market value at the end of year 7 and will be shown as cash inflows at that point. George also decides that of the original $750,000 cash outflow for working capital, 80 percent will be recovered as cash at the end of year 7 (some accounts receivable will not be collectible, and some inventory will be obsolete). The 20 percent loss will be tax-deductible.

George now prepares his worksheet, shown as Table 14.1. The column labeled "Constant" contains the parameters established originally. (These constant parameters can be changed if different assumptions are to be used. A change in one of these will alter the entire line. This technique will be used in Chapter 15 when we examine how any change in the assumptions will affect the results. The detailed explanation of the Lotus program used for the solution to this project may be found on the diskette furnished to your instructor.) Most of the numbers in this table are self-explanatory, but a few comments should help. The startup expense of $750 is tax-deductible; thus, the cash outflow is $450. The cost of the plant is $3.5 million (50 percent of the purchase price plus $1 million for renovation). The cost of equipment is $3 million (40 percent of the original purchase price plus $1 million for new machinery). Land ($500,000) is assumed not to appreciate.

When the cash flows are obtained and discounted at the 15 percent required rate of return, the resulting NPV is a positive $3,552,000. The internal rate of return is 24.20 percent—considerably above the required rate.

George can therefore recomment the acceptance of this expansion proejct. However, since all of the cash flows are estimates into the future, there is probably considerable uncertainty about their accuracy. We will revisit this project in Chapter 15 and will show how risk and uncertainty can be accomodated in our analysis.

(Continued)

Table 14.1 Expansion Project (000)

	Constant	*Year 0*	*Year 1*	*Year 2*	*Year 3*	*Year 4*	*Year 5*	*Year 6*	*Year 7*
Total market	4.0%			100,000	104,000	108,160	112,486	116,986	121,665
Market share				1.0%	2.0%	3.0%	4.0%	5.0%	5.0%
Company sales				1,000	2,080	3,245	4,499	5,849	6,083
Expenditures		−5,000	−2,000						
Working capital			−750						
Start-up expense	−750		−450						
Sales	5.00			5,000	10,400	16,224	22,497	29,246	30,416
Product cost	2.50			2,500	5,200	8,112	11,248	14,623	15,208
Distribution cost	0.60			600	1,248	1,947	2,700	3,510	3,650
G&A exp. (fixed)	500			500	500	500	500	500	500
G&A exp. (var.)	3.0%			150	312	487	675	877	912
Advertising exp.	5.0%			250	520	811	1,125	1,462	1,521
Deprec. (plant)	3,500			111	111	111	111	111	111
Deprec. (equip.)	3,000			420	750	510	390	300	270
Total cost & exp.				4,531	8,641	12,478	16,749	21,383	22,172
Net earnings before taxes				469	1,759	3,746	5,748	7,863	8,244
Income tax	40.0%			188	704	1,498	2,299	3,145	3,298
Net earnings after taxes				281	1,055	2,248	3,449	4,718	4,946
Add depreciation				531	861	621	501	411	381
Oper. cash flow				812	1,916	2,869	3,950	5,129	5,327
Remaining values									
Land									500
Plant	1.00								2,833
Equipment	1.00								360
Working capital	80.0%								660
Total cash flow		−5,000	−3,200	812	1,916	2,869	3,950	5,129	9,680
Net present value	15.0%								3,552
IRR									24.2%

Project 2: Depalletizer Replacement

The original cash outflow at time 0 is $100,000. But if the investment in the new machine is made, the old one will be sold for $12,000. Since its book value is only $10,000, there would be a profit from the disposal of used equipment of $2,000. The tax rate being 40 percent, the company would have to pay an income tax of $800 on this profit; so the cash inflow from the sale of the old depalletizer would be $11,200.

The annual increase in operating cash flows would be $18,000. The new machine would be depreciated over seven years straight-line. The annual depreciation would, therefore, be $14,286. The annual operating cash flow statement would be as follows:

Revenue less cost	$18,000
Depreciation	14,286
Net profit before taxes	$ 3,714
Income tax	1,486
Net profit after taxes	$ 2,228
Depreciation	14,286
Net cash flow	$16,514

(Continued)

These cash flows would occur during the first seven years of operations. In years 8–10, there would be no depreciation tax shield. Thus, the annual operating cash flows would be:

Revenue less cost	$18,000
Income tax	7,200
Net cash flow	$10,800

One additional piece of information must be included. If Global Foods had kept the old machine, it would be depreciated in years 1 and 2 at $5,000 annually. Since the tax rate is 40 percent, Global would save $2,000 each year in taxes—a cash inflow. If the old machine is sold, this depreciation tax shield will no longer be available. Consequently, the cash flows would be decreased by the present value of the two after-tax depreciation deductions.

Original investment at $t = 0$	−100, 000
Cash proceeds from old machines at $t = 0$	11, 200
Annual cash flow from operations, years 1–7, at PV of annuity factor, 7 years at 12%: 16,514 × 4.5638	75, 363
Annual operating cash flows, years 8–10:	
Year 8 10,800 × .4039	4, 362
Year 9 10,800 × .3606	3, 894
Year 10 10,800 × .3220	3, 478
Depreciation of old machine forgone: 5,000 × .4 × 1.6091	−3, 380
Net present value	$ − 5, 083

Now the proposal can be put together: The IRR calculation would have given us 10.5 percent.

The result is a negative net present value (and an IRR less than the cost of capital). Acquisition of the new depalletizer is not indicated at this time. This is the recommendation the Capital Planning Department will make. However, the decision could be reconisdered if any of the cash flow estimates should change.

Summary

In this chapter we expanded the economic concept of profit maximization to multiperiod projects.

Capital budgeting involves the evaluation of projects in which initial expenditures provide streams of cash inflows over a significant period of time. The process of evaluating capital proposals includes:

1. Estimating all incremental cash flows resulting from the project
2. Discounting all flows to the present
3. Determining whether a proposal should or should not be accepted

Two methods were recommended for evaluating capital budgeting proposals–net present value and internal rate of return. These two criteria were compared as to their validity. It was found that, from a theoretical viewpoint, net present value is the more valid. However, there is much to recommend the use of IRR, and business, in fact, favors this technique. In most cases, both methods lead to the same answer.

The concept of the cost of capital was then developed, and methods of arriving at a weighted cost of capital were discussed.

Finally, using the economist's marginal revenue–marginal cost approach, it was shown that, to maximize its total value, a firm should accept any project whose IRR exceeds the marginal cost of capital.

Important Concepts

Accounting rate of return: Also known as the *return on investment* (ROI) or *return on assets* (ROA), a method for evaluating capital projects. It is obtained by dividing the average annual profit by the average investment.

Capital asset pricing model (CAPM): A financial model specifying relationships between risk and return. A major part of the CAPM is the development of beta, which measures the market risk of a security and is a necessary ingredient in determining a stock's required rate of return.

Capital budgeting: An area of business decision making that concerns undertakings whose receipts and expenses continue over a significant period of time.

Capital rationing: The practice of restricting capital expenditure to a certain amount, possibly resulting in the rejection of projects that have a positive net present value and should be accepted to maximize the company's value.

Cost of capital: Also often referred to as the required rate of return, the hurdle rate, or the cutoff rate, the rate of return a company must earn on its assets to justify the using and acquiring of funds.

Discount rate: The rate at which cash flows are discounted. It is the required rate of return or cost of capital.

Dividend growth model: A method to arrive at the value of a security. Given the price of the security, it calculates the company's cost of equity as the dividend divided by the current stock price plus the growth rate in dividends (assumed to be constant). It is an alternative method to CAPM in calculating the equity cost of capital.

Independent projects: A situation in which the acceptance of one capital project does not preclude the acceptance of another project. (See *mutually exclusive projects*.)

Internal rate of return (IRR): One method of evaluating capital projects by discounting cash flows. The IRR is the interest rate that equates the present value of inflows with the present value of outflows, or, in other words, causes the net present value of the project to equal zero.

Mutually exclusive projects: A situation in which the acceptance of one project precludes the acceptance of another.

Net present value: A method of evaluating capital projects in which all cash flows are discounted at the cost of capital, to the present and the present value of all outflows is subtracted from the present value of all inflows.

Payback: A method of evaluating capital projects in which the original investment is divided by the annual cash flow. It tells management how many years it will take for a project's cash inflows to repay the original investment.

Time value of money: Very basically, this means that a dollar today is worth more than a dollar tomorrow, since today's dollar will earn interest and increase in value.

Questions

1. What is the objective of capital budgeting?
2. Name five types of decisions that utilize the capital budgeting method.
3. Define the time value of money.
4. What are the advantages and disadvantages of the payback method? The accounting rate of return on investment method?
5. How is net present value calculated? What is the decision rule for net present value?
6. How is the internal rate of return calculated? What is the decision rule for IRR?
7. The relationship between net present value and the internal rate of return is such that the IRR of a project is equal to the firm's cost of capital when the NPV of the project is $0. True of false? Explain.
8. Under which circumstances can the NPV and IRR calculations lead to conflicting results? What is the major reason for the difference? Which of the two methods is preferable? Why?
9. What are the major types of cash flows to be included in a capital budgeting analysis? Describe each.
10. Why is depreciation important in the analysis of a capital budgeting proposal?
11. Should a reallocation of fixed costs from other projects to the project being analyzed be included in the project's cash flows, if there is no net increase in cash outflow to the company? Why or why not?
12. How is the company's optimal capital budget determined? Does the decision-making process in this case resemble the procedure used in determining the price and quantity of output? How?
13. How is the weighted cost of capital determined?
14. Discuss the two methods by which the costs of equity can be determined.

Problems

1. The Warwick Company is reviewing three projects for potential investment. The cash outflows and cash inflows for each are shown.

Year	Project A	Project B	Project C
0	−100	−100	−100
1	60	40	60
2	40	60	40
3	20	20	20
4	20	20	20
5	0	0	20
6	0	0	20

a. Calculate the payback period for each project.
b. Based on the payback calculation, which of the three projects would be preferred (if only one can be accepted)?
c. Critique the results you obtained.

2. An investment requires an initial cash outlay of $200,000 and has a life of 10 years. The average annual before-tax cash flow during these years is $50,000. The tax rate is 40 percent, and 10-year straight-line depreciation (with zero salvage) is used. What is the accounting rate of return?
3. Jay Wechsler agrees to purchase a car from a local dealer, the Con Car Co. The purchase price is $15,000. Jay has the cash to pay the entire amount and wants to do so. Con's sales manager uses the following argument to convince him to finance the car: "All we require is a down payment of $3,000. Then you can borrow the $12,000 from our finance company at 12 percent. You will make monthly payments of $266.93 for five years (60 months), a total of $16,015.80. If you do that, you get to keep your $12,000. Now suppose you keep this money in a money market account that pays you 8 percent compounded quarterly. In five years the $12,000 will grow to $17,831.40. That means that you will be better off by $1,815.60 than if you pay the $12,000 in cash."

   Assume that all the numbers are correct. Does the offer sound too good to be true? Why? (This is an argument often used by automobile dealers. One of the authors encountered it not too long ago.)
4. Your firm has an opportunity to make an investment of $50,000. Its cost of capital is 12 percent. It expects after-tax cash flows (including the tax shield from depreciation) for the next five years to be as follows:

Year 1	$10,000
Year 2	20,000
Year 3	30,000
Year 4	20,000
Year 5	5,000

a. Calculate the net present value.
b. Calculate the internal rate of return (to the nearest percent).
c. Would you accept this project?

5. As a capital budgeting analyst for the Georgian Corporation, you have been asked to analyze two proposed projects. Each involves an initial investment of $15,000, and the company's cost of capital is 10 percent. The projects have the following (after-tax) cash flows:

Year	*Project A*	*Project B*
0	($15,000)	($15,000)
1	9,000	7,000
2	6,000	7,000
3	5,000	7,000

a. For each project, calculate
   (1) Payback
   (2) Accounting rate of return, assuming that the original investment will be depreciated on a straight-line basis to zero at the end of the three years
   (3) Net present value
   (4) Internal rate of return
b. Which project would you select under each of the four measures, if the projects are mutually exclusive?

6. The Glendale Construction Company is considering the purchase of a new crane. Its cost would be $500,000. If it were to make the purchase, the company would sell its old crane, which still has a book value of $100,000 and which it could probably sell in the second-hand market for $70,000. If the tax rate is 40 percent, what would be the actual cash investment in the new crane?
7. As capital investment analyst for the Parkhurst Printing Corporation, you have been asked to evaluate the advisability of purchasing a new printing press to accommodate projected increases in demand. This new machine is expected to last five years, and you will be calculating the cash flows of the project for that period.

The purchase price of the press is expected to be $140,000; in addition, it will cost $10,000 to install it. The press will be depreciated on a straight-line basis over five years to a zero salvage value. However, it is expected to have a salvage value of $10,000 at the end of five years.

The press is expected to generate the following cash revenues and cash costs and expenses:

	Year 1	*Year 2*	*Year 3*	*Year 4*	*Year 5*
Cash revenue	$50,000	$80,000	$80,000	$80,000	$40,000
Cash cost and expenses	25,000	40,000	40,000	40,000	20,000

Because of increased production, additional working capital of $15,000 will be needed at $t = 0$ (today) and will be returned at the end of the project (five years from now). The income tax rate is 40 percent, and the company's cost of capital is 12 percent. Calculate the net present value. Should the press be purchased?

8. The Colgate Distributing Company has the choice of furnishing its sales representatives with a car or paying a mileage allowance for the use of the representatives' own cars. If the company furnishes the car, it will pay all expenses connected with it, including gasoline for business mileage. The estimates are as follows:

   Cost of car: $15,000

   Estimated life: Four years

   Depreciation method: Straight-line over four years (assuming no salvage value)

   Expected sales value of car at end of four years: $2,500

   Estimated annual operating costs:

Gasoline	$900
License and insurance	600
Garaging	300
Maintenance	
Year 1	250
Year 2	350
Year 3	450
Year 4	600

   If the sales representatives use their own cars, the company will reimburse them at 35 cents per mile; the company estimates that each representative will drive 18,000 miles per year for business purposes. The company's cost of capital is 10 percent, and its income tax rate is 40 percent.

   Should the company buy cars for its sales representatives or pay them a mileage allowance? Use the NPV method in your calculation.

9. The Manchester Tool Company is considering the replacement of an existing machine by a more efficient machine. The new machine costs $1,200,000 and requires installation costs of $150,000.

   The present machine is 4 years old. It originally cost $800,000 and is being depreciated straight-line over 10 years to a zero salvage value. Its market value today is $400,000. It can be used for the next 6 years; at that time, its salvage value will be zero.

   The new machine has an expected life of 6 years and will be depreciated on a straight-line method over 5 years to a salvage value of zero. However, it is expected to have a market value of $200,000 at the end of 6 years.

   The new machine will reduce operating costs by $250,000 per year. The company's income tax rate is 40 percent, and its cost of capital is 9 percent. Would you recommend that the old machine be replaced?

10. A company's common stock is currently selling at $40 per share. It pays a dividend of $1.60, and the financial community expects that its dividend will

grow at 10 percent per year in the foreseeable future. What is the company's equity cost of retained earnings? If the company sells new common stock to finance new projects and must pay $2 per share in flotation costs, what is the cost of equity?

11. A company has 1,000,000 shares of common stock outstanding, and the current market price is $50 per share. The company has also issued 20,000 bonds ($1,000 maturity value each), which are presently selling in the market at $980 each. The bonds are selling at a yield of 11 percent; the company expects to pay a dividend of $3 per share in the coming year, and the dividend is expected to grow at 8 percent per year. The company is in the 40 percent tax bracket. What is the weighted cost of capital?
12. A company has a beta of 1.3. The risk-free interest rate today is 8 percent, and the return on a market portfolio of stocks is 14 percent. (Therefore, the market risk premium is 6 percent, the difference between the market return and the risk-free return.)
    a. What is the required return (equity cost) on the company's stock?
    b. If the risk-free rate rises to 9 percent, what will be the required rate of return on the company's stock?
    c. If the beta of this company were 0.8, what would be its required rate of return?

APPENDIX 14A
Calculations for Time Value of Money

In this appendix, a brief explanation of the computation of the time value of money is given for readers not familiar with this subject. Modern technology has made these calculations very easy. Many computer programs have built-in time-value functions, and a large assortment of hand-held calculators will solve these problems using special keys. However, some people who use these methods do not understand the rationale for the answers and merely accept the results.

At the other extreme, the calculations could be made using exponentials and/or logarithms. Such a procedure may provide a thorough learning experience, but it is tedious and time-consuming. Compound interest tables have been developed to provide a relatively easy tool for solving time-value problems. They will be found in the appendix at the end of this book. Here we will walk through four types of calculations, each representing one of the four tables.

The Future Value of a Single Sum

If you deposit $1,000 in a savings account that pays 7 percent interest annually, and you do not withdraw this interest, the original amount will keep growing. (In real life, bank interest is usually compounded more frequently than once a year, but annual compounding will be assumed here. In other words, the 7 percent will be credited to the account once a year, at the end of the year.) One year later, $70 of interest will be added to the account, making the total balance $1,070. In mathematical terms, this occurrence can be written as follows: If i equals the annual interest rate, then the amount of interest paid in one year equals A times i, where A is the original amount deposited. Thus, B, the ending balance in the account, will be

$$B = A + (A \times i) \quad \text{or} \quad \mathrm{B} = \mathrm{A}(1 + i)$$

In the present case, this will compute as

$$B = 1{,}000(1 + .07) = 1{,}000(1.07) = 1{,}070$$

Now, if $1,070 is left in the account for another year, interest will be paid on the $1,070:

$$B = 1{,}070(1.07) = 1{,}144.90$$

We could also find the answer in the following way:

$$B = 1{,}000 \times 1.07 \times 1.07 = 1{,}144.90$$

This expression simplifies to $1{,}000(1.07)^2$. Thus, in general terms,

$$\mathrm{FV} = \mathrm{PV}(1 + i)^n$$

where FV = Future value
PV = Present value
i = Rate of interest
n = Number of periods over which compounding takes place.

Table A.1*a* at the end of this book presents the $(1 + i)^n$ factors for a large number of periods and interest rates. Thus, if you wish to find out how much your original $1,000 will grow in eight years, you can look it up by moving down the leftmost (period) column to 8 and then moving to the right until you hit the 7 percent column. You will obtain an answer of 1.7182. Substituting into the general formula,

$$\begin{aligned} \mathrm{FV} &= 1{,}000(1.7182) \\ &= 1{,}718.20 \end{aligned}$$

This table can also be used if you know the beginning and ending amounts and want to find the rate of interest it took to go from the first to the last amount. The formula for future value can be easily transformed to solve for the interest rate. If we refer to the number that appears in the table as "factor," then

$$\begin{aligned} \mathrm{FV} &= \mathrm{PV}(\mathrm{Factor}) \\ \mathrm{Factor} &= \mathrm{FV}/\mathrm{PV} \end{aligned}$$

Assume that you are saving for a particular purpose. You put aside $1,000 today and want to have $2,000 five years from now:

$$\text{Factor} = \frac{2{,}000}{1{,}000} = 2$$

To find the answer, enter the table at five periods and move to the right until the number nearest to 2 is reached. This happens at 15 percent, where the $(1 + i)^n$ factor equals 2.0114. Thus, you would have to earn approximately 15 percent interest to double your amount in five years.[24]

This type of calculation is employed frequently to obtain compound growth rates, a very popular concept in business.

The Future Value of an Annuity

In the previous section we dealt with the compounding of a single sum. But suppose that a uniform amount is set aside each period (e.g., each year), and we want to know how much will be in the account after several years?

For example, suppose five annual deposits of $500 each will be made to an account paying 7 percent annually, starting a year from now. What will be the amount at the end of five years? A simple diagram will illustrate:

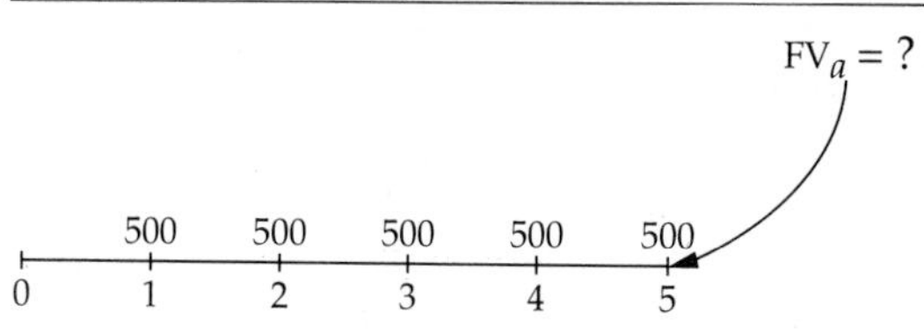

The first $500 will collect interest for four years; the second for three years and so on. This problem could be solved by making all the separate calculations and adding the items:

$$FV_a = A(1 + i)^{n-1} + A(1 + i)^{n-2} + \cdots + A(1 + i)^0$$

where FVa = Future value of the annuity
A = Annuity

This expression simplifies to

$$\frac{(1 + i)^n - 1}{i}$$

Again, a table has been constructed to ease the effort involved in this calculation. Table A.1*b* at the end of the book shows the *sum of an annuity*. For the question posed here the answer is:

---

[24] If more exact results are needed, linear interpolation should be used. We will not explain interpolation here. An explanation can be found in any basic mathematics text.

$$\begin{aligned} FV_a &= A(\text{Factor}) \\ &= 500(5.7507) \\ &= 2{,}875.35 \end{aligned}$$

where "factor" is found in Table A.1*b*.

The preceding calculation solves for the future value of the annuity. But suppose we have a problem stated in the following form:

To finance the college education of a just-born child, the parents expect they will need \$200,000 18 years from now. They believe that they can earn 7 percent on their savings. How much should they put aside each year? The future-value formula can be transposed to solve for the annuity, A:

$$\begin{aligned} A &= FV_a/\text{Factor} \\ &= 200{,}000/33.999 \\ &= 5{,}883 \end{aligned}$$

The parents will have to deposit \$5,883 per year to have \$200,000 in 18 years.

Table A.1*b* presents factors for ordinary annuities, which means that the first payment is made at the end of the first period and the last payment occurs on the final date. But suppose the payments are to start right now, and the last payment will occur at the beginning of the last period. Such a series of payments is usually referred to as an *annuity due,* and the diagram for such an arrangement, using data from the first example of this section, is:

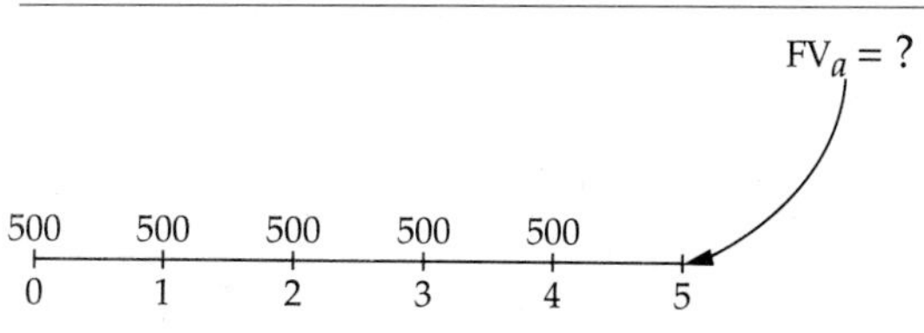

Table A.1*b* can still be applied, with one small change. The ordinary annuity factor in Table A.1*b* must be multiplied by $(1 + i)$. With interest again at 7 percent, the "annuity due" factor become 5.7507 times 1.07, or 6.1532. Thus, the result is

$$\begin{aligned} FV_a &= 500(6.1532) \\ &= 3{,}077 \end{aligned}$$

Note that the amount accumulated at the end of five years is considerably larger than in the first example. The reason? Each of the contributions has an extra year to compound.

Present Value of a Single Sum

Suppose you are to receive a sum of \$500 three years from now. You would like to receive the money today, and you would be willing to accept less, since an amount deposited today with interest would grow to a larger sum in three years. The question can be stated as follows: How much money accepted today would be equivalent to \$500 three years from now? That depends, of course, on the rate of interest you earn on your money. As with our previous example, let us use a 7 percent interest rate.

Remember from our discussion of compounding a single sum that $FV = PV(1 + i)^n$. We are now attempting to solve the opposite problem: we know the future value and wish to find the present value. Therefore,

$$PV = \frac{FV}{(1 + i)^n}$$

Since

$$\frac{1}{(1 + i)^n} = (1 + i)^{-n}$$

this simple equation can be written as

$$PV = FV(1 + i)^{-n}$$

The number can be found in Table A.1*c*. We look up the three-year factor at 7 percent and find it to be .8163. Thus,

$$\begin{aligned} PV &= 500(.8163) \\ &= 408 \end{aligned}$$

Incidentally, the present-value factors (Table A.1*c*) are reciprocals of the future-value factors (Table A.1*a*). Thus, if you have only one of these tables available, you can still do both future-and present-value calculations. For the preceding case, if only table A.1*a* were available, the solution would be as follows:

$$\begin{aligned} FV &= PV(1 + i)^n \\ PV &= \frac{FV}{(1 + i)^n} \\ &= \frac{500}{1.225} \\ &= 408 \end{aligned}$$

Present Value of an Annuity

Suppose that instead of receiving just one amount in the future, you expect to receive a series of uniform payments annually for four years starting a year from now (an ordinary annuity), or, as an alternative, you can receive a lump sum today. The single amount that would be equivalent to the annuity again depends on the interest rate you can earn. Assume that you are to receive four annual payments of $2,000. This is illustrated as follows:

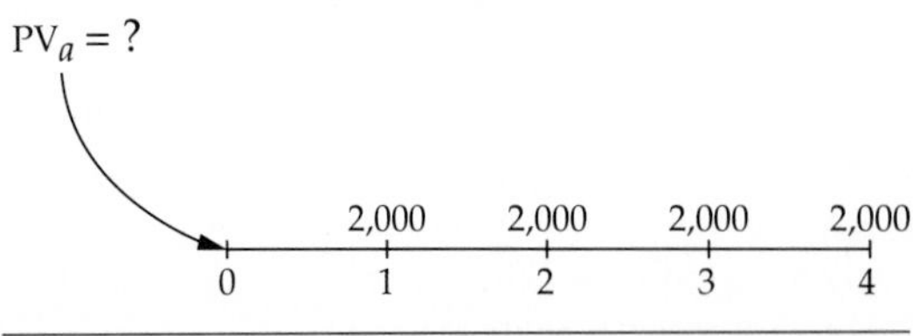

The solution could be obtained by calculating the present value of each payment using Table A.1*c* and totaling the results. The first $2,000 would be discounted one year, the second two years, and so on. Using Table A.1*d*, however, avoids this time-consuming method. The factors contained in this table already include the discounting and summation of all the individual numbers. Thus, if the interest rate to be used is 8 percent, then

$$\begin{aligned} PV_a &= A(Factor) \\ &= 2{,}000(3.3121) \\ &= 6{,}624 \end{aligned}$$

where "factor" is found in Table A.1*d*. You would be indifferent between receiving a sum of $6,624 today and a series of four annual payments of $2,000.

The preceding calculations apply to an ordinary annuity. If the first payment is to be received today, a relatively simple adjustment must be made to the factors of Table A.1*d*.

A very relevant example of the present value of an annuity due is the case of a state lottery. You certainly have seen a banner headline such as "John P. Oliver Wins $5 Million in the Lottery." True, Mr. Oliver will receive $5 million (before he pays his taxes), but not all at one time. State lotteries frequently pay the winners in 20 equal installments; the first payment is received today and the other 19 are received annually starting one year from today. To convert the calculation to an annuity due, the ordinary annuity factor in Table A.1*d* must be multiplied by $(1 + i)$. For 20 payments of $250,000 each, using an 8 percent interest rate, the 20-year factor is 9.8181 which, when multiplied by 1.08, becomes 10.6035. The calculation is as follows:

$$\begin{aligned} PV_a &= A(10.6035) \\ &= 250{,}000(10.6035) \\ &= 2{,}650{,}875 \end{aligned}$$

Obviously, this amount is much less than the $5 million that was announced as Mr. Oliver's winning ticket. Still, more than $2.5 million dollars is not that bad.

There is one more exercise that should be examined in this section. Suppose we know the present value of the annuity and the interest rate, but the annuity payment is unknown. Assume that you wish to borrow $20,000 to be paid back over five years in equal installments at an interest rate of 9 percent. What will your annual payments be? The factors in Table A.1*d* are again applicable, but we must reverse the formula:

$$\begin{aligned} PV_a &= \text{A(Factor)} \\ A &= \frac{PV_a}{\text{Factor}} \\ &= \frac{20{,}000}{3.8897} \\ &= 5{,}142 \end{aligned}$$

More Frequent Compounding

All of the preceding examples were in terms of years—annual compounding. But compounding may occur more frequently. Banks advertise that they compound interest on savings accounts quarterly, monthly, or even daily. The more frequent the compounding, the greater the effect of the time value of money.

In the first section of this appendix, compounding of a single sum was discussed. The formula was

$$FV = PV(1+i)^n$$

If compounding occurs more often than n—for instance, m times n—then the compounding formula is revised as follows:

$$FV = PV(1 + i/m)^{mn}$$

Suppose a deposit of $10,000 pays an annual interest rate of 8 percent compounded semiannually, and the time elapsed is five years. The equation would be:

$$\begin{aligned} FV &= 10,000(1 + .08/2)^{5\times 2} \\ &= 10,000(1.04)^{10} \\ &= 10,000(1.4802) \\ &= 14,802 \end{aligned}$$

If compounding had been annual, the resulting amount would have been lower: 10,000(1.4693) = 14,693.

On the other hand, with quarterly compounding:

$$\begin{aligned} FV &= 10,000(1.02)^{20} \\ &= 10,000(1.4859) \\ &= 14,859 \end{aligned}$$

The more frequent the compounding, the larger will be the future value.

Bond Values and Perpetuities

One more application of present-value calculations will be discussed here. A corporate or government bond pays periodic interest and then repays the face value on the maturity date. Interest payments are generally fixed for the life of the bond and are expressed as a percentage of the face value. Whether market interest rates rise or fall during the life of the bond, the periodic interest paid will not change. However, the price of the bond will change so that the yield corresponds to the interest rate paid in the market for bonds of a similar risk class and length of life.[25]

[25]The riskier, or less safe, a bond, the higher will be the interest that the market will require. The longer the length of life of the bond, the higher will be the required interest, under normal circumstances.

As an example, we will take a bond with a face and maturity value of $1,000 (the usual amount in which bonds are denominated). It will mature in 20 years (it was originally a 30-year bond, issued 10 years ago), and the stated interest rate is 8 percent. Thus, the annual interest payment is $80.[26]

Interest rates have risen recently, and today bonds with 20-year maturities yield 10 percent. But since the interest payment of $80 per year on the bond cannot be changed, the market value of the bond (the price someone would be willing to pay for it today) will have to decline. This situation is quite obvious. If bonds are now yielding 10 percent, a potential buyer of a $1,000 bond would require $100 of annual interest. The bond in our example pays $80 per year, with a final payment of $1,000 at maturity. To obtain its value when the current market yield is 10 percent, we compute the present value of a 20-year annuity of $80 at a 10 percent discount rate and add to it the present value of the maturity value, $1,000, also discounted to the present at 10 percent:

$$\begin{aligned} P_0 &= 80(8.5136) + 1,000(.1486) \\ &= 681 + 149 = 830 \end{aligned}$$

At $P_o = 830$, representing the market price of the bond today, and a yield of 10 percent to maturity, this bond is equivalent to a bond selling today for $1,000 that pays $100 annually and will mature 20 years hence at $1,000.

Had interest rates dropped to 6 percent, the bond of our example, still paying $80 a year, would rise in price above its maturity value:

$$\begin{aligned} P_o &= 80(11.4699) + 1,000(.3118) \\ &= 918 + 312 = 1,230 \end{aligned}$$

Perpetual bonds do not exist in the United States. However, they have been issued elsewhere, for example in the United Kingdom. Such bonds never mature, but they promise to pay a stated interest amount forever. If

$$\begin{aligned} P_0 &= \text{Price of the bond today} \\ I &= \text{Annual interest paid} \\ i &= \text{Market interest rate} \end{aligned}$$

then

$$i = \frac{I}{P_0}$$

and

$$P_0 = \frac{I}{i}$$

If the bond pays $80 a year and the market rate is 8 percent, the price of the bond today will be its face value of $1,000. However, should the market rate of interest for bonds of this type rise to 10 percent, the bond paying $80 per year

[26]Bond interest is usually paid semiannually, but for this example, annual payments are assumed.

will be worth

$$P_0 = \frac{80}{.1} = 800$$

A bond selling for $800 and paying $80 a year yields precisely 10% in perpetuity.

Fluctuations in bond prices will be greater for any change in the market interest rate, the longer the period to maturity. The price of a bond that matures one year hence will not decrease much when market interest rates rise. On the other hand, the price of a perpetuity will fluctuate very significantly with changes in market interest yields.

APPENDIX 14B
Mutually Exclusive Projects and Capital Rationing

Net Present Value and Internal Rate of Return in the Evaluation of Mutually Exclusive Projects

When projects are independent, either the net present value or the internal rate of return criterion will give the correct signal as to whether a project should be accepted or rejected. Therefore, under most circumstances (except in the case of nonconventional cash flows, when the IRR computation results in multiple solutions), either of the two measures can be used.

However, when two (or more) projects are mutually exclusive (i.e., only one of the alternatives can be accepted), the two measures can give conflicting results. As mentioned in the chapter, this can be caused by a difference in project size. Table 14B.1 shows such a case. Two mutually exclusive projects are presented. Project A involves an original outlay of $1,500; its cash inflows are $580 per year for four years. Project B (which is a substitute for A) is somewhat less expensive—only $1,000—but the four cash inflows are also smaller, at $400 each. Each project has a four-year life and no salvage value. Proceeding in the normal way, we find that the IRR of project B is higher than that of project A—21.9 percent against 20.1 percent. If we were to go no further, basing our choice on a comparison of IRRs, project B would be selected. But if we perform an NPV calculation (at the company's cost of capital of 15 percent), project A tops B's NPV by $14, (i.e., $156 against $142). The IRR tells us to adopt project B, but if we want to maximize net present value, we should implement project A.

To resolve this dilemma, we calculate the NPV and IRR for an "incremental" (or *delta*) project. That is, we take the differences between the two project cash flows and create a delta project. If we undertake A rather than B, we must incur an additional original cash outflow (at $t = 0$) of $500 and receive in turn additional cash inflows of $180 for each of the next four years. Such a project, evaluated separately, would have an NPV of $14 and an IRR of 16.4 percent. This means that the additional outlay of $500 provides an incremental positive NPV ($14) and an internal rate of return (16.4 percent) that exceeds the 15 per-

Table 14B.1 Two Mutually Exclusive Projects that Differ in Size

Project	t=0	t=1	t=2	t=3	t=4
A	−1500	580	580	580	580
B	−1000	400	400	400	400

Cost of capital 15.0%

	Internal Rate of Return	Net Present Value
Project A	20.1%	156
Project B	21.9%	142

Delta Project

	t=0	t=1	t=2	t=3	t=4
(A−B)	−500	180	180	180	180

Net Present Value 14 Internal Rate of Return 16.4%

Project evaluation at several discount rates

	0.0%	5.0%	10.0%	15.0%	20.0%	25.0%
Project A	820	557	339	156	1	−130
Project B	600	418	268	142	35	−55

cent cost of capital. Thus, both criteria indicate that the additional investment of $500 is worthwhile. It follows that the NPV rule, which suggested project A, was the correct indicator, and that project A should be chosen over project B.

Figure 14B.1 illustrates the relationship between the two projects. At the bottom of Table 14B.1, the two projects have been evaluated at six different discount rates, and their respective NPVs have been plotted on the graph. When the discount rate is 0, the NPV is merely the sum of all the cash flows (for project A, $-1,500 + 580 + 580 + 580 + 580 = 820$). This is shown on the vertical axis. On the horizontal axis, the projects' NPVs become 0 at their respective IRRs (20.1 percent for A and 21.9 percent for B). The two projects' NPVs cross at $111, at a discount rate of 16.4 percent, which is the IRR of the incremental project. To the left of the Fisher intersection,[27] project's a NPV exceeds that of project B, which creates a conflict, since project B's IRR (21.9 percent) is always higher than project A's (20.1 percent). Had the cost of capital been higher than 16.4 percent, project B would have been preferred under both methods, since it would now have the higher NPV.

Another instance when the two measures give conflicting rankings is when the shapes of the cash inflow streams differ significantly. Although the initial

[27]Named for the American economist Irving Fisher, who was a pioneer in developing the economic theory of interest.

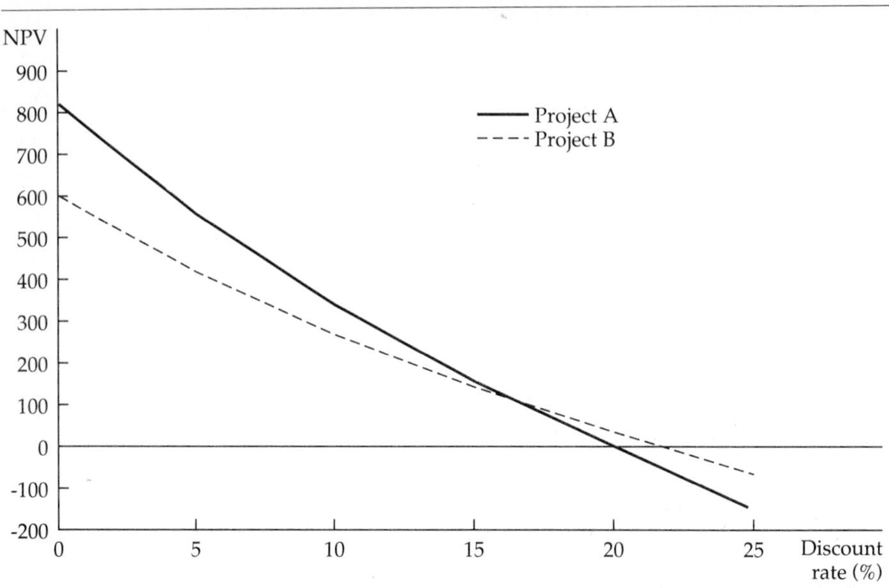

Figure 14B.1 Net Present Value Profiles for Projects of Different Size (with Fisher Intersection)

outlays for both mutually exclusive projects are the same, one of the projects has a cash flow pattern that starts slowly and builds up, whereas the other has cash inflows that are initially large but decline over time. Table 14B.2. shows the data for projects A and B; both start with a $5,000 investment.

A's cash inflows rise significantly over the three years of project duration, whereas B's decline. The cost of capital is 10 percent. Again, the NPV and IRR solutions give opposite signals. Project B has the higher IRR, but project A's NPV is significantly larger.

The solution can again be accomplished by calculating the NPV and IRR for the incremental project. The delta project has a positive net present value of $406 ($1,277 minus $872, with a $1 difference due to rounding). The internal rate of return of the incremental project is a very acceptable 17.6 percent. Thus, project A would be chosen, since the net present value of the incremental cash flows is considerably larger than for project B. Figure 14B.2 can be interpreted in the same way as Figure 14B.1. The intersection of the plots occurs at 17.6 percent, the IRR of the incremental project.

We discussed in the body of the chapter the fact that the internal rate of return is the preferred measure in today's corporations, but it is worthwhile to reiterate here the reason for the theoretical superiority of the NPV rule. A firm should accept all projects that have a positive net present value, if and when they are available. When a company obtains a positive net present from undertaking a project, the NPV amount increases the value of the company. Since a company's objective is to maximize its value (or shareholders' wealth), it should accept all those projects that will add up to the largest total net present value. This can

Table 14B.2 Two Mutually Exclusive Projects with Different Cash Inflow Streams

Project	t=0	t=1	t=2	t=3
A	−5000	500	2500	5000
B	−5000	3500	2800	500
Cost of capital			10.0%	

	Internal Rate of Return	Net Present Value
Project A	20.4%	1277
Project B	22.4%	882

Delta Project

	t=0	t=1	t=2	t=3
(A−B)	0	−3000	−300	4500

Net Present Value ,406 Internal Rate of Return 17.6%

Project evaluation at several discount rates

	0.0%	5.0%	10.0%	15.0%	20.0%	25.0%
Project A	3000	2063	1277	613	46	−440
Project B	1800	1305	872	489	150	−152

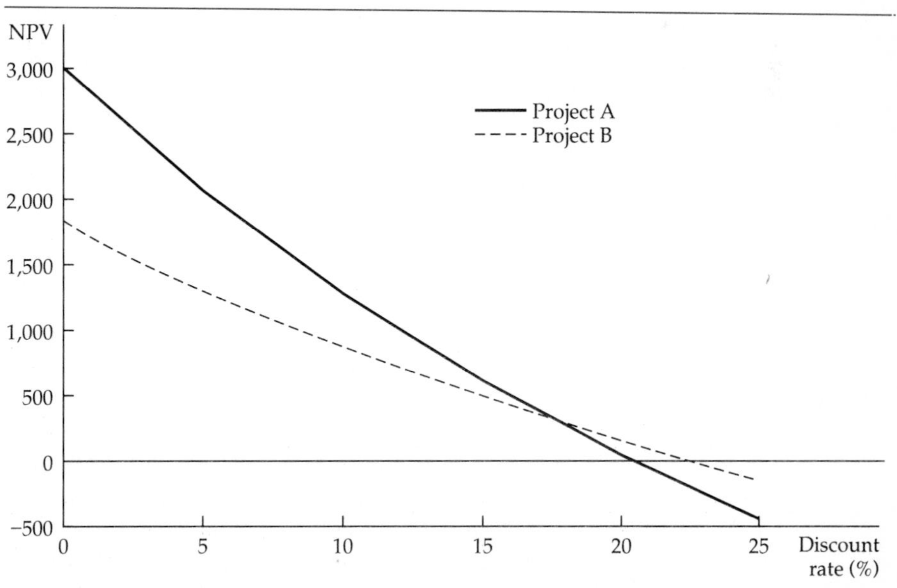

Figure 14B.2 Net Present Value Profiles for Projects with Different Cash Inflow Patterns (with Fisher Intersection)

Table 14B.3 Investment Choices under Capital Rationing

Project	*Original Investment*	*Net Present Value*
A	$50	$25
B	70	30
C	20	25
D	30	10
E	80	30

be achieved only if all projects are evaluated by the NPV criterion. Using the IRR when there are mutually exclusive projects would not necessarily, as we have seen, lead to the creation of maximum value.

We have concluded that a company should invest funds as long as there is a positive net present value being derived from the projects. However, there are situations that deviate from this prescription. One important deviation is capital rationing, which will be discussed next.

Capital Rationing

The term *capital rationing* signifies that a company has imposed an absolute (and arbitrary) limit on the amount of investment it is willing to undertake at a given time. We have stressed over and over again that any project with a positive net present value should be undertaken. However, under capital rationing conditions, a company may have to reject otherwise acceptable projects to remain within its expenditure limit.

Assume that a corporation has evaluated five independent capital projects, with the results shown in Table 14B.3. Each of the projects has a positive net present value and therefore should be undertaken under the usual rule. To embark on these five projects, the company would have to incur cash outflows of $250 and would obtain a net present value of $120.

However, the management of this firm has decreed that only $100 will be spent on capital projects at this time. Obviously, the company will not be able to maximize its net present value at $120. Which projects should it select? To create the most value it can under the circumstances, it will choose the combination of projects that will give the highest net present value within the spending constraint. This leads to the selection of projects A, C, and D. These three projects together will require an outlay of just $100 and will have a combined net present value of $60. No other combination of projects within the $100 spending constraint will achieve a net present value as high as $60.

Although the imposition of capital rationing does not appear to be rational maximizing behavior, it nevertheless occurs quite frequently. Many reasons can be given for such action, but basically it comes down to management's being too cautious with its borrowing policies and/or unwilling to issue additional stock if cash is not available. The final judgment on capital rationing is that it does not permit a company to achieve its maximum value.

Problems

1. Two mutually exclusive alternatives, projects C and D, have the following investments and cash flows:

	Project C	*Project D*
Investment at period $t = 0$	\$40,000	\$40,000
Cash inflow at $t = 1$	10,000	20,500
Cash inflow at $t = 2$	10,000	20,500
Cash inflow at $t = 3$	47,000	20,500

   a. Calculate the net present value and internal rate of return of each project. The company's cost of capital is 12 percent.
   b. Which of the two projects would you accept? Explain.
   c. Sketch the two projects' NPV profiles.

2. The Berkshire Resort Hotel has planned several improvement projects. However, it has decided to restrict its capital expenditures to \$340,000 during the next year. The following are the projects it has on its drawing board:

	Original Investment	*Net Present Value*
Additional tennis court	\$ 20,000	\$ 5,500
Kitchen renovation	50,000	14,000
New children's playground	60,000	12,500
New bungalows	100,000	22,500
New golf clubhouse	120,000	32,500
Olympic-size swimming pool	140,000	45,000
New theater arena	150,000	40,000

   Which projects should it undertake?

CHAPTER 15

Risk and Uncertainty

The Situation

When George Kline completed his analysis of the expansion proposal,[1] he concluded that the company's plan for extending its activities into a new geographical region was desirable. He had calculated a net present value that was positive and, consistently, an internal rate of return that exceeded the required rate of return (cost of capital).

He discussed his findings with his immediate manager, the company's treasurer. The treasurer agreed that the estimates used were the best available, and that even if some of them turned out to be overly optimistic, the project would still be acceptable. However, he indicated management's awareness that expanding into new, relatively untested territory was a rather perilous undertaking. He believed that more should be done to examine the economic risk characteristics of the project. Therefore, he asked George to perform additional risk analyses. George informed him that there are various techniques available, some of which involve statistical concepts. The Treasurer suggested that George keep his analysis on a relatively simple level, but that it should be extensive enough that the vice president of finance and others who will be present when the proposal is presented can be comfortable with this important decision.

[1]See "Solution" in Chapter 14.)

Introduction

This chapter would be unnecessary if we were living in a world of perfect knowledge, where all future events could be determined with complete certainty.

Throughout this text, all quantities have been treated as if they were certain. Demand curves showed specific quantities that would be sold at specific prices. Cost curves showed definite dollar amounts of costs for specific quantities. In the preceding chapter, on capital budgeting, the various estimates of cash flows for projects were treated as if they were known with certainty. In the real world, of course, most future events are not known with any degree of certainty. Managers must make decisions daily, relying on estimates they believe are reasonably reliable but by no means certain. Dealing with uncertainty and recognizing that future results may differ from well-constructed plans is a reality in the business world.

Although risk or uncertainty was not explicitly considered in the calculation of cash flows in the preceding chapter, there were several references to risk. For example, the replacement project was evaluated at a lower discount rate than the expansion project because the latter was considered to be more risky. Risk and uncertainty also played an important role in Chapter 6, on forecasting. However, risk or uncertainty was not considered explicitly in any of the discussions. In this chapter, the meaning of the words *risk* and *uncertainty* will be explained, and the various methods of incorporating these concepts into economic analysis will be explored.

Risk versus Uncertainty

In economic or financial theory, the two terms *risk* and *uncertainty* have somewhat different meanings, even though they are often used interchangeably.[2] Although no future events are known with certainty, some events can be assigned probabilities, and others cannot. Where future events can be defined and probabilities assigned, we have a case of risk. If, for instance, a company's sales manager estimates that next year's sales of diet cola could be 5, 6, or 7 million cases and that the probabilities are 25 percent that 5 million will be sold, 50 percent that 6 million will be sold, and 25 percent that 7 million cases will be sold, we are describing a risk situation. If there is no way to assign any probabilities to future random events, we are addressing pure uncertainty.

Even though this distinction is theoretically important, many writers omit it as a matter of convenience. We will follow this practice. Of course, students will understand that whenever probabilities are assigned to future events, a risk situation is being discussed.

How are probabilities obtained? There are at least two ways. In the terminology of economist Frank Knight, probabilities can be classified as *a priori* or

[2] An early discussion of this distinction can be found in Frank H. Knight's *Risk, Uncertainty and Profit* (Boston: Houghton Mifflin, 1921, reprinted as no. 16 in a series of reprints by the London School of Economics and Political Science.) Knight made the distinction as follows: "The essential fact is that 'risk' means in some cases a quantity susceptible of measurement, while at other times it is something distinctly not of this character . . . It will appear that a 'measurable' uncertainty, or 'risk' proper, as we shall use the term, is so far different from an unmeasurable one that it is not in effect an uncertainty at all" (pp. 19–20).

statistical.[3] The former can be obtained by repetition. Thus, if a true two-sided coin is flipped an infinite number of times, tails will come up on half the tosses and heads on the other half. When two dice are thrown, there are 36 possible combinations of numbers. There is only one way to obtain a 2 (a 1 on each die). On the other hand, there are six different ways to obtain a 7. If the two dice were to be thrown an infinite number of times, a 2 would appear, on the average, once in every 36 throws, and a 7 would come up six times every 36 throws, on the average. Instead of throwing the coin or dice an infinite number of times, we can specify the frequency based on general mathematical principles.

In everyday business, a priori probabilities cannot be specified. To assign probabilities to various outcomes, businesspeople must rely on statistical probabilities. These may be obtained empirically, based on past events. For instance, if a particular event has occurred once every 10 times in the past, a 10 percent probability would be assigned to it. If probabilities of future events are assigned based on the past, then we are assuming that the future is a mirror of the past (which in itself could be construed to be an a priori judgment). Alternatively, probabilities obtained from past events can be adjusted to reflect changed expectations for the future.

Sources of Business Risk

Before discussing how risk should be treated in economic analysis, it is important that we first explain the reasons a businessperson faces an uncertain future. What are some of the sources of business risk?[4]

First, there are general economic conditions. Firms face rising and declining phases of business cycles. Some success can be attained in forecasting economic fluctuations, but the timing of changes and the volatility of economic activity are never known with certainty. Moreover, the effects of movements in general economic activity on a specific firm or a specific product are not known ahead of time. Thus, a firm does not have the ability to completely prepare for these changes.

In addition to uncertainty with respect to the economy as a whole, there are fluctuations in specific industries, which are at least as uncertain and may not always coincide with those of the overall economy.

But fluctuations in the economy or in a specific industry are not the only sources of uncertainty faced by a firm. The actions of a company's competition are certainly not known perfectly. Closely related to competitive actions are changes in technology. If a competitor effectively introduces an improved product, sales of a particular company or even an industry may suffer. For in-

[3] *Ibid.*, pp. 224–225. The names *objective* and *subjective* probabilities, respectively, can also be used.

[4] We will discuss only business risk in this chapter. In finance texts other types of risk are also explored. For instance, there is "financial" risk, which is a function of a firm's capital structure, or the relationship between debt and stockholder equity. Usually, the higher the fraction of the business that is financed with debt, the greater is the financial risk.

stance, the introduction of fax machines has cut into the overnight delivery business and one-hour film development has hurt Polaroid's business. On the other hand, a firm's own technological breakthrough may bring about considerably increased sales.

The vagaries of consumer demand create another source of risk for the businessperson. Successful products of one year or one season may become the discarded, unwanted items of the next. It is easy to find examples of such products. Cabbage Patch dolls—hot items for a year or two—met their demise suddenly. The fashion industry is notorious for changes in styles and skirt lengths from one year to another.[5] The great boom in bowling in the 1960s disappeared some years later and caused serious dislocations for the leading companies in the industry.

Not all sources of uncertainty stem from the demand side. In the process of decision making, a company must also consider costs and expenses. When estimates of future expenditures are made, the company cannot be sure what the prices of its factors of production will be (unless they are stipulated in contracts into which a company has entered). Thus, the prices of materials, such as sugar, corn starch, and flavorings, can change, and so can the costs of electricity and other services. Labor costs and the cost of benefits are also subject to change unless union contracts are in existence.

To summarize our discussion, it is easy to see that almost any future business event is attended by uncertainty. Both revenues and costs per period as well as the length of life of a product are uncertain. Obviously, this greatly complicates the jobs of managers.

The Measures of Risk

When outcomes are uncertain, two measures that take risk into consideration are used.

First, not just one outcome but a number of outcomes is possible. Each potential result will have a probability attached to it. In making estimates of a future cash inflow, for example, the analyst must decide on the probability of each possible result. He or she must construct a probability distribution.

A probability distribution describes, in percentage terms, the chances of all possible occurrences. When all the probabilities of the possible events are added up, they must total 1, because all possibilities together must equal certainty. Thus, we may assign probabilities to various possible cash flows as shown in Table 15.1.

The interpretation of Table 15.1 is as follows: We estimate that possible cash flows from a project during the coming year will be \$3,000, \$4,000, \$5,000, \$6,000 or \$7,000. Which of the five possible flows actually occurs will depend,

[5] Some of these changes are brought about by the leading designers in the industry. In these cases, the consumers are influenced—or sometimes actually dictated to—by the industry.

Table 15.1 Probability Distribution for Cash Inflows

Cash Inflow	*Probability*
3,000	.1
4,000	.2
5,000	.4
6,000	.2
7,000	.1

for instance, on general economic conditions, the conditions in the industry, and the action of the competition. If all factors are favorable to the project, the cash flow will be $7,000; if unfavorable conditions prevail, the cash flow will be only $3,000. One of the other outcomes will emerge if some factors work to our benefit and others are unfavorable. Table 15.1 can also be translated into a bar chart, shown in Figure 15.1.

The assigned probabilities indicate that there is only a 10 percent chance that all the unfavorable predictions will materialize. Similarly, there is only 1 chance in 10 (i.e., 10 percent) that all of the favorable conditions will prevail. It is much more likely that some favorable and some unfavorable influences will ensue. Therefore, the probabilities for the intermediate cash flows are the highest.

Once we have established a probability distribution, we are ready to calculate the two measures used in decision making under conditions of risk.

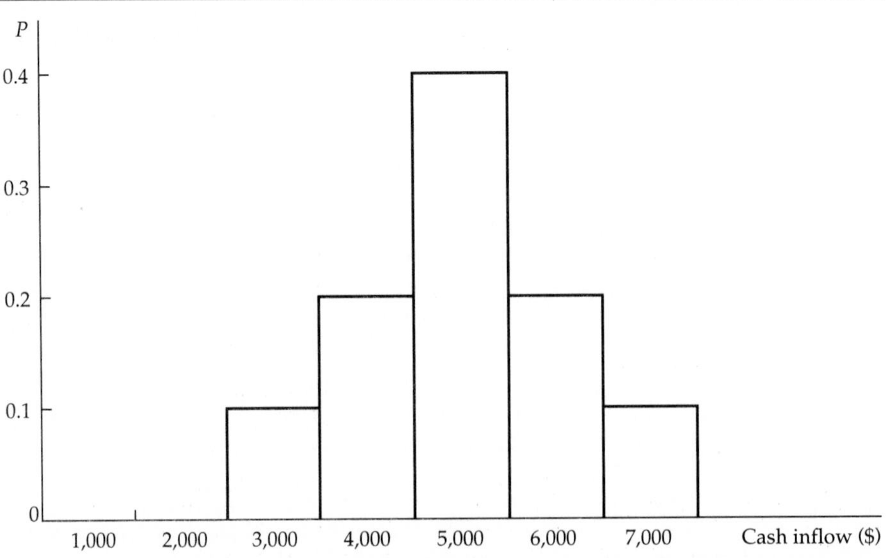

Figure 15.1 Bar Graph of Data from Table 15.1

Expected Value

Whereas only one possible cash flow has been designated in past chapters, where risk was not considered, we must now address several possible flows, each with a given probability. From this distribution, it is necessary to calculate a single value for cash flow. This is accomplished by computing the *expected value* of the possible outcomes. The expected value is simply the average of all possible outcomes weighted by their respective probabilities. Using the numbers from Table 15.1,

$$\begin{aligned}\overline{R} &= (3{,}000 \times .1) + (4{,}000 \times .2) + (5{,}000 \times .4) + (6{,}000 \times .2) + (7{,}000 \times .1) \\ &= 300 + 800 + 2{,}000 + 1{,}200 + 700 \\ &= 5{,}000\end{aligned}$$

where R represents the expected value. The generalized expression for expected value is as follows:

$$\overline{R} = \sum_{i=1}^{n} R_i p_i$$

where $\overline{R}$ = Expected value
R_i = Value in case i
p_i = Probability in case i
n = Number of possible outcomes

Now that the weighted average—the expected value—has been obtained, we can determine the second measure, the one that specifies the extent of the risk.

The Standard Deviation

In economics and finance, risk is considered to be the dispersion of possible outcomes around the mean outcome, the expected value. The greater the potential differences from the average, the greater the risk. Thus, to measure risk, we must find some yardstick that reflects the variation of possible outcomes from this average. A concept prominent in elementary statistics is used for this purpose—the standard deviation.[6]

The standard deviation is the square root of the weighted average of the squared deviations of all possible outcomes from the expected value:

$$\sigma = \sqrt{\sum_{i=1}^{n} (R_i - \overline{R})^2 p_i}$$

where σ is the standard deviation. For the example in Table 15.1, the standard deviation is calculated in Table 15.2.

[6]If you wish to review the concept of standard deviations, any college textbook can be consulted, for instance, Heinz Kohler, *Statistics for Business and Economics*, Glenview, Ill: Scott, Foresman, 1985, pp. 115ff.

Table 15.2 Calculation of Standard Deviation for Table 15.1

R_i	$(R_i - \overline{R})$	$(R_i - \overline{R})^2$	p_i	$(R_i - \overline{R})^2 p_i$
3,000	−2,000	4,000,000	.1	400,000
4,000	−1,000	1,000,000	.2	200,000
5,000	0	0	.4	0
6,000	1,000	1,000,000	.2	200,000
7,000	2,000	2,000,000	.1	400,000
				1,200,000

$$\sigma = \sqrt{1,200,000} = 1,095$$

What is the meaning of a standard deviation of 1,095? First of all, since our probability distribution is symmetric, there is a 50 percent chance that the outcome will be larger than the expected value and a 50 percent chance that it will be less. The chance of a particular outcome occurring depends on how many standard deviations it is removed from the mean. Based on statistical theory describing the normal curve (which will be discussed more fully later), about 34 percent of all possible occurrences will be within one standard deviation of the mean, on each side of the mean, 47.7 percent within two standard deviations, and 49.9 percent within three standard deviations. Thus, given the expected value of 5,000 and standard deviation of 1,095, we conclude the following: There is 34 percent probability that the cash flow will fall between 5,000 and $5,000 - 1,095$, or 3,905. In other words, there is a 16 percent probability that our cash flow will be 3,905 or lower. Further, since two standard deviations are equal to 2,190, there is a 2.3 percent probability (50 percent − 47.7 percent) that the cash flow will be 2,810 or lower. And it is almost certain that the cash flow will not fall below 1,715 (5,000 minus three standard deviations, or 3,285). The same reasoning leads us to conclude that chances are almost nil that the cash flow will exceed 8,285. There is a 16 percent probability that it will exceed 6,095, and so on.

The combination of the expected value and the standard deviation aids in making a decision between two projects. Suppose that we have to choose between project 1 (shown in Tables 15.1 and 15.2) and another, called project 2. Data for project 2 are shown in Table 15.3, and Figure 15.2 is the bar chart for this project.

Since the expected values of the two proposals are identical, the decision will be made on the basis of the standard deviation. Which of the two projects is riskier? Project 2, with the greater standard deviation (1,710), is the riskier of the two. Generally, businesspeople are risk-averse; therefore, project 1, which has the lower risk, would usually be accepted.

As already stated, there is a 16 percent chance that the outcome for project 1 will be less than 3,905. However, for project 2, the 16 percent probability holds for an outcome of less than 3,290. In addition, chances are just about nil that project 1 will show a result less than 1,715, which is three standard deviations

Table 15.3 Data for Project 2

R_i	p_i	$(R_i - \overline{R})$	$(R_i - \overline{R})^2$	$(R_i - \overline{R})^2 p_i$
2,000	.10	−3,000	9,000,000	900,000
3,500	.25	−1,500	2,250,000	562,500
5,000	.30	0	0	0
6,500	.25	1,500	2,250,000	562,500
8,000	.10	3,000	9,000,000	900,000
				2,925,000

$$\overline{R} = 5,000$$
$$\sigma = \sqrt{2,925,000} = 1,710$$

below the mean. But for project 2, there is a small chance that the result will actually be negative (three standard deviations equal 5,130). It is quite evident which is the riskier project.[7]

Discrete versus Continuous Distributions and the Normal Curve

The frequency distributions that have been discussed so far are known as discrete.[8] The potential outcomes have been limited to just five numbers (3,000,

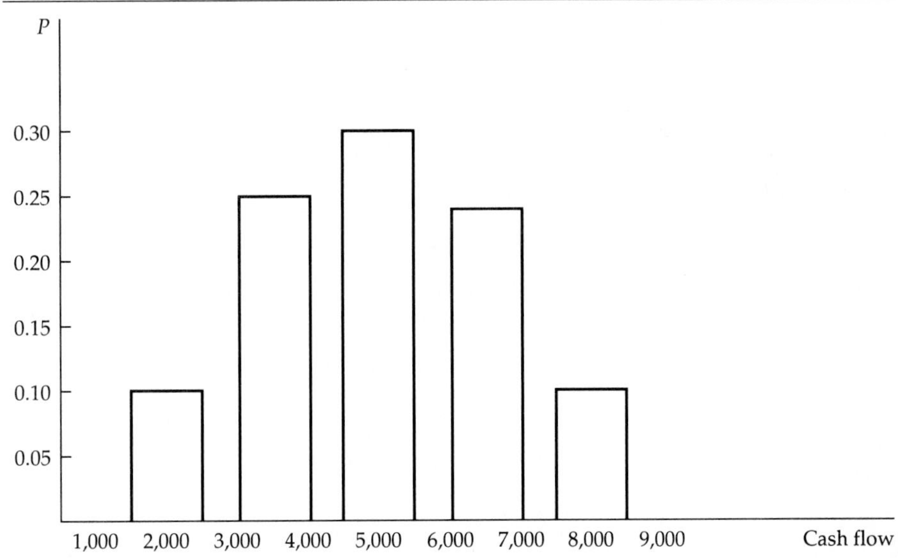

Figure 15.2 Bar Chart of Data from Table 15.3

[7]Of course, project 2 has the potential to achieve a larger final result (5,000 + 3 × 1,710) than project 1, but for a risk-averse businessperson, it is the low end of the distribution that is important.

[8]They are also symmetrical, which means that the observations to the left and to the right of the mean have the same probabilities and the same deviations from the mean.

4,000, 5,000, 6,000 and 7,000 for project 1; and 2,000, 3,500, 5,000, 6,500 and 8,000 for project 2). However, it is quite likely that other outcomes could occur—for instance, 4,679 or 6,227. If all possible outcomes are considered, we have a continuous distribution. The possible outcomes on a continuous distribution are often described by a bell-shaped curve, referred to as a *normal curve*. It is only on this type of curve that the properties of the standard deviation previously explained apply strictly. The normal curve, shown in Figure 15.3, peaks at the center, at the expected value, and is symmetrical on either side. Actually, the curve approaches but does not reach zero at either end of the X-axis. Curves of this kind are called *asymptotic*.

With projects 1 and 2 drawn as continuous standard normal probability functions, Project 1 exhibits a tighter curve, whereas project 2's curve is spread out over a much larger horizontal distance. Since project 1's standard deviation is 1,095, 34 percent of the area under its curve is between 5,000 and 3,905 (and also between 5,000 and 6,095). For project 2, whose standard deviation is 1,710, 34 percent of the area under the curve can be found between 5,000 and 3,290 (and also between 5,000 and 6,710).

The probabilities for any other range of numbers can be easily obtained from a table of values of the areas under the standard normal distribution function, (see Table A.2 at the end of this text). If, in assessing project 1, we wish to find the probability that the cash flow will be between, for example, 3,200 and 5,000, we can apply the following formula:

$$Z = \frac{X - \bar{R}}{\sigma}$$

where Z = Number of standard deviations from the mean
X = Variable in which we are interested

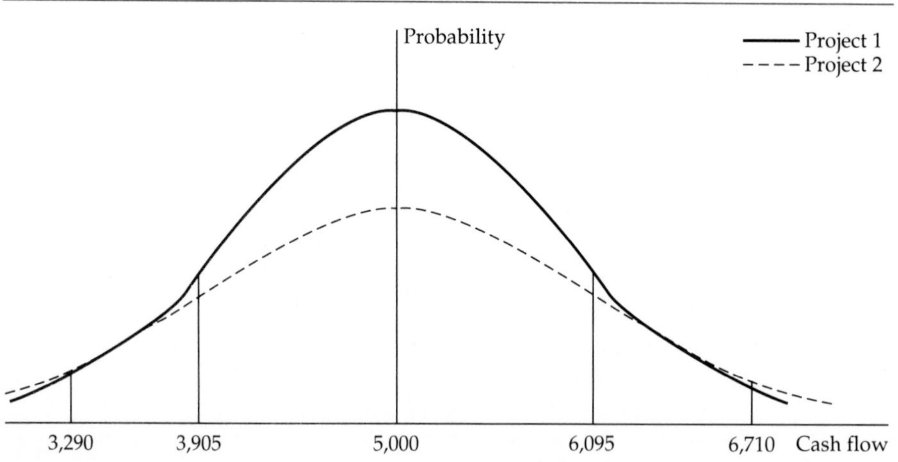

Figure 15.3 Continuous Distributions for Projects 1 and 2

Thus,

$$Z = \frac{3{,}200 - 5{,}000}{1{,}095} = \frac{-1{,}800}{1{,}095} = -1.64$$

The quantity 3,200 is 1.64 standard deviations below the mean. Looking up 1.64 in Table A.2, we find the value to be .4495. Thus, the probability that the cash flow will be between 3,200 and 5,000 is 45 percent. Since the left half of the normal curve represents 50 percent of all probabilities, we can also state that the chance of the cash flow being below 3,200 is 5.0 percent.

The Coefficient of Variation

When the expected values of two projects are equal, or at least close to one another, the standard deviation is a proper measure of risk. But since the standard deviation is an absolute measure, it may not serve our purposes if the two projects being compared have divergent expected values. For example, compare the two following hypothetical projects:

	Expected Value	*Standard Deviation*
Project A	100	30
Project B	50	20

Project A has both the larger expected value and the larger standard deviation.

Since the expected values of the two projects are so dissimilar, an absolute measure of risk may not give an adequate answer. In such cases, another concept is introduced, the *coefficient of variation*, which measures risk relative to expected value. The simple formula for the coefficient of variation is

$$CV = \sigma/\overline{R}$$

For the two projects,

$$CV_A = 30/100 = .30$$
$$CV_B = 20/50 = .40$$

The coefficient of variation is greater for project B. Thus, despite the fact that project A's standard deviation is higher in absolute terms, its relative risk is lower. Since project A's expected value is greater and relative risk is smaller, project A is preferable.

The coefficient of variation will provide a satisfactory solution in most cases. However, when it does not, the businessperson will have to make a choice based on the perception of whether the risk is worth the potential return.[9]

Capital Budgeting Under Conditions of Risk

So far the discussion of expected value and risk has been limited to the results of one period only. However, the assessment of risk is even more important when plans span a term of several years. So we now turn to the question of how to deal with a capital investment proposal in which an initial outlay of funds promises to return cash flows over some period into the future. In Chapter 14, the analysis of capital projects was discussed, but risk was not considered explicitly.

The first task is to calculate the net present value of the expected values obtained in each year, or the expected net present value. For a three-year project with one initial investment, we can use the following equation:

$$\overline{\text{NPV}} = \frac{\overline{R}_1}{1 + r_f} + \frac{\overline{R}_2}{(1 + r_f)^2} + \frac{\overline{R}_3}{(1 + r_f)^3} - O_0$$

or, in more general terms,

$$\overline{\text{NPV}} = \sum_{t=1}^{n} \frac{\overline{R}_t}{(1 + r_f)^t} - O_0$$

where $\overline{\text{NPV}}$ = Expected net present value

$\overline{R}_t$ = Expected values of the annual cash inflows

O_0 = Initial investment

r_f = Riskless interest rate

It should be noted that the expected cash flows are discounted at the riskless interest rate. Since risk is considered separately (in calculating the standard

[9]The economic theory of the marginal utility of money can also provide a way to incorporate risk in decision making. Although such an approach is quite elegant, it is somewhat doubtful that it can be utilized in most practical situations. To apply this approach, one would have to know the utility function of the decision maker, or of the stockholders the decision maker represents. This appears to be a rather monumental task. However, in the final analysis, it is the decision maker's perception of risk that determines the shape of the utility function. Thus, the decision is a subjective one. For a more detailed explanation of utility, see for example, Haim Levy and Marshall Sarnat, *Capital Investment and Financial Decisions*, 4th ed. Hertfordshire, England: Prentice Hall International, 1986, pp. 195ff. This exposition is based on the famous work of John Von Neumann and Oskar Morgenstern, *Theory of Games and Economic Behavior*, 2d. ed. Princeton, N.J.: Princeton University Press, 1953.

deviation), discounting at a rate that includes a risk premium could result in double-counting risk.[10]

The standard deviation of the present value is

$$\sigma = \sqrt{\sum_{t=1}^{n} \frac{\sigma_t^2}{(1 + r_f)^{2t}}}$$

where σ = Standard deviation of NPV

σ_t = Standard deviation of each year's cash flow

Note that the exponent in the denominator of the expression is $2t$. Thus, the first year's σ will be discounted at $(1 + r_f)^2$, the second at $(1 + r_f)^4$, and so on.

Table 15.4 Capital Budgeting Under Risk

Expected Value

	headYear 0	Year 1		Year 2	
	p	R	p	R	
	−500	.2	300	.25	400
		.6	500	.50	500
		.2	700	.25	600
$\overline{R}$			500		500

$$r = .05$$

$$\overline{\text{NPV}} = 500/1.05 + 500/1.05^2 - 500$$
$$= 476 + 454 - 500 = 430$$

Standard Deviation

Year 1				Year 2			
p	$(R - \overline{R})$	$(R - \overline{R})^2$	$(R - \overline{R})^2 p$	p	$(R - \overline{R})$	$(R - \overline{R})^2$	$(R - \overline{R})^2 p$
.2	−200	40,000	8,000	.25	−100	10,000	2,500
.6	0	0	0	.50	0	0	0
.2	+200	40,000	8,000	.25	+100	10,000	2,500
			16,000				5,000

$$\sigma = \sqrt{16,000/1.05^2 + 5,000/1.05^4}$$
$$= \sqrt{14,512 + 4,114} = \sqrt{18,626} = 136$$

[10] Actually, the use of the proper discount rate is subject to some controversy. In discounting at the risk-free rate, we have followed the method recommended in several books, Levy and Sarnat, op. cit. pp. 215–16; and James C. Van Horne, *Financial Management and Policy*, 8th ed. Englewood Cliffs, N.J.: Prentice-Hall. 1989. pp. 160–62. However, other authors suggest that the company's (or the specific unit's or project's) risk-adjusted discount rate is more appropriate. See, for example, Lawrence J. Gitman, Michael D. Joehnk, and George E. Pinches, *Managerial Finance*, New York: Harper & Row, 1985, pp. 582–83; and Eugene F. Brigham and Louis C. Gapenski, *Intermediate Financial Management*, 3d ed., Hinsdale, Ill.: Dryden, p. 350. Using the lower, risk-free rate will increase the project's net present value and make it more acceptable.

A simple numerical example will conclude this section. Table 15.4 shows that for a two-year project with a cash flow distribution and probabilities as specified, and with an initial investment of \$500, the expected net present value is \$430, and the standard deviation is 136. From these results we can conclude that chances are almost zero that NPV will be less than 22 (430 minus three standard deviations of 136) or more than 838 (430 plus three standard deviations of 136).

The preceding calculations are generally valid when the cash flows over the years are independent, that is, if in the case depicted in Table 15.4, the results in year 2 are not influenced by those of year 1.

Two Other Methods for Incorporating Risk

Up to this point, two measures have been used in connection with the evaluation of risk. The first was the expected value, or the expected net present value of a project spanning a period of time. The second was the standard deviation, which represents a gauge of the extent of the risk. Given these two yardsticks, the decision maker has to determine whether the profitability of a project is sufficient to offset the risk involved.

Two other techniques of accounting for risk are commonly used. Both of these make the risk adjustment within the present-value calculation, so that the final result is just one number: the net present value adjusted for risk. The two methods are:

1. The risk-adjusted discount rate (RADR), in which the risk adjustment is made in the denominator of the present-value calculation.
2. The certainty equivalent, in which the numerator of the present-value calculation is adjusted for risk.

The Risk Adjusted Discount Rate (RADR)

RADR is probably the most practical risk adjustment method and is the one most frequently used in business. In fact, we employed this technique in Chapter 14, in the discussion of the cost of capital. The discount rate at which capital project flows are discounted to the present comprises two components, the riskless (or risk-free) rate, r_f, and the risk premium, RP:

$$k = r_f + \text{RP}$$

The risk-free rate is, in the ideal sense, the pure time value of money. Since such a rate is very difficult—if not impossible—to establish, it is usually represented by yields on short-term U.S. Treasury securities.[11] The risk premium represents a judgment as to the additional return necessary to compensate for additional risk.

[11] Of course, even the shortest of U.S. Treasuries, the three-month bill, includes an inflation factor in its yield.

For example, assume that the risk-free rate is 6 percent, but that a corporation uses a cost of capital of 10 percent for projects which are thought to carry average risk. The risk premium is 4 percent. The firm is not, however, limited to using the 10 percent rate for all of its projects or, for that matter, for all of its divisions. A company may be composed of a number of divisions or subsidiaries, each of which may represent a different level of risk.[12] In such a case, the parts of the company that sell products in markets not considered to be very risky may be discounted at 8 percent, while areas engaged in the production of more risky goods or services could carry a discount rate of 12 percent. Furthermore, the discount rates within a particular division can differ from project to project if some projects appear to be subject to greater risk than others.

As a matter of fact, it is very important that appropriate discount rates be used for individual parts of the company or individual projects. A correct specification of the discount rate is necessary to achieve the optimal allocation of company resources. As an example, assume that a company is composed of two divisions, the Risk division and the Sure division. The company's overall cost of capital has been estimated to be 12 percent. If no differentiation between the two divisions is made, then all projects with internal rates of return of 12 percent or more[13] should be accepted. However, if the Risk division's cost of capital should really be 14 percent, there is the possibility that projects that do not earn the Risk division's required return will be implemented if the company applies its average cost of capital of 12 percent and does not distinguish the two divisions. On the other hand, the Sure division's appropriate discount rate may be 10 percent. In this case, a project with an internal rate of return of 11.5 percent proposed by the Sure division would be rejected if the overall 12 percent hurdle rate were applied across the board. A recent study shows that about 70 percent of a sample of companies drawn from the Fortune 1,000 either individually measure project risk or group projects into risk classes.[14]

Of course, it must be recognized that developing risk-adjusted discount rates involves a large amount of judgment. But even if such adjustments are necessarily judgmental, they are very important. Companies with staffs capable of such refinements have developed some methods for differentiating discount rates.[15]

Certainty Equivalents

In calculating the risk-adjusted discount rate, the inclusion of risk in the calculation of present value is accomplished by altering the discount rate or the cost

---

[12]For instance, a hypothetical company may have two operating divisions, a supermarket chain and an electronics enterprise.

[13]Or an NPV no less than zero when all cash flows are discounted at the cost of capital.

[14]Lawrence J. Gitman and Vincent A. Mercurio, "Cost of Capital Techniques Used by Major U.S. Firms: Survey and Analysis of Fortune's 1000," *Financial Management*, Winter 1982, pp. 21–29.

[15]See, for instance, Benton E. Gup and Samuel W. Norwood III, "Divisional Cost of Capital: A Practical Approach," *Financial Management*, Spring 1982, pp. 20–24.

of capital, that is, the denominator of the discounting equation.[16] Another technique for including risk in the calculation of present values is to work through the numerator of the cash flow fraction; that is, the cash flow itself is adjusted to account for risk. Basically, this is accomplished by applying a factor to the cash flow to convert a risky flow into a riskless one. Since, as was said before, businesspeople tend to be risk-averse, they are expected to prefer a smaller cash flow that is certain (riskless) over one that is attended by risky conditions. To accomplish this, the risky cash flow must be reduced by some amount, or multiplied by a number smaller than 1. We will refer to this adjustor as the *certainty equivalent factor*.

However, assigning a size to the certainty equivalent factor is fraught with at least as many problems as estimating the risk premium. Again, the economic theory of utility would be useful in obtaining certainty equivalents.[17] But when all is said and done, the size of the certainty equivalent factor depends on the decision maker's attitude toward risk. Thus, if he or she decides that a specific risky cash flow (or the expected value of the risky cash flow) of $500 is equivalent to a riskless cash flow of $450, the certainty equivalent factor, a_t, equals .9:

$$.9 \times 500 = 450$$

So, for each risky cash flow, R_t, a certainty equivalent factor is assigned. If risk increases as a function of time, the certainty equivalent factors will decrease as we move into the future. For instance, a project could have the following cash flows and certainty equivalent factors:

Period	R_t	a_t	a_tR_t
1	100	.95	95
2	200	.90	180
3	200	.85	170
4	100	.80	80

[16] In other words, the discounted cash flows can be expressed as follows:

$$PV = \sum_{t=1}^{n} \frac{\overline{R}_t}{(1 + r_f + RP)^t}$$

The risk is included in the formula by increasing the denominator for different level of RP.

[17] A simple illustration should suffice. Suppose you are faced with the opportunity to receive either $1,000 or nothing and the probabilities are 50 percent for each event. The expected value, therefore, is $500. You are asked how much you would be willing to pay for this investment. If you say $500, you are considered risk-indifferent. If you are risk-averse, you will offer less than $500 for this investment. Suppose you offer $400. This means that you consider a risky expected value of $500 to be worth $400; in other words, the certainty equivalent factor, a_t, is .8 (since $a_tR_t = \$400$).

The risk-free cash flows, $a_t R_t$, are obviously smaller than the risky flows, R_t, as would be expected for a risk-averse investor. These riskless cash flows are then discounted at the risk-free interest rate to obtain the present value of the cash flows.

RADR versus Certainty Equivalents

Two methods of accounting for risk without specifically calculating a standard deviation have just been presented. Which of the two is preferable? The certainty equivalent technique appears to be more sophisticated and is often recommended by people in academia. Businesspeople prefer RADR, which is by far the more frequently used technique. The reason for this preference is fairly obvious. It is considerably easier to make a rough estimate of the cost of capital than to specifically calculate each cash flow's certainty equivalent factor. However, it can be shown that the two methods arrive at identical results if the calculations and adjustments are made in a consistent and correct manner.

The present value of a risky cash flow discounted at the risk-adjusted discount rate can be written as follows:

$$\frac{R_t}{(1+k)^t}$$

On the other hand, the present value of a risk-adjusted cash flow discounted at the risk-free rate is:

$$\frac{a_t R_t}{(1+r_f)^t}$$

If the two discounted cash flows are to be equal, then:

$$\frac{R_t}{(1+k)^t} = \frac{a_t R_t}{(1+r_f)^t}$$

$$a_t = \frac{(1+r_f)^t}{(1+k)^t}$$

Thus, the certainty equivalent factor is equal to $(1 + r_f)$ divided by $(1 + k)$, each term raised to the appropriate power.

Sensitivity Analysis

Sensitivity analysis is a very pragmatic way to estimate project risk. It involves identifying the key variables that affect the results (the NPV of a project or its internal rate of return), and then changing each variable (and sometimes a combination of variables) to ascertain the size of the impact. Since the outcomes of a sensitivity analysis can be displayed and presented in a very simple and straightforward manner, it is a method quite frequently used in business.

To explain and illustrate the concept of sensitivity analysis, we will utilize the data that were presented in Table 14.1 of the previous chapter. However, we will simplify the worksheet by combining product and distribution costs, which are a function of the number of cases shipped; by combining expenses, which are a percentage of dollar revenue; and by combining all the fixed costs. This is shown in Table 15.5.

We must now decide which of the lines in the projected cash flow statement will have the gratest impact on results. The following four items are probably key factors:

1. Number of cases sold
2. Sales price
3. Product and distribution costs
4. Variable expenses

Since the amount of capital expenditures is fairly certain, fixed costs will not be used as a test variable. Nor will the remaining book values, because they are expected to occur in the rather distant future, and thus their present value would have a relatively minor effect on net present value.

Next, a decision must be made on the range of the changes in the variables. The changes will be tested at 10 percent intervals between −40 percent and +40 percent. Admittedly, these are very wide ranges, and the extremes would represent very serious deviations from the best estimates. However, using such wide ranges is quite useful in pointing out by how much the forecasters would have had to miss their estimates to convert a positive NPV into a negative one. Furthermore, should a particular percentage point in between appear to be important for the analysis, it could easily be computed and added to the table of numbers. The results are summarized in Table 15.6.

Of the four variables selected for closer scrutiny, sales price appears to have the most serious impact. NPV turns negative if the price per case drops by a little over 10 percent. Of course, this will occur only if production and distribution costs do not decrease concurrently. But there is no reason that they should, unless the price decrease follows a cost decrease. Prices could decline for other reasons, such as intense competition.

Since a large amount of variable costs and expenses can be saved if sales quantities do not come up to the best estimate, a drop in sales of about 35 percent below estimated levels would have to occur before NPV would become negative. On the other hand, an increase of between 10 and 20 percent in production and distribution costs would make the NPV unacceptable. An error in the estimate of the relationship of variable expenses to revenue would not have a significant impact on net present value.

One other analysis should also be performed: the effect of an error in the assumed discount rate. Fifteen percent was the risk-adjusted rate that was employed. Since the internal rate of return on the project was 24.2 percent, it would take an increase of more than 9 percentage points to reverse the recommendation. That appears to be too large a margin to occur within any reasonable assumptions.

The results of the sensitivity analysis can also be shown in graphical form, as in Figure 15.4. The effect on net present value, shown on the vertical axis, can be related to each of the percentage changes in a given variable shown on the

Table 15.5 Expansion Project: Sensitivity Analysis Worksheet (000)

	Constant	*Year 0*	*Year 1*	*Year 2*	*Year 3*	*Year 4*	*Year 5*	*Year 6*	*Year 7*
Total market	4.0%			100,000	104,000	108,160	112,486	116,986	121,665
Market share				1.0%	2.0%	3.0%	4.0%	5.0%	5.0%
Company sales	1.00			1,000	2,080	3,245	4,499	5,849	6,083
Expenditures		−5,000	−2,000						
Working capital			−750						
Start-up expense	750		−450						
Sales	5.00			5,000	10,400	16,224	22,497	29,246	30,416
Prod. & dist. cost	3.10			3,100	6,448	10,059	13,948	18,133	18,858
Variable expenses	8.0%			400	832	1,298	1,800	2,339	2,433
Fixed costs				1,031	1,361	1,121	1,001	911	881
Total cost & exp.				4,531	8,641	12,478	16,749	21,383	22,172
NEBT				469	1,759	3,746	5,748	7,863	8,244
Income tax	40.0%			188	704	1,498	2,299	3,145	3,298
NEAT				281	1,055	2,248	3,449	4,718	4,946
Add depr.				531	861	621	501	411	381
Oper. cash flow				812	1,916	2,869	3,950	5,129	5,327
Remaining values									
Land									500
Plant									2,833
Equipment									360
Working capital	1.00								660
Total cash flow		−5,000	−3,200	812	1,916	2,869	3,950	5,129	9,680
Net present value	15.0%								3,552
IRR									24.2%

Note: This table and the calculations involved are included on the Lotus diskette furnished to your instructor.

Table 15.6 Results of Sensitivity Analysis: Expansion Project (NPV in $000)

Change (%)	*Sales*	*Sales Price*	*Cost*	*Variable Expenses*
+40	7,524	15,731	−4,655	2,493
+30	6,531	12,687	−2,603	2,758
+20	5,538	9,642	−552	3,023
+10	4,545	6,597	1,500	3,287
0	3,552	3,552	3,552	3,552
−10	2,559	507	5,604	3,817
−20	1,567	−2,537	7,656	4,082
−30	574	−5,582	9,708	4,347
−40	−419	−8,627	11,760	4,611

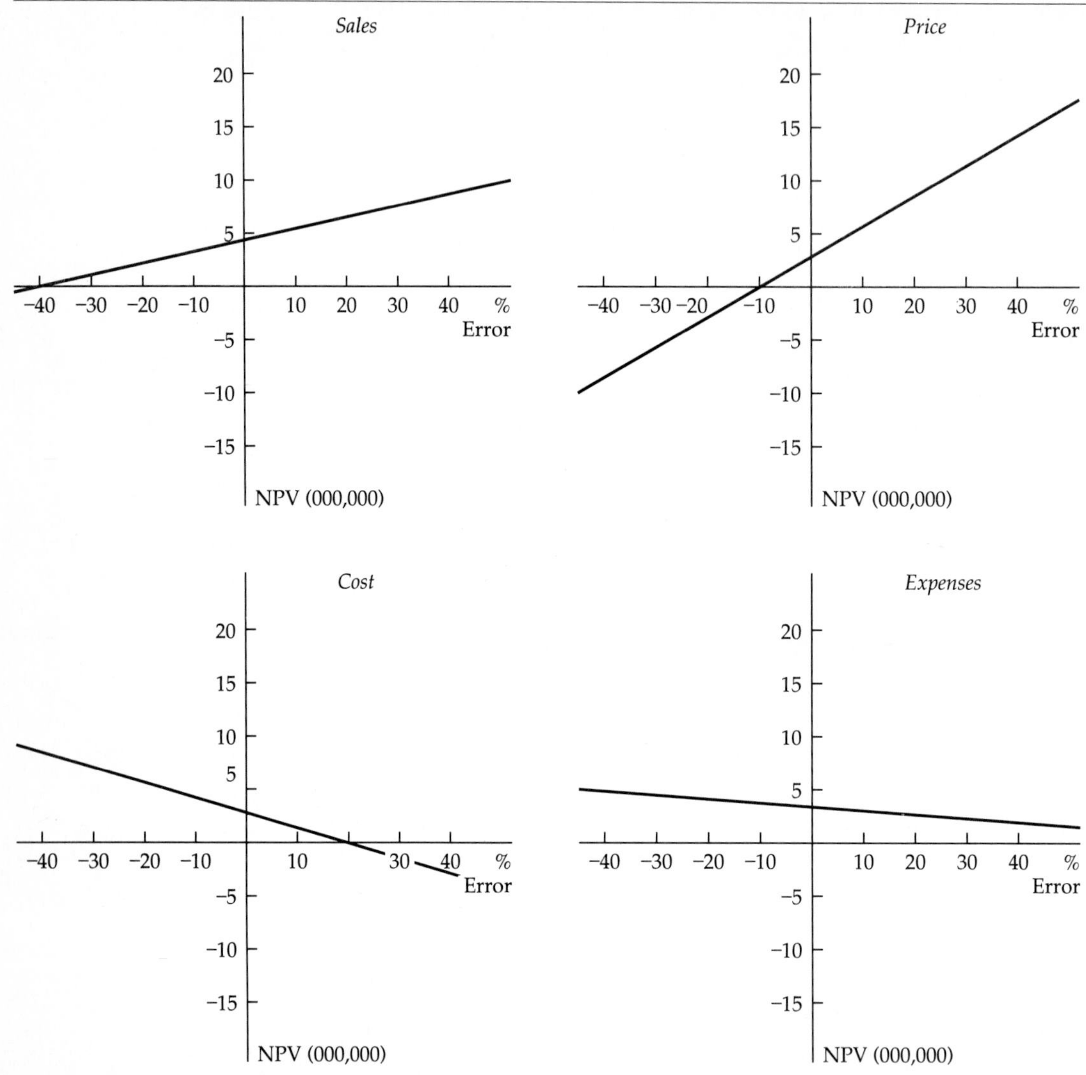

Figure 15.4 Results of Sensitivity Analysis

horizontal axis. In addition, it is quite easy to combine the changes in several variables by recomputing the numbers in the table.

Simulation

Although the sensitivity analysis technique is popular with business, it does not make use of probability distributions. But there is one method that does: simulation. In simulation analysis, each of the key variables is assigned a probability distribution. Thus, for instance, the sales variable of our previous example could be given the following distribution:

Deviation from estimate value (%)	*Probability*	*Cumulative Probability*
−30	.1	.1
−15	.2	.3
0	.4	.7
+15	.2	.9
+30	.1	1.0

The column of cumulative probabilities indicates that there is a 10 percent chance that sales will be 30 percent lower than the best case. Furthermore, the probability is 30 percent that sales will be at least 15 percent below the base case, 70 percent that sales will not exceed the best estimate, and so on. Similar distributions would be estimated for the other important variables.

The device of random numbers is used to "simulate" a possible outcome. Suppose a random number generator with numbers from 1 to 100 is utilized. For this case, we can assign numbers from 1 to 10 to represent the −30 percent case. Any number between 11 and 30 (which has a 20 percent chance of being drawn) would stand for a −15 percent sales situation. All numbers between 31 and 70 would represent 0 percent deviation (the base case estimate) and so on.

We will also assign probability distributions to the other three variables considered to have significant impacts on net present value. The next step is to generate a random number for each of these four key variables, obtain the appropriate values, and calculate a NPV figure. This process will then be repeated a large number of times, each time generating another NPV figure. The NPVs thus generated will form a probability distribution and also enable the analyst to calculate a standard deviation as well as a z-statistic.[18]

To show how each NPV can be obtained, we will calculate one iteration with the distributions shown in Table 15.7. Suppose the random numbers generated turn out to be 24, 37, 69, and 29, respectively. These numbers are associated with sales 15 percent below expectations, sales price and costs at expected values (i.e. 0 percent deviation), and variable expenses 5 percent below the best estimates. They result in a net present value of 2,175 and an internal rate of return of 20.9 percent. (These numbers were derived from the Lotus program included on the accompanying diskette.) If we repeat this operation a large number of times—say one thousand—we will obtain a frequency distribution of NPVs. Such a procedure appears to be very time-consuming and cumbersome. However, thanks to the existence of computers, a large number of iterations can be obtained quickly and effortlessly.

---

[18]The simulation procedure discussed here is based on a technique introduced by David B. Hertz in "Risk Analysis in Capital Investment," *Harvard Business Review*, January–February 1964, pp. 95–106, and "Investment Policies that Pay Off," *Harvard Business Review*, January–February 1968, pp. 96–108.

Table 15.7 Simulation Analysis

Sales:					
Deviation from expected value (%)	−30	−15	0	+15	+30
Probability	.1	.2	.4	.2	.1
Cumulative probability	.1	.3	.7	.9	1.0
Sales price:					
Deviation from expected value (%)	−20	−10	0	+10	+20
Probability	.1	.25	.3	.25	.1
Cumulative probability	.1	.35	.65	.90	1.0
Production and distribution costs:					
Deviation from expected value (%)	−10	−5	0	+5	+10
Probability	.1	.15	.5	.15	.1
Cumulative probability	.1	.25	.75	.9	1.0
Variable expenses:					
Deviation from expected value (%)	−10	−5	0	+5	+10
Probability	.1	.2	.4	.2	.1
Cumulative probability	.1	.3	.7	.9	1.0

Simulation can be a good tool for decision making. However, the illustration used here is severely simplified and may not be sufficient for the solution of complex business problems. In obtaining the preceding solution, we made at least two assumptions that, although making the calculations rather straightforward, may have omitted some important relationships among the variables. First, we assumed that the deviations obtained with the use of random numbers remain the same in each year for which estimated cash flows were calculated. This need not be the case. A set of different random number calculations for each year may have been more appropriate. With the use of a computer, such calculations could have been taken care of quite efficiently.

Even more important, it has been assumed here that the four variables are statistically independent. As may have already occurred to you, it is much more likely that the various factors are interrelated. For example, a shortfall in market demand may have a negative effect on the price of each case of soft drinks. An unexpected increase in sales may have an effect on costs: in the short run, cost per unit may rise as plant employees work overtime at increased wages. If such interdependencies actually exist, they must be included in the simulation model. Such a model would, of course, be considerably more complex. A large number of estimates relating to these relationships would have to be made. And even though such a model would present the manager with a significant amount of useful information, the final decision, as in all cases, would still have to be based on the decision maker's judgment. In other words, no amount of data and information will substitute for mature business thinking.

Decision Trees

One other method for making decisions under conditions of risk is the decision tree. This technique is especially suitable when decisions have to be made sequentially, for instance, if a decision two years hence depends on the outcome of an action undertaken today. Such decision making can be extremely complex, and the use of a tree diagram facilitates the process because it illustrates the sequence in which decisions must be made. It also compares the values (e.g., net present values) of the various actions that can be undertaken.

The best way to explain the technique is to use a relatively uncomplicated example. To manufacture a new product, a company must decide whether to buy a larger, more expensive, and more productive machine or a smaller, less expensive, and less productive one. If the demand for this new product turns out to be at the high end of the forecast, the purchase of the larger machine may turn out to be profitable; the smaller machine does not possess sufficient capacity to produce large quantities efficiently, and its purchase would require an additional machine to be purchased to satisfy the high demand. On the other hand, should the optimistic forecast turn out to be wrong, then the larger machine, if it were the one originally acquired, would not be used to capacity. The smaller machine, in this case, would be able to produce the quantities needed efficiently and profitably.

Such a scenario could be played out over several years, but we will assume that the life of this project, as well as of the machines, is just two years. The market and cash flow forecasts have been put together, and the decision tree analysis can begin. To simplify our task here, and also to save steps involving familiar calculations, we will assume that all flows occurring in the future (i.e., years 1 and 2) have already been converted to present values.

Table 15.8 shows all the probabilities and forecasts, and Figure 15.5 illustrates the decision tree with the resulting calculations. The first step in the analysis is to set up all the "branches" of the decision tree. As we move from left to right on the diagram, we are faced with decision points (e.g., acquire the large machine versus the small machine) and with chance events (e.g., the probabilities are 50/50 that the demand will be high/low). On the diagram, decision points are designated with squares and chance events with circles. When the entire tree is completed, the procedure is to move back from right to left, calculate the value of each branch, and where appropriate combine or eliminate branches.

Starting in the upper right, if the large machine is acquired and year 1 demand is high, there is a 75 percent probability that the second-year (present-value) cash flow will be \$500 and a 25 percent probability that it will be \$100. The expected value is, therefore, \$400. If the first-year demand is high, cash flow will be \$150 in year 1, so the present value of the cash flow of years 1 and 2 combined will be \$550. If first-year demand is low, the expected value of the second set of branches will be \$−37.50 (.25 × 300 + .75 × −150). The cash flow in year 1 when demand is low is \$−50, so the present value of the two cash flows combined will be \$−87.50. Since the probabilities are 50/50 that first-year demand will be high/low, the present value of cash flows, if the large machine is purchased, is \$231.25 (.5 × 550 + .5 × −87.50). Now the original investment of \$250 must be deducted, and the result is an NPV of \$−18.75.

If the small machine is acquired, a decision must be made at the end of year 1 if demand in that year is high: Should a second machine be purchased? If first-year demand is high and the second machine is acquired, then the present value of the year 2 cash flow is \$320 (.75 × 400 + .25 × 80). If the second machine

Table 15.8 Decision Tree Inputs

Demand Forecasts

Year 1: High 50% Low 50%

Year 2:

If year 1 is high: High 75% Low 25%

If year 1 is low: High 25% Low 75%

Cost of Machine

Large $250 Small $150

Cash Flows (present values)

If large machine is acquired:

Year 1:

If demand is high: $150

If demand is low: $−50

Year 2:

If year 1 demand is high:

If demand is high: $500

If demand is low: $100

If year 1 demand is low:

If demand is high: $300

If demand is low: $−150

If small machine is acquired:

Year 1:

If demand is high: $100

If demand is low: $30

Year 2:

If year 1 demand is high and second machine is acquired:

If demand is high: $400

If demand is low: $80

If year 1 demand is high and second machine is not acquired:

If demand is high: $250

If demand is low: $120

If year 1 demand is low:

If demand is high: $150

If demand is low: $0

is not acquired, the cash flow is $217.50 (.75 × 250 + .25 × 120). Since it would cost $150 to obtain the second small machine, the NPV of the former result is only $170 compared to $217.50. Therefore, the decision at this point would be not to expand productive capacity. We put an X over the "additional machine" branch in the tree to signify that we will ignore this branch as we continue our evaluation. So, if first-year demand is high with a cash flow of $100, the present value of the upper branch will be $217.50 + $100, or $317.50.

One more branch needs to be addressed. If the small machine is selected and demand is low in the first year, then the second-year expected value of the cash

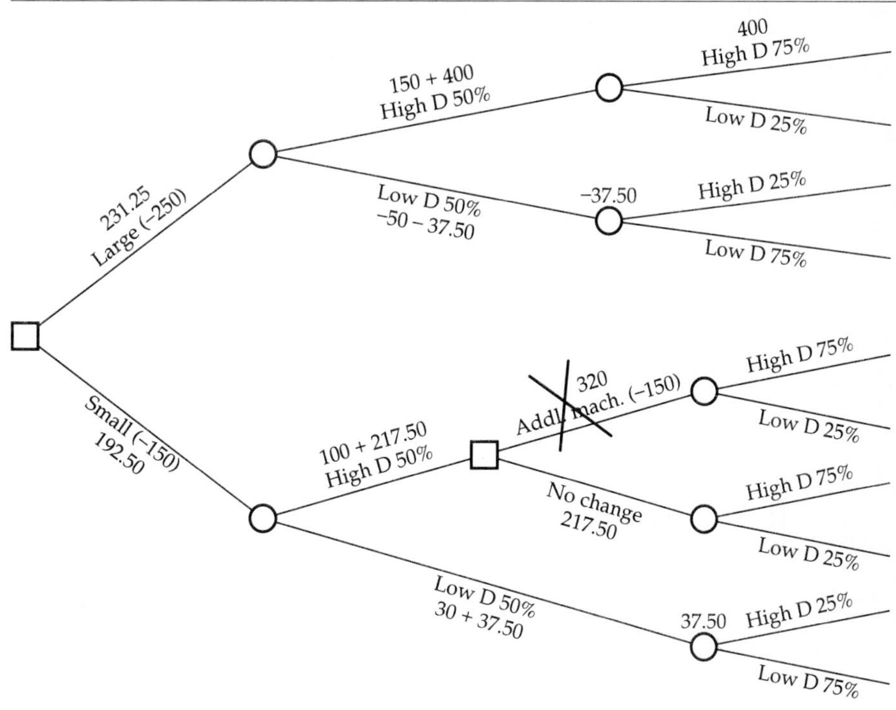

Figure 15.5 Decision Tree Analysis

flow will be \$37.50 (.25 × 150 + .75 × 0). Adding the first-year cash flow to this branch, we obtain \$67.50 (\$37.50 + \$30). To complete the calculation of the net present value for the small-machine alternative, each of the two present values must be multiplied by .5, since this is the probability that the first year's demand will be high/low: .5 × 317.50 + .5 × 67.50 equals \$192.50. Subtracting the cost of the smaller machine, \$150, we find that the net present value is \$42.50. The final step is to compare the expected net present values of the two alternatives. The expected NPV if the large machine is acquired is \$−18.75; if the smaller machine is selected, it is \$42.50. Thus, it is obvious that the smaller machine is the better choice. Indeed, the large machine would have been unacceptable in any case, since its net present value is negative.

The preceding solution is not quite complete, since the decision is being made on the basis of expected net present value alone. There has been no calculation of standard deviations, so we have, in effect, ignored the differences in risk between the large- and small-machine alternatives. As mentioned previously, risk can also be measured by the use of utility analysis. Each of the outcomes could have been assigned an expected utility, and instead of maximizing net present value, as we did in this example, the objective would have been to maximize utility.

The Solution

George Kline is now preparing to perform the risk analysis on the expansion project as requested by the treasurer. Although he is quite familiar with the various risk adjustment techniques, he heeds the treasurer's suggestion to stay away from statistical refinements. He decides to use sensitivity analysis for his presentation. (Since we used the expansion project data in explaining sensitivity analysis, we will now continue with the same data.)

George gives some thought to how to simplify Table 15.6 and show a combination of changes. He decides that he will present three summary estimates: worst case, base case, and best case. The base case will, of course, be the original analysis (developed in Chapter 14). The worst case will show all variables on the unfavorable side, and the best case will be the opposite. He tries out several combinations. He believes that certain variables are more likely to contain larger errors than others. For instance, he postulates that production and distribution costs, with which the company has experience in other geographic areas, is a fairly good estimate. However, since this new market is not well known, sales price and quantity are more likely to involve significant error, especially on the down side. Because of severe competition, a considerably higher sales price should not be expected. Also, since the company is attempting to penetrate a new market, the chances of falling short of the base estimate appear to be greater than those of surpassing it. He finally settles on the ranges shown in Table 15.9, which also include the resulting net present values and internal rates of return.

The worst case turns out to have a very negative NPV and an internal rate of return close to zero. To prepare for the presentation, George calculates several cases for which NPV is near zero and the internal rate of return is about 15 percent which, of course, is the required rate. He is thus able to show the magnitude of the errors that would cause the company to be indifferent to this proposal. Three combinations that provide such results are shown in Table 15.10. Many other calculations could have been made, but at this point George feels that he has a good handle on the presentation.

When the time for the presentation to top management arrived, George, accompanied by the treasurer, brought all of his charts to the conference room. George proceeded with his discussion, summarizing the forecasts and estimates and arriving at the recommended solution. He reviewed with management his sensitivity analysis, and the treasurer completed the presentation by recommending that the company go ahead and begin production in the new region.

(Continued)

Table 15.9 Three Possible Scenarios

	Worst Case	*Base Case*	*Best Case*
Percentage differences:			
Sales	−20	0	+20
Sales price	−15	0	+5
Prod. & distr. costs	+10	0	−10
Variable expenses	+10	0	−10
Net present value	−3, 909	3,552	10, 161
Internal rate of return	1.6%	24.2%	37.7%

Table 15.10 Additional Scenarios

	Case 1	*Case 2*	*Case 3*
Percentage differences:			
Sales	−10	−5	−7
Sales price	−6	−7	−5
Prod. & distr. costs	+5	+7	+7
Variable expenses	0	+5	+4.5
Net present value	−8	−2	0
Internal rate of return	15.0%	15.0%	15.0%

George felt that his presentation went well, and the treasurer commended him for a good job. But a few days later, the treasurer called George into his office and told him that management had, at least for the time being, decided not to go ahead with expansion. He explained that management felt that this was not the right time to expand, given the economy's somewhat cloudy future. Also, they considered the strength of their competition and decided that this was not the time to make the investment. Sensing George's disappointment, the treasurer assured him that he did an excellent job with the data he had. Actually, he said, the vice president of finance had told him to commend George for his substantial effort. "But that's the way things go in a large corporation," he continued. "You see, decisions are not always made on the basis of figures, however thoroughly they were developed. You must remember that in business, once the data have been put together, there is still the judgment factor that must be applied by management. After all, that's what top management gets paid for. I am sure that in the future, this or a similar project will be considered again."

Summary

In this chapter the emphasis has been on incorporating risk into the capital budgeting process. After we explained the differences between risk and uncertainty and examined some of the sources of business risk, the discussion concentrated on different techniques to measure risk. The most common measure of risk in economic and financial literature is the standard deviation, which measures the dispersion around the mean of a distribution of possible outcomes. The coefficient of variation, which puts the standard deviation on a relative basis, helps in comparing projects with unequal expected net present values. The Z-statistic is used to ascertain probabilities of an outcome being below a certain amount, above a certain amount, or within a range of amounts.

The calculation of the expected net present value and standard deviation for multiperiod projects under conditions of statistical independence was also discussed.

In real business situations, these calculations are often not employed because of their complexity. Instead, the discount rate is frequently adjusted to incorporate risk; the risk-adjusted discount rate (RADR) is a technique that is dominant in business. Another method of accounting for risk, the certainty equivalent, can give results identical to those obtained using the RADR; however, because of its greater theoretical complexity and the difficulty of defining certainty equivalents, this method is not very popular in business.

Additional techniques were discussed. One whose use is quite widespread—sensitivity analysis—was used in solving the situation presented at the beginning of the chapter. Although it doesn't consider the probabilities of occurrence, this method calculates answers to a series of what-if questions. It pinpoints the specific variables (on either the revenue or the cost side) that will have large and small impacts on the results.

The two other techniques explained in this chapter were the simulation and decision tree analyses. Both are fairly sophisticated procedures, and both leave much to be desired. The former becomes extremely complex if the interrelationships among variables are taken into account. Assuming the variables to be independent makes the analysis much more simple but ignores the importance of interdependencies. The decision tree method lends itself to sequential decision making. However, specifying sequences and the effects of one decision on another is extremely difficult. In addition, the results appear as expected net present values and do not explicitly include the analysis of risk.

Although many techniques of accounting for risk were discussed in this chapter, it is obvious that none of these methods is completely satisfactory. However, the important lesson of this chapter is that risk is ever present in business, and anyone engaging in business planning must be aware of the dangers of risky outcomes and be able to cope with the uncertainty of future events. Thus, the awareness of a risky situation may be more important than familiarity with any of the specific methods illustrated in this chapter.

Important Concepts

Certainty equivalent: A certain cash flow that would be acceptable as opposed to the expected value of a risky cash flow.

Coefficient of variation: A measure of risk relative to expected value that is used to compare standard deviations of projects with unequal expected values.

Decision tree: A method used with sequential decision making in which a diagram points out graphically the order in which decisions must be made and compares the value of the various actions that can be undertaken.

Expected value: An average of all possible outcomes weighted by their respective probabilities.

Probability: An expression of the chance that a particular event will occur.

Probability distribution: A distribution indicating the chances of all possible occurences.

Risk: Refers to a situation in which possible future events can be defined and probabilities assigned.

Risk-adjusted discount rate (RADR): A value equal to the riskless (risk-free) interest rate plus a risk premium. The riskless rate ideally is the pure time value of money, and the risk premium represents a judgment as to the additional return necessary to compensate for additional risk.

Sensitivity analysis: A method for estimating project risk that involves identifying the key variables that affect results and then changing each variable to measure the impact.

Simulation analysis: A method that assigns a probability distribution to each of the key variables and uses random numbers to simulate a set of possible outcomes to arrive at an expected value and dispersion.

Standard deviation: The degree of dispersion of possible outcomes around the mean outcome or expected value. It is the square root of the weighted average of the squared deviations of all possible outcomes from the expected value.

Uncertainty: Refers to situations in which there is no viable method of assigning probabilities to future random events.

Questions

1. Distinguish risk and uncertainty. Distinguish a priori and statistical probabilities.
2. Enumerate causes of business risk.
3. The following are the probabilities and outcomes for a certain event:

Probability	*Outcome*
.25	3,000
.50	4,000
.25	5,000

Does the table represent a discrete or a continuous distribution? Distinguish the two.

4. If two projects have different expected values, can the standard deviations be used to determine differences in risk?
5. Would a risk-averse person prefer a project whose distribution of potential outcomes can be drawn as a continuous normal curve with a very high peak and a steep decline around the peak?
6. Of what use is the table of values of areas under the standard normal distribution in determining the risk level of a project?
7. Define the coefficient of variation.
8. "All our projects are discounted at the same interest rate," says the treasurer of a large company. Would you dispute the advisability of such a procedure?
9. Why do companies use the RADR method much more frequently than the certainty equivalent method? Can the two methods arrive at the same result?
10. Is a person who regularly goes to horse races (and places bets) and has insured his house against fire acting inconsistently?
11. Describe and give examples of:
    a. Sensitivity analysis
    b. Simulation analysis
12. Explain the use of the decision tree in risk analysis. Is this a useful method? Is it the appropriate method for all types of analyses?

Problems

1. The Quality Office Furniture Company has compiled the year's revenue expectations and their probabilities:

Sales ($000)	*Probabilities*
240	.05
280	.10
320	.70
360	.10
400	.05

Calculate:

a. The expected revenue
b. The standard deviation
c. The coefficient of variation

2. If the probabilities in problem 1 had been .15, .2, .3, .2, and .15, recalculate the expected revenue, standard deviation, and coefficient of variation. Which of the two projections (in problem 1 and this problem) represents a riskier situation? Explain. Draw a bar graph for each situation.
3. The Learned Book Company has a choice of publishing one of two books on the subject of Greek mythology. It expects the sales period for each to be extremely short, and it estimates profit probabilities as follows:

Book A		Book B	
Probability	*Profit*	*Probability*	*Profit*
.2	2,000	.1	1,500
.3	2,300	.4	1,700
.3	2,600	.4	1,900
.2	2,900	.1	2,100

Calculate the expected profit, standard deviation, and coefficient of variation for each of the books. If you were asked which of the two to publish, what would be your advice?

4. Suppose you can make an investment with the following possible rates of return:

Probability	*Rate of Return*
.2	−10%
.6	10%
.2	30%

On the other hand, you can invest in a U.S. Treasury bill that earns a certain 7 percent. Evaluate the alternatives.

5. The Cactus Corporation is considering a two-year project, project A, involving an initial investment of $600 and the following cash inflows and probabilities:

Year 1		Year 2	
Probability	*Cash Flow*	*Probability*	*Cash Flow*
.1	700	.2	600
.4	600	.3	500
.4	500	.3	400
.1	400	.2	300

a. Calculate the project's expected NPV and standard deviation, assuming the discount rate to be 8 percent.
b. The company is also considering another two-year project, project B, which has an expected NPV of $320 and a standard deviation of $125. Projects A and B are mutually exclusive. Which of the two projects would you prefer? Explain.

6. The Grand Design Corporation uses the certainty equivalent approach in making capital budgeting decisions. You are given the following data for a particular project:

Year	*Cash Flow*	*Certainty Equivalent Factor*
0	$−20,000	1.00
1	5,000	.90
2	5,000	.90
3	5,000	.90
4	15,000	.70

The risk-free discount rate is 4 percent, and the risk-adjusted discount rate is 12 percent. Calculate the net present value. Would you accept this project?

7. You have just been employed in the finance department of the Mahler Transportation Corporation. The first task you have been assigned is to recommend a method for evaluating risky projects. You have studied both the risk-adjusted discount rate (RADR) method and the certainty equivalent method, and you have been asked to evaluate the following project using both methods.

A four-year project involves an original cash outflow of $30,000; there will be (after-tax) cash inflows of $10,000 in each of the first three years and an inflow of $20,000 in the fourth year. You estimate that the risk-free interest rate is 8 percent and the project's risk premium is 4 percent.

a. Calculate the net present value using the RADR.
b. Now calculate net present value using the certainty equivalent method, and show that the two methods give identical answers.

8. Project A has an expected net present value of $500 and a standard deviation of $125. Project B has a standard deviation of $100 and an expected net present value of $300. Which of the two projects would you select? Explain why.

9. Global Industries has calculated the return on assets (ROA) for one of its projects using the simulation method. By simulating the operations 1,000 times, they obtained an ROA of 16.7 percent and a standard devia-

tion of 6.2. The results of the simulation conform quite closely to a normal curve.

a. Draw a probability distribution using the given data.
b. The company's objective is to achieve an ROA of 12 percent. What is the probability that the project will achieve at least that level?
c. What is the probability of ROA being nonnegative?

CHAPTER 16

The Role of Government in the Market Economy

The Situation

Bill Adams, the director of data and voice communications for Global Foods, Inc., was pleasantly surprised when he received a call from the marketing representative of the local telephone company serving the city in which Global's corporate headquarters were located. "This is pretty unusual," he thought. "In most instances we have to call them if we have a problem with our phone lines. Not only did the phone company initiate the call, but they also are offering some services that are pretty price-competitive."

Based on the initial call and a series of meetings with the representative, Bill decided to present a proposal to Global Foods' vice president for administration, Carl James, to use the switching services of the phone company rather than the private switching facilities (private branch exchange, or PBX) that the company was currently using.

Bill's proposal was a big surprise to James. "I didn't think that they could give us a price that was even in the same ballpark with our present telecommunications setup," Carl remarked. "Right now, we use a combination of a PBX and a private company to hook us up with our long-distance carrier. Bill, are you trying to tell me that the phone company can offer us comparable service at competitive prices? What is going on? There must be some sort of deregulation occurring that enables them to have more flexibility in their pricing. I don't quite understand it all, but I like what I am hearing so far. Tell me more."

Introduction

The primary objective of this chapter is to discuss the impact of government policies on managerial decision making. In the United States, the government is involved in the economy in a number of different ways, including the regulation of such industries as telecommunications. In this chapter, we will explore the different ways in which government involvement in the market process affects managerial decisions. Particular attention will be paid to the regulation and subsequent deregulation of airlines, commercial banking, and telecommunications. These three industries provide a rich source of examples of how management decisions are influenced by government policies and actions.

There is a saying in management that "you get what you reward." Throughout this text, we have assumed that management decisions about the allocation of scarce resources were based on the anticipated reward of a profit. Consequently, in the short run we expect managers to select the least costly combination of inputs, to determine a profit-maximizing or cost-minimizing output level in perfectly competitive markets, and to select a profit-maximizing or cost-minimizing price in markets where they have control over their product's price. In the long run, we also expect managers to decide whether to enter or leave the market for a particular good or service based on their ability to earn at least a "normal" level of profit. Moreover, we expect that management decisions about the allocation of funds for fixed assets such as machinery, equipment, and factories are based on the potential for these assets to generate a positive net present value, adjusted where appropriate for a certain level of risk. In short, because of the reward of profit, we expect that managerial decisions about the allocation of scarce resources will result in economic and allocative efficiency. And efficiency is the main advantage of the market process over the command and traditional processes.

When the government is involved in the market economy, it generally controls the behavior of buyers and sellers through a process of "indirect command." That is, rather than ordering buyers and sellers to allocate resources in a particular way, the government uses market incentives or disincentives. This "visible hand" of the government can take such forms as price controls, rules and regulations, taxes, and subsidies. In using the incentive of profit or the disincentive of a loss, the government does not change the basic system of rewards and punishments used in the market process. Instead, it simply alters the reward structure of a laissez-faire market so that resources are allocated more in accordance with government policy than with the actions of individual buyers and sellers in the market. The government can make certain kinds of activities more profitable for producers (e.g., by offering subsidies or by establishing price floors) or less profitable (e.g., by imposing taxes or by establishing price ceilings). For example, rather than let the market decide whether to produce more "butter" or more "guns," Congress in the late 1980s and early 1990s decided to cut back on defense expenditures, thereby reducing the resources that privately owned defense contractors allocate to this activity.

The Rationale for Government Involvement in a Market Economy

There are five major functions the government can perform in a market economy such as that of the United States.[1] First, it provides a legal and social framework within which market participants buy and sell the goods and services produced from the economy's scarce resources. To ensure that all parties deal with each other in a fair and orderly manner, laws are established that define the legal status of a business, the rights of private ownership, and the enforcement of contracts. Other laws seek to protect consumers from being exploited by sellers who may engage in unfair, unsafe, or unethical business practices. For example, the Food and Drug Administration (FDA) seeks to ensure that food and pharmaceutical companies sell products that meet certain standards of safety and quality.

The second function of government is to maintain competition in markets for specific goods and services. The two most important pieces of legislation to deal with anticompetitive or monopolistic behavior were passed around the turn of the century. In 1890, Congress passed the Sherman Anti-Trust Act. According to this act, such monopolistic actions as price fixing by collusion and the formal division of markets among competitors were declared illegal and subject to various penalties. The Clayton Anti-Trust Act of 1914 sought to strengthen the Sherman Act by specifically outlawing such anticompetitive activities as price discrimination not based on cost differences and the formation of interlocking directorates (whereby a member of the board of directors of one firm is also on the board of a direct competitor). This act also prohibited the practice of a firm's selling a particular good or service on the condition that the customer buy other products only from this same firm, and not from any of its competitors.

The third basic function of government in a market economy is the redistribution of income.[2] One means used by the government to help rectify income inequality is the progressive personal income tax. This tax structure requires people with higher incomes to pay a proportionately greater amount of taxes than those with lower incomes. Another means of redistributing income are government transfer payments, such as veteran's benefits, unemployment benefits, aid to dependent children, and food stamp payments. Government subsidies also result in a redistribution of society's income. One of the most commonly cited government subsidies is the farm price support program. However, there are many other ways in which the government can subsidize a particular

[1]More complete introductory discussions of the role of government in the market process can be found in most economics principles texts. For example, see Campbell McConnell, *Economics*, New York: McGraw-Hill, 1987, Chapter 6. The division of the role of the government into five basic functions is based on the ideas discussed in that chapter.

[2]There are those who might argue that this function is not a basic responsibility of government in a market economy. To be sure, very little, if anything, was done by the United States government in this capacity until the early 1900s. However, we believe that its current involvement in the redistribution of income is so extensive that it has become de facto a basic function.

interest group. For example, the ability to deduct the interest payments on residential mortgages represents a subsidy to homeowners and results in a redistribution of after-tax income in their favor. The costly bailout of failed savings and loan companies (estimated in 1990 to cost taxpayers well over $500 billion) is another example of how government assistance redistributes income in favor of a particular group (in this case, the depositors, management and workers of these banks).

The fourth market-related function of government is the reallocation of resources. According to economic theory, a misallocation of resources results whenever a market has certain externalities or spillovers. That is, some of the benefits or costs associated with the production or consumption of a particular product accrue to parties other than the buyers or sellers of the product.

Let us start by explaining the concept of benefit externalities. Suppose one of your neighbors has a beautiful rose garden, which is admired by all passersby in the area. The entire community's enjoyment of this one person's flowers can be termed a "benefit externality." One household paid for its purchase and upkeep, but many "third parties" (i.e., those other than the buyer or seller of the product) benefit from this purchase. On the other hand, when this same neighbor bought a 32-inch color TV set in order to enjoy the Super Bowl, others in the neighborhood could not benefit, except by invitation to the Super Bowl party. Thus, the purchase of the TV set provides "private" or exclusive benefits. Other, more important examples of goods or services that provide spillover or nonexclusive benefits to third parties are bridges, roads, tunnels, parks, libraries, national defense, and education. But regardless of the example, the inability of the market to deal with the existence of such benefit externalities leads to the same problem: the misallocation of resources, or, more specifically, the *underallocation* of society's scarce resources in the production of these types of goods and services.

To clarify this point, let us resume our example of the neighbor with the rose garden. Suppose your neighbor gets the brilliant idea that since the whole community is enjoying his garden, he will ask everyone who passes by to make a donation for its upkeep. After all, since the admirers are enjoying its beauty, why should they not pay for its benefits in the same way that they would have to pay admission to a movie or a concert? Absurd, you say. Certainly, but why? Because even though these people did not help to pay for the garden's upkeep, there is nothing to prevent them from continuing to enjoy its beauty. Furthermore, if some spectators agreed to contribute to its upkeep, they would in effect be subsidizing the benefits of those members of the community who refused to help defray the owner's expenses. Thus, in markets where there are external benefits, the demand for a good or service tends to be understated because of the reluctance of people to pay for products that provide nonexclusive benefits to the buyers.

The concept of benefit externalities can be illustrated with the use of supply-and-demand diagrams. In Figure 16.1*a*, demand line D_t represent the "true" market demand for a product, reflecting the true desire by consumers for the product. In our flower example, it would represent the willingness of people to pay for the upkeep of their neighbor's garden on the basis of their enjoyment of its beauty. Demand line D_a represents the actual demand line, given the

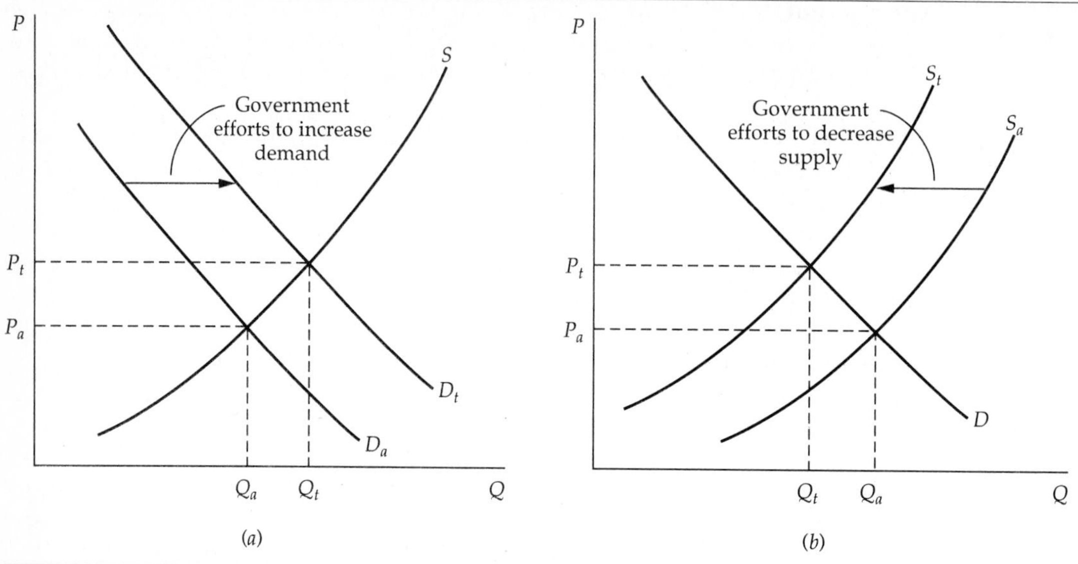

Figure 16.1 (a) Benefit Externalities and (b) Cost Externalities

reluctance of people to pay for goods that provide external benefits. In terms of supply and demand, the actual price understates the "true" price. Consequently, the actual quantity of the product is less than the "true" quantity.

When benefit externalities are present in the market, the government may intervene in order to express society's true demand for this product. It would generally do so by taxing the population and then paying a price that would be closer to the theoretically "true" price for the product. Regardless of this price, the purpose would be to increase the amount of resources devoted to the production of this type of good or service. The arrow in Figure 16.1*a* shows the direction of change in the demand for goods with external benefits as a result of government intervention.

The concept of cost externalities is similar to that of benefit externalities, except that these lead to an *overallocation* of a society's resources in a market for a particular good or service. A cost externality is a cost incurred in the production of a good or service that is not paid for directly and entirely by the producers and consumers of the product. The best example of this is environmental pollution. Suppose a chemical company decides to reduce its costs by dumping its industrial waste into a lake. Let us assume that this cost reduction enables them to sell their products at a lower price to consumers. In a sense, it is difficult to fault a company that chooses to reduce its cost in this manner because it thereby increases its possibilities of earning a greater profit. In other words, the market process actually provides an incentive for a firm to pollute the environment if the firm is thus able to reduce its cost. Unfortunately, the economic saying "there is no such thing as a free lunch" applies here because although the producers and consumers of the chemicals do not pay entirely and directly for the cost of disposing of the industrial waste, eventually everyone in the society must pay. For example, the public must pay for it directly in the form of taxes if the government wants to take the responsibility for cleaning up the lake. If the government does not wish to impose an out-of-pocket expense on taxpayers for this purpose, society still incurs an opportunity cost. For example, the lake may be lost for recreational uses (e.g., swimming and fishing). If a thriving resort area had developed around the lake, it would mean a loss of business for the restaurants, hotels, and shops catering to vacationers.[3]

From the perspective of supply-and-demand analysis, the presence of cost externalities tends to increase the supply and lower the price of a product. Thus, the quantity of the product will generally be greater than it would be without this type of externality. Figure 16.1*b* illustrates this. By dumping the industrial waste into the lake, producers lower their costs. This in turn causes the actual supply of the product to be greater than the "true" supply, where by "true" we mean the supply that is truly reflective of all costs incurred in the making of the chemicals, including the cost of using the lake. A greater actual supply causes a lower actual price and an overallocation of resources in this particular market.

If the government decides to "internalize" the cost externalities, it may impose certain penalties or fines on those firms caught polluting the lake. It may also impose certain regulations on the ways in which firms may dispose of their industrial wastes. This would have the effect of increasing the sellers' cost of production. Supply would be cut back, price would rise, and there would be fewer resources allocated to production in this market (see arrow in Figure 16.1*b*).

The fifth major function of government in a market economy is the stabilization of the aggregate economy. The market economy is prone to periodic upswings and downswings in economic activity. Downswings in the cycle are accompanied by reductions in output, jobs, and income, and upswings in the cycle are often accompanied by inflation. The United States government over the second half of this century has used fiscal and monetary policy in an attempt to control the volatility of the American business cycle. The governments of other developed countries, including England, Germany, and Japan, have also employed fiscal and monetary policies to stabilize their macro economies.

One government function that does not quite fit into any the five main categories is the regulation of "natural monopolies." The economic definition of a natural monopoly is an industry in which a single firm can serve customers more efficiently than many competing firms because of the predominance of economies of scale. Examples of natural monopolies are electricity and gas utilities and telephone services. In exchange for granting a legal monopoly to these types of firms, the government regulates certain key aspects of their business, such as the prices they charge and the amount of profit they may earn. A more

---

[3]You can probably cite instances of this problem in your own locality. A good example near the place of residence of one of the authors occurred in the summer of 1988, when many businesses on the Jersey Shore (New Jersey) were hurt because the dumping of industrial waste forced the closing of many the area's beaches.

detailed account of this particular government function is found in a later section of this chapter.

The Impact of Government on Managerial Decision Making

Over the years, a sizable (some would say overwhelming) number of federal laws and regulations and regulatory agencies have been established to carry out the five functions just noted. Table 16.1 lists the major regulatory agencies of the federal government.

The Center for the Study of American Business of Washington University found that between 1900 and 1988, the number of federal regulatory agencies grew from around 10 to almost 60.[4] It also found that the total expenditures of 54 federal agencies grew from $1.6 billion in 1970 to an estimated $9 billion in 1986.[5] Furthermore, there have been a considerable number of laws passed by Congress regulating various aspects of business. Between 1962 and 1988, Congress passed 52 such laws. Among them are the Cigarette Labeling and Advertising Act (1965), the Flammable Fabric Act (1967), the Age Discrimination in Employment Act (1967), the Noise Pollution and Control Act (1972), the Surface Mining and Reclamation Act (1977), the Insider Trading Sanctions Act (1984), and the Asbestos Hazard Emergency Response Act (1988).[6]

The main purpose of this chapter is not to go into detail about the federal

Table 16.1 Major Federal Regulatory Agencies

Consumer Product Safety Commission
Environmental Protection Agency
Equal Employment Opportunity Commission
Federal Communications Commission
Federal Deposit Insurance Corporation
Federal Energy Regulatory Commission
Federal Reserve System
Federal Trade Commission
Food and Drug Administration
Interstate Commerce Commission
National Labor Relations Board
Occupational Safety and Health Administration
Securities and Exchange Commission

Source: Federal Regulatory Directory, 5th ed., Washington, D.C.: Congressional Quarterly, Inc., 1986.

[4]Murray L. Weidenbaum, *Business, Government, and the Public*. Englewood Cliffs, N.J.: Prentice Hall, 1990. p. 21.

[5]*Federal Regulatory Directory*, 5th ed., Washington, D.C.: Congressional Quarterly, Inc., 1986, p. 4.

[6]A complete listing of all 52 laws along with a brief description of each is provided in Weidenbaum, op. cit., pp. 39–44.

regulatory process, but to examine the impact of government on managerial decision making. In doing so, we shall continue to assume that the managers of a firm are competing in a market economy and are guided primarily by the market incentive of profit. Thus, government involvement, whatever form it takes, is either an aid or a deterrent to a firm's quest for profit. In other words, government policies and actions can affect either the revenues or the costs associated with a particular good or service. Under these conditions, we expect profit-seeking managers to incorporate in their decisions the quantitative or qualitative impact of government policies and actions. Let us explore a series of examples to illustrate this point.

Increased Cost of Doing Business

Without a doubt, government regulation costs businesses a considerable amount of money. In 1977, the Commission on Federal Paperwork found that it cost private industry between $25 and $32 billion to fill out all the paperwork required by the federal government. In 1987, the Office of Management and Budget estimated that the American public spent 1.7 billion hours filling out government forms. About 61 percent of these hours were spent by businesses and not-for-profit organizations.[7]

A good example is the pharmaceutical industry. On the average, it takes a company in this industry about 10 years and $100 million to develop and bring to market a new drug.[8] Much of this initial outlay of funds is related to satisfying the requirements of the Food and Drug Administration. The paperwork required by the FDA for the approval of a new drug has been known to exceed 100,000 pages of documentation.

The requirements of other government regulatory agencies can be equally costly. For example, it was noted in a 1984 Supreme Court ruling that Monsanto spent $23.6 million to compile the data on its pesticide products to meet the requirements of the Environmental Protection Agency.[9] Such requirements are obviously made for the protection of consumers. Nonetheless, compliance with these types of government regulations can increase substantially both the out-of-pocket and the opportunity costs of doing business.[10]

Table 16.2 gives an idea of what it costs a firm to comply with the regulatory standards of the Environmental Protection Agency and the Occupational Safety and Health Administration (OSHA). These are actual numbers for a unit of a company that wished to remain anonymous.[11] The table shows that the costs for this company of meeting new governmental safety standards increased nearly tenfold, from $70,000 in 1988 to $652,000 in 1989.

---

[7]See Louis Rukeyser, ed., *Business Almanac*, New York: Simon & Schuster, 1988.

[8]This estimate is based on the decade of the 1980s.

[9]Rukeyser, op. cit., p. 160.

[10]For more examples of the impact of regulation on the cost structure of a firm, see Robert A. Leone, *Who Profits: Winners, Losers, and Government Regulation*, New York: Basic Books, 1986.

[11]The authors are grateful to one of their graduate students for providing these data.

Table 16.2 Expenditures Required to Comply with EPA Regulations, 1988 and 1989

Activity	*1988*	*1989*	*Comments*
Hazardous waste pickup	$70,000	$110,000	Same quantity dumped; increase due to higher dumping charges
Monitoring of waste water	—	12,000	New regulation
Employee safety training	—	90,000	New law—employers must comply or face stiff penalty
Storage of chemicals	—	250,000	New regulation on how "spent" and "virgin" chemicals must be stored
General improvements (eyewash, safety showers)	—	40,000	Required to meet OSHA standards
Fuel tank removal	—	150,000	New regulation concerning removal of fuel storage tanks not in use

A Firm's Optimal Combination of Inputs

In addition to increasing the cost of doing business, government policies and actions can affect the combination of inputs that a business uses in its production process. For example, government import quotas have kept the price of sugar above the free market price in the United States. This has provided the incentive for soft drink producers to substitute high-fructose corn syrup for sugar.

A similar example of input substitution resulting from government policy is found in the automobile industry. In the late 1980s, American automakers began to use robots to paint the assembled automobiles. By itself, this capital for labor substitution increased slightly the cost of production. However, an important economic incentive for using machines instead of people was prompted by a new law regarding the disposal of excess paint in the auto factories. Although relatively more expensive than labor, robots are able to apply the paint to cars far more efficiently; virtually no paint is wasted when they are used. The savings in not having to dispose of wasted paint according to the standards of the Environmental Protection Agency more than compensated auto manufacturers for the added cost of using the robots.[12] Figure 16.2 illustrates this example with the use of the production isoquant. As GM moved from point a to b, production costs were reduced from C_2 to C_1.

The Demand for a Particular Good or Service

Government regulations may influence the demand for a product. They might even create a demand for a product that did not exist prior to the government action, thereby creating an entirely new market. For example, government health

[12]This example was provided by a student who works as a plant engineer for General Motors. At his request, the actual amount of cost savings is not presented.

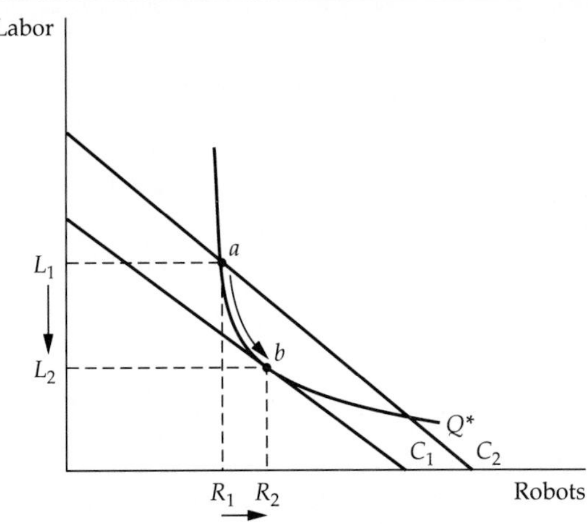

Figure 16.2 Production Isoquant for GM: Labor versus Roberts.

warnings and regulations on smoking (e.g., the surgeon general's findings and the banning of smoking on airline flights) have probably reduced the demand for cigarettes. As a result, cigarette manufacturers have had to make various types of resource allocation decisions to counter this fall in demand. One decision has been to increase their marketing resources in international markets, where government and consumer concern about the hazards of smoking are not as strong as in the United States.[13]

Another example of how the government's influence on demand can affect business decisions pertains to stricter government auto emission standards. These have forced automakers to equip their cars with catalytic converters, a decision that has increased manufacturing cost as well as the price of cars to the consumer. But this in turn has created a demand (i.e., a derived demand) for catalytic converters. Prior to this government regulation, this particular product was not available on the market.

Price

In Appendix 4A, we discussed various ways in which supply-and-demand analysis can be applied to certain market situations. One topic was the ways in which government involvement in the market can affect the market price. As demonstrated in this appendix, the government's control of market price is based on its ability to affect market supply or demand. For example, we showed that government price supports were affected either by acreage control (i.e., limiting the supply of an agricultural product) or by purchasing any surplus resulting from price controls (i.e., eliminating excess demand). We also

[13]However, governments in Western Europe are stepping up their efforts to warn people about the dangers of smoking. Again, this will probably have an adverse effect on demand. Perhaps of greater importance, more and more restaurants in Europe are introducing nonsmoking areas.

showed that such government actions as the establishment of quotas on imports effectively raised their prices by limiting their supply in the market. This type of government policy would obviously have an impact on a firm's ability to compete. For example, American manufacturers who are protected by import quotas (e.g., steel producers and automakers) have less incentive to be cost-efficient. They may also be able to raise their prices higher than they could without the import quotas. In the case of American farmers, prices that are supported at above-free-market levels enable less efficient farmers to compete in the marketplace.

The Cases of Commercial Banks and Airlines

Two industries that had been strictly regulated by the government until the late 1970s and early 1980s are commercial banking and airlines.[14] A brief look at the management decisions of banks and airlines while they were subject to strict government regulation and a comparison with decisions now made in a deregulated environment provide important insight into how the government shapes management decisions.

Commercial Banking

In the wake of the banking crisis during the Great Depression, several laws were passed by Congress in an effort to prevent further bank failures and to restore the serious decline of public confidence in the banking system. The most important piece of legislation passed was the Banking Act of 1933 (commonly referred to as the Glass-Steagall Act). Essentially, this act divided financial activities into two basic functions: commercial banking and investment banking. Financial institutions at that time were forced to choose which activity they wished to engage in. The former conducted the usual deposit-taking and lending activities that we associate with commercial banks, whereas the latter could underwrite, distribute, and deal in stocks, bonds, and other financial instruments. The only instruments that commercial banks were allowed to underwrite, distribute, and deal in were federal government bonds, certain types of municipal bonds, and certificates of deposit.[15] In addition, this act introduced federal deposit insurance, prohibited the payment of interest on demand deposits, and set ceilings on the interest rates that could be paid by commercial banks on savings and time deposits.

There is an immense amount of detailed information about the various legislative acts that established the regulatory framework for banks and the rest of the financial services industry; such a comprehensive background is clearly

---

[14] There are numerous surveys available on both of these industries. In particular, see William G. Shepherd, "The Airline Industry," and Arnold A. Heggestad, "The Banking Industry," in Walter Adams, *The Structure of American Industry,* New York: MacMillan, 1990.

[15] Actually, negotiable certificates of deposit were introduced in the early 1960s. The point is that at that time the Glass-Steagall Act did not prohibit banks from issuing and dealing in this new financial instrument.

beyond the scope of our text. However, let us simply state that because of legislation such as the Glass-Steagall Act, banks were essentially constrained by regulation in the following three areas of business:

- *Products and services*: Commercial banks could not engage in investment banking and also could not offer any insurance services.
- *Pricing of products and services*: The prohibition of interest payments on demand deposits and the ceiling on interest payments of time deposits represented a form of price control on commercial banks. In addition, state usury laws prevented banks from charging interest rates on their loans above certain levels.
- *Geographic location*: The McFadden Act of 1927 and various state statutes restricted interstate banking by prohibiting out-of-state branches for national and state-chartered banks. Later legislation permitted holding companies to acquire or establish banks in other states only if permitted by state laws. Up until the 1980s, very few states allowed this.

From the standpoint of managerial decision making, the important question to consider is: If you were a commercial bank manager before the deregulation of the financial services industry began, how would you compete? What kinds of management decisions would earn your bank the most profit, given the fact that you were limited by the kinds of services you could offer, the prices you could charge for these services, and the places you could offer them?

Prior to deregulation, commercial banks competed primarily on the basis of what economists call *nonprice competition*. Every effort was made by a bank to differentiate itself from the competition. One important way in which to differentiate a bank is service and one aspect of service is convenience. Hence, banks, such as Bank of America in California, began to build huge networks of branches all across their states of residence. Figure 16.3 shows the growth in the number of bank branches relative to the number of banks from 1915 to the mid-1980s.

Did banks use formal capital budgeting techniques such as those discussed in Chapter 14 before deciding whether to build an additional branch? Some did, perhaps, but many probably did not. Extending a branch network was one of the few ways that the highly regulated commercial banks could compete with one another. If one bank started building more branches, others had to follow just to stay in the competition.

Another highly publicized way in which the banks competed on a nonprice basis was to offer customers all kinds of gifts, such as toasters, blankets, dishware, and irons. (Back in the 1960s, a customer stepping into a bank branch might think that he or she mistakenly walked into a retail store.) All this product differentiation cost money. But cost competition was not as important as product differentiation. Furthermore, the control of the prices of commercial bank services such as the interest rate on savings accounts at least provided banks with a certain maximum cost of a major source of their funds. It also guaranteed that their competitors could not compete on a price basis for the deposits. It is one thing to give a customer matching pillowcases and bed sheets;

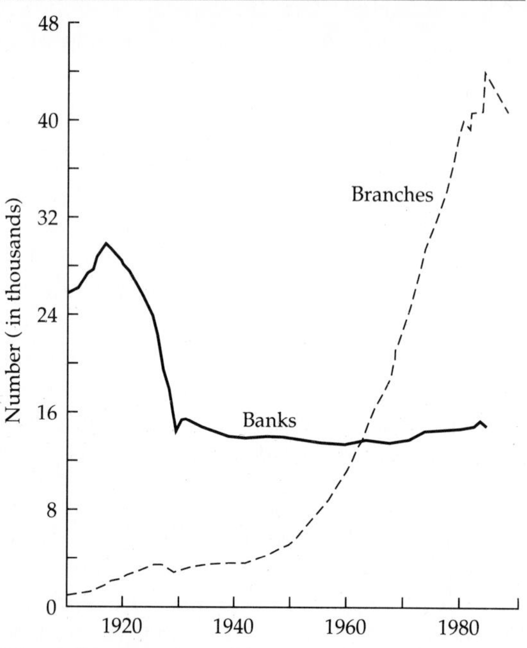

Figure 16.3 Number of Commercial Banks and Branches, 1915–1986 (*Source*: Board of Governors of the Federal Reserve System, *1987 Historical Chart Book)*

it is quite another to have to pay higher interest rates on deposits to lure depositors into a bank.

During the 1970s and early 1980s, certain key developments in the deregulation of financial institutions took place that loosened the constraints placed on commercial bank products, pricing, and geographic location. A key piece of legislation was the Monetary Control Act of 1980. This was quickly followed by another act, the Depository Institutions Act of 1982 (Garn–St. Germain Act). With the passage of these two acts, the walls of regulation in the financial services industry began crumbling. The commercial banks were particularly affected. As a result of these pieces of legislation, ceilings on deposit rates were gradually phased out. By 1986, banks were free to offer any interest rate they wished to attract depositors. The ceiling on interest rates and the interest rate differentials between commercial banks and savings and loan institutions (a previous law had allowed thrift institutions to pay at least one-quarter of a percentage point more than commercial banks for savings accounts) were eliminated. Furthermore, with a few minor exceptions, commercial banks were no longer limited by state usury laws on the interest rates they could charge to borrowers. Especially important to banks was the lifting of the ceiling on mortgage rates. Banks were also able to begin offering various kinds of products, such as checking accounts, that paid depositors interest. Geographical restrictions were also relaxed to some extent. Banks were allowed to make out-of-state acquisitions of any type of failing depository institution. Moreover, during the 1980s, many states passed laws allowing out-of-state banks within their borders. Table 16.3 summarizes the principal developments from 1972 to 1983 in the deregulation of financial institutions.

Beginning in the mid-1980s, depository institutions began to fail in increasing numbers at considerable cost to American taxpayers, as well as the insurance funds that were financed by the financial industry. Most of the attention by the media has been given to the mismanagement and outright fraud that have led many thrift institutions to fail. However, commercial banking is also in serious

Table 16.3 Principal Developments in Deregulation of Financial Institutions, 1972–1983

Year	Development
1972	NOW accounts were authorized for thrift institutions in Massachusetts. In the next few years, all New England thrifts were allowed to issue NOW accounts.
1973	The "wild card experiment": the first use of ceiling-free, small-denomination certificates of deposit. The certificate had a minimum maturity of four years; the experiment lasted four months. All depository institutions were allowed to participate.
1975	California state-chartered savings and loans were authorized to issue variable-rate mortgages. At the same time, a few national banks in California began to issue variable-rate mortgages.
1978	Six-month money market certificates were authorized nationally for all depository institutions. California federally chartered savings and loans were authorized to issue variable-rate mortgages.
1980	Authorization of the 2½-year small savers' certificate for all depository institutions. Passage of the Depository Institutions Deregulation and Monetary Control Act (DIDMCA). Extension of reserve requirements to all depository institutions. Creation of the Depository Institutions Deregulation Committee (DIDC). Allowed thrifts to invest 20 percent of assets in consumer loans. Allowed mutual savings banks to make business loans and accept business deposits.
1981	Introduction of nationwide NOW accounts, ceiling-free Individual Retirement Accounts (IRAs), and tax-exempt all-savers certificates of deposit.
1982	Several new accounts paying market-related rates were introduced: 91-day money market certificates, 3½-year ceiling-free deposits, and 7–31-day time deposits. Passage of the Garn-St. Germain Act. Capital assistance for ailing thrifts. Authorized the money market deposit account. Increased allowable consumer loan percentage at thrifts to 30 percent. Authorized savings and loans to issue business loans and accept business deposits.
1983	Introduction of the Super NOW accounts, a lowering of minimum deposit on short-term certificates of deposit to $2,500, and the elimination of ceiling rates on remaining time deposits.

Source: Economic Review, Federal Reserve Bank of Kansas City, July–August 1983, p. 35.

trouble. Table 16.4 shows the growing problem posed by both types of financial intermediaries.

Bad loans, particularly in the slumping commercial real estate market, have been a major cause of the banks' problems. However, bank executives believe that a key reason for all of the troubles in their industry is the regulatory constraint that prohibits them from fully competing with other types of financial institutions. At the heart of this constraint is the Glass-Steagall Act, which bars them from engaging in investment banking activities such as the underwriting of stocks, corporate bonds, and most other financial instruments in the private credit market. (Banks have always been able to underwrite and sell securities issued by federal, state, and local governments.) Since the passage of the 1982 Garn–St. Germain Act, there has been no major piece of federal legislation concerning banking, particularly one that would allow banks to expand their operation into activities outside of the usual lending, deposit-taking, and demand-deposit services. In 1989, five large bank holding companies were granted authority by the Federal Reserve to affiliate with securities firms that underwrote and dealt with a small amount of corporate bonds.[16]

Table 16.4 Problem Banks and Thrifts

	Failed Banks[a]	*Problem Banks*[b]	*Problem Banks as Percent of Total*	*Failed Thrifts*[c]	*Problem Thrifts*[d]	*Problem Thrifts as Percent of Total*
1980	10	217	1.5%	11	16	0.4%
1981	10	223	1.5	28	53	1.4
1982	42	369	2.5	71	222	6.6
1983	48	642	4.4	52	281	8.8
1984	78	848	5.7	28	434	13.7
1985	116	1,140	7.7	34	449	14.0
1986	138	1,484	10.1	49	460	14.3
1987	184	1,575	11.1	48	505	16.0
1988	200	1,394	10.6	205	364	12.3

[a] Includes commercial banks and FDIC-insured savings banks that were liquidated or sold to other banks. Does not include banks granted FDIC assistance in order to remain open.

[b] Banks on the FDIC's official "problem bank list."

[c] Savings and loan associations and FSLIC-insured savings banks that were liquidated or sold with financial assistanc from FSLIC. Does not include "supervisory" mergers or thrifts kept open under the FSLIC Management Consignment Program.

[d] Thrifts whose net worth as a percentage of assets, measured by generally accepted accounting principles, was less than zero.

Sources: FDIC, Federal Home Loan Bank Board. Reported in *Congress and the Nation*, Washington, D.C.: Congressional Quarterly, Inc. 1985–88, vol VII, p. 121.

[16] An excellent summary of financial regulation in the 1980s is found in *Congress and the Nation*, Washington, D.C.: Congressional Quarterly, Inc., 1985–88, vol. VII, pp. 109–36.

In recent years, Congress has been considering legislation that would clearly define the ground rules for competition among all parties (i.e., commercial banks, thrifts, insurance companies, investment banks, and nonbank corporations). This legislation is also considered to be a top priority of the Bush administration. Just prior to the printing of this text, the House Banking Committee voted to recommend a bill that would result in sweeping changes in the financial industry. The major parts of the bill will permit interstate banking, the industrial ownership of banks, and the full affiliation of commercial banks with investment banks.[17]

Regardless of the outcome of the bill recommended by the House Banking Committee, it is clear that deregulation up to this point has presented a considerable challenge to the managers of commercial banks and the entire financial services industry. This challenge essentially came from the increased competition fostered by deregulation. However, competition in the financial services industry also increased during the 1980s because of factors other than government legislation. The emergence of "nonbank" banks, whose innovative and aggressive actions were focused on meeting customer needs, greatly affected the market shares of commercial banks in their traditional lines of business. In fact, loopholes in the law have enabled nonbanks such as the Ford Motor Company and American Express to buy savings and loans and state banks that were not members of the Federal Reserve System. Sears, General Motors Acceptance Corporation, the Ford Credit Corporation, and a number of other large credit companies greatly increased their lending activities to households and businesses. Brokerage houses such as Merrill-Lynch developed cash management accounts, which were very much like the commercial banks' demand deposit products but enabled customers to earn very competitive interest rates.

Perhaps one of the most adverse factors to banks was the growth of the commercial paper market. Large firms with strong credit ratings (such as the Fortune 500 companies) bypassed the lines of credit that their commercial bankers had always offered and instead issued their own IOUs or commercial paper in the money market. Many banks were forced to seek business in the "middle market" (commonly defined as businesses with \$10 to \$250 million in annual sales) and in the "retail market" (household accounts). Moreover, those American banks that continued to compete in the upper end of the commercial lending market found themselves pitted against very price-competitive foreign banks, particularly Japanese banks. Figure 16.4 summarizes some of the competitive pressures that faced the commercial banks in the 1980s and also indicates some of the businesses they were unable to compete in because of regulatory restrictions.

Another important reason for the increased competition during the past few decades was the tremendous progress made in information processing technology, which led to the creation and tracking of newly developed financial services. For example, the proliferation of credit cards was made possible by the use of large mainframe computers. Also, a high degree of technological

[17]"House Panel Backs Broad Changes in Bank Rules," *New York Times*, June 20, 1991.

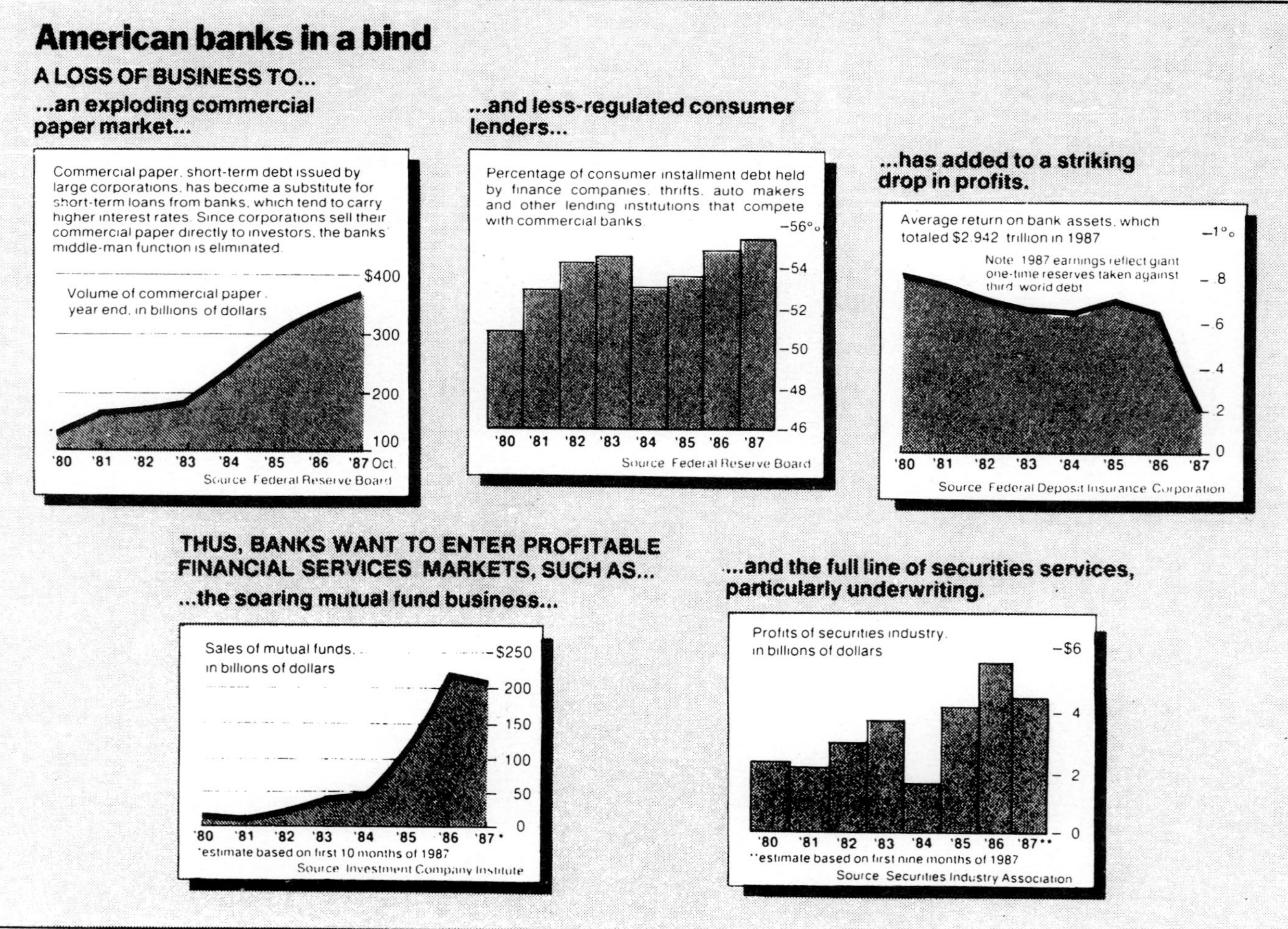

Figure 16.4 Pressures Facing Banks in the 1980s (*Source:* "After 55 years, is it Time to Deregularate the Banks", *New York Times*, January 3, 1988)

sophistication as well as a considerable cost is involved in establishing and maintaining a network of automated teller machines (ATMs).

We can summarize the competitive situation of commercial banks by stating that regulation prevented managers from competing on the basis of price, variety of product offerings, and geographic location. Deregulation, new technology, and innovative and tough competitors in the form of nonbank financial firms forced commercial banks to compete in ways more generally associated with the kinds of businesses we have used in our economic models throughout this text. Thus, banks today must be more aware of their cost structure in the short run and long run, of possible economies of scale in their operations, of the pricing of products according to such guidelines as the MR = MC rule, and of such techniques as NPV and IRR in the making of capital budgeting decisions. It was not that commercial bankers did not know about these decision-making techniques; it was just that because of the restraints of a regulatory environment and the lack of nonbank competition, there was no incentive for their use among commercial bank managers. As a reflection of this, consider a quote by the CEO of a major bank in California:

> The days when we could sit back and benefit from low-cost deposits, from no competition, from offering only whatever products we wanted to offer, are gone. You know darn well the clients can go anywhere they want to go. I've got to make life in the world of finance easier for them or I won't have any customers.
>
> [I've also made] my branches leaner and keener. Full-time equivalents have been reduced 20 percent and [I've used] part-timers to bolster peak-time support. This permitted the branch platform staff to be more sales and service oriented.[18]

The Airline Industry

The rationale for regulating the airline industry was similar to that used for commercial banking: consumer safety and financial stability. The Civil Aeronautics Act of 1938 sought to prevent unduly high airfares and also to prevent "competing carriers from engaging in rate wars which would be disastrous to all concerned." It also wanted to end the "chaotic situation of the air carriers [which] has shake[n] the faith of the investing public in the financial stability [of this industry].[19] The Civil Aeronautics Board (CAB), created by this act, set domestic airfares and established the condition of entry of airlines and the routes they served. The CAB set the overall rate structure on the basis of the average cost of the entire industry. The aim was to reward those airlines whose cost structures were below the industry average and to penalize those whose cost structures exceeded the average. Furthermore, the CAB long-distance rates were set to provide a profit margin to the airlines that was about 25 percent higher than the margin on short-distance fares. In effect, the long-haul profits were supposed to subsidize the short-haul profits. Presumably, the demand for short-haul flights was more price-elastic than for long-haul flights because of

---

[18] "A Banker's Prescription for Making Retail Pay," *Wall Street Journal*, February 6, 1990.

[19] As quoted in Paul W. MacAvoy, *The Regulated Industries and the Economy*, New York: W. W. Norton, 1979, p. 20.

the greater availability of substitutes. Thus, to expand markets, the price had to be set below the average cost, causing airlines to incur losses on their short-haul service.[20] Price controls in the airline industry fostered the same type of nonprice competition witnessed in commercial banking. Instead of toasters and blankets, airlines offered steak and champagne dinners and similar amenities.

Much of the pressure to deregulate the airline industry came from the airlines themselves. Because the CAB kept a rather tight lid on the rate structure, airline companies found it difficult to keep up with the inflation that began in the late 1960s and continued through the 1970s. Rising oil prices caused by the OPEC cartel hit the airline industry particularly hard because fuel costs are a major part of its cost structure. In 1978, after a brief period in which the CAB experimented with various types of flexible pricing, Congress passed the Airline Deregulation Act. This act phased out controlled airfares over the period 1979–1983. Restrictions on the entry of airlines into various routes were also gradually eliminated.

Once the airlines were deregulated, the focus of management decisions shifted from nonprice to price competition. People Express entered the airline industry as a low-priced competitor and quickly began to take market share from the established carriers. However, various management control problems emerged when the company reached a certain size. This, along with matched price cuts by the major air carriers, proved to be the fledgling airline's downfall.

Today airlines compete on the basis of both price and nonprice competition. The airfare structure is complex and rapidly changing. The pricing strategy among the airlines is based on the simple but important concept discussed in Chapter 4: price elasticity. Because the marginal cost of an additional passenger is minimal, any additional revenues gained through the maximization of passenger load pass directly down to the "bottom line." Quite simply, airlines have divided their market into a "price-insensitive/schedule-sensitive" group (usually business travelers) and a "price-sensitive/schedule-insensitive" group (usually vacation travelers). The idea is to fill as many seats as possible with the category of full-fare customers and fill the balance of the load with the price-sensitive passengers, who pay discount fares. The full-fare passengers travel primarily for business reasons. A good way to maximize the number of such passengers is to have a flight network with connecting hubs in and around cities in which most business is conducted (e.g. New York, Chicago, Atlanta, St. Louis). Another way to keep the loyalty of these frequent-flying, full-fare passengers is to offer bonus trips and other incentives based on mileage accumulated on a particular airline.

A useful summary of the type of price competition that currently exists in the airline industry is contained in the following quotation from a 1991 article in *USA Today*:

> American and United are... planning to raise fares and increase restrictions on some fares after April 8. . . .

---

[20] Ibid., p. 40.

> Other airlines are still mulling whether [to] match United's and American's fares for after April 8. If they don't, United and American will have to back off. But, typically when one plan to raise fares fails, airlines keep proposing new ones until they hit on one everyone can support.[21]

It should be evident that the domestic airline industry has evolved into a textbook example of an oligopoly. Interdependence and price leadership govern the way in which prices are set. American Airlines and United Airlines, the nation's two largest carriers, are the price leaders. The article implies that they set their prices with the anticipation of a reaction by the other carriers. If the other carriers do not follow their lead, the prices are rolled back. In most cases, however, the others follow suit. To be sure, supply and demand conditions play a role in the pricing policies of the leaders. During the Gulf Crisis in 1990–91, airline fuel costs rose rapidly, causing sudden increases in air fares. As the recession and increased fears of flying by passengers began to hurt air travel demand, air fares started to decrease.

The increased competition in price and frequent flier bonuses that has arisen because of deregulation is very visible to the general public. Not so apparent but equally important in the postregulation era are certain types of nonprice competition, such as the ownership of a computerized reservations system (CRS). Most major airlines are part owners in CRSs. However, a recent government study found that most of the benefits of these systems go to the two majority owners of the two dominant CRSs, American and United. Estimates taken from 1986 data show that

> The lack of effective competition in the CRS industry allows the CRSs controlled by American and United each to receive over $300 million per year, in excess of the costs of the service provided (including a reasonable profit) from other carriers in the industry, most of which are financially weaker.[22]

Another form of nonprice competition is the limitation of access to airport gates and other facilities. The current practice is for airports to lease gates and facilities to airlines on a long-term and exclusive basis. The same government study just noted found that at some airports a single airline controlled most of the gates and passenger waiting rooms. It also found that a related practice, called the "majority-in-interest clause," is equally effective in limiting competition. This provision in a typical airport use agreement gives airlines that provide a majority of the operations at an airport the right to disapprove capacity expansion projects under certain conditions. It is not surprising that this government study found that "carriers charge significantly higher fares on routes to airports

---

[21]Doug Carroll, "Snap up Deals for Summer Flights Now," *USA Today*, March 26, 1991.

[22]*Airline Competition: Weak Financial Structure Threatens Competition,* "Report to the Chairman, Subcommittee on Aviation, Committee on Public Works and Transportation," House of Representatives USGAO, Washington D.C.: (GAO/RECD-91-1110), April 1991, p. 4.

where a single carrier controls a large portion of the gates or where a majority-in-interest clause is in effect."[23]

Table 16.5 shows the results of the intensive price and nonprice competition that has ensued in the wake of deregulation. Notice the increasing concentration of the two major carriers, American and United. Also notice the turmoil implied by the data for the rest of the airlines. The bankrupt People Express is not listed for 1989. Of those on the list for 1989, Eastern has gone out of business entirely, and Continental and Pan American have both filed for protection from their creditors under Chapter 11 of the Bankruptcy Code. One of the airlines included in "others," America West Airlines, has also recently filed for bankruptcy court protection. In fact, a recent news article on this filing cited that America West was one of the few remaining airlines out of the 100 or so that opened for business after deregulation.[24]

The benefits to the consumer of airline deregulation are still hotly debated. On the one hand, consumers are able to obtain much lower fares on particular routes at certain times than when the industry was fully regulated. On the other hand, some customers have found it far less convenient to fly between certain cities because of the spoke and hub networks that the major airlines have built around the key business cities in the United States. Furthermore, there is a growing feeling among consumers that airline transportation is not as comfortable as before deregulation.[25] But regardless of the pros and cons for the consumer, deregulation has changed the "rules of the game" for the competing airlines and has thus changed the way in which their managers make decisions about the use of their scarce resources.

Table 16.5 Market Share in the Airline Industry (Based on Revenue Passenger Miles)

1989 Rank	*Company*	*Percent Market Share*	*1985 Rank*	*Company*	*Percent Market Share*
1	American	17.0	1	American	13.3
2	United	16.1	2	United	12.5
3	Delta	13.7	3	Eastern	10.0
4	Northwest	10.6	4	TWA	9.6
5	Continental	8.9	5	Delta	9.0
6	TWA	8.1	6	Pan Am	8.1
7	USAir	7.8	7	NWA	6.7
8	Pan Am	6.7	8	Continental	4.9
9	Eastern	2.7	9	People Express	3.3
	Others	8.4	10	Republic	3.2
				Others	19.4

Source: Department of Transportation, and Standard & Poors', *Industry Surveys*, vol. 1, April 1991.

[23] Ibid.

[24] "A Young Airline's Battle to Survive Lean Times," *New York Times*, June 29, 1991.

[25] Paul Dempsey, "Deregulation Has Spawned Abuses in Air Transportation," *Aviation Week and Space Technology*, 129, 21 (November 21, 1988).

The Breakup of AT&T

Besides airlines and commercial banking, other key industries that have been regulated are highway freight services (trucking), natural gas, telephone services, railroad transportation, and electricity generation. In the late 1970s, Congress mandated the decontrol of railroad rates and natural gas prices along with its deregulation of airline fares. Electricity rates continue to be regulated by various state commissions.

Perhaps the most important deregulation of an industry in the history of the United States is the breakup of the national telephone monopoly of AT&T. It is important simply because of the size of the company (as measured by the value of the assets and profits and by the number of employees). However, we have devoted a good portion of this chapter to this case because the transition of the telephone industry from a regulated monopoly to a more competitive type of business is extremely instructive as to how management decisions are affected by the government command process.

A Natural Monopoly

The history of how AT&T became a regulated national monopoly and the reasons it was broken up in 1984 are well beyond the scope of this text.[26] But at the time the executives of AT&T sought to convince the government to grant it a monopoly on telephone service, their main argument was that it should be considered a "natural monopoly." According to economic theory, a natural monopoly exists when one firm can serve customers more efficiently than many competing firms because of the cost savings resulting from its economies of scale. The theory states that it is better for the government to allow the one firm to supply all the services while regulating the prices this legal monopoly charges to its customers.

However, the regulation of a natural monopoly presents something of a dilemma, as depicted in Figure 16.5. Figure 16.5*a* shows the idealized long-run cost structure of a natural monopoly. The LRAC line has been drawn to show that relatively high levels of output are required for the firm to reap the benefits of scale economies. In Figure 16.5*b*, we add a line indicating some "average" demand (D_a) for the monopoly's services. Notice that the line intersects the LRAC curve slightly to the left of its lowest point. This represents the fact that a monopoly should have excess capacity to handle peak loads of demand. Peak demand is represented by the line to the right of the average demand for the service, D_p. The way we have drawn the average and peak demand lines in relation to the cost curves assumes that the firm is able to handle peak demand at its most efficient level of operation (i.e., at the lowest point on the AC curve).

[26] There are numerous books on the subject. Among the best is Leonard S. Hyman, Richard C. Toole, and Rosemary M. Avellis, *The New Telecommunications Industry: Evolution and Organization*, 2 vols. Arlington, VA: Public Utilities Reports, Inc., 1987. Also see W. Brooke Tunstall, *Disconnecting Parties*, New York: McGraw-Hill, 1985; Steve Coll, *The Deal of the Century: The Breakup of AT&T*, New York: Atheneum, 1986; and Robert W. Crandall, *After the Breakup: U.S. Telecommunications in a More Competitive Era*, Washington D.C.: Brookings Institution, 1991.

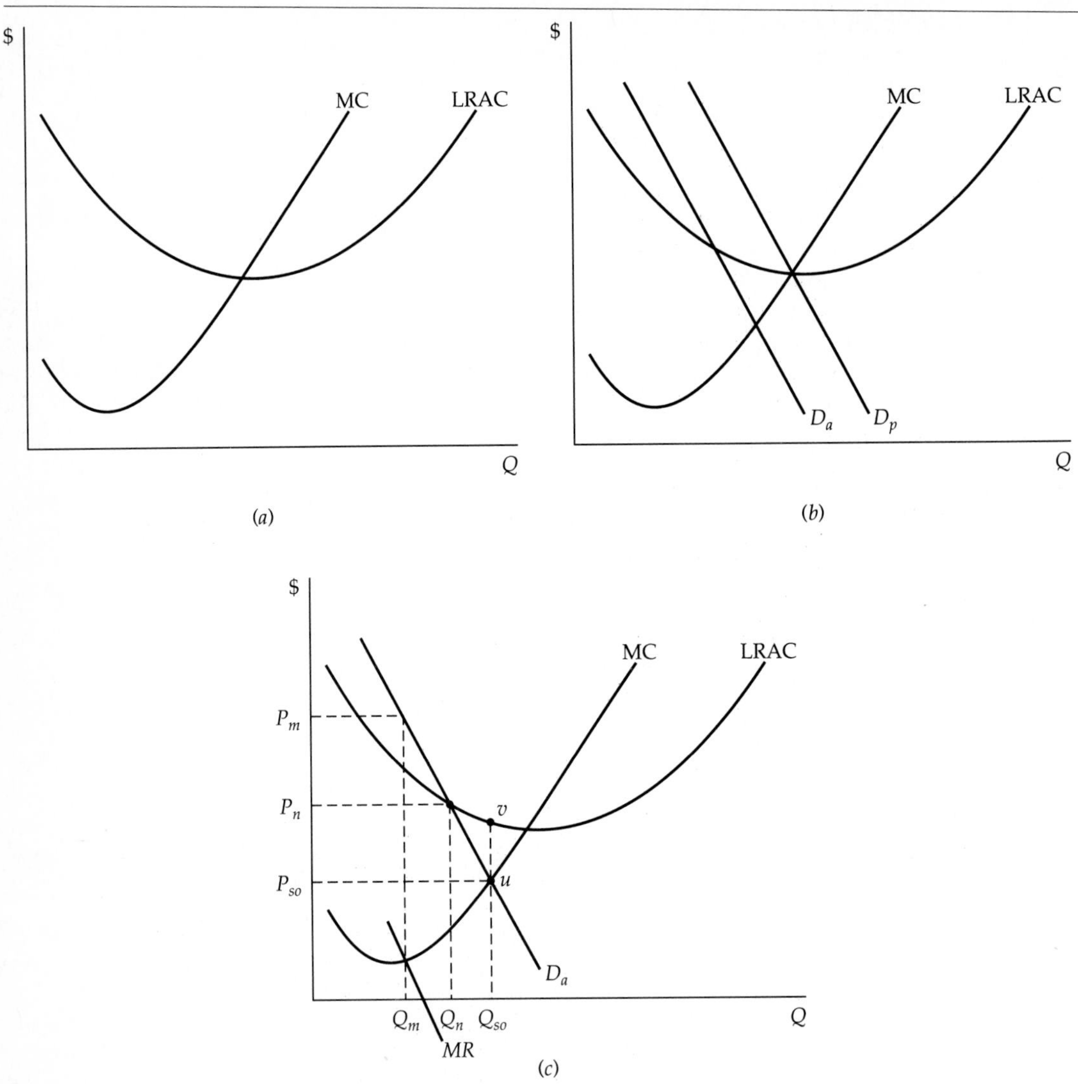

Figure 16.5 Costs and Demanding Structure for a Natural Monopoly

In Figure 16.5*c*, we show the long-run cost structure, average demand, and marginal revenue for the monopoly. Based on this graph we can say that an unregulated monopoly of this kind would set its price at P_m if it wanted to maximize its profit. This is because at P_m, the quantity demanded, Q_m, enables the firm to follow the MR = MC rule. However, in exchange for allowing a firm to be a natural monopoly, the government regulates its ability to set prices. The term regulated monopoly is generally used in reference to this type of arrangement. If the regulator wants the monopoly to earn no more than normal profit, it will tell the firm to set the price at P_n. In this case, we assume that opportunity cost is included in the firm's cost structure, as we did in previous chapters.

There is an alternative price that the regulators might want the firm to charge. This is referred to by economists as the *socially optimal* price, P_{so}. According to economic theory, this is the price that equals the firm's marginal cost of production.[27] In Figure 16.5*c*, we observe that if the firm is forced by the regulators to charge this price, it would lose money. (The per-unit loss is shown as the difference between and points *u* and *v*.) In comparing the normal price with the socially optimal price, we see the regulators' dilemma. On the one hand, if the regulators want the monopoly to charge the socially optimal price, the government must provide some sort of subsidy to cover the monopoly's losses. On the other hand, a price that allows a monopoly to earn normal profit is greater than the socially optimal price; consumers would thus be forced to pay a price for the monopoly's product that is greater than the value of the product that society forgoes in producing the additional unit of the monopoly's product (i.e., its marginal cost).

Let us leave the question of whether regulators should require natural monopolies to charge a "normal" price or a "socially optimal" price to economic theorists. From a practical standpoint, most natural monopolies have been allowed by regulators to charge a price that lets them earn a normal profit. The key point is that from the perspective of business decision making, the establishment of a "normal" price presents the management of a regulated monopoly with a set of challenges rather different from those faced by the managers of an unregulated firm. This was precisely the case with the managers of AT&T when it was a regulated provider of national telecommunications services, and it is still the case to a large extent for the seven regional Bell operating companies formed when AT&T's monopoly was broken up in 1984. To explain this, let us discuss briefly how the pricing and profits of the telecommunications industry are actually regulated. What we will describe also applies to other types of regulated monopolies, such as water and electric companies.

Essentially, natural monopolies such as the telephone and electric utilities are subject to a practice called rate-base regulation. Figure 16.6 shows an idealized balance sheet of a regulated monopoly. A very high proportion of the company's assets are in fixed plant and equipment. In the case of the telephone companies, a tremendous amount of investment is needed to build and maintain a communications network. The funding for the assets, shown on the right-hand side of the balance sheet, comes from three basic sources: (1) non-interest-bearing liabilities (NIBL), such as accounts and wages payable, (2) interest-bearing debt both short-term and long-term and, (3) equity. The rate base of a regulated monopoly is the dollar value of the net property, plant, and equipment (gross value minus accumulated depreciation). As you can see from Figure 16.6, the rate base of

[27]Standard microeconomic theory considers marginal cost as the cost of society's scarce resources that must be used to produce one additional unit of some commodity. It is also considered to be the value of resources that would be saved by producing one fewer unit of that commodity. When a product's price is equal to its marginal cost of production, its purchase by consumers implies that they are willing to pay an amount for it equal to what they are willing to forgo in the way of another product, that is, the "socially optimal price."

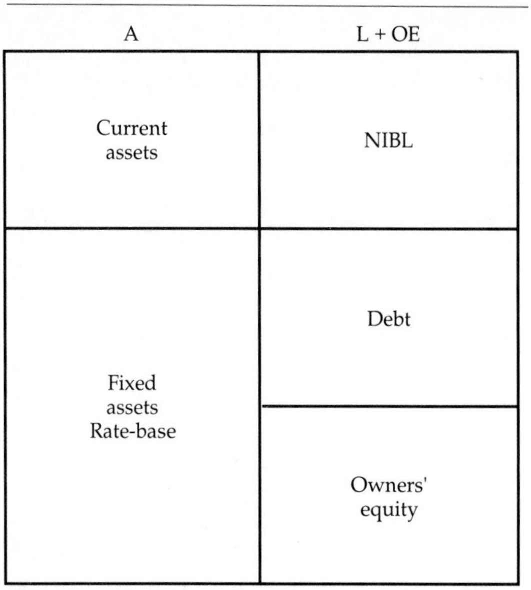

A	L + OE
Current assets	NIBL
Fixed assets Rate-base	Debt
	Owners' equity

Figure 16.6 Idealized Balance Sheet for a Natural Monopoly

net property, plant, and equipment is essentially funded by the debt and equity of the firm. Rate base regulation provides a means for the lenders and owners of the firm (i.e., the holders of the debt and the equity) to earn a reasonable return on the funds they have agreed to tie up in the company's fixed plant and equipment.

The regulated return on the rate base is:

$$\text{Rate of return} = \frac{\text{Profit}}{\text{Rate base}}$$

Given the size of the rate base, the rate of return depends on the amount of profit that a firm is able to earn. Profit in turn is determined by the amount of revenues that a firm earns relative to its expenses.

The concept of rate base regulation may seem simple enough, but it is not so easy to implement because of the many different ways in which the terms in the equation can be defined or interpreted. For one thing, there are at least seven different ways to define "rate base."[28] For another, there are ways to influence and determine the actual percentage return that lenders and owners are allowed to earn on their investment in the company. Calculating the return on debt is

[28] According to Hyman, Toole, and Avelis, they are: (1) net original cost rate base, (2) fair value, (3) average rate base, (4) end-of-period rate base, (5) used and useful rate base, (6) telephone plant under construction in the rate base and interest during construction included in the income, (7) telephone plant under construction in rate base (*The New Telecommunications Industry*, op. cit., pp. 212–13).

easy enough. For this, regulators use the interest rate paid on a bond by a borrower with a risk comparable to that of a regulated monopoly, such as the U.S. Treasury, or a highly rated unregulated corporation (AAA or AA). But the method of determining the appropriate return on equity is not as clearly established. One that is commonly employed is the *discounted cash flow* (DCF) method or the Gordon model.[29] Under this method, the amount of profit that a monopoly is allowed to earn relative to its equity is computed as

$$k = \frac{D_1}{P_0} + g$$

where k = Expected return on investment in stock
D_1 = Dividend per share
P_0 = Price of stock
g = Expected annual growth in dividend or market price of stock

Also,

$$g = br$$

where b = Earnings retention rate (1 − Dividend payout ratio)
r = Expected return on book equity

There are other methods for determining the allowable return on equity. One is the *comparable earnings* method, in which some average return on equity for a sample of firms with similar risks are used as the basis for determining the allowed rate for the regulated monopoly. Another method is based on the capital asset pricing model.[30]

Once a suitable, mutually agreeable method for determining the rate of return has been selected, there remains the question of regulating the revenues and expenses in such a way as to give the natural monopoly a reasonable chance to earn an allowable return (i.e., some sort of normal profit) on its rate base. In this matter, regulators focus primarily on the revenue side of the issue. For example, suppose the rate base of the monopoly is \$100, and the regulators allow the firm to earn up to 12 percent on this rate base. This means that it is allowed a profit of \$12 (.12 × \$100). This also means that whatever its expenses are, the total revenue of the regulated monopoly must be \$12 greater. As you well know, total revenue is price times quantity (TR = $P \times Q$). Since the regulators cannot actually control quantity (e.g., the amount of telephone service demanded by the public), it must regulate the amount of revenue that a monopoly earns by controlling the prices for its services.

At last we arrive at the heart of the regulation of natural monopolies: the pricing of their services. In effect, we are back to the graphical illustration of the regulated natural monopoly shown in Figure 16.5. But now you should have a better idea of why pricing is so important to the regulatory process. You

---

[29]This model was discussed in greater detail in Chapter 14.

[30]See Chapter 14 for a discussion of this model.

should also have a better appreciation for the rationale of certain management decisions in such a regulated environment.

To begin with, the managers of a regulated monopoly have an obligation to provide customers with a certain level of service at prices dictated by the regulatory commission. In the case of the Bell system monopoly, this meant that AT&T provided "end-to-end" universal service (from the caller to the receiver of the call) for all customers throughout the country.[31] All telephone rates for varying distances and for different times of the day or week were determined by regulators. The Federal Communications Commission (FCC) set long-distance rates, and the state regulatory commissions set rates within their respective states. A key measure of managerial performance was the "service index," which indicated the degree of satisfaction of customers with AT&T's provision of telephone service. Table 16.6 compares the management objectives and decisions under conditions of regulation and unregulated competition.

One key difference between the two types of firms is the incentive (or lack of incentive) to use resources in an efficient manner. This is not because managers of regulated monopolies are less capable than managers of unregulated competitors in making optimal decisions about their resources. It is simply that the differing reward structures encourage different types of management decisions. Put yourself in the place of a manager of a firm operating under conditions of rate base regulation. If you earn a profit above the allowable rate of return, your firm may be asked to "give back" the extra profit to rate payers in the form of reduced telephone rates. If your costs increase to the point that it is difficult to earn the allowable rate of return, you may be able to convince the regulators that these costs are needed to provide an acceptable level of universal service, and you may then be able to obtain "regulatory relief" in the form of higher prices for your services. (The increase in prices is based on the assumption that the demand for certain types of telephone services is inelastic and therefore will result in an increase in the firm's revenues.)

Factors Precipitating the AT&T Breakup

One of the most telling statistics about the lack of cost-effectiveness of a management that operates in a regulated environment is the number of people employed in the telephone industry before and after the breakup of AT&T. Just prior to the January 1, 1984, breakup, AT&T employed about 1 million people. By the end of the decade, AT&T and the seven regional Bell operating companies (RBOCs) formed at divestiture together employed about two-thirds that many people. To be sure, advances in technology made it possible to run the telecommunications network with fewer people. (In fact, as we discuss next, it was the advances in telecommunications technology that helped to convince government regulators that the maintenance of AT&T's monopoly no longer was in the best interest of the public.) However, a large number of jobs were

[31] Although AT&T provided most of the telephone service for the country, there were and still are a number of independent phone companies such as General Telephone of California (a subsidiary of GTE).

Table 16.6 Management Objectives and Decisions about Resource Allocation under Regulation and Unregulated Competition

	Regulated Monopoly	*Unregulated Competitor*
Objectives	Earn a profit sufficient to reach the allowable return on the rate base.	Earn as much profit as possible (profit maximization).
Cost structure	Incur whatever costs are needed to achieve an acceptable level of universal service. Costs will most likely be covered by the rate structure set by regulation.	Incur whatever costs are needed to meet the demands of the customers. If costs are too high relative to revenue, losses will be incurred.
Pricing policy	Prices are subject to regulation. However, every effort is made to get the regulators to agree on a pricing structure that will enable the firm to generate revenues that exceed its costs sufficiently to earn the firm an allowable return on its rate base.	Policy is based on the MR = MC rule or some cost-plus price that helps it to achieve its profit-maximizing objective. Policy may also include consideration of competitors' reactions.
Capital budgeting policy	Use discounted cash flow techniques such as NPV and IRR to justify capital expenditures. However, forecasts regarding future cash flows (either from revenue increases or cost savings) may be given an upward bias to justify capital spending. This is because any increase in capital spending adds to the regulated monopoly's rate base of property, plant, and equipment and may be covered in future regulatory rate cases.	Use discounted cash flow techniques such as NPV and IRR to justify capital expenditures. However, any errors in the forecast will penalize the firm by adding under-utilized assets to its balance sheet or by not having sufficient assets to support revenues.

eliminated because of the more competitive environment in which AT&T and the RBOCs were operating when the Bell system monopoly was broken up.

The economic rationale for AT&T's monopoly in telecommunications was that it was a natural monopoly. As such, its economies of scale would presumably cost consumers less than if they were served by many different telecommunications companies. Furthermore, the early history of the telephone business showed that many different telephone companies might use different equipment and communications standards, making it difficult to establish a universal network. A national monopoly would ensure the provision of end-to-end service for all consumers throughout the nation. Much of the cost of setting up and maintaining a national telecommunications franchise resides in what telecommunications people call the "local loop." This is the distance between an end point (e.g., a home or office) and some station—called the "central office"—that switches calls to and from the other end of the line.

If callers were charged based on the actual costs directly attributable to the provision of their service (i.e., some form of marginal cost pricing), then local calls would be fairly expensive, and long-distance calls would be relatively inexpensive. Prior to AT&T's breakup, regulators deliberately set the prices of local calls below their marginal cost and the prices of long-distance calls above their marginal cost. Thus, the average residential customer, who makes a higher proportion of local calls, was subsidized by the business customer, who makes a higher proportion of long-distance calls. The regulators thus made telephone service more accessible and reasonably priced for the "little guy."[32]

The system of a national telephone monopoly offering universal service at prices set above cost for business customers and below cost for residential customers worked quite well—until rapid changes in technology began to expose its weaknesses. In 1963, Microwave Communications, Inc. (later called MCI), filed with the FCC for permission to build a private-line microwave system between Chicago and St. Louis. Several telephone companies fought against this application, but finally, in 1969, the FCC ruled that this offering would be beneficial to customers who did not need the full-service offerings of AT&T. Also around this time, satellite communication became a practical means of transporting information over long distances. AT&T could not extend its monopoly over this medium of telecommunications because of a law passed by Congress in 1962.[33]

Several other major developments in technology also helped to change the fundamental nature of the telecommunications industry. Digital switches replaced analog switches, enabling a far greater number of calls to be routed considerably faster through central offices. Fiber-optic cable, carrying light generated by lasers, enabled much more information to be sent at a considerably faster rate from the calling point to the receiving point. Copper wire, the transmission medium used by AT&T for decades, was rapidly becoming outmoded. Moreover, the price-performance ratio of digital switching and fiber-optic cables meant that the start-up cost of a telecommunications network was within the reach of many more entrepreneurs. High start-up capital and economies of scale could no longer be used to justify a national telephone monopoly.

In 1979, The Department of Justice began an antitrust case against AT&T because it believed that the monopoly was creating unfair barriers to entry by competitors. Finally, on January 8, 1982, after a long legal battle, AT&T agreed to settle with the Department of Justice. Basically, the terms of the settlement were as follows:

- AT&T would divest itself of all fully owned Bell Telephone companies.

---

[32]This subsidization of local calls from long-distance profits is very similar to the regulation of the airline industry, whereby the profits from the longer flights subsidized the cost of providing flights of shorter distance.

[33]For a complete discussion of these early inroads in technology, see Hyman, Toole, and Avelis, op. cit., pp.123–26.

- AT&T would keep Western Electric (its manufacturing arm), Long Lines, Bell Labs, terminal equipment, Yellow Pages, and all assets related to interexchange services. (Subsequently, Yellow Pages were given to the regional Bell Telephone companies.)
- AT&T could enter any business, but it could not buy stock in assets of a local Bell operating company. (A 1956 consent decree prevented AT&T from entering the computer business. The 1982 settlement meant that it could now enter this market.)
- The Bell operating companies had to guarantee all interexchange carriers equal access to the local network (besides AT&T, other major carriers today are MCI and Sprint).[34]

In the latter part of 1983, each of the newly formed Bell operating companies—Pacific Telesis, Bell South, NYNEX, Bell Atlantic, U.S. West, Ameritech, and Southwestern Bell—began issuing stock. On January 1, 1984, the biggest company in the world was broken up, and a new era in telecommunications began.

RBOCs

To understand how management decision making was required to change when the telecommunications industry moved from a regulated to a less regulated or unregulated environment, let us look at the seven regional Bell operating companies (RBOCs). The bulk of their business is to provide local telephone service and access to long-distance carriers. In fact, about 80 percent of their revenue comes from (1) local service, (2) toll service (local calls that are made beyond the local calling area), and (3) access to long-distance service. This core business is still subject to rate base regulation, as in the old Bell system. The rest of their business is unregulated, and the RBOCs are essentially free to price these services as they see fit. The settlement between AT&T and the Justice Department (called the "Modified Final Judgment," or MFJ) still prevents the RBOCs from pursuing certain key types of businesses. For example, they are forbidden to manufacture telecommunications equipment and to provide information services (e.g., home shopping, stock market quotations, airline fares). Aside from certain restrictions, they do have quite a bit of leeway in starting unregulated businesses. Some have started leasing companies; others have bought software development firms. Perhaps the most successful of their unregulated businesses is cellular telephone service.[35]

Beginning in the late 1980s, the RBOCs' core business of providing local service and access to long-distance service has been gradually moving from rate base regulation to some form of "incentive regulation." Rate base regulation provides a relatively secure environment in which, in exchange for an acceptable level of service, companies are allowed to earn a certain amount of profit

---

[34]These terms are summarized in Hyman, Toole, and Avelis, op., cit. pp. 157–78.

[35]Currently, cellular telephone service is regulated in terms of the entry of firms into a particular market. The FCC permits only two cellular companies per market area. This is what economists call a "duopoly," not to be confused with a 1950s rock group.

relative to their rate base. But since divestiture, the RBOCs have found that even regulation cannot protect them from aggressive competitors armed with the latest in telecommunications technology. Just as in the case of commercial banks, the regional telephone companies' largest customers are able to "bypass" their services. (Recall that in the case of commercial banks, the big customers issued commercial paper and thus did not require as much of the banks' traditional lending services.) In the case of the RBOCs, their largest customers have been setting up their own means of gaining access to long-distance carriers, avoiding the need to use the local loop services of the public telephone companies. Indeed, some very large companies (e.g., Sears, IBM, American Express) have established private telephone networks that are completely independent of public carriers. One of the best examples of the competitive pressures on RBOCs is Teleport, a subsidiary of the Merrill-Lynch Corporation.[36] Teleport is particularly active in New York City, where the physical setup for bypass facilities is ideal. Let us say a company has its corporate headquarters in one of the skyscrapers located in lower Manhattan. Teleport will provide the company with a hook-up directly to the toll switches of a long-distance carrier chosen by the customer. All it takes is a microwave tower on the top of the building, and presto! The New York Telephone Company network is bypassed.

In addition to basic telephone services (e.g., dial tone and call connections), the RBOCs offer "enhanced services." You may have some of these in your own home. They include call forwarding, call waiting, and three-way conference calling. These services, grouped under the generic name of "centrex services," are controlled by switches, located in the RBOC's central offices. However, companies can also bypass these services by installing their own private switches, called private branch exchanges (PBXs). PBXs existed for quite some time and were sold by AT&T prior to divestiture. AT&T continues to sell this product, but since AT&T and the RBOCs are no longer one company, this represents direct competition to the RBOCs' centrex services. Today PBXs are available for small and medium-size companies as well as for large ones. Small PBX systems can provide customers who have between 10 and 50 telephone lines with many of the leading-edge features once available only to large customers. RBOCs now find themselves competing for enhanced services in all segments of the business market.

Besides the rapidly changing technology, the most important factor promoting bypass of the RBOCs is their regulated pricing structure. As part of rate base regulation, RBOCs are allowed to earn a certain amount of revenue relative to their cost and their rate base. Their revenue is also affected by the prices that the regulators allow them to charge for their services. The problem is that once prices are set by the regulators, the RBOCs have no power to raise or lower them. From the standpoint of customers, the most important reason for bypassing the local network is cost savings. An independent provider of telephone services such as Teleport is able to connect a big business to a long-distance carrier for far less than the local phone company. Similarly,

---

[36] Another major company engaging in bypass activities is Metropolitan Fiber Systems (MFS).

potential customers of centrex services might determine that the cost of purchasing and maintaining a PBX is less than that of using the RBOC's centrex services. The RBOCs can counter by offering reliability and continuous upgrading of the centrex services, but very often price wins out.[37]

At this time, bypass affects the RBOCs' business customers but not their residential customers. However, because of higher local loop costs and lower phone usage by people in their homes, most of the RBOCs' profit is in the business segment of the market. Now put yourself in the place of the managers of the RBOCs. What should you do about this? The logical thing to do is to ask for more pricing flexibility from the regulators so that you can try to be more price-competitive with those firms trying to get your customers to bypass you. But, as you know, the control of prices is at the heart of rate base regulation. Thus, the only avenue ultimately available to these regulated phone companies is to seek deregulation. In the opinion of the authors of this text, it is only a matter of time before most of the telecommunications services offered by the RBOCs will be deregulated. At the time of this writing almost all the regulatory commissions in the states served by the seven RBOCs have implemented or are considering implementing incentive regulation. To illustrate this concept, let us take the case of Pacific Bell of California.

PACIFIC BELL Pacific Bell is the operating subsidiary of Pacific Telesis, one of the seven regional Bell companies formed at AT&T's divestiture in 1984. In 1987, the company submitted a proposal to the California Public Utilities Commission (CPUC) called the California Plan for Rate Stability (CPRS). Phase I of this plan was approved and implemented in 1988. Among other things, this aspect of the plan gave Pacific Bell greater flexibility in the pricing of its centrex services so that it could more effectively compete in the telecommunications marketplace. Phase II was adopted in late 1989. Its provisions included substantial modification of rate base regulation and greater pricing flexibility on a full range of Pacific Bell's telephone services. Two key details of this phase of the plan are:

- Pacific Bell is allowed to earn up to a 13 percent return on its rate base. Between a 13 percent and 16 percent rate of return, it will be able to keep half of the profits earned; the other half will be retuned to its customers in the form of reduced telephone rates. Any return above 16 percent will return in full to its customers.
- Pacific Bell can lower its prices to whatever level it considers appropriate. It will not be allowed to raise its price above a level dictated by the following formula:

$$\begin{array}{c}\text{Percentage increase}\\ \text{in price}\end{array} = \begin{array}{c}\text{Increase in price index}\\ \text{minus 4.5 percent}\end{array}$$

The first aspect of this phase does not do away with rate base regulation, but it does certainly provide a greater incentive for Pacific Bell to increase profits,

---

[37]Many PBXs were out out of commission after the 1989 California earthquake. However, none of Pacific Bell's centrex services were adversely affected.

either by increasing revenues or by reducing costs. The second aspect, known in the telecommunications industry as "price cap" regulation,[38] makes it imperative that Pacific Bell contain its costs in order to earn a profit. For example, suppose that the annual rate of inflation (as measured by the price index) is 5 percent. Given the preceding formula, Pacific Bell, if it so chooses, can raise its prices only by 0.5 percent to offset the effects of inflation on its costs (5 percent minus 4.5 percent = 0.5 percent). The 4.5 percent in the formula is called the *productivity factor.* That is, to account for the full 5 percent effect of inflation, the productivity of Pacific Bell will have to improve by 4.5 percent. To cite an extreme case, if inflation is zero, then Pacific Bell will have to lower its prices by 4.5 percent. The management of Pacific Bell is fully aware that this does away with the good old days of regulatory relief, when regulators often granted them permission to raise prices in the face of rising costs. However, given the increasing competition from bypass and PBX technology, they also realize that it might be difficult to raise prices anyway.

Pacific Bell illustrates the specific challenges faced by managers in moving from a deregulated to a competitive environment. It also is presented to show the arbitrariness involved when the command process is used instead of the market process. For example, the index selected to measure the rate of inflation was the GNP deflator. Why not use the consumer price index or the producer price index? Furthermore, a 4.5 percent productivity factor is in fact higher than the national average. Can Pacific Bell be expected to be more productive than the average American company? To earn a profit above its allowable limit, it may well have to be.

In any event, institution of this type of plan throughout the country is now being considered. The management of all the RBOCs will soon be dealing with key management decisions that are much closer to the right column in Table 16.6 than to the left column. More precisely, here are some of the economic issues they face:

- *Cost structure.* At divestiture, Pacific Bell employed over 100,000 people. At the start of 1990, this number had been reduced to about 65,000. In early 1990 the company announced its intention to reduce its work force by an additional 10,000 over the next five years. Cost improvements stem from force reductions, but they also result from productivity improvements. The management of Pacific Bell will have to reduce costs in both ways. This includes finding optimal combinations of labor and capital (substitution of capital for labor or vice versa, as illustrated by isoquant-isocost analysis and linear programming analysis), taking full advantage of economies of scale and the experience curve factor, and increasing productivity through investments in the training and education of the work force. The last point

[38]In 1988, the FCC established price caps for AT&T. Shortly thereafter, it established price caps on the rates charged by local exchange carriers to long-distance carriers for access to the local network. The structure of the price caps is similar to that one the applies to Pacific Bell. The differences pertain to the productivity factor and the range of rates of return in which profit sharing occurs.

is particularly important because within a short period of time, the entire telecommunications industry has moved from the electromechanical world of analog switches and copper wire to the digital world of computer hardware and software and fiber-optic cable.

- *Pricing Policy.* Managers must have a thorough understanding of the nature of the demand for their various telecommunications products. Reliable estimates of price, income, and cross-price elasticity will be critical. Downward flexibility in pricing is important, but if prices are lowered when demand is inelastic, more harm than good will result.
- *Competition.* Marketing managers must find and implement effective ways to differentiate the products of the RBOCs from those of their competitors. A monopoly, particularly one whose franchise is protected by law, is not accustomed to differentiating its products in a competitive marketplace. The RBOCs already have an inkling of the importance of maintaining product differentiation in such services as pay-phone operations. Throughout the country, independent companies are free to set up pay phones wherever they can under any terms and conditions mutually agreeable to the company and the managers of the premises (e.g., non-RBOC pay phones set up in laundromats). Do customers really know or care who provides this service? If not, will this also be the case when the entire telecommunications industry is deregulated?[39]

In conclusion, managers of telecommunications companies will have to consider carefully all of the factors that we have discussed in this text. They may have already done so to some extent prior to the divestiture of AT&T and the gradual deregulation of the telecommunications industry. However, they will have to do even more of this now that their potential rewards and penalties are a lot closer to those confronting the manager of a firm in a competitive market environment.

The Solution

After listening to Bill Adams' presentation, Carl James was extremely impressed. He discovered by listening to Bill that the local phone company was now able to offer central office-based switching services (i.e., centrex) at more competitive prices be-

(Continued)

[39]For an excellent summary of the changing nature of competition in telecommunications, see "The Baby Bells Learn a Nasty New Word: Competition," *Business Week,* March 25, 1991, pp. 96–101.

cause of the greater pricing flexibility made possible by the recent ruling of the state public utilities commission. The price that it offered was still slightly higher than the present cost of Global's telecommunications set up. However, Carl felt that the phone company offered greater reliability and the opportunity to keep Global Food up to date with the latest technological advances in voice and data communications. In particular, Carl was excited about the prospect of having the phone company set up a system that would allow Global to transport data, voice, and video all on one line (referred to in the industry as "integrated services digital network," or ISDN).

Bill was elated that Carl had accepted his proposal. By bringing in the services of the phone company, he believed that his network would benefit from the latest technology and would also be more reliable and of a higher quality than the present system. What amazed Bill most was how different the phone company was compared to the days when it was a national monopoly. "I guess competition really affects the way people do business," he concluded.

Summary

Although the United States relies on the market process to allocate its scarce resources, the American economy is considered a "mixed economy" because there is also substantial use of the government's command process to answer the basic questions of *what, how,* and *for whom.* Thus, managers of companies competing in the United States must be fully aware of the influence government has on the resource allocation process and must factor this influence into their decisions about the allocation of their own company's resources. As we have shown in this chapter, this is particularly true for companies that are subject to heavy government regulation.

Important Concepts

Benefit externalities: Benefits that accrue to individuals other than those who have paid for a particular good or service, also referred to as *spillover benefits, third-party benefits,* and *social benefits.* The demand for products with external benfits tend to be understated in the market.

Cost externalities: Costs incurred by individuals other than those who produce a particular good or service, also referred to as *spillover costs* and *social costs.* The supply of goods whose production involves cost externalities tends to be overstated in the market. A good example of cost externalities is environmental pollution.

Federal regulatory agencies: Agencies of the federal government responsible for the enforcement of laws regulating the prices and services of certain industries, the health and saftey of workers, the quality of the environment, and the practices of financial institutions.

Internalizing market externalities: The process of government intervention in the market process to reallocate resources in a manner believed to be more reflective of the true costs and benefits of a good. For example, the government "internalizes" external costs by establishing laws against the pollution of the environment and by fining or taxing those parties found to be guilty of violating such laws. It "internalizes" external benefits by taxing the general public and then spending an amount for a particular social good that is more reflective of the true demand of the population.

Natural monopoly: An industry in which a single large firm can serve customers more efficiently than many smaller ones because of economies of scale.

Normal price: The price a regulated company is allowed to charge that gives a normal return on its investment (i.e., the price that is equal to its average total cost of production.) This is the price that is usually agreed on under rate base regulation.

Price caps: A method of deregulating companies subject to rate base regulation by allowing them to earn a rate of return on their investment that is above the usual regulated rate in exchange for their agreeing not to raise prices above a certain level.

Rate base regulation: The regulation of a company in a manner that allows it to earn an amount of profit equal to some percentage of a predetermined "rate base" such as the net book value of the property, plant, and equipment employed by the company. Also referred to as *rate of return regulation*.

Socially optimal price: The price of a good or service that is equal to its marginal cost of production. The dilemma often faced by regulators is that if regulated companies were forced to charge the socially optimal price, they could not earn a normal profit on investment, and in fact may actually lose money. This being the case, the regulated firm that charges the socially optimal price may well need to be supported by government subsidies.

Questions

1. What is the rationale for government involvement in the market economy? (Cite the five points presented at the outset of this chapter.)
2. Define *market externalities*. Explain why situations involving benefit externalities tend to result in an underallocation of society's scarce resources, and why situations involving cost externalities tend to result in an overallocation of society's scarce resources.
3. What is the role of government in dealing with benefit externalities? Cost externalities?
4. When government regulation either controls prices or limits price changes in a particular industry, the firms in the industry try to compete on a basis other than price. Cite examples of this nonprice competition that occurred in the airline and commercial banking industries when they were more heavily subjected to government regulation.

5. Suppose a chemical company was fined for violating certain antipollution laws. As the spokesperson for the Environmental Protection Agency, how would you explain the economic reasons for these actions to angry customers of this company who were forced to pay more for the chemicals as a result of this government action?
6. "The reason the government has to step in and 'internalize' benefit and cost externalities is because people are basically selfish." Do you agree with this statement? Explain.
7. Part of the basic dilemma of regulation is that if the regulators force the monopoly to charge the socially optimal price (i.e., $P = MC$), the government may eventually have to subsidize the firm. Explain why.
8. Under the Bell system monopoly, the United States had the best telephone system in the world. However, the U.S. government decided to break up this system. Briefly cite some of the economic justifications for this drastic change in policy.
9. A common saying in the telecommunications business is that much of the job of regulating the industry is now done by competition instead of the public utilities commission. What is meant by this? Cite specific examples if possible.

Appendix

Table A.1*a* Future Value of $1 at the End of *n* Periods

Period	*1%*	*2%*	*3%*	*4%*	*5%*	*6%*	*7%*	*8%*	*9%*	*10%*
1	1.0100	1.0200	1.0300	1.0400	1.0500	1.0600	1.0700	1.0800	1.0900	1.1000
2	1.0201	1.0404	1.0609	1.0816	1.1025	1.1236	1.1449	1.1664	1.1881	1.2100
3	1.0303	1.0612	1.0927	1.1249	1.1576	1.1910	1.2250	1.2597	1.2950	1.3310
4	1.0406	1.0824	1.1255	1.1699	1.2155	1.2625	1.3108	1.3605	1.4116	1.4641
5	1.0510	1.1041	1.1593	1.2167	1.2763	1.3382	1.4026	1.4693	1.5386	1.6105
6	1.0615	1.1262	1.1941	1.2653	1.3401	1.4185	1.5007	1.5869	1.6771	1.7716
7	1.0721	1.1487	1.2299	1.3159	1.4071	1.5036	1.6058	1.7138	1.8280	1.9487
8	1.0829	1.1717	1.2668	1.3686	1.4775	1.5938	1.7182	1.8509	1.9926	2.1436
9	1.0937	1.1951	1.3048	1.4233	1.5513	1.6895	1.8385	1.9990	2.1719	2.3579
10	1.1046	1.2190	1.3439	1.4802	1.6289	1.7908	1.9672	2.1589	2.3674	2.5937
11	1.1157	1.2434	1.3842	1.5395	1.7103	1.8983	2.1049	2.3316	2.5804	2.8531
12	1.1268	1.2682	1.4258	1.6010	1.7959	2.0122	2.2522	2.5182	2.8127	3.1384
13	1.1381	1.2936	1.4685	1.6651	1.8856	2.1329	2.4098	2.7196	3.0658	3.4523
14	1.1495	1.3195	1.5126	1.7317	1.9799	2.2609	2.5785	2.9372	3.3417	3.7975
15	1.1610	1.3459	1.5580	1.8009	2.0789	2.3966	2.7590	3.1722	3.6425	4.1772
16	1.1726	1.3728	1.6047	1.8730	2.1829	2.5404	2.9522	3.4259	3.9703	4.5950
17	1.1843	1.4002	1.6528	1.9479	2.2920	2.6928	3.1588	3.7000	4.3276	5.0545
18	1.1961	1.4282	1.7024	2.0258	2.4066	2.8543	3.3799	3.9960	4.7171	5.5599
19	1.2081	1.4568	1.7535	2.1068	2.5270	3.0256	3.6165	4.3157	5.1417	6.1159
20	1.2202	1.4859	1.8061	2.1911	2.6533	3.2071	3.8697	4.6610	5.6044	6.7275
21	1.2324	1.5157	1.8603	2.2788	2.7860	3.3996	4.1406	5.0338	6.1088	7.4002
22	1.2447	1.5460	1.9161	2.3699	2.9253	3.6035	4.4304	5.4365	6.6586	8.1403
23	1.2572	1.5769	1.9736	2.4647	3.0715	3.8197	4.7405	5.8715	7.2579	8.9543
24	1.2697	1.6084	2.0328	2.5633	3.2251	4.0489	5.0724	6.3412	7.9111	9.8497
25	1.2824	1.6406	2.0938	2.6658	3.3864	4.2919	5.4274	6.8485	8.6231	10.834
26	1.2953	1.6734	2.1566	2.7725	3.5557	4.5494	5.8074	7.3964	9.3992	11.918
27	1.3082	1.7069	2.2213	2.8834	3.7335	4.8223	6.2139	7.9881	10.245	13.110
28	1.3213	1.7410	2.2879	2.9987	3.9201	5.1117	6.6488	8.6271	11.167	14.421
29	1.3345	1.7758	2.3566	3.1187	4.1161	5.4184	7.1143	9.3173	12.172	15.863
30	1.3478	1.8114	2.4273	3.2434	4.3219	5.7435	7.6123	10.062	13.267	17.449
40	1.4889	2.2080	3.2620	4.8010	7.0400	10.285	14.974	21.724	31.409	45.259
50	1.6446	2.6916	4.3839	7.1067	11.467	18.420	29.457	46.901	74.357	117.39
60	1.8167	3.2810	5.8916	10.519	18.679	32.987	57.946	101.25	176.03	304.48

Table A.1*a* (*continued*)

Period	*12%*	*14%*	*15%*	*16%*	*18%*	*20%*	*24%*	*28%*	*32%*	*36%*
1	1.1200	1.1400	1.1500	1.1600	1.1800	1.2000	1.2400	1.2800	1.3200	1.3600
2	1.2544	1.2996	1.3225	1.3456	1.3924	1.4400	1.5376	1.6384	1.7424	1.8496
3	1.4049	1.4815	1.5209	1.5609	1.6430	1.7280	1.9066	2.0972	2.3000	2.5155
4	1.5735	1.6890	1.7490	1.8106	1.9388	2.0736	2.3642	2.6844	3.0360	3.4210
5	1.7623	1.9254	2.0114	2.1003	2.2878	2.4883	2.9316	3.4360	4.0075	4.6526
6	1.9738	2.1950	2.3131	2.4364	2.6996	2.9860	3.6352	4.3980	5.2899	6.3275
7	2.2107	2.5023	2.6600	2.8262	3.1855	3.5832	4.5077	5.6295	6.9826	8.6054
8	2.4760	2.8526	3.0590	3.2784	3.7589	4.2998	5.5895	7.2058	9.2170	11.703
9	2.7731	3.2519	3.5179	3.8030	4.4355	5.1598	6.9310	9.2234	12.166	15.916
10	3.1058	3.7072	4.0456	4.4114	5.2338	6.1917	8.5944	11.805	16.059	21.646
11	3.4785	4.2262	4.6524	5.1173	6.1759	7.4301	10.657	15.111	21.198	29.439
12	3.8960	4.8179	5.3502	5.9360	7.2876	8.9161	13.214	19.342	27.982	40.037
13	4.3635	5.4924	6.1528	6.8858	8.5994	10.699	16.386	24.758	36.937	54.451
14	4.8871	6.2613	7.0757	7.9875	10.147	12.839	20.319	31.691	48.756	74.053
15	5.4736	7.1379	8.1371	9.2655	11.973	15.407	25.195	40.564	64.358	100.71
16	6.1304	8.1372	9.3576	10.748	14.129	18.488	31.242	51.923	84.953	136.96
17	6.8660	9.2765	10.761	12.467	16.672	22.186	38.740	66.461	112.13	186.27
18	7.6900	10.575	12.375	14.462	19.673	26.623	48.038	85.070	148.02	253.33
19	8.6128	12.055	14.231	16.776	23.214	31.948	59.567	108.89	195.39	344.53
20	9.6463	13.743	16.366	19.460	27.393	38.337	73.864	139.37	257.91	468.57
21	10.803	15.667	18.821	22.574	32.323	46.005	91.591	178.40	340.44	637.26
22	12.100	17.861	21.644	26.186	38.142	55.206	113.57	228.35	449.39	866.67
23	13.552	20.361	24.891	30.376	45.007	66.247	140.83	292.30	593.19	1178.6
24	15.178	23.212	28.625	35.236	53.108	79.496	174.63	374.14	783.02	1602.9
25	17.000	26.461	32.918	40.874	62.668	95.396	216.54	478.90	1033.5	2180.0
26	19.040	30.166	37.856	47.414	73.948	114.47	268.51	612.99	1364.3	2964.9
27	21.324	34.389	43.535	55.000	87.259	137.37	332.95	784.63	1800.9	4032.2
28	23.883	39.204	50.065	63.800	102.96	164.84	412.86	1004.3	2377.2	5483.8
29	26.749	44.693	57.575	74.008	121.50	197.81	511.95	1285.5	3137.9	7458.0
30	29.959	50.950	66.211	85.849	143.37	237.37	634.81	1645.5	4142.0	10143.
40	93.050	188.88	267.86	378.72	750.37	1469.7	5455.9	19426.	66520.	*
50	289.00	700.23	1083.6	1670.7	3927.3	9100.4	46890.	*	*	*
60	897.59	2595.9	4383.9	7370.1	20555.	56347.	*	*	*	*

* > 99,999

Table A.1*b* Sum of an Annuity of $1 per Period for *n* Periods

Number of Periods	*1%*	*2%*	*3%*	*4%*	*5%*	*6%*	*7%*	*8%*	*9%*	*10%*
1	1.0000	1.0000	1.0000	1.0000	1.0000	1.0000	1.0000	1.0000	1.0000	1.0000
2	2.0100	2.0200	2.0300	2.0400	2.0500	2.0600	2.0700	2.0800	2.0900	2.1000
3	3.0301	3.0604	3.0909	3.1216	3.1525	3.1836	3.2149	3.2464	3.2781	3.3100
4	4.0604	4.1216	4.1836	4.2465	4.3101	4.3746	4.4399	4.5061	4.5731	4.6410
5	5.1010	5.2040	5.3091	5.4163	5.5256	5.6371	5.7507	5.8666	5.9847	6.1051
6	6.1520	6.3081	6.4684	6.6330	6.8019	6.9753	7.1533	7.3359	7.5233	7.7156
7	7.2135	7.4343	7.6625	7.8983	8.1420	8.3938	8.6540	8.9228	9.2004	9.4872
8	8.2857	8.5830	8.8923	9.2142	9.5491	9.8975	10.259	10.636	11.028	11.435
9	9.3685	9.7546	10.159	10.582	11.026	11.491	11.978	12.487	13.021	13.579
10	10.462	10.949	11.463	12.006	12.577	13.180	13.816	14.486	15.192	15.937
11	11.566	12.168	12.807	13.486	14.206	14.971	15.783	16.645	17.560	18.531
12	12.682	13.412	14.192	15.025	15.917	16.869	17.888	18.977	20.140	21.384
13	13.809	14.680	15.617	16.626	17.713	18.882	20.140	21.495	22.953	24.522
14	14.947	15.973	17.086	18.291	19.598	21.015	22.550	24.214	26.019	27.975
15	16.096	17.293	18.598	20.023	21.578	23.276	25.129	27.152	29.360	31.772
16	17.257	18.639	20.156	21.824	23.657	25.672	27.888	30.324	33.003	35.949
17	18.430	20.012	21.761	23.697	25.840	28.212	30.840	33.750	36.973	40.544
18	19.614	21.412	23.414	25.645	28.132	30.905	33.999	37.450	41.301	45.599
19	20.810	22.840	25.116	27.671	30.539	33.760	37.379	41.446	46.018	51.159
20	22.019	24.297	26.870	29.778	33.066	36.785	40.995	45.762	51.160	57.275
21	23.239	25.783	28.676	31.969	35.719	39.992	44.865	50.422	56.764	64.002
22	24.471	27.299	30.536	34.248	38.505	43.392	49.005	55.456	62.873	71.402
23	25.716	28.845	32.452	36.617	41.430	46.995	53.436	60.893	69.531	79.543
24	26.973	30.421	34.426	39.082	44.502	50.815	58.176	66.764	76.789	88.497
25	28.243	32.030	36.459	41.645	47.727	54.864	63.429	73.105	84.700	98.347
26	29.525	33.670	38.553	44.311	51.113	59.156	68.676	79.954	93.323	109.18
27	30.820	35.344	40.709	47.084	54.669	63.705	74.483	87.350	102.72	121.09
28	32.129	37.051	42.930	49.967	58.402	68.528	80.697	95.338	112.96	134.20
29	33.450	38.792	45.218	52.966	62.322	73.639	87.346	103.96	124.13	148.63
30	34.784	40.568	47.575	56.084	66.438	79.058	94.460	113.28	136.30	164.49
40	48.886	60.402	75.401	95.025	120.79	154.76	199.63	259.05	337.88	442.59
50	64.463	84.579	112.79	152.66	209.34	290.34	406.52	573.76	815.08	1163.9
60	81.669	114.05	163.05	237.99	353.58	533.12	813.52	1253.2	1944.7	3034.8

Table A.1*b* ***(continued)***

Number of Periods	*12%*	*14%*	*15%*	*16%*	*18%*	*20%*	*24%*	*28%*	*32%*	*36%*
1	1.0000	1.0000	1.0000	1.0000	1.0000	1.0000	1.0000	1.0000	1.0000	1.0000
2	2.1200	2.1400	2.1500	2.1600	2.1800	2.2000	2.2400	2.2800	2.3200	2.3600
3	3.3744	3.4396	3.4725	3.5056	3.5724	3.6400	3.7776	3.9184	4.0624	4.2096
4	4.7793	4.9211	4.9934	5.0665	5.2154	5.3680	5.6842	6.0156	6.3624	6.7251
5	6.3528	6.6101	6.7424	6.8771	7.1542	7.4416	8.0484	8.6999	9.3983	10.146
6	8.1152	8.5355	8.7537	8.9775	9.4420	9.9299	10.980	12.135	13.405	14.798
7	10.089	10.730	11.066	11.413	12.141	12.915	14.615	16.533	18.695	21.126
8	12.299	13.232	13.726	14.240	15.327	16.499	19.122	22.163	25.678	29.731
9	14.775	16.085	16.785	17.518	19.085	20.798	24.712	29.369	34.895	41.435
10	17.548	19.337	20.303	21.321	23.521	25.958	31.643	38.592	47.061	57.351
11	20.654	23.044	24.349	25.732	28.755	32.150	40.237	50.398	63.121	78.998
12	24.133	27.270	29.001	30.850	34.931	39.580	50.894	65.510	84.320	108.43
13	28.029	32.088	34.351	36.786	42.218	48.496	64.109	84.852	112.30	148.47
14	32.392	37.581	40.504	43.672	50.818	59.195	80.496	109.61	149.23	202.92
15	37.279	43.842	47.580	51.659	60.965	72.035	100.81	141.30	197.99	276.97
16	42.753	50.980	55.717	60.925	72.939	87.442	126.01	181.86	262.35	377.69
17	48.883	59.117	65.075	71.673	87.068	105.93	157.25	233.79	347.30	514.66
18	55.749	68.394	75.836	84.140	103.74	128.11	195.99	300.25	459.44	700.93
19	63.439	78.969	88.211	98.603	123.41	154.74	244.03	385.32	607.47	954.27
20	72.052	91.024	102.44	115.37	146.62	186.68	303.60	494.21	802.86	1298.8
21	81.698	104.76	118.81	134.84	174.02	225.02	377.46	633.59	1060.7	1767.3
22	92.502	120.43	137.63	157.41	206.34	271.03	469.05	811.99	1401.2	2404.6
23	104.60	138.29	159.27	183.60	244.48	326.23	582.62	1040.3	1850.6	3271.3
24	118.15	158.65	184.16	213.97	289.49	392.48	723.46	1332.6	2443.8	4449.9
25	133.33	181.87	212.79	249.21	342.60	471.98	898.09	1706.8	3226.8	6052.9
26	150.33	208.33	245.71	290.08	405.27	567.37	1114.6	2185.7	4260.4	8233.0
27	169.37	238.49	283.56	337.50	479.22	681.85	1383.1	2798.7	5624.7	11197.9
28	190.69	272.88	327.10	392.50	566.48	819.22	1716.0	3583.3	7425.6	15230.2
29	214.58	312.09	377.16	456.30	669.44	984.06	2128.9	4587.6	9802.9	20714.1
30	241.33	356.78	434.74	530.31	790.94	1181.8	2640.9	5873.2	12940.	28172.2
40	767.09	1342.0	1779.0	2360.7	4163.2	7343.8	22728.	69377.	*	*
50	2400.0	4994.5	7217.7	10435.	21813.	45497.	*	*	*	*
60	7471.6	18535.	29219.	46057.	*	*	*	*	*	*

* > 99,999

Table A.1*c* Present Value of $1 Received at the End of *n* Periods

Period	*1%*	*2%*	*3%*	*4%*	*5%*	*6%*	*7%*	*8%*	*9%*	*10%*
1	.9901	.9804	.9709	.9615	.9524	.9434	.9346	.9259	.9174	.9091
2	.9803	.9612	.9426	.9246	.9070	.8900	.8734	.8573	.8417	.8264
3	.9706	.9423	.9151	.8890	.8638	.8396	.8163	.7938	.7722	.7513
4	.9610	.9238	.8885	.8548	.8227	.7921	.7629	.7350	.7084	.6830
5	.9515	.9057	.8626	.8219	.7835	.7473	.7130	.6806	.6499	.6209
6	.9420	.8880	.8375	.7903	.7462	.7050	.6663	.6302	.5963	.5645
7	.9327	.8706	.8131	.7599	.7107	.6651	.6227	.5835	.5470	.5132
8	.9235	.8535	.7894	.7307	.6768	.6274	.5820	.5403	.5019	.4665
9	.9143	.8368	.7664	.7026	.6446	.5919	.5439	.5002	.4604	.4241
10	.9053	.8203	.7441	.6756	.6139	.5584	.5083	.4632	.4224	.3855
11	.8963	.8043	.7224	.6496	.5847	.5268	.4751	.4289	.3875	.3505
12	.8874	.7885	.7014	.6246	.5568	.4970	.4440	.3971	.3555	.3186
13	.8787	.7730	.6810	.6006	.5303	.4688	.4150	.3677	.3262	.2897
14	.8700	.7579	.6611	.5775	.5051	.4423	.3878	.3405	.2992	.2633
15	.8613	.7430	.6419	.5553	.4810	.4173	.3624	.3152	.2745	.2394
16	.8528	.7284	.6232	.5339	.4581	.3936	.3387	.2919	.2519	.2176
17	.8444	.7142	.6050	.5134	.4363	.3714	.3166	.2703	.2311	.1978
18	.8360	.7002	.5874	.4936	.4155	.3503	.2959	.2502	.2120	.1799
19	.8277	.6864	.5703	.4746	.3957	.3305	.2765	.2317	.1945	.1635
20	.8195	.6730	.5537	.4564	.3769	.3118	.2584	.2145	.1784	.1486
25	.7798	.6095	.4776	.3751	.2953	.2330	.1842	.1460	.1160	.0923
30	.7419	.5521	.4120	.3083	.2314	.1741	.1314	.0994	.0754	.0573
40	.6717	.4529	.3066	.2083	.1420	.0972	.0668	.0460	.0318	.0221
50	.6080	.3715	.2281	.1407	.0872	.0543	.0339	.0213	.0134	.0085
60	.5504	.3048	.1697	.0951	.0535	.0303	.0173	.0099	.0057	.0033

Table A.1*c* ***(continued)***

Period	*12%*	*14%*	*15%*	*16%*	*18%*	*20%*	*24%*	*28%*	*32%*	*36%*
1	.8929	.8772	.8696	.8621	.8475	.8333	.8065	.7813	.7576	.7353
2	.7972	.7695	.7561	.7432	.7182	.6944	.6504	.6104	.5739	.5407
3	.7118	.6750	.6575	.6407	.6086	.5787	.5245	.4768	.4348	.3975
4	.6355	.5921	.5718	.5523	.5158	.4823	.4230	.3725	.3294	.2923
5	.5674	.5194	.4972	.4761	.4371	.4019	.3411	.2910	.2495	.2149
6	.5066	.4556	.4323	.4104	.3704	.3349	.2751	.2274	.1890	.1580
7	.4523	.3996	.3759	.3538	.3139	.2791	.2218	.1776	.1432	.1162
8	.4039	.3506	.3269	.3050	.2660	.2326	.1789	.1388	.1085	.0854
9	.3606	.3075	.2843	.2630	.2255	.1938	.1443	.1084	.0822	.0628
10	.3220	.2697	.2472	.2267	.1911	.1615	.1164	.0847	.0623	.0462
11	.2875	.2366	.2149	.1954	.1619	.1346	.0938	.0662	.0472	.0340
12	.2567	.2076	.1869	.1685	.1372	.1122	.0757	.0517	.0357	.0250
13	.2292	.1821	.1625	.1452	.1163	.0935	.0610	.0404	.0271	.0184
14	.2046	.1597	.1413	.1252	.0985	.0779	.0492	.0316	.0205	.0135
15	.1827	.1401	.1229	.1079	.0835	.0649	.0397	.0247	.0155	.0099
16	.1631	.1229	.1069	.0930	.0708	.0541	.0320	.0193	.0118	.0073
17	.1456	.1078	.0929	.0802	.0600	.0451	.0258	.0150	.0089	.0054
18	.1300	.0946	.0808	.0691	.0508	.0376	.0208	.0118	.0068	.0039
19	.1161	.0829	.0703	.0596	.0431	.0313	.0168	.0092	.0051	.0029
20	.1037	.0728	.0611	.0514	.0365	.0261	.0135	.0072	.0039	.0021
25	.0588	.0378	.0304	.0245	.0160	.0105	.0046	.0021	.0010	.0005
30	.0334	.0196	.0151	.0116	.0070	.0042	.0016	.0006	.0002	.0001
40	.0107	.0053	.0037	.0026	.0013	.0007	.0002	.0001	*	*
50	.0035	.0014	.0009	.0006	.0003	.0001	*	*	*	*
60	.0011	.0004	.0002	.0001	*	*	*	*	*	*

* The factor is zero to four decimal places.

Table A.1*d* Present Value of an Annuity of $1 per Period for *n* Periods

Number of Payments	1%	2%	3%	4%	5%	6%	7%	8%	9%
1	0.9901	0.9804	0.9709	0.9615	0.9524	0.9434	0.9346	0.9259	0.9174
2	1.9704	1.9416	1.9135	1.8861	1.8594	1.8334	1.8080	1.7833	1.7591
3	2.9410	2.8839	2.8286	2.7751	2.7232	2.6730	2.6243	2.5771	2.5313
4	3.9020	3.8077	3.7171	3.6299	3.5460	3.4651	3.3872	3.3121	3.2397
5	4.8534	4.7135	4.5797	4.4518	4.3295	4.2124	4.1002	3.9927	3.8897
6	5.7955	5.6014	5.4172	5.2421	5.0757	4.9173	4.7665	4.6229	4.4859
7	6.7282	6.4720	6.2303	6.0021	5.7864	5.5824	5.3893	5.2064	5.0330
8	7.6517	7.3255	7.0197	6.7327	6.4632	6.2098	5.9713	5.7466	5.5348
9	8.5660	8.1622	7.7861	7.4353	7.1078	6.8017	6.5152	6.2469	5.9952
10	9.4713	8.9826	8.5302	8.1109	7.7217	7.3601	7.0236	6.7101	6.4177
11	10.3676	9.7868	9.2526	8.7605	8.3064	7.8869	7.4987	7.1390	6.8052
12	11.2551	10.5753	9.9540	9.3851	8.8633	8.3838	7.9427	7.5361	7.1607
13	12.1337	11.3484	10.6350	9.9856	9.3936	8.8527	8.3577	7.9038	7.4869
14	13.0037	12.1062	11.2961	10.5631	9.8986	9.2950	8.7455	8.2442	7.7862
15	13.8651	12.8493	11.9379	11.1184	10.3797	9.7122	9.1079	8.5595	8.0607
16	14.7179	13.5777	12.5611	11.6523	10.8378	10.1059	9.4466	8.8514	8.3126
17	15.5623	14.2919	13.1661	12.1657	11.2741	10.4773	9.7632	9.1216	8.5436
18	16.3983	14.9920	13.7535	12.6593	11.6896	10.8276	10.0591	9.3719	8.7556
19	17.2260	15.6785	14.3238	13.1339	12.0853	11.1581	10.3356	9.6036	8.9501
20	18.0456	16.3514	14.8775	13.5903	12.4622	11.4699	10.5940	9.8181	9.1285
25	22.0232	19.5235	17.4131	15.6221	14.0939	12.7834	11.6536	10.6748	9.8226
30	25.8077	22.3965	19.6004	17.2920	15.3725	13.7648	12.4090	11.2578	10.2737
40	32.8347	27.3555	23.1148	19.7928	17.1591	15.0463	13.3317	11.9246	10.7574
50	39.1961	31.4236	25.7298	21.4822	18.2559	15.7619	13.8007	12.2335	10.9617
60	44.9550	34.7609	27.6756	22.6235	18.9293	16.1614	14.0392	12.3766	11.0480

Table A.1*d* ***(continued)***

Number of Payments	*10%*	*12%*	*14%*	*15%*	*16%*	*18%*	*20%*	*24%*	*28%*	*32%*
1	0.9091	0.8929	0.8772	0.8696	0.8621	0.8475	0.8333	0.8065	0.7813	0.7576
2	1.7355	1.6901	1.6467	1.6257	1.6052	1.5656	1.5278	1.4568	1.3916	1.3315
3	2.4869	2.4018	2.3216	2.2832	2.2459	2.1743	2.1065	1.9813	1.8684	1.7663
4	3.1699	3.0373	2.9137	2.8550	2.7982	2.6901	2.5887	2.4043	2.2410	2.0957
5	3.7908	3.6048	3.4331	3.3522	3.2743	3.1272	2.9906	2.7454	2.5320	2.3452
6	4.3553	4.1114	3.8887	3.7845	3.6847	3.4976	3.3255	3.0205	2.7594	2.5342
7	4.8684	4.5638	4.2883	4.1604	4.0386	3.8115	3.6046	3.2423	2.9370	2.6775
8	5.3349	4.9676	4.6389	4.4873	4.3436	4.0776	3.8372	3.4212	3.0758	2.7860
9	5.7590	5.3282	4.9464	4.7716	4.6065	4.3030	4.0310	3.5655	3.1842	2.8681
10	6.1446	5.6502	5.2161	5.0188	4.8332	4.4941	4.1925	3.6819	3.2689	2.9304
11	6.4951	5.9377	5.4527	5.2337	5.0286	4.6560	4.3271	3.7757	3.3351	2.9776
12	6.8137	6.1944	5.6603	5.4206	5.1971	4.7932	4.4392	3.8514	3.3868	3.0133
13	7.1034	6.4235	5.8424	5.5831	5.3423	4.9095	4.5327	3.9124	3.4272	3.0404
14	7.3667	6.6282	6.0021	5.7245	5.4675	5.0081	4.6106	3.9616	3.4587	3.0609
15	7.6061	6.8109	6.1422	5.8474	5.5755	5.0916	4.6755	4.0013	3.4834	3.0764
16	7.8237	6.9740	6.2651	5.9542	5.6685	5.1624	4.7296	4.0333	3.5026	3.0882
17	8.0216	7.1196	6.3729	6.0472	5.7487	5.2223	4.7746	4.0591	3.5177	3.0971
18	8.2014	7.2497	6.4674	6.1280	5.8178	5.2732	4.8122	4.0799	3.5294	3.1039
19	8.3649	7.3658	6.5504	6.1982	5.8775	5.3162	4.8435	4.0967	3.5386	3.1090
20	8.5136	7.4694	6.6231	6.2593	5.9288	5.3527	4.8696	4.1103	3.5458	3.1129
25	9.0770	7.8431	6.8729	6.4641	6.0971	5.4669	4.9476	4.1474	3.5640	3.1220
30	9.4269	8.0552	7.0027	6.5660	6.1772	5.5168	4.9789	4.1601	3.5693	3.1242
40	9.7791	8.2438	7.1050	6.6418	6.2335	5.5482	4.9966	4.1659	3.5712	3.1250
50	9.9148	9.3045	7.1327	6.6605	6.2463	5.5541	4.9995	4.1666	3.5714	3.1250
60	9.9672	8.3240	7.1401	6.6651	6.2492	5.5553	4.9999	4.1667	3.5714	3.1250

Table A.2 Areas under the Normal Curve

Z	.00	.01	.02	.03	.04	.05	.06	.07	.08	.09
0.0	.0000	.0040	.0080	.0120	.0160	.0199	.0239	.0279	.0319	.0359
0.1	.0398	.0438	.0478	.0517	.0557	.0596	.0636	.0675	.0714	.0753
0.2	.0793	.0832	.0871	.0910	.0948	.0987	.1026	.1064	.1103	.1141
0.3	.1179	.1217	.1255	.1293	.1331	.1368	.1406	.1443	.1480	.1517
0.4	.1554	.1591	.1628	.1664	.1700	.1736	.1772	.1808	.1844	.1879
0.5	.1915	.1950	.1985	.2019	.2054	.2088	.2123	.2157	.2190	.2224
0.6	.2257	.2291	.2324	.2357	.2389	.2422	.2454	.2486	.2517	.2549
0.7	.2580	.2611	.2642	.2673	.2704	.2734	.2764	.2794	.2823	.2852
0.8	.2881	.2910	.2939	.2967	.2995	.3023	.3051	.3078	.3106	.3133
0.9	.3159	.3186	.3212	.3238	.3264	.3289	.3315	.3340	.3365	.3389
1.0	.3413	.3438	.3461	.3485	.3508	.3531	.3554	.3577	.3599	.3621
1.1	.3643	.3665	.3686	.3708	.3729	.3749	.3770	.3790	.3810	.3830
1.2	.3849	.3869	.3888	.3907	.3925	.3944	.3962	.3980	.3997	.4015
1.3	.4032	.4049	.4066	.4082	.4099	.4115	.4131	.4147	.4162	.4177
1.4	.4192	.4207	.4222	.4236	.4251	.4265	.4279	.4292	.4306	.4319
1.5	.4332	.4345	.4357	.4370	.4382	.4394	.4406	.4418	.4429	.4441
1.6	.4452	.4463	.4474	.4484	.4495	.4505	.4515	.4525	.4535	.4545
1.7	.4554	.4564	.4573	.4582	.4591	.4599	.4608	.4616	.4625	.4633
1.8	.4641	.4649	.4656	.4664	.4671	.4678	.4686	.4693	.4699	.4706
1.9	.4713	.4719	.4726	.4732	.4738	.4744	.4750	.4756	.4761	.4767
2.0	.4772	.4778	.4783	.4788	.4793	.4798	.4803	.4808	.4812	.4817
2.1	.4821	.4826	.4830	.4834	.4838	.4842	.4846	.4850	.4854	.4857
2.2	.4861	.4864	.4868	.4871	.4875	.4878	.4881	.4884	.4887	.4890
2.3	.4893	.4896	.4898	.4901	.4904	.4906	.4909	.4911	.4913	.4916
2.4	.4918	.4920	.4922	.4925	.4927	.4929	.4931	.4932	.4934	.4936
2.5	.4938	.4940	.4941	.4943	.4945	.4946	.4948	.4949	.4951	.4952
2.6	.4953	.4955	.4956	.4957	.4959	.4960	.4961	.4962	.4963	.4964
2.7	.4965	.4966	.4967	.4968	.4969	.4970	.4971	.4972	.4973	.4974
2.8	.4974	.4975	.4976	.4977	.4977	.4978	.4979	.4979	.4980	.4981
2.9	.4981	.4982	.4982	.4983	.4984	.4984	.4985	.4985	.4986	.4986
3.0	.4987	.4987	.4987	.4988	.4988	.4989	.4989	.4989	.4990	.4990

Table A.3*a* Critical Values for the *F*-Distribution (α = .05)

Degrees of Freedom for Denominator	Degrees of Freedom for Numerator								
	1	*2*	*3*	*4*	*5*	*6*	*8*	*10*	*15*
1	161.4	199.5	215.7	224.6	230.2	234.0	238.9	241.9	245.9
2	18.51	19.00	19.16	19.25	19.30	19.33	19.37	19.40	19.43
3	10.13	9.55	9.28	9.12	9.01	8.94	8.85	8.79	8.70
4	7.71	6.94	6.59	6.39	6.26	6.16	6.04	5.96	5.86
5	6.61	5.79	5.41	5.19	5.05	4.95	4.82	4.74	4.62
6	5.99	5.14	4.76	4.53	4.39	4.28	4.15	4.06	3.94
7	5.59	4.74	4.35	4.12	3.97	3.87	3.73	3.64	3.51
8	5.32	4.46	4.07	3.84	3.69	3.58	3.44	3.35	3.22
9	5.12	4.26	3.86	3.63	3.48	3.37	3.23	3.14	3.01
10	4.96	4.10	3.71	3.48	3.33	3.22	3.07	2.98	2.85
11	4.84	3.98	3.59	3.36	3.20	3.09	2.95	2.85	2.72
12	4.75	3.89	3.49	3.26	3.11	3.00	2.85	2.75	2.62
13	4.67	3.81	3.41	3.18	3.03	2.92	2.77	2.67	2.53
14	4.60	3.74	3.34	3.11	2.96	2.85	2.70	2.60	2.46
15	4.54	3.68	3.29	3.06	2.90	2.79	2.64	2.54	2.40
16	4.49	3.63	3.24	3.01	2.85	2.74	2.59	2.49	2.35
17	4.45	3.59	3.20	2.96	2.81	2.70	2.55	2.45	2.31
18	4.41	3.55	3.16	2.93	2.77	2.66	2.51	2.41	2.27
19	4.38	3.52	3.13	2.90	2.74	2.63	2.48	2.38	2.23
20	4.35	3.49	3.10	2.87	2.71	2.60	2.45	2.35	2.20
21	4.32	3.47	3.07	2.84	2.68	2.57	2.42	2.32	2.18
22	4.30	3.44	3.05	2.82	2.66	2.55	2.40	2.30	2.15
23	4.28	3.42	3.03	2.80	2.64	2.53	2.37	2.27	2.13
24	4.26	3.40	3.01	2.78	2.62	2.51	2.36	2.25	2.11
25	4.24	3.39	2.99	2.76	2.60	2.49	2.34	2.24	2.09
26	4.23	3.37	2.98	2.74	2.59	2.47	2.32	2.22	2.07
27	4.21	3.35	2.96	2.73	2.57	2.46	2.31	2.20	2.06
28	4.20	3.34	2.95	2.71	2.56	2.45	2.29	2.19	2.04
29	4.18	3.33	2.93	2.70	2.55	2.43	2.28	2.18	2.03
30	4.17	3.32	2.92	2.69	2.53	2.42	2.27	2.16	2.01
40	4.08	3.23	2.84	2.61	2.45	2.34	2.18	2.08	1.92
50	4.03	3.18	2.79	2.56	2.40	2.29	2.13	2.03	1.87
60	4.00	3.15	2.76	2.53	2.37	2.25	2.10	1.99	1.84
70	3.98	3.13	2.74	2.50	2.35	2.23	2.07	1.97	1.81
80	3.96	3.11	2.72	2.49	2.33	2.21	2.06	1.95	1.79
90	3.95	3.10	2.71	2.47	2.32	2.20	2.04	1.94	1.78
100	3.94	3.09	2.70	2.46	2.31	2.19	2.03	1.93	1.77
125	3.92	3.07	2.68	2.44	2.29	2.17	2.01	1.91	1.75
150	3.90	3.06	2.66	2.43	2.27	2.16	2.00	1.89	1.73
200	3.89	3.04	2.65	2.42	2.26	2.14	1.98	1.88	1.72
∞	3.84	3.00	2.60	2.37	2.21	2.10	1.94	1.83	1.67

Table A.3*b* Critical Values for the *F*-Distribution (α = .01)

Degrees of freedom for denominator	Degrees of Freedom for Numerator								
	1	*2*	*3*	*4*	*5*	*6*	*8*	*10*	*15*
1	4052.	4999.	5403.	5625.	5764.	5859.	5981.	6056.	6157.
2	98.50	99.00	99.17	99.25	99.30	99.33	99.37	99.40	99.43
3	34.12	30.82	29.46	28.71	28.24	27.91	27.49	27.23	26.87
4	21.20	18.00	16.69	15.98	15.52	15.21	14.80	14.55	14.20
5	16.26	13.27	12.06	11.39	10.97	10.67	10.29	10.05	9.72
6	13.75	10.92	9.78	9.15	8.75	8.47	8.10	7.87	7.56
7	12.25	9.55	8.45	7.85	7.46	7.19	6.84	6.62	6.31
8	11.26	8.65	7.59	7.01	6.63	6.37	6.03	5.81	5.52
9	10.56	8.02	6.99	6.42	6.06	5.80	5.47	5.26	4.96
10	10.04	7.56	6.55	5.99	5.64	5.39	5.06	4.85	4.56
11	9.65	7.21	6.22	5.67	5.32	5.07	4.74	4.54	4.25
12	9.33	6.93	5.95	5.41	5.06	4.82	4.50	4.30	4.01
13	9.07	6.70	5.74	5.21	4.86	4.62	4.30	4.10	3.82
14	8.86	6.51	5.56	5.04	4.69	4.46	4.14	3.94	3.66
15	8.68	6.36	5.42	4.89	4.56	4.32	4.00	3.80	3.52
16	8.53	6.23	5.29	4.77	4.44	4.20	3.89	3.69	3.41
17	8.40	6.11	5.19	4.67	4.34	4.10	3.79	3.59	3.31
18	8.29	6.01	5.09	4.58	4.25	4.01	3.71	3.51	3.23
19	8.18	5.93	5.01	4.50	4.17	3.94	3.63	3.43	3.15
20	8.10	5.85	4.94	4.43	4.10	3.87	3.56	3.37	3.09
21	8.02	5.78	4.87	4.37	4.04	3.81	3.51	3.31	3.03
22	7.95	5.72	4.82	4.31	3.99	3.76	3.45	3.26	2.98
23	7.88	5.66	4.76	4.26	3.94	3.71	3.41	3.21	2.93
24	7.82	5.61	4.72	4.22	3.90	3.67	3.36	3.17	2.89
25	7.77	5.57	4.68	4.18	3.85	3.63	3.32	3.13	2.85
26	7.72	5.53	4.64	4.14	3.82	3.59	3.29	3.09	2.81
27	7.68	5.49	4.60	4.11	3.78	3.56	3.26	3.06	2.78
28	7.64	5.45	4.57	4.07	3.75	3.53	3.23	3.03	2.75
29	7.60	5.42	4.54	4.04	3.73	3.50	3.20	3.00	2.73
30	7.56	5.39	4.51	4.02	3.70	3.47	3.17	2.98	2.70
40	7.31	5.18	4.31	3.83	3.51	3.29	2.99	2.80	2.52
50	7.17	5.06	4.20	3.72	3.41	3.19	2.89	2.70	2.42
60	7.08	4.98	4.13	3.65	3.34	3.12	2.82	2.63	2.35
70	7.01	4.92	4.07	3.60	3.29	3.07	2.78	2.59	2.31
80	6.96	4.88	4.04	3.56	3.26	3.04	2.74	2.55	2.27
90	6.93	4.85	4.01	3.53	3.23	3.01	2.72	2.52	2.24
100	6.90	4.82	3.98	3.51	3.21	2.99	2.69	2.50	2.22
125	6.84	4.78	3.94	3.47	3.17	2.95	2.66	2.47	2.19
150	6.81	4.75	3.91	3.45	3.14	2.92	2.63	2.44	2.16
200	6.76	4.71	3.88	3.41	3.11	2.89	2.60	2.41	2.13
∞	6.63	4.61	3.78	3.32	3.02	2.80	2.51	2.32	2.04

Table A.4 Critical Values for the *t*-Distribution

One-tailed α =	.10	.05	.025	.01	.005
Two-tailed α =	.20	.10	.05	.02	.01
df = 1	3.078	6.314	12.706	31.821	63.657
2	1.886	2.920	4.303	6.965	9.925
3	1.638	2.353	3.182	4.541	5.841
4	1.533	2.132	2.776	3.747	4.604
5	1.476	2.015	2.571	3.365	4.032
6	1.440	1.943	2.447	3.143	3.707
7	1.415	1.895	2.365	2.998	3.499
8	1.397	1.860	2.306	2.896	3.355
9	1.383	1.833	2.262	2.821	3.250
10	1.372	1.812	2.228	2.764	3.169
11	1.363	1.796	2.201	2.718	3.106
12	1.356	1.782	2.179	2.681	3.055
13	1.350	1.771	2.160	2.650	3.012
14	1.345	1.761	2.145	2.624	2.977
15	1.341	1.753	2.131	2.602	2.947
16	1.337	1.746	2.120	2.583	2.921
17	1.333	1.740	2.110	2.567	2.898
18	1.330	1.734	2.101	2.552	2.878
19	1.328	1.729	2.093	2.539	2.861
20	1.325	1.725	2.086	2.528	2.845
21	1.323	1.721	2.080	2.518	2.831
22	1.321	1.717	2.074	2.508	2.819
23	1.319	1.714	2.069	2.500	2.807
24	1.318	1.711	2.064	2.492	2.797
25	1.316	1.708	2.060	2.485	2.787
26	1.315	1.706	2.056	2.479	2.779
27	1.314	1.703	2.052	2.473	2.771
28	1.313	1.701	2.048	2.467	2.763
29	1.311	1.699	2.045	2.462	2.756
30	1.310	1.697	2.042	2.457	2.750
40	1.303	1.684	2.021	2.423	2.704
50	1.299	1.676	2.009	2.403	2.678
60	1.296	1.671	2.000	2.390	2.660
70	1.294	1.667	1.994	2.381	2.648
80	1.292	1.664	1.990	2.374	2.639
90	1.291	1.662	1.987	2.368	2.632
100	1.290	1.660	1.984	2.364	2.626
125	1.288	1.657	1.979	2.357	2.616
150	1.287	1.655	1.976	2.351	2.609
200	1.286	1.653	1.972	2.345	2.601
∞	1.282	1.645	1.960	2.326	2.576

Table A.5*a* Durbin-Watson Statistic: Significance Points for d_l and d_u (One-Tailed Test, α = .05)

	$k = 1$		$k = 2$		$k = 3$		$k = 4$		$k = 5$	
n	d_l	d_u	d_l	d_u	d_l	d_u	d_l	d_u	d_l	d_u
15	1.08	1.36	0.95	1.54	0.82	1.75	0.69	1.97	0.56	2.21
16	1.10	1.37	0.98	1.54	0.86	1.73	0.74	1.93	0.62	2.15
17	1.13	1.38	1.02	1.54	0.90	1.71	0.78	1.90	0.67	2.10
18	1.16	1.39	1.05	1.53	0.93	1.69	0.82	1.87	0.71	2.06
19	1.18	1.40	1.08	1.53	0.97	1.68	0.86	1.85	0.75	2.02
20	1.20	1.41	1.10	1.54	1.00	1.68	0.90	1.83	0.79	1.99
21	1.22	1.42	1.13	1.54	1.03	1.67	0.93	1.81	0.83	1.96
22	1.24	1.43	1.15	1.54	1.05	1.66	0.96	1.80	0.86	1.94
23	1.26	1.44	1.17	1.54	1.08	1.66	0.99	1.79	0.90	1.92
24	1.27	1.45	1.19	1.55	1.10	1.66	1.01	1.78	0.93	1.90
25	1.29	1.45	1.21	1.55	1.12	1.66	1.04	1.77	0.95	1.89
26	1.30	1.46	1.22	1.55	1.14	1.65	1.06	1.76	0.98	1.88
27	1.32	1.47	1.24	1.56	1.16	1.65	1.08	1.76	1.01	1.86
28	1.33	1.48	1.26	1.56	1.18	1.65	1.10	1.75	1.03	1.85
29	1.34	1.48	1.27	1.56	1.20	1.65	1.12	1.74	1.05	1.84
30	1.35	1.49	1.28	1.57	1.21	1.65	1.14	1.74	1.07	1.83
31	1.36	1.50	1.30	1.57	1.23	1.65	1.16	1.74	1.09	1.83
32	1.37	1.50	1.31	1.57	1.24	1.65	1.18	1.73	1.11	1.82
33	1.38	1.51	1.32	1.58	1.26	1.65	1.19	1.73	1.13	1.81
34	1.39	1.51	1.33	1.58	1.27	1.65	1.21	1.73	1.15	1.81
35	1.40	1.52	1.34	1.58	1.28	1.65	1.22	1.73	1.16	1.80
36	1.41	1.52	1.35	1.59	1.29	1.65	1.24	1.73	1.18	1.80
37	1.42	1.53	1.36	1.59	1.31	1.66	1.25	1.72	1.19	1.80
38	1.43	1.54	1.37	1.59	1.32	1.66	1.26	1.72	1.21	1.79
39	1.43	1.54	1.38	1.60	1.33	1.66	1.27	1.72	1.22	1.79
40	1.44	1.54	1.39	1.60	1.34	1.66	1.29	1.72	1.23	1.79
45	1.48	1.57	1.43	1.62	1.38	1.67	1.34	1.72	1.29	1.78
50	1.50	1.59	1.46	1.63	1.42	1.67	1.38	1.72	1.34	1.77
55	1.53	1.60	1.49	1.64	1.45	1.68	1.41	1.72	1.38	1.77
60	1.55	1.62	1.51	1.65	1.48	1.69	1.44	1.73	1.41	1.77
65	1.57	1.63	1.54	1.66	1.50	1.70	1.47	1.73	1.44	1.77
70	1.58	1.64	1.55	1.67	1.52	1.70	1.49	1.74	1.46	1.77
75	1.60	1.65	1.57	1.68	1.54	1.71	1.51	1.74	1.49	1.77
80	1.61	1.66	1.59	1.69	1.56	1.72	1.53	1.74	1.51	1.77
85	1.62	1.67	1.60	1.70	1.57	1.72	1.55	1.75	1.52	1.77
90	1.63	1.68	1.61	1.70	1.59	1.73	1.57	1.75	1.54	1.78
95	1.64	1.69	1.62	1.71	1.60	1.73	1.58	1.75	1.56	1.78
100	1.65	1.69	1.63	1.72	1.61	1.74	1.59	1.76	1.57	1.78

Note: n = number of observations, k = number of regressors.

Table A.5*b* Durbin-Watson Statistic: Significance Points for d_l and d_u (Two-Tailed Test, α = .05)

	$k = 1$		$k = 2$		$k = 3$		$k = 4$		$k = 5$	
n	d_l	d_u	d_l	d_u	d_l	d_u	d_l	d_u	d_l	d_u
15	0.95	1.23	0.83	1.40	0.71	1.61	0.59	1.84	0.48	2.09
16	0.98	1.24	0.86	1.40	0.75	1.59	0.64	1.80	0.53	2.03
17	1.01	1.25	0.90	1.40	0.79	1.58	0.68	1.77	0.57	1.98
18	1.03	1.26	0.93	1.40	0.82	1.56	0.72	1.74	0.62	1.93
19	1.06	1.28	0.96	1.41	0.86	1.55	0.76	1.72	0.66	1.90
20	1.08	1.28	0.99	1.41	0.89	1.55	0.79	1.70	0.70	1.87
21	1.10	1.30	1.01	1.41	0.92	1.54	0.83	1.69	0.73	1.84
22	1.12	1.31	1.04	1.42	0.95	1.54	0.86	1.68	0.77	1.82
23	1.14	1.32	1.06	1.42	0.97	1.54	0.89	1.67	0.80	1.80
24	1.16	1.33	1.08	1.43	1.00	1.54	0.91	1.66	0.83	1.79
25	1.18	1.34	1.10	1.43	1.02	1.54	0.94	1.65	0.86	1.77
26	1.19	1.35	1.12	1.44	1.04	1.54	0.96	1.65	0.88	1.76
27	1.21	1.36	1.13	1.44	1.06	1.54	0.99	1.64	0.91	1.75
28	1.22	1.37	1.15	1.45	1.08	1.54	1.01	1.64	0.93	1.74
29	1.24	1.38	1.17	1.45	1.10	1.54	1.03	1.63	0.96	1.73
30	1.25	1.38	1.18	1.46	1.12	1.54	1.05	1.63	0.98	1.73
31	1.26	1.39	1.20	1.47	1.13	1.55	1.07	1.63	1.00	1.72
32	1.27	1.40	1.21	1.47	1.15	1.55	1.08	1.63	1.02	1.71
33	1.28	1.41	1.22	1.48	1.16	1.55	1.10	1.63	1.04	1.71
34	1.29	1.41	1.24	1.48	1.17	1.55	1.12	1.63	1.06	1.70
35	1.30	1.42	1.25	1.48	1.19	1.55	1.13	1.63	1.07	1.70
36	1.31	1.43	1.26	1.49	1.20	1.56	1.15	1.63	1.09	1.70
37	1.32	1.43	1.27	1.49	1.21	1.56	1.16	1.62	1.10	1.70
38	1.33	1.44	1.28	1.50	1.23	1.56	1.17	1.62	1.12	1.70
39	1.34	1.44	1.29	1.50	1.24	1.56	1.19	1.63	1.13	1.69
40	1.35	1.45	1.30	1.51	1.25	1.57	1.20	1.63	1.15	1.69
45	1.39	1.48	1.34	1.53	1.30	1.58	1.25	1.63	1.21	1.69
50	1.42	1.50	1.38	1.54	1.34	1.59	1.30	1.64	1.26	1.69
55	1.45	1.52	1.41	1.56	1.37	1.60	1.33	1.64	1.30	1.69
60	1.47	1.54	1.44	1.57	1.40	1.61	1.37	1.65	1.33	1.69
65	1.49	1.55	1.46	1.59	1.43	1.62	1.40	1.66	1.36	1.69
70	1.51	1.57	1.48	1.60	1.45	1.63	1.42	1.66	1.39	1.70
75	1.53	1.58	1.50	1.61	1.47	1.64	1.45	1.67	1.42	1.70
80	1.54	1.59	1.52	1.62	1.49	1.65	1.47	1.67	1.44	1.70
85	1.56	1.60	1.53	1.63	1.51	1.65	1.49	1.68	1.46	1.71
90	1.57	1.61	1.55	1.64	1.53	1.66	1.50	1.69	1.48	1.71
95	1.58	1.62	1.56	1.65	1.54	1.67	1.52	1.69	1.50	1.71
100	1.59	1.63	1.57	1.65	1.55	1.67	1.53	1.70	1.51	1.72

Note: n = number of observations, k = number of regressors.

Index

F

G

H

I

J

K

L

R

S